Borland® C++ 2.0 Programming

Ben Ezzell

Addison-Wesley Publishing Company, Inc.

Reading, Massachusetts Menlo Park, California New York
Don Mills, Ontario Wokingham, England Amsterdam Bonn
Sydney Singapore Tokyo Madrid San Juan
Paris Seoul Milan Mexico City Taipei

Many of the designations used by manufacturers and sellers to distinguish their products are claimed as trademarks. Where those designations appear in this book and Addison-Wesley was aware of a trademark claim, the designations have been printed in initial capital letters.

Library of Congress Cataloging-in-Publication Data
Ezzell, Ben.
    Borland C++ 2.0 programming / Ben Ezzell.
        p.   cm.
    Includes index.
    ISBN 0-201-56781-4
    1. C++ (Computer program language)   2. Turbo C++ (Computer
program)   3. Microsoft Windows (Computer programs) I. Title.
II. Title: Borland C plus plus 2.0 programming.
QA76.73.C153E98   1991
005.4'3--dc20   91-12226
                                                             CIP

Managing Editor: Amorette Pedersen
Set in 10.5-point Palatino by Benchmark Productions

1 2 3 4 5 6 7 8 9-MW-9594939291
First Printing, June 1991

Dedication

While the first computer was built shortly after World War II, for several decades afterwards, computers remained rare devices, tended by a strangely mixed crew of electronic technicians and mathematicians. Slowly, a new occupation came into existance with various titles such as systems analyst and programmer. But most practitioners of this new field did not begin as software specialists. Indeed, most of us have come to this industry from fields so diverse that a list of origins would read like an encyclopedia of occupations.

But this is always the case when a new occupation is born and there is no established infrastructure to determine who may enter and how. And, with this freedom, the best of the best come from a host of backgrounds with a host of talents to create and breathe life into something for which no single occupation could serve as parent.

This has happened in the past as well.

In the mid-15th century, at a time in Europe when guilds controlled virtually every occupation and skills were taught only by rote, a thirty-year-old goldsmith fell afoul of his guild and other political forces in Mainz, Germany and, as a result, began a series of experiments which changed the entire world. In the end, while it was not the developer's aim, his processes resulted in destroying the power not only of the guilds but the entire political, social, and religious structures of the time—not merely in Europe but throughout the world.

The echos of this event are still being heard today. Loud and clear!

In the 1450's, Johann Gutenberg created a revolution in communications with the development of practical moveable type which was first used to print school grammar books, indulgences, and a Bible. He took books from the hands of scribes and placed them in the hands of the populace. And the world has not stood silent since!

Just as printing began the revolution of communication, computers continue the destruction of the old order, making information available to all.

Because communications—first in printed form—brought about the Reformation and, later, the Declaration of Liberty (and, more recently, the fall of the Berlin Wall). The future is in your hands, just as the tools for communications rest in your hands at this moment—because communications come in many forms.

Some years ago, my wife remarked—with great satifaction—that *"the power of the press belongs to she who has one."* But, as the students in Tieneman Square taught us, using an underground network of fax machines, the power of the press is simply one form of the power of communications ... just as Windows 3.0 is another.

This volume—which is also an example of the power of the press—is respectfully dedicated to one of our first communicators:

Johann Gutenberg
1394—1468
The Father of Communications

Table of Contents

Acknowledgments

Too often, when finishing a book like this (after proofreading, correcting, and other far from minor but perniciously aggravating details), the author is often only too happy to allow the entire subject to sink into a sea of oblivion. In doing so, he or she may forget to say a heart-felt and well-deserved "Thank You" to others who have also spent more than a little time and effort in the preparation of the book.

Therefore, lest I forget, I am taking this opportunity to acknowledge several individuals who have also expended sweat, blood, and (sometimes) tears in putting this book together. These individuals include:

Chris Ohlsen at Borland International, who has provided technical review as well as many valuable comments and to whom I am very much indebted.

Nan Borreson, also with Borland International, for expediting all manner of details and for her constant and careful attention to even my stupidest inquiries.

And, not least, Chris Williams, Amy Pedersen, and Ann Radwan with Benchmark Productions for their patience.

To each of you—collectively and individually—thank you very sincerely!

Ben Ezzell
May, 1991

## Part 1

An Introduction To Programming For Windows 3.0

For many programmers, writing applications for Windows 3.0 will constitute an abrupt departure from familiar and accustomed practices—a departure which may even leave some wondering if they are actually writing in C, or if they have been suddenly catapulted into some strange, almost-parallel universe.

For others, particularly those who may have worked with earlier versions of Windows, or with OS/2, these new practices may seem less strange, or may even be welcome as old friends.

Whether those with previous Windows or OS/2 experience will have any advantage over those who have never programmed in a multitasking environment, is, however, a moot point.

This assertion is made partially because of the changes and enhancements incorporated in Windows 3.0, which will require even experienced Windows programmers to learn new skills. More important, because the Borland C++ compiler and the Whitewater Resources Toolkit provide features and capabilities which greatly shift the emphasis from Windows experience back to general planning/programming skills, i.e., with Borland C++, how experienced you are in the intracacies of Windows programming becomes less important than your overall skills as a programmer.

All of which is not to say or suggest that you will be able to program Windows without understanding Windows; just that Windows programming will be easier for you to learn and understand while the tools (the compiler and toolbox) take care of the dirty work for you.

The emphasis, however, will still be on understanding how Windows programming works; which means, of course, understanding how Windows works.

Therefore, in Part 1, I'll begin by helping you to set up your BC++ complier and the Toolkit for Windows. Later, I'll introduce the basics of preparing displays for Windows, show you how mouse operations are used, and discuss the principles of programming in a message-controlled enviroment.

If you are ready, we will proceed.

## Chapter 1

Installing C/C++ for Windows 3.0

Installing Borland C/C++ on your system hard disk is perhaps the simplest task you will ever accomplish on your computer. Simply insert the installation disk and type A:>**INSTALL**. Then just follow the directions on your screen.

Installing C/C++ for Windows 3.0, however, is slightly more complicated. Before going into the installation requirements, I'll begin by explaining that installation is optional because the C/C++ compiler can be executed from DOS or from MS/Windows using the File Manager without installing C/C++ as an MS/Windows application. Also, MS/Windows application programs can be compiled under either DOS or Windows, though any compiled MS/Windows program can only be executed within the Window environment. Non-Windows programs can, of course, be compiled and executed in the normal fashion. As an alternative, any program can be compiled using the command-line compiler; using either BCC for 8086/80286 systems or BCCX for '386 protected-mode. For the present, however, I will assume that you, like most users, prefer to use the Borland C/C++ Integrated Development Environment for both your Windows and non-Windows applications and, consequently, would like to have the compiler readily available from within MS/Windows.

Protected Mode C++

Windows 3.0 provides three modes of operation: Real, Standard, and 386 Enhanced. Further, Windows 3.0 detects its hardware environment and loads the mode appropriate for the hardware. That mode, however, may not necessarily be the mode appropriate for your requirements.

For computers with less than 1 MB of RAM, Windows automatically loads itself in Real mode providing full compatibility with Windows 2.x applications. Windows can be called in Real mode on any system by appending the /r switch as:

```
C:\WIN >win \r.
```

For 80286 CPU systems with more than 1 MB and less than 2 MB of RAM, Windows 3.0 loads in Standard mode providing access to extended memory. Standard mode can also be used with 80386/486 systems regardless of the amount of memory installed and is called as:

```
C:\WIN >win \s.
```

For 80386/486 systems with more than 2 MB of RAM, Windows loads by default in 386 Enhanced mode, using the 80386's virtual memory capability. The Borland C++ IDE compiler (BC or BCX), however, does not operate under Windows Enhanced mode and either Real or Standard modes must be selected before the IDE can operate.

For further details on Windows 3.0, refer to *Windows 3.0: A Definitive Guide For DOS Users*, by Michael Vose, available from Addison-Wesley Publishing Company.

Installing C++ as a Windows Application

While Borland C/C++ is not an MS/Windows application (i.e., it does not operate within MS/Windows except under the DOS shell) C/C++ can still be installed as a Windows application. To do so conveniently requires three steps: first, create a .PIF file, second, modify the Windows SETUP.INF file to recognize the C/C++ application and, third, call the Windows SetUp Applications utility.

The first step, creating a .PIF file, is accomplished within MS/Windows by calling the PIF Editor from the Accessories menu. The PIF Editor is shown in

Figure 1-1. Only a few items are required to create the .PIF file: the location of the C/C++ compiler, the icon/window title desired, and the startup directory. The startup directory may be the same as the compiler directory or may be any other drive and/or directory desired. The **Advanced** button at the bottom of the window calls a second window with a variety of options and settings, but these may be left as the default values/settings for most applications.

Figure 1-1: Creating a .PIF File

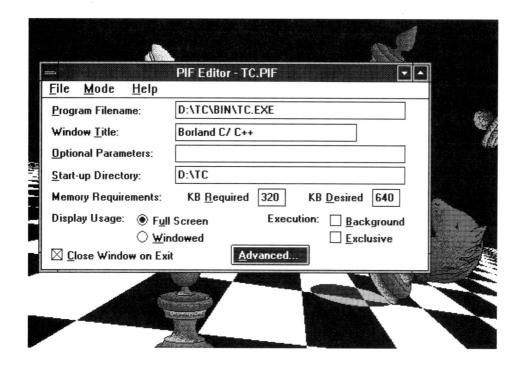

The second step is to insert a line in the SETUP.INF file which is located in the d:\WINDOWS\SYSTEM directory. SETUP.INF contains a variety of information which is used to install MS/Windows and to install Window applications. Beginning around line 470, you should find the notation [pif]. Following this line, each line item refers to an application that may be present on your system and can be installed as a Window (or non-Window) application. Unfortunately, Borland C/C++ is not included in this list. A correction, however, can easily provide it as shown in Figure 1-2. The options settings are explained in detail in the MS/Windows documentation and may be modified as desired. The settings shown here are adequate for normal operations.

The third step is to call Window's SetUp Applications utility to install the compiler as a non-windows application. For this utility, begin by calling the Main menu from the Program Manager and select the Windows Setup utility. Next, from the Windows Setup utility, select the Options menu item. Then select the SetUp Applications item from the submenu.

Figure 1-2: Excerpt from SETUP.INF

```
The [pif] list begins at approximately        background bit set
line 470 in the SETUP.INF file located           faste_paste
in d:\WINDOWS\SYSTEM                                 com
                                              graphics
                                     minimum memory
                  optional command-line paramters
description              exe file        pifname

"Sidekick Plus",       skplus.com,     skplus.pif,  "", 384, g, n, n, n, 2
"Borland C/C++",       bcx.exe         bc.pif,      "", 320, n, n, p, n, 6
"Turbo Pascal",        turbo.exe       turbo.pif,   "", 320, g, n, p, n, 6
"Ventura Publisher",   vp.bat,         vp.pif,      "", 512, g, n, n, n, 2
```

At this point, you may select either the drive where the C/C++ application is installed, or all drives so that the SetUp Applications utility will search for programs that match the list in the SETUP.INF file. When finished, a display appears similar to Figure 1-3.

The SetUp Applications display will probably provide a rather lengthy list of applications found (left window), many of which you will not want installed as Windows applications. This list may even include some complete surprises. For example, the fortran compiler which MS/Windows appears to believe it has found is, actually, an entirely unrelated program and, only coincidentally, has a file name which SETUP.INF identifies as a fortran compiler.

Unless you are accidentally fortunate, the best approach at this time is to select those applications which you know that you wish to install, beginning with the C/C++ compiler. At the same time, it's also a good idea to go ahead and install the Turbo Debugger (TDW), the Whitewater Resource Toolkit (which may be incorrectly identified as *Actor Version 3.0*) and any other utilities which you may need. The WRT will definitely be needed and will be covered in Part 2 of this book.

Alternatively, any of these can be installed at a later time.

Select one or more items in the left-hand window, then click on the Add button. Items in the right-hand window can also be deselected. After making your selections, click on the **Ok** button (or press Enter) and the selected items will be installed as Window (or non-Window) applications.

Figure 1-3: The SetUp Applications Display

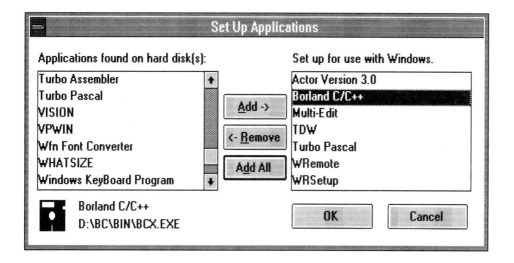

When installation is complete, the selected items will appear in the Windows Applications menu (not shown) or the Non-Windows Applications menu (Figure 1-4). The nature of the application determines which of the two menus an item appears on. But, if desired, applications can be moved between the two menus using MS/Windows facilities or by simply clicking on the icon and dragging it to the desired menu window. For example, instead of the C/C++ application appearing in the Non-Windows Applications menu and the WRT and Turbo Debugger applications appearing in the Windows Applications menu, you may prefer to create a new Windows menu entitled Compilers (Figure 1-5) in which all three of these applications can be installed.

Also, since most non-Windows applications lack custom icon images, default icon images are used as shown in Figure 1-4. However, a custom icon for Borland C/C++ can be installed as shown presently.

Still, at this point, Borland C/C++ is ready for use under either Windows or under DOS .

Figure 1-4: Non-Window Applications with Icons

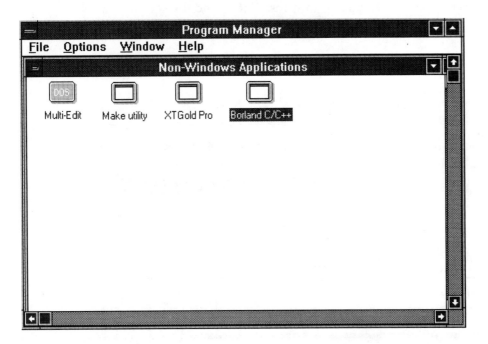

Installing A New Icon

Even when an application runs in the DOS window and lacks a screen icon for display in the Windows menu, the Icon Editor in the Resource Toolbox can be used to design any icon desired. Some DOS applications do provide icons , as Borland C/C++ does, as a separate .ICO file.

In either case, however, the icon must be assigned to the application in the menu. This is accomplished by clicking once on the current application icon in the menu.

Figure 1-5: Compilers Menu

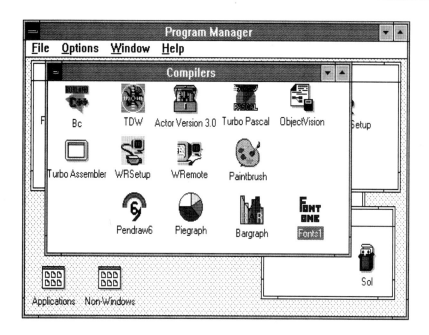

Next, select **Files/Properties**, from the Program Manager menubar, and click on the Change **I**con button. This will call a dialog box for the application showing the current icon, if any, and, in an edit box, the drive/path/name (if applicable) of the icon file (.ICO).

If the icon displayed is the default DOS box icon, then click the View **N**ext button and enter the drive/path/filename specification for the .ICO file desired.

Click on the OK button until you are back to the Program Manager menu and the new icon image should be displayed.

In other cases, some Windows applications may have more than one icon available(within the .EXE program, not as separate .ICO files) and these can be selected simply by clicking the View **N**ext button.

In any case, whether external .ICO files are supplied, internal icon images are available, or you have created your own custom icon image, these are certainly much more convenient for visual identification than a string of DOS icons with small labels below.

The choice is yours.

Incidental note: This is also your opportunity—if desired—to change the caption displayed below the icon as, for example, changing "Actor Version 3.0" to read "WRT" or "Resources" or "Toolkit".

QEMM-386 Version 5.1

QEMM is an expanded memory manager. Among other features, on 80386/80486 systems, QEMM permits loading TSR utilities into high memory (the memory addresses between 640K and 1024K). While this area in memory is traditionally reserved for system hardware, normally only a portion of this area is actually used. Unused space is available where TSRs such as your mouse driver, ANSI.SYS and other drivers or utilities can be relocated, freeing memory in the lower 640K for use by your principal applications, such as your compiler(s), or by Windows.

Unfortunately, earlier versions of QEMM-386 have not been 100% compatible with Windows, thus necessitating provisions for alternate boot configurations for DOS and Windows 3.0.

Quarterdeck has recently released a new version of QEMM-386 which is compatible with Windows 3.0. Upgrading to QEMM-386 verion 5.1 (or later) offers all the advantages of loading DOS TSRs in high memory and, at the same time, does not require separate boot configurations for DOS and Windows.

In most cases, QEMM-386 will install itself in a fully Windows 3.0 compatible format and, together with the OPTIMIZE utility, requires little or no revision for appropriate operation.

Unfortunately, most cases are not all cases and, depending on your video system, you may, get the message: *Cannot run Windows because of video device conflict* when you attempt to load Windows 3.0,

There is also a solution. You may revise your CONFIG.SYS file to exclude specific memory areas from use by QEMM-386's memory management. As installed, the first line in CONFIG.SYS should look something like this:

```
DEVICE=C:\QEMM\QEMM386.SYS RAM
```

In the case of a video conflict with Windows 3.0, Quarterdeck suggests the following revision:

```
DEVICE=C:\QEMM\QEMM386.SYS RAM X=0000-3FFF X=A000-C7FF
X=F000-FFFF
```

The balance of the CONFIG.SYS file might look like this:

```
BREAK=ON
STACKS=0,0
BUFFERS=25 /X
FILES=30
LASTDRIVE=E
SHELL=C:\DOS\COMMAND.COM /P /E:256
DEVICE=C:\QEMM\LOADHI.SYS /R:1 C:\DOS\ANSI.SYS
INSTALL=C:\QEMM\LOADHI.COM /TSR /R:1 C:\DOS\FASTOPEN.EXE
C:=(50,25)
DEVICE=C:\QEMM\LOADHI.SYS /R:1 D:\WINDOWS\SMARTDRV.SYS 256
```

Note that HIMEM.SYS (installed by Windows) has been removed and the memory sizes used by SMARTDRV.SYS have been reduced.

These are optional changes, however, and the important revisions are the eXclusion statements in the first line. Three areas in the first megabyte of memory have been excluded as:

- X=0000-3FFF—optional, this excludes the Low Memory area which is normally used by DOS, in part, for system services and, in part, by applications. This does not effect QEMM-386 or LOADHI operations in any fashion and does not effect normal DOS operations but may prevent some Windows conflicts.
- X=A000-C7FF—essential, this excludes the entire video memory area. This blanket exclusion does cover some regions which might otherwise be used by LOADHI to relocate some TSR utilities. It does, specifically, prevent the video conflict which may prevent Windows 3.0 from loading.

You might fine-tune this by using the Manifest utility from Quarterdeck to examine exactly which areas within this range are used and test different exclusions against both normal DOS operation and for conflicts with Windows 3.0.

- X=F000-FFFF—optional, this excludes the high memory area normally used by the system ROM (ROM data/code may be remapped to this area in RAM for improved speed). This exclusion may prevent some Windows 3.0 conflicts.

Table 1-1 shows a typical usage for the first meg of RAM as reported by Quarterdeck's MANIFEST, with additional notes on excluded memory areas.

Table 1-1:   Memory Usage (DOS Active)

System Memory Area	Memory Size	Description	Notes
0000 - 003F	1K	Interrupt Area	*exclude X=0000-3FFF*
0040 - 004F	0.3K	BIOS Data Area	*excluded*
0050 - 006F	0.5K	System Data	*excluded*
0070 - 0CEF	50K	DOS (ver 4.01)	*excluded*
0CF0 - 1720	40K	Program Area	*excluded*
1721 - 9FFF	547K	[Available]	*excluded through 3FFF*
Conventional memory ends at 640K (9FFF:0000)			
A000 - AFFF	64K	VGA Graphics	*exclude X=A000-C7FF*
B000 - B7FF	32K	Unused	*excluded*
B800 - BFFF	32K	VGA Text	*excluded*
C000 - C5FF	24K	Video ROM	*excluded*
C600 - C7FF	8K	Unused	*excluded*
C800 - DFFF	96K	High RAM	*available*
E000 - EFFF	64K	Page Frame	
F000 - FFFF	64K	System ROM	*exclude X=F000-FFFF*

Using C/C++ — Windows or DOS

Now that I've shown you how to install Borland C/C++ as a Windows application, I'd like to briefly explain the tradeoffs between running the compiler under DOS and running the compiler under Windows.

For many programmers, DOS and Windows are almost entirely separate operating systems, requiring a warm reboot to switch between the two configurations. This situation can occur because of several reasons; but the most common is usually that a 386 memory manager such as QEMM-386 is used which is incompatible with Windows. Happily, these conflicts will be corrected in the near future as new memory-handling standards are written by joint agreement between most, if not all, of the major software developers in the industry.

Still, these conflicts do exist with DOS and Windows, particularly with more sophisticated systems, being treated as separate configurations,imposing a minimum of inconvenience when switching between the two. Those of you who are experienced Turbo C/C++ users and are familiar with Borland's Integrated Development Environment are most likely accustomed to the convenience of executing and testing applications from within the compiler. If, of course, your previous experience is limited to using a command-line compiler and .MAK files, then you may not feel so inconvenienced when creating MS/Windows applications. The point is that any window application program can be compiled from the DOS environment. The only restriction is that the MS/Windows application cannot be run from the DOS environment or from within the C/C++ IDE, whether the compiler is being run under DOS or under Windows' DOS shell.

With the C/C++ compiler installed as a non-Windows application, the compiler is available to make revisions or corrections to the source code for a Windows application and to recompile the application without leaving Windows. The inconvenience of switching to a DOS shell for development and then back to Windows-proper for testing the application is minimal and certainly a minor trade-off measured against the convenience of using the Borland C++ IDE for program development. The primary trade-off, however, is speed because the compile/link process under DOS is considerably faster than under Windows (enhanced mode, specifically). For an example, an application project requiring some 16.20 seconds to compile and link under DOS (on a 33 Mhz 386 system), required 261.63 seconds to compile and link under Windows, some sixteen times slower.

Of course, only minimal imagination is required to surmise that some future version of Borland C/C++ will operate directly as a Windows application with all of the same conveniences that have been considered commonplace under DOS with Turbo C/C++. But, for the moment, even these minimal inconveniences remain a tremendous improvement over command-line compilers.

To demonstrate just how much more convenient the Borland IDE really is, the first Window program is presented in both command-line and IDE compiler formats.

Environments and Terminology

While Windows 3.0 operates within the DOS environment, DOS and Windows will often be contrasted within this book as though they were separate and independent operating environments . While technically inaccurate, this contrast is used to recognize the effective reality as it affects users, programmers, and programming language conventions.

Compiling Programs for Windows

Because compiling for the Windows environment is different than compiling for DOS, an explanation of the steps required to compile a Windows program is presented before introducing a program example.

Figure 1-6 diagrams the steps required to compile a Windows application. If you are familiar with OS/2 programming, this diagram may strike a chord in your memory. This is not accidental; OS/2 and Windows programming have a lot of similarities.

Figure 1-6: Steps in Compiling a Windows Application

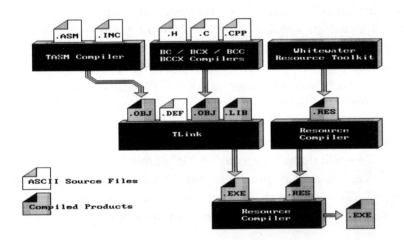

The first step in compiling a Windows application involves a .C or .CPP source file and a .H header file which BCC (or BCCX) will compile to a .OBJ file. Or, using the IDE compiler, BC, or BCX, the .H header file will be omitted. And, optionally, .OBJ files can also be compiled by TASM from .ASM and .INC source files. Once the .OBJ file(s) are created, TLINK is invoked together with the .DEF file and library file(s) to create an .EXE program.

Up to this point, this process should be familiar to all C/C++ programmers. For Windows, the .EXE file exists, and might even execute, but the process is not finished.

This brings us to the second leg of the compiler process which begins with WRT (Whitewater Resource Toolkit). WRT will be explained in detail in Part 2 of this book. For the moment, WRT is used to create window icons, bitmapped images, menus, resource and dialog script files, and application hotkey assignments. And, while many, though not all, of these resources could be created by writing ASCII text source files, WRT provides considerable convenience and saves more than a little time in development as an interactive utility for creating and testing resources.

The .RC resource file created by WRT is compiled to a .RES file (roughly the equivalent of an .EXE file) created by the .RC resource compiler before the resource compiler is invoked a second time to combine the .EXE and .RES files, thus producing an executable Windows application program.

The .MAK file, which normally provides the instructions for compiling the various sections, can be omitted entirely when using the Borland C/C++ IDE. The IDE compiler can handle this entire process, including recompiling and updating any necessary program segments, without separate Make instructions.

Aside from this introductory overview of the compiler process, this will be the last time you need to be concerned with the multiple compiler steps; unless, of course, you prefer to use the command-line compiler, BCC, instead of the integrated compiler version, BC. Still, there may be occasions when memory requirements imposed by very large programs require using the command-line compiler. For most purposes, the BC/BCX compiler is considerably more convenient and will be more than adequate for all of the examples in this book.

WinHello — An Introductory Windows Program

Traditionally, a "Hello, World" message has been the introductory C example. For Windows, however, the traditional example will still serve as an example but will be somewhat longer than usual, requiring more like 70 lines instead of the customary half-dozen lines of source code.

In both the traditional example, "Hello.C", and the new Windows version, "WinHello.C", the program objective is quite simple: to write a message to the screen. And, for the traditional version, this is a simple task requiring little more than a *printf* statement. In the traditional environment, irrespective of the operating system, any application program was considered to own the entire system, whether the output device was a teletype, printer, or CRT.

With Windows, however, the output device is a shared display. Any application, not just the present example, has to share the display (as well as other system resources) with all other active applications. The principal difference in size between the traditional and Windows examples is simply the overhead necessary for coexistence in a multi-tasking environment.

In the traditional "Hello.C" program, the program consisted of a single main procedure with a single simple instruction:

```
main()
{   printf( 'Hello, World' );   }
```

In traditional C programming, the entry point for a program has always been titled *main*; but, for Windows, the entry point is now titled *WinMain* and begins with four parameters supplied by Windows:

```
int PASCAL WinMain( HANDLE hInstance,
                    HANDLE hPrevInstance,
                    LPSTR lpszCmdParam, int nCmdShow )
```

The calling parameters are actually supplied by the start-up code segment which is supplied by the C/C++ compiler. But, this definition can be considered standard for all Windows programs, using the PASCAL calling sequence and returning an integer termination message to the start-up code. The type identifiers for the four calling parameters, together with notational conventions, identifiers, and Windows-specific data types and data structures, will be explained shortly. The more general structure of the program will be discussed first.

The four calling parameters for the *WinMain* procedure begin with the *Hinstance* parameter which is a unique identifier referred to as the "instance handle" and uniquely identifies a specific program instance under Windows. Unlike the conventional DOS environment, where only one program (TSRs excepted) can be operating at any time, several separate instances of many programs can be operating simultaneously under Windows, and, therefore, require unique identification supplied by the Windows system. This is comparable to a "task ID" or "process ID" commonly used in multitasking operating systems.

The second parameter, *hPrevInstance* (previous instance), is the identifier of the most recent instance of an application which is currently running. Of course, if no other instances are operating, then a null or 0 parameter argument will be supplied. Usage for this parameter will be demonstrated momentarily.

The *lpszCmdParam* parameter is a long or far pointer to a null-terminated (ASCIIZ) string that contains any command-line parameters passed to this program instance. These parameters could be supplied through the Run dialog box invoked from the Program Manager or the File Manager, or could be included in the SetUp.INF instructions discussed previously. In most Windows applications, command-line parameters are avoided in favor of interactive dialog boxes within the program itself, but provisions still exist for this format.

The final entry parameter is *nCmdShow*, which is an integer message argument provided by the calling application; normally Windows itself. This parameter indicates whether the newly launched program will be displayed as a normal window or will initially be minimized. While the application instance does not normally need to test the value of this parameter, the two usual messages are SW_SHOWNORMAL (value 1) or SW_SHOWMINNOAC-TIVE (value 7), both of which are defined in Windows.H.

Within the *WinMain* procedure, four local variables are defined:

```
{
    static  char  szAppName[] = "WinHello";
    HWND          hWnd;
    MSG           msg;
    WNDCLASS      wc;
```

The *szAppName* is a string variable with the application class name; *hWnd* is a window handle; *msg* is a message variable; and *wc* is a window class structure defined in Windows.H as:

```
typedef struct tagWNDCLASS
    ( WORD       style;
      LONG       ( FAR PASCAL *lpfnWndProc ) ( );
      int        cbClsExtra;
      int        cbWndExtra;
```

```
    HANDLE    hInstance;
    HICON     hIcon;
    HCURSOR   hCursor;
    HBRUSH    hbrBackground;
    LPSTR     lpszMenuName;
    LPSTR     lpszClassName;
)   WNDCLASS;
```

The Windows environment manages multiple application or application instances by passing messages to specific application instances. Before Windows can pass messages, each application type, not each instance, must be registered as a *window class*. This identifies the application procedure that processes messages sent to the application window.

Registering a Window Class

In *WinMain*, if no previous instance of this application has registered as a window class (i.e., *hPrevInstance* is null or 0) then initial values are assigned to the WNDCLASS structure (*wc*).

Note: The second and last fields in this record structure are the most important, with the second field providing the address of the window procedure used for all window creation and window message handling. The last field supplies the name of the window class, which is normally the same as the program name. The remaining eight fields describe characteristics used for each window instance.

```
if( ! hPrevInstance )
{
    wc.style          = CS_HREDRAW | CS_VREDRAW;
```

The *style* record field is assigned two "class style" identifiers which are OR'd bit-wise. The CS_ identifiers are defined in Windows.H as 16-bit constants with one flag bit set in each. The CS_HREDRAW and CS_VREDRAW flags indicate that window instances are to be completely redrawn anytime the horizontal or vertical window size changes. When WinHello is resized, for example, the display is redrawn with the message string recentered in the new window display.

```
wc.lpfnWndProc    = WndProc;
```

The *WndProc* procedure handles all window messages that are sent to instances of this window type. The type prefix *lpfn* identifies this field as a "long pointer to function". These prefix conventions are provided for the benefit of programmers and do not affect the compiler; except, of course, that these particular record fields are predefined.

The following two record fields are integer fields that are reserved for the application's use, but since they are unused here, they are initialized as 0:

```
wc.cbClsExtra = 0;
wc.cbWndExtra = 0;.
```

The *cb* prefix stands for "count of bytes".

The *hInstance* field is simply the instance handle of the program that was also one of the parameters passed to *WinMain*:

```
wc.hInstance     = hInstance;
```

The *hIcon* and *hCursor* fields accept values returned by the *LoadIcon* and *LoadCursor* procedures and, for the moment, use the default IDI_APPLICA-TION icon (a white square with a black border) and the default IDC_ARROW cursor (the slanted arrow cursor):

```
wc.hIcon = LoadIcon( NULL, IDI_APPLICATION );
wc.hCursor = LoadCursor( NULL, IDC_ARROW );.
```

Later, custom icon and mouse cursor images will be introduced, but defaults are used here for simplicity .

The *h* prefix in the preceding three fields is simply shorthand for handle.

The *hbrBackground* field controls the background color and pattern for the client area of each application instance:

```
wc.hbrBackground=GetStockObject(WHITE_BRUSH);
```

The *hbr* prefix stands for "handle to brush" where brush is a graphics term referring to the pattern of pixel colors used to fill an area. Standard or stock brushes defined by Windows will be discussed later.

Since WinHello has no menu, the *lpszMenuName* field is assigned a null value:

```
wc.lpszMenuName  = NULL;.
```

lpszClassName, the last field in this structure, is the name of the windows class and is normally the same as the application name as stored in the *szappname* variable:

```
wc.lpszClassName = szAppName;.
```

After the values are assigned, the *RegisterClass* function is called with a pointer to the structure *wc*:

```
    RegisterClass( &wc );
}
```

Subsequent instances of the application will not need to register as window classes because the first class registered (and the initial values) are available to all class instances.

Creating an Application Window

While registering the window class has defined several general characteristics for all windows of this class (i.e., all instances of this application), the window is not yet created; only the default characteristics are established. Registering the window class is done only by the first instance of the application and is not called by any subsequent instances. Every window instance needs to call the *CreateWindow* function to create its own actual screen window, while the *Hwnd* window handle returned will be subsequently used to address operations within this window instance. Unlike *RegisterClass*, *CreateWindow* is called with a parameter list instead of a record structure. The first two parameters are the application name (*szAppName* or window class name) and the window caption which will appear at the top of the window:

```
hWnd = CreateWindow(
      szAppName,
      ""Hello, World - Windows Style"",
```

The third parameter is a window style message which, for most applications, will be WS_OVERLAPPEDWINDOW:

```
WS_OVERLAPPEDWINDOW.
```

The next four parameters are the initial X and Y axis window positions that specify the position of the upper-left corner of the window, and the X and Y axis window sizes. The CW_USEDEFAULT message instructs Windows to use the default values for an overlapped window:

```
CW_USEDEFAULT,
CW_USEDEFAULT,
CW_USEDEFAULT,
CW_USEDEFAULT,
```

These default conditions position successive overlapped windows at stepped horizontal and vertical offsets from the upper-left of the display with the right window border at the right of the screen and the bottom border above the icon display area. Thus, with several sequential instances, each subsequent window will be somewhat smaller but with the lower right corner of each window at the same position on the screen.

The next two parameters are null in this case because this application window is not associated with a parent window. If, on the other hand, this window were a child-window, then the parent window handle would be used so that the child window would appear on the surface of the parent. For an example of child windows, call the Windows' File Manager program and observe the layout of the child window as you step down through a directory tree. Since this application has no menu, a second null parameter is passed for the window menu handle:

```
NULL,
NULL,
```

The program instance handle should never be passed as a null parameter but is always passed as the *hInstance* parameter which was originally passed to *WinMain* by the setup code:

```
hInstance,
```

The final parameter is another null value in this example but, in other cases, would be a pointer to some type of data that might be used by the application window or by subsequent processes:

```
NULL  );
```

After *CreateWindow* has been called, the application window is created internally in Windows but has not yet been written to the screen display. And, therefore, the returned *hWnd* window handle is used in calling the *Show-Window* procedure together with the *nCmdShow* parameter which was passed as a calling parameter to *WinMain*:

```
ShowWindow( hWnd, nCmdShow );
```

If the value of *nCmdShow* is SW_SHOWMINNOACTIVE (7), the application window is initially displayed as an icon.

The *UpdateWindow* procedure is called to update the client area of the window:

```
UpdateWindow( hWnd );
```

This is necessary because *ShowWindow* does not repaint the interior of the window, only the frame, sidebars (if any), and captions, and it is left to the *UpdateWindow* call to create the interior of the window display.

This completes the process of creating the window and updating the screen display. The message "Hello, World!" is finally displayed. This, however, is not the end of *WinMain*'s task processing.

The Message Handling Loop

The *WinMain* function still has one very important task required for all window applications: the message handling loop, which processes keyboard and mouse events.

Windows creates and manages a message queue for each current Windows program instance. Thus, when a keyboard or mouse event occurs, Windows translates the event into a message value that is inserted into the program's message and must be subsequently retrieved by the application for handling.

The message handling loop begins by calling the *GetMessage* function which, as long as the retrieved message is anything except WM_QUIT (0x0012), will return a non-zero value, and causes the loop to continue:

```
while( GetMessage( &msg, NULL, 0, 0 ) )
    {
```

The GetMessage Function

The syntax for the *GetMessage* function is defined as:

```
BOOL GetMessage( lpMsg, hwnd, wMsgFilterMin, wMsgFilterMax )
```

In most cases, only the first parameter is actually used and the remaining three are passed as NULL or zero.

The initial parameter returns a pointer to the message structure to be retrieved and, in most cases, will be passed on to the *TranslateMessage* and *DispatchMessage* functions. If no message is available, *GetMessage* yields control to other applications until a message becomes available. The second parameter is a window handle specifying the window whose messages are to be retrieved. When passed as NULL, as in the example, *GetMessage* retrieves messages for any window belonging to the application making the call. However, the *GetMessage* function does not retrieve messages for windows belonging to other applications.

The third and fourth parameters provide a filter capability restricting the message types that are returned. When *wMsgFilterMin* and *wMsgFilterMax* are both zero, *GetMessage* returns all available messages (no filtering is performed). Alternatively, the constants WM_KEYFIRST and WM_KEYLAST can be used as filter values to retrieve all messages related to keyboard input and the constants WM_MOUSEFIRST and WM_MOUSELAST can be used to retrieve all mouse-related messages.

The return value specifies the outcome of the function. It is nonzero if a message other than WM_QUIT is retrieved and zero if the WM_QUIT message is retrieved. This return value is normally used to decide whether or not to terminate the application's main loop and exit the program.

In addition to yielding control to other applications when no messages are available, the *GetMessage* and *PeekMessage* functions yield control when WM_PAINT or WM_TIMER messages for other tasks are available. Also, the message functions *GetMessage*, *PeekMessage*, and *WaitMessage* provide other applications with their share of the CPU time to execute. If your application does not call any of these functions for long periods of time, other applications cannot run.

In the example program, however, as long as the message (*msg*) is not WM_QUIT, the message value is passed first to Windows' *TranslateMessage* procedure for any keystroke handling that may be specific to this application, and then to Windows' *DispatchMessage* handler for further dispatching to the next appropriate message handling procedure:

```
    TranslateMessage( &msg );
    DispatchMessage( &msg );
}
```

When the message processing loop terminates, the *wParam* from the message record is returned to the calling application, which, in this case, is Windows itself.

```
    return( msg.wParam );
}
```

Message Programming or Event-Driven Programming

Message programming, often referred to as event-driven programming, is not new, but may still be unfamiliar to many programmers because previous appearances in OS/2, in earlier versions of Windows and, most recently, in Borland's Turbo Vision have received only limited exposure. Whether you refer to this process as message programming or event-driven programming, it is a concept that is an integral part of Windows programming and is also becoming increasingly common in non-Windows applications as well.

In its simplest form, message programming is a process by which various subapplications communicate with each other. In Windows, it is the process by which Windows itself is able to manage a multitasking system and share keyboard, mouse, and other input information between different applications or application instances. Thus, in Windows, keyboard and mouse events are received by the actual applications but are intercepted by Windows and translated, if necessary, by the *TranslateMessage* procedure and parcelled out in the form of message records by the *DispatchMessage* procedure to the appropriate processes.

This process is not limited to the keyboard and mouse events, but also includes all input devices as well as messages that can be generated by application processes and addressed either to other applications, child processes or, most frequently, to Windows itself. Since an abstract description of this process does not really give you much of an idea of how to use message programming, the real explanations will be reserved for demonstration with hands-on examples.

One point to notice right now is that the *WinMain* procedure does not at any point call or pass information to the *WndProc* function in WinHello where much of the actual processing of this program occurs. And, in subsequent examples, this divergence from conventional programming practices will be even more obvious as large sections of the application execute with no apparent connection within the program structure.

Before going further into how messages are handled, even in this very simple example, it will help to see how messages are organized.

The Message Record Structure

The MSG message type is a record structure defined in Windows.H as:

```
typedef struct tagMSG
   (  HWND   hWnd;
      WORD   message;
      WORD   mParam;
      LONG   lParam;
      DWORD  time;
      POINT  pt;    )   MSG;
```

The POINT data type is a second structure, also defined in Windows.H as:

```
typedef struct tagPOINT
   (  int  x;
      int  y;   )  POINT;
```

The following message (event) fields are used:

- *hWnd*—the handle of the window where the message is directed. In WinHello, this is the handle of the client window; but, if multiple windows have been created in other applications, this is the handle of the selected or active window or, for mouse events, the window where the mouse cursor appears.

- *message*—a sixteen-bit value identifying the message. Constants corresponding to all message values are defined in Windows.H and begin with the WM_ prefix ("window message"). For a mouse left-button

event, for example, the message value might be WM_LBUTTON-
DOWN.

- *wParam*—a sixteen-bit message parameter with the value and meaning dependent on the specific event message.
- *lParam*—a 32-bit message parameter with the value and meaning dependent on the specific event message.
- *time*—the time the message was placed in the message queue.
- *pt*—the mouse coordinates at the time the message was placed in the message queue (irrespective of the message event type or origin).

As you will soon see, many or most of these event messages will normally be handled by Windows' default message handler. Even when a program exercises specific message handling provisions, many of these message fields may quite validly be ignored as irrelevant to the response; or, in other cases, they may be quite relevant.

The WndProc Procedure

The *WndProc* procedure in WinHello.C provides local response to two event messages: WM_PAINT and WM_DESTROY. All other event messages are handled, by default, by Windows itself.

One very important aspect of Windows programming, however, is that in any application there is no direct connection between the *WndProc* procedure and the *WinMain* procedure. While this is completely contrary to conventional programming practices, where one routine calls another routine, passing parameters and accepting responses; in an event-driven, multi-tasking environment, this lack of direct connection is perfectly normal because there is an indirect connection!

In the *WinMain* procedure, the address of the *WndProc* subroutine was passed to Windows as:

```
wc.lpfnWndProc = WndProc;.
```

Given this address, Windows is able to call *WndProc* directly, passing event messages to *WndProc* in the form of four parameters:

```
long FAR PASCAL WndProc( HWND hWnd,    WORD message,
                         WORD wParam, LONG lParam )
```

The four calling parameters begin with the window handle and identify the window to which the message applies. In the case of WinHello, of course, there is only one window involved; but this will not always be the case. The second calling parameter is obviously the 16-bit value identifying the event message, while the third and fourth parameters are the 16- and 32-bit message parameters described previously. The *time* and *pt* (mouse) portions of the message record are not passed to *WndProc*, but are used by Windows to determine where the specific message should be addressed and to resolve any conflicts that might occur over the order of events.

WndProc declares three local variables as:

```
{
    HDC          hdc;
    PAINTSTRUCT  ps;
    RECT         rect;
```

The *hdc* variable is short for **h**andle **d**evice **c**ontext and provides a handle to the output device; in this case, the CRT. The *ps* variable contains information for painting the screen and will be discussed later. The *rect* variable is a rectangular structure with four integer fields: *left, top, right* and *bottom*.

Most messages that might be directed to the WinHello program can be handled by default processing (i.e., handled by Windows). This includes resizing and repositioning the application window, reducing the application to an icon, or closing the application window. There are still two messages for which most applications must provide some specific handling: the WM_PAINT and WM_DESTROY messages. Within the WndProc procedure, a simple *switch* statement is used to process messages and provide the appropriate responses to each:

```
    switch( message )
    {
```

The first message that requires a response is the WM_PAINT message. This message is issued anytime an application window is moved, resized, restored from an icon, uncovered by a change in another application window, or anything else that invalidates the client area of the present application.

When WinHello's *style* field in the *winclass* structure was given the CS_HREDRAW and CS_VREDRAW flags, Windows was directed to invalidate the entire window anytime a size change occurred. This caused the

WM_PAINT message to be issued as an instruction to redraw the client window. Also, when an application window is reduced to an icon, the client area image information is not retained. In any graphic display environment, saving even a single screen image requires an excessive amount of memory. With multiple application windows, system memory could easily be exhausted if attempts are made to save screen images. In like fashion, when an application window is overlapped by another window, the overwritten portion of the screen is not saved. Instead, in any of these cases, when the application client window is revealed, moved, or resized, the WM_PAINT message is sent to the application as an instruction to update the contents of the invalid client window.

Updating the application window frame, captions, etc, is handled automatically by Windows without intervention by the application; but, at the same time, Windows erases the invalidated client window area by repainting the area using the brush specified in the *hbrBackground* field in WINCLASS.

Response to the WM_PAINT message always begins by calling *BeginPaint* which returns a handle to the output device (*hdc*) and loads the *ps* structure with information about the client area colors and brush information. The handle, *hdc*, will be released when finished by calling *EndPaint*.

```
case WM_PAINT:
    hdc = BeginPaint( hWnd, &ps );
    GetClientRect( hWnd, &rect );
```

After retrieving the device handle, the *GetClientRect* procedure is called to return the *rect* structure with coordinates for the client window. The *left* and *top* fields are returned as 0s and the *right* and *bottom* fields are returned as the current width and height of the client window (in pixels). Once the client window information is available, the next step is specific to the WinHello program. It consists of an instruction creating the display, in this case, using the *DrawText* instruction:

```
DrawText( hdc, "Hello, World!", -1, &rect,
          DT_SINGLELINE | DT_CENTER | DT_VCENTER );
```

DrawText is called beginning with the *hdc* variable which provides access to the display, then the string (text) to be drawn, followed by a third parameter, –1, which indicates that the string is null-terminated. The final parameter is a combination of flags defined in Windows.H which, in this case, instructs that the string should be written as a single line of text, centered vertically and horizontally.

The *EndPaint* procedure is called last to release the *hdc* and validate the restored client area, thus completing the response to the WM_PAINT message.

```
EndPaint( hWnd, &ps );
return( 0 );
```

The final *return(0)* instruction simply ends this *case* statement and returns processing to Windows. In other cases, instead of a *return*, a *break* may be used.

In all responses to the WM_PAINT message, the *BeginPaint*, *GetClientRec*, and *EndPaint* procedure calls are stock provisions even though the actual screen painting instructions vary according to the requirements of the application. The second message that all applications need to respond to is the WM_DESTROY message:

```
case WM_DESTROY:
    PostQuitMessage( 0 );
    return( 0 );
}
```

The stock response, however, is quite simple: calling *PostQuitMessage* to place a WM_QUIT message in the program's message queue. In response, the *GetMessage* provision in *WinMain* will receive a zero, allowing the loop to terminate and the program to exit.

Since the *switch..case* decision structure responds only to two of the possible messages that may be sent to the application's *WndProc* procedure for handling, a default alternative is required to insure correct processing. This default is provided along with a final instruction to first call the *DefWindow-Proc* function with the same four parameters that were initially passed to the *WndProc* procedure, and then to return the result to the Windows calling process:

```
return( DefWindowProc( hWnd, message, wParam, lParam ) );
}
```

This last provision should also be considered standard for all *WndProc* message handler procedures.

Notations, Constants, and Variables

Many OS/2 and Windows programmers use a variable naming convention commonly known as Hungarian notation, apocryphally named in honor of Microsoft programmer, Charles Simonyi.

With Hungarian notation, variable names begin with one or more lowercase letters that denote the variable data type, thus providing built-in identification. For example, the prefix *h* identifies a handle as in *hWnd* which is a handle to a window, while the prefix *lpsz* identifies a *long pointer* to a null-terminated string (ASCIIZ).

This inherent type notation helps to prevent errors caused by mismatched data types. Common prefixes are shown in Table 1-2.

Table 1-2: Hungarian Notation Conventions

Prefix	Data Type
b	BOOL (boolean, int)
by	BYTE (unsigned char)
c	char
cx, cy	short used as X or Y length
dw	DWORD (double word or unsigned long)
fn	function
h	handle
i	int
l	LONG
n	short or int
s	string
sz	ASCIIZ (null-terminated) string
w	WORD (unsigned int)
x, y	short used as X or Y coordinates

Windows also uses an extensive list of predefined constants that are employed as messages, flag values, or other operational parameters. These constant values are always uppercase and most include a two- or three-letter prefix set off by an underscore:

CS_HREDRAW	CS_VREDRAW	CW_USEDEFAULT
DT_CENTER	DT_SINGLELINE	DT_VCENTER
IDC_ARROW	IDI_APPLICATION	WM_DESTROY
WM_PAINT	WS_OVERLAPPEDWINDOW	

The prefix indicates the general category of the constant as shown in Table 1-3.

Table 1-3: Constant Prefix Identifiers

Prefix	Category
CS	class style
IDI	icon id
IDC	cursor id
WS	window style
CW	create window
WM	window message
DT	draw text

There are also several new data-type identifiers defined in Windows.H as shown in Table 1-4.

Table 1-4: Window Data Types

Data Type	Meaning
FAR	same as *far*
PASCAL	same as *pascal*
WORD	unsigned integer (16 bit)
DWORD	double word, unsigned long integer (32 bit)
LONG	signed long integer (32 bit)
LPSTR	long (far) pointer to char string

The five data structures displayed in Table 1-5, again defined in Windows.H, appear in the WinHello program.

Table 1-5: Five Window Structures

Structure	Meaning
MSG	message structure
PAINTSTRUCT	paint structure
PT	point structure (mouse position)
RECT	rectangle structure
WNDCLASS	window class structure

Four handles are also defined with uppercase identifiers as shown in Table 1-6.

Table 1-6: Four Handle Identifiers

Handle	Meaning
HANDLE	handle, generic
HWND	handle, window
HDC	handle, device context (CRT)
HBRUSH	handle, paint brush

A complete list of types, structures, constants, and macros declared in the Windows header file appears in Appendix A.

Using the Command-Line Compiler

For those who are dedicated to using the command-line compiler, compiling a Windows application in C/C++ is initially no different than compiling any other type of application, but, as shown Figure 1-6, does include a couple of additional steps.

First, of course, you must begin by creating the WinHello.C and Win-Hello.DEF files (complete listings follow). The command-line version of the C/C++ compiler is then invoked from either DOS or from Windows as:

```
C:\BC >bcc -W winhello.c.
```

Note: The **-W** directive calls for a Windows application. Other directives, in the form **-Wxxx**, provide the compiler with more specific instructions on compilation and code generation; for example, **-WD** creates a Windows .DLL file. A complete list of directives can be found in the *Borland C++ Version 2.0 User's Guide*.

The preceding command-line compiler directive compiles to a .EXE program. Sometimes, however, you may prefer to compile only to an .OBJ file, leaving the link operation for a separate step, which can be accomplished by including a **-c** directive in the original invocation.

If this is done, the linker can be invoked separately as:

```
C:\BC >TLINK /Tw /v /c:\bc\lib\cOws winhello, winhello, ,
c:\bc\lib\cwins c:\bc\lib\cs c:\bc\lib\import, winhello
```

Since the link instructions are too long to fit on screen, the command-line wraps to a second line.

The TLINK command-line is composed of link options followed by five groups of filenames (object files, execute files, map files, library files and definition files) with each group separated by a comma. Beginning with the link options, the **/Tw** command indicates that the link target is a Windows application, the **/v** instruction includes debugging information, and the **/c** instruction forces case recognition in public and external symbols.

The first group of filenames are the .OBJ files to be linked. C0WS is the initialization module for small memory models and should always be the first .OBJ. WinHello is the program module. The extension .OBJ is assumed in both cases.

The second group of filenames has only one file, WinHello, which is the file name desired for the executable file. The .EXE extension is assumed for execution files and .DLL for dynamic link libraries. (The .DEF file, introduced later, would include a LIBRARY statement to create a .DLL output file.)

The third group, omitted from this example, is the output .MAP file name. If no file name is specified, TLINK assumes the same name as the .EXE specification but with the .MAP extension. MAP files are created only if explicitly directed by a flag passed to TLINK.

The fourth group is a list of library files beginning with the CWINS.LIB small memory model run time library for Windows, CS.LIB as the regular run time library, and IMPORT.LIB providing access to the built-in Windows functions. The .LIB extension is assumed for all library files.

The fifth and final group consists of the module definition file(s), WinHello.DEF. The .DEF extension is assumed for all files.

After the application is linked to an .EXE file, the resource file must be compiled and then combined with the executable program. No resource file has been created for the WinHello program yet. Creating resources using WRT will be demonstrated later in Part 2. The resource compiler would be invoked as:

```
C:\BC >rc -R winhello.rc.
```

This will produce a .RES file with the **-R** option instructing not to combine the result with the corresponding .EXE file. The .RES file would be combined with the .EXE file in a separate step by invoking the RC resource compiler a second time as:

```
C:\BC >rc winhello.res winhello.exe.
```

These last two steps could be combined as a single operation,

```
C:\BC >rc winhello.
```

In this form, compiling and combining is accomplished in a single step and no file name is specified for the .EXE program, which is assumed to have the same name as the .RC file.

To load Windows and run the application, assuming that you are compiling from DOS, simply type:

```
C:\BC >win winhello.
```

The .DEF Module Definition File

The .DEF module definition file is, in part, redundant under Borland C/C++ because IDE options provide many of the settings previously controlled by parameters in the .DEF file. Still, the .DEF file is required for Windows programs. The structure is relatively simple, beginning with the NAME declaration and followed by an optional descriptive title:

```
NAME           WINHELLO
DESCRIPTION    "Windows Hello, World Program"
```

The EXETYPE statement declares this application to be a Windows program, while the STUB statement provides for inclusion of the stub program, WINSTUB.EXE.

```
EXETYPE        WINDOWS
STUB           "WINSTUB.EXE"
```

WINSTUB.EXE is a brief utility segment that does absolutely nothing under Windows but, under DOS displays a message informing the user that the application requires Windows for execution. Programs can be compiled and executed without including WINSTUB, but as a courtesy to the user, you should include this feature.

The next two instructions set flag conditions for CODE and DATA handling. These instructions state that the Code segment of the program should be preloaded, can be moved in memory as required, and can be discarded as necessary.

```
CODE        PRELOAD MOVEABLE DISCARDABLE
DATA        PRELOAD MOVEABLE MULTIPLE
```

For the Data segment, the MULTIPLE flag states that more than one copy of the data segment can be created for use by multiple copies of the program. In this case, the flag is definitely an affectation since the data is not altered by the program. The HEAPSIZE and STACKSIZE instructions state memory requirements, again, affectations for such a simple program.

```
HEAPSIZE    1024
STACKSIZE   8192
```

The EXPORTS statement lists application functions that are declared exportable and will be called by external applications; in this case, by Windows:

```
EXPORTS     WndProc
```

An IMPORTS statement may also be used to declare functions that will be imported from external libraries such as .DLL modules. The present applications, however, can be compiled without requiring a .DEF file by using the integrated compiler, BC or BCX, the **P**roject options, and by setting any special memory requirements through menu options.

Compiling with a MAKE File

Even if you prefer to use the command-line compiler, you would probably prefer to not type the full command line instructions for BCC and TLINK each time an application is compiled. The makefile, therefore, provides a way to automate this process.

The makefile, WinHello.MAK, is provided for the WinHello program and appears as:

```
winhello.exe : winhello.obj, winhello.def, winhello.res
    tlink /Tw /v /r /c:\bc\lib\c0ws winhello, \
        winhello, \
        , \
        c:\bc\lib\cwins c:\bc\lib\cs c:\bc\lib\import, \
        winhello
```

Since .MAK files contain instructions in the reverse order of their execution, the first instruction specifies the WinHello. , .DEF, .OBJ, and .RES files as source files for linking the final .EXE file. Presently, however, the .RES file should be omitted from actual practice. The second instruction, which is broken into several lines, provides the link instructions that specify the sources and directories for the command-line entry format as discussed previously.

The third instruction calls the resource compiler to combine the .RES and .EXE files, as:

```
rc winhello.res
```

But, before these instructions can be executed, the fourth instruction tells MAKE how to create .OBJ files from .C source files (or from .CPP source files). The options specified here are **-W** for a Windows application, **-c** calling for compile-only, **-ms** for the small memory model, and **-v** for debugging:

```
.c.obj :
    bcc -c -ms -W -v winhello.c
```

The final instruction, which is executed first, tells MAKE to create the required .RES file(s) from the .RC file(s) of the same name:

```
.rc.res :
    rc -r -ic:\bc\include winhello.rc
```

The **-r** command, as shown above, calls for compiling the resources, but without combining them with the executable file that has not yet been created. The WinHello.MAK file is invoked as:

```
C:\BC >make -fwinhello.mak
```

Using the Integrated Compiler

The simplest method of both compiling an application and of writing the source code file(s) for the application is using the Borland C/C++ IDE. The only drawback in using the IDE is that the total system memory is reduced and, therefore, some applications may need to use the command-line compiler (with or without .MAK files) for the actual compile/ link process. Most of the time, however, the IDE provides both speed in compiling, and convenience in correcting and debugging. Please note, however, that the .MAK file is unnecessary with the IDE and, instead, a .PRJ (project) file will be created within the IDE.

The first step is to start the compiler by invoking BC or BCX (protected mode version) from the DOS command-line or from Windows, and then enter the WinHello.C and WinHello.DEF files, as shown below, or you can copy these files from the program example disk which may be ordered using the coupon in the back of this book. Within the IDE, change to the directory where the .C and .DEF files are located using the **File/ Change dir** menu options.

To create the .PRJ file, select **Project/Open** project from the IDE menu, then enter *WinHello.PRJ* in the Project Name box. Press *Enter* or click on the **Ok** button to open a new project.

Now select **Project/ Add** item and enter *WinHello.** in the Name box to display a list of all WinHello files (see Figure 1-7). Select WinHello.C for the application (later, when resources are added, the WinHello.RC resource script file will also be selected) and close the Project dialog box when finished.

This is all that is necessary to create a Project file. But, what about the options that were set using the command-line entry or using the .MAK file? Particularly what about selecting Windows applications and .DLLs?

Under the IDE, instead of command-line flags, application selections are made through the Set Applications Options dialog box (see Figure 1-8) called from the IDE menu as **Options/ Applications**. Four buttons at the bottom of the dialog box select DOS Standard, DOS Overlay, Windows App, and Windows DLL, while a window in the dialog box displays settings for the Linker output, Prolog/Epilog, memory model, and other options. For the present, simply select Windows App.

To compile the application, from the IDE menu, select **Compile/Build**. That's it!

Of course, in order to test a Windows application after compiling, you will need to exit from Borland C/C++ and, from DOS, load Windows as:

```
win winhello.
```

If you are running the compiler from Windows' DOS Shell, then the application can be loaded in the same fashion as any Windows application, as, for example, through the File Manager.

Figure 1-7: Building a Project File

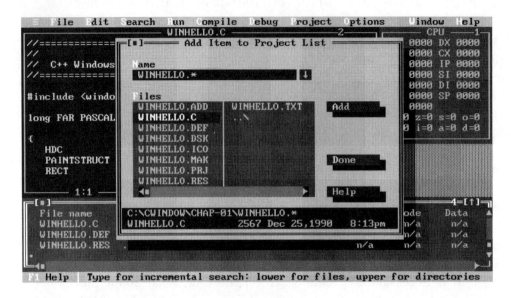

Figure 1-8: Setting the Primary Compiler Options

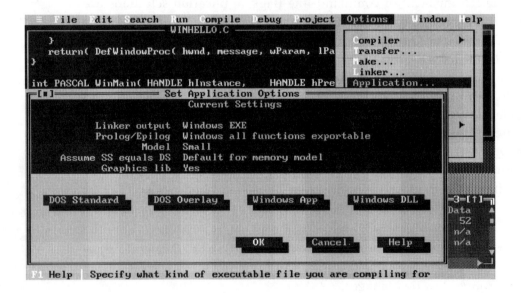

Other Compiler Options

The Set Applications Options dialog box provides a convenient means of switching between DOS, Overlay, Windows, and DLL compilation. But there are other compiler options that you will want to set for various applications. These options are controlled within the IDE through four menu selections:

- *Code Generation*—sets memory models, selects usage for pre-compiled headers, etc. Select **O**ptions/ **C**ompiler/ **C**ode generation.
- *Entry/Exit Code*—selects compiler options for prolog and epilog code generation and export options. Select **O**ptions/ **C**ompiler/ **E**ntry/Exit Code.
- *Make* —the Make dialog box, selected as **O**ptions/ **M**ake, offers access to the Generate Import Library options. This permits creating an import library for a DLL, making it possible to declare all of the functions in a DLL as imports to another model without using a module definition file.
- *Linker*—the Linker dialog box, selected as **O**ptions/ **L**inker, sets options for the output type desired from TLINK including the DOS .EXE, Windows .EXE, DOS overlay, Windows .DLL, and others.

These compiler options are discussed in greater detail in *Borland C++ User's Guide* but are mostly self-explanatory. However, familiarizing yourself with all of the menu options and dialog boxes presented by the IDE would be time well spent.

Summary

While Borland C/C++ provides its own installation utility that creates directories and copies file to your system, installing the compiler as a Windows application requires some special provisions in modifying the SETUP.INF file. But, the C/C++ compiler can be used to compile Windows applications even if it is run from DOS. Trade-offs between developing under DOS and under Windows were also discussed.

Following installation, an initial Window application, WinHello.C, was demonstrated together with an explanation of the principal features and basic requirements of Windows programming.

Three methods of compiling(using command-line instructions, using .MAK files, and using the IDE) offered a choice of processes for developing applications. In the future, however, when compiler operations are mentioned, the IDE will be the default development process for both Windows .EXE applications and .DLL files for the simple reason that the IDE is the most convenient and the fastest environment for development.

In subsequent chapters, the primary topics will show how to develop Windows applications, with compiler requirements occurring as a secondary topic only when relevant to the applications developed. At the same time, details on using the IDE Editor, performing file operations, and other peripheral features will not be discussed here but can be found in the *Borland C++ Version 2.0 User's Guide*.

While Borland C/C++ offers integrated debugging, since the compiler does not at this time operate as a Windows application, the integrated debugger has little application to Windows programs. Of course, the Turbo Debugger which accompanies the Borland C/C++ compiler, does operate under Windows, can be used for debugging and will be discussed in Part 5 of this book.

For now the principal topic will continue to be developing applications for Windows and the special requirements of programming for the Windows environment since there is little point in debugging applications until they have been created.

```
//==========================================//
//                 WinHello.C               //
//   C++ Windows HELLO WORLD == Version 1   //
//==========================================//

#include windows.h

long FAR PASCAL WndProc( HWND  hWnd,   WORD message,
                         WORD wParam, LONG lParam )
{
    HDC          hdc;
    PAINTSTRUCT ps;
    RECT         rect;

    switch( message )
    {
      case WM_PAINT:
          hdc = BeginPaint( hWnd, &ps );
          GetClientRect( hWnd, &rect );
```

```
        DrawText( hdc, ""Hello, World!"", -1, &rect,
                  DT_SINGLELINE | DT_CENTER | DT_VCENTER );
        EndPaint( hWnd, &ps );
        return( 0 );

    case WM_DESTROY:
        PostQuitMessage( 0 );
        return( 0 );
    }
    return( DefWindowProc( hWnd, message, wParam, lParam ) );
}

int PASCAL WinMain( HANDLE hInstance, HANDLE hPrevInstance,
                    LPSTR lpszCmdParam, int nCmdShow )
{
    static char szAppName[] = "WinHello";
    HWND        hWnd;
    MSG         msg;
    WNDCLASS    wc;

    if( ! hPrevInstance )
    {
        wc.style         = CS_HREDRAW | CS_VREDRAW;
        wc.lpfnWndProc   = WndProc;
        wc.cbClsExtra    = 0;
        wc.cbWndExtra    = 0;
        wc.hInstance     = hInstance;
        wc.hIcon         = LoadIcon( NULL, IDI_APPLICATION );
        wc.hCursor       = LoadCursor( NULL, IDC_ARROW );
        wc.hbrBackground = GetStockObject( WHITE_BRUSH );
        wc.lpszMenuName  = NULL;
        wc.lpszClassName = szAppName;
        RegisterClass( &wc );
    }
    hWnd = CreateWindow(
        szAppName,                     // window class name      //
        "Hello, World - Windows Style",    // window caption    //
        WS_OVERLAPPEDWINDOW,           // window style           //
        CW_USEDEFAULT,                 // initial X position     //
        CW_USEDEFAULT,                 // initial Y position     //
        CW_USEDEFAULT,                 // initial X size         //
        CW_USEDEFAULT,                 // initial Y size         //
        NULL,                          // parent window handle   //
        NULL,                          // window menu handle     //
        hInstance,                     // program instance handle //
        NULL );                        // creation parameters    //
```

```
        ShowWindow( hWnd, nCmdShow );
        UpdateWindow( hWnd );
        while( GetMessage( &msg, NULL, 0, 0 ) )
        {
            TranslateMessage( &msg );
            DispatchMessage( &msg );
        }
        return msg.wParam;
}


        ;=====================================;
        ;   WinHello.DEF module definition file  ;
        ;=====================================;

NAME            WINHELLO
DESCRIPTION     "Windows Hello, World Program"
EXETYPE         WINDOWS
STUB            "WINSTUB.EXE"
CODE            PRELOAD MOVEABLE DISCARDABLE
DATA            PRELOAD MOVEABLE MULTIPLE
HEAPSIZE        1024
STACKSIZE       8192
EXPORTS         WndProc


            #===========================#
            #   WinHello.MAK make file  #
            #===========================#

#   alternate — no resource file(s) included at this time
#   winhello.exe : winhello.obj, winhello.def, winhello.res
winhello.exe : winhello.obj, winhello.def
    tlink /Tw /v /r /c c:\bc\lib\cOws winhello, \
            winhello, \
            , \
            c:\bc\lib\cwins c:\bc\lib\cs c:\bc\lib\import, \
            winhello

#   omit — no resource file(s) included at this time
#   rc winhello.res

.c.obj :
    bcc -c -ms -W -v winhello.c

#   omit — no resource file(s) included at this time
#   .rc.res :
#       rc -r -ic:\bc\include whello.rc
```

## Chapter 2

Transporting Text Applications to Windows

Textual displays are integral to virtually all applications with very few, if any, exceptions. Even graphic games generally employ some text even if only to report scores.

In conventional, non-graphics environments, text output is relatively simple using the *gotoxy* function for position and the *printf* function (or a variation) to format and print the string information.

Even in a graphics environment, the text output isn't much more complicated, particularly if you create a graphic counterpart to the *printf* function. In both cases, your application "owns" the display and simply writes the desired output, then forgets it. See Chapter 8, *Graphics Programming in Turbo C++*, for examples of *gprintf* and associated functions.

In the Windows environment, however, there are other factors to consider that will affect the design and execution of your program.

Design for Uncertain Circumstances

Under Windows, your application's output is limited to its own client window, but once the client window is written, the display is not inviolate. Under Windows, an application does not "own" the display. Other applications or resident popups may assume the focus and partially or completely overwrite your display. And, your own application may create dialog boxes or pulldown menus which may also overwrite the client window. When any of these intruders are removed, or when an overwritten application is brought to the front (i.e., receives the focus of operations), a Windows application must be able to recreate an invalidated screen display.

In a text environment, many TSRs and applications using pop-up dialog boxes or pull-down menus save a memory copy of the existing display on activation and restore the display before exiting. In a text environment, this is a relatively simple matter because less than 8K are necessary to save an entire 50 X 80 text screen since 2 bytes per cell (one character, one attribute) are needed.

For a graphics display, however, the corresponding operation would require nearly 300K for a 16 color, 640 X 480 screen without data compression, which is not practical in most systems.

In spite of memory requirements, there are circumstances when Windows may still attempt to save a portion of the display, such as when a dialog or message box is created or when a menu is pulled down, restoring the application image when the operation is finished. This may or may not, however, be successful, and, if it is not, the application will need to recreate the screen display.

There are two cases in which Windows does save overwritten display areas: when the display is overlaid by a cursor image or when an icon is dragged across a client area. In these circumstances, no screen update is required. But, in all other cases, Windows notifies applications whose screen displays have been invalidated when it is time to update the client window (and, of course, updates the application's frame at the same time).

The WM_PAINT Message

The WM_PAINT message is posted to an application as notification that an invalidated screen display needs to be restored. Thus when a window has been hidden entirely, or is partially resized (assuming that CS_HREDRAW and CS_VREDRAW are set), or when *ScrollWindow* is called to scroll the client area (vertically or horizontally), Windows issues a WM_PAINT message, notifying the application to update its own display.

There are also circumstances when an application may need to issue its own WM_PAINT message.

Most applications call the *UpdateWindow* function during initialization before entering the message processing loop. This instructs Windows to return a WM_PAINT message which, subsequently, after the message loop begins, is processed by the application's *WinProc* function and creates the initial client window display. Or, in other circumstances, an application may call the *InvalidateRect* or *InvalidateRgn* function which explicitly generates WM_PAINT messages with information describing the area needing to be updated.

While sending a message to Windows asking for a message to be sent back to the application in order to accomplish a specific task may sound rather round-about as well as contrary to normal programming customs, in actual practice it works quite smoothly as it provides Windows with the opportunity to intercede as necessary. This smooths potential conflicts that might otherwise occur in a multitasking environment. The actual program structures required are also quite simple.

To accommodate the requirement of being ready and able to rewrite (paint) the client window area on demand, an application must take a different approach to writing the screen display. Instead of the write-the-output-and-forget-it approach, Windows applications must be structured to accumulate the output information, and to write-on-demand and rewrite-on-demand as well.

Invalidated Window Areas

Windows maintains the paint information structure, PAINTSTRUCT, for each application window. PAINTSTRUCT is defined in Windows.H as:

```
typedef  struct  tagPAINTSTRUCT
{  HDC      hdc;
   BOOL     fErase;
   RECT     rcPaint;
   BOOL     fRestore;
   BOOL     fIncUpdate;
   BYTE     rgbReserved[16];   }   PAINTSTRUCT;
```

While the first three fields of this structure are available for use by applications, the remaining fields are used internally by Windows only. The *hdc* field is simply a handle to the device context, Windows redundancy, since this value is also returned by the *BeginPaint* function that would be called before any screen update operations commence. The *fErase* field is a flag value. FALSE indicates that Windows needs to erase the background of an invalidated rectangle and TRUE indicates that the background area has been erased.

For our current purposes, however, it is the *rcPaint* field which is most important. This field consists of a RECT structure which is also defined in Windows.H as:

```
typedef struct tagRECT
{  int   left;    int   top;
   int   right;   int   bottom;   }   RECT;
```

Anytime an application's client window has been overwritten, whether by an overlying dialog box, by a pull-down menu, by another application's display, or by a Windows' message box, Windows keeps track of the "damage" to the application's display. It does this by recording the invalidated rectangle's coordinates in the paint information structure maintained for each application; specifically in the *rcPaint* record fields. Any time another application or another screen element belonging to the current application overlies an application's client window, Windows records the upper-left and lower-right corners of the overwritten area. Or, if an invalidated rectangle has already been recorded and a second rectangle is invalidated, the information is updated as a single larger rectangle including both areas, if necessary.

When the application is finished processing a WM_PAINT message (by calling *EndPaint*), the invalidated rectangle is reset. This validates the entire client window. Then, if any portion of the client window is still overwritten by another application or dialog box, a new invalidated rectangle is calculated. When any window is moved, closed, or resized, Windows checks for other affected applications by sending WM_PAINT messages to each Window as necessary.

But why all this trouble to repaint windows selectively? The main reason, of course, is simply that it is faster to update a portion of the screen than to repaint the entire screen or even to repaint an entire window. Further, while text-based displays can afford less-than-optimum updates without being visually apparent, optimum updating is essential in presenting a smooth, visually seamless display for a graphics display such as Windows which simply takes longer to recreate.

At the same time, *rcpaint* operates as a clipping rectangle as well as an invalidation rectangle, allowing Windows to restrict painting to the necessary area. There are also times when an application will need to set its own areas for update. This can be done with the *InvalidateRect* as:

```
InvalidateRect( hwnd, NULL, TRUE );
```

The first parameter is a window handle. The second parameter, NULL in this example, invalidates the entire client area; otherwise, an HRGN parameter provides a handle to a data structure that specifies the rectangle to invalidate. The third parameter erases the background for the region if passed as TRUE, and leaves the current background as is if passed as FALSE.

Processing WM_PAINT Messages

While Windows is normally responsible for issuing WM_PAINT messages, the application is responsible for responding to the message and creating or recreating the client window as necessary. But, before an application can write (paint) anything to a client window, there is another essential precursor operation: getting the Device Context Handle.

In the previous demo program, WinHello.C, the *BeginPaint* function was called as:

```
hdc = BeginPaint( hwnd, &ps );
```

In this example, the *BeginPaint* function returns both the device context handle (*hdc*) and the PAINTSTRUCT structure (*ps*) which was passed as a variable parameter. This is the form that will commonly be used in response to WM_PAINT messages. A *BeginPaint* function is always matched with a corresponding *EndPaint* function call to release the *hdc*, as:

```
EndPaint( hwnd, &ps );
```

A second method of accessing the device context is :

```
hdc = GetDC( hwnd );
```

The *GetDC* function is normally used in any context in which immediate client window paint operations are desired without waiting to respond to a message WM_PAINT. For an example, the Clock program distributed with Windows needs to repaint its client window regularly, not just when a WM_PAINT message is issued. This is a typical use of *GetDC* rather than *BeginPaint*. The *GetDC* function, however,is not restricted to paint operations.

It is also used when an application needs to retrieve information from the device context, such as text metrics, as shown later.

GetDC, requires the following corresponding end statement:

```
ReleaseDC ( hwnd, hdc );.
```

Note: *EndPaint* must always be used in response to a *BeginPaint* function call, while *ReleaseDC* must always close *GetDC* function call operations.

- Caution: mixing these functions incorrectly will have undesirable effects on your program's execution.

So, why the two different forms? Because there are two principal differences between the two formats. First, a call to *BeginPaint* returns an invalidated (clipping) rectangle that was set by Windows in response to some overlying display, or as a result of an application call to the *InvalidateRect* function. However, unless specific provisions are made, such as calling *InvalidateRect*, the clipping rectangle may restrict drawing operations undesirably. A call to *GetDC* returns a clipping rectangle equal to the entire client window area; imposing no restrictions whatsoever on subsequent drawing operations.

Second, while *EndPaint* validates any invalid rectangles, *ReleaseDC* does not reset existing invalidations and inadvertently clears information that might be needed later to insure correct restoration of an obscured area.

Note: Even though *GetDC* does permit drawing operations over the entire client window area, it does not mean that drawing operations will overwrite other Window applications that overlay the client window. Windows will restrict the actual screen operations to the visible portion of the client window even though the clipping rectangle extends over the entire client window.

Device Context Handles are only one part of creating a Windows display and, for a graphics-based text display, there are a few other considerations.

Graphic Text Display Elements

Within the Windows environment, there are four principal elements which must be taken into account when creating a text display:

- *Position*—in Windows, window-relative positions replace screen-absolute positions and use pixel coordinates rather than character cell coordinates. Positioning must take into consideration the font metrics (text sizing), horizontal and vertical scrolling, and variable window limits.

- *Text size*—in conventional displays, characters are fixed size and are determined by the active text mode. In Windows, as in other graphic environments, not only can text size and font styles be varied, but different fonts and sizes can be mixed in a single display. And, regardless of the font chosen (fixed-width fonts excepted), individual characters may vary in width.

- *Scrolling*—most conventional displays are limited to vertical scrolling. Scrolling is accomplished by text line. Even when horizontal scrolling is used, movements are based on character cells. In Windows, both vertical and horizontal scrolling are always common; both adjustments can be made in single pixel steps. But, since text display sizes can vary as can hardware video resolutions, any type of scrolling must take into consideration both display and hardware variables.

- *Window limits* —along with scrolling, text displays (and non-text displays) must conform to window limits, both vertical and horizontal. If a string is too long for the window or screen in conventional, nongraphic displays, the display can automatically wrap to the next line.

In a graphics window, text displays do not normally wrap at the windows borders. Provisions can, however, be made to reformat text per window limits. Instead, in most cases, text is allowed to flow beyond the window limits while scrolling the active display over a larger, virtual display.

Note: While a fixed-size window could be created and text windowwrapped, this approach is not common and would still require essentially the same handling as a variable-sized window.

In Windows, these four elements are not entirely separate considerations but are interrelated or synergistic in their effects. But, Windows also saves you many of the problems that would otherwise be a part of the process of sharing a screen display with other applications. First, since all display operations are window-relative (i.e., relative to the limits of the client window), window applications can be moved around the screen without the application (i.e., the programmer) making any special provisions for repositioning. The real point, however, is that Window applications must take a different approach to writing screen displays of any type than applications operating in a DOS environment.

Windows' Font Metrics

In WinHello.C (Chapter 1), text output was limited to a single brief line that was passed to the *DrawText* function with flags centering the output in the client window. This was a rather restricted output and probably will not form the heart of most applications.

A different approach is required for displays with multiple lines of text because there are at least two critical pieces of information required in a graphics display before multiple lines of text can be displayed: vertical line spacing and horizontal line length. Both vertical line spacing and horizontal line length are characteristics that will vary depending upon the font used. But, for present uses, the Windows 3.0 default system font, the font used for text in caption bars, menus, and dialog boxes, will also be used for text displays.

Under earlier Windows versions, the system font was a fixed-width font, similar to the character font used under DOS. With Windows 3.0, however, while the system font remains a "raster," or bit-mapped font, the widths of individual characters are variable with "W" as the widest character in the font and " I " as the narrowest.

System font characteristics are not the same for all computer systems because the Windows installation selects from seven system fonts with various size characteristics to match different video display adapters. At the same time, video board manufacturers may design and distribute their own system font(s). The only guarantee is that the system font is designed to display at least 25 lines of 80 characters.

Even when using the system font, applications must treat this as a variable font and ask for the available font size information through the *GetTextMetrics* function:

```
TEXTMETRICS  tm;

hdc = GetDC( hwnd );
GetTextMetrics( hdc, &tm );
ReleaseDC( hwnd, hdc );
```

This is also an example of using the *GetDC* function instead of the *BeginPaint* function. In this case, no screen paint operations are executed; only a retrieval of device context information. The TEXTMETRICS data structure is defined in Windows.H and appears in full in Appendix A.

This information is used in determining how text will be displayed. Figure 2-1 illustrates seven of the 20 values available in the TEXTMETRIC data structure; five of which are concerned with font vertical characteristics.

Figure 2-1: Windows' Font Metrics

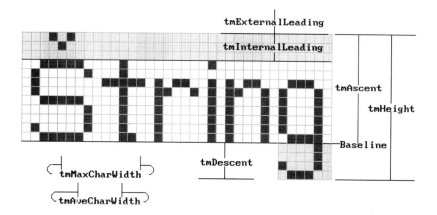

Beginning at the top, the values are as follows:

- *tmExternalLeading*—the font designers suggested interlinear spacing because the white space between lines makes the text readable.
- *tmInternalLeading*—the space allocated for accent marks above characters as shown by the "Š" character with the caret accent. Note: while accents are not commonly used in English, many other languages depend heavily on these forms and these are supported by most extended ASCII character fonts.
- *tmAscent*—the height of an uppercase character including the *tmInternalLeading* space.
- *tmDescent*—the space provided for character descenders as in the "g", "j", "p", "q" and "y" characters.
- *tmHeight*—the overall height of the font, including *tmAscent* and *tmDescent* but not incorporating *tmExternalLeading*.

In the present application, the vertical line spacing, *cyChr*, will be calculated as:

```
cyChr = tm.tmHeight + tm.tmExternalLeading;
```

The length of a line of text is not as easily calculated. TEXTMETRICS supplies two values for character width:

- *tmAveCharWidth*—a weighted average of the lowercase character widths.
- *tmMaxCharWidth*—the width of the widest character(s) in the font, usually the "W" and/or "M" characters.

In some cases it may help to have a third value for the average width of uppercase (capital) letters which can be approximated, for most fonts, as 150% of *tmAveCharWidth*.

Since this font information will not change during program execution unless the application changes fonts, the simplest method of determining text spacing is to get the text metric information when the application is initiated. And, the best place for initialization code is in response to the WM_CREATE message, the first message the *WinProc* procedure receives. The PrinText.C program shows how this information is retrieved:

```
case WM_CREATE:
    hdc = GetDC( hwnd );
    GetTextMetrics( hdc, &tm );
    ReleaseDC( hwnd, hdc );
    cxChr = tm.tmAveCharWidth;
    cxCap = cxChr * 2 / 3;
    cyChr = tm.tmHeight + tm.tmExternalLeading;
    return( 0 );
```

This provides three values for determining text size, though only *cxChr* and *cyChr* will actually be needed. However, a variation of the PrinText program, which displays strings of uppercase characters, will need the *cxCap* variable later.

Window Limits

Before taking the application's output further, a few comments on the organization of an application window and on window coordinates will clarify explanations that follow. If, of course, you have worked with graphics and graphics windows in the past, what follows may well be old news but, for those who have not, here's how a graphics window is organized.

Figure 2-2 shows an application window overlying one of Windows "wallpaper" displays. Within the application's client window, the window coordinates begin at 0,0 in the upper left corner of the window and increases down and to the right. These coordinates are window-relative, not screen relative, and the origin remains at the 0,0 point regardless of the place on the screen at which this particular application appears. The application does not know, and does not need to know, where on the overall screen the client window is located, or even where its own frame window is located. Granted, the absolute screen position includes information that Windows has, but it is not information that the application needs nor should it have any reason to access it.

How are screen paint operations carried out if the application doesn't know where its client window is located in the "real" world? The answer is quite simple. Properly behaved Windows applications do not write directly to the screen. Instead, they call Windows functions with directions for screen output. Windows then adjusts for the absolute screen position and clips the output to the active or exposed client window limits. Thus, if an application's window is overlaid by another application or by its own dialog box or menu, but the screen display is still updating, as in the Clock program example, its Windows task is to prevent the update operations from painting the overlying window(s). At the same time, the application itself proceeds as though its entire client window were active and draws its images without worrying about possible conflicts.

There are other advantages in operating within a windowed graphic environment. Graphic operations may also operate at coordinates outside the window limits but may paint only within the currently valid display area. This is no small advantage as will be demonstrated by the PainText.C program, discussed shortly.

Figure 2-2: Window Coordinates and Invalidated Areas

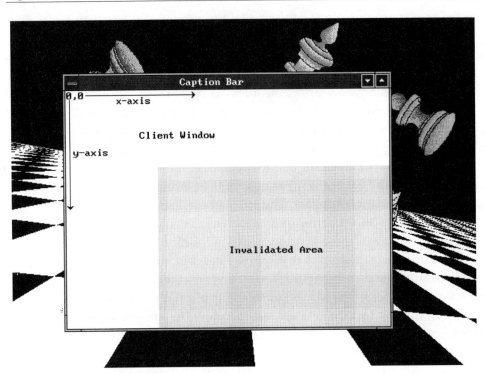

Windowing Text Output

After retrieving the TEXTMETRIC information and deriving height and width information for the system font, text output to the application's client window is the next obvious step. In WinHello.C, the function *DrawText* sufficed for a single, brief line that was centered in the client window; but, in PaintText.C, a more sophisticated display is the intention. The WinProc response to the WM_PAINT message is still the occasion for writing the screen and begins again with the *BeginPaint* function to retrieve the device context handle, *hdc*, and the PAINTSTUCT information, *ps*:

```
case WM_PAINT:
    hdc = BeginPaint( hwnd, &ps );
```

This time the application needs additional information and begins by calculating two values from information contained, in part, in *ps*. The field value *ps.rcPaint.top* is the top limit of the invalidated rectangle area while *ps.rc-Paint.bottom* is the bottom limit. These are client window relative values. What the application needs for *cBeginPaint* and *cEndPaint* are line numbers referring to the text to be displayed:

```
cBeginPaint = max( 0,
            cyScrlPos + ps.rcPaint.top / cyChr );
cEndPaint   = min( NumLines,
            cyScrlPos + ps.rcPaint.bottom / cyChr );
```

In PainText, a vertical scrollbar has been enabled because the display is too long for a single screen display and the scrollbar position, *cyScrlPos*, is also a factor in the equation.

Note: The *cyScrlPos* (vertical) variable is not measured in pixels but in text lines, and the *cxScrlPos* (horizontal) variable is also not measured in pixels but in character widths using the average character width read from the *tm* font metrics.

In order to forestall errors in calculation, the two macros, *min* and *max*, insure that *cBeginPaint* is never less than 0 and *cEndPaint* cannot be greater than *NumLines*. Once beginning and ending text lines have been calculated, set text alignment before writing to the screen. Since *TA_LEFT* and *TA_TOP*, meaning that the left-top of the characters will be aligned at the output coordinates, are the default text alignment values, calling *SetTextAlign* may be unnecessary but is still good practice:

```
SetTextAlign( hdc, TA_LEFT | TA_TOP );
for( i = cBeginPaint; i <= cEndPaint; i++ )
{
    x = cxChr * ( i - cxScrlPos + 1 );
    y = cyChr * ( i - cyScrlPos + 1 );
```

The x-axis/y-axis screen (client window) positions are calculated for each line output. Normally, for left-aligned text, the *x* position would be equal to *cxChr*, supplying a one-character width inset from the client window frame and only the y-axis position would need calculation. But, there are two factors relevant here. First, each successive line is stepped to the right to provide a display that is deliberately wider than any normal display terminal can handle. This is done, in part, to allow demonstration of horizontal scrolling but, also, to demonstrate a subtle but unusual error. The error, however, will be deferred for a later discussion.

Second, the *x* and *y* window positions are calculated taking into account the scrollbar positions. Either or both may be negative integers, indicating that the current text line begins outside of the client window. This is not an error and there is no problem in beginning a paint operation outside of the window limits because the actual screen paint operations that do appear are clipped, in this case, by the invalidated rectangle limits which will never fall outside the window limits.

The alternative, in this example, is to calculate the part of the written string which actually falls within the window and then clip or truncate the output string before writing to the window. In text-based, rather than graphic-based environments, such an approach is possible and sometimes necessary.

For a graphics-based environment, and particularly when a variable width font is being used, the only reasonable approach is to simply calculate relative positions that may lie outside the actual window limits. Then pass only those pixel operations whose coordinates fall within the valid display. In this fashion, a line or curve can begin anywhere but will appear on screen only within the active window or, in this example, within the application's client window. But, and this is important, the application does not need to worry about clipping; that is Windows' job. Instead, as described previously, the application simply treats output operations as if they were operating in a larger virtual window, leaving clipping to the actual display window; or, more accurately, to the invalidated rectangle, for Windows to handle.

Some applications that are using intensive graphic calculations, may perform better by restricting their own operations to approximate the active window area; but the actual clipping should be left to Windows, and not duplicated by the application.

The TextOut Function

In conventional C, formatted text output is a simple matter using the *printf* function (or any of the equivalent forms):

```
gotoxy( x, y );
printf( ""This is line %d being displayed at X:%d / Y:%d",,
        i, x, y );
```

For Window C, however, output is somewhat more complicated. The *Text-Out* function is called with five parameters:

```
TextOut( HDC, int xpos, int ypos,
         LPSTR szBuffer, int cStrlen );
```

The first parameter is the usual device context handle while the second and third parameters are integer arguments (signed) that specify the window relative coordinates at which output (paint operations) begins. The fourth parameter, LPSTR, is defined in Windows.H as a FAR pointer to **char**. It is a pointer to the buffer space at which the output string is located. However, unlike conventional C, an ASCIIZ (null-terminated) string is not enough and thus a fifth parameter, *TextOut*, is required which specifies the number of characters in the string.

In one respect, this is similar to the Pascal string convention in which the string length is stored as the first (0th) byte of the character array instead of depending upon a null-terminator character. Here, however, the string length is not available automatically and must be calculated by calling a C function using the string as an argument.

Rather than entering all strings in a string table (a topic which will be introduced later) so that they can be referenced first by *strlen* to find their length and then passed to *TextOut* for display, the *sprintf* and *wsprintf* functions can substitute within the *TextOut* function call, thus:

```
TextOut( hdc, x, y, szbuffer, wsprintf( szbuffer,
""This is line %d being displayed at X:%d / Y:%d",",
i, x, y ) );
```

The *szbuffer* text buffer is still, as the identifier suggests, a conventional null-terminated string buffer. Both the *sprintf* and *wsprintf* functions write the formatted string argument to the buffer, returning an integer that specifies the length of the finished string.

There is, however, one difference. *wsprintf*, defined in Windows.H, does not handle floating-point values but it does have the advantage of being a part of Windows and, therefore, does not increase the size of .EXE applications or .DLL libraries. On the other hand, if floating-point values are needed in the formatted string, *sprintf* will serve quite well.

Note: The savings of approximately 1.75K are quite significant.

Scrollbars

Scrollbars provide an effective, intuitive device for adjusting window views. They are not limited to graphic displays and are increasingly common in text-based displays as you may have noticed when using the Borland C/C++ IDE. Perhaps the only drawback to scrollbars are that they cannot be operated without a mouse; at least, not conveniently. However, a computer mouse is no longer an exception and few, if any, Windows users will not have a system mouse. Therefore, there is certainly no reason not to use scrollbars in your applications; and every reason, including programming convenience, for using them.

Scrollbars are not completely automatic, however. Some provisions within the application are necessary in order to respond to scrollbar messages. Figure 2-3 illustrates a window application with vertical and horizontal scrollbars and diagrams displaying the seven scrollbar messages that will be returned by mouse clicks at various positions on the scrollbar. Both scrollbars return SB_LINEUP messages when the mouse is clicked (button down) on the top or left endpads, and SB_LINEDOWN messages from the bottom or right endpads.

Also, if the mouse button is held down while the mouse cursor remains on the thumbpad, a series of SB_LINEUP or SB_LINEDOWN messages are generated, providing continuous scrolling by line (or character, horizontally). In either case, an SB_ENDSCROLL message is returned when the mouse button is released; but, normally, these SB_ENDSCROLL messages are simply ignored.

SB_PAGEUP messages are generated when the mouse is clicked (button down) anywhere above or to the left of the current thumbpad position and SB_PAGEDOWN when the mouse is anywhere below or to the right of that position. As with the endpads, as long as the mouse button is held down and the mouse cursor remains on the scrollbar, a series of SB_PAGEUP or SB_PAGEDOWN messages are generated, providing continuous scrolling by page. In either case, a SB_ENDSCROLL message is returned when the mouse button is released.

The scrollbar thumbpad presents a different response set. It returns a series of SB_THUMBTRACK messages when the mouse button is held down and during which movement occurs; but, only when the mouse button is subsequently released and the mouse cursor is still on the scrollbar does it generate a SB_THUMBPOSITION message that indicates movement is complete and that a new thumbpad position has been set. While the mouse button is held down, even if the SB_THUMBTRACK messages are ignored, an outline of the thumbpad image is generated which follows the mouse cursor.

Windows documentation states that SB_TOP and SB_BOTTOM messages can be generated to indicate that the scrollbar has reached minimum or maximum positions. Neither message is returned by scrollbars that are created by application windows, and handling for these two cases may safely be omitted.

Figure 2-3: Scrollbar Messages

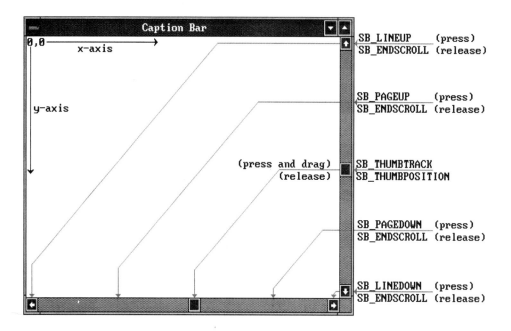

Handling Scrollbar Messages

Because these SB_xxxx messages are secondary messages, applications must begin by responding to either a WM_VSCROLL or WM_HSCROLL message, indicating the mouse action in the vertical or horizontal scrollbar respectively. Either message is accompanied by the *wPARAM* value that contains the secondary message information; but it is the primary event message to which your application's *WinProc* procedure must initially respond. In PainText.C, both vertical and horizontal scrollbars are enabled. But, since both respond to their secondary messages in essentially the same fashion, the *WM_VSCROLL* message response will illustrate both:

```
case WM_VSCROLL:
    switch( wPARAM )
    {
```

The response structure for the *WM_VSCROLL* message is simply a subsidiary *switch...case* statement that lists the scrollbar messages to be handled and the response appropriate for each.

While the order in which these are handled is not important, the first two are the event messages generated by the endpads, SB_LINEUP and SB_LINEDOWN:

```
case SB_LINEUP:   cyScrlStp = -1;  break;
case SB_LINEDOWN: cyScrlStp =  1;  break;
```

In both cases, the appropriate response is quite simple: to select a movement of one line up or down. And, since the thumbpads will generate repeated messages if the mouse button is held down, virtually any range of movement desired is available without complex provisions. For the SB_PAGEUP and SB_PAGEDOWN messages, the handling is slightly more complex. It establishes a minimum movement of one line up or down but attempts to set a more reasonable movement step based upon the vertical font size and the vertical window size. (Or the average character width and window width for the horizontal scrollbar.)

```
case SB_PAGEUP:
    cyScrlStp = min( -1, -cyWin / cyChr );
    break;
case SB_PAGEDOWN:
    cyScrlStp = max(  1,  cyWin / cyChr );
    break;
```

While the line and page scroll messages are relatively simple, responding to the thumbpad messages requires the information above the thumbpad position provided in the low word of the *Lparam* value:

```
case SB_THUMBTRACK:
    cyScrlStp = LOWORD( LPARAM ) - cyScrlPos;
```

```
        break;
  case SB_THUMBPOSITION:
        cyScrlStp = LOWORD( LPARAM ) - cyScrlPos;
        break;
```

The macro LOWORD, defined in Windows.H (see Appendix A), returns a word value within the minimum..maximum range for the scrollbar position. In this example, *cyScrlStp* is calculated as the difference between the new thumbpad position and the current *cyScrlPos* position.

Normally, an application would respond only to the SB_THUMBPOSITION or the SB_THUMBTRACK message, but not to both. In most cases, the SB_THUMBPOSITION message, which is returned when the mouse button is released, would be the preferred choice. This allows the application to respond with a single screen update instead of attempting to track continuous movement of the scrollbar. Or, as an alternative, an application could offer a choice of scrollbar configurations as a menu or installation option, permitting either form of response with the scrollbar message code appearing something like this:

```
  case SB_THUMBTRACK:
        if (! TrackContinuous) break;
  case SB_THUMBPOSITION:
        cyScrlStp = LOWORD( lParam ) - cyScrlPos;
        break;
```

In this form, a boolean flag, *TrackContinuous*, would prevent a response to the SB_THUMBTRACK message if false or, if true, would allow the response to fall through to the SB_THUMBPOSITION case, providing continuous window updates as the thumbpad is moved.

The drawback, of course, is that a slow system may not be able to keep up with rapid movement of the scrollbar thumbpad, resulting in a jerky response and a rough program appearance. On the other hand, continuous tracking can also provide finer control by permitting the user to see precisely where a scrollbar adjustment reaches.

The choices to use and the way in which they are implemented will depend upon your applications' needs, but testing should always be done using extreme conditions.

Returning to the example program, a default provision is made that sets *cyScrlStp* to zero or no movement:

```
        default:      cyScrlStp = 0;
    }
```

After responding to the scrollbar messages, however, there remain a few tasks to be handled within the WM_VSCROLLBAR message response. One is to test the new step value for a valid range result:

```
    if( cyScrlStp = max( -cyScrlPos,
                    min( cyScrlStp,
                        cyScrlMax - cyScrlPos ) ) )
    {
```

If no scrollbar movement was selected, i.e., the thumbpad ends exactly where it was when the process began, a *cyScrlStp* value of zero causes the *if* test to fail and no subsequent actions are necessary. The test statement also imposes conditions on any step value set to insure that movements remain within the valid scrollbar ranges.

Note: Depending on compiler warning settings, this code statement may prompt the warning message "Possibly incorrect assignment in ...". This happens because the compiler normally expects to see a statement in the form $a == b$ as the test condition within an *if* statement. But, in this case, this is not an error, simply a valid but alternative programming form.

After checking the movement value, it is still the application's responsibility to first set a new value for *cyScrlPos*; second, scroll the window; and, third, adjust the scrollpad position:

```
        cyScrlPos += cyScrlStp;
        ScrollWindow( hwnd, 0, -cyChr * cyScrlStp,
                    NULL, NULL );
        SetScrollPos( hwnd, SB_VERT, cyScrlPos, TRUE );
```

While the first step is simple, the second step requires calling the *Scroll-Window* function with parameters instructing Windows how to scroll the client window and how much movement desired.

In this example, the second parameter is zero, specifying no horizontal movement. The third parameter specifies the vertical movement. A positive value for *cyScrlStp* (scrolling down) becomes a negative argument to scroll the present window display upwards. Negative values scroll left or up and positive values scroll right or down.

The final two parameters, each passed as NULL, are pointers to RECT data structures.

The first pointer is to a RECT data structure that sets a portion of the client area to be scrolled. If NULL, the entire client area is scrolled.

The second pointer indicates a RECT data structure containing data that specifies the clipping rectangle to be scrolled. Only bits inside this rectangle are scrolled. If NULL, the entire window is scrolled.

Note: Additional details on *ScrollWindow* operations as well as other Windows functions can be called within the Borland C++ IDE by pressing Ctrl-F1. See the *C++ User's Guide* for additional details on using the help features or, within the Help screen, press F1 again for Help on Help.

The last task is to call *UpdateWindow* which instructs Windows to return a WM_PAINT message to the application, causing the window to be updated:

```
        UpdateWindow( hwnd );
    }
    return( 0 );
```

Remember, the *ScrollWindow* function call causes Windows to set invalidated rectangle parameters that correspond to the area revealed by the scroll operation. Thus, when the WM_PAINT message is returned, only the region uncovered by scrolling is repainted. This is much faster than repainting the entire window.

The response provisions for the WM_HSCROLLBAR message from the horizontal scrollbar in PainText.C are essentially the same, though the vertical and horizontal scrollbars could, when needed, respond in entirely different manners.

Window Sizing/Resizing

While *PrinText* has been written deliberately to extend beyond the normal window limits, thus necessitating the use of both vertical and horizontal scrollbars, provisions are still required in order to respond to window resizing operations.

The WM_SIZE message is sent to an application anytime the window frame and, therefore, the client window are resized. The WM_SIZE message preceding the first WM_PAINT message is also sent when the application is created to paint the initial display. In WinHello.C in Chapter 1, the WM_SIZE message was not handled by the application but was left for default handling by Windows. Here, however, the application has become somewhat more sophisticated and several operations are necessary. The first operations are to retrieve new *cyWin* and *cxWin* values which are available as the high and low word values in *Lparam*:

```
case WM_SIZE:
    cyWin = HIWORD( lParam );
    cxWin = LOWORD( lParam );
```

Once the new window size is available, the scrollbar needs to be reset to match. This is done by calculating a new *cyscrlmax* to correspond to the number of lines that can be displayed in the resized window:

```
cyScrlMax = max( 0, NumLines + 2 - cyWin / cyChr );
cyScrlPos = min( cyScrlPos, cyScrlMax );
```

A check is also in order to insure that the present scrollbar thumbtab position remains valid.

The next two steps are the critical operations because they insure that the scrollbar matches the resized window and that the thumbpad is correctly positioned.

The *SetScrollRange* function sets minimum (0) and maximum (*cyScrMax*) ranges for either the horizontal or vertical scrollbar as specified by the *nBar* (2nd) parameter. The limits set are integer arguments and, in this application, refer to text lines vertically or to characters (using the average character width) horizontally. The final, boolean parameter, if true, instructs Windows to redraw the scrollbar image based on the new range:

```
SetScrollRange( hwnd, SB_VERT, 0, cyScrlMax, FALSE );
```

Since the scrollbar range does not change during execution of this program, the *SetScrollRange* function could have been called in the WM_CREATE response. Alternately, in any application in which the vertical or horizontal range does change, there may be more appropriate circumstances when this task should be executed. The remaining task always needs execution in response to a resize operation: calling *SetScrollPos* to update the thumbpad position:

```
SetScrollPos( hwnd, SB_VERT, cyScrlPos, TRUE );
```

While resizing an application does not change the position within the display, resizing does change the scale of the scrollbar display. Happily, however, Windows is responsible for the actual position calculations within the scrollbar image. The only information that needs to be passed, except the application handle (*hwnd*) and the scrollbar identifier (*SB_VERT* or *SB_HORZ*), is the current position, *cyScrlPos*. The final boolean parameter, when true, simply instructs Windows to redraw the image as well as update the scrollbar's coordinates. These same instructions are repeated for the horizontal scrollbar as well.

Scrolling Errors

The PainText example program was created primarily to demonstrate how to write text to a virtual display larger than the application window and to demonstrate the scrollbar controls and scroll operations that provide a means of moving the active window to view any part of the virtual display. PainText also demonstrates a rather unusual error which few applications will ever encounter, but which is still worth being aware of.

Figure 2-4 shows an enlarged snapshot of a corner of PainText's client window with a box drawn around several characters which are, in this example, illegible. In the same illustration, a shaded bar at the bottom of the window shows the area that was redrawn in response to the last WM_PAINT message which followed a one-line vertical scroll operation. The error that appears in the last three lines in Figure 2-4 results from the display line being drawn in two halves and the reported information having changed in the interlude between the two paint operations. In each of the three error lines shown, the top half of the line was drawn with the y-axis origin reported corresponding to the last line on the screen. However, only the top half of the line falls within the client window's display area. After the screen is scrolled up, the bottom half of the line is drawn, but is now attempting to report a different y-axis origin.

Okay, this is hardly a typical application; but it does demonstrate a potential error that can occur when the written information changes between paint operations. This same discrepancy can also be observed during some horizontal scroll operations.

If it is necessary for an application to guard against this type of error, of course, the *InvalidateRect* or *InvalidateRgn* functions could be called during scrollbar message handling to insure that critical areas are always included in the subsequent paint operations. But, in reality, this is not likely to be a frequent concern.

Figure 2-4: Redraw Errors—When the Information Changes

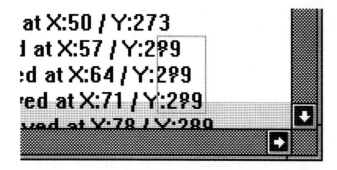

Summary

Thus far, text output to an application's client window has been demonstrated as have scrollbar operations used to control the client window position as a view into a larger virtual display. The present demonstration, however, has limited operations to using the default Windows font and the default display mapping mode, a topic to be introduced later.

Elementary mouse operations have also been demonstrated, if only indirectly; and this is another topic that will receive further discussion later.

Because the keyboard is still the primary user interface, the next topic will be keyboard operations.

Below is the complete source code for the PainText.C program, the Pain-Text.DEF definition file, and a .MAK file. A partial program listing, Pain-Txt2.C, is also included to show the changes necessary to incorporate the SysMets.H file, which will report the system metrics information for your computer.

```
//==========================//
//          PainText.C      //
//  C++ Windows Paint Text  //
//==========================//


#include <windows.h>


int   NumLines = 99;


long FAR PASCAL WndProc( HWND hwnd,    WORD message,
                         WORD wParam, LONG lParam )
{
    static short cxChr, cxCap, cyChr, cxWin, cyWin,
                 cyScrlPos, cxScrlPos, cyScrlMax, cxScrlMax;
    short        i, x, y, cyScrlStp, cxScrlStp,
                 cBeginPaint, cEndPaint;
    HDC          hdc;                PAINTSTRUCT ps;
    RECT         rect;              TEXTMETRIC  tm;
    char         szBuffer[180];


    switch( message )
    {
        case WM_CREATE:
            hdc = GetDC( hwnd );
            GetTextMetrics( hdc, &tm );
            cxChr = tm.tmAveCharWidth;
            cxCap = cxChr * 2 / 3;
            cyChr = tm.tmHeight + tm.tmExternalLeading;
            ReleaseDC( hwnd, hdc );
            return( 0 );


        case WM_SIZE:
            cyWin = HIWORD( lParam );
            cxWin = LOWORD( lParam );
                // setup vertical scrollbar //
            cyScrlMax = max( 0, NumLines + 2 - cyWin / cyChr );
            cyScrlPos = min( cyScrlPos, cyScrlMax );
            SetScrollRange( hwnd, SB_VERT, 0,
                            cyScrlMax, FALSE );
            SetScrollPos(   hwnd, SB_VERT,
                            cyScrlPos, TRUE );
                // setup horizontal scrollbar //
            cxScrlMax = max( 0, NumLines + 60 - cxWin / cxChr );
            cxScrlPos = min( cxScrlPos, cxScrlMax );
            SetScrollRange( hwnd, SB_HORZ, 0,
```

```
                         cxScrlMax, FALSE );
    SetScrollPos(    hwnd, SB_HORZ,
                         cxScrlPos, TRUE );
    return( 0 );

case WM_PAINT:
    hdc = BeginPaint( hwnd, &ps );
    cBeginPaint = max( 0,
                cyScrlPos + ps.rcPaint.top / cyChr );
    cEndPaint   = min( NumLines,
                cyScrlPos + ps.rcPaint.bottom / cyChr );
    SetTextAlign( hdc, TA_LEFT | TA_TOP );
    for( i = cBeginPaint; i <= cEndPaint; i++ )
    {
        x = cxChr * ( i - cxScrlPos + 1 );
        y = cyChr * ( i - cyScrlPos + 1 );
        TextOut( hdc, x, y, szBuffer, wsprintf( szBuffer,
        "This is line %d being displayed at X:%d / Y:%d",
        i, x, y ) );
    }
    EndPaint( hwnd, &ps );
    return( 0 );

case WM_VSCROLL:
    switch( wParam )
    {
        case SB_PAGEUP:
            cyScrlStp = min( -1, -cyWin/cyChr );
            break;
        case SB_LINEUP:
            cyScrlStp = -1;
            break;
        //================================================//
        // case SB_THUMBTRACK:                            //
        //     cyScrlStp = LOWORD( lParam ) - cyScrlPos;  //
        //     break;                                     //
        //================================================//
        case SB_THUMBPOSITION:
            cyScrlStp = LOWORD( lParam ) - cyScrlPos;
            break;
        case SB_LINEDOWN:
            cyScrlStp = 1;
            break;
        case SB_PAGEDOWN:
            cyScrlStp = max( 1, cyWin/cyChr );
            break;
```

```
        default:     cyScrlStp = 0;
    }
    if( cyScrlStp = max( -cyScrlPos,
                     min( cyScrlStp,
                          cyScrlMax - cyScrlPos ) ) )
    {
        cyScrlPos += cyScrlStp;
        ScrollWindow( hwnd, 0, -cyChr * cyScrlStp,
                      NULL, NULL );
        SetScrollPos( hwnd, SB_VERT, cyScrlPos, TRUE );
        UpdateWindow( hwnd );
    }
    return( 0 );

case WM_HSCROLL:
    switch( wParam )
    {
        case SB_PAGEUP:
            cxScrlStp = min( -1, -cxWin/cxChr );
            break;
        case SB_LINEUP:
            cxScrlStp = -1;
            break;
    //==================================================//
    // case SB_THUMBTRACK:                              //
    //     cxScrlStp = LOWORD( lParam ) - cxScrlPos;   //
    //     break;                                       //
    //==================================================//
        case SB_THUMBPOSITION:
            cxScrlStp = LOWORD( lParam ) - cxScrlPos;
            break;
        case SB_LINEDOWN:
            cxScrlStp = 1;
            break;
        case SB_PAGEDOWN:
            cxScrlStp = max( 1, cxWin/cxChr );
            break;
        default:     cxScrlStp = 0;
    }
    if( cxScrlStp = max( -cxScrlPos,
                     min( cxScrlStp,
                          cxScrlMax - cxScrlPos ) ) )
    {
        cxScrlPos += cxScrlStp;
        ScrollWindow( hwnd, -cxChr * cxScrlStp, 0,
                      NULL, NULL );
```

```
            SetScrollPos( hwnd, SB_HORZ, cxScrlPos, TRUE );
        }
        return( 0 );

    case WM_DESTROY:
        PostQuitMessage( 0 );
        return( 0 );
    }
    return( DefWindowProc( hwnd, message, wParam, lParam ) );
}

int PASCAL WinMain( HANDLE hInstance,
                    HANDLE hPrevInstance,
                    LPSTR  lpszCmdParam, int    nCmdShow )
{
    static char szAppName[] = "Paint Text";
    HWND        hwnd;
    MSG         msg;
    WNDCLASS    wc;

    if( ! hPrevInstance )
        wc.lpfnWndProc   = WndProc;
    wc.cbClsExtra     = 0;
    wc.cbWndExtra     = 0;
    wc.hInstance      = hInstance;
    wc.hIcon          = LoadIcon( NULL, IDI_APPLICATION );
    wc.hCursor        = LoadCursor( NULL, IDC_ARROW );
    wc.hbrBackground  = GetStockObject( WHITE_BRUSH );
    wc.lpszMenuName   = NULL;
    wc.lpszClassName  = szAppName;
    RegisterClass( &wc );
    }
    hwnd = CreateWindow( szAppName,
            "Painting text in Windows",
            WS_OVERLAPPEDWINDOW | WS_VSCROLL | WS_HSCROLL,
            CW_USEDEFAULT, CW_USEDEFAULT,
            CW_USEDEFAULT, CW_USEDEFAULT,
            NULL, NULL, hInstance, NULL  );
    ShowWindow(  hwnd, nCmdShow );
    UpdateWindow( hwnd );
    while( GetMessage( &msg, NULL, 0, 0 ) )
    {
        TranslateMessage( &msg );
        DispatchMessage(  &msg );
    }
```

```
    return msg.wParam;
}



              //==============================//
              //            PainTxt2.C         //
              //  revisions to use sysmets.h   //
              //   and display system metrics  //
              //==============================//

#include <windows.h>
#include "sysmets.h"                    // add include statement

//   int   NumLines = 99;              // delete NumLines statement

long FAR PASCAL WndProc( ...
{
    static short cxMax;                 // add cxMax declaration

    switch( message )
    {
    case WM_CREATE:
        ...
        cxMax = 40*cxChr+18*cxCap;      // add cxMax definition
        return( 0 );
    case WM_SIZE: ...                           // no changes
    case WM_PAINT:
        ...
        SetTextAlign( hdc, TA_LEFT | TA_TOP );
        for( i = cBeginPaint; i <= cEndPaint; i++ )
        {
            TextOut( hdc, cxChr, cyChr*i,
                sysmetrics[i].szLabel,
                lstrlen( sysmetrics[i].szLabel ) );
            TextOut( hdc, cxChr+18*cxCap, cyChr*i,
                sysmetrics[i].szDescript,
                lstrlen( sysmetrics[i].szDescript ) );
            SetTextAlign( hdc, TA_RIGHT | TA_TOP );
            TextOut( hdc, cxChr+18*cxCap+40*cxChr, cyChr*i,
                szBuffer, wsprintf( szBuffer, "%5d",
                GetSystemMetrics( sysmetrics[i].nIndex ) ) );
            SetTextAlign( hdc, TA_LEFT | TA_TOP );
        }
        EndPaint( hwnd, &ps );
        return( 0 );
```

```
      case WM_VSCROLL: ...                        // no changes
      case WM_HSCROLL: ...                        // no changes
      case WM_DESTROY: ...                        // no changes
   }
   return( DefWindowProc( hwnd, message, wParam, lParam ) );
}


int PASCAL WinMain( ...                           // no changes



   //=============================================//
   // SysMets.H == System Metrics Display Struct //
   //=============================================//

#define NumLines (sizeof sysmetrics / sizeof sysmetrics[0] )

struct
{ int   nIndex;
  char  *szLabel;
  char  *szDescript; } sysmetrics[] =
{
   SM_CXSCREEN,        "SM_CXSCREEN",
      "Screen width in pixels",
   SM_CYSCREEN,        "SM_CYSCREEN",
      "Screen height in pixels",
   SM_CXVSCROLL,       "SM_CXVSCROLL",
      "Vert scroll arrow width",
   SM_CYHSCROLL,       "SM_CYHSCROLL",
      "Horz scroll arrow height",
   SM_CYCAPTION,       "SM_CYCAPTION",
      "Caption bar height",
   SM_CXBORDER,        "SM_CXBORDER",        "Border width",
   SM_CYBORDER,        "SM_CYBORDER",        "Border height",
   SM_CXDLGFRAME,      "SM_CXDLGFRAME",
      "Dialog window frame width",
   SM_CYDLGFRAME,      "SM_CYDLGFRAME",
      "Dialog window frame height",
   SM_CXHTHUMB,        "SM_CXHTHUMB",
      "Vert scroll thumb height",
   SM_CYVTHUMB,        "SM_CYVTHUMB",
      "Horz scroll thumb height",
   SM_CXICON,          "SM_CXICON",          "Icon width",
   SM_CYICON,          "SM_CYICON",          "Icon height",
   SM_CXCURSOR,        "SM_CXCURSOR",        "Cursor width",
   SM_CYCURSOR,        "SM_CYCURSOR",        "Cursor height",
```

```
SM_CYMENU,            "SM_CYMENU",              "Menu bar height",
SM_CXFULLSCREEN,  "SM_CXFULLSCREEN",
    "Client window width",
SM_CYFULLSCREEN,  "SM_CYFULLSCREEN",
    "Client window height",
SM_CYKANJIWINDOW, "SM_CYKANJIWINDOW",
    "Kanji window height",
SM_MOUSEPRESENT,  "SM_MOUSEPRESENT",
    "Mouse present flag",
SM_CYVSCROLL,     "SM_CYVSCROLL",
    "Vert scroll arrow height",
SM_CXHSCROLL,     "SM_CXHSCROLL",
    "Horz scroll arrow width",
SM_DEBUG,         "SM_DEBUG",
    "Debug version flag",
SM_SWAPBUTTON,    "SM_SWAPBUTTON",
    "Mouse buttons swapped flag",
SM_RESERVED1,     "SM_RESERVED1",           "Reserved",
SM_RESERVED2,     "SM_RESERVED2",           "Reserved",
SM_RESERVED3,     "SM_RESERVED3",           "Reserved",
SM_RESERVED4,     "SM_RESERVED4",           "Reserved",
SM_CXMIN,         "SM_CXMIN",
    "Minimum window width",
SM_CYMIN,         "SM_CYMIN",
    "Minimum window height",
SM_CXSIZE,        "SM_CXSIZE",
    "Min/max icon width",
SM_CYSIZE,        "SM_CYSIZE",
    "Min/max icon height",
SM_CXFRAME,       "SM_CXFRAME",
    "Window frame width",
SM_CYFRAME,       "SM_CYFRAME",
    "Window frame height",
SM_CXMINTRACK,    "SM_CXMINTRACK",
    "Min tracking width",
SM_CYMINTRACK,    "SM_CYMINTRACK",
    "Min tracking height",
SM_CMETRICS,      "SM_CMETRICS",
    "Number of system metrics"{
```

Chapter 3

Keyboard, Caret, and Scrollbars

While applications of all types, not just those that execute under Windows, are becoming increasingly mouse interactive, the keyboard is still the user's primary input device; either in the form of the standard 89-key or the enhanced 101/102-key keyboards. Even in a graphic environment, there are few applications that do not depend, at least in part, on a text output display. Therefore, even under Windows, keyboard input and text output remain central to all types of application programming and are the principal topics in this chapter. I'll begin first with the handling of input from the keyboard.

Keyboard Drivers

The earliest PCs were strictly mono-lingual, supporting only the English alphabet, thus imposing chauvinistic constraints on all non-English speakers. But now computers are international in nature and, in recognition, Windows 3.0 includes several keyboard drivers and .DLL libraries to support international (principally European) keyboard configurations.

The Windows SETUP program is responsible for choosing the appropriate KEYBOARD.DRV driver. When Windows is started, SETUP saves the original 09h interrupt vector (the hardware keyboard interrupt address), redirecting the interrupt vector to routines supplied by the driver. When a key is pressed on the keyboard, an Interrupt 09h is generated that suspends execution of the current program and passes control to the Interrupt 09h handler.

Routines supplied by Windows decode the key events storing them as queued messages. After the hardware event has been interpreted, control is restored to the interrupted program which can subsequently retrieve the key event messages through a *GetMessage* request.

The principal difference between a DOS application retrieving keyboard events from the keyboard queue (using interrupts 16h and 21h) and a Windows application retrieving keyboard events through a *GetMessage* request, is the amount of information available under Windows. For example, when the "a" key is pressed, the DOS keyboard queue would simply contain the character "a". Under Windows, three key event messages are generated: a WM_KEYDOWN event reporting the key being pressed, a WM_CHAR event message reporting character code, and a WM_KEYUP event after the key is released.

Windows reports eight different keyboard event messages in all. These messages are identified as WM_xxxx, and each message is accompanied by the *wParam* and *lParam* variables; thus comprising a total of eight separate pieces of information about each key event. Fortunately, applications are not required to use all of the information provided by these messages; but the information is there if and when it is needed.

The WM_xxxx Event Message

The first piece of information provided with each key event is the window message; which can be either application messages (non-system keystrokes) as WM_KEYDOWN, WM_KEYUP, WM_CHAR and WM_DEADCHAR or system keystroke messages as WM_SYSKEYDOWN, WM_SYSKEYUP, WM_SYSCHAR and WM_SYS-DEADCHAR.

The system keystroke messages, which contain "SYS" in their identifiers, are generally more important to Windows than to applications and are normally passed to *DefWindowProc* for handling. These would include ALT key combinations such as Alt-Tab or Alt-Esc used to switch the active window or system menu accelerators (Alt-function key combinations are discussed in Part 2).

The WM_KEYUP and WM_KEYDOWN messages are also normally ignored by applications. These messages are generated by keys that are pressed or released without the Alt key but are ignored by Windows.

The two "DEAD" key messages are also normally ignored. These are generated by non-U.S. keyboards whereby certain keys are designated to add an accent or diacritic to a letter, but are called "dead" because they do not, by themselves, generate characters. And, for most applications, these messages can be ignored.

This leaves the WM_CHAR message as the single keyboard message that most applications will need to process because this is where the character code, the keyboard letter, is actually found.

But, I said that there were a total of eight pieces of information contained in the keyboard message and the character code is only one of these. So what else is available?

In DOS, in addition to character and scan codes, it is also possible to retrieve keyboard shift-state information which contains the status of the left and right Shift keys, the Ctrl and Alt key states, and the CapsLock and NumLock shift states as well as the normally ignored Scroll Lock and Insert status. For enhanced keyboards, the right and left Ctrl and Alt keys are identified separately and the key positions (as well as toggle state) of the ScrollLock, Num-Lock, CapsLock, and SysReq keys are reported. Key up and key down events, however, are not reported as separate events under DOS. And, while similar information is available under Windows (see *GetKeyState*), a different type of information accompanies each keyboard event message, contained in the *wParam* and *lParam* variables.

The wParam and lParam Variables

The *wParam* variable reports a virtual key code which, for a WM_CHAR message, provides the character code, but, as discussed in the list below, may also contain much more.

First, the *lParam* variable is broken down into three fields: the repeat count, the OEM scan code, and the flag bits as illustrated in Figure 3-1.

■ *Repeat Count*—gives the number of keystrokes represented by the event message and, in most cases, is one. However, when a key is held down and an application cannot process key-down messages fast enough (the default typematic rate is approximately 10-characters-per-second), Windows will combine multiple WM_KEYDOWN, WM_SYSKEYDOWN, WM_CHAR, and WM_SYSCHAR messages into a single message, increasing the repeat count appropriately. For WM_KEYUP or WM_SYSKEYUP event messages, the repeat count is always one.

The *KeyCodes.C* demo program, even on fast (386/33MHz) systems, will demonstrate typematic overruns simply because of the time required to write a full-line screen message for each key event. This does not mean that all applications are likely to be overwritten. There are cases, however, when applications may prefer to ignore the repeat count in order to reduce the potential for overscrolling—a problem that is not specific to Windows, but has often been encountered in DOS as typematic keystrokes piled up in the keyboard buffer faster than applications could respond. This is an area in which experimentation is the best guide. An application option could be provided to allow toggling or variable responses for repeat counts reported by certain keys.

- *OEM Scan Code*—the keyboard scan code generate by the system hardware which identifies the physical key that was pressed. For example, on an enhanced keyboard, a "1" could be generated by the normal number key in the top row of characters or by the keypad, but each physical key returns a different and unique scan code. In other cases, different scan codes may be generated by the same physical key under different Alt, Ctrl or Shift states. Windows applications normally ignore the scan code information, using other approaches to derive this information.

- *Extended Key*—set (1) if the keystroke derives from one of the additional keys on the enhanced keyboard. These keys include the separate (non-keypad) cursor and page keys (including the Insert and Delete keys), the slash (/) and Enter keys on the keypad, and the NumLock key.

- *Context Code* (Alt-Key)—set (1) if the Alt key is pressed. Also, the context code is always set for WM_SYSKEYUP and WM_SYS-KEYDOWN messages and cleared (0) for WM_KEYUP and WM_KEY-DOWN messages—with two exceptions:

  (1) Some non-English keyboards use combinations of Shift, Ctrl, and Alt keys with conventional keys to generate special characters. For these characters, *lParam* has the context code flag set (1), but these are not reported as *system* keystroke messages.

(2) When the active window is an icon, it does not receive the input focus. Therefore, all keystrokes generate WM_SYS-KEYUP and WM_SYSKEYDOWN messages so that the active window (icon) does not process these strokes. The context code flag is set only if the Alt key is down.

- *Prior Key State*—reports the prior state of the current key. For WM_CHAR, WM_CHARDOWN, WM_SYSCHAR, and WM_SYS-CHARDOWN messages, the prior key state flag is set (1) if the same key was previously down, or cleared (0) if the key was previously up. For WM_KEYUP or WM_SYSKEYUP messages, the prior key state flag is always set (since, obviously, the key had to already be down before it could be released).

- *Transition State*—virtually a redundancy and cleared (0) if a key is being pressed (WM_KEYDOWN or WM_SYSKEYDOWN), and set (1) if the key is being released (WM_KEYUP or WM_SYSKEYUP). The Transition State flag is also cleared for WM_CHAR or WM_SYSCHAR messages, but means nothing at all in such a case.

Figure 3-1: The lParam Message Variable

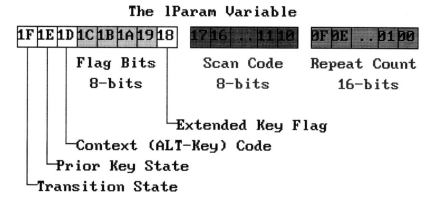

Figure 3-2 shows a series of key event messages captured by the *KeyCodes.C* program. The program has added an additional half-line space after each WM_KEYUP or WM_SYSKEYUP message to provide a degree of grouping to the keyboard event messages reported. But, as you may observe, the _KEY-

DOWN, _CHAR and _KEYUP messages for a specific key do not always appear in sequential order.

Figure 3-2: Virtual Key Codes

Keyboard Event Messages										
Message	Code	Key	Char	Cnt	Scan	Ext	ALT	Prv	Trs	
WM_KEYDOWN	28h			1	50h	√		↑	↓	
WM_KEYUP	28h			1	50h	√		↓	↑	Down Arrow
WM_KEYDOWN	26h			1	48h	√		↑	↓	
WM_KEYUP	26h			1	48h	√		↓	↑	Up Arrow
WM_KEYDOWN	54h			1	14h			↑	↓	
WM_CHAR		74h	t	1	14h					
WM_KEYDOWN	48h			1	23h			↑	↓	
WM_CHAR		68h	h	1	23h					
WM_KEYUP	54h			1	14h			↓	↑	
WM_KEYUP	48h			1	23h			↓	↑	
WM_KEYDOWN	49h			1	17h			↑	↓	
WM_CHAR		69h	i	1	17h					
WM_KEYDOWN	53h			1	1Fh			↑	↓	
WM_CHAR		73h	s	1	1Fh					
WM_KEYUP	49h			1	17h			↓	↑	
WM_KEYUP	53h			1	1Fh			↓	↑	
WM_KEYDOWN	20h			1	39h			↑	↓	
WM_CHAR		20h		1	39h					Spacebar
WM_KEYUP	20h			1	39h			↓	↑	
WM_KEYDOWN	49h			1	17h			↑	↓	call to
WM_CHAR		69h	i	1	17h					screen
WM_KEYUP	49h			1	17h			↓	↑	capture
WM_KEYDOWN	7Ah			1	57h			↑	↓	F11 program

For example, the "t" character WM_KEYUP message appears after the "h" WM_KEYDOWN and WM_CHAR messages, not because of any defect in Windows, but simply because, as a speedy touch-typist, I had not yet released the "t" at the time I was pressing the "h" key. A similar mixed ordering appears for the "i" and "s" characters for the same reasons. Also, notice the last line in the illustration where the WM_KEYDOWN message appears without a corresponding WM_KEYUP message. This occurred in the example program because the keydown event was received by the demo program, but the key pressed was the F11 key, which was used as a hot key to summon the screen capture program used to produce this snapshot and, naturally, transferred the keyboard focus to the new program (see Keyboard Focus, below).

Since the KeyCodes application did hold the keyboard focus at the time the F11 key was pressed, it did receive the WM_KEYDOWN message. But, after reporting this fact, the key event message was passed back to Windows using the *DefWindowProc* function. Since Windows then called the capture utility, transferring the focus, the KeyCodes application did not receive the WM_KEYUP release event message.

Notice also that the Up Arrow and Down Arrow key events, identified by comments added to the illustration, do not generate WM_CHAR messages; only key down and key up event messages.

The listing for the KeyCodes demo program appears at the end of this chapter and can be used to view most, but not all, keyboard event messages.

Virtual Key Codes

While the *lParam* variable may contain information useful in specialized cases, the virtual key codes contained in the *wParam* variable comprise the principal identifiers for key events. These codes do not include all keyboard characters, only the principal characters that might be used for controls or menu selections. Thus, the **VK_xxxx** definitions are a means of identifying specific key codes in a device-independent format.

In Table 3-1, the column labeled "Req," ("Required") indicates by asterisks (*) the keys which are required for all Windows implementations and which will always be available. The remaining **VK_xxxx** definitions, unless labeled as *not supported*, are found on most conventional or enhanced keyboards. **VK_xxxx** definitions listed as *not supported* are not implemented on IBM/compatible keyboards but may be supported by other manufacturers' keyboards.

Note: For text input, file names, or data of any type, character codes should be used, not the **VK_xxxx** key codes.

Table 3-1: Virtual Key Codes (Defined in Windows.H)

Hex	Dec	Constant	Req	Keyboard	Comments
01h	1	VK_LBUTTON			(mouse emulation)
02h	2	VK_RBUTTON			(mouse emulation)
03h	3	VK_CANCEL	*	Ctrl-Break	same code as Ctrl-C
04h	4	VK_MBUTTON			(mouse emulation)
08h	5	VK_BACK	*	BackSpace	
09h	9	VK_TAB	*	Tab	
0Ch	12	VK_CLEAR		numeric keypad 5	NumLock OFF
0Dh	13	VK_RETURN	*	Enter	CR
10h	16	VK_SHIFT	*	Shift	
11h	17	VK_CONTROL	*	Ctrl	

Table 3-1: *Virtual Key Codes (Defined in Windows.H) (cont.)*

Hex	Dec	Constant	Req	Keyboard	Comments
12h	18	VK_MENU	*	Alt	
13h	19	VK_PAUSE		Pause	
14h	20	VK_CAPITAL	*	Caps Lock	
1Bh	27	VK_ESCAPE	*	Esc	
20h	32	VK_SPACE	*	Spacebar	
21h	33	VK_PRIOR	*	Page Up	
22h	34	VK_NEXT	*	Page Down	
23h	35	VK_END		End	
24h	36	VK_HOME	*	Home	
25h	37	VK_LEFT	*	Left Arrow	
26h	38	VK_UP	*	Up Arrow	
27h	39	VK_RIGHT	*	Right Arrow	
28h	40	VK_DOWN	*	Down Arrow	
29h	41	VK_SELECT			not supported
2Ah	42	VK_PRINT			not supported
2Bh	43	VK_EXECUTE			not supported
2Ch	44	VK_SNAPSHOT		Print Screen	
2Dh	45	VK_INSERT	*	Insert	
2Eh	46	VK_DELETE	*	Delete	
2Fh	47	VK_HELP			not supported
30h..39h	48..57		*	0..9	main keyboard
41h..5Ah	65..90		*	A..Z, a..z	main keyboard
60h	96	VK_NUMPAD0		numeric keypad 0	NumLock ON
61h	97	VK_NUMPAD1		numeric keypad 1	NumLock ON
62h	98	VK_NUMPAD2		numeric keypad 2	NumLock ON
63h	9	VK_NUMPAD3		numeric keypad 3	NumLock ON
64h	100	VK_NUMPAD4		numeric keypad 4	NumLock ON
65h	101	VK_NUMPAD5		numeric keypad 5	NumLock ON
66h	102	VK_NUMPAD6		numeric keypad 6	NumLock ON
67h	103	VK_NUMPAD7		numeric keypad 7	NumLock ON
68h	104	VK_NUMPAD8		numeric keypad 8	NumLock ON
69h	105	VK_NUMPAD9		numeric keypad 9	NumLock ON
6Ah	106	VK_MULTIPLY		numeric keypad *	enhanced kbd
6Bh	107	VK_ADD		numeric keypad +	enhanced kbd
6Ch	108	VK_SEPARATOR			not upported
6Dh	109	VK_SUBTRACT		numeric keypad -	enhanced kbd
6Eh	110	VK_DECIMAL		numeric keypad .	

Table 3-1: Virtual Key Codes (Defined in Windows.H) (cont.)

Hex	Dec	Constant	Req	Keyboard	Comments
6Fh	111	VK_DIVIDE		numeric keypad /	enhanced kbd
70h	112	VK_F1	*	function key F1	
71h	113	VK_F2	*	function key F2	
72h	114	VK_F3	*	function key F3	
73h	115	VK_F4	*	function key F4	
74h	116	VK_F5	*	function key F5	
75h	117	VK_F6	*	function key F6	
76h	118	VK_F7	*	function key F7	
77h	119	VK_F8	*	function key F8	
78h	120	VK_F9	*	function key F9	
79h	121	VK_F10	*	function key F10	
7Ah	122	VK_F11		function key F11	enhanced kbd
7Bh	123	VK_F12		function key F12	enhanced kbd
7Ch	124	VK_F13			not supported
7Dh	125	VK_F14			not supported
7Eh	126	VK_F15			not supported
7Fh	127	VK_F16			not supported
90h	144	VK_NUMLOCK		Num Lock	

The VK_LBUTTON, etc key codes are not returned by keystroke messages but do correspond to mouse button messages.

The virtual key definitions do not include punctuation and/or symbols. Instead virtual key codes in the range 80h..FFh (128..255) are used but assigned values in this range may vary on non-English keyboards. Therefore, applications should not depend on keystroke values not defined in Windows.H.

Virtual key definitions listed as ***not supported*** are not found on IBM/compatible keyboards but may be supported by some variant keyboards.

The GetKeyState Function

While the *wParam* and *lParam* variables contain considerable information, they do not include specific shift-key information. The current state of any of the defined virtual keys can be queried by the *GetKeyState* function which is customarily used to query the shift keys (Shift, Ctrl and Alt keys) and the toggle keys (CapsLock and NumLock). This does not, however, provide the status of a specific shift key since no differentiation is made between the right and left Alt keys.

This latter type of query has been normally used under DOS for TSR applications that install their own Interrupt 09h handlers; and, under Windows, there are other methods of providing hot-key selections. The *GetKey State* function can be used, for example, to query the state of the shift key(s):

```
if( GetKeyState( VK_SHIFT ) != 0 ) ....
```

This example returns TRUE if either shift key is down, or FALSE if both shift keys are up. The *GetKeyState(VK_SHIFT)* function, however, returns a negative value if either shift key is down, and zero if both are up.

In other cases, as with the NumLock and CapsLock keys, *GetKeyState* reports on the toggled state set by the key. Thus the query:

```
if( GetKeyState( VK_NUMLOCK ) != 0 ) ) ...
```

returns TRUE if NumLock is toggled ON or FALSE if it is OFF because the function call, *GetKeyState(VK_NUMLOCK)* returns with the low-bit set (positive) if the corresponding system flag is set.

The *GetKeyState* function can also be used with the VK_LBUTTON, VK_RBUTTON and VK_MBUTTON virtual key codes to query a mouse button status; even though this is unnecessary because the mouse event messages, as shown in Chapter 4, contain complete key status information.

Caution: This is not a "real-time" keyboard status check. It is a test of the keyboard status at the time the last keyboard event message was retrieved by the application. Thus, *GetKeyState* cannot be used in *while* control loops because the application must retrieve the event message from the queue before *GetKeyState* can query the status. Ergo, the example:

```
while( GetKeyState( VK_NUMLOCK ) != 0 ) ...
```

could wait forever since no change in status would ever be detected. But the alternative:

```
do ... while( GetKeyState( VK_NUMLOCK ) != 0 );
```

could viably execute as long as the message queue is queried within the loop.

Responding to Keyboard Messages

The *KeyCodes* program, which demonstrates interception and reporting keyboard event messages, also shows some of the hazards of attempting to process every message received. As suggested earlier, if an application is not fast enough to process all messages, Windows will combine duplicate messages using the *repeat count* field in the *lParam* variable. But, processing all keyboard messages is neither necessary nor desirable.

First, WM_SYS messages are intended for Windows systems functions, not for the application to handle, and can be safely ignored.

Second, WM_KEYDOWN and WM_KEYUP messages are largely duplicates and most Windows applications confine themselves to watching for WM_KEYDOWN messages and ignore the WM_KEYUP events.

Third, even when WM_KEYDOWN messages are processed by applications, they are generally confined to cursor and special key events and should not be used to retrieve conventional character key strokes. For conventional characters, only the WM_CHAR messages should be used.

Finally, repeating an earlier caution, Windows applications should not attempt to rely on special key combinations since they may easily be quite different on non-English keyboards (and non-English keyboard drivers). While this may appear to invalidate a number of favorite "tricks", there are more than a few alternatives. Not relying on deciphering such key combinations can considerably reduce the time required for processing keyboard messages.

Note: Under Windows, the capability of processing messages is paralleled by the capability of generating and sending messages. This will be demonstrated in Chapter 4 when the cursor keys are used to generate mouse messages.

Character Event Messages

Most applications dealing with text input depend upon processing WM_CHAR character event messages. As stated previously, the WM_CHAR messages do not always correspond to the familiar ASCII codes. So, what is available and dependable? First, Windows does provide translation services. This has been incorporated in all program examples presented thus far in the code segment in *WinMain*:

```
while( GetMessage( &msg, NULL, 0, 0 ) )
{  TranslateMessage( &msg );
   DispatchMessage( &msg );    }
```

This *while* loop retrieves messages from the message queue, then passes them for processing through the *TranslateMessage* function before dispatching the translated messages for further action by the application's *WndProc* procedures.

However, it is the *TranslateMessage* function that converts keystroke messages into character messages which are recognizable and usable by the application. The keyboard, per se, generates only keystroke information that is interpreted by the keyboard driver into WM_KEYDOWN, WM_KEYUP, WM_SYSKEYDOWN, and WM_SYSKEYUP messages. It is the translation process that generates the four character messages: WM_CHAR and WM_DEADCHAR messages derived from WM_KEYDOWN messages, and WM_SYSCHAR and WM_SYSDEADCHAR messages derived from WM_SYS-KEYDOWN messages.

This translation process includes processing shift-key information to generate upper- and lower-case characters, checking toggle states for CapsLock and NumLock and, in the end, generating WM_CHAR or WM_DEADCHAR messages. In the resulting WM_CHAR messages, the *lParam* variables are simply the same as the keystroke messages that generate the character message. But, the *wParam* variables are the important thing here and contain the ASCII codes for the characters.

In Figure 3-2, the WM_KEYDOWN message shows a keycode of 54h (ASCII "T"), but the generated WM_CHAR message has an ASCII code of 74h ("t"). In one instance shown (the spacebar) the WM_KEYDOWN, and WM_CHAR message codes are the same, 20h, but this is not always the rule even though most keycodes do correspond to one of the ASCII codes generated by most English-language keyboards. The scan codes, of course, report the physical key pressed but these are keyboard dependent codes and also vary internationally.

In contrast, the up arrow key shows a keycode of 28h which would be an ASCII '('. The scan code of 50h does identify the up arrow key except that an enhanced keyboard has two up arrow keys with two different scan codes. One of these may be attempting to generate an ASCII "8" instead of a cursor instruction.

The point is that the WM_CHAR messages should be relied on for character information and the VK_xxxx message parameters used for all function and cursor key identification. Examples will be shown in the demo program, *Editor.C* .

The KeyCodes Program

The *KeyCodes.C* program provides a window to examine keyboard event messages, but introduces very little in terms of Windows programming. Most of the actual program is copied directly from previous examples with the exceptions of the *ShowKey* subprocedure and the addition of eight case statements that call *ShowKey* in response to keyboard WM_xxxx messages.

There are, however, a few other provisions. Since this display will be formatted, the default proportionally spaced character font would be difficult to use, so the WM_CREATE response calls *GetStockObject* to select a fixed-width font instead:

```
case WM_CREATE:
   . . .
    SelectObject( hdc, GetStockObject(OEM_FIXED_FONT) );
   . . .
```

The fonts available under Windows will be discussed presently but the OEM_FIXED_FONT, which is the familiar DOS system font, was selected for this example in order to use a few of the extended ASCII character symbols not available in other fonts. A second special provision is found in the WM_PAINT response:

```
case WM_PAINT:
   . . .
SetBkMode( hdc, TRANSPARENT );
TextOut( hdc, cxChr, 1, szCapt, (sizeof szCapt)-1 );
TextOut( hdc, cxChr, 5, szUnLn, (sizeof szUnLn)-1 );
SetBkMode( hdc, OPAQUE );                // restore default mode //
   . . .
```

The two string definitions, *szCapt* and *szUnLn*, provide a column caption in the client window but are written, effectively, on top of each other. The default paint mode used by *TextOut* emulates a character-based display and paints the character background. The result is that the second string displayed overwrites (erases) the first. By calling *SetBkMode* with the instruction TRANS-

PARENT, *TextOut* paints only the character, leaving the background unchanged. When this is finished, *SetBkMode* is called a second time with the OPAQUE instruction to reset the default conditions.

The eight WM_xxxx keyboard event messages then each call the *ShowKey* procedure, passing, in addition to the window handle (*hwnd*), two flag parameters, a string identifying the message and, finally, the *wParam* and *lParam* variables:

```
case WM_KEYDOWN:
    ShowKey( hwnd, 0, 0, WM_KEYDOWN, wParam, lParam );

    return(0);

case WM_KEYUP:
    ShowKey( hwnd, 0, 1, WM_KEYUP, wParam, lParam );

    return(0);

case WM_CHAR:
    ShowKey( hwnd, 1, 0, WM_CHAR, wParam, lParam );

    return(0);

case WM_DEADCHAR:
    ShowKey( hwnd, 1, 0, WM_DEADCHAR, wParam, lParam );

    return(0);

case WM_SYSKEYDOWN:
    ShowKey( hwnd, 0, 0, WM_SYSKEYDOWN, wParam, lParam );

    break;

case WM_SYSKEYUP:
    ShowKey( hwnd, 0, 1, WM_SYSKEYUP, wParam, lParam );

    break;

case WM_SYSCHAR:
    ShowKey( hwnd, 1, 0, WM_SYSCHAR,  wParam, lParam );
    break;


case WM_SYSDEADCHAR:
ShowKey( hwnd, 1, 0, WM_SYSDEADCHAR,
```

```
            wParam, lParam );
break;
```

The four WM_SYSxxxx message cases each end with a *break* statement rather than a *return* statement. This insures that these messages are passed, after review, to *WndDefaultProc* for any necessary handling by Windows. The two character messages and the WM_KEYDOWN and WM_KEYUP messages end here, needing no further processing.

The flag parameters following *hwnd* identify, first, the format that *ShowKey* will use to display the event message and, second, a provision for additional line spacing following the display of WM_...KEYUP messages.

The subprocedure *ShowKey* is essentially self-explanatory, breaking the *lParam* values down according to the field shown in Figure 3-1 and displaying these in a formatted arrangement. Since the *lParam* values for the WM_...CHAR messages are the same as the WM_...KEYDOWN messages that cause the *TranslateMessage* function to generate the character messages, these fields are only displayed for the WM_...KEYDOWN and WM_...KEYUP messages, not for the character messages.

There is one other item worth noting:

```
TextOut( hdc, cxChr, cyWin - step, szBuff,
         wsprintf( szBuff, szFormat[iType],
         (LPSTR) szMsg, ...
```

In *ShowKey*, the *wsprintf* function is called with the typecasting instruction LPSTR preceeding the *szMsg* parameter. LPSTR is defined in Windows.H as a far pointer to a string. This explicit typecasting is necessary, in this case, because *szMsg* has already been passed as a local pointer reference from the *WndProc* procedure and must be redefined from a local to a far pointer. On the other hand, the first two string pointer parameters, *szBuff* and *szFormat[...]*, are pointer references to variables declared within the *ShowKey* procedure and, therefore, are automatically passed to *wsprintf* as the far pointer references expected. Still, when in doubt, typecasting pointers shouldn't hurt.

Text Input Handling

A majority of applications, even without being word processor/editor programs, are text oriented and must process text input as well as display text characters. While processing text input can range from input boxes that display a few words or a single line to full screens of unstructured text, there are a few basics that apply to any type of text input. Also, when using Windows a few differences exist as well. These differences are discussed below.

Caret vs Cursor

In Windows, the word **cursor** is reserved for the mouse cursor: i.e., the bitmapped image representing the mouse position and, frequently, indicating the type of action the mouse will control. But what about the old, familiar DOS text cursor? That ubiquitous blinking underline character that has so reliably guided our interactions for so many years?

Well, the text cursor, under Windows, is now known as the **caret**; perhaps a poor choice of terms since caret is also the name of that funny little hat-shaped character (^) that C uses as the bitwise XOR operator (and that other *human* languages use as an accent as in the characters Â, Ê, Î, Ô, Û and a,e,i,o,u). Still, under windows, the caret is the new text cursor and can be a horizontal line, a character-sized block, a vertical line, or a bitmapped image.

An underline caret is, of course, equivalent to the standard DOS cursor, while the box or caret has been used by a variety of editor/word processor applications. The vertical line caret, however, has not been a familar element in DOS except in the case of graphics-based programs such as paint or typesetting programs. This latter caret (cursor) is preferred, however, whenever proportional typefaces (fonts) are used because underline and box carets can not vary their widths conveniently to match varying character widths.

Caret Functions

Because the caret (text cursor) is a system resource, individual applications can not create and destroy their own carets any more than they can create and destroy the system mouse cursor. And, like the mouse cursor, there is only one caret in the system.

Applications can, however, borrow the system caret as needed but can do so only while they hold the system (input) focus. An application can modify the caret, thus changing the caret type and, of course, modifying the caret position.

An application must first know when it has or loses the system focus. This is established by receipt of WM_SETFOCUS and WM_KILLFOCUS messages. These messages are always issued in pairs, i.e., a WM_KILLFOCUS message is never sent to an application unless it has already received a WM_SETFO-CUS message; and a WM_KILLFOCUS message is always sent to an application before the system focus is removed.

Receipt of a WM_SETFOCUS or WM_KILLFOCUS message does not mean that an application is being created or destroyed. It only means that the focus is being shifted to or from the current application. A WM_CREATE message, however, always follows a WM_SETFOCUS message and a WM_DESTROY message precedes a WM_KILLFOCUS message. Also, an application always receives an equal number of WM_SETFOCUS and WM_KILLFOCUS messages during its active life.

Thus, to use the caret, an application calls *CreateCaret* in response to the WM_SETFOCUS messages and calls *DestroyCaret* in response to WM_KILLFOCUS messages:

```
case WM_SETFOCUS:
    CreateCaret( hwnd, 1, cxChr, cyChr );
    SetCaretPos( xCaret * cxChr, yCaret * cyChr );
    ShowCaret( hwnd );
    return( 0 );
```

When *CreateCaret* is called, the caret is always invisible and its position within the client window is indeterminate. Therefore, *SetCaretPos* is needed to set the caret position and *ShowCaret* is needed to make the caret visible.

```
case WM_KILLFOCUS:
    HideCaret( hwnd );
    DestroyCaret();
    return( 0 );
```

The *HideCaret* function should be called before *DestroyCaret* to conceal the caret . Refer to the notes below on individual caret functions.

CreateCaret/DestroyCaret When the system caret is called by an application using the *CreateCaret* function, the application can first set the shape and type of caret used. Since any call to *CreateCaret* automatically destroys the previous caret shape, if any, assigning caret parameters is absolutely necessary before

ShowCaret can be called to reveal the caret; no matter which window owned the caret.

The parameters for *CreateCaret* are:

- *hwnd* —identifies window owning the new caret
- *hBitmap*—identifies the bitmap that defines the caret shape; NULL selects a solid caret, and 1 selects a gray caret. Bitmapped caret shapes will be discussed later.
- *nWidth*—specifies caret width in logical units
- *nHeight*—specifies caret height in logical units

Examples of three popular caret styles include:

```
CreateCaret( hwnd, 1, cxChr, cyChr );    // gray block caret //
CreateCaret( hwnd, 0, cxChr, 1 );        // underscore caret //
CreateCaret( hwnd, 0, 1, cyChr );        // vertical var caret //
```

The *DestroyCaret* function is called without parameters.

SetCaretPos/GetCaretPos   *SetCaretPos* moves the caret to the position specified in logical coordinates by the X/Y parameters. Coordinates are client window-relative and are affected by the window's mapping mode. So, the exact position in pixels depends upon this mapping mode. *SetCaretPos* moves the caret only if it is owned by a window in the current task but is not affected by the caret being hidden.

Note: The caret is a shared resource and an application window should not move the caret if it does not own the caret.

GetCaretPos retrieves the caret's current position, in screen coordinates, copying the values to a POINT structure addressed by the *lpPoint* parameter. The caret position is always given in the client coordinates of the window which contains the caret.

ShowCaret/HideCaret   *ShowCaret* and *HideCaret* are complementary functions that reveal or conceal the caret only if the window indicated by the *hwnd* parameter owns the caret. If *hwnd* is NULL, the function shows or hides the caret only if a window in the current task owns the caret. *ShowCaret* and *HideCaret* are also cumulative. Thus, if *HideCaret* has been called five times in a row, *ShowCaret* must be called five times before the caret will be visible.

SetCaretBlinkTime/GetCaretBlinkTime *SetCaretBlinkTime* sets the caret blink rate as elapsed milliseconds between flashes and is called with a WORD parameter setting. The caret flashes on or off with each *wMSeconds* milliseconds, making the total flash cycle (on-off-on) 2 * wMSeconds.

The complementary *GetCaretBlinkTime* returns the blink rate (*wMSeconds*) as a WORD value.

Caret (Cursor) Positioning

The *Editor.C* program used for demonstration creates a gray-block caret (see Figure 3-3) suitable for use with the SYSTEM_FIXED_FONT (fixed-width) character set. Since this editor uses a fixed-width font, cursor positioning becomes quite simple. Begin by watching for the WM_KEYDOWN message:

```
case WM_KEYDOWN:
    switch( wParam )
    {
```

Many of the WM_KEYDOWN messages simply will be ignored, but the *wParam* message parameter will identify messages which correspond to the cursor and page control keys:

```
        case VK_HOME:   xCaret = 0;                 break;
        case VK_END:    xCaret = cxBuff - 1;        break;
        case VK_PRIOR:  yCaret = 0;                 break;
        case VK_NEXT:   yCaret = cyBuff - 1;        break;
        case VK_LEFT:
        xCaret = max( 0, xCaret-1 );                break;
        case VK_RIGHT:
        xCaret = min( cxBuff-1, xCaret+1 );         break;
        case VK_UP:
        yCaret = max( 0, yCaret-1 );                break;
        case VK_DOWN:
        yCaret = min( cyBuff-1, yCaret+1 );         break;
```

Repositioning the cursor is fairly straight-forward in most cases but could be elaborated to provide wrapping at screen margins plus other features not supported here. For other non-character keys, a more elaborate response is required. The VK_DELETE message produced by the Delete key is an example:

```
case VK_DELETE:
    for( x=xCaret; x<cxBuff-1; x++ )
        Buffer(x,yCaret) = Buffer(x+1,yCaret);
    Buffer( cxBuff-1, yCaret ) = ' ';
```

In this case, the response for the indicated line begins by copying each character from one position beyond the delete position to the end of the line back one position, i.e., deleting the current character by shifting the remainder of the line left and adding a blank at the end of the line. This much is fairly simple since no wrapping or other editor elaborations are attempted. But, in addition to deleting a character from the buffer, the process also executes an immediate screen update:

```
HideCaret( hwnd );
hdc = GetDC( hwnd );
SelectObject( hdc,
    GetStockObject( SYSTEM_FIXED_FONT ) );
TextOut( hdc, xCaret*cxChr, yCaret*cyChr,
        &Buffer( xCaret, yCaret ),
        cxBuff-xCaret );
ShowCaret( hwnd );
ReleaseDC( hwnd, hdc );
break;
}
```

Figure 3-3: A Simple Windows Editor

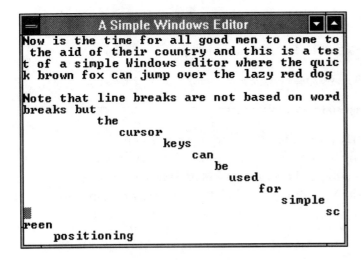

Notice that the *HideCaret* function is called before the screen is updated and the *ShowCaret* function is called afterwards to restore the caret. This is a necessary process anytime a screen paint operation is executed. It is needed to insure that the caret does not interfere with the paint operations. Similar precautions are exercised when the mouse cursor is active.

Before the WM_KEYDOWN message handling exits, *SetCaretPos* is called to update the caret position, even though most of the WM_KEYDOWN messages have no effect on the caret position:

```
SetCaretPos( xCaret * cxChr, yCaret * cyChr );
return( 0 );                        // end cursor / keypad keys //
```

The WM_CHAR message is also subject to several types of processing. But, since a single WM_CHAR message may be responsible for several keystrokes on a single character, handling begins with a loop using the repeat count value from the *lParam* variable:

```
case WM_CHAR:
   for( i=0; i<LOWORD(lParam); i++ )
   {
```

And, within the loop, the *wParam* variable contains the character code:

```
   switch( wParam )
   {
```

The order in which the characters are handled is not particularly important, but the '\b' or backspace character is a special case:

```
      case '\b':                    // backspace             //
         if( xCaret > 0 )
         {
            xCaret;
            SendMessage( hwnd, WM_KEYDOWN,
                     VK_DELETE, 1L );
         } break;
```

To respond to a backspace character which, unlike the Delete key, appears as a standard character instead of a WM_KEYDOWN message with a VK_xxxx identifier, the *SendMessage* function is called after testing and adjusting the caret position (*xCaret*). This generates a WM_KEYDOWN, VK_DELETE message, thus allowing the earlier handling to delete the character and update the display. The tab key also uses the *SendMessage* function to generate a series of WM_CHAR space character messages:

```
case '\t':                        // tab                    //
    do SendMessage( hwnd, WM_CHAR, ' ', 1L );
    while( xCaret % 8 != 0 );
    break;
```

The next two special character codes simply change the caret position in this application:

```
case '\r':                        // carriage return        //
    xCaret = 0;                   // falls through to '\n'  //
case '\n':                        // linefeed               //
    if( ++yCaret == cyBuff ) yCaret = 0;
    break;
```

Rather than duplicating the linefeed provisions for the carriage return case, the carriage return case is not given a *break* statement. This allows it to fall through for additional handling by the linefeed statement.

The ESCape key resets the entire text buffer which also happens in this example anytime the screen is resized. It is provided here with a dialog box to query the action before execution:

```
case '\x1B':                      // escape                 //
    if( MessageBox( hwnd, Reset text buffer?,
        Editor Query,
        MB_ICONEXCLAMATION | MB_OKCANCEL |
        MB_DEFBUTTON2 ) == IDOK )
    {
        for( y=0; y<cyBuff; y++ )
            for( x=0; x<cxBuff; x++ )
                Buffer( x, y ) = ' ';
        xCaret = 0;    yCaret = 0;
        InvalidateRect( hwnd, NULL, FALSE );
    }
            break;
```

Dialog boxes will be discussed at greater length in Part 2.

For every character that was not handled by one of the preceding special cases, which will include most text entries, the *default* case inserts the character in the buffer; then, as before, hides the caret, updates the screen and restores the caret (text cursor).

```
    default:                          // all other characters  //
        Buffer( xCaret, yCaret ) = (char) wParam;
        HideCaret( hwnd );
        hdc = GetDC( hwnd );
        SelectObject( hdc,
              GetStockObject(SYSTEM_FIXED_FONT) );
        TextOut( hdc, xCaret*cxChr, yCaret*cyChr,
                 &Buffer( xCaret, yCaret ), 1 );
        ShowCaret( hwnd );
        ReleaseDC( hwnd, hdc );
        if( ++xCaret == cxBuff )
        {
            xCaret = 0;
            if( ++yCaret == cyBuff ) yCaret = 0;
        }
        break;
  }  }
```

The default case also has provisions to recalculate, i.e., advance, the caret position. And, since other preceding provisions may also have affected the caret position, the WM_CHAR message handling also ends with a call to *SetCaretPos*:

```
SetCaretPos( xCaret * cxChr, yCaret * cyChr );
return( 0 );
```

As editors go, this example is an idiot editor and has no provisions for anything except the simplest of input and display with elementary positioning and revision capabilities. Still, this example does show how WM_KEYDOWN and WM_CHAR messages can be handled, and demonstrates the basic caret functions.

The SendMessage Function

The flip-side of processing keyboard messages is the ability to send your own messages that request actions. The *SendMessage* function provides this capability. The *SendMessage* function is called with the same four parameter types that were passed to the WndProc procedure:

```
SendMessage( HWND hwnd,    WORD msg,
             WORD wParam, LONG lParam );
```

SendMessage passes its message parameters to Windows which is then responsible for placing the message in the message queue for the window procedure identified by *hwnd*. This destination could be the same window procedure that posted the message, another window procedure belonging to the same application or an entirely different application.

As another example, the program *PainText.C* in Chapter 2 demonstrated scrollbars that responded only to mouse events. There are still some computers that lack a mouse and rely on the keyboard to operate Windows applications. Therefore, to demonstrate the *SendMessage* function, *PainText.C* will be modified to provide an alternative means of scrolling the client window using the keyboard.

Rather than attempting to actually emulate the mouse using the keyboard, it's easier for this application to directly generate scrollbar messages in response to the *left, right, up*, and *down* arrow keys. This can be accomplished by adding a WM_KEYDOWN response:

```
switch( message )
{
   ...
   case WM_KEYDOWN:
      switch( wParam )
      {
         case VK_LEFT:
            SendMessage( hwnd, WM_HSCROLL, SB_LINEUP,   0L );
            break;
         case VK_RIGHT:
            SendMessage( hwnd, WM_HSCROLL, SB_LINEDOWN, 0L );
            break;
         case VK_UP:
            SendMessage( hwnd, WM_VSCROLL, SB_LINEUP,   0L );
            break;
         case VK_DOWN:
            SendMessage( hwnd, WM_VSCROLL, SB_LINEDOWN, 0L );
            break;
      }
      return(0);
   ...
```

In this fashion, the four arrow keys generate scrollbar messages equivalent to clicking on the arrow keys at the ends of the scrollbars. Or, for faster scrolling, the PageUp, PageDown, Home, and End keys could be added to generate SB_PAGEUP and SB_PAGEDOWN messages. The *SendMessage* function is capable of sending almost any type of message, not just keystroke, character, or scrollbar messages. These messages will be discussed further in future examples.

Fonts and Character Sets

Thus far, most of the examples have used a fixed-width font either for simplicity in formatting output or for simplicity in positioning the cursor. However, Windows supplies several character sets (fonts) as well as supporting the hardware character set that is embedded in the ROM chips in video adapters, printers, and BIOS system chips. But, as you will see, these are two quite different character sets.

International Character Sets

In the very early days of computers, several keyboard translation schemes were used, ranging from the early EBCDIC coding to the old 7-bit ASCII. Even the original teletype code is still embedded, fossil-fashion, in the ASCII codes 00h..1Fh. And, even today, when 8-bit character codes are effectively standard, few keyboards directly generate the extended keyboard characters, 80h..FFh. Both screen and printer character sets in this range are roughly as standardized as automobile models; all have similarities, but are very far from identical. As computers have become more and more international, the built-in character set for most computers sold in Euro-American nations has been expanded beyond the familiar English/American alphabet. It now includes the superscripted characters illustrated in the two character sets displayed in Figure 3-4.

The first character set, SYSTEM_FIXED_FONT, omits the frame or box-drawing characters that appear in the DOS character set OEM_FIXED_FONT. This is natural enough since, in Windows, the box-drawing characters are not needed because in a graphics environment it is easier and more flexible to draw lines where they are needed than it is to display strings of box characters. The Greek alphabet and mathematical characters provided in the old extended ASCII set are also omitted in favor of the accented letters used in many European languages. The old ROM-coded character set is still supported and is available. In many countries, such as Thailand (to cite a first-hand example), non-Roman alphabets are often installed as ROM chips that provide local supplementary character fonts.

Figure 3-4: Two Character Sets

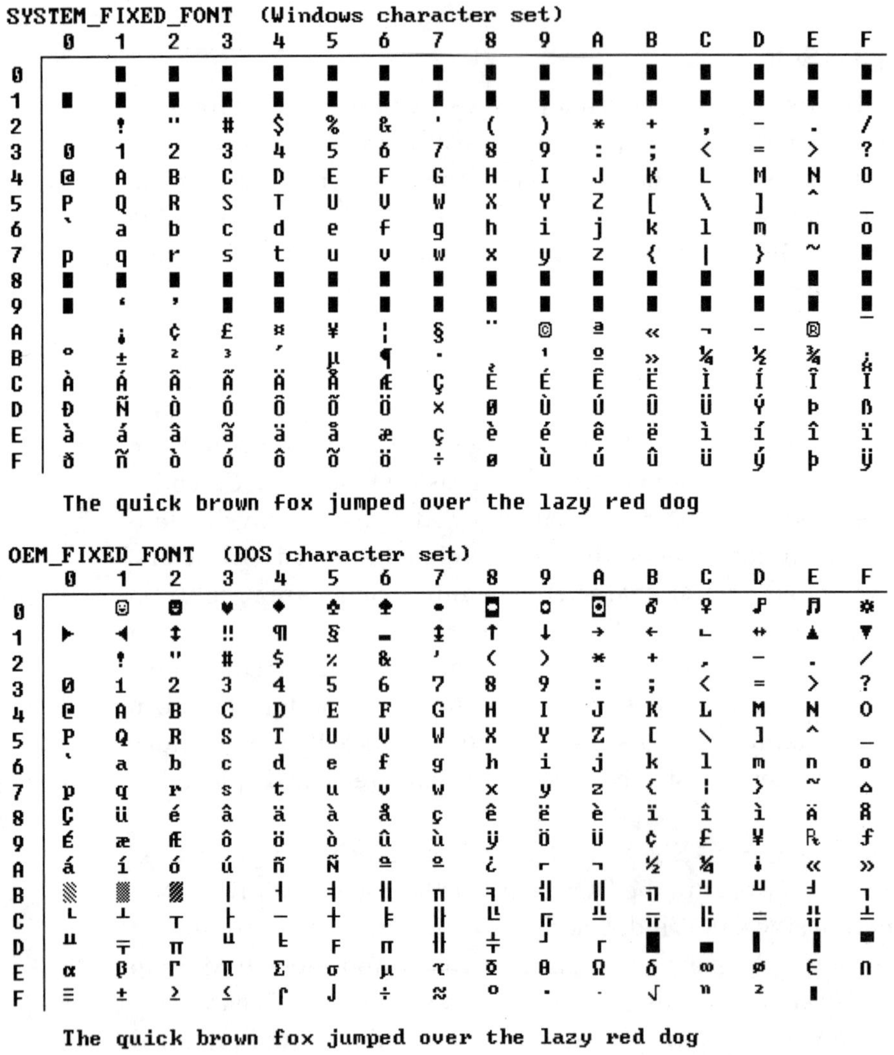

SYSTEM_FIXED_FONT   (Windows character set)

	0	1	2	3	4	5	6	7	8	9	A	B	C	D	E	F
0		■	■	■	■	■	■	■	■	■	■	■	■	■	■	■
1	■	■	■	■	■	■	■	■	■	■	■	■	■	■	■	■
2		!	"	#	$	%	&	'	(	)	*	+	,	-	.	/
3	0	1	2	3	4	5	6	7	8	9	:	;	<	=	>	?
4	@	A	B	C	D	E	F	G	H	I	J	K	L	M	N	O
5	P	Q	R	S	T	U	V	W	X	Y	Z	[	\	]	^	_
6	`	a	b	c	d	e	f	g	h	i	j	k	l	m	n	o
7	p	q	r	s	t	u	v	w	x	y	z	{	|	}	~	■
8	■	■	■	■	■	■	■	■	■	■	■	■	■	■	■	■
9	■	'	'	■	■	■	■	■	■	■	■	■	■	■	■	■
A		¡	¢	£	¤	¥	¦	§	¨	©	ª	«	¬	-	®	
B	°	±	²	³	´	µ	¶	·		¹	º	»	¼	½	¾	¿
C	À	Á	Â	Ã	Ä	Å	Æ	Ç	È	É	Ê	Ë	Ì	Í	Î	Ï
D	Ð	Ñ	Ò	Ó	Ô	Õ	Ö	×	Ø	Ù	Ú	Û	Ü	Ý	Þ	ß
E	à	á	â	ã	ä	å	æ	ç	è	é	ê	ë	ì	í	î	ï
F	ð	ñ	ò	ó	ô	õ	ö	÷	ø	ù	ú	û	ü	ý	þ	ÿ

The quick brown fox jumped over the lazy red dog

OEM_FIXED_FONT   (DOS character set)

	0	1	2	3	4	5	6	7	8	9	A	B	C	D	E	F
0		☺	☻	♥	♦	♣	♠	•	◘	○	◙	♂	♀	♪	♫	☼
1	►	◄	↕	‼	¶	§	▬	↨	↑	↓	→	←	∟	↔	▲	▼
2		!	"	#	$	%	&	'	(	)	*	+	,	-	.	/
3	0	1	2	3	4	5	6	7	8	9	:	;	<	=	>	?
4	@	A	B	C	D	E	F	G	H	I	J	K	L	M	N	O
5	P	Q	R	S	T	U	V	W	X	Y	Z	[	\	]	^	_
6	`	a	b	c	d	e	f	g	h	i	j	k	l	m	n	o
7	p	q	r	s	t	u	v	w	x	y	z	{	|	}	~	⌂
8	Ç	ü	é	â	ä	à	å	ç	ê	ë	è	ï	î	ì	Ä	Å
9	É	æ	Æ	ô	ö	ò	û	ù	ÿ	Ö	Ü	¢	£	¥	₧	ƒ
A	á	í	ó	ú	ñ	Ñ	ª	º	¿	⌐	¬	½	¼	¡	«	»
B	░	▒	▓	│	┤	╡	╢	╖	╕	╣	║	╗	╝	╜	╛	┐
C	└	┴	┬	├	─	┼	╞	╟	╚	╔	╩	╦	╠	═	╬	╧
D	╨	╤	╥	╙	╘	╒	╓	╫	╪	┘	┌	█	▄	▌	▐	▀
E	α	ß	Γ	π	Σ	σ	µ	τ	Φ	Θ	Ω	δ	∞	φ	ε	∩
F	≡	±	≥	≤	⌠	⌡	÷	≈	°	∙	·	√	ⁿ	²	■	

The quick brown fox jumped over the lazy red dog

Both character sets illustrated are fixed-width fonts and, for characters 20h..7Eh are essentially the same. The Windows 3.0 fonts, however, lack the symbol characters 01h..1Fh as well as the boxdrawing characters B3h..D8h but expand the available international characters and symbols. The specific characters in the extended ASCII set may vary according to national language requirements.

Happily, in this last category, Windows should prove especially popular because it is easier to create, display, and interpret a new Windows software font than firmware fonts.

The ANSI Character Set and Windows Fonts

The extended character set used by Windows and Windows programs is called the "ANSI character set" and is supported by several fonts distributed with Windows as shown in Figure 3-5. By default, applications use the proportional-spaced SYSTEM_FONT for window captions, messages, menus, and dialog boxes as well as all other text output unless another font is explicitly selected. As you can see, the SYSTEM_FONT has the advantage of providing smooth, readable text using less space than a fixed-width font such as SYSTEM_FIXED_FONT or OEM_FIXED_FONT.

SYSTEM_FIXED_FONT is the same font as the previous Windows version's SYSTEM_FONT, and is roughly the same as the OEM_FIXED_FONT, except that it supports the ANSI character set rather than the extended ASCII character set. The ANSI_FIXED_FONT is another fixed-width font that has essentially the same characters spacing as does the SYSTEM_FIXED_FONT, but is a light typeface approximating the Elite or 10-point (12 characters per inch) typeface which is popular on many printers and typewriters. The ANSI_VAR_FONT is a clean, sans-serif font that supports high-density text display with only a minimal loss of clarity. Finally, the DEVICE_DEFAULT_FONT approximates the 12-point Courier (10 characters per inch) typeface which is standard on typewriters and older printers.

Supporting the ANSI Character Set

While still limited to variations on the Roman alphabet, the ANSI character set provided by Windows has established a departure from the chauvanisticly English-only character sets that were standard on earlier systems. This broadening of languages, however, has also invalidated a number of assumptions and a few standard C functions.

First, when a WM_CHAR message is received by a Windows application, the *wParam* variable may quite legitimately contain values above 7Fh (127). It would be a prime mistake to "trim" the high-bit or to assume that higher values are invalid. While many word processor programs have established proprietary notions about using the high-bit on character values, this is another mistake that will not be valid in the Windows environment. In the past, this has also prevented many such editors from being adapted in other countries.

Figure 3-5: Six Fonts

```
SYSTEM_FIXED_FONT
The quick brown fox jumped over the lazy red dog

SYSTEM_FONT
The quick brown fox jumped over the lazy red dog

ANSI_FIXED_FONT
The quick brown fox jumped over the lazy red dog

ANSI_VAR_FONT
The quick brown fox jumped over the lazy red dog

DEVICE_DEFAULT_FONT
The quick brown fox jumped over the lazy red dog

OEM_FIXED_FONT
The quick brown fox jumped over the lazy red dog
```

The familiar C functions, *toupper* and *tolower*, are no longer valid because they operate correctly only for characters in the 41h..5Ah and 61h..7Ah range. They are not valid for characters in the (European) C0h..FFh range (see Figure 3-4). Instead, Windows supplies two string-oriented functions, *AnsiUpper* and *AnsiLower*, both requiring null-terminated strings:

```
AnsiUpper( pStr );
```

These strings can also be used for single characters but do require typecasting to insure that the high-order word of the parameter is null (0):

```
ch = AnsiLower( (LPSTR) (LONG) (BYTE) ch );
```

While this typecasting may seem rather extreme, converting a char value to a byte value first, then to a long value, and finally to a long pointer to a string, it does work. And, in this form, the *AnsiLower* and *AnsiUpper* functions return 32-bit (LPSTR) values that contain the converted character in the low byte of the low word, i.e., in the 8 least significant bits. If *ch* is a BYTE value, no explicit typecasting is required on the returned value. Or, for character strings that are not null-terminated, the *AnsiUpperBuff* and *AnsiLowerBuff* functions can be called as:

```
AnsiUpperBuff( pStr, nLen );
```

AnsiUpperBuff and *AnsiLowerBuff* return a word value of the converted string length.

Other conversions include the *AnsiToOem*, *AnsiToOemBuff*, *OemToAnsi*, and *OemToAnsiBuff* functions for conversions between the ANSI character sets and the extended-ASCII (OEM) character sets. These functions are principally useful in converting non-English string arguments or text strings between ANSI and OEM formats. Applications would include output to printers that do not support the ANSI character arrangements, non-English file/directory names, or converted textual data between DOS and Windows formats. Also, in several non-European languages (Japanese is a primary example) character sets require two bytes for some characters. The *AnsiNext* and *AnsiPrev* functions provide an alternative to conventional C pointer arithmetic for scanning a string. *AnsiNext* and *AnsiPrev* accept a far pointer to a string and, after consulting the keyboard/language driver, return a far pointer that has been properly incremented or decremented for 2-byte character codes.

Generating ANSI (Extended-ASCII) Characters

While the familiar English-language keyboard does not provide keys for direct entry of character codes above 7Fh (127), these character codes can be generated by using the Alt-Keypad combination and by entering the appropriate 3-digit decimal value. Windows provides this same facility in two forms: first, using ASCII character codes that are converted to ANSI codes and, second, entering ANSI codes directly. In both cases, of course, the resulting character is the ANSI value, not OEM ASCII value.

The first form duplicates the DOS entry format but processes the entered value through the *OemToAnsi* function before generating the WM_CHAR message. Holding down the Alt key and entering 142 on the keypad (8Eh— ASCII) is processed through the *OemToAnsi* function to generate a WM_CHAR message with the character value 196 (C4h). This will display the ANSI character "Ä".

The second form also uses the Alt-Keypad combination, but begins with Alt-0 (keypad zero) in the entry of a four digit ANSI code 0196. This also generates a WM_CHAR message displaying the ANSI character "A". In this form, the *OemToAnsi* function is not invoked for translation.

The shorter form uses the three-digit ASCII character codes and fits established habits, while the longer form provides entry of international characters that do not appear in the OEM character sets (such as Å, Ä, À, Ã, Á, Â).

If you would like to experiment with the Alt-Keypad entry form using the KeyCodes program to demonstrate these effects, change the OEM_FIXED_FONT entries to SYSTEM_FIXED_FONT. (This will invalidate the checkmark and arrow symbols used but will show the ANSI characters.)

Alternatively, the Editor program can be used, without modification, to show both forms of entry.

Note: In either form, accidental entry of more than three digits (four with a leading 0) results in the last three digits being used as the character value. Likewise, decimal values above 255 are truncated as byte values (NNN mod 256).

Summary

While Windows keyboard messages are initially a bit more complicated than simply retrieving characters from the keyboard buffer, responding to WM_KEYDOWN and WM_CHAR messages provides a much more convenient method of handling mixed cursor and character keyboard entry.

Also, while less elaborate than WYSIWYG typesetting word processors, the option of changing from fixed-width fonts to proportionally-spaced fonts provides a major improvement in text presentation.

Less immediate, but more important in the long run, the ANSI character set provides greater flexibility in reaching many international markets, while future drivers can be expected which will provide even wider access to non-English-speaking users.

```
//==============================//
//           KeyCodes.C         //
//   C++ Windows Keyboard Test  //
//==============================//

#include <windows.h>

RECT   rect;

short cxChr, cyChr, cxWin, cyWin;

void ShowKey( HWND   hwnd,    int    iType,    BOOL EndRpt,
              char *szMsg,  WORD   wParam,  LONG lParam )
{
    static char *szFormat[2] =
        { "%-15s %02Xh              %3d   %02Xh"
          "  %c   %c   %c   %c",
          "%-15s        %02Xh     %c   %3d   %02Xh"   };
    char   szBuff[80];     PAINTSTRUCT   ps;
    HDC    hdc;               short         step;
    WORD   ChCnt, ChScan, ChFlags;

    if( EndRpt ) step = 3*cyChr/2; else step = cyChr;
    ChCnt   = LOWORD( lParam );
    ChScan  = HIWORD( lParam ) & 0x00FF;
    ChFlags = HIWORD( lParam ) & 0xFF00;
    ScrollWindow( hwnd, 0, -step, &rect, &rect );
    hdc = BeginPaint( hwnd, &ps );
    SelectObject( hdc, GetStockObject( OEM_FIXED_FONT ) );
    if( ! iType )
    TextOut( hdc, cxChr, cyWin - step, szBuff,
            wsprintf( szBuff, szFormat[iType],
            (LPSTR) szMsg,              // message constant //
                    wParam,            // key code value   //
                    ChCnt,             // repeat char count //
                    ChScan,            // keyboard scan code //
            (BYTE)( ChFlags & 0x0100 ? '√' : '
' ),
            (BYTE)( ChFlags & 0x2000 ? '√' : '
' ),
            (BYTE)( ChFlags & 0x4000 ? '↓' : '↑'
),
            (BYTE)( ChFlags & 0x8000 ? '↑' : '↓'
) ) );
    else
    TextOut( hdc, cxChr, cyWin - step, szBuff,
```

```
                wsprintf( szBuff, szFormat[iType],
                   (LPSTR) szMsg,                   // message constant   //
                           wParam,                  // key code value     //
                           ChCode,                  // character or space //
                           ChCnt,                   // repeat char count  //
                           ChScan ) );              // keyboard scan code //
      EndPaint( hwnd, &ps );
      ValidateRect( hwnd, NULL );
   }

   long FAR PASCAL WndProc( HWND hwnd,    WORD message,
                            WORD wParam, LONG lParam )
   {
           // Prv = Prior key state / Trs = Transition key state
     //
      static char szCapt[] =
         "Message          Code  Key  Char  Cnt  Scan   "
         "Ext ALT Prv Trs";
      static char szUnLn[] =
         "_____ ____ ___ ____ ___ ____  "
         "___ ___ ___ ___";
      HDC          hdc;      PAINTSTRUCT  ps;
      TEXTMETRIC   tm;

      switch( message )
      {
         case WM_CREATE:
            hdc = GetDC( hwnd );
            SelectObject( hdc, GetStockObject(OEM_FIXED_FONT)
   );
            GetTextMetrics( hdc, &tm );
            cxChr = tm.tmAveCharWidth;
            cyChr = tm.tmHeight + tm.tmExternalLeading;
            ReleaseDC( hwnd, hdc );
            rect.top = 2 * cyChr;
            return( 0 );

         case WM_SIZE:
            cxWin = LOWORD( lParam );              // window width  //
            cyWin = HIWORD( lParam );              // window height //
            rect.right  = cxWin;
            rect.bottom = cyWin;
            UpdateWindow( hwnd );
            return( 0 );

         case WM_PAINT:
```

```
          InvalidateRect( hwnd, NULL, TRUE );
          hdc = BeginPaint( hwnd, &ps );
          SelectObject( hdc, GetStockObject(OEM_FIXED_FONT)
);
          SetBkMode( hdc, TRANSPARENT );
          TextOut( hdc, cxChr, 1, szCapt, (sizeof szCapt)-1
);
          TextOut( hdc, cxChr, 5, szUnLn, (sizeof szUnLn)-1
);
          SetBkMode( hdc, OPAQUE );    // restore default mode //
          EndPaint( hwnd, &ps );
          return( 0 );

     case WM_KEYDOWN:
          ShowKey( hwnd, 0, 0, "WM_KEYDOWN,"wParam, lParam );;

          return(0);

     case WM_KEYUP:
          ShowKey( hwnd, 0, 1, "WM_KEYUP",wParam, lParam );

          return(0);

     case WM_CHAR:
          ShowKey( hwnd, 1, 0, "WM_CHAR",wParam, lParam );

          return(0);

     case WM_DEADCHAR:
          ShowKey( hwnd, 1, 0, "WM_DEADCHAR",wParam, lParam );

          return(0);

     case WM_SYSKEYDOWN:
          ShowKey( hwnd, 0, 0, "WM_SYSKEYDOWN",wParam, lParam );

          break;

     case WM_SYSKEYUP:
          ShowKey( hwnd, 0, 1, "WM_SYSKEYUP",wParam, lParam );

          break;

     case WM_SYSCHAR:
          ShowKey( hwnd, 1, 0, "WM_SYSCHAR",wParam, lParam );

          break;
```

```
      case WM_SYSDEADCHAR:
          ShowKey( hwnd, 1, 0, "WM_SYSDEADCHAR"wParam, lParam};

          break;

      case WM_DESTROY:
          PostQuitMessage( 0 );      return( 0 );
   }
   return( DefWindowProc( hwnd, message, wParam, lParam )
);
}

int PASCAL WinMain( HANDLE hInstance,
                    HANDLE hPrevInstance,
                    LPSTR  lpszCmdParam,
                    int    nCmdShow )
{
   static char szAppName[] = "Keyboard Codes";
   HWND        hwnd;
   MSG         msg;
   WNDCLASS    wc;

   if( ! hPrevInstance )
   {
       wc.style         = CS_HREDRAW | CS_VREDRAW;
       wc.lpfnWndProc   = WndProc;
       wc.cbClsExtra    = 0;
       wc.cbWndExtra    = 0;
       wc.hInstance     = hInstance;
       wc.hIcon         = LoadIcon( NULL, IDI_APPLICATION );
       wc.hCursor       = LoadCursor( NULL, IDC_ARROW );
       wc.hbrBackground = GetStockObject( WHITE_BRUSH );
       wc.lpszMenuName  = NULL;
       wc.lpszClassName = szAppName;
       RegisterClass( &wc );
   }
   hwnd = CreateWindow( szAppName, "Keyboard Event Messages",
                        WS_OVERLAPPEDWINDOW,
                        CW_USEDEFAULT, CW_USEDEFAULT,
                        CW_USEDEFAULT, CW_USEDEFAULT,
                        NULL, NULL, hInstance, NULL  );
   ShowWindow(   hwnd, nCmdShow );
   UpdateWindow( hwnd );
   while( GetMessage( &msg, NULL, 0, 0 ) )
   {
       TranslateMessage( &msg );
```

```
        DispatchMessage( &msg );
    }
    return( msg.wParam );
}


        ;==========================================;
        ;  KeyCodes.DEF module definition file  ;
        ;==========================================;

NAME           KEYCODES
DESCRIPTION    "Windows KeyBoard Program"
EXETYPE        WINDOWS
STUB           "WINSTUB.EXE"
CODE           PRELOAD MOVEABLE DISCARDABLE
DATA           PRELOAD MOVEABLE MULTIPLE
HEAPSIZE       1024
STACKSIZE      8192
EXPORTS        WndProc



        //===========================//
        //          Editor.C         //
        //   C++ Windows Editor Demo //
        //===========================//

#include <windows.h>

#define Buffer( x, y ) *( pBuffer + y * cxBuff + x )

long FAR PASCAL WndProc( HWND hwnd,   WORD message,
                         WORD wParam, LONG lParam )
{
    static char   *pBuffer = NULL;
    static int    cxChr,  cyChr,  cxWin,  cyWin,
                  cxBuff, cyBuff, xCaret, yCaret;
         int     i, x, y;
    HDC          hdc;
    PAINTSTRUCT  ps;
    TEXTMETRIC   tm;

    switch( message )
    {
       case WM_CREATE:
          hdc = GetDC( hwnd );
          SelectObject( hdc,
```

```
                    GetStockObject(SYSTEM_FIXED_FONT) );
        GetTextMetrics( hdc, &tm );
        cxChr = tm.tmAveCharWidth;
        cyChr = tm.tmHeight;
        ReleaseDC( hwnd, hdc );
        return( 0 );

    case WM_SIZE:
        cyWin = HIWORD( lParam );      // window pixel height //
        cxWin = LOWORD( lParam );      // window pixel width  //
        cxBuff = max( 1, cxWin / cxChr );
        cyBuff = max( 1, cyWin / cyChr );
        if( pBuffer != NULL )
            free( pBuffer );        // free any existing buffer //
        if( (LONG) cxBuff * cyBuff > 65535L ||
            ( pBuffer = malloc( cxBuff*cyBuff ) ) == NULL
)
            MessageBox( hwnd,
                "Insufficient memory - reduce window size!",
                "Editor Report",
                MB_ICONEXCLAMATION | MB_OK );
        else
            for( y=0; y<cyBuff; y++ )
                for( x=0; x<cxBuff; x++ ) Buffer(x,y) = ' ';
        xCaret = 0;
        yCaret = 0;
        if( hwnd == GetFocus() )
            SetCaretPos( xCaret * cxChr, yCaret * cyChr );

    case WM_SETFOCUS:
        CreateCaret( hwnd, 1, cxChr, cyChr );
                                    // gray caret (cursor) //
        SetCaretPos( xCaret * cxChr, yCaret * cyChr );
        ShowCaret( hwnd );
        return( 0 );

    case WM_KILLFOCUS:
        HideCaret( hwnd );
        DestroyCaret();
        return( 0 );

    case WM_KEYDOWN:
        switch( wParam )
        {
            case VK_HOME:
                xCaret = 0;                              break;
            case VK_END:
```

```
          xCaret = cxBuff - 1;                          break;
     case VK_PRIOR:
          yCaret = 0;                                   break;
     case VK_NEXT:
          yCaret = cyBuff - 1;                          break;
     case VK_LEFT:
          xCaret = max( 0,          xCaret-1 );  break;
     case VK_RIGHT:
          xCaret = min( cxBuff-1, xCaret+1 );  break;
     case VK_UP:
          yCaret = max( 0,          yCaret-1 );  break;
     case VK_DOWN:
          yCaret = min( cyBuff-1, yCaret+1 );  break;
     case VK_DELETE:
          for( x=xCaret; x<cxBuff-1; x++ )
             Buffer(x,yCaret) = Buffer(x+1,yCaret);
          Buffer( cxBuff-1, yCaret ) = ' ';
          HideCaret( hwnd );
          hdc = GetDC( hwnd );
          SelectObject( hdc,
             GetStockObject( SYSTEM_FIXED_FONT ) );
          TextOut( hdc, xCaret*cxChr, yCaret*cyChr,
                   &Buffer( xCaret, yCaret ),
                   cxBuff-xCaret );
          ShowCaret( hwnd );
          ReleaseDC( hwnd, hdc );
          break;
     }
     SetCaretPos( xCaret * cxChr, yCaret * cyChr );
     return( 0 );                // end cursor / keypad keys //

  case WM_CHAR:
     for( i=0; i<LOWORD(lParam); i++ )
     {
        switch( wParam )
        {
        case '\b':                // backspace                //
            if( xCaret > 0 )
            {
                xCaret;
                SendMessage( hwnd, WM_KEYDOWN,
                             VK_DELETE, 1L );
            } break;
        case '\t':                // tab                      //
            do SendMessage( hwnd, WM_CHAR, ' ', 1L );
            while( xCaret % 8 != 0 );
```

```
                 break;
              case '\r':            // carriage return      //
                 xCaret = 0;        // falls through to '\n' //
              case '\n':            // line feed             //
                 if( ++yCaret == cyBuff ) yCaret = 0;
                 break;
              case '\x1B':          // escape                //
                 if( MessageBox( hwnd, "Reset text buffer?",
                       "Editor Query",
                       MB_ICONEXCLAMATION | MB_OKCANCEL |
                       MB_DEFBUTTON2 ) == IDOK )
                 {
                    for( y=0; y<cyBuff; y++ )
                       for( x=0; x<cxBuff; x++ )
                          Buffer( x, y ) = ' ';
                    xCaret = 0;   yCaret = 0;
                    InvalidateRect( hwnd, NULL, FALSE );
                 }
                 break;
              default:             // all other characters  //
                 Buffer( xCaret, yCaret ) = (char) wParam;
                 HideCaret( hwnd );
                 hdc = GetDC( hwnd );
                 SelectObject( hdc,
                       GetStockObject(SYSTEM_FIXED_FONT)
);
                 TextOut( hdc, xCaret*cxChr, yCaret*cyChr,
                       &Buffer( xCaret, yCaret ), 1 );
                 ShowCaret( hwnd );
                 ReleaseDC( hwnd, hdc );
                 if( ++xCaret == cxBuff )
                 {
                    xCaret = 0;
                    if( ++yCaret == cyBuff ) yCaret = 0;
                 }
                 break;
           }  }
           SetCaretPos( xCaret * cxChr, yCaret * cyChr );
           return( 0 );

      case WM_PAINT:
         hdc = BeginPaint( hwnd, &ps );
         SelectObject( hdc,
                  GetStockObject(SYSTEM_FIXED_FONT)
);
         for( y=0; y<cyBuff; y++ )
            TextOut( hdc, 0, y*cyChr,
```

```
                            &Buffer( 0, y ), cxBuff );
            EndPaint( hwnd, &ps );
            return( 0 );

        case WM_DESTROY:
            PostQuitMessage( 0 );
            return( 0 );
    }
    return( DefWindowProc( hwnd, message, wParam, lParam )
);
}

int PASCAL WinMain( HANDLE hInstance,
                    HANDLE hPrevInstance,
                    LPSTR  lpszCmdParam,
                    int    nCmdShow )
{
    static char szAppName[] = "Editor";
    HWND        hwnd;
    MSG         msg;
    WNDCLASS    wc;

    if( ! hPrevInstance )
    {
        wc.style         = CS_HREDRAW | CS_VREDRAW;
        wc.lpfnWndProc   = WndProc;
        wc.cbClsExtra    = 0;
        wc.cbWndExtra    = 0;
        wc.hInstance     = hInstance;
        wc.hIcon         = LoadIcon( NULL, IDI_APPLICATION );
        wc.hCursor       = LoadCursor( NULL, IDC_ARROW );
        wc.hbrBackground = GetStockObject( WHITE_BRUSH );
        wc.lpszMenuName  = NULL;
        wc.lpszClassName = szAppName;
        RegisterClass( &wc );
    }
    hwnd = CreateWindow( szAppName,
                         "A Simple Windows Editor",
                         WS_OVERLAPPEDWINDOW,
                         CW_USEDEFAULT, CW_USEDEFAULT,
                         CW_USEDEFAULT, CW_USEDEFAULT,
                         NULL, NULL, hInstance, NULL );
    ShowWindow( hwnd, nCmdShow );
    UpdateWindow( hwnd );
    while( GetMessage( &msg, NULL, 0, 0 ) )
    {
```

```
      TranslateMessage( &msg );
      DispatchMessage(  &msg );
   }
   return( msg.wParam );
}
         ;=======================================;
         ; Editor.DEF module definition file     ;
         ;=======================================;

NAME            EDITOR
DESCRIPTION     "Windows Editor Program"
EXETYPE         WINDOWS
STUB            "WINSTUB.EXE"
CODE            PRELOAD MOVEABLE DISCARDABLE
DATA            PRELOAD MOVEABLE MULTIPLE
HEAPSIZE        1024
STACKSIZE       8192
EXPORTS         WndProc
```

Chapter 4

The Mouse in Windows

As you must certainly realize, MS/Windows is heavily mouse oriented even though, unlike the keyboard, the mouse remains an optional device. Most Windows programs can be controlled from the keyboard and, whenever practical, your own applications should provide at least a minimal keyboard interface. This is not to suggest in any way, shape, or fashion that the mouse should be ignored! Even if the mouse is not essential it is still, in many if not all cases, the most convenient interface in Windows as well as many non-Windows applications.

Mouse Types, Yesterday, and Today

Originally, mouse devices were single-button (left only) pointing devices. This form is still found today on Apple computers, but is virtually obsolete on contemporary MSDOS/Windows systems. Even so, some sources suggest that single button mice should still be considered the minimal standard. Observing this restriction is rather like writing applications to conform to the 25x40 text-only video standards because, today, virtually all mice, Apple systems excepted, have two buttons (left /right) while many even support three (left/ right/middle). While Windows supports two- and three-button mice, support is also provided as mouse emulation for joysticks or lightpens which are necessarily treated as single-button mice. Common usage continues to emphasize the left mouse button, even when a three-button mouse is installed, although Windows has provided support for south-paws, permitting the left and right buttons to be swapped as a system default rather than an application option.

There are also newer devices, such as track-ball pointers; but these emulate two- or three-button mice without requiring special treatment. And, of course, there are still newer devices, such as control gloves, which sense spacial motion and, eventually, may not only type on truly "virtual" (or possibly holographic) keyboards, but may eventually—as Brer Rabbit phrased it — read writin'. These are, however, still in the experimental stage and, for the present, can be safely ignored.

Restrictions aside, most applications will find it sufficient to recognize two-buttons (right and left) while reserving the third (middle) button for optional short-cuts.

Is There a Mouse in the House?

Mouse-critical applications especially need to test the system and insure that a mouse is present. This can be done by using the *GetSystemMetrics* function:

```
if( GetSystemMetrics( SM_MOUSEPRESENT ) ) ...
```

If a mouse is installed (and working, of course), *GetSystemMetrics* will return TRUE (non-zero). If a mouse is not installed, a FALSE (zero) result is reported.

The Mouse3.C program, demonstrated later, shows one response indicating the absence of a mouse by presenting a dialog box, and then issues a WM_QUIT message. The way in which your application should respond to the absence of a mouse depends on the application. Unfortunately, no method is provided by Windows to determine the number of buttons present on an installed mouse.

The Mouse Cursor

As explained in Chapter 3, under Windows, the text cursor is now known as the "caret" while the mouse cursor is simply called the cursor. While the mouse cursor actually points at a single pixel, the cursor proper is a bit-mapped image that is tracked across the display preserving the background image. Within the cursor image, one pixel serves as the "hot spot" and is the actual pointer location.

Windows provides eleven predefined cursor images, but, by default, uses the slanted arrow (IDC_ARROW). Applications, however, may define any of the standard cursors as their own defaults, may change cursors according to tasks or window areas, or may define their own custom cursors. This last topic will be reserved for Part 2 where WRT (Whitewater Resource Toolkit) makes cursor creation convenient.

Mouse Actions   Three types of interaction are defined for mice:

- *Clicking*—pressing (and releasing) a mouse button
- *Double-clicking*—clicking a mouse button twice in quick succession
- *Dragging*—moving the mouse while holding a button down

Some applications also use a drag-and-release interaction that involves clicking on an object and then using a second click to release the object. This permits dragging the object without holding down the button. This form is also popular for drawing programs and reduces "mouse-wrist" injuries (muscle and tendon strains caused by holding and dragging a mouse in tasks requiring fine positioning control).

Mouse Messages

Twenty-four mouse event messages are defined in Windows.H. Two of these messages have values that duplicate other mouse messages and are, apparently, provided for compatibility with earlier versions of Windows. The other twelve are normally handled by Windows through the *WndDefProc* function. The first nine of the remaining mouse event messages concern mouse button events as shown in Table 4-1.

Table 4-1: Mouse Button Messages

Button Pressed	Released	Double-clicked	
Left	WM_LBUTTONDOWN	WM_LBUTTONUP	WM_LBUTTONDBLCK
Right	WM_RBUTTONDOWN	WM_RBUTTONUP	WM_RBUTTONDBLCK
Middle	WM_MBUTTONDOWN	WM_MBUTTONUP	WM_MBUTTONDBLCK

A WM_xBUTTONDOWN or WM_xBUTTONUP message is issued only once when the mouse button is pressed or released, and a WM_xBUTTONDBLCK message is issued in response to a rapid double click (down-up-down). However, no button messages of any kind are issued by holding a mouse button down.

All working mice, whether they have one, two, or three buttons (or lightpen or joystick devices), generate WM_LBUTTONxxxx messages. WH_RBUTTONxxxx messages are generated by two- or three-button mice while WH_MBUTTONxxxx messages are generated only by three-button mice.

Double-Click Messages

WM_xxxxDOWN and WM_xxxxUP messages are generated automatically but WM_xxxxDBLCK messages (double-click) are generated only if the class definition of the client window includes the double-click enabling flag:

```
wc.style = CS_HREDRAW | CS_VREDRAW | CS_DBLCLKS;
```

If CS_DBLCLKS is not included in the window style (or child-window style) specification, a double-click is received as four separate messages: WM...DOWN, WM...UP, WM...DOWN, and WM...UP. When CS_DBLCLKS is included, a double-click is received as WM...DOWN, WM...UP, WM...DBLCLK, and WM...UP with the double-click message replacing the second button-down message.

Caution: If it is necessary to double click in order to perform a very different task from a single click message, your message processing could become quite complex because a single button-down message will always be received before the double-click message.

An example of compatible single and double-click handling is found in the Windows File Manager. A single click on a subdirectory listing changes directories, but a double-click calls a new directory window that displays the selected directory. The result is that accidental entries perform essentially, if not exactly, the same task.

Mouse Movement Messages

The tenth mouse message, WM_MOUSEMOVE, is issued every time the mouse moves within the client window. Movement is not reported per screen pixel but per unit of physical mouse motion, i.e., one message per mickey, subject to the processing speed of the window procedure handling the movement message.

Note: A mickey is not a joke. It is the basic unit of mouse movement and, depending on the physical mouse, movement may be reported in increments of 200 to 320 mickeys per inch.

With rapid mouse movement, WM_MOUSEMOVE messages may be reported at various screen spacings as will be demonstrated by the Mouse1.C program. With slower mouse movement, WM_MOUSEMOVE message may be received at contiguous pixel positions but this cannot be guarenteed, regardless of system (CPU) and program speeds. Also, WM_MOUSEMOVE messages are issued only while the mouse cursor remains within the application's client window. The same is true of the mouse button messages.

Additional Information in Mouse Messages

In addition to the mouse event message itself, every mouse message provides complete mouse position and button status information in the *lParam* and *wParam* variables. At the time the mouse event message is issued, the mouse position is contained in the *lParam* variable. This can be extracted as x-coordinate /y-coordinate values using the LOWORD and HIWORD macros defined in Windows.H:

```
xCord = LOWORD( lParam );
yCord = HIWORD( lParam );
```

The x and y coordinate values are the coordinates of the mouse cursor's hot spot relative to the client window area as offsets (positive values only) from the upper-left corner of the window (0,0). The *wParam* variable contains the state of the mouse button(s) as well as the Shift and Ctrl keys. The state of these keys can be tested using the MK_xxxx bit masks defined in Windows.H (MK stands for "mouse key" even though two of these are keyboard status bits). Key status can be tested as:

```
if( wParam & MK_LBUTTON ) ...        // left button down     //
if( wParam & MK_MBUTTON ) ...        // middle button down   //
if( wParam & MK_RBUTTON ) ...        // right button down    //
if( wParam & MK_SHIFT   ) ...        // Shift key down        //
if( wParam & MK_CONTROL ) ...        // Ctrl key down         //
```

Mouse Events in Windows

Mouse events in Windows can be a bit different than those in other environments. First, because the Windows environment is shared, mouse button events are not always paired; a button down event might occur in one window with only the release event reported to the application—or vice versa. Even if the application occupies the entire screen, the application's caption bar, control buttons, and frame each constitute separate windows. Only those events that occur within the client window area are reported to the application's client window message procedure.

Second, a window procedure can capture the mouse and continue to receive all mouse messages even when the mouse is outside the client window area.

Third, if a system-model message or dialog box is active, no other application window can receive any mouse messages. System-model message and dialog boxes prohibit switching to any other window or application until exited. Awareness of these special circumstances aside, normally there are no restrictions or extraordinary provisions required for handling Windows mouse event messages.

Mouse1: Mouse Tracking

The Mouse1.C program demonstrates how WM_MOUSEMOVE messages are generated by plotting a single pixel at the reported coordinates of each message received. Plotting is toggled on/off by pressing the left mouse button. For this purpose, only two mouse messages are handled: WM_MOUSEMOVE and WM_LBUTTONDOWN:

```
switch( message )
{
    case WM_LBUTTONDOWN:
        fPaint = fPaint ^ 1;
        MessageBeep(0);
        return(0);
```

The WM_LBUTTONDOWN message toggles *fPaint*, a static boolean variable, by XORing it with one, thus enabling and disabling the WM_MOUSE-MOVE response. The WM_MOUSEMOVE response is about as simple and as fast as possible, and passes the mouse position reported to *SetPixel* to plot a single screen pixel as a black dot:

```
case WM_MOUSEMOVE:
   if( fPaint )
   {
      hdc = GetDC( hwnd );
      SetPixel( hdc, LOWORD( lParam ),
                     HIWORD( lParam ), 0L );
      ReleaseDC( hwnd, hdc );
   }
   return(0);
```

This example is enough to demonstrate tracking the mouse movement through WM_MOUSEMOVE messages. Notice particularly, however, that rapid mouse movements are reported as widely spaced dots, while slow movements may or may not generate a completely continuous line.

Complete listings for Mouse1.C appear at the end of this chapter.

Mouse2: Mouse Cursors

The Mouse2 demo creates ten child windows within the application's client window area; each appearing as a simple outline with a white background. These client windows are secondary to the main purpose of this demo which is to show ten predefined mouse cursor shapes. As the mouse is moved, each of these client windows tracks the WM_MOUSEMOVE event messages to load a different mouse cursor image. Using client windows requires some additional provisions that did not appear in previous examples, beginning in the *WinMain* procedure, in which a second child window class is declared:

```
if( ! hPrevInstance )
{
   ...
   RegisterClass( &wc );          // register parent class //
   ...                            // define child window class //
   wc.lpfnWndProc   = ChildWndProc;
   wc.cbWndExtra    = sizeof( WORD );
```

The *cbWndExtra* field is a provision for two bytes of additional data which, while not used in this example, will be needed in Mouse3 to hold flag values:

```
wc.hIcon         = NULL;
wc.hCursor       = NULL;
```

For the purposes of this demonstration the *hCursor* field must be declared as NULL. In other circumstances no specification of any kind is required if the default cursor will be used by the client window. Or, a specific cursor, either predefined or custom, may be selected for this window class using the *Load-Cursor* function:

```
    wc.lpszClassName = szChildClass;
    RegisterClass( &wc );
}
```

The child window class is registered in the same fashion as the parent window class. Note, however, that this is only the class declaration and does not create any instances of the class.

Creating and Sizing Child Windows

The actual child windows are declared by a static array in the *WndProc* procedure:

```
static HWND  hwndChild[5][2];
```

In this example, ten child window instances will be used in a 2x5 array. Since the child window instances belong to the main application window, they are created in response to the WM_CREATE message in *WndProc*:

```
case WM_CREATE:
    for( x=0; x<5; x++ )
        for( y=0; y<2; y++ )
            hwndChild[x][y] =
                CreateWindow( szChildClass, NULL,
                WS_CHILDWINDOW | WS_VISIBLE,
                0, 0, 0, 0, hwnd,
                x | y << 8,                   // child window id //
                GetWindowWord( hwnd, GWW_HINSTANCE ),
                NULL );
    return(0);
```

The *CreateWindow* function is called for each of the child window instances, following the same pattern as in *WinMain* for the application's client window, with three principal differences. First, each child window receives the *hwnd* variable indicating the parent window. For the parent window, of course, this value was NULL.

Second, each child window requires a unique ID; a WORD value defined by x | y<< 8. This parameter was declared as NULL again in the declaration of the application client window. This child window ID will be used later in *ChildWndProc* , the example which will set the cursor image for each instance. Even if it is not used directly within the application, it is still necessary.

Third, the child window instance parameter is supplied by calling the *GetWindowWord* function while, for the application client window, this parameter was supplied by Windows as the *hInstance* parameter. In each case, a unique instance handle is required and must be supplied either directly or indirectly by Windows.

There are other differences in the absence of a window title (declared as NULL) as well as the window style flags used, but they may vary depending upon the type of child window desired. Also, within *WndProc*, the WM_SIZE message response has provisions for resizing the child windows which, incidentally, are not defined to receive individual WM_SIZE messages:

```
case WM_SIZE:
    cxWin = LOWORD( lParam ) / 5;
    cyWin = HIWORD( lParam ) / 2;
    for( x=0; x<5; x++ )
        for( y=0; y<2; y++ )
            MoveWindow( hwndChild[x][y],
                        x*cxWin, y*cyWin,
                        cxWin, cyWin, TRUE );
    return(0);
```

When the client window is resized, the child windows are individually repositioned by the *MoveWindow* function and at the same time are given new size parameters to fit the resized client window. This completes the handling provided by the client window for the child window instances. Handling is also provided for individual child window instances within the *ChildWndProc* process.

Cursor Operations in ChildWndProc

The *ChildWndProc* responds to WM_MOUSEMOVE messages and sets a new cursor image when the mouse is moved from one child window to another. In a previous example, the WM_SETFOCUS and WM_KILLFOCUS messages were used to create, show, hide, and destroy the text caret, but child windows do not receive these messages. Instead, the mouse movement message is used because it is reported only to the client or child window at which the mouse is located. An individual child window receives this message if, and only if, the mouse is in that window. To set a different cursor shape for each of these ten child windows, the child window ID is needed to identify it. This is retrieved by using the *GetWindowWord* function:

```
case WM_MOUSEMOVE:
    switch( GetWindowWord( hwnd, GWW_ID ) )
    {
        case 0x0000:
```

The formula x | y << 8 was used to generate the child window ID values. Here, it's certainly easier to use constants, particularly since variables are not accepted in *case* statements. The child window ID values generated were 0x0000..0x0004 and 0x0100..0x0104. The *switch..case* structure simply assigns one of the predefined cursors using the *SetCursor* and *LoadCursor* functions:

```
SetCursor( LoadCursor( NULL, IDC_xxxxx ) );
```

The *LoadCursor* function is called with two parameters beginning with an *hInstance* parameter indicating the .EXE file that contains the cursor resource. Normally, for a custom cursor, this would be the same *hInstance* variable that Windows uses to identify the application. Or, as in this example, the variable is NULL because the cursor is a predefined resource.

The second parameter is the resource identifier. For the predefined cursor images, this is actually a macro defined as MAKEINTRESOURCE(...) which contains an ID value for the specified cursor image. The IDC_xxxx macros are listed in Appendix A and defined in Windows.H. The custom cursors topic will be covered further in Part 2.

The *SetCursor* function uses the *hCursor* handle returned by *LoadCursor* to make this the new active cursor. While consideration might suggest that this code would result in slow operation that repeatedly reloads the cursor image each time the WM_MOUSEMOVE message was received, this is not actually the case. First, *LoadCursor* loads the cursor resource into memory only if it has not been loaded previously. Otherwise, it retrieves a handle to the existing resource. Second, *SetCursor* executes only if the new cursor shape, indicated by *hCursor*, is different from the current cursor. Otherwise, *SetCursor* simply returns without action.

There is, however, one circumstance where both *LoadCursor* and *SetCursor* execute repeatedly. Before the child window class was registered, the *wc.h-Cursor* field was defined as NULL. If this definition is commented out, or if a specific cursor is defined for the child window class, a very different execution of this example program may be observed. The cursor images for the child windows would then be quite jerky as the new images continually reload and reset to replace the default image. This undesired effect can be easily observed by commenting out the *wc.hCursor* assignment in the child window definitions in Mouse2.C, and then recompiling the program. Or, you could create separate versions with and without this provision and compare them directly.

The Default Cursor

While the default cursor image will reappear anytime the mouse cursor moves outside child window areas, provisions have also been made for the WM_LBUTTONDOWN to load the default cursor. This is identified by IDC_ARROW:

```
case WM_LBUTTONDOWN:
    SetCursor( LoadCursor( NULL, IDC_ARROW ) );
    return(0);
```

Any subsequent mouse movement results in the child window's cursor being reloaded. This type of handling can be used to load one cursor as a mouse button is held down, and another cursor restored when the button is released. A counterpart to this type of response is shown next.

Hiding the Mouse Cursor

In examples in Chapter 3, the text caret (cursor) was hidden before a screen paint operation was executed and then revealed again afterwards. For the mouse cursor, this appears less important (i.e., appears to be handled automatically) but there may still be other occasions when an application may prefer to conceal the mouse cursor. For this purpose, the *ShowCursor* function is called with a boolean argument; FALSE (zero) to hide the mouse cursor, or TRUE (non-zero) to reveal it. In Mouse2.C, the right mouse button conceals the cursor when down, showing the cursor when the button is released:

```
case WM_RBUTTONDOWN:   ShowCursor(0);   return(0);
case WM_RBUTTONUP:     ShowCursor(1);   return(0);
```

Complexities are also possible here because the mouse cursor visibility state is not a simple boolean flag but is an integer variable. Repeated calls to *ShowCursor(FALSE)* decrement the variable while multiple calls to *ShowCursor(TRUE)* increment it. Thus, multiple sequential calls to *ShowCursor(FALSE)* will require multiple sequential calls to *ShowCursor(TRUE)* to make the cursor visible again. And, in like fashion, multiple calls to *ShowCursor(TRUE)* require multiple calls to *ShowCursor(FALSE)* to hide the cursor again.

Normally this does not happen and shouldn't be a problem. But, if for any reason, multiple calls of either type could occur, there is another way to insure that the mouse cursor is turned on or off cleanly. To do this use the value returned by *ShowCursor* which is the cursor visiblity setting:

```
while( ShowCursor(0) >= 0 );
while( ShowCursor(1) <  0 );
```

These two algorithms insure that the mouse cursor is immediately visible or hidden by repeating the show or hide instruction until the desired condition is reported. However, when either form is called, the *ShowCursor* instruction is always invoked at least once and, therefore, could still increment or decrement the counter so that conventional processes would require multiple *ShowCursor* calls.

Mouse3: Hit Testing

The Mouse3 example program demonstrates hit testing by creating a cruciform grid (see Figure 4-1) composed of squares within a single client window. The actual grid is a 7x7 array, but four grid elements from each corner of the array have been flagged as invalid and will not be included in paint operations. The remaining grid elements each have a corresponding boolean *fState* flag which is initially FALSE.

To demonstrate mouse hit testing, the location of each WM_L-BUTTON-DOWN message is tested against the grid coordinates for a match and a corresponding *fState* flag is inverted, toggling the grid state on or off. Mouse hits that fall outside of the grid area or correspond to a grid area and are flagged as invalid trigger a beep message. Then, when WM_PAINT is called, each valid grid element is drawn as a white square with a black outline. Grid elements whose *fState* flag is set have two diagonal lines added. Other than the form and demonstrating mouse hits, Mouse3 does not introduce any new program elements requiring explantion. This topic will be discussed again later in further demonstrations.

Figure 4-1: A Cruciform Grid for Mouse Hit Testing

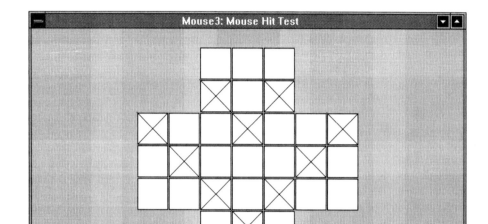

Non-Client-Window Messages

All mouse operations thus far have occured within the application's client window or within child windows belonging to the client window. However, outside of the client window, a different series of "non-client-window" mouse messages are generated. Normally these messages are ignored by applications and are passed back to Windows for handling via the *WndDefProc* function. Eleven of these messages are non-client-window mouse messages, beginning with the nine button messages shown in Table 4-2.

Table 4-2: Non-Client-Window Mouse Button Messages

Button Pressed	Released		Double-clicked
Left	WM_NCLBUTTONDOWN	WM_NCLBUTTONUP	WM_NCLBUTTONDBLCK
Right	WM_NCRBUTTONDOWN	WM_NCRBUTTONUP	WM_NCRBUTTONDBLCK
Middle	WM_NCMBUTTONDOWN	WM_NCMBUTTONUP	WM_NCMBUTTONDBLCK

These nine button messages correspond in function to the client-window mouse button messages discussed earlier. The WM_NCMOUSEMOVE message corresponds to WM_MOUSEMOVE and only reports mouse movement outside of the client window area. These ten mouse messages, however, do not correspond to their earlier counterparts in their accompanying information variables.

Non-Client Area Mouse Parameters

The *wParam* variable that accompanies a non-client area mouse button or movement message returns a WinWhere() Area Code that indicates the non-client area at which the message was generated instead of containing the button and keyboard shift state information that accompanies client area messages. Constants for these areas as defined in Windows.H are listed in Appendix A. All of these 26 area codes begin with HT (Hit Test) and include such designations as HTERROR (-2), HTTRANSPARENT (-1, corresponding to a window covered by another window), HTNOWHERE (0, not on any window), HTCLIENT (1, client window), or HTHSCROLL (6, horizontal scrollbar).

The *lParam* variable that accompanies a non-client area mouse button or movement message does, as with the client area messages, still contain coordinate information except that now the x and y coordinates are screen relative instead of client-window relative. The 0,0 origin point for the coordinates reported begins at the upper-left corner of the screen and increases down and right, as within a client window.

Coordinate Conversion

Screen and client-window coordinates can be converted from one form to the other using the *ScreenToClient* and *ClientToScreen* functions:

```
ScreenToClient( hwnd, lpPoint );
ClientToScreen( hwnd, lpPoint );
```

The address variable *lpPoint* is a long pointer to an instance of the POINT record structure that contains the integer values for the x and y coordinates. Remember, coordinates for a point lying to the left or above the client window origin will contain negative values if converted to client window coordinates. Likewise, since application windows can be moved "off-screen" to the left and up, client window coordinates converted to screen window coordinates might also contain negative values. The MAKEPOINT macro can be used to convert *lParam* values to a POINT structure.

The Hit-Test Message

The WM_NCHITTEST message is a special case and, strictly speaking, is not a non-client area message despite the NC designation. Instead, this message is generated before any other mouse messages, client area and non-client area, and is sent to the window that contains the cursor (or a window using *GetCapture* to capture the mouse input) every time the mouse is moved.

The *wParam* value that accompanies WM_NCHITTEST is not used. The *lParam* value contains the x and y cursor position values as screen coordinates. Normally, applications pass this message to Windows through the *Def-WindowProc* function where Windows will generate all other mouse messages based on the mouse coordinates and mouse button information. When the resulting message generated is a client area message, the screen coordinates are converted to client-window coordinates for the new message. Also, intercepting WM_NCHITTEST messages, e.g.,

```
case WM_NCHITTEST:   return( (LONG) HTNOWHERE );
```

will effectively disable all mouse messages both within the current application's client area and outside of the client window. The mouse buttons will simply work anywhere on the screen as long as this interception is in effect. Use this with extreme caution, if at all.

A Final Mouse Message

The 20-second mouse message is defined as WM_MOUSEACTIVATE and occurs when the cursor is in an inactive window and any mouse button is pressed. The parent receives this message only if the child passes it to the *DefWindowProc* function. In this event, the *wParam* variable contains a handle to the topmost parent window of the window being activated. The *lParam* variable then contains the hit-test area code in the low-order word and the mouse message number in the high-order word. The mouse cursor coordinates are not included in the message parameters.

Normally, the child window passes this message to the *DefWindowProc* function which passes the message to the window's parent window before any further processing occurs. If the parent window returns TRUE, processing is halted.

Duplicated Mouse Messages

Windows.H includes two duplicate mouse message definitions: WM_MOUSEFIRST, corresponding to WM_MOUSEMOVE, and WM_MOUSELAST, corresponding to WM_MBUTTONDBLCLK. These duplicate messages are included in Appendix A but do not provide different results. Reasons for their inclusion are uncertain.

Summary

Mouse operations under Windows are, in general, more convenient than in conventional graphics environments. Three example programs have demonstrated mouse operations within the client window area, including hit testing, changing mouse cursors, and mouse tracking.

Other, non-client area mouse messages have also been discussed but not demonstrated because they should normally be handled by default message processing. These are messages intended for other applications and are not intended for local handling.

Because the mouse is integral to Windows operations, mouse operations will continue to appear in later chapters.

The source listings for the Mouse1, Mouse2 and Mouse3 demo programs follow.

```
//============================//
//          Mouse1.C          //
//   Windows Mouse Tracking   //
//============================//

#include <windows.h>

long FAR PASCAL WndProc( HWND hwnd,   WORD message,
```

```
                              WORD wParam, LONG lParam  )
{
   HDC           hdc;
   PAINTSTRUCT   ps;
   static BOOL   fPaint = 0;

   switch( message )
   {
      case WM_MOUSEMOVE:
         if( fPaint )
         {
            hdc = GetDC( hwnd );
            SetPixel( hdc, LOWORD( lParam ),
                           HIWORD( lParam ), OL );
            ReleaseDC( hwnd, hdc );
         }
         return(0);

      case WM_LBUTTONDOWN:
         fPaint = fPaint ^ 1;
         MessageBeep(0);
         return(0);

      case WM_PAINT:
         hdc = BeginPaint( hwnd, &ps );
         EndPaint( hwnd, &ps );
         return(0);

      case WM_DESTROY:
         PostQuitMessage( 0 );
         return( 0 );
   }
   return( DefWindowProc( hwnd, message, wParam, lParam ) );
}

int PASCAL WinMain( HANDLE hInstance,
                    HANDLE hPrevInstance,
                    LPSTR  lpszCmdParam,
                    int    nCmdShow )
{
   static char szAppName[] = "Mouse1";
   HWND        hwnd;
   MSG         msg;
   WNDCLASS    wc;
   if( ! hPrevInstance )
   {
      wc.style          = CS_HREDRAW | CS_VREDRAW;
```

```
    wc.lpfnWndProc    = WndProc;
    wc.cbClsExtra     = 0;
    wc.cbWndExtra     = 0;
    wc.hInstance      = hInstance;
    wc.hIcon          = LoadIcon( NULL, IDI_APPLICATION );
    wc.hCursor        = LoadCursor( NULL, IDC_ARROW );
    wc.hbrBackground  = GetStockObject( WHITE_BRUSH );
    wc.lpszMenuName   = NULL;
    wc.lpszClassName  = szAppName;
    RegisterClass( &wc );
}
hwnd = CreateWindow( szAppName, "Mouse1: Tracking Demo",
                     WS_OVERLAPPEDWINDOW,
                     CW_USEDEFAULT, CW_USEDEFAULT,
                     CW_USEDEFAULT, CW_USEDEFAULT,
                     NULL, NULL, hInstance, NULL  );
ShowWindow(   hwnd, nCmdShow );
UpdateWindow( hwnd );
while( GetMessage( &msg, NULL, 0, 0 ) )
{
    TranslateMessage( &msg );
    DispatchMessage(  &msg );
}
return( msg.wParam );
}


        ;=======================================;
        ;  Mouse1.DEF module definition file   ;
        ;=======================================;

NAME           MOUSE1
DESCRIPTION    "Mouse1: Demonstrates Mouse Tracking"
EXETYPE        WINDOWS
STUB           "WINSTUB.EXE"
CODE           PRELOAD MOVEABLE DISCARDABLE
DATA           PRELOAD MOVEABLE MULTIPLE
HEAPSIZE       1024
STACKSIZE      8192
EXPORTS        WndProc


              //=====================//
              //      Mouse2.C       //
              //  Windows Mouse Test //
              //=====================//


#include <windows.h>
```

```
char    szChildClass[] = "Mouse2_Child";

long FAR PASCAL ChildWndProc( HWND hwnd,    WORD msg,
                                WORD wParam, LONG lParam   )
{
    HDC             hdc;
    PAINTSTRUCT     ps;
    RECT            rect;
    HCURSOR         hCursor;

    switch( msg )
    {
        case WM_MOUSEMOVE:
            switch( GetWindowWord( hwnd, GWW_ID ) )
            {
                case 0x0000:
                    SetCursor( LoadCursor( NULL, IDC_CROSS ) );
                    break;
                case 0x0001:
                    SetCursor( LoadCursor( NULL, IDC_IBEAM ) );
                    break;
                case 0x0002:
                    SetCursor( LoadCursor( NULL, IDC_ICON ) );
                    break;
                case 0x0003:
                    SetCursor( LoadCursor( NULL, IDC_UPARROW ) );
                    break;
                case 0x0004:
                    SetCursor( LoadCursor( NULL, IDC_WAIT ) );
                    break;
                case 0x0100:
                    SetCursor( LoadCursor( NULL, IDC_SIZE ) );
                    break;
                case 0x0101:
                    SetCursor( LoadCursor( NULL, IDC_SIZEWE ) );
                    break;
                case 0x0102:
                    SetCursor( LoadCursor( NULL, IDC_SIZENWSE ) );
                    break;
                case 0x0103:
                    SetCursor( LoadCursor( NULL, IDC_SIZENS ) );
                    break;
                case 0x0104:
                    SetCursor( LoadCursor( NULL, IDC_SIZENESW ) );
                    break;
            }
```

```
            return(0);

        case WM_LBUTTONDOWN:
            SetCursor( LoadCursor( NULL, IDC_ARROW ) );
            return(0);

        case WM_RBUTTONDOWN:
            ShowCursor(0);        // while( ShowCursor(0) >= 0 ); //
            return(0);

        case WM_RBUTTONUP:
            ShowCursor(1);        // while( ShowCursor(1) < 0 );  //
            return(0);

    //====================================================//
    // option = omit WM_PAINT for plain gray background //
    //          or include to show child window outlines //
    //====================================================//

        case WM_PAINT:
            hdc = BeginPaint( hwnd, &ps );
            GetClientRect( hwnd, &rect );
            Rectangle( hdc, 0, 0, rect.right, rect.bottom );
            EndPaint( hwnd, &ps );
            return(0);
    }
    return DefWindowProc( hwnd, msg, wParam, lParam );
}

long FAR PASCAL WndProc( HWND hwnd,   WORD message,
                         WORD wParam, LONG lParam  )
{
    static HWND   hwndChild[5][2];
    short         cxWin, cyWin, x, y;

    switch( message )
    {
        case WM_CREATE:
            for( x=0; x<5; x++ )
                for( y=0; y<2; y++ )
                    hwndChild[x][y] =
                        CreateWindow( szChildClass, NULL,
                        WS_CHILDWINDOW | WS_VISIBLE,
                        0, 0, 0, 0, hwnd,
                        x | y << 8,              // child window id //
                        GetWindowWord( hwnd, GWW_HINSTANCE ),
                        NULL );
```

```
            return(0);

        case WM_SIZE:
            cxWin = LOWORD( lParam ) / 5;
            cyWin = HIWORD( lParam ) / 2;
            for( x=0; x<5; x++ )
                for( y=0; y<2; y++ )
                    MoveWindow( hwndChild[x][y],
                                x*cxWin, y*cyWin,
                                cxWin, cyWin, TRUE );
            return(0);

        case WM_LBUTTONDOWN:
            MessageBeep(0);
            return(0);

        case WM_DESTROY:
            PostQuitMessage( 0 );
            return( 0 );
    }
    return( DefWindowProc( hwnd, message, wParam, lParam ) );
}

int PASCAL WinMain( HANDLE hInstance,
                    HANDLE hPrevInstance,
                    LPSTR  lpszCmdParam,
                    int    nCmdShow )
{
    static char szAppName[] = "Mouse2";
    HWND        hwnd;
    MSG         msg;
    WNDCLASS    wc;

    if( ! hPrevInstance )
    {
        wc.style         = CS_HREDRAW | CS_VREDRAW;
        wc.lpfnWndProc   = WndProc;
        wc.cbClsExtra    = 0;
        wc.cbWndExtra    = 0;
        wc.hInstance     = hInstance;
        wc.hIcon         = LoadIcon( NULL, IDI_APPLICATION );
        wc.hCursor       = LoadCursor( NULL, IDC_ARROW );
        wc.hbrBackground = GetStockObject( LTGRAY_BRUSH );
        wc.lpszMenuName  = NULL;
        wc.lpszClassName = szAppName;
        RegisterClass( &wc );
```

```
       //*** new elements for child window class ***//
       wc.lpfnWndProc   = ChildWndProc;
       wc.cbWndExtra    = sizeof( WORD );
       wc.hIcon         = NULL;
       wc.hCursor       = NULL;                    // essential!!! //
       wc.lpszClassName = szChildClass;
       RegisterClass( &wc );
   }
   hwnd = CreateWindow( szAppName, "Mouse2: Stock Cursors",
                        WS_OVERLAPPEDWINDOW,
                        CW_USEDEFAULT, CW_USEDEFAULT,
                        CW_USEDEFAULT, CW_USEDEFAULT,
                        NULL, NULL, hInstance, NULL  );
   ShowWindow(   hwnd, nCmdShow );
   UpdateWindow( hwnd );
   while( GetMessage( &msg, NULL, 0, 0 ) )
   {
       TranslateMessage( &msg );
       DispatchMessage(  &msg );
   }
   return( msg.wParam );
}


          ;====================================;
          ;  Mouse2.DEF module definition file  ;
          ;====================================;

NAME          MOUSE2
DESCRIPTION   "Mouse2: Demonstrates Child Windows and Cursors"
EXETYPE       WINDOWS
STUB          "WINSTUB.EXE"
CODE          PRELOAD MOVEABLE DISCARDABLE
DATA          PRELOAD MOVEABLE MULTIPLE
HEAPSIZE      1024
STACKSIZE     8192
EXPORTS       WndProc


             //==========================//
             //           Mouse3.C       //
             //  Windows Mouse Hit Test  //
             //==========================//

#include <windows.h>

#define xPos( x ) ( (x) * cxGrid + cxOff )
#define yPos( y ) ( (y) * cyGrid + cyOff )
```

```
long FAR PASCAL WndProc( HWND hwnd,    WORD message,
                         WORD wParam, LONG lParam )
{
   static BOOL  fState[7][7], fValid[7][7];
   static short cxGrid, cyGrid, cxWin, cyWin, cxOff, cyOff;
   HDC          hdc;        POINT       point;
   RECT         rect;       PAINTSTRUCT ps;
   short        x, y;

   switch( message )
   {
      case WM_CREATE:
         if( ! GetSystemMetrics( SM_MOUSEPRESENT ) )
         {
            MessageBox( hwnd,
               "Mouse not found! This application can"
               " not operate without a working mouse!",
               "Mouse Hit Test",
               MB_ICONSTOP | MB_OK );
            SendMessage( hwnd, WM_DESTROY, 0, 0L );
         }
         for( x=0; x<7; x++ )
            for( y=0; y<7; y++ )
            {  fValid[x][y] = 1;
               fState[x][y] = 0;  }
         for( x=0; x<2; x++ )
            for( y=0; y<2; y++ )
               fValid[ x ][ y ] = fValid[x+5][ y ] =
               fValid[ x ][y+5] = fValid[x+5][y+5] = 0;
         return(0);

      case WM_SIZE:
         cxWin = LOWORD( lParam );
         cyWin = HIWORD( lParam );
         cxGrid = cyGrid = min( cxWin, cyWin ) / 8;
         cxOff = ( cxWin - ( cxGrid * 7 ) ) / 2;
         cyOff = ( cyWin - ( cyGrid * 7 ) ) / 2;
         return(0);

      case WM_LBUTTONDOWN:
         x = ( LOWORD( lParam ) - cxOff ) / cxGrid;
         y = ( HIWORD( lParam ) - cyOff ) / cyGrid;
         if( x < 7 && y < 7 && fValid[x][y] )
         {
            fState[x][y] ^= 1;
            rect.left   = xPos( x );
```

```
                    rect.top    = yPos( y );
                    rect.right  = xPos(x+1);
                    rect.bottom = yPos(y+1);
                    InvalidateRect( hwnd, &rect, FALSE );
             } else   MessageBeep(0);
             return(0);

        case WM_PAINT:
             hdc = BeginPaint( hwnd, &ps );
             for( x=0; x<7; x++ )
                for( y=0; y<7; y++ )
                   if( fValid[x][y] )
                      {
                         Rectangle( hdc, xPos(x)+1, yPos(y)+1,
                                         xPos(x+1), yPos(y+1) );
                         if( fState[x][y] )
                         {
                            MoveTo( hdc, xPos( x ), yPos( y ) );
                            LineTo( hdc, xPos(x+1), yPos(y+1) );
                            MoveTo( hdc, xPos( x ), yPos(y+1) );
                            LineTo( hdc, xPos(x+1), yPos( y ) );
                      } }
             EndPaint( hwnd, &ps );
             return(0);

        case WM_DESTROY:
             PostQuitMessage( 0 );     return( 0 );
    }
    return( DefWindowProc( hwnd, message, wParam, lParam ) );
}

int PASCAL WinMain( HANDLE  hInstance,
                    HANDLE  hPrevInstance,
                    LPSTR   lpszCmdParam,
                    int     nCmdShow )
{
    static char szAppName[] = "Mouse3";
    HWND        hwnd;
    MSG         msg;
    WNDCLASS    wc;

    if( ! hPrevInstance )
    {
        wc.style          = CS_HREDRAW | CS_VREDRAW;
        wc.lpfnWndProc    = WndProc;
        wc.cbClsExtra     = 0;
        wc.cbWndExtra     = 0;
```

```
    wc.hInstance      = hInstance;
    wc.hIcon          = LoadIcon( NULL, IDI_APPLICATION );
    wc.hCursor        = LoadCursor( NULL, IDC_ARROW );
    wc.hbrBackground  = GetStockObject( LTGRAY_BRUSH );
    wc.lpszMenuName   = NULL;
    wc.lpszClassName  = szAppName;
    RegisterClass( &wc );
}
hwnd = CreateWindow( szAppName, "Mouse3: Mouse Hit Test",
                     WS_OVERLAPPEDWINDOW,
                     CW_USEDEFAULT, CW_USEDEFAULT,
                     CW_USEDEFAULT, CW_USEDEFAULT,
                     NULL, NULL, hInstance, NULL  );
ShowWindow(   hwnd, nCmdShow );
UpdateWindow( hwnd );
while( GetMessage( &msg, NULL, 0, 0 ) )
{
    TranslateMessage( &msg );
    DispatchMessage(  &msg );
}
return( msg.wParam );
}


        ;======================================;
        ;   Mouse3.DEF module definition file  ;
        ;======================================;
NAME          MOUSE3
DESCRIPTION   "Mouse3: A Mouse Hit Test Program"
EXETYPE       WINDOWS
STUB          "WINSTUB.EXE"
CODE          PRELOAD MOVEABLE DISCARDABLE
DATA          PRELOAD MOVEABLE MULTIPLE
HEAPSIZE      1024
STACKSIZE     8192
EXPORTS       WndProc
```

## Chapter 5

Child Windows and Control Elements

In Chapter 4, child windows were demonstrated with provisions to show different mouse cursors in each. Another example created an array of squares and responded to mouse clicks by showing crossed diagonals in the appropriate box. Both examples could have been created with or without using child windows.

One of the principal uses of child windows is "child window controls". These are child windows that process mouse (and keyboard) messages and notify the parent window when the child window's state has changed. This can be accomplished without the need for an elaborate *ChildWndProc*, as demonstrated previously, if you use a number of predefined window classes.

Windows Buttons

These predefined "child windows" are commonly referred to as buttons or control buttons, but also include edit and list boxes, combo boxes, and scrollbars. Of course, this last category has already appeared in earlier program examples, but scrollbars do have applications other than scrolling windows.

Control buttons will be covered in this chapter, leaving the other buttons to be discussed in subsequent chapters. If you have used Windows at all, you've already encountered a number of these control elements and should already be aware of their convenience for the user. These are also convenient for the programmer because, in Windows, you do not need to worry about the mouse logic or about making the control features change state or "flash" when clicked. Instead, all that is necessary is to define the desired controls and then wait for a WM_COMMAND message to be returned. This message provides notification that a control has been selected.

In the previous Mouse2 example, a child window class was defined and registered. Then, individual instances of the window class were created by calling *CreateWindow* and were positioned by calling *MoveWindow*. For instances of the predefined window classes used as control elements, however, the process is much simpler. The classes already exist as "button", "combobox", "edit", "listbox", "scrollbar", or "static", and the *CreateWindow* function, using the predefined class, simply sets the size, position, and function of the child window control, including, of course, the appropriate labels if desired. Dialog boxes also use control button elements but, as will be shown in Part 2, these function at a different level and are isolated from direct interaction with the program. For now, child window controls will be demonstrated using direct interactions, beginning with button controls.

Button Types

Windows provides eleven predefined button types in three principal groups: push buttons, checkboxes, and radio buttons. A fourth type, called a group box, does not respond to mouse or keyboard events but is used to group other buttons. Two other special "types" will be covered later. The standard Windows button types are illustrated in Figure 5-1.

Pushbuttons

Pushbutton controls are rectangular boxes that display a centered text label and a light outline that simulate a raised button (3-D shading). When a button is clicked, the outline vanishes to simulate a (physically) depressed button. Pushbutton controls are used principally to initiate an immediate action without retaining or displaying any type of status (on/off) information.

- *BS_PUSHBUTTON*—control button containing a given text label, which sends a message to its parent window whenever clicked (by a mouse or arrow key selection followed by pressing the Enter key).

- *BS_DEFPUSHBUTTON*—same as BS_PUSHBUTTON but with a bold border representing the default user response.
- *BS_PUSHBOX*—displays a label only until selected (receives the input focus), then displays an outline which is the same as BS_PUSHBUTTON, but with the label highlighted. The outline remains until another pushbutton or control is selected and the input focus is lost.

Figure 5-1: Button Control Styles

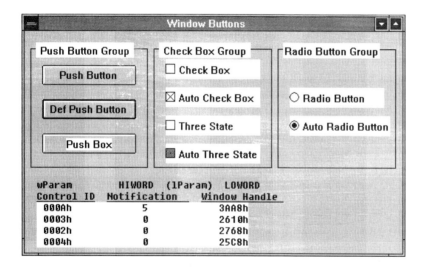

Radio Buttons

Radio buttons are small circular buttons with text (labels) that appear to the right (see also BS_LEFTTEXT). Customarily, two or more radio buttons are grouped together, representing mutually exclusive choices and permitting only one button in a group to be checked at any time. Clicking a radio button a second time does not change the button status.

The set condition is shown as a solid center (see Figure 5-1) and a default or initial choice is normally shown set when the group is first displayed.

- *BS_RADIOBUTTON*—displays a bold border when clicked. Set condition is not displayed automatically but must be set by the owner.

- *BS_AUTORADIOBUTTON*—same as BS_RADIOBUTTON, except that once a button is checked, a BM_CLICKED message notifies the application and checkmarks are removed from any other radio buttons in the group. The set or clear condition is displayed automatically.

Check Boxes

Check boxes are small square or rectangular buttons with text appearing to the right of the button. Checked state is shown by crossed diagonals.

- *BS_CHECKBOX*—displays a bold border when the button is checked. State must be set by the owner and is not displayed automatically.
- *BS_AUTOCHECKBOX*—same as BS_CHECKBOX, except that the button state is automatically toggled when selected.
- *BS_3STATE*—same as BS_CHECKBOX, except that three states can be toggled: clear, checked, or grayed. State must be set by the owner. The grayed state is typically used to show that a check box has been disabled.
- *BS_AUTO3STATE*—same as BS_3STATE, except that the button automatically toggles its own state when clicked.

Specials

- BS_GROUPBOX—designates a rectangle that groups other buttons. Any text or label is displayed in the rectangle's upper-left corner. The groupbox size and position must be specified appropriately to enclose the desired buttons. The groupbox does not respond directly to any mouse events; it does not return any WM_COMMAND messages.
- *BS_LEFTTEXT*—causes text to appear on the left side of the radio button or check-box button. Used with BS_CHECKBOX, BS_RADIOBUTTON, or BS_3STATE, but not with BS_PUSHBUTTON (not illustrated).

- *BS_OWNERDRAW*—designates an owner-draw button. The parent window is notified when the button is clicked. Notification includes requests to paint, invert, and disable the button. No default image or label is displayed (not illustrated).

Button Operations

The button operations demonstrated by Button1.C, shown in Figure 5-1, are fairly restricted because these child window controls respond only to the mouse. No provisions are made to permit movement from one control to another using the Tab or cursor keys nor do any of these, including the default pushbutton, respond to pressing the Enter key. Except for the BS_AU-TOCHECKBOX, BS_AUTO3STATE, and BS_AUTORADIOBUTTON styles, none of these controls display any change of state aside from the immediate selection "flash" when the mouse button is held down. And, less obvious in the example program but still relevant, these child window controls can obtain the input focus but do not, once acquired, release the input focus to the parent window.

These buttons do, however, send a WM_COMMAND message to the parent window when clicked with the mouse. And, in this demo, the *WndProc* function displays the *wParam* and *lParam* values from the command message at the bottom of the screen.

The Button1 example has been written with a gray background to make the full button (child window) visible. In the pushbutton examples, it's obvious that the entire button area is an active hit area. The button or checkbox image is not the sole target region for the checkbox and radiobutton controls. A mouse click anywhere in the white child window region is accepted.

Creating the Buttons

Individual buttons are created using the *CreateWindow* function in response to the WM_CREATE message in *WndProc*. In this example, three groups of buttons have been created to group the types using BM_GROUPBOX child windows.

Each button, including the group boxes, are created by their own *Create-Window* function calls using the following parameters:

- *lpClassName*—points to an ASCIIZ character string naming the window class. In these examples, "button" is used, but this must be either one of the predefined class names or a registered custom class. An error in this field does not cause an error to appear. It prevents the erroneous class object from being displayed.
- *lpWindowText*—points to an ASCIIZ character string and provides a label.
- *dwStyle*—a double word value specifying a combination of window styles and control styles. In the example program, these are WS_CHILD | WS_VISIBLE | BS_*buttonstyle*.
- *X*—an integer value specifying the initial x-position of the button class. The X and Y coordinates are relative to the parent window origin (*hWndParent*) whether the parent is the application client window or a groupbox child window.
- *Y*—an integer value specifying the initial y-position of the button class.
- *nWidth*—an integer value specifying the width (in device units) of the control button.
- *nHeight*—an integer value specifying the height (in device units) of the control button.
- *hWndParent*—identifies the parent or owner of the window being created.
- *hMenu*—a menu or child window identifier (HMENU). In this example it is a unique integer identifying each control button.
- *hInstance*—identifies the module instance associated with the child window control. In this example, the lParam variable contains a pointer to a structure of type CREATESTRUCT which contains a member of *hInstance*. The LPCREATESTRUCT macro is used for type casting. Alternatively, in *WinMain*, a global variable *hInst* could be assigned as hInst = hInstance; and is subsequently used as the argument. Or *GetWindowWord(...)* could be used to retrieve an instance reference as needed.
- *lpParam*—a pointer to any extra parameters that are passed as a LPSTR pointer. In this example, the field is another *CreateWindow* function or NULL to terminate. For an example, the following code creates a groupbox and two child window control buttons using second and

third *CreateWindow* functions as *lpParam* arguments before terminating the chain with NULL:

```
hwndGroup3 =
   CreateWindow
   (  "button", "Radio Button Group",
      BStyle | BS_GROUPBOX,
      BIndent3 - 2 * cxChr, cyChr,
      4 * cxChr + BWidth, 11 * cyChr,  hwnd, 9,
      ((LPCREATESTRUCT)lParam) -> hInstance,
   CreateWindow
   (  "button", "Radio Button",
      BStyle | BS_RADIOBUTTON,
      BIndent3, BVStep2 * 2,  BWidth,  BHeight,
      hwnd, 10, ((LPCREATESTRUCT)lParam) -> hInstance,
   CreateWindow
   (  "button", "AutoRadio Button",
      BStyle | BS_AUTORADIOBUTTON,
      BIndent3, BVStep2 * 3,  BWidth,  BHeight,
      hwnd, 11, ((LPCREATESTRUCT)lParam) -> hInstance,
      NULL
   )  )  );
```

This particular format is valid and is used in the Button1.C example. This format has one drawback—the created control buttons do not belong to the groupbox in which they're displayed because the groupbox and the individual buttons all have the same parent window specification (*hwnd*)—the application client window. For this same reason, the coordinates for each of the buttons are specified as offsets from the application client window origin, not from the groupbox origin.

For the purposes of this demonstration, this is also an advantage because the event messages generated by each button are reported directly back to the application. But it is also a disadvantage because an array of radio buttons declared in this form are not grouped by the groupbox outline enclosing them. Instead, all such radiobuttons belong to the application client window, even if they appear in different groupboxes. This means that clicking any one of the radiobuttons would reset all others regardless of your intention in grouping them. Button2.C illustrates another more practical means of grouping buttons. It uses the groupbox element as the parent window:

```
hwndAPB[0] =
   CreateWindow
```

```
(  "button", "Radio Button Group",
   BStyle | BS_GROUPBOX,
   43 * cxChr, cyChr, 4 * cxChr + BWidth, 13 * cyChr,
   hwnd, 9, hInst, NULL );
```

In this example, the groupbox window is created as a child of the application client window (*hwnd*) before a loop is used to create four autoradio buttons using the groupbox (*hwndAPB[0]*) as the parent.

```
for( i=1; i; i++ )
{
   wsprintf( szBuff, "AutoRadio #%d", i );
   hwndAPB[i] =
      CreateWindow
      ( "button", szBuff, AutoStyle,
        2 * cxChr, BVStep2 * i, BWidth, BHeight,
        hwndAPB[0], i+10,  hInst, NULL );
}
```

This format creates four autoradio buttons that belong to the groupbox and are, therefore, isolated from any other radio buttons.

There is, however, still a flaw in this particular format. These child window buttons report not to the application client window but to the groupbox. The groupbox itself does not report these events to its parent or handle them in any fashion. Instead, in an actual application, the groupbox should be created as a child window with a child window message function similar to the *ChildWndProc* functions demonstrated in other examples. But, for the moment, this format will be used in Button2.C to demonstrate other aspects of child window buttons.

Button Control Communications: to and from

The Button1.C program demonstrates how submessages are received from child window button controls as the *wParam* and *lParam* variables that accompany the WM_COMMAND event message. The *wParam* variable contains the control button ID (child window ID) that was assigned as a parameter in the *CreateWindow* function call. The *lParam* variable contains two values: the child window handle in the low word value and the notification code in the high word. The child window handle value is returned from Windows by the *CreateWindow* function call. The notification code, *HIWORD(lParam)*, is a submessage code used by the child window to inform the parent window precisely what event has occurred. The values of these submessage codes are shown in Table 5-1.

Table 5-1: Control Button Notification Codes

Code Constant	Value	Code Constant	Value
BN_CLICKED	0	BN_UNHILITE	3
BN_PAINT	1	BN_DISABLE	4
BN_HILITE	2	BN_DOUBLECLICKED	5

In the example program Button1 only two submessage codes will be returned: 0 or 5. The second, BM_DOUBLECLICKED, can only be returned by the BS_RADIOBUTTON style controls, but not by BS_AUTORADIOBUTTON. Control notification codes 1..4 are only returned by custom control buttons styled as BS_USERBUTTON, which are not illustrated in the present example program.

Sending Messages to Control Buttons

The Button2 example program demonstrates four groupboxes with sets of child window button controls. Unlike Button1.C, in this example, the groupboxes are actually parents to the controls they enclose. As your own experimentation will show, setting an autoradio button in one group will not affect the settings in the other. This example shows several other aspects of control button programming that involve messages sent to the control buttons by the application.

There are five button-specific messages defined in Windows.H, each beginning with the prefix "BM_" for "button message".

Table 5-2: Button Control Messages

Code Constant	Value	Code Constant	Value
BM_GETCHECK	WM_USER+0	BM_SETSTATE	WM_USER+3
BM_SETCHECK	WM_USER+1	BM_SETSTYLE	WM_USER+4
BM_GETSTATE	WM_USER+2		

The WM_USER identifier is provided so that programs can define their own messages. WM_USER has a value of 0x0400 which permits each window class to have its own set of messages unique to that class. Also, predefined child window controls can have their own messages defined in terms of WM_USER.

Note: All WM_msg values below 0x0400 are reserved. See Appendix A.

The BM_SETCHECK and BM_GETCHECK messages are sent by the parent window to a child window control button to set or retrieve the check state of checkboxes and radio buttons. In Button2.C, as shown in Figure 5-2, the BM_SETSTATE message has been sent to three of the checkboxes and to three of the radiobuttons in the group *RadioButtons 1*. Using the BM_SETCHECK message to set more than one box is valid and appropriate for the checkboxes, and would be used the initial state for a series of them.

For the radio buttons, however, the BM_SETCHECK message has established an anomalous state of affairs. Three radiobuttons in the group are checked, where as in normal operations—as you can discover first hand—clicking on one button would turn off any other button in the group that was set. Remember, normal behavior for radio buttons is to have only one in a group turned on at a time. But, likewise, one button is a group and is always on. This is when the BM_SETCHECK message would be used correctly. The BM_SETCHECK message was sent as:

```
SendMessage( hwnd..., BM_SETCHECK, 1, OL );
```

Or, to clear the checkstate of a button, another message could be sent as:

```
SendMessage( hwnd..., BM_SETCHECK, O, OL );
```

The first parameter is the handle of the child window (control button), the second is the message identifier, and the third parameter is a boolean value explicitly setting or clearing a flag state. The fourth parameter is not used and is passed as 0 (zero).

The single radio button in the second checked group was turned on by clicking the mouse, not by a BM_SETCHECK message. And, in the first group, clicking on any of these buttons will restore the normal state of one button on and all others off.

The BM_SETSTATE message is slightly different than the BM.SETCHECK message. The BM.SETCHECK message simulates the pushbutton "flash" that occurs when a button is clicked by the mouse or, after receiving the focus, by pressing the spacebar. In the checkboxes shown in Figure 5-2, the 2nd through 4th checkboxes have been sent BM_SETSTATE messages in the same fashion as the BM_SETCHECK messages, as shown by the heavy outlines. The third "set" message is slightly different because this message permits changing the style of button on-the-fly, so to speak. Two examples of this message type have been incorporated in Button2.C. It first changes the third pushbutton (left group) from BS_PUSHBUTTON to BS_DEFPUSHBUTTON:

```
SendMessage( hwndPB[3], BM_SETSTYLE,
              BStyle | BS_DEFPUSHBUTTON, OL );
```

Figure 5-2: Grouped Button Controls

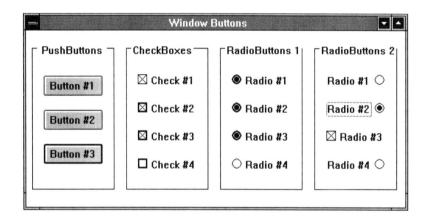

The BM_SETSTYLE message, unlike the other button messages, uses the fourth parameter and passes a non-zero argument to request that the control button be immediately redrawn. A zero argument does not redraw the control. In this example, these messages were all sent during the WM_CREATE response and, therefore, did not require a redraw instruction. In like fashion, the third control element in the right-hand group (shown in Figure 5-2) was originally created as an autoradio button, then revised with a BM_SETSTYLE message:

```
SendMessage( hwndARB2[3], BM_SETSTYLE, CheckStyle, OL );
```

Once this has been done, the control button behaves exactly like any other checkbox control while remaining a member of the *RadioButton 2* group.

Using BM_GETSTATE and BM_GETCHECK Messages

The BM_GETSTATE and BM_GETCHECK messages are sent as information requests to specific button controls. They then return the state or check status of the button; TRUE if the button is depressed or checked, or FALSE if it is normal. For the pushbutton controls, which do not retain checked (on/off) information, the BM_GETCHECK message is not relevant. The status of a checkbox control could be toggled using get and set messages for checkboxes, for example:

```
SendMessage( hwnd..., BM_SETCHECK,
             (WORD) ! SendMessage( hwnd..., BM_GETCHECK,
                                   0, OL ), OL );
```

Notice the negation operator (!) that precedes the second *SendMessage* instruction to return the current state after inversion. More often, however, the AUTOxxxx styles would be used to relieve the application of the need for updating the button status (as in Button2.C). In these cases, only the get message would be needed to inquire about the current status:

```
fStatus = SendMessage( hwnd..., BM_GETCHECK, 0, OL );
```

Button (Window) Labels

The text labels displayed within a pushbutton beside checkboxes and/or radio buttons or as window captions can be changed at any time by calling the *SetWindowText* function:

```
SetWindowText( hwnd, lpszString );
```

Hwnd is a handle to the window of whatever type while the string specification is a long or far pointer to an ASCIIZ string.

The current text label can also be retrieved from any window type using the *GetWindowText* function:

```
nLen = GetWindowText( hwnd, lpszBuff, nMaxLen );
```

The buffer must be large enough to hold the string returned while the *nMaxLen* specification places a limit on the length copied. At the same time, the *GetWindowTextLength* function can be used to determine the text length:

```
nLen = GetWindowTextLength( hwnd );
```

Part 2

Introducing the Whitewater Resource Kit

Examples in the first section of this book have been a mixture of conventional C programming code with calls to Windows-specific functions in order to demonstrate Windows programming. In Chapter 5, child window control buttons were introduced, including pushbuttons, checkboxes, and radio buttons. These were created using conventional C programming even though Windows-specific functions accomplished much of the programming tasks. At the same time, more than a little of the actual processing was handled by Windows, not by provisions within the example programs.

In addition to control buttons and group boxes, brief mention was made of other child window controls such as edit boxes, list boxes, scrollbars, and icons as well as custom controls. None of these have yet been illustrated by examples except for scrollbars used in a text window.

Collectively, all of these control elements as well as bitmaps, keyboard accelerators, menus, and strings are known as "program resources"—a term denoting the fact that they are used by programs but, in Windows particularly, are not necessarily provided directly within the source code. In some cases, as with menus and keyboard accelerators, these resources cannot be created within the application source code (whether C or Pascal) but are created through resource scripts and become part of the finished application, when they are compiled by the resource compiler (RC) shown in Figure 1-6, shown on page 14.

Resource Scripts

Having mentioned resource scripts—which Windows and OS/2 programmers will already be familiar with—a brief explanation is in order for those programmers who are new to Windows.

A resource script is an ASCII text script used by the resource compiler in preparing menus and other program resources that interface to Windows. The source code, however, is not written in C, Pascal, or assembly language but in a relatively simple high level language as shown below:

```
SolitronMenu MENU
BEGIN
    POPUP "&MENU"
    BEGIN
        MENUITEM "&Reset...\t^N",   Sol_Menu_Reset
        MENUITEM SEPARATOR
        MENUITEM "&Quit...\t^Q",   Sol_Menu_Quit
    END
```

And, for a dialog box:

```
101 DIALOG DISCARDABLE LOADONCALL PURE MOVEABLE
    70, 90, 170, 70 STYLE WS_POPUP | WS_CAPTION
BEGIN
    CONTROL "" "EDIT", WS_CHILD | WS_VISIBLE | WS_TABSTOP |
        0X80L, 10, 32, 130, 12
    CONTROL "" "STATIC", WS_CHILD | WS_VISIBLE | WS_GROUP,
        11, 5, 140, 18
    CONTROL "&Ok" 1, "BUTTON", WS_CHILD | WS_VISIBLE |
        WS_TABSTOP | 0X1L, 32, 50, 32, 14
    CONTROL "&Cancel" 2, "BUTTON", WS_CHILD | WS_VISIBLE |
        WS_TABSTOP, 99, 50, 32, 14
END
```

Using Borland C++, however, you are not required to learn and write resource scripts.

Developing Resources—Not Source Code

The Whitewater Resource Toolkit distributed with Borland C++ contains a variety of resource tools for creating and/or editing keyboard accelerators, bitmaps, cursors, icons, dialog boxes, menus, and string resources.

More important, while all of these resources could be created by other utilities or by writing script files, independently constructed resources and particularly script files must be compiled and linked before they can be tested. Instead, using the Resource Toolkit editors, these user-interface resources can be created and tested directly. In an interactive development process they eliminate the tediously slow edit-compile-link-test-edit cycle. And, most importantly, interactive development changes the emphasis from writing source code (scripts) to directly creating the application.

At the same time, because the Resource Toolkit creates these resources directly in binary format, compile and link time for applications using the resources are also reduced.

Last, but far from least, the Resource Toolkit is not limited to creating new applications but is also used to access and edit resources in existing applications. This feature is not practical, or often even possible, in the conventional development cycle. Further, while this last feature may initially sound interesting, if somewhat frivolous, reasons and uses that are not frivolous will be discussed later.

Resource Toolkit Components

The Resource Toolkit consists of eight interactive utilities, each of which will be discussed in more detail in this section. These eight utilities are:

- *Resource Manager*—the central control program that organizes groups of resources and provides access to the several toolkit editors. It also permits copying resources from other files or from existing applications.
- *Dialog Box Editor*—creates new dialog boxes and/or edits existing dialog boxes while providing tools to create combo boxes and owner-draw controls. Combo boxes are a combination of edit controls and a list box. Owner-draw controls are customized control elements that normally require maintenance by the application.
- *Bitmap, Cursor, Icon Editors*—supports and edits Windows bitmap formats; also maintains color tables for these formats.
- *Menu Editor*—supports hierarchic pop-up menus introduced in Windows 3.0. Hierarchic menus permit creating multiple pop-up menu levels for each menu item.

- *Accelerator Editor*—creates and edits accelerator resources that provide hot keys for commands.
- *String Editor*—creates and edits string resources that are test strings used by applications for messages or window captions.

The Resource Toolkit utilities are not the end-all and be-all of application programming, but they do relieve you of much of the work in writing the Windows-compatible interface portion of any application. This is no small portion of the overall task.

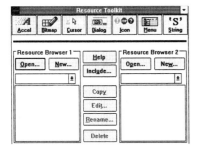

Chapter 6

Application Resources and Resource Files

Windows applications are composed of a variety of elements, textual menus, combined graphic and textual dialog displays, and purely graphic bitmaps, icons, and cursors. Individual applications may contain large numbers of each of these as multiple menus and dialog boxes, scores of bitmaps, and a dozen cursor images that represent different operational modes.

Instead of explicitly coding these elements within the application code, resources are elements that are loaded by the application as needed. This reduces the memory demands of the application and makes these resources editable and reusable.

In general, resources describe visual characteristics of program elements, including text strings, but do not define functional elements of the application. For example, they do not describe how the application responds to controls or menu selections.

Note: The actions/responses of visual elements such as button controls are controlled by Windows, not by the application.

Because these resources are separate from the application's execute code, the user interactive elements defined by the resources can be changed without access to the source code.

For an example, the Solitaire program distributed with Windows 3.0 contains 75 bitmaps including a full deck of 52 card faces with a choice of a dozen backs while the Whitewater Resource Toolbox provided with Borland C++ uses 31 hotkey accelerators, 11 cursors, 19 bitmaps, 26 dialogs, nine icons, seven menus, and several hundred strings. In either application, defining all of these elements within the source code would not only make the .EXE program too large for execution, it would also be unnecessarily unwieldy.

Keyboard Resources: Accelerators

An accelerator is a key or key combination used as an alternative to choosing a menu item that invokes a command such as pressing *Shift-Ins* instead of pulling down an Edit menu and selecting the Paste option. Using the editor, accelerator keys are defined as substitutions for defined menu options and can subsequently be identified in the menu as alternative invocations.

The Whitewater Resource Toolkit supports three types of resource images: bitmaps (.BMP), cursors (.CUR), and icons (.ICO). The simplest image type is the bitmap image which is a pixel image of any size using up to 16 colors. Individual bitmap images may be as large as in the full screen, as the CHESS.BMP desktop image; medium, as in the tilable desktop images or the Solitaire card deck; or small, as used in the REVERSI game or in icons and cursors. Unlike cursor and icon images, however, bitmap images consist only of a foreground image and overwrite any background display.

A cursor is also a bitmap image, but is a specialized type of image that is confined to a specific 32x32 pixel size and is used to select graphic elements or to locate an insertion position. Cursor resources contain two 32x32 pixel images. One describes the cursor image and the second describes the image's interaction with the existing background. For example, cursors can be partially or largely transparent or may interact with background colors. Also, each cursor image contains a single "hot spot" location which is a pixel coordinate within the cursor image defining the exact screen (pixel) location of the cursor.

Icons, the third type of bitmap, are used to select or activate an application. Like cursor bitmaps, icon images can define a combination of foreground and background colors, permitting the icon appearance to change as it is moved across existing images. Also, like cursor bitmaps, icons are normally 32x32 pixels using up to 16 colors.

The bitmap editor is a sophisticated paint program that provides a variety of tools for creating and editing bitmap, cursor, and icon images. And, while essentially the same bitmap editor is used for all three forms, the editor's facilities are changed somewhat according to the the needs of the image type being edited.

Individual bitmapped resources are stored as separate files prior to compilation and contain a single bitmap image and type identified by the appropriate extensions.

Dialog Boxes

Dialog boxes are input windows that provide the ability to select program options through graphic control elements including push buttons, checkboxes, radio buttons, list boxes, scrollbars, and entry fields. The Dialog Box editor permits interactive construction of dialog screens, showing them exactly as they will appear within the application. Tools are included for drawing, positioning, aligning, sizing, and moving dialog box controls.

Menus

Menus provide lists of available program options that can be executed either as immediate actions or by calling submenus with additional options. The Menu editor defines menu resources and allows construction and testing of pull-down menus. Hot key shortcuts for menu items are defined by the Accelerator menu.

Strings

Strings are text strings that are displayed by an application in its menus, dialog boxes, error messages, and so on. By defining strings as resources, applications can easily be revised or customized for international use without requiring source code revisions (or distribution). Also, defining strings as resources makes it easier to improve and edit application messages. For example, an ambiguous message can be revised without altering the application's source code.

Editable vs. Untouchable

Most of the resource items in an application, including all of the preceding resource types, can be edited, viewed, or copied for use by other applications, as well as renamed or deleted. There are, however, a few resources that can be copied, renamed, or deleted, but cannot be edited or revised. These include fonts used by the application to display text, raw data resources (.RC data files), and user-defined resources (included in the executable file).

Files and File Types

The Resource Toolkit can create or edit most resource files used by Windows, including executable files that contain resources. Editable file types are shown in Table 6-1.

Table 6-1: Resource Toolkit File Types

File	Type	Description
EXE	executable	executable program code containing application resources and compiled program code
RES	resource	compiled (binary) resource file
DLL	executable	executable (dynamic link library) module containing application resources and compiledprogram code
H	source code	header file containing symbolic names for defined resources
ICO	resource	icon resource file
CUR	resource	cursor resource file
BMP	resource	bitmap resource file

Two other file types can be generated by the Resource Toolkit but must be compiled by the Microsoft Resource Compiler to create .RES or .EXE files. These (see Table 6-2) can not be edited directly by the Resource Toolkit.

Table 6-2: Resource Files Requiring Microsoft's Resource Compiler

File	Type	Description
DLG	resource script	dialog box resource script containing a single dialog box resource definition in text format
RC	resource script	ASCII resource script containing a list of all of an application's defined resources

Since the Resource Toolkit can save resources directly as .RES or .EXE files, Microsoft's Resource Compiler is not required to compile resources or to include compiled resources in the .EXE file. Thus, .DLG and .RC file types are not required nor is the Microsoft Resource Compiler.

Two final file types can be copied, renamed, or deleted but cannot be created, browsed, or edited using the Resource Toolkit.

Table 6-3: Uneditable Resource Types

File	Type	Description
FON	resource	fonts used to display text
DAT	resource	raw data resources

Linking Resources

Normally, the Resource Toolkit compiles resources directly to an .RES (binary) file and then links the .RES file into the .EXE file. But, when editing an existing .EXE or .DLL file, the Resource Toolkit does not create a .RES file, but writes the resources directly to the runtime program. However, there are still reasons for having the intermediate .RES file rather than compiling all resources directly to the .EXE or .DLL files. The principal reason is that a .RES file needs to be compiled only once and is not subject to subsequent changes in the program code.

After this, when C compiles an application's source code, the first step involves updating any .OBJ files whose sources have changed. And, with this step finished, the linker converts the .OBJ code to .EXE code, links the run-time and Windows libraries, and, finally, links the .RES code to produce the finished executable program. After an application has been compiled to runtime, the application interface, i.e., the resource elements, can be modified directly through the Resource Toolkit without recompiling the application.

Dynamic Link Libraries

Dynamic link libraries (.DLL) are executable modules that may contain both Windows application functions (compiled source code) and application resources. A .DLL (or "dill") is similar in construction to a run-time library except that it is not linked to the application during the compile process. Instead, a .DLL is linked during execution whenever another module calls a function contained in the .DLL.

In brief, .DLLs have two principal strengths. First, .DLL libraries can be accessed by more than one application without being duplicated in each application. Second, routines in .DLL libraries can be modified without recompiling the programs using the library. The .DLL resources, like .EXE resources, can be modified without recompiling the dynamic link library or the applications using the library.

Header Files

Windows resources, like the constants defined in Windows.H, are identified by numbers. A series of dialog box resources, for example, might use the identifiers 1000, 1001, 1002, 1003, and so on. Windows applications use these same numbers to identify the individual control elements.

A typical application may require several hundred such identifiers. The previous example, Resource Toolkit, has 11 cursors, 19 bitmaps, and nine icons, all with corresponding numerical identifiers. It has seven menus with multiple menu options and several hundred strings which all have identifiers. And, there are 26 dialog windows with every dialog box and control element within the dialog requiring identifiers. Some of them, such as the icon identifiers, are not normally used by the application directly, but most, including the dialog box, menu, and string elements, are.

The actual number of identifiers required is immaterial. The point here is that remembering these numbers is easy for the computer but quite impractical (as well as pointless) for the programmer. Instead, header files (.H) are used to assign symbolic names to these identifying numbers allowing you, the programmer, to work with names instead of attempting to maintain a confusing list of reference numbers. The compiler, of course, translates these symbolic names to their corresponding number values (and, eventually, to addresses or offsets).

Maintaining such a header file is not a difficult task because the Resource Toolkit, through the relevant editors, creates and maintains the symbolic references required for the .H file as shown in the following example:

```
/* D:\BC\SOLITRON.H 1/19/1991 18:44*/
#define   Sol_Main_Menu        0x3E9
#define   Sol_Main_Quit        0x3EB
#define   Sol_Main_New         0x3EA
#define   Sol_Inst             0x3EC
#define   Sol_Inst_Object      0x3ED
```

```
#define   Sol_Inst_Moves        0x3ED
#define   Sol_Inst_About        0x3EF
```

In the .H example shown, the numerical constants (identifiers) appear in hexidecimal format but can also be generated, if desired, in decimal format. Naturally, to the computer, the difference is immaterial.

The Resource Manager

The Resource Manager, shown in Figure 6-1, is central to the Resource Toolkit. This provides access to existing resources as well as the seven resource editors.

Figure 6-1: The Resource Manager

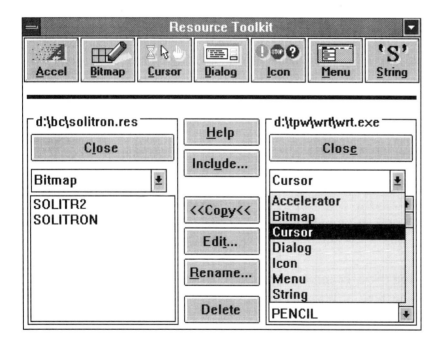

The Resource Manager does not support any menus. It is designed for mouse operation which activates features by clicking the button or by pressing the key that corresponds to the underscored letter in each button's caption, i.e., pressing *N* to select the *Include* button or *A* for the *Accel* icon.

Following the handling patterns established for Windows applications, the *Tab* key can be used to cycle to a button or field shown by a heavy border. The button or field can be activated by pressing the *Enter* or *spacebar* keys. Resource Manager facilities are used to:

- Start any of the Resource Toolkit editors
- Access existing resources to copy, edit, or delete
- Create new resource files
- Close resource files after editing, copying, or deleting

The principal features of the Resource Manager include the editor buttons, the resource browsers, and the include button.

The Editor Buttons   The Editor buttons appear at the top of the Resource Toolkit in the form of seven editor icons for the Accelerator, Bitmap, Cursor, Dialog, Icon, Menu, and String editors. The Resource Editors can be used to open individual resource files (of the appropriate type), or resources can be selected for editing through the Resource Browsers.

Resource Browsers   Two resource browsers are provided that permit the creation of resource groups. They also permit copying, deleting, or editing individual resources within a group. The two browsers provide a means of simultaneously opening two resource files to copy individual resources from one source to another, including copying to or from .EXE files.

Individual resources within a group can be selected for editing and new resources can be incorporated into existing resource groups. The Resource Manager will select the appropriate editor and load the resource automatically. Figure 6-1 shows two resource groups; Solitron.RES on the left and WRT.EXE (the Resource Toolkit) on the right. In the right hand Resource Browser, the resource type list is called (as a pull-down display) by clicking on the down arrow in the type window. From this list of included types, resources belonging to the selected type are displayed in the lower window (partially covered in the right example). In the lower left-hand window, Solitron.RES shows two bitmap images. Of course, a cursor image copied from WRT.EXE to Solitron.RES would automatically appear in the cursor listings, not among the bitmap listings that are currently displayed.

The Include Button   The Include button calls a dialog box listing all resource types, shown in Figure 6-2, that can be edited or copied. This dialog box includes both the editable and uneditable resource types. Any combination of resources types can be selected and will be displayed, if present, in any open file(s). The Include dialog can be used at any time to include or exclude resource types (but not source file types) by checking the desired resource types or unchecking the types to be excluded. The *Select all* button selects all resource types regardless of the previously checked status. The *Unselect all* button clears all selections.

Figure 6-2: Resource Type Selection

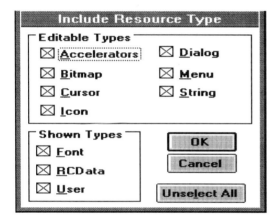

Accessing and Creating Resources

New resource elements can be created in three fashions. First, with an existing resource file open, from the Resource Manager, initiate an editor by clicking on the appropriate button. Or, second, from within an editor, choose **File/ New** to create a new resource element.

To open a new resource file, click on the **New** button above an unopened resource browser from the Resource Manager. This will initiate a new file where resource elements can be created or copied from existing resource files.

Existing resources can be accessed in two fashions: from within an editor or from the Resource Manager.

From within any editor, selecting **File/ Open** will call a dialog box with a list of resource file types appropriate to the editor. From the Cursor editor, for example, the dialog box will permit the selection of .CUR, .DLL, .EXE, or .RES sources.

After choosing the source type, a file selection dialog will present a list of files of that type. Select the file desired and, for a .DLL, .EXE, or .RES source, a list of corresponding resources will be displayed. Following the example, if the selection type is a .CUR file, the resource will be loaded immediately.

From the Resource Manager, begin by using the Include button to select the resource types to be displayed from an opened file. If the default has not been changed, all resources will be displayed.

After selecting the resource file (a DLL, RES, EXE or an explicit resource file), a single resource element can be selected for edit, or multiple resource elements can be selected for copy or delete. If an .EXE or .DLL source that does not contain Windows resources (or is a non-Windows file) is selected, the Resource Manager beeps, indicating that the selected file cannot be opened. The Resource Editor automatically makes a backup copy of the original file, replacing the first letter of the type extension with a tilde (~).

Copying Resources

Resource elements can be copied from one file to another using the Resource Manager (but not within the resource editors). Use one resource browser to open the source file and the other to open the destination file. The destination can be a new or existing file.

From the source file's edit field, select the desired resource type and then, in the list box, select one or more resource elements to be copied.

Next, click the Copy button.

Note: The arrows on the copy button show the copy direction, pointing from the browser from which resources were selected, to the destination browser.

When the Copy button is clicked, a dialog box (Figure 6-3) appears for each item selected, displaying the options to either rename resource items (to match application expectations) or to change the resource attributes (discussed later).

To change the resource name, simply type a new name in the dialog's Name input field. Or, to change attributes, click the radio buttons and/or checkbox to reflect the settings desired.

The Defaults button can be used to select the default resource options as shown in Figure 6-3. If no changes are desired, simply click the OK button.

Figure 6-3: Resource Attributes Dialog

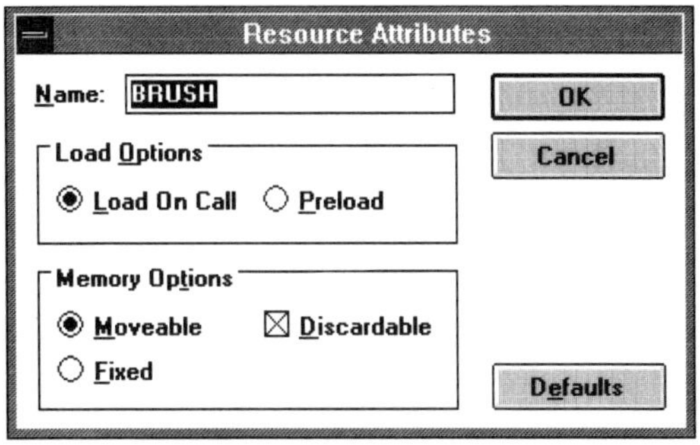

Renaming Resources/Changing Attributes

Resource elements can also be renamed without copying them by opening the source file, as described previously, and selecting one or more resource element before clicking the **Rename** button instead of the **Copy** button. The Resource Attributes dialog display, discussed previously, will be called for each resource selected. Within a resource editor, resource items may be renamed by selecting File/Save as.

Deleting Resources

Resource elements can be deleted in the same fashion as copying or renaming; by opening the source file, selecting the elements to delete, and clicking the Delete button.

Note: Deleted resources are immediately cleared from the source file! Use caution when selecting resources for deletion.

Closing a Resource File

When the Resource Manager is used to open a new or existing file, the resource browser's Open and New buttons are replaced by a single Close button. Immediately clicking the Close button saves all changes made, and closes and saves the resource file.

Files can also be closed from within a resource editor by choosing the Close option from the editor's control menu (upper left corner of the editor).

Summary

The Resource Manager is central to the Resource Toolkit. It provides a variety of functions ranging from allowing access to the individual resource editors to including a means of gathering, maintaining, and copying resource elements as well as providing for editing and revising resource elements in compiled applications. This will be discussed further in subsequent chapters.

The Resource Toolbox provides more than just resource editor utilities. It also maintains collected application resources as binary (i.e., compiled) resources ready for linking to applications without further processing.

The Resource Manager can also create header files, which provide a link between the numerical values returned by control and resource elements and mnemonic constants for use by the programmer.

In Chapters 7 through 12, the Resource Toolbox editors will be demonstrated. At the end of each chapter, these editors will be used to recreate resources which, when finished, will be used by working example program FileView.C, which appears in Chapter 13.

Chapter 7

Bitmaps, Cursors, and Icons

While the Bitmap, Cursor, and Icon editors are represented in the Resource Manager by separate buttons and the three resource types receive separate file extensions, these three editors accomplish essentially the same tasks. They create and edit graphic images and share most tools and features.

At the same time, since these three editors provide tool sets that follow the general styles and patterns of other popular "paint" utilities, much of the operation of these editors will be familiar and require relatively little explanation.

Each of these three types of bitmapped images serves a different function in an application and, in two cases, have device-specific default sizes and/or size limitations. Before discussing elements specific to individual editors and resource types, the majority of the elements in any of the three graphics editors are common to all of them.

The Graphics Editors

All three graphics editors; bitmap, cursor, and icon, appear essentially the same and provide features common to most paint programs, including color palettes, tools, editing and view windows, rulers, and resource statistics. Figure 7-1 shows the Bitmap editor with the image Ribbons.BMP loaded. The 16-color palette appears vertically at the left with the current (selected) color shown in a block above the palette. The tools palette appears across the top, just below the menu bar.

Figure 7-1: The Bitmap Editor Display

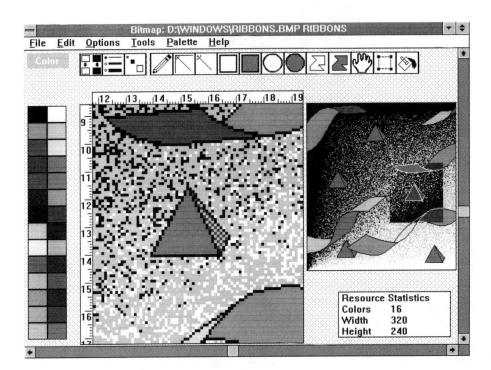

Two windows occupy the majority of the screen. The larger edit window shows a X4 blow-up while the smaller view window shows the entire bitmap image. The area in the view window that corresponds to the edit window display appears here in reverse video.

At the top, left of the edit window, rulers show the exact cursor position within the full bitmap. A small dialog box (lower right) shows resource statistics, including the width and height in screen units (pixels) and the number of colors in the palette.

The vertical and horizontal scrollbars at the right and bottom of the display are used to adjust the edit window position within the view window. For smaller bitmaps and for icon and cursor images, when the edit window shows the entire bitmap image, the scrollbars are omitted.

The Color Palette

The color palette is shown at the left of the editor window and, for the Bitmap editor, a single color box above it shows the selected color. For the Cursor and Icon editors, the single color box is supplemented by two additional boxes that show *Screen* and *Inverse* color modes.

- *Color*—selects colors that overpaint the background and do not change regardless of background screen color, i.e., are permanent colors. This is the only color mode supported for bitmap images.
- *Screen*—selects a background color showing how the icon or cursor image will appear against a similar background. Any lines drawn using Screen mode take the background color—i.e., become transparent.
- *Inverse*—does not actually select colors, but specifies a color that is always the inverse of the background (screen) color. It changes according to the underlying color value. Because lines and areas drawn as Inverse are always the inverse of the background, these lines are always visible regardless of the cursor or icon position. Inverse mode is especially useful for outlining to insure that cursor or icon images are always visible against any screen background.

Palette entry selections in either the Screen or Inverse color modes each change the other. Thus, changing the Screen color changes the color shown for the Inverse mode, and any lines drawn using Inverse mode also change accordingly.

When multiple color modes are supported, the mode currently in effect is indicated by a heavy border around the color mode button. To select colors, click on the mode box to be set, then click on the palette color desired.

In 16-color mode, the color palette shows 28 entries with the first 16 entries showing "pure" colors and the lower twelve showing "dithered" colors. For 2-color mode, the palette consists of black, white, and 26 shades of gray.

For cursors, only black and white are available for drawing the cursor image as required by Windows. A 16 entry palette is available for screen and inverse colors. These may be dithered colors if required by video device capabilities.

For icons, the color palette varies according to the video device capabilities (selected from WRT.DAT when the image is initially created). In some cases, the icon editor may support only a single color for all three color modes or may have two palettes with the top palette providing drawing colors and the bottom palette supplying screen and inverse colors. Again, depending on device capabilities, some may be dithered colors.

- *Pure Colors*—colors generated directly by the output device. For EGA/VGA systems, 16 pure colors are supported as combinations of red, blue, and green. All lines drawn by the graphics tools require pure colors.
- *Dithered Colors*—a mixture of pixels of two or more pure colors, rather like the half-tone colors used in the color comics. These are best suited for coloring areas. Because these are simulated colors created by mixed dot patterns, they cannot be used by the line drawing tools. When a dithered color is selected for line drawing, the closest possible pure color is used instead. Further disadvantages are found in changes in the appearance of dithered colors from one device to another and, in some environments, Windows may switch from dithered colors to pure colors which may result in changing the image presented.
- *Customizing Colors/Palettes*—offers the options both of customizing individual colors and loading and saving custom color palettes (the Cursor and Icon editors use only the Windows color palette).

Individual colors are edited by first selecting a color entry from the palette, then choosing **Palette/Edit** color from the menu to call the color edit dialog box, (shown in Figure 7-2). All color entries are set as RBG color combinations with the red, blue, and green fields accepting values in the range 0..255. These can be adjusted either by the red, blue, and green scrollbars or by entering numerical values directly in each edit field. The combined color result is shown in the rectangle to the right of the scrollbars.

Note: Both the scrollbar and edit fields are updated whenever the other is changed, while the scrollbar backgrounds show the relative intensity of each color component, i.e., the scrollbar backgrounds scale from pure color (255) to black (0).

The **Accept**, **Cancel**, and **Default** buttons either accept the new color settings, restore the previous color setting, or restore the palette's default color entry which may or may not be the original color before this operation began.

Dithered palette colors can also be adjusted but continue to appear as mixtures of pure palette entries.

For 2-color bitmaps, the color editor can also be used, but only the **A**ccept and **C**ancel options are offered.

Figure 7-2: The Color Editor Dialog

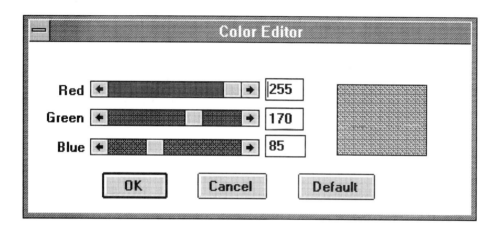

Saving and Loading Color Palettes   Color entries within a palette must be customized individually but, after this is done, the revised palettes can be saved through the **P**alette/**S**ave color menu option. Or, a previously saved palette can be retrieved through the **P**alette/**G**et color option. Both options open a dialog box for selection of directory and palette names. Palette file extensions are always .PAL.

The Graphic Editor Tools

The 15 graphics tools that appear as icons in Figure 7-1 are supported by all three of the graphics editors while the Cursor editor adds a 16th, hotspot tool. Any of these tools can be selected by clicking on the tool symbol while the selected symbol is shown inverted (white on black). In many cases, the mouse cursor is also changed to reflect the current task.

Color Toggle—toggles drawing colors as the inverse of the selected color when on; off by default. The toggle tool works only with the Pencil.

 Line Thickness—provides three line widths: 1 pixel, 3 pixel, and 5 pixel. The selected thickness is shown by the solid bullet (dot) next to one of the three lines pictured. Clicking on the tool icon cycles through the three settings. The **O**ptions menu can also be used to select line widths.

 Magnification—three settings for the edit window are offered as the actual size, four times the actual size, and eight times the actual size. The selected magnification is indicated by the filled (solid) square in the icon and can be cycled through the three settings by clicking on the tool icon or by calling the **O**ptions menu to select magnification. The default setting is four times the actual size.

When the edit window is magnified, the bitmapped graphic may be too large to display within the edit area. When this happens, the horizontal and vertical scrollbars can be used to adjust the edit area. Alternatively, the Dragging tool can be clicked anywhere in the edit area and dragged in any direction with the same effect as using the scrollbars, only faster.

The left mouse button can be clicked anywhere in the View window to reveal the current area shown in the Edit window by inverting the colors in the corresponding area. To change viewpoints, click the right mouse button anywhere in the View window. The Edit window will then center, as closely as possible, on the point clicked in the View window.

 Pencil—used to draw freeform lines and shapes or to edit individual pixels within an image. To draw with the Pencil, hold down the left mouse button and drag the image. Release the mouse button to cease drawing. Use the Pouring tool to fill large areas.

 Line Tool—used to draw straight lines horizontally, vertically, or diagonally (45° increments). To draw, press the left mouse button to anchor the beginning of the line, then move the pointer to the desired endpoint and release to create the line.

Constrained Line —used to draw straight lines at any angle. To begin, press the left mouse button to anchor the line, move the pointer to the desired endpoint, and release to create the line.

Rectangles, Hollow or Filled—used to draw rectangles by pressing the left mouse button at the first corner position desired and then moving to the diagonally-opposite corner before releasing the button. A hollow rectangle may be filled with a contrasting color using the Pouring tool. Filled rectangles are drawn solid using the current drawing color.

Ellipses, Hollow or Filled—used to draw hollow or filled ellipses. Ellipses are drawn by specifying the corners of an enclosing, but invisible, rectangle in the same fashion as the rectangle tools. Hollow ellipses may be filled with a contrasting color using the Pouring tool. Filled ellipses are drawn solid using the current drawing color.

Polygons, Hollow or Filled—used to draw hollow or filled polygons. The mode of operation, however, is rather different than with the rectangle or ellipse tools. Polygons are drawn as a series of sides, beginning by pressing the left mouse button to start the first line, then dragging the mouse to the desired position to end this side of the polygon.

Release the mouse button, then, before moving the mouse further, press the button again. Repeat this process for the subsequent sides of the polygon. The final side of the polygon may be drawn or may be completed automatically by double-clicking the mouse. The left mouse button must be double-clicked to complete the figure. Open figures are not permitted, all polygons must be closed. Polygon figures, rectangles and ellipses may be hollow or filled.

Dragging Tool—used in two fashions: first, to move the edit area by holding the mouse button and moving the drag icon outside of the edit window or, second, to move or copy a portion of a bitmap that has been selected using the Area Selection tool.

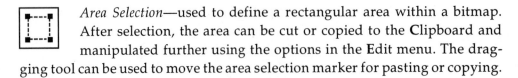

Area Selection—used to define a rectangular area within a bitmap. After selection, the area can be cut or copied to the Clipboard and manipulated further using the options in the Edit menu. The dragging tool can be used to move the area selection marker for pasting or copying.

Pouring (Color Fill)—used to fill continuous areas with the currently selected pure or dithered color. The hotspot for the pouring tool is located at the tip of the spill. The pouring tool is used to fill large areas with color and will fill any bounded region by clicking within the bounded area. Alternatively, any continuous region of an existing color can be changed by clicking the pouring tool within the colored area or line. When the pouring tool is clicked, the pixel color at the hotspot location is read and the pouring action replaces all contiguous cells with the same initial color, stopping only when a cell of a different color value is reached.

Note: Pouring does not work well when replacing a ditthered color because of the mixture of pixel colors encountered.

Hotspot (Cursor Only)—available only in the Cursor editor and is used to set the hotspot position within a cursor image. If no hotspot is set, the default position is the upper left corner of the grid.

The Options Menu

The Options menu duplicates the line width, toggle, and magnification selections that appear as icons in the tool bar and operate in the same fashion.

In the Bitmap editor, the Options menu offers the additional Combination mode feature. This feature calls a dialog box that determine how colors in Clipboard bitmaps will be combined with existing bitmaps during pasting.

By default, Combination mode pastes bitmaps precisely as they were saved, overwriting existing images. The Combination mode settings permit various pixel combination effects but are better understood by experimentation than explanation. One hint, however: reversing all settings inverts the colors of the stored image.

The Tools Menu

The Tools menu offers an alternative means of selecting the tools represented by icons. Tool operations are the same regardless of where the choice of tool is exercised.

Images and Image Sources

The three graphic editors can edit and save images to and from resource files (.RES), executable files (.EXE), and dynamic link libraries (.DLL) as well as individual bitmap files of three types: bitmap (.BMP), cursor (.CUR), and icon (.ICO). New resources can be saved directly to .RES files, to .EXE files, or to individual files.

Bitmap Resources

Bitmap resources most closely approach conventional bitmapped images and describe a picture or illustration but possess no Windows-interactive functions. The bitmapped resource provides a display element but does not respond directly to mouse or keyboard events. Some applications, of course, may provide their own indirect responses. The Solitaire program which provides movement of bitmapped card images in response to program inputs is an example.

Bitmapped images can be created in 2-or 16-color formats with no specific size limitations imposed, except available memory. Individual .BMP files contain only one bitmap image while .RES files may contain any number of files of one or more types.

Note: The Bitmap editor may import OS/2-format images but this capability is not officially supported nor fully tested. Windows bitmapped images, however, are not created in OS/2-compatible formats.

Cursor Resources

Cursor resources (or mouse pointers) are a specialized form of bitmap providing three elements: a pointer image that indicates general function as well as mouse tracking, a screen image that governs interaction with background images and, a hotspot that indicates the absolute screen position. In general, the cursor image is the primary concern with different shapes used to indicate selected functions such as I-beams for text editing, a pencil for drawing or a hand with the index finger extended to punch buttons.

When designing cursor images (see Figure 7-3) only black and white are available for drawing. The second, lower palette provides sixteen screen colors, allowing the cursor image to be checked against different backgrounds.

Figure 7-3: The Cursor Editor

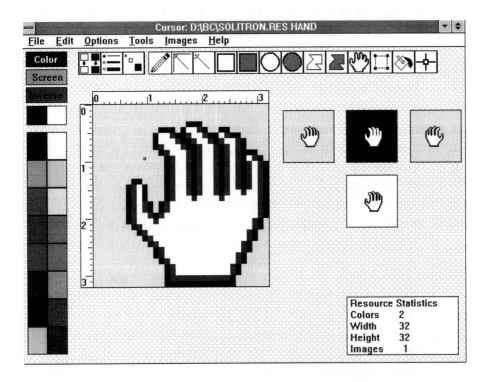

Below the Color block, the Screen block shows the current background color while the Invert block shows the inverse of the Screen color. Any of these three can be selected as the active drawing color with selection indicated by a heavy black border. But, only the Color block actually sets color pixels in the cursor image.

When the Screen block is selected, drawing resets pixels to the background (screen) color by making them transparent. When Inverse is selected, the pixels are set to invert the background color. In both cases, the areas drawn change according to changes in the background selected. The cursor image will interact with the existing screen image in the same fashion, either as transparent pixels allowing the background to show through or by inverting the background pixels.

The cursor illustrated shows a hand image outlined in black, then traced inside the outline with inverted pixels and, finally, filled with white. As can be seen in the small illustrations immediately to the right, this inverted trace allows the cursor to stand out easily against any background. This is important in any application.

The fourth cursor image, far right, is simply a left-handed version of the cursor that matches the Windows option of swapping right and left buttons. After all, roughly $^1/_7{}^{th}$ of the population is left-handed and there's no sense in being parity chauvinistic.

Note: The three right-most cursor images do not appear in the Cursor editor but have been added to this illustration to show contrast against different backgrounds.

The hotspot tool at the right end of the toolbar is used to set the cursor hotspot that is indicated in the edit window as a small concentric square between the thumb and forefinger.

The Resource Statistics show details about the current cursor image as well as the number of cursor images contained in this file for different video capacities. Thus far, only one cursor version has been created. However, individual .CUR files may contain multiple cursor images designed for display on different devices that vary in pixel dimensions and colors according to the capacities of different video displays.

Cursor and Icon Resolutions

The file WRT.DAT contains data for four display device types: VGA, EGA, Monochrome, and CGA video devices. Both the Cursor and Icon editors permit creating multiple images under a single name (and single file) for each display resolution. All modes presently use 32x32, 2-color cursors as shown in Table 7-1, but this may change with the introduction of new video devices. The information in WRT.DAT may be modified, as necessary.

Table 7-1: Cursor and Icon Resolutions (from WRT.DAT)

Device Name	IconColors	— Cursor — Width	Height	— Icon — Width	Height
4-Plane	16	32	32	32	32
3-Plane	8	32	32	32	32
Monochrome	2	32	32	32	32
CGA	2	32	32	32	16

When a cursor or icon is loaded, Windows selects the cursor or icon image appropriate to the device driver.

Icon Resources

 Icon resources are used to represent applications, system re-sources or, as in the resource toolkit, subsystems within an application. Under Windows, icons are most commonly dis-played on screen or in Program Manager windows to repre-sent minimized programs. In general, these are static images, though some applications create their own custom icons such as the Clock program distributed with Windows.

Custom icons aside, however, conventional icons are either 32x32 or 32x16 bit images using 16, 8, or 2 colors.

The Icon editor illustrated in Figure 7-4 shows the same 28-color palette discussed previously, offering 16 "pure" colors and 12 "dithered" colors. Icons can be drawn using any of these colors or any combination of them or, like the cursor images, can also use transparent (Screen) or inverted pixels. In the icon illustrated, the single letter (S) was drawn using inverted pixels, making this portion of the icon readily visible against any background. The grid was outlined in alternating black and white pixels, again providing maximum visibility.

The main point in this illustration is to present a caution. While there is great temptation to create elaborate icons as in this one, too much detail is quickly lost in the actual icon images shown at the right. And, in general, a simpler, less detailed icon will be easier to recognize, as shown in Figure 7-5.

Figure 7-4: The Icon Editor

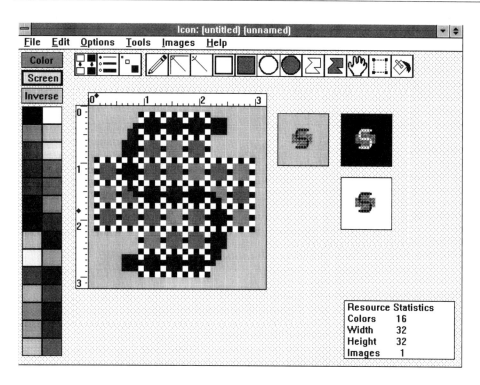

Exactly how you design an icon for your application is, of course, a matter of personal esthetics. This is not a course in commercial art design. Remember, however, that your application is not going to stand or fall on the basis of your icon unless, perhaps, you have a very unusual application.

Don't forget that not all systems can support elaborate multi-color icons. This doesn't necessarily mean that you must design a separate icon for each video because, on a monochrome system, for example, Windows will dither all colors except black and white.

As a last ditch solution, a simple design drawn largely or entirely as inverse and screen pixels will always be visible as shown in the two examples in Figure 7-6.

Figure 7-5: A Simpler Icon Design

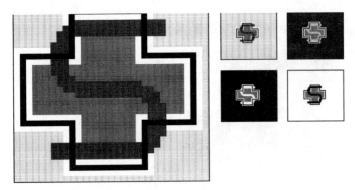

Two Icons for FileView.C

The first two resource items for FileView.C, appearing in Chapter 13, will be
a pair of icons shown in Figure 7-6. The primary application icon is shown on
the right while a secondary icon, which will be used by one of the dialog boxes,
appears on the left. Both icons were designed to stand out against any background. They begin with a background drawn using the inverse brush, while
the letters use the screen brush with an outline in light blue. The details of the
two icons can be varied according to your own tastes, but both icons will be
needed by the example program. These icons should be created in File-
View.RES with the titles FILEVIEW and FILETYPE.

Figure 7-6: Two Icons Used By FileView.C

Summary

Bitmapped images are integral to Windows even if the only bitmaps used are a cursor and an icon. The three graphic editors, Bitmap, Cursor, and Icon included in the Resource Toolkit make creating these resources a relatively simple task. The Resource Toolkit can also be used to revise existing bitmaps, cursors, and icons in other applications or to copy existing resources from one application to another.

Windows provides a number of predefined icon images such as MB_ICON-HAND, MB_ICONQUESTION, and MB_ICONASTERISK which are invoked in quite a different manner, as shown in Chapter 14, Message Boxes.

Chapter 8

The Dialog Box Editor

Dialog boxes provide a wealth of resources for applications. They allow the presentation of everything from elaborate error message popups to list boxes, selection buttons, and help windows; virtually anything you can choose to imagine. This is important simply because dialog boxes introduce a flexibility in program design which, previously, was only manageable with elaborate coding and special provisions for saving overlaid screen information. Of course, these same elements have been used in conventional (DOS) programming but not with the convenience afforded under Windows.

The Dialog Box editor provides a matching convenience by offering a visually-interactive platform for designing and editing dialog box resources. Using the Dialog Box editor is as simple and is nearly as instinctive as using a paint program. Tools are provided for creating and/or editing all types of controls from buttons and checkboxes to listboxes and edit fields.

The Dialog Box editor also provides several special capabilities because dialog box resources can be edited from and saved to resource files (.RES), executable files (.EXE), and dynamic link libraries (.DLL). It can also be saved as dialog box resource scripts (.DLG) as well as opening header files (aka include files) to create lists of mnemonic symbols correlated with dialog box resources.

The Dialog Box Editor

The Dialog Box editor provides two resource palettes, the Tools palette and the Alignment palette. Both are shown in Figures 8-3 and 8-5.

The Tools palette consists of 11 icons that represent dialog element types or features. Five of these icons toggle through one to four changes for a total of 22 dialog elements or styles. The Alignment palette consists of nine icons, that offer provisions to adjust the alignment and arrangement of controls within the dialog box. By default, the two palettes are located at the top of the Dialog Box editor, immediately below the menu bar. The Tools palette is to the left and the Alignment palette to the right. Since both palettes may not be visible in their entirety, the **D**ialog menu provides the **S**wap Palettes option, exchanging the positions of the two palettes.

A second option, the **D**ialog/Palettes option on the Bottom, positions both palettes at the bottom of the window below the dialog box edit area. The alternate option, the **D**ialog/Palettes option on the To**p**, restores the Tool and Alignment palettes to the default (upper) position.

The Dialog Box editor shown in Figure 8-1 opens with a blank dialog box which can be resized by dragging on the corner blocks (which also show that the dialog box is the currently active edit resource) or moved as desired. Other features, including the style of the dialog box and the caption, can be revised by calling the menu option **D**ialog/**A**ttributes. The default Captioned dialog box can be changed to an Uncaptioned dialog box by double-clicking on the dialog box icon in the Tools menu.

Dialog Menu Options

The Dialog Box editor menu also provides options that set dialog attributes (discussed below), show control tab order, control ID numbers, and show logical groups among the controls. Each option is described below:

- *Show Tab Order*—displays the order in which the Tab key steps the focus through the dialog box controls. Tab order is displayed as red numbers in the upper-left corner of each control item, beginning with one and progressing sequentially. Tab order can be changed for individual items using the Controls menu.
- *Show Item ID*—displays the ID value for each control item in blue in the lower-left corner of each control. ID numbers are assigned auto-

matically beginning with 101 but can be changed by using the **Controls** menu.

- *Show Item Group*—uses patterned rectangles to overlay grouped controls with each element in a group shown using a matching pattern. Logical group arrangements can be redefined using the **Controls** menu.
- *Grid Items*—permits setting grid resolution controlling the placement of controls. Grid spacing is expressed as an integer value and corresponds to pixel coordinates. A grid setting of two, for example, limits placement to even coordinate values within the dialog box window.
- *Show Header menu*—calls the header-file editor if a header file has been opened through the **File/Open Header** menu option. Alternatively, if the header file is already displayed, this option hides the header file editor.

Figure 8-1: Captioned and Uncaptioned Dialog Boxes

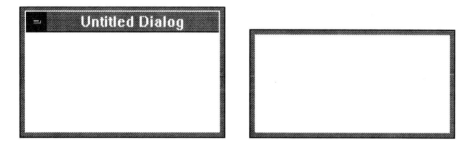

Dialog Attributes

The Dialog Attributes dialog box shown in Figure 8-2 provides access to a variety of features for customizing the style (performance) of the dialog box, editing the caption title, and setting menu and class fields.

The dialog box position within the application client window can be set as X/Y coordinates or, the Windows defaults can be selected via the check box. The dialog box size is subject to the same options; either a specific size (in pixels) or a Windows default.

Figure 8-2: Dialog Attributes and Fonts

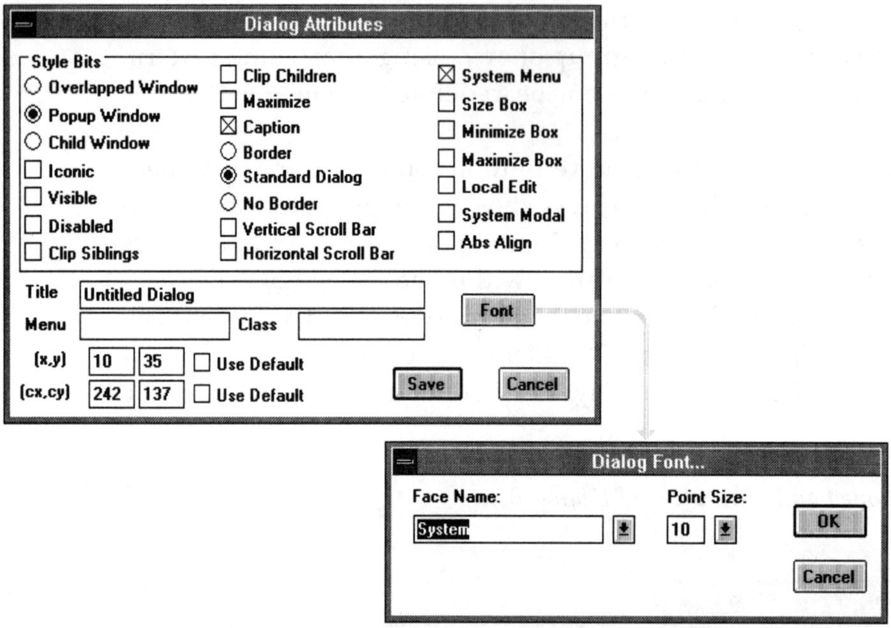

The various options are largely self-explanatory but, if not, can be more easily understood by experimentation than explanation.

The default selections shown are: Popup Window, Caption, Standard Dialog, and System Menu. Of these options, the Caption option can be unchecked here or, as mentioned previously, by double-clicking on the dialog box icon in the toolbar. All other options must be explicitly selected or deselected.

The System Menu option is represented by the icon in the upper-left corner that calls the system menu. This feature is frequently disabled when an explicit response, usually in the form of a pushbutton control, is expected. With the System menu disabled, the dialog box cannot be exited except by responding in the expected manner.

A Standard dialog box can not be move or resized (by the user) while a Captioned dialog box is not subject to these restrictions. This does not, of course, prevent resizing or movement within the Dialog Box editor.

The Fonts button, lower right, calls another dialog box from which two pull-down listboxes allow selection of typefaces and type size. Six fonts are normally available: System, Terminal, Helv (Helvetica), Courier (typewriter), TmsRmn (Times-Roman) and DIGITAL. Alternatively, any font type can be typed in the combo box's edit field and doesn't necessarily need to be listed or installed in the present machine.

The dialog box font selection is applied to all controls (and labels) within the current dialog box but may vary between dialog boxes. Font changes should be minimized for consistency of appearance.

Font sizes vary according to the typeface selected, but range from 8 to 14 points. Also, fonts may or may not be available even though they are listed. If the font is not available, the system font or default font will normally be substituted by Windows.

Operating The Dialog Box Resources

The Dialog Box editor is principally a mouse-interactive editor. This means that most operations are accomplished using the mouse pointer to select, position, or operate resource tools. As an alternative, menus are also provided that duplicate the selections shown in the Tool and Alignment palettes and that offer some selections that are not represented by icons. In general, however, the Dialog Box editor is mouse operated.

For mouse operations, primarily while positioning or sizing a control or dialog element, mouse movement can be restricted to a single dimension (i.e., vertical or horizontal movement). To restrict mouse movement, hold down the Shift key, then move the mouse horizontally or vertically. This will restrict movement to the selected direction until the Shift key is released.

Dialog Box Tools

The Dialog Box Tool palette shown in Figure 8-3 consists of a bar containing 11 icons. Several of these icon controls can be toggled through two, three, or four related variations by double-clicking on the icon. They are illustrated here vertically as unfolded icon sets. The various dialog tools are discussed and illustrated on the next page.

Figure 8-3: The Dialog Box Tool Palette

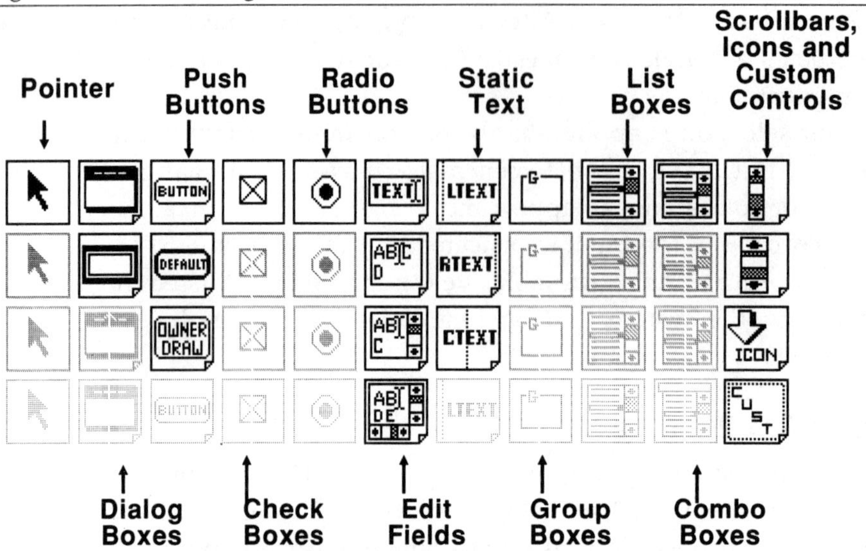

The Pointer—a general purpose mouse pointer. It is the default item in the tool palette and is automatically activated after operations are completed with any other tool. For example, selecting the radio button tool permits 'drawing' a radio button by specifying position and size but, once completed, the pointer tool is reactivated automatically.

Dialog Boxes—used to create either a captioned dialog box (default) or a standard dialog box to change the style by double-clicking on the toolbar icon. Existing dialog box styles can be changed through the Dialog Attributes dialog box discussed below. Remember, however, that captioned dialog boxes are moveable within an application and uncaptioned dialog boxes are immobile.

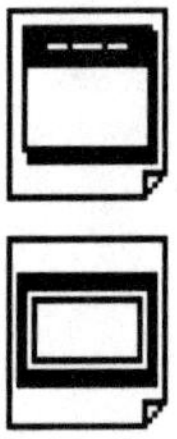

Control Elements

The Dialog Box tool palette provides three types of control elements: push buttons, check boxes, and radio buttons.

Push Buttons—controls that execute an immediate response when activated (clicked) but do not maintain on/off status information. Either standard, default, or owner-draw push buttons can be selected by double-clicking on the toolbar icon.

A standard pushbutton (which is the default tool selection) must be selected before it can be activated, either by clicking with the mouse or by Tabbing until the button is highlighted. It is then activated by pressing the Enter or Spacebar key.

The default pushbutton appears with a heavy border that indicates it is the default selection and will be activated immediately by pressing the Enter or Spacebar key. Only one default pushbutton should be defined for a dialog box.

Owner-draw pushbuttons require support for button appearance and operation within the application, instead of being handled by Windows. As an example, the editor buttons displayed by the Resource Manager are owner-draw buttons that use bitmapped displays. With owner-draw buttons, the parent window is notified when a button is selected and receives requests to paint, invert, or disable the button. This requires support within the application to handle these functions. For more information on owner-draw buttons, refer to Microsoft's Software Development Kit.

Check Boxes—provide multiple and independent selections, allowing each to be selected (checked) or turned off (cleared) without affecting other checkboxes. For example, a checkbox to enable/disable sound effect prompts would be completely independent of a second checkbox that selects a timed save operation and a third that enables/disables backup files. Check boxes can be enclosed to appear as visual groups, with or without group captions, using the Group Box tool.

Radio Buttons—always defined as logical groups as demonstrated in Chapter 6. Only one radio button in a group can be selected at any time. Customarily, a default radio button is set within the application, as shown in Chapter 6.

To define radio buttons as a logical group, the Controls menu provides the Start Group control. Radio buttons can be enclosed, appearing as visual groups, with or without group captions, using the Group Box tool.

Text Fields

Two text field types are provided: static text fields which are used for information or labels, and edit fields which are used for user entries and response.

Edit Fields—used for text entry but sometimes used to display default text. Four styles of edit fields are provided and are selected by double-clicking on the toolbar icon. The four edit field types are: a single-line edit field, a multi-line edit field, a multi-line edit field with vertical scrolling, and a multi-line edit field with both vertical and horizontal scrolling. Single-line edit fields are commonly used for brief entries but can accommodate entries longer than the entry field box (the outlined area) by scrolling horizontally. This does not require a horizontal scrollbar because the entry display automatically scrolls in response to keyboard entries or in response to the left and right arrow keys. An I-beam cursor is supplied automatically when the edit field is active. The three multi-line edit fields operate in essentially the same fashion except multiple lines of text can be entered.

When an edit field is created, a default text entry is also supplied as "EDIT" but can be cleared entirely. Or, another default entry can be supplied through the menu options: Controls/ Attributes which are discussed for both Edit and Static Text fields.

Static Text—normally used to display information, offer error prompts, ask questions, explain the consequences of proposed actions or, frequently, to provide labels for edit fields. Three format options are supplied: left-justified, right-justified, and centered text.

When a text field is created, a default text label is supplied as "LTEXT", "RTEXT", or "CTEXT" according the justification style. Since these are static labels, a new label is entered via the Controls/ Attributes option from the menu bar, which also offers access to other features.

   Caution: Static text fields are limited to 255 characters and multiple static text fields may conceal all or part of each other if their positions overlap.

The Controls Menu

The Controls menu offers a variety of options specific to individual control elements within the dialog box, including attributes, tabstops, and logical groups. To use the Controls menu, begin by selecting the desired control element by clicking with the mouse. The four black corner blocks indicate the selected control element.

Controls/Attributes opens an attributes dialog box for the selected control element. Figure 8-4 begins by illustrating an Item Attribute dialog box (top left) that was called for an edit box entry. For other control types, the details will differ, but initially they have a similar appearance.

The EDIT Attributes dialog provides edit boxes for a default text display, an Item ID and position, and size parameters. For an edit box, as used for this example, the text field might well be left blank but, for other types such as pushbuttons, checkboxes, radiobuttons, and static text displays, the text entry field would be used to label the control or to enter a text message. The remaining edit box fields, for the Item ID and position and size parameters, have already been set by the Dialog Box editor but can be revised as desired.

Figure 8-4: Control Attributes Menu

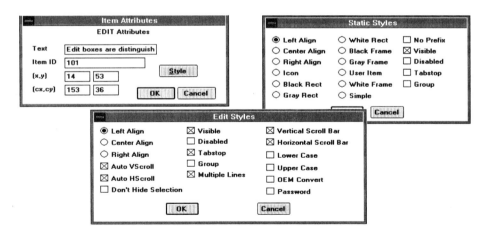

The Style button calls a second dialog box with two examples shown at top right and bottom for a static text field and an edit entry field respectively. In each case, the settings shown are defaults established by the control style selection when the control element was created. A variety of other settings are available to customize the appearance and/or performance of individual control elements.

Notice that a variety of appearances for the Static Styles (upper right) are controlled by radio buttons and, while not shown by group boxes, are actually divided into several groups, i.e., more than one radio button style feature can be selected, but only one from each group.

In the check box options, notice that checkboxes are provide for Tabstop and Group flags. These do duplicate, in effect, menu options which will be discussed below.

The Tabstop and Group checkboxes also appear for the Edit Styles (bottom). Make particular note of the Lower Case, Upper Case, and OEM Convert checkboxes which can be enabled to convert keyboard to displayed characters. The Password checkbox prevents keyboard entry from being echoed to the screen.

Controls/Set Tabstop toggles the tab stop bit for the selected control. This is equivalent to checking or unchecking the Stoptab option in the Attributes menu.

The tab stop flag is set, by default, for all new controls except static text, group boxes, icons, and custom controls. When the tab stop flag is set, the control item is allowed to receive the focus when the Tab key is pressed.

Controls/Move Forward and Move Backward move the selected control one tab stop (position) forward or backward in the tab order. The remainder of the order is unaffected.

Controls/To Top of Tab Order and To Bottom of Tab Order move the selected control to the first or last of the tab order, leaving the remainder of the order unaffected.

Controls/Start Group defines the current control element as the first control in a new group. All controls created subsequently are defined as members of this group, unless of course, another new group is started. This is equivalent to setting the Group flag (checkbox) in the Controls/ Attributes/ Style dialog. To change or redefine existing groups, use the Group Together option.

Controls/Group Together creates a new control group. To define the control group, select the desired controls by clicking each group while holding down the shift key, then selecting Group Together from the Controls menu. This associates the selected controls as a group, moving them to the top of the tab order.

Note: This operation will not work if more than one control in the group has the Group flag (checkbox) on. The best option is to turn off the Group flags for all of the selected controls before selecting the controls to be grouped.

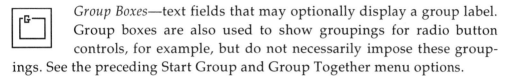

Group Boxes—text fields that may optionally display a group label. Group boxes are also used to show groupings for radio button controls, for example, but do not necessarily impose these groupings. See the preceding Start Group and Group Together menu options.

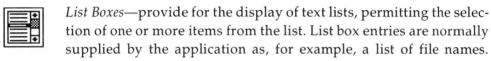

List Boxes—provide for the display of text lists, permitting the selection of one or more items from the list. List box entries are normally supplied by the application as, for example, a list of file names. When lists are too long for the allocated display space, a built-in scrollbar appears for vertical scrolling.

Custom List Boxes—can also be defined as *owner-draw list boxes*. These boxes have the general characteristics of conventional list boxes but are functionally supported by the application rather than by Windows.

To define a custom list box, begin by creating a standard list box, then, either press the Alt key and double-click on the list box, or select the list box and choose **Controls/ Attributes/ S**tyles. Next, from the Styles dialog box, select Owner Draw Fixed or Owner Draw Variable. Fixed requires that all items in the list box be of equal height. Variable permits items to vary in height. One advantage of a custom list box is that bitmaps as well as text strings can be displayed. Refer to Microsoft's Software Development Kit for more information on supporting owner-draw list boxes.

Combo Boxes—combine the features of edit boxes and list boxes. They permit selection from a list of items or use of an entry field. While the toolbar supplies only one tool icon for combo boxes, there are three styles of combo box supported: simple, drop-down, and drop-down list combo boxes. Combo box styles and other options are selected through the **Controls/ Attributes** menu. Alternatively, the Style dialog box can be called by creating a simple combo box (the default style), then holding down the Alt key while double-clicking on the combo box.

Simple Combo Boxes—displays both the list box and edit area features, each behaving exactly like the corresponding control elements except that selection can be made by either typing an entry in the edit box or by selecting an item from the list box. Typed entries in simple and drop-down combo boxes are not required to correspond to list box items.

Drop-Down Combo Boxes—behaves in the same fashion as the simple combo boxes except that only the edit box portion is displayed initially and the list box appears only when the down arrow to the right of the list box is clicked.

The list box portion of the drop-down combo box is sized in the same fashion as a simple combo box but, by not appearing initially, permits tighter spacing of controls. Examples of drop-down combo boxes appear in the Font dialog box in Figure 8-4 as the Font Name and Point Size boxes.

Drop-Down Combo List Boxes—similar to drop-down combo boxes but differ in the behavior of their edit box areas. For a drop-down combo list box, entries can be made in the edit box, but must correspond to items included in the list box.

Custom Combo Boxes—can also be created as *owner-draw combo boxes* and are defined in the same fashion as custom list boxes described on page 195.

Scrollbars, Icons, and Custom Controls   Scrollbars, Icons, and custom controls are grouped together under a single, toggled toolbar icon, but provide three quite different tools:

Scrollbars—used to create standalone scroll bars within the dialog box. The edit controls, list boxes, and combo boxes have their own integrated and attached scrollbars and do not require the creation of separate scrollbars. Standalone scrollbars are used in a variety of ways and can be created in either vertical or horizontal varieties. More than one vertical or horizontal scrollbar can be created and can be used to control anything, not just window display coordinates.

For an example, the bitmap editor in the Resource Toolkit uses three horizontal scrollbars to mix intensities of red, green, and blue to customize a palette color. Four or more scrollbars might be used in a MIDI control application to set tone, voice, fade, and reverberation. Anything else in an application that needs scaler control could be set using one or more scrollbars.

Scrollbar controls are provided in two versions: standard scrollbars which may vary in size but cannot vary in width, or variable-width scrollbars which may be any width desired.

Icon Controls—creates a box in which an icon can be displayed. Since Windows handles the box sizing automatically, only the box position needs to be set.

 Custom Controls—require a dynamic-link library (DLL) that defines the Windows procedure for the control as well as functions that interact with the Dialog Box editor. For further details on custom controls, refer to Microsoft's Software Development Kit.

Aligning, Positioning and Sizing Control Elements

While controls can be positioned and sized by using the mouse or by entering values directly in the Attributes dialog boxes, the Alignment palette offers a selection of tools that provide a very welcome convenience. These tools also permit adjustments and alignments for groups of controls and can be selected either from the Alignment palette or from the Alignment menu. The tools provided allow adjustments to the position of a selected set of controls with alignments relative to the *top, bottom, left, right* or *center* of one control within the set. They also provide for evenly spacing a set of controls vertically or horizontally. Sizes can also be adjusted for a set of controls, setting all elements within a selected set to the same size. The first control selected is either used as the standard or is a reference anchor for all adjustments, i.e., if three controls are selected for Make Same Size, the second and third items will be sized to match the first item selected.

Note: Alignment and sizing selections are independent of any control element functional groupings.

The Alignment palette (toolbar) shown in Figure 8-5 provides nine alignment tools. Individual adjustment tools are described below.

 Align Left—aligns the selected controls relative to the anchor control's left border. Both horizontal and vertical size and vertical positions are unaffected. Variations in horizontal size do not affect alignment.

 Center on Vertical—centers each of the selected controls horizontally on the anchor control's vertical axis. Both horizontal and vertical size and vertical positions are unaffected.

Figure 8-5: The Alignment Tool Palette

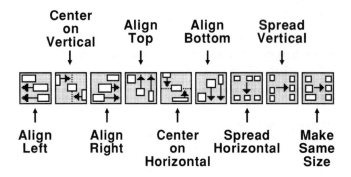

A single control can be centered within the dialog box by clicking on the dialog box as the anchor element, selecting the control, and then selecting Center on Vertical. Multiple controls spread horizontally, however, will be stacked one on top of the other. If this happens, the mouse can be used to individually drag these controls apart, and then to select and realign the controls as appropriate. Multiple controls spread vertically will be centered horizontally within the dialog box.

Align Right—aligns the selected controls relative to the anchor control's right border. Both horizontal and vertical size and vertical positions are unaffected.

Variations in horizontal size do affect the resulting alignment appearance, particularly with radio buttons or check boxes when the size of the label portion of the control is not visually apparent. As an alternative, the Styles dialog box for each control in the group can be called to set Left Text, placing the button or checkbox images to the right of the labels.

Align Top—aligns the top of the selected controls relative to the anchor control's top border. Both horizontal and vertical size and horizontal positions are unaffected.

Center on Horizontal—centers each of the selected controls vertically on the anchor control's horizontal axis. Both horizontal and vertical size and horizontal positions are unaffected. A single control can be centered within the dialog box by clicking on the dialog box as the anchor element, selecting the control, and then selecting Center on Horizontal.

Multiple controls spread vertically, however, will be stacked one on top of the other. If this happens, the mouse can be used to individually drag these controls apart, and then to select and realign the controls as appropriate. Multiple controls spread horizontally will be centered vertically within the dialog box.

 Align Bottom—aligns the bottom of the selected controls relative to the anchor control's bottom border. Both horizontal and vertical size and horizontal positions are unaffected.

Variations in vertical size will result in irregular appearance. This can be corrected by using the Make Same Size tool. However, this has the disadvantage of adjusting both horizontal as well as the vertical sizes.

 Spread Horizontal—spaces the selected controls evenly between the left-most and right-most controls but does not center controls horizontally within the dialog box client window.

The horizontal positions of the left-most and right-most controls are unaffected as are the vertical positions and horizontal and vertical sizes of any of the selected controls.

 Spread Vertical—spaces the selected controls evenly between the top-most and bottom-most controls but does not center controls vertically within the dialog box client window. The vertical positions of the top-most and bottom-most controls are unaffected as are the horizontal positions and horizontal and vertical sizes of any of the selected controls.

 Make Same Size—makes all selected controls the same size, both vertically and horizontally, as the anchor control. Positions, both vertical and horizontal, are not affected.

Dialog Boxes with Menus

Dialog box menus are not displayed in the Dialog Box editor but must be created, tested, and revised using the Menu editor. At the same time, the client area in the Dialog box appears larger vertically than it actually is because space is reserved at the top of the client window for the menu bar which is not displayed.

Header Files

Header files (aka include files) can be opened while defining dialog box resources by selecting **File/Open Header** or **New Header** from the Dialog Box editor menu. Once a header file has been opened, the **Dialog/Show Header** and **Hide Header** menu options reveal and conceal the header-file editor. Editing and creating header files will be discussed further in Chapter 12.

Three Dialogs for the FileView Application

The FileView program requires three dialog boxes: About, FileType, and OpenFile. These three dialog boxes are illustrated and explained below but need to be created as dialog box resources in FileView.RES for later use by the FileView.C application (the subject of Chapter 13).

The About dialog shown in Figure 8-6 consists of a captioned dialog box without a system menu entitled About FileView. Three dialog elements are shown inside the dialog box: a centered text line, an icon box, and a single button.

The dialog ID values appear below each dialog element but only the pushbutton, with a value of one, returns a value when activated. Since no header file is open for this resource, only the numeric value is shown. The value one corresponds to the message constant IDOK which is defined in Windows.H but will also later be duplicated in FileView.H.

Figure 8-6: A Simple Dialog Box with an Icon

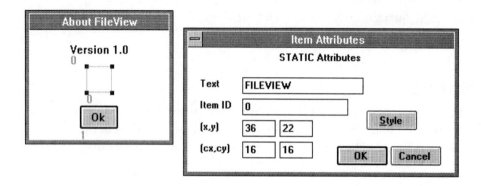

In this illustration, the icon box in the center is selected while the Item Attributes dialog box (from the Dialog Editor) at the right shows the attributes for the icon dialog element. Since the icon entitled FILEVIEW is the icon that should be displayed when this dialog box is active, the icon name has been entered in the edit field labeled Text. Perhaps the label Item Attributes dialog would be more appropriate than About FileView dialog for this dialog box, but this same dialog box is also used for text display and text edit fields. None-the-less, for icons, the icon name used in the resource file should appear here in order for the icon to appear when this dialog box is active in the application.

The Item ID field, immediately below, has a value of zero since the icon is not a selectable item and does not return a message value. The actual value used here is not important but there is one potential problem with "null" values.These problems will be discussed in the section entitled Idiocyncracies and Possible Problems.

The **(x,y)** coordinate fields were set automatically when the icon box was drawn. They show the coordinates of the upper-left corner of the icon box relative to the dialog box client window. The **(cx,cy)** size field for icon boxes are irrelevant since icons are sized automatically and any values entered here are simply ignored.

Caution: The **(cx,cy)** size fields can be zero and often are when .RC script files are used to specify dialog boxes. This presents a small problem in making it impossible to select or change the icon box, using the Dialog Box editor. Once the icon size is set to zero, the icon box will still function but cannot be moved, deleted, or otherwise edited. A standard size of 16,16 is recommended.

The Style button summons a further dialog box that permits revisions to the dialog element style, i.e., to change a radio button to an autoradio button or even to a checkbox, a pushbutton, or an icon box. In this instance, however, there are no relevant alternative styles.

Idiocyncracies and Possible Problems

Dialog boxes that have been created using .RC resource scripts often use a value of -1 for controls that are not expected to return a message value. The Dialog Box editor also permits entering a -1 value—except that there is a catch. When the resource file is saved and loaded again, or when resources that were created through a .RC file are loaded, -1 values are converted to word values as 65535—the maximum value possible for an (unsigned) word variable. In Figure 8-7, this value appears on three dialog box elements: the dialog box label (a text field), the icon box, and the group box. This presents a deliberate illustration of the error.

Figure 8-7: The Select File Type Dialog Box

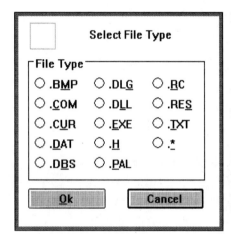 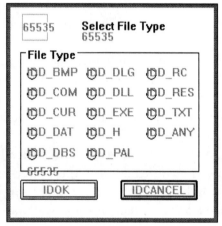

The catch occurs when a new element is added to an existing dialog box because the Dialog Box editor automatically assigns an initial value that is one higher than the highest existing element ID. And, if any element has a value of 65535, the new ID value assigned is 65536. This is an illegal value as you will discover the moment you attempt to call **Control/Attributes** for any reason, such as assigning a preferred value to the control. And, the result? Quite simply, Windows will terminate the Resource Toolkit and display a system violation error message!

Ergo: Use zero values for non-control elements, but do not assign -1 or 65535 as values. If you call an existing resource that already has a -1 or 65535 value, check by selecting **Dialog/Show Item ID**, before adding any new control (or display) elements, use **Control/ Attributes** to change each to a zero value (or double-click on the dialog element to call the Item Attributes dialog).

The File Type Dialog

The File Type dialog box uses an uncaptioned dialog box and displays the second icon, FILETYPE, to the left of the title text. The icon box is created in the same fashion as that in the About dialog except that the icon name is entered in the Item Attributes dialog. The File Type dialog box appears in Figure 8-7 on the left with a duplicate box on the right showing the ID constants for each control element.

Note: The ID constants can be displayed only if they are defined in a .H header file and if the header file has been opened for this resource. Different resources may have different constants with the same values. The ID constant that is shown for a resource depends upon the order within the header file. However, even if the wrong resource ID constant is shown here, it does not mean that an error will occur in the application.

The purpose of the File Type dialog is found in the fourteen autoradio buttons, each labeled with a different file extension (concluding with a wildcard extension option). Most of the file extensions used are common to Windows applications but were chosen here simply for an example of a radio button list. The autoradio button style has been used for all of these controls, freeing the application from the responsibility of checking and unchecking the button display each time a control is selected. In most cases, this will be the preferred approach. The radio buttons are enclosed here in a group box, but the group box does not control the grouping. Groupings are established by setting the group attributes or by clicking on the controls to be grouped (while holding the Shift key down) and then selecting Control/Group Together.

The box on the right in Figure 8-7 shows the ID constants defined in the VIEWFILE.H header file. Header files can be created using an ASCII editor, but may produce compiler problems if the file is terminated with an EOF (0x1A) character. If so, simply load the .H file using the BC editor and then save it again. This will remove the offending EOF tag. The editor used to create the header file will be discussed in Chapter 12.

The File Selection Dialog

The File Selection dialog is the last of the three dialogs for the FileView example. It is also the most complicated and most important of the three because it is the dialog that file names are entered into or selected from the list box for display in the main application window (which is not created as a dialog box). The File Selection dialog shown in Figure 8-8 consists of two edit boxes (with text labels), one list box (unlabeled), three buttons, and one icon box (displaying the FileView icon). The ID constant values for each of these control elements are shown at the right. They are the values (or constants) that will be used by the application to enter and retrieve information from these dialog elements.

Figure 8-8: The File Selection Dialog Box

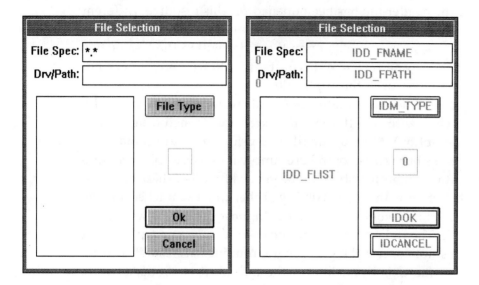

The first edit field, labeled *File Spec:* and identified as IDD_FNAME, is shown here with a default text display. This default text, however, will immediately be overwritten by the application when the dialog box is created and, therefore, is actually irrelevant.

The second edit field, labeled *Drv/Path:* and identified as IDD_FPATH, does not show a default text display and will also be filled in by the application with the default drive/path when the dialog box is created. The list box, identified as IDM_LIST, will be filled by the application with a list of file names that match the file specification shown in IDD_FNAME in the directory shown in IDD_FPATH. If the list is longer than the list box, a vertical scrollbar is generated and maintained automatically.

The icon box displays the FILEVIEW icon while the Ok and Cancel buttons are essentially stock controls that return IDOK and IDCANCEL messages. The remaining button control returns the message IDM_TYPE which is defined in FileView.H and will be received by the application as a request to call the File Type dialog box.

ID Constants and Values

The values and ID constants required for the three dialog boxes are:

Table 8-1: Dialog Constants/Values

Constant	Value	Constant	Value
IDD_FNAME	16	IDD_DLG	206
IDD_FPATH	17	IDD_DLL	207
IDD_FLIST	18	IDD_EXE	208
IDM_TYPE	104	IDD_H	209
IDD_BMP	201	IDD_PAL	210
IDD_COM	202	IDD_RC	211
IDD_CUR	203	IDD_RES	212
IDD_DAT	204	IDD_TXT	213
IDD_DBS	205	IDD_ANY	214

These values and constants also appear in the header listing FileView.H (Chapter 12) but will be needed as control element IDs while creating the three dialog boxes illustrated.

Summary

While dialog boxes are integral to Windows applications, and the Dialog Box editor is a tremendous convenience, dialog boxes do not exist and operate in a vacuum. As mentioned a moment ago, the Dialog Box editor does not even directly support dialog box menus that must be created by the Menu editor described in the next chapter.

Several mentions have been made of custom dialog box controls and owner-draw styles, with reference to Microsoft's Software Development Kit for more information. While these custom features are possible and practical, they also require additional programming skills and provisions that go beyond the scope of topics covered in this volume and are not needed or desired by the majority of applications.

While interesting, custom controls cannot only expend an inordinate amount of programming time, but may also distract from program execution or even confuse the user. Use these controls with care.

Chapter 9

The Menu Editor

The Menu editor provides full facilities for creating, editing, and testing dialog box menu resources. Menu resources can be edited from resource files (.RES), executable programs (.EXE), and dynamic link libraries (.DLL). Menu resources can also be saved to a new .RES file or saved to (but not loaded from) a resource script file (.RC). Resource script files, as explained previously, must be compiled by Microsoft's Resource Compiler.

The Menu editor, like the Dialog Box editor, can also open a header file (aka: include file), correlating symbolic constants with the menu resource. When a header file is opened, a Symbol column is added to the menu table and the Header editor is called. Symbol values can be edited directly from the menu table or through the Header editor detailed in Chapter 12.

Using the Menu Editor

The Menu Editor operates by constructing a menu table consisting, initially, of two columns: Item Text and Value. A third column, Symbol, is added when a header file is opened to show the symbolic name, if any, for each menu item.

- *Item Text field*—(left column) contains the menu text as it appears in the actual menu. Text may include any alphanumeric characters with the exception of the ampersand (&) which is used to define and underscore activation characters and \t which is used for the tab character.

- *Value field* —contains the ID number for the menu item in the Item Text field. This is the value the menu item returns when selected and is used in the source code to identify each item. Additionally, a symbol name can be defined for each item in the Symbol column.

- *Symbol field*—optionally defines a constant that corresponds to the Value field and writes to the header file. If no header file is open, this column does not appear in the Menu editor.

Below the menu table, a set of style and attribute fields permit defining menu styles for individual menu entries. Above the menu table, four arrow buttons are used to set a menu item's level in the menu hierarchy (right and left) and a menu item's position in the menu (up and down). This will be explained below. Above the menu table, a test window is provided for interactively testing a menu.

The Item Text Field

The menu text to appear on the actual menu is entered in the Item Text field exactly as it should appear on the menu. Entries may consist of any alphanumeric characters including the extended ANSI (international) characters. Do not use characters in the range 00h..1Fh.

The ampersand character, (&), is a special purpose character used to indicate and underscore the activation character for each menu entry. An Item Text entry specified as "Select &File" appears in the menu as "Select File", and "F" becomes the activation key for the entry. By default, Windows uses the first letter in each item as the activation key but does not identify the activation key unless the ampersand is used to specify the key character. If more than one ampersand occurs in a menu definition, only the last ampersand is recognized.

The tab character is supplied by the character pair "\t" and is commonly used to identify accelerator keys for menu options. The right tab character aligns the items following the tab. However, tabbed entries should not be included in primary menu items, only in the pull-down submenus. Also, accelerator keys designated in menu entries must still be defined using the Accelerator editor (Chapter 10).

Caution: While entries up to 255 characters are permitted by the editor, it does nothing for the menu's capacity to display such strings. Carriage return and line feed characters do not enable the display of multi-line menu entries.

The Value Field

The Value Field is the message value returned by a menu item, identifying the menu option selected. Values assigned must be unsigned integers in the range 0..65,535. Each new item (row) created has an initial value of 0. ID numbers for menu items in each window class must be unique, even though the same ID numbers can be used within another window class. A series of ID numbers defined in the Menu editor for menu items can be duplicated by string table IDs without conflict, but cannot be duplicated for elements in a dialog box using the menu.

Menu items that call pop-up menus (submenus) do not return values and, therefore, all items with submenus can have the same value field entry (zero, for instance). However, after the submenu has been created, the item's Value field is grayed out. Thus, values may be assigned and, after the item's submenu entries are created, the value is simply ignored, but is still present if the submenu is removed or if the menu is tested before the submenus are created.

Defining Menu Levels

Each line in the menu table represents a menu option and indentations in the Item Text column (left column) indicate successive menu levels. Item indentation is not provided by leading spaces but is controlled by the right and left arrow buttons above the menu table at the left. Flush-left menu items appear on the primary menu, the menu bar at the top of a dialog box client window, while successively indented groups appear as submenus. The menu item list appears in Figure 9-1:

| **Edit**
| **Cut**
| **Copy**
| **Paint**
| **Search**
| **Find**
| **Replace**

| **Clear Clipboard**
| **Print**
| **File**

The items Edit, Print, and File are primary menu items while Cut, Copy, Paint, Search, and Clear Clipboard are submenu items under Edit. Find and Replace are submenu items under Search. The menu created by this structure is shown in the menu test window at the top of Figure 9-1.

Figure 9-1: The Menu Editor

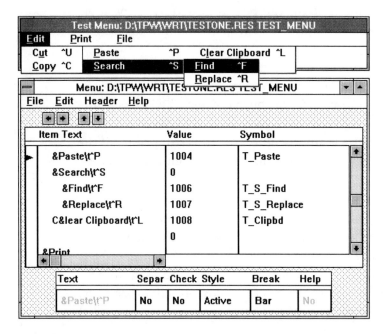

The right-arrow button indents the selected item one step, one level in the menu hierarchy, while the left-arrow button outdents the selected item one step. The Alt← and Alt→ keys substitute for the arrow buttons.

The order of menu items can also be revised by using the up and down arrow buttons by moving a selected item up or down in the menu order. If the selected item has submenu entries, they are moved as a block. Further, if the selected item is a submenu entry, it cannot be moved outside of its submenu range, i.e., the Paint entry in the preceding example could be moved before

Cut or after Clear Clipboard but could not precede its parent menu entry Edit, or be moved to appear under the menu headings Print or File.

Menu Design

Windows menus consist of a menu bar that shows top level menu options that is always visible. Submenu selections are always pull-down menus activated by selection of a primary menu option either by mouse or underscored hot-key. Submenu entries may call additional submenus with the only practical limit being the display capacity of the screen. Or, of course, a primary level menu item may immediately activate a selection or option without calling any submenus.

Primary level menus are normally single line menus. They can have extra spacing between items by inserting blank separators, or may extend over more than one line, if necessary, as shown in Figure 9-2. This latter format, however, is not recommended. The help attribute can be assigned to one primary level menu item by typing "Yes" in the help attribute box. Since this causes the menu item to be right-justified on the menu bar, it should be the last menu on the menu bar.

Figure 9-2: A Multiline Primary Menu

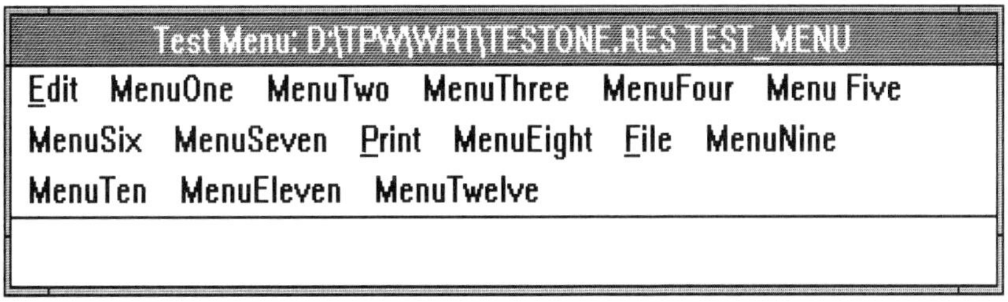

For submenu entries, but not for primary level menu entries, several style and attribute features can be defined, including:

- Horizontal separator lines between menu items
- Blank separators between menu items
- Multi-column menus
- Vertical separator lines between columns

- Checkmarks indicating menu item status
- Inactive and grayed-out item status

Horizontal Separators

A separator is a division that groups menu items in visual categories. Within a submenu column, these items may be either blank lines or horizontal bar separators. For a blank separator, simply create a blank menu entry at the desired location, give the menu item a value of zero, and flag the item as Inactive.

More commonly, however, a separator bar is used, by inserting a blank menu entry and then typing "Yes" in the Separator field. All other style and attributes fields become inactive and the menu item appears as a horizontal bar which cannot be selected in any fashion. Any entry in the Item Text field will be grayed out and will not appear in the menu.

Vertical Separators

The Break attribute field for all menu items has a default setting of **None** but can be used to separate menu items into columns by providing two types of breaks: **C**olumn breaks and **B**ar breaks.

- *Column*—indicates that the item begins a new column and that all menu items at the current level following the break item are aligned in the new column, unless, of course, a subsequent break item is set. (See Figure 9-3.)
- *Bar*—begins a new column, but inserts a vertical bar between columns, further emphasizing the break.

Figure 9-3: Column and Bar Settings

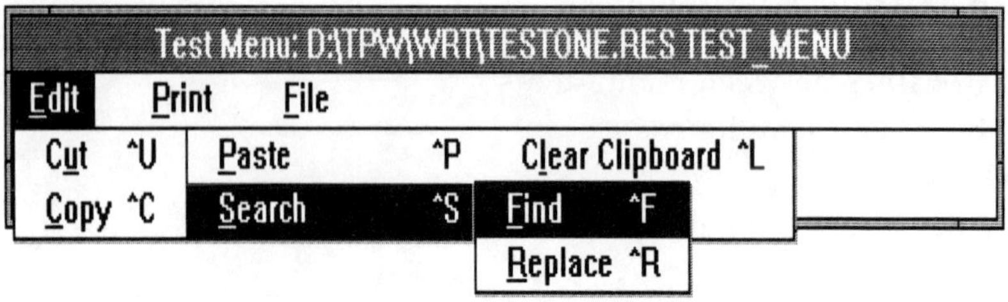

Checkmarks

Pull-down menu items may either offer independent options that are toggled on/off or exclusive options which, like radio buttons, can be selected one at a time. In either situation, a checkmark can be enabled by typing "**Yes**" in the item's Check field to indicate if an option is in effect.

The Check option provides an initial setting that displays a checkmark beside the menu option when it's enabled. However, it is the application's responsibility to maintain check flag status to continue to reflect the appropriate settings.

Item Status: Inactive/Grayed-Out

The default Style attribute for each item is **A**ctive but can also be initialized as Inactive or Gray. Inactive items cannot be selected, i.e., they do not return a value when selected even though they are displayed in the same fashion as active items. This is most useful during development for items that are not presently supported but will be provided later in the development process. Gray flags an item as temporarily unavailable, showing the menu selection in gray text. Like inactive, no response is returned when the item is selected. The Style attribute is only an initial setting. The application source code is responsible for determining when and if these settings should change, making a gray or inactive item active or vice versa.

Menu Testing

Figure 9-4 shows the Menu test window after clicking on the File option. The client window shows both the numeric return value and, since the Header file for the menu is open, the corresponding symbolic constant.

Figure 9-4: Testing a Menu

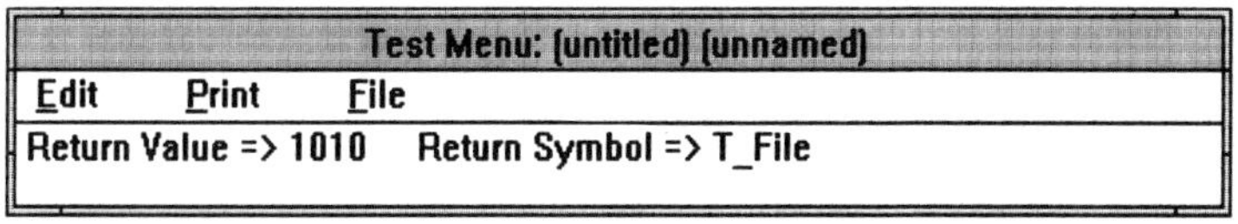

Clicking on the Edit entry displays the Edit submenu as shown in Figure 9-3, continuing to pull-down submenus until an active menu entry is selected.

Menus can be tested using both the mouse and the active keys (underscored). But, the accelerator keys shown (if any) cannot be tested here since they must be defined using the Accelerator editor.

Creating a Menu for FileView

The FileView application, discussed in Chapter 13, uses a relatively simple menu consisting of one pulldown menu with four entries. Figure 9-5 shows the Menu editor with the FileView menu in the menu test window at the top. In the illustration, the header file is opened showing the symbolic constant names defined in FileView.H as well as the menu item values. This menu will be expected in the FileView.RES resource file with the menu name the same as the application name, FILEVIEW.

Figure 9-5: The FileView Menu Resource

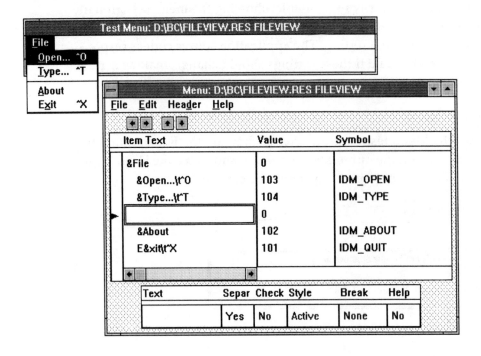

Summary

The Menu editor permits creating, defining, and testing dialog menus using the Header editor symbolic names for the menu items. Accelerator keys can also be shown as part of the menu item text, but must be defined separately using the Accelerator editor. This is discussed in Chapter 10.

Chapter 10

The Accelerator Editor

The Accelerator editor is used to create and edit accelerator resources which are hot keys for issuing application commands. While conventional (DOS) programs often provide similar services or, sometimes use TSR utilities to translate individual keystrokes or key combinations into command sequences, accelerator keys take a different form and do not depend on processing by the application under Windows.

Because all keyboard events are handled by Windows in the first instance and only keyboard messages are passed to the applications instead of raw key data, Windows acquires the accelerator key information from each active application. It then responds to hot key events by issuing the appropriate command messages to the application just as if a corresponding control button or other control feature had been activated.

However, it remains the programmer's responsibility to define hot keys and to prepare this information in a form acceptable for Windows to interpret. This is the purpose of the Accelerator editor.

Defining Accelerators (Hot Keys)

The Accelerator editor stores accelerator key and code information in an application resource called an accelerator table. The accelerator table consists of seven columns of data with an eighth column added when editing a header file.

■ *Type*—toggles between Virtkey (Virtual Key) and ASCII, indicating the accelerator type. The type flag is toggled by pressing the Spacebar or by typing *V* or *A* while the Type field is active. Virtkey uses the virtual key definitions in Window.H (see Appendix A), while *ASCII* defines the accelerator as an ASCII value. Thus, Ctrl-S is defined either as S with the Ctrl field set or as ASCII ^S (see Figure 10-1). Toggling the Type field will show that the first two entries shown here are actually the same even though the definitions appear different.

Caution: Not all accelerators can be converted from Virtual to ASCII and vice versa. For example, the function keys F1 through F12, Home, etc, do not have ASCII equivalents while some ASCII values such as the exclamation point (!) have no Virtkey equivalent.

■ *Key*—shows the accelerator key selection. These are entered simply by pressing the key or key combination. For example, Shift-Del would be entered by holding down the shift key and pressing the Del key. Entering an accelerator key produces a beep. It is invalid for the format indicated in the Type field.

The strings shown in this field may vary, depending upon how the accelerator is defined. For example, as shown in Figure 10-1, Ctrl-S is defined as a Virtkey and displays an *S* in the Key field. When defined as ASCII, the field appears as ^*S*. When the key entry is made, all of the fields for this key, with the exception of the Value field, are automatically set.

■ *Code*—gives the accelerator's keyboard scan code and is entered automatically when the Key field is defined. The displayed value varies depending upon the selection of VirtKey or ASCII in the Type field but is not entered directly.

■ *Shift*—indicates whether the Shift key is needed to activate the accelerator specified in the Key field, but is used only when Virtkey is selected in the Type field. This value is assigned automatically when the Key field is defined, but can be toggled using the Spacebar or by entering **Yes** or **No**. The Shift field is blank when ASCII is selected in the Type field.

- *Ctrl*—indicates whether the Ctrl key is needed to activate the accelerator specified in the Key field but is used only when Virtkey is selected in the Type field. This value is assigned automatically when the Key field is defined, but can be toggled using the Spacebar or by entering Yes or No. The Ctrl field is blank when ASCII is selected in the Type field.
- *Value*—provides an ID number (integer values only) for the accelerator defined in the Key field. Either this value or the symbolic name will be used in the application source code to load the accelerator. These ID values may duplicate ID values used by other resources, such as controls in a dialog box, without conflicts because the ID value is interpreted within the context of the presently active resource.
- *Invert*—can be **Yes** or **No** and indicates whether the menu item associated with the accelerator should be highlighted when the accelerator key is pressed.
- *Symbol*—appears only if a header file is opened and shows the symbolic constant defined as corresponding to the Value field in the header file. By opening a header file while developing the Accelerator tables, symbolic names can also be defined and are added directly to the header file without requiring a second step and consequent cross-referencing. The symbolic names shown in Figure 10-1 are examples only and do not follow any particular conventions or standards.

Figure 10-1: The Accelerator Editor

Type	Key	Code	Shift	Ctrl		Value	Symbol	Invert
Virtkey	S	83	No	Yes	No	2001	VK_S	Yes
Ascii	^S	19				2002	CTRL_S	Yes
Ascii	S	83				2003	UPCASE_S	Yes
Virtkey	S	83	No	No	No	2004	JUST_S	Yes
Ascii	s	115				2006	LOCASE_S	Yes
Virtkey	F1	112	No	No	No	2007	KEY_F1	Yes
Virtkey	F1	112	Yes	No	No	2008	SHIFT_F1	Yes
Virtkey	F1	112	No	Yes	No	2009	CTRL_F1	Yes

Accelerator: D:\TPW\WRT\TESTING.RES A_RESOURCE

File   Edit   Header   Help

Accelerators for FileView

While the FileView application lacks any extensive need for accelerator keys, three accelerator key definitions are supplied so that accelerator key handling can be demonstrated in Figure 10-2.

Figure 10-2: Accelerator Keys for FileView

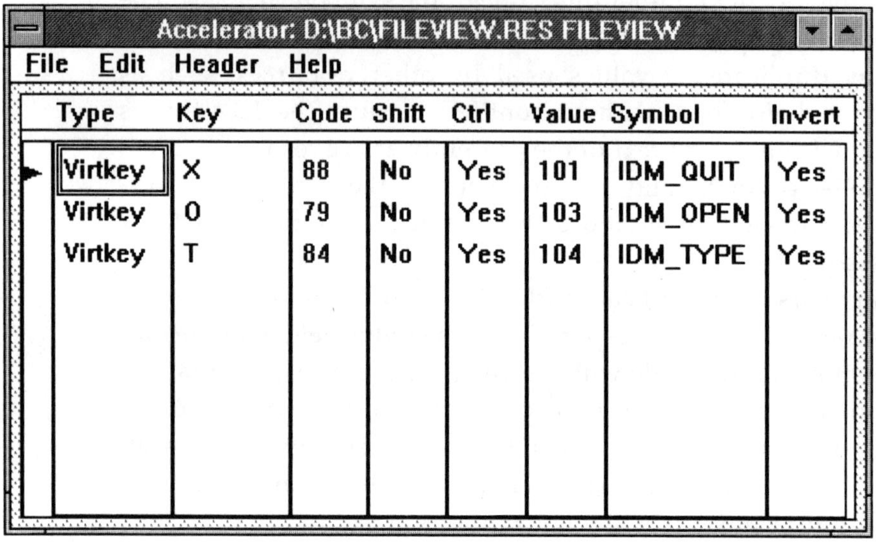

The three accelerator key definitions used are:

- Ctrl-O, defined as IDM_OPEN (value 103) and calls the File Open dialog.
- Ctrl-T, defined as IDM_TYPE (value 104) and calls the File Type dialog.
- Ctrl-X, defined as IDM_QUIT (value 101) and calls the exit routine.

A single accelerator table (containing these three key definitions) will be expected in FileView.RES with the accelerator table name FILEVIEW.

Summary

Accelerator key definitions are used by many applications and, depending on the application, different accelerator key tables may be loaded at different times for different purposes. In general, however, accelerator keys provide simple short-cut alternatives to complex menus. They will be greatly appreciated by those using your applications. The routines for using the accelerator keys will be demonstrated in the File-View.C discussed in Chapter 13.

Chapter 11

Editing String Resources

The String editor is a distinct departure from conventional programming in grouping strings used by applications as string resources instead of having them scattered through the application's source code. Many compilers have always gathered such scattered data together in the compiled program, usually toward the end of the .EXE file, along with other static data elements. Defining strings directly as resources that are separate from the execution program is a distinct difference.

This provides two advantages. First, string data is not automatically maintained in memory as with conventional .EXE programs and, second, as resources, string data can be edited, translated, or customized without recompiling the application.

Defining Strings

String resources may consist of any string data including error, status and general system messages, window captions, and even brief explantions displayed by dialog windows. Button and control captions are not normally included in the string resources because they can be edited directly through the Dialog editor. Likewise, menu strings can be edited through the Menu editor. Individual strings may contain up to 255 characters in length while the maximum size of the string table is 64K bytes. Only one string table can be defined for an application.

The String Editor

The string table is displayed by the String editor in a three-column format (see Figure 11-1). The first column shows the string ID as an integer value, while the second column shows the string proper. If a header file is opened, a new column appears between the Value and String Text columns, showing the symbolic name corresponding to the string ID.

Figure 11-1: The String Editor

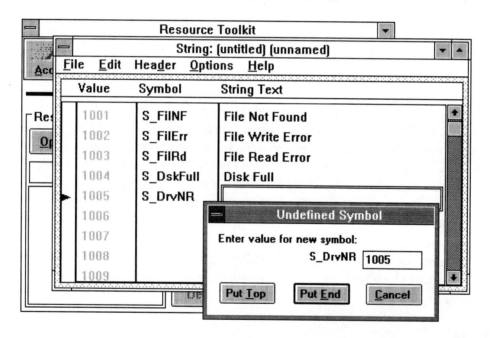

The Value field's (left column) contents are already assigned as integers in the range 0..65,534. Obviously, if all of these slots were used, each string could be a maximum of one character long; not very practical. As a corrolary, rows cannot be inserted, moved, or deleted from the string table. Instead, strings are entered in the desired row in the String Text field. For example, if you want a string numbered 61234, move down (drag the scrollbar) to this slot to enter the string.

Within the String editor, a row indicator appears as an arrow head (left margin) that shows the currently selected row, while a field indicator, a double outlined box, shows the active field. The field indicator can be moved within the String Text column by using the arrow keys or by clicking with the mouse. It cannot be moved to the Value column. If a header file is opened, the field indicator can also be moved to the Symbol column.

The String Text Field

Strings are entered without quotation marks since quotation marks will be treated as part of the string. The entry field will scroll to permit entry of up to 255 characters. The entry field will beep when more than 255 characters are entered; the excess characters do not appear. Strings are normally displayed as a single line, but a line feed can be inserted using octal format as \012. Thus, the string entry, "This is the first line\012and this is the second", will display as:

> This is the first line
> and this is the second

The Symbol Field

When a header file is opened, the Symbol Field appears as the second column and symbolic constants can be entered directly. One drawback, however, is that the String ID value is established by the row in which the string is entered. As Figure 11-1 shows, a dialog box appears requesting a numerical value for the symbolic constant. If the value entered does not match the row number, the symbol string will be moved to the row that corresponds to the entry, but the string definition will not. Since the ID values are determined here by the row values, an improved version of this utility would enter these header values automatically. This is a small flaw in an otherwise convenient utility.

Grouping Strings

String resources are loaded in 16 string segments. Thus, when an application requests string 10, Windows loads all strings in the ID range zero through 15. For this reason, grouping associated strings within hexidecimal blocks permits Windows to execute fewer loads and reduces memory overhead used during execution. Otherwise, there are no restrictions on the values used to define string text. When the string resource is saved, only the rows containing data are included in the resource file. But, when the resource file is loaded into memory again, blank rows are inserted for all unused values. This permits new strings to be defined.

Resource Attributes

When a string resource table is saved, a resource attributes dialog appears as shown in Figure 11-2. Unless there are strong reasons to the contrary, string resources should always be loaded on demand, and be moveable and discardable.

Figure 11-2: The Resource Attributes Dialog

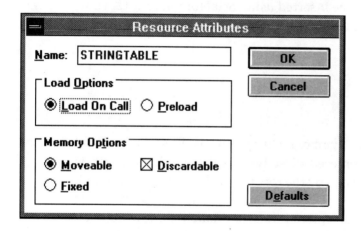

String Editor Controls

In addition to the scrollbar, the String editor menu offers a few shortcuts for locating particular locations in the table. This is partially because of the sheer length of the editable string table. These controls can be called either from the menu bar or by keyboard entry.

- *PgUp*—moves up one page.
- *PgDn*—moves down one page.
- *Ctrl-PgUp*—moves up to next page with defined strings.
- *Ctrl-PgDn*—moves down to next page with defined strings.
- *Ctrl-L*—calls dialog box for a row number, then moves directly to the row number entered.

A Stringtable for FileView

The FileView application (Chapter 13) has virtually no use for a string table simply because the application title that appears in the caption bar at the top of the main window is the only string which is not already present in a resource component (and, therefore, editable directly). The Stringtable editor appears with a single entry in Figure 11-3.

Figure 11-3: A Stringtable for Fileview

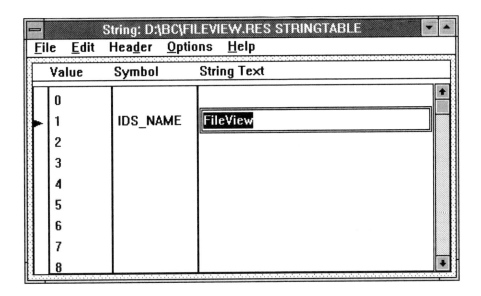

Note: Since only one stringtable is permitted in a Resource file, the stringtable name in the .RES file is already fixed as, quite simply, "STRINGTABLE".

Summary

While string resources are a bit less convenient than simply entering strings within the application source code, they do have the advantages of providing easy revision and/or conversion to other languages. They also reduce the amount of string information that must be held in memory while an application executes.

Chapter 12

The Header Editor

The Header editor provides a convenient means of defining symbolic constants for resource ID numbers. Normally, they are entered indirectly through the various resource editors by opening a header file while creating the resource. But, once the header file is opened, the header editor can be used directly.

The Accelerator, Dialog Box, Menu and String editors include menu options such as File/ New Header or File/ Open Header that automatically call the Header editor. The Bitmap, Cursor, and Icon editors do not include, or require, Header options.

Once the header is opened, the Header editor appears as a child window of the resource editor. It can be hidden by clicking the Header/ Hide option. If the associated editor is closed or reduced to an icon, the Header editor is also closed or minimized. Only one header file can be opened at a time.

Since the symbols included in the header file become global constants when the application is compiled, the symbols (strings) must be unique within each application. The symbolic values, however, need only be unique within their resource types because Windows interpets these ID values within the context of the resource presently being used in the application.

Note: Even though separate resources may have the same ID numbers (with different symbolic names), the header file does not distinguish between which constants belong to which resource type. The Header editor is shown in Figure 12-1. A sample header file that uses C-style define statements appears here:

```
/* D:\BC\TESTMENU.H 1/27/1991 17:05*/
#define   T_Edit        1001
#define   T_Cut         1002
#define   T_Copy        1003
#define   T_Paste       1004
#define   T_Search      1005
#define   T_S_Find      1006
#define   T_S_Replace   1007
#define   T_Clipbd      1008
#define   T_Print       1009
```

The header file (.H) created by the Resource Toolkit editors are barebones entries except for the filename and date-time stamp which appears as a comment at the top of the file. However, header files can be edited with any ASCII text editor and can be revised and rearranged as desired. Comments can also be added using the conventional delimiters /*, */ and //.

Figure 12-1: The Header Editor

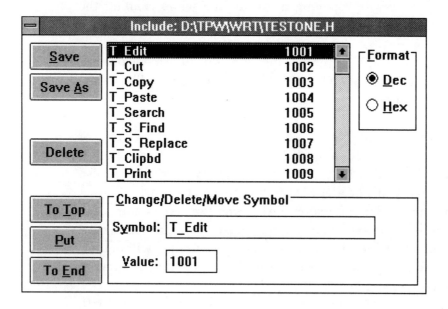

Chapter 13

Putting It All Together:
The Fileview Application

In Chapters 6 through 12, the various Resource Toolkit editors and the Header editor were discussed. Each chapter ended with one or more sample resources for use by the FileView application. It is now time to put all of these fragments together by creating the application itself.

The FileView program opens a file of any type, displaying the file contents in hexadecimal format with the file offset address display at the left and an ASCII string display at the right. The main purpose of this application is to demonstrate the several resources created by the Resource Toolkit editors and to show how they are called on by an application.

Figure 13-1 shows a composite of the FileView application and the several dialog boxes. The complete source code listings for FileView.C, FileView.DEF, and FileView.H appear at the end of this chapter. The fourth component, FileView.RES, must be created using the Resource Toolbox following the directions in previous chapters.

Preventing Compiler Warning Messages

Many Windows application functions, when compiled, cause the compiler to generate warning messages which are actually irrelevant; usually they result from arguments that have been passed to the functions, such as Windows message parameters, that are not used by the function. Because of this, you may notice that in the source listing, the following code line precedes several functions: *#pragma argsused*. This pragma command prevents the compiler from generating an unused parameter message for the function immediately following. The pragma directive applies only to a single function and must precede the function declaration.

Figure 13-1: The FileView Application and Dialog Window

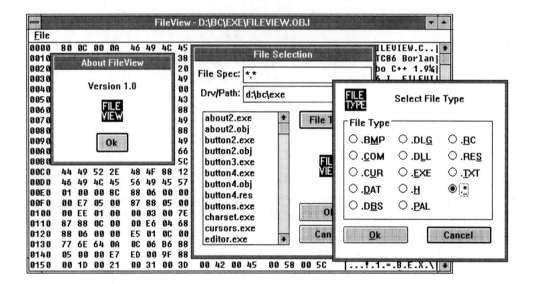

Loading Resources in WinMain

Several of the resource elements defined in ViewFile.RES are loaded during the execution of WinMain when the first instance of the application is created. Others will be loaded when individual dialog boxes are created and, when the dialog boxes are finished and released from memory. The Accelerator resource is also loaded within the WinMain procedure but not during the instance initialization.

ViewFile.C uses only one string from the Stringtable resource; the application title. This is retrieved in WinMain during the initialization of the application's first instance:

```
LoadString( hInstance, IDS_NAME, (LPSTR) szAppName, 10 );
```

The constant IDS_NAME identifies the desired string resource. The string is copied from the stringtable to the global variable *szAppName* with the final argument, 10, specifying the size of the data transferred.

In other circumstances, multiple strings might be loaded as needed, during dialog initialization. The only menu resource created belongs to the main application window, but requires an assignment instead of a Load statement.

```
wc.lpszMenuName   = (LPSTR) szAppName;
```

The icon resource also receives a load instruction:

```
wc.hIcon = LoadIcon( hInstance, szAppName );
```

This specific instruction, however, only provides the icon for the application itself; it is used when the application is reduced to icon size. Alternatively, the various icons used in dialog boxes are not affected by this instruction. They execute their own icon loads without requiring provisions in the source code for icon handling.

Notice that each of the resources loaded has the same name as the application, which is also the same as the stringtable resource loaded to szAppName. If desired, other "names" could have been used. When multiple resources are used more than one name is obviously essential. At the same time, these names are often supplied simply as numeric identifiers, but a simple string suggesting the resource identity is usually easier to work with.

The remaining instance initialization is essentially the same as that shown in previous examples.

Initializing Settings

Following the instance initialization, provisions are also made to set a default file type and to copy the default type string to szFileExt:

```
iFileType = IDD_ANY - IDD_BMP;
strcpy( szFileExt, szFileType[iFileType] );
```

These two provisions, however, do not set either dialog box. Only global variables are affected at this point and additional specific provisions are required when the affected dialog boxes are called.

Loading the Keyboard Accelerator

When the Accelerator resource is used, it requires a few special provisions, beginning with a Load instruction:

```
hAccel = LoadAccelerators( hInst, szAppName );
```

The LoadAccelerators function returns a handle to the Accelerator table. Different accelerator tables can be loaded to provide services that correspond to different menus or dialogs. Simply loading the accelerator is only half the trick because the *TranslateAccelerator* function is necessary to provide the actual processing:

```
while( GetMessage( &msg, NULL, 0, 0 ) )
{
    if( !TranslateAccelerator( hWndMain, hAccel, &msg ) )
    {
        TranslateMessage( &msg );
        DispatchMessage( &msg );
} }
```

Most of this loop should be familiar enough from previous examples but now has the additional provision of translating accelerator key messages into application messages. Simply put , this function intercepts any key events that are defined as accelerator keys and, in turn, issues a new message in the form provided by the accelerator table.

Creating the Dialogs

Three dialog boxes are used in the FileView application. They are called through the WndProc function in response to WM_COMMAND messages with wParams of IDM_ABOUT, IDM_TYPE or IDM_OPEN. The IDM_ABOUT message is handled directly:

```
lpProc = MakeProcInstance( About, hInst );
DialogBox( hInst, "ABOUT", hwnd, lpProc );
FreeProcInstance( lpProc );
```

This initiates the dialog by making an instance of the dialog and returning a handle (*lpProc*). It then calls the DialogBox function to display and operate the dialog box. In this case, only one response is expected, an IDOK message, which will also exit the dialog and, therefore, no further handling is necessary.

For the second dialog box, in response to IDM_TYPE, a local subprocedure is called:

```
CallFileTypeDlg( hInst, hwnd );
```

The provision within CallFileTypeDlg are essentially the same as those used for the ABOUT dialog. They create the dialog and then discard it when finished. Any return value is simply ignored because the real operations of this dialog consist of setting the global variable *iFileType*.

In the third case, in response to an IDM_OPEN message, the task is somewhat more complex because an initial search path, file specification, and file type are required before calling the CallFileOpenDlg subprocedure. A resulting file path and file name will be expected on return.

After the subprocedure returns the file specification, this case statement also has the task of opening the indicated file and displaying the results. This portion of the task, however, is essentially conventional programming, while the Windows-specific provisions will be found, in part, in the CallFileOpen-Dlg procedure, but principally in the exported FileOpenDlgProc procedure. This will be discussed later. However, initializing these dialogs is, in some instances, critical.

Initiating Dialogs

The FileTypeDlgProc and FileOpenDlgProc functions provide a variety of services but, for the moment, the two responses to the WM_INITDIALOG messages are the principal topic.

In FileTypeDlgProc, when the dialog box receives the WM_INITDIALOG message, only one initialization provision is required; setting the initial state of the grouped radio buttons:

```
CheckRadioButton( hDlg, IDD_BMP, IDD_ANY,
                  IDD_BMP+iFileType );
```

The CheckRadioButton function is called with the dialog box handle (*hDlg*), the first and last (range) radio button IDs to set and, finally, an ID value indicating which member of the group should presently be turned on (set).

Since the radio button controls in this dialog have been declared as autoradio buttons, no further provisions—within the application source code —will be made for changing their state. However, this initial setting is necessary as is a later provision to determine which has been set (see the WM_COM-MAND message response in FileTypeDlgProc).

The FileOpenDlgProc has a slightly more extensive response to the WM_IN-ITDIALOG message because there are three elements in the File Open dialog that require initialization: two edit boxes and a list box. The first task sends a message to the file name edit box, IDD_FNAME:

```
SendDlgItemMessage( hDlg, IDD_FNAME, EM_LIMITTEXT,
                    80, 0L );
```

The gist of the message is to "limit the length of text input" (EM_LIMITTEXT) with a set limit of 80 characters. This is a reasonable length for a file specification. It does not provide a display in the edit box, but does set a control on what can be entered.

The SendDlgItemMessage function can be used in a variety of fashions, depending upon the control element addressed and the message type. This is equivalent to obtaining a handle to the control element and then calling the SendMessage function.

The next task fills both the list box and the file path edit box in a single step, using the *DlgDirList* function:

```
DlgDirList( hDlg, szFileSpec, IDD_FLIST,
            IDD_FPATH, wFileAttr );
```

The DlgDirList function is called with the handle for the dialog box (hDlg), a drive/path/file specification (szFileSpec), the list box and path (edit) box identifiers, and a file attribute flag (wFileAttr). When called, DlgDirList fills the list box with a list of files that match the specification and fill in the current drive/directory in the edit box.

Subdirectories are shown enclosed in square brackets ([subdir]) while drives are shown in the format [-x-] with x replaced by the drive letter. The file attribute flag, wFileAttr, limits the types of file entries displayed as shown in Table 13-1.

Table 13-1: DOS File Attributes

Attribute	Meaning
0x0000	Read/write data files with no additional attributes
0x0001	Read-only files
0x0002	Hidden files
0x0004	System files
0x0010	Subdirectories
0x0020	Archives
0x2000	LB_DIR flag (note 1)
0x4000	Drives
0x8000	Exclusive (note 2)

Note 1 If LB_DIR is set, messages generated by DlgDirList are sent to the application's queue, otherwise messages are sent directly to the dialog function.

Note 2 The exclusive bit lists only files of the type(s) specified, otherwise normal files are listed as well.

The final task during initialization is to write the file specification to the filename edit box by calling SetDlgItemText:

```
SetDlgItemText( hDlg, IDD_FNAME, szFileSpec );
```

While Windows provides a rather powerful and comprehensive function for directory lists, other types of lists are also needed and would be created using the SendMessage function:

```
SendMessage( hDlg, LB_ADDSTRING, 0, (LPSTR) szString );
```

The LBS_SORT style for the list box will sort the entries. LB_INSERTSTRING can be used to insert items in a specific order with the third parameter (zero in the preceding example) specifying the list position.

In the case of the FileOpenDlgProc, the DlgDirList, and the SetDlgItemText functions are called in essentially the same context in response to other item selection messages. The majority of the dialog box interactions, however, are carried out without intervention by the application, including scrolling the file list and inverting (high lighting) selections.

Summary

In this chapter, the resources created using the Resource Toolkit editors in previous chapters are actually brought into play in the FileView application.

Many of the resources created, such as the menu and the icons, required little
or no intervention within the application source code, while others were only
partially autonomous in their actions. The complete listing for FileView appears below.

```
//=================================================//
//                    FileView.C                   //
//   demonstrates Resource Toolkit interactions     //
//=================================================//

#include <windows.h>
#include <dir.h>
#include <stdio.h>
#include "fileview.h"

#define   wFileAttr  0x4010                  // file attribute flag

HANDLE    hInst,                    // hInstance of application
          hAccel,                    // handle of accelerator
          OrgFont,                   // handle of original font
          NewFont;                   // handle of new fixed font
HWND      hWndMain;                    // hwnd of main window
LOGFONT   FontLog;                      // font structure
int       ChrX, ChrY, ChrV,             // character size
          WndX, WndY,                 // client window size
          VScrlMax, HScrlMax,            // scroll ranges
          VScrlPos, HScrlPos,         // current scroll positions
          VInc, HInc,                  // scroll increments
          FilLines,                  // number of lines in file
          WndWidth,                   // width of display format
          WndHeight,                   // max lines on screen
          iFileType;                       // file type
char      szAppName[10],                 // application name
          szFileSpec[64],         // file spec for initial search
          szFileExt[5],               // default extension
          szFileName[64],                  // file name
          szFilePath[64],                  // file path
          szFName[64];              // file to display
WORD      wStatus;                       // status of search
FILE      *hFil;                     // handle of open file
LONG      FilSz,                          // size of file
          HDisplay;                  // display width (LONG)

char      *szFileType[14] = { ".BMP", ".COM", ".CUR",
          ".DAT", ".DBS", ".DLG", ".DLL", ".EXE", ".H",
```

```
                 ".PAL", ".RC",  ".RES", ".TXT", ".*" };

  //============== function prototypes ==============//

        int        PASCAL WinMain( HANDLE hInstance,
                                   HANDLE hPrevInstance,
                                   LPSTR  lpszCmdLine,
                                   int    cmdShow );

  //============== exported procedures ==============//

        BOOL FAR PASCAL About( HWND hDlg,   WORD msg,
                               WORD wParam, LONG lParam );
        long FAR PASCAL WndProc( HWND hwnd,   WORD msg,
                                 WORD wParam, LONG lParam);
extern BOOL FAR PASCAL FileOpenDlgProc(
        HWND hDlg, WORD msg, WORD wParam, LONG lParam );
extern BOOL FAR PASCAL FileTypeDlgProc(
        HWND hDlg, WORD msg, WORD wParam, LONG lParam );

  //============== end declarations ==================//

  //==================================================//
  //  CloseFV: used to clean up application instance  //
  //==================================================//

void CloseFV() { }

  //==================================================//
  // SetScrlRange: sets vertical and horizontal scroll //
  //               ranges based on number of lines in  //
  //               file and width of display           //
  //       returns: nothing, sets global values        //
  //==================================================//

void SetScrlRange( HWND hwnd )
{
   VScrlMax = max( 0, FilLines + 1 - (int)( WndY / ChrY ) );
   VScrlPos = min( VScrlPos, VScrlMax );
   HScrlMax = max( 0, WndWidth - WndX / ChrX );
   HScrlPos = min( HScrlPos, HScrlMax );
   SetScrollRange( hwnd, SB_VERT, 0, VScrlMax, FALSE );
   SetScrollPos(   hwnd, SB_VERT,    VScrlPos, TRUE  );
   SetScrollRange( hwnd, SB_HORZ, 0, HScrlMax, FALSE );
   SetScrollPos(   hwnd, SB_HORZ,    HScrlPos, TRUE  );
   WndHeight = min( FilLines, WndY / ChrY );
}
```

```
//========================================================//
// FormatLine: formats 8/16 bytes per line for           //
//             display, beginning with file offset,       //
//             hex values grouped by fours and ASCII      //
//             text at end.                               //
//      returns: pointer to szBuff                        //
//========================================================//
char *FormatLine( char *szBuff, LPSTR lpMem,
                  int    iLen,   char *LnOfs )
{
   int             i, j;
   unsigned char   chr, szTemp1[80], szTemp2[80];

   *szBuff = 0;
   i = j = 0;
   sprintf( szTemp1, "%04X   ", LnOfs );            // line offset
   strcpy( szBuff, szTemp1 );                       // add to buff
   for( i=0; i<min(iLen,HDisplay); i++ )
   {
      chr = *lpMem++;
      if( (i+1) % 4 )
          sprintf( szTemp1, "%02X ",  chr );    // write hex in
      else sprintf( szTemp1, "%02X   ", chr );  // clmn of four
      strcat( szBuff, szTemp1 );                  // add hex to buff
      if( ( chr >= 0x20 && chr <= 0x7E ) ||
          ( chr >= 0xA0 && chr <= 0xFE ) ) szTemp2[i] = chr;
                                       else szTemp2[i] = '.';
   }
   szTemp2[i] = 0;                                  // add null
   for( j=i; j<HDisplay; j++ )
   {
      if( (j+1) % 4 ) strcat( szBuff, "   " );       // pad hex
                 else strcat( szBuff, "     " );
      strcat( szTemp2, " " );                        // pad ASCII
   }
   sprintf( szTemp1, " |%s|", szTemp2 );           // format ASCII
   strcat( szBuff, szTemp1 );                      // add ASCII
   return( szBuff );
}
```

```
//==========================================================//
// PaintFile: if FilLines is greater than zero,            //
//            reads and displays some portion of the //
//            file according to the size and scroll  //
//            position.                               //
//    return: nothing                                      //
//      note: file is opened, read and closed. Files //
//            should not remain open over multiple    //
//            Window messages.                        //
//==========================================================//

void PaintFile( HWND hwnd )
{
    PAINTSTRUCT   ps;
    HDC           hdc;
    LONG          lFilOfs;
    int           i, iFilSz, iTxtSz, hFile, lPos;
    char          szBuff[128];
    HANDLE        hBuff;
    LPSTR         lpStr1, lpStr2;

    BeginPaint( hwnd, (LPPAINTSTRUCT) &ps );
    hdc = ps.hdc;
    SelectObject( hdc, NewFont );          // use fixed font in DC
    if( FilLines )
    {
        if( ( hFile = _lopen( szFName, OF_READ ) ) != -1 )
        {
            iFilSz = WndHeight * HDisplay;     // buffer for data
            hBuff = GlobalAlloc( GMEM_MOVEABLE,
                                 (DWORD) iFilSz );
            if( hBuff )
            {
                lpStr1 = GlobalLock( hBuff );       // lock buffer
                if( lpStr1 )
                {                      // get offset in file to start
                    lFilOfs = (LONG) VScrlPos * HDisplay;
                    if( _llseek( hFile, lFilOfs, 0 ) != -1L )
                    {
                        iTxtSz = _lread( hFile, lpStr1, iFilSz );
                        if( iTxtSz != -1 )
                        {
                            lPos = 0;
                            lpStr2 = lpStr1;
                            for( i=VScrlPos;
                                 i<(VScrlPos+WndHeight); i++ )
```

```
                          {
                              if( iTxtSz > HDisplay )
                                      iFilSz = HDisplay;
                              else iFilSz = iTxtSz;
                              iTxtSz -= iFilSz;
                              FormatLine( szBuff, lpStr2, iFilSz,
                                          (char *) (i * HDisplay) );
                              TextOut( hdc, ChrX * (-HScrlPos + 0),
                                          ChrY * lPos++, szBuff,
                                          strlen( szBuff ) );
                              lpStr2 += HDisplay;
                      } } }
                      GlobalUnlock( hBuff );
                  }
                  GlobalFree( hBuff );
              }
              _lclose( hFile );
      } }
      EndPaint( hwnd, (LPPAINTSTRUCT) &ps );
}

  //==========================================================//
  // CallFileOpenDlg: invokes FileOpenDlgProc to get   //
  //                  name of file to open             //
  //      parameters: szFileSpecIn  - init file path   //
  //                  szFileExtIn   - init file ext     //
  //      (returned)  szFilePathOut - selected path     //
  //      (returned)  szFileNameOut - selected file     //
  //            return: TRUE if file selected           //
  //==========================================================//

int CallFileOpenDlg( HANDLE hInst,          HWND   hwnd,
                     char   *szFileSpecIn, char *szFileExtIn,
                     char   *szFilePathOut,
                     char   *szFileNameOut )
{
    FARPROC    lpProc;
    int        iReturn;

    strcpy( szFileSpec, szFileSpecIn);     // save init file spec
    strcpy( szFileExt, szFileExtIn);
    lpProc =
        MakeProcInstance( FileOpenDlgProc, hInst );
    iReturn = DialogBox( hInst, "OPENFILE", hwnd,
                         lpProc );
    FreeProcInstance( lpProc );
```

```
      strcpy( szFilePathOut, szFilePath );      // ret new filepath
      strcpy( szFileNameOut, szFileName );      // ret new filename
      return( iReturn );
}

  //=======================================================//
  // CallFileTypeDlg: invokes FileTypeDlgProc             //
  //           return: TRUE if type selected             //
  //=======================================================//

int CallFileTypeDlg( HANDLE hInst, HWND hwnd )
{
    FARPROC    lpProc;
    int        iReturn;

    lpProc =
       MakeProcInstance( FileTypeDlgProc, hInst );
    iReturn = DialogBox( hInst, "FILETYPE", hwnd,
                         lpProc );
    FreeProcInstance( lpProc );
    return( iReturn );
}

  //=============== export procedures ===================//

  //=======================================================//
  //    About: About dialog procedure                    //
  //=======================================================//

#pragma argsused            // prevents unused parameter message //

BOOL FAR PASCAL About( HWND hDlg, WORD msg, WORD wParam, LONG
lParam )
{
    switch( msg )
    {
        case WM_INITDIALOG: return( TRUE );
        case WM_COMMAND:
           switch( wParam )
           {
               case IDOK: EndDialog( hDlg, TRUE );
                          return( TRUE );
               default: return( TRUE );
    }        }
    return( FALSE );
}
```

```
//=======================================================//
//  WndProc: handles application messages              //
//=======================================================//
long FAR PASCAL WndProc( HWND hwnd,    WORD msg,
                         WORD wParam, LONG lParam )
{
   static char szTmpFilePath[64];
   static char szTmpFileExt[5];
   static char szTmpFileSpec[64];
   static char szTmpFileName[64];

   FARPROC  lpProc;                        // pointer to dialog box
   char     szBuff[128];                        // temp buffer
   int      i;
   FILE     *hFil;

   switch( msg )
   {
      case WM_CREATE:
         getcwd( szTmpFilePath, sizeof(szTmpFilePath) );
         strcat( szTmpFilePath, "\\" );
         strcpy( szTmpFileExt,  szFileType[iFileType] );
         strcpy( szTmpFileName, "" );
         HDisplay = 16L;
         return( DefWindowProc( hwnd, msg, wParam, lParam ));
      case WM_COMMAND:
         switch( wParam )
         {
            case IDM_ABOUT:
               lpProc = MakeProcInstance( About, hInst );
               DialogBox( hInst, "ABOUT", hwnd, lpProc );
               FreeProcInstance( lpProc );
               break;
            case IDM_TYPE:
               CallFileTypeDlg( hInst, hwnd );
               break;
            case IDM_OPEN:                 // set initial search path
               strcpy( szTmpFileSpec, szTmpFilePath );
               strcat( szTmpFileSpec, "*" );
               strcat( szTmpFileSpec, szFileType[iFileType]);
               if( CallFileOpenDlg( hInst, hwnd,
                                    szTmpFileSpec,
                                    szFileType[iFileType],
                                    szTmpFilePath,
                                    szTmpFileName ) )
```

```
        {
            strcpy( szFName, szTmpFilePath );
            strcat( szFName, szTmpFileName );
            sprintf( szBuff, "%s - %s",
                     szAppName, szFName );
            SetWindowText( hwnd, szBuff );
            hFil = fopen( szFName, "r+b" );
            if( hFil )             // determine file size, etc
            {
                FilSz = filelength( fileno( hFil ) );
                FilLines = (int)( (FilSz+HDisplay-1L)
                                  / HDisplay );
                FormatLine( szBuff, szFName,
                            HDisplay, NULL );
                WndWidth = strlen( szBuff );
                                        // get display width
                VScrlPos = HScrlPos = 0;
                fclose(hFil);
            }
            else                   // if file open failed
            {
                SetWindowText( hwnd, "FileView" );
                FilLines = WndWidth = 0;
            }
            SetScrlRange( hwnd );
            InvalidateRect( hwnd, NULL, TRUE );
            UpdateWindow( hwnd );
        } break;
        case IDM_QUIT:
            PostMessage( hwnd, WM_CLOSE, 0, OL );
            break;
        default: break;
    } break;
    case WM_SIZE:
        if( lParam )
        {
            WndY = HIWORD( lParam );            // save vert size
            WndX = LOWORD( lParam );            // save horiz size
            WndY = ( WndY / ChrV + 1 ) * ChrV;
            if( ( WndX / ChrX ) < 60 ) HDisplay =  8L;
                             else  HDisplay = 16L;
            FilLines = (int)((FilSz + HDisplay-1L)/HDisplay);
            SetScrlRange( hwnd );            // set scroll range
            lParam = MAKELONG( WndX, WndY );
            return(DefWindowProc(hwnd,msg,wParam,lParam));
        } break;
```

```
case WM_VSCROLL:
   switch( wParam )
   {
      case SB_TOP:
              VInc = -VScrlPos;                          break;
      case SB_BOTTOM:
              VInc =  VScrlMax - VScrlPos;       break;
      case SB_LINEUP:
              VInc = -1;                                 break;
      case SB_LINEDOWN:
              VInc =  1;                                 break;
      case SB_PAGEUP:
              VInc = -max( 1, WndY / ChrY );     break;
      case SB_PAGEDOWN:
              VInc =  max( 1, WndY / ChrY );     break;
      case SB_THUMBPOSITION:
              VInc = LOWORD(lParam) - VScrlPos; break;
      case SB_THUMBTRACK:
              VInc = LOWORD(lParam) - VScrlPos; break;
      default: VInc = 0;
   }
   VInc = max( -VScrlPos,
               min( VInc, VScrlMax - VScrlPos ) );
   if( VInc )
   {
      VScrlPos += VInc;
      ScrollWindow( hwnd, 0, -ChrY*VInc, NULL, NULL );
      SetScrollPos( hwnd, SB_VERT, VScrlPos, TRUE );
      UpdateWindow( hwnd );
   } break;
case WM_HSCROLL:
   switch( wParam )
   {
      case SB_TOP:
              HInc = -HScrlPos;                          break;
      case SB_BOTTOM:
              HInc =  HScrlMax - HScrlPos;       break;
      case SB_LINEUP:
              HInc = -1;                                 break;
      case SB_LINEDOWN:
              HInc =  1;                                 break;
      case SB_PAGEUP:
              HInc = -8;                                 break;
      case SB_PAGEDOWN:
              HInc =  8;                                 break;
      case SB_THUMBPOSITION:
```

```
                    HInc = LOWORD(lParam) - HScrlPos; break;
        case SB_THUMBTRACK:
                    HInc = LOWORD(lParam) - HScrlPos; break;
        default: HInc = 0;
    }
    HInc = max( -HScrlPos,
                min( HInc, HScrlMax - HScrlPos ) );
    if( HInc )
    {
        HScrlPos += HInc;
        ScrollWindow( hwnd, -ChrX*HInc, 0, NULL, NULL );
        SetScrollPos( hwnd, SB_HORZ, HScrlPos, TRUE );
        UpdateWindow( hwnd );
    } break;
case WM_KEYDOWN:
            // translate keydown msg to horiz/vert messages
    switch( wParam )
    {
        case VK_HOME:
            SendMessage(hwnd,WM_HSCROLL,SB_TOP,0L);
            SendMessage(hwnd,WM_VSCROLL,SB_TOP,0L);
            break;
        case VK_END:
            SendMessage(hwnd,WM_HSCROLL,SB_BOTTOM,0L);
            SendMessage(hwnd,WM_VSCROLL,SB_BOTTOM,0L);
            break;
        case VK_PRIOR:
            SendMessage(hwnd,WM_VSCROLL,SB_PAGEUP,0L);
            break;
        case VK_NEXT:
            SendMessage(hwnd,WM_VSCROLL,SB_PAGEDOWN,0L);
            break;
        case VK_UP:
            SendMessage(hwnd,WM_VSCROLL,SB_LINEUP,0L);
            break;
        case VK_DOWN:
            SendMessage(hwnd,WM_VSCROLL,SB_LINEDOWN,0L);
            break;
        case VK_LEFT:
            SendMessage(hwnd,WM_HSCROLL,SB_PAGEUP,0L);
            break;
        case VK_RIGHT:
            SendMessage(hwnd,WM_HSCROLL,SB_PAGEDOWN,0L);
            break;
    } break;
case WM_PAINT:
```

```
                    PaintFile( hwnd );                 break;
        case WM_CLOSE:
                    DestroyWindow( hwnd );             break;
        case WM_DESTROY:
                    CloseFV();  PostQuitMessage(0); break;
        case WM_QUERYENDSESSION:
                    CloseFV();  return( (LONG) TRUE );
        default: return(DefWindowProc(hwnd,msg,wParam,lParam));
    }
    return( 0L );
}

  //========================================================//
  // FileOpenDlgProc - get the name of a file to open  //
  //========================================================//
BOOL FAR PASCAL FileOpenDlgProc( HWND hDlg,    WORD msg,
                                 WORD wParam, LONG lParam )
{
    static char    OrgPath[64];
    char           cLastChar;
    int            nLen;
    struct ffblk   fileinfo;

    switch (msg)
    {
        case WM_INITDIALOG:
            getcwd( OrgPath, sizeof(OrgPath) );
            SendDlgItemMessage( hDlg, IDD_FNAME, EM_LIMITTEXT,
                              80, 0L );
              // fill list box with files from starting file spec.
            DlgDirList( hDlg, szFileSpec, IDD_FLIST,
                        IDD_FPATH, wFileAttr );
            SetDlgItemText( hDlg, IDD_FNAME, szFileSpec );
                                            // show init filespec
            return( TRUE );
        case WM_COMMAND:
            switch( wParam )
            {
                case IDM_TYPE:
                    if( CallFileTypeDlg( hInst, hDlg ) )
                    {
                        strcpy( szFileSpec, "*" );
                        strcat( szFileSpec, szFileType[iFileType]);
                        DlgDirList( hDlg, szFileSpec, IDD_FLIST,
                                    IDD_FPATH, wFileAttr );
```

```
            SetDlgItemText( hDlg, IDD_FNAME,
                            szFileSpec );
            MessageBeep(0);
        }
        break;
    case IDD_FLIST:
        switch( HIWORD(lParam) )
        {
            case LBN_SELCHANGE:
                if( DlgDirSelect( hDlg, szFileName,
                                  IDD_FLIST ) )
                    strcat( szFileName, szFileSpec );
                SetDlgItemText( hDlg, IDD_FNAME,
                                szFileName );
                break;
            case LBN_DBLCLK:
                if( DlgDirSelect( hDlg, szFileName,
                                  IDD_FLIST ) )
                {
                    strcat( szFileName, szFileSpec );
                    DlgDirList( hDlg, szFileName,
                        IDD_FLIST, IDD_FPATH, wFileAttr );
                    SetDlgItemText( hDlg, IDD_FNAME,
                                    szFileSpec );
                }
                else
                {
                    SetDlgItemText( hDlg, IDD_FNAME,
                                    szFileName );
                    SendMessage( hDlg, WM_COMMAND,
                                 IDOK, 0L );
                } break;
        } break;
    case IDD_FNAME:
        if( HIWORD(lParam) == EN_CHANGE )
        {
            EnableWindow( GetDlgItem( hDlg, IDOK ),
                    (BOOL) SendMessage( LOWORD(lParam),
                           WM_GETTEXTLENGTH, 0, 0L ) );
        } break;
    case IDOK:
        GetDlgItemText( hDlg, IDD_FNAME,
                        szFileName, 80 );
        nLen  = strlen( szFileName );
        cLastChar = *AnsiPrev( szFileName,
                                szFileName + nLen );
```

```
         if( cLastChar == '\\' || cLastChar == ':' )
            strcat( szFileName, szFileSpec );
         if( strchr( szFileName, '*' ) ||
             strchr( szFileName, '?' ) )
         {
            if( DlgDirList( hDlg, szFileName,
                   IDD_FLIST, IDD_FPATH, wFileAttr ) )
            {
               strcpy( szFileSpec, szFileName );
               SetDlgItemText( hDlg, IDD_FNAME,
                               szFileSpec );
            }
            else MessageBeep(0);
            break;
         }
         if( DlgDirList( hDlg, szFileName,
             IDD_FLIST, IDD_FPATH, wFileAttr ) )
         {
            strcpy( szFileSpec, szFileName );
            SetDlgItemText( hDlg, IDD_FNAME,
                            szFileSpec );
            break;
         }
         szFileName[nLen] = '\0';
                            // szFileName not search path
         if( findfirst( szFileName, &fileinfo, 0 ) )
         {
            strcat( szFileName, szFileExt );
            if( findfirst( szFileName, &fileinfo, 0 ) )
            {                   // if file doesn't exist
               MessageBeep(0);    break;
         }  }
         GetDlgItemText( hDlg, IDD_FPATH,
                         szFilePath, 80 );
         strupr( szFilePath );
         if( szFilePath[strlen(szFilePath)-1] != '\\' )
            strcat( szFilePath, "\\" );
         strcpy( szFileName, fileinfo.ff_name );
                                   // return filename
      chdir( OrgPath );             // reset directory
      EndDialog( hDlg, TRUE );        // end dialog box
      break;
   case IDCANCEL:
      chdir( OrgPath );             // reset directory
      EndDialog( hDlg, FALSE );       // end dialog box
      break;
```

```
            default:  return( FALSE );
        }  break;
      default: return( FALSE );
   }
   return( TRUE );
}

//========================================================//
// FileTypeDlgProc - get file type to open               //
//========================================================//

#pragma argsused          // prevents unused parameter message //

BOOL FAR PASCAL FileTypeDlgProc( HWND hDlg,    WORD msg,
                                 WORD wParam, LONG lParam )
{
   int  OrgFileType;

   switch (msg)
   {
      case WM_INITDIALOG:
         CheckRadioButton( hDlg, IDD_BMP, IDD_ANY,
                           IDD_BMP+iFileType );
         OrgFileType = iFileType;
         return( TRUE );
      case WM_COMMAND:
         switch( wParam )
         {
            case IDD_BMP:       case IDD_COM:
            case IDD_CUR:       case IDD_DAT:
            case IDD_DBS:       case IDD_DLG:
            case IDD_DLL:       case IDD_EXE:
            case IDD_H:         case IDD_PAL:
            case IDD_RC:        case IDD_RES:
            case IDD_TXT:       case IDD_ANY:
               iFileType = wParam - IDD_BMP;   // set file type
               strcpy( szFileExt, szFileType[iFileType] );
                                               // set extension
               return( TRUE );
            case IDOK:
               EndDialog( hDlg, TRUE );        // end dialog box
               break;                          // fall through?
            case IDCANCEL:
               iFileType = OrgFileType;
               EndDialog( hDlg, FALSE );       // end dialog box
               break;
            default:  return( FALSE );
```

```
            }  break;
       default: return( FALSE );
    }
   return( TRUE );
}

 //=======================================================//
 // WinMain - ViewFile main                               //
 //=======================================================//

#pragma argsused          // prevents unused parameter message //

int PASCAL WinMain(HANDLE hInstance,    HANDLE hPrevInstance,
                   LPSTR  lpszCmdLine, int    cmdShow )
{
    MSG         msg;
    HDC         hdc;
    WNDCLASS    wc;
    TEXTMETRIC  tm;

    if( !hPrevInstance )    // if no prev instance, this is first
    {
        LoadString( hInstance, IDS_NAME,
                    (LPSTR) szAppName, 10 );
        wc.lpszClassName = szAppName;
        wc.hInstance     = hInstance;
        wc.lpfnWndProc   = WndProc;
        wc.hCursor       = LoadCursor( NULL, IDC_ARROW );
        wc.hIcon         = LoadIcon( hInstance, szAppName );
        wc.lpszMenuName  = (LPSTR) szAppName;
        wc.hbrBackground = GetStockObject( WHITE_BRUSH );
        wc.style         = CS_HREDRAW | CS_VREDRAW;
        wc.cbClsExtra    = 0;
        wc.cbWndExtra    = 0;
        RegisterClass(&wc);
    }
    else GetInstanceData( hPrevInstance,
                          (PSTR) szAppName, 10 );
    iFileType = IDD_ANY - IDD_BMP;              // initial file type
    strcpy( szFileExt, szFileType[iFileType] );
                                        // set default extension
    hInst = hInstance;   // global: save for use by window procs
    hWndMain =
        CreateWindow( szAppName, szAppName,
                WS_OVERLAPPEDWINDOW | WS_HSCROLL | WS_VSCROLL,
                CW_USEDEFAULT,  0, CW_USEDEFAULT,  0,
                NULL, NULL, hInstance, NULL );
```

```
hdc = GetDC( hWndMain );
FontLog.lfHeight         =  6;
FontLog.lfWidth          =  6;
FontLog.lfEscapement     =  0;
FontLog.lfOrientation    =  0;
FontLog.lfWeight         =  FW_NORMAL;
FontLog.lfItalic         =  FALSE;
FontLog.lfUnderline      =  FALSE;
FontLog.lfStrikeOut      =  FALSE;
FontLog.lfCharSet        =  ANSI_CHARSET;
FontLog.lfOutPrecision   =  OUT_DEFAULT_PRECIS;
FontLog.lfClipPrecision  =  CLIP_DEFAULT_PRECIS;
FontLog.lfQuality        =  DEFAULT_QUALITY;
FontLog.lfPitchAndFamily =  FIXED_PITCH | FF_DONTCARE;
strcpy( FontLog.lfFaceName, "System" );
NewFont = CreateFontIndirect( (LPLOGFONT) &FontLog );
OrgFont = SelectObject( hdc, NewFont );
GetTextMetrics( hdc, &tm );
ChrX = tm.tmAveCharWidth;
ChrY = tm.tmHeight + tm.tmExternalLeading;
ChrV = tm.tmHeight;
ReleaseDC( hWndMain, hdc );
ShowWindow( hWndMain, cmdShow );
UpdateWindow( hWndMain );
hAccel = LoadAccelerators( hInst, "FILEVIEW" );
while( GetMessage( &msg, NULL, 0, 0 ) )
{
    if( !TranslateAccelerator( hWndMain, hAccel, &msg ) )
    {
        TranslateMessage( &msg );
        DispatchMessage( &msg );
}   }
return(msg.wParam);
}



                    ;================;
                    ;  FileView.DEF  ;
                    ;================;

NAME         FileView

DESCRIPTION 'Windows FileView Program'

STUB         'WINSTUB.EXE'
```

```
CODE            PRELOAD MOVEABLE DISCARDABLE
DATA            PRELOAD MOVEABLE MULTIPLE

EXETYPE         WINDOWS

SEGMENTS
        _RES    PRELOAD MOVEABLE DISCARDABLE

HEAPSIZE        128
STACKSIZE       8192

EXPORTS
                WndProc
                About
                FileOpenDlgProc
                FileTypeDlgProc


                      //==============*/
                      // FileView.H  //
                      //==============//

#define  IDS_NAME       1           // string table ID        //

#define  IDD_FNAME      16          // edit and list box IDs  //
#define  IDD_FPATH      17
#define  IDD_FLIST      18

#define  IDM_QUIT       101         // menu item IDs          //
#define  IDM_ABOUT      102
#define  IDM_OPEN       103
#define  IDM_TYPE       104

#define  IDD_BMP        201         // radio button IDs       //
#define  IDD_COM        202
#define  IDD_CUR        203
#define  IDD_DAT        204
#define  IDD_DBS        205
#define  IDD_DLG        206
#define  IDD_DLL        207
#define  IDD_EXE        208
#define  IDD_H          209
#define  IDD_PAL        210
#define  IDD_RC         211
#define  IDD_RES        212
#define  IDD_TXT        213
#define  IDD_ANY        214
```

Chapter 14

Message Box Dialogs

Before leaving the topic of dialog boxes, which have certainly been a major feature in several preceeding chapters, I would like to mention one additional type of dialog box which does not require the Resource Toolkit to prepare: the Message Dialog Box.

Message dialog boxes are designed to present a brief message. These messages may be a warning, caution, error, or simply informational. They may also return a response to the application. At the same time, four icons can be displayed together with up to three of seven buttons in six combinations as well as three modal settings.

The message dialog box function (*MessageBox*) is called with four parameters, beginning with a HWND parameter that indicate the window owning the message box. The second parameter, an ASCIIZ (null-terminated) string, contains the message to display. This message will be wrapped to fit the message box, but Windows will also size the message box to fit the message.

When a system-modal message box is created to indicate low memory, strings passed as text and caption parameters should not be taken from a resource file because an attempt to load the resource may fail.

The third parameter is also an ASCIIZ string that provides the dialog box caption. If the caption parameter is NULL, the default caption "Error" is used. The fourth parameter is a WORD value that specifies the icon, button, and mode settings as shown in Table 14-1.

Table 14-1: Message Box Types

Icons

Symbolic Constant	Value	Meaning
MB_ICONSTOP	0x0010	stop sign icon
MB_ICONHAND	same as	MB_ICONSTOP
MB_ICONQUESTION	0x0020	question-mark icon
MB_ICONEXCLAMATION	0x0030	exclamation-point icon
MB_ICONINFORMATION	0x0040	displays a lowercase i in a circle
MB_ICONASTERISK	same as	MB_ICONINFORMATION

Icons cannot be combined. Only one icon can be specified for a Message Box. If two icons are combined (using the OR operator), either one or no icon is displayed. (i.e., MB_ICONSTOP | MB_ICONQUESTION would be interpeted as MB_ICONEXCLAMATION.)

Pushbuttons

Symbolic Constant	Value	Meaning
MB_OK	0x0000	single pushbutton: Ok
MB_OKCANCEL	0x0001	two pushbuttons: OK, Cancel.
MB_ABORTRETRYIGNORE	0x0002	three pushbuttons: Abort, Retry, Ignore
MB_YESNOCANCEL	0x0003	three pushbuttons: Yes, No, Cancel
MB_YESNO	0x0004	two pushbuttons: Yes, No
MB_RETRYCANCEL	0x0005	two pushbuttons: Retry, Cancel

Only one button combination can be selected; combining button values (i.e., MB_ABORTRETRYIGNORE | MB_YESNOCANCEL, for example, would be interpeted simply as MB_YESNOCANCEL). Other combinations might simply result in invalid flag values.

Default Button

Symbolic Constant	Value	Meaning
MB_DEFBUTTON1	0x0000	first button is default
MB_DEFBUTTON2	0x0100	second button becomes default
MB_DEFBUTTON3	0x0200	third button becomes default

The first button is always the default unless MB_DEFBUTTON2 or MB_DEFBUTTON3 are specified. Only one button can be selected as default.

Table 14-1: Message Box Types (cont.)

Mode Settings		
Symbolic Constant	*Value*	*Meaning*
MB_APPLMODAL	*0x0000*	*(default)*

—The user must respond to the message box before continuing work in the window identified by the *hWndParent* parameter. However, the user can move to the windows of other applications and work in those windows. MB_APPLMODAL is the default if neither MB_SYSTEMMODAL nor MB_TASKMODAL are specified.

MB_SYSTEMMODAL   *0x1000*

— All applications are suspended until the user responds to the message box. Unless the application specifies MB_ICONHAND, the message box does not become modal until after it is created; consequently, the parent window and other windows continue to receive messages resulting from its activation. System-modal message boxes are used to notify the user of serious, potentially damaging errors that require immediate attention (for example, running out of memory).

MB_TASKMODAL   *0x2000*

— Same as MB_APPMODAL except that all the top-level windows belonging to the current task are disabled if the hWndOwner parameter is NULL. This flag should be used when the calling application or library does not have a window handle available, but it still needs to prevent input to other windows in the current application without suspending other applications.

When an application calls *MessageBox* specifying the MB_ICONSTOP and MB_SYSTEMMODAL flags, Windows will display the resulting message box regardless of available memory. It limits the length of the message-box text to one line. If a message box is created when a dialog box is present, use the handle of the dialog box as the *hWndParent* parameter. The *hWndParent* parameter should not identify a child window, such as a dialog-box control. The return value specifies the outcome of the function, returning zero if there is insufficient memory to create the message box. Otherwise, the value returned will be shown in Table 14-2.

Table 14-2: Dialog Box Command IDs

Symbol	*Value*	*Meaning*
IDOK	1	OK button pressed
IDCANCEL	2	Cancel button pressed
IDABORT	3	Abort button pressed

Table 14-2: Dialog Box Command IDs (cont.)

Symbol	Value	Meaning
IDRETRY	4	Retry button pressed
IDIGNORE	5	Ignore button pressed
IDYES	6	Yes button pressed
IDNO	7	No button pressed

If a message box has a Cancel button, the IDCANCEL value will be returned if either the Escape key or Cancel button is pressed. Otherwise the escape key has no effect.

Figure 14-1 shows a demonstration program with four message box dialogs called through the menu for convenience. The illustration is a composite because multiple dialog boxes would not normally be displayed. The general format for handling a dialog box is to use either an *if* statement, if only one return message will be tested:

```
if( MessageBox( hwnd, "Exit application?", "Exit?",
          MB_ICONQUESTION | MB_YESNOCANCEL
          | MB_DEFBUTTON2 ) == IDYES ) ...
```

Or, use a *switch..case* statement to test all possible return values:

```
switch( MessageBox( hwnd, "Exit application?", "Exit?",
          MB_ICONQUESTION | MB_YESNOCANCEL
          | MB_DEFBUTTON2 ))
{ case      IDYES: ...
  case       IDNO: ...
  case IDCANCEL: ...   }
```

The case values, of course, must match the specified button settings. Alternatively, if the message box is for information purposes only, the return values may simply be ignored (as shown in four of the examples in MsgBoxes.C, below.)

Note: The menu resource for MsgBoxes must be created using the Resource Toolbox Menu editor. The application icon, not shown, is optional.

Figure 14-1: Message Boxes

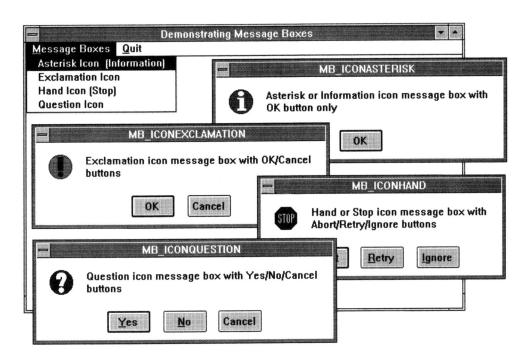

```
//==============================//
//         MsgBoxes.C           //
//   C++ Windows Editor Demo    //
//==============================//

#include (windows.h)
#include "msgboxes.h"

long FAR PASCAL WndProc( HWND hwnd,    WORD message,
                         WORD wParam, LONG lParam )
{
   switch( message )
   {
      case WM_COMMAND:
         switch( wParam )
         {
            case IDM_ASTERISK:
               MessageBox( hwnd, "Asterisk or Information",
```

```
                        " icon message box with OK button only",
                        "MB_ICONASTERISK",
                        MB_ICONASTERISK | MB_OK );
                    return( 1 );
                case IDM_EXCLAMATION:
                    MessageBox( hwnd, "Exclamation icon message"
                        " box with OK/Cancel buttons",

                        "MB_ICONEXCLAMATION",
                        MB_ICONEXCLAMATION | MB_OKCANCEL );
                    return( 1 );
                case IDM_HAND:
                    MessageBox( hwnd, "Hand or Stop icon message"
                        " box with Abort/Retry/Ignore buttons",
                        "MB_ICONHAND",
                        MB_ICONHAND | MB_ABORTRETRYIGNORE );
                    return( 1 );
                case IDM_QUESTION:
                    MessageBox( hwnd, "Question icon message box "
                        "with Yes/No/Cancel buttons",
                        "MB_ICONQUESTION",
                        MB_ICONQUESTION | MB_YESNOCANCEL );
                    return( 1 );
                case IDM_QUIT:
                    if( MessageBox( hwnd, "Exit application?",
                        "Exit?", MB_ICONQUESTION | MB_YESNOCANCEL
                                | MB_DEFBUTTON2 ) == IDYES )
                        PostQuitMessage( 0 );
                    return( 1 );
            }
        case WM_DESTROY:
            PostQuitMessage( 0 );
            return( 0 );
    }
    return( DefWindowProc( hwnd, message, wParam, lParam ) );
}

#pragma argsused

int PASCAL WinMain( HANDLE hInstance,
                    HANDLE hPrevInstance,
                    LPSTR  lpszCmdParam, int    nCmdShow )
{
    static char szAppName[] = "MSGBOXES";
    HWND        hwnd;
    MSG         msg;
```

```
    WNDCLASS     wc;

    if( ! hPrevInstance )
    {
        wc.hInstance      = hInstance;
        wc.lpfnWndProc    = WndProc;
        wc.cbClsExtra     = 0;
        wc.cbWndExtra     = 0;
        wc.lpszClassName  = szAppName;
        wc.hIcon          = LoadIcon( hInstance, szAppName );
        wc.lpszMenuName   = (LPSTR) szAppName;
        wc.hCursor        = LoadCursor( NULL, IDC_ARROW );
        wc.hbrBackground  = GetStockObject( WHITE_BRUSH );
        wc.style          = CS_HREDRAW | CS_VREDRAW;
        RegisterClass( &wc );
    }
    hwnd = CreateWindow( szAppName,
                         "Demonstrating Message Boxes",
                         WS_OVERLAPPEDWINDOW,
                         CW_USEDEFAULT, CW_USEDEFAULT,
                         CW_USEDEFAULT, CW_USEDEFAULT,
                         NULL, NULL, hInstance, NULL  );
    ShowWindow(   hwnd, nCmdShow );
    UpdateWindow( hwnd );
    while( GetMessage( &msg, NULL, 0, 0 ) )
    {
        TranslateMessage( &msg );
        DispatchMessage(  &msg );
    }
    return( msg.wParam );
}


        ;=======================================;
        ;  MsgBoxes.DEF module definition file  ;
        ;=======================================;

NAME          MSGBOXES
DESCRIPTION   "Windows Message Box Program"
EXETYPE       WINDOWS
STUB          "WINSTUB.EXE"
CODE          PRELOAD MOVEABLE DISCARDABLE
DATA          PRELOAD MOVEABLE MULTIPLE
HEAPSIZE      1024
STACKSIZE     8192
EXPORTS       WndProc
```

```
//=================================//
// D:\BC\MSGBOXES.H 2/10/1991 12:33 //
//=================================//

#define   IDM_ASTERISK       101
#define   IDM_EXCLAMATION    102
#define   IDM_HAND           103
#define   IDM_QUESTION       104
#define   IDM_QUIT           106
```

Part 3

Graphics Programming In Windows

The Graphics Device Interface is a bridge between an application and one or more output devices, whether video display, printer or plotter. For example, video displays vary greatly in size, resolution, and color capabilities. For a text (DOS) display, however, any application could assume that the display was 80 characters wide and 25 lines vertical, without worrying about the pixel size of individual characters or making any provisions for mapping text differently for a 200 pixel vertical resolution or a 480 pixel vertical resolution.

In effect, DOS and ROM (BIOS) services combine to provide "translation" services between the virtual world manipulated by the application and the physical world of the video monitor. In Windows' graphic environment, the GDI provides these same "translation" services for applications, allowing the applications to operate in a "virtual" environment and mapping the application's output to the physical hardware display, whether a CRT or a hard-copy device.

Thus far, the GDI has been used only in a limited respect to display text information with a brief mention of fonts and text alignment. It is now time to look at the GDI from a more general standpoint before, in subsequent chapters, manipulating colors, images, and graphic/text combinations.

The GDI does far more than mapping output images from a virtual display to a real display, and one of the first items which we will look at is how the GDI permits Windows to determine, from the output drivers, what hardware capabilities are present and can be used to handle all or part of the video processing tasks.

For example, if the hardware where an application executes includes a graphics coprocessor (as many of the newer video boards do), the GDI will allow the display device to calculate points composing an ellipse, line, or polygon. If not, then the GDI module executes the necessary calculations itself.

The overall intention of the GDI is to make applications independent of the variety of peripheral devices. Thus, as new graphic devices appear, either Windows or the hardware developers will supply appropriate drivers which the GDI will use to adapt the application's output for display appropriate to the device.

To use another example, Windows can run on both color and monochrome systems, but Windows applications are not required to make separate provisions for each because Windows, on a monochrome device, will translate colors into shades of gray.

If an application has been written to use colors supported by an 8514/A but is executed on an EGA system with only 16 colors, the missing colors may be simulated by dithering (mixing primary colors to provide shades not directly available).

Of course, at the same time, your application may ask the system about the color resolution of the attached output device and make optimum use of whatever capacities are available. However, there are limitations because the GDI does not have the capacity for all possible demands which might be placed on a graphics environment. Items which are not supported, for example, are three-dimensional hidden-line calculations, animation, or object-rotation.

Still, while not omniscient, the GDI does provide a variety of graphic resources, including both virtual and vectored coordinate systems and adjustments for varying screen resolutions, combining text and graphics and even scalar fonts while still maintaining a high degree of device independence.

## Chapter 15

Introducing Graphics Device Interface

At the heart of the GDI graphics system is the ***device context***, commonly abbreviated simply as *DC*. Under Windows, before anything can be drawn on the screen, the application must begin by obtaining a handle to the device context.

Unlike DOS, where applications own the entire video display, or printer or other device, under Windows the output device is a shared resource, and the device context is a method allowing peaceful coexistence between applications sharing an output display.

Asking Windows for a handle to a device context is, in effect, the equivalent of asking permission to use the output device. After obtaining permission, the handle is included as a parameter to the GDI output functions, telling Windows which output device is needed.

The device context handle (*hDC*) is more than a single parameter. It is actually a pointer that not only indicates a device, but also an information structure detailing device (graphic) settings. For an example, a call to the function *TextOut* does not include font and color information because these have already been set for the device context (or are simply using default settings). Each application has its own set of colors and fonts for display, but does not need to respecify these as parameters for each output operation. Instead, only the coordinates (position) and the text information are passed as parameters. To change context attributes, a separate function call is used and affects subsequent *TextOut* operations.

Thus the device context is both a handle to the actual display and a body of information about how the display should be created, including font selections, character spacing, line width, and foreground and background colors.

Accessing The Device Context

Access to the device context has already been demonstrated in preceding examples, using the *BeginPaint* and the *GetDC* functions and using the *End-Paint* and *ReleaseDC* functions to release the device context when finished. What you should remember, however, is that any application should not attempt to hold on to a device context beyond the immediate operation, particularly since Windows has only five device context handles to share among all executing applications.

Instead, a device context should always be released or deleted as soon as the immediate output operation is finished. Of course, after releasing the handle, the device context is no longer valid.

When calling *BeginPaint*, a second parameter was included as:

```
hdc = BeginPaint( hwnd, &ps );
```

The *EndPaint* function also includes the *ps* parameter:

```
EndPaint( hwnd, &ps );
```

The *ps* parameter is a structure variable of type *PAINTSTRUCT,* and contains a rectangle structure indicating the invalidate region within the window client area and, specifying the region to be updated. Thus, with *BeginPaint*, drawing operations are limited to the indicated region. The *ps* parameter (and *BeginPaint*) are used in response to *WM_PAINT* messages when only a portion of a screen needs to be updated. The *GetDC* and *GetWindowDC* are also used to retrieve a handle to the device context. The *GetDC* function is used for operations on the entire client window area and released using the *ReleaseDC* function. *GetWindowDC* provides access not just to the client window, but to the entire window—including the caption bar, menu, scrollbars, and frame as well as the client window area. It does not, however, provide access outside of the application window. Again, the *ReleaseDC* function is used when finished.

There are two other methods of obtaining a handle to the device context: the *CreateDC* and *CreateIC* functions. The first function, *CreateDC*, is commonly used to obtain a device context allowing operations outside of an application's client window area as, for example, for a screen capture utility. The handle is obtained as:

```
hdc = CreateDC( "DISPLAY", NULL, NULL, NULL );
```

The second function, *CreateIC*, is used to obtain an *information context* rather than a device context. The difference is that an information context, unlike a device context, does not provide a handle for output operations, but does provide a handle that can be used to obtain information about the output device.

Selecting The Device

The first step in accessing device information is to determine which device information will be requested about.

For the video display—the CRT—information is accessible by creating an information context using the default specification, *"DISPLAY"*, as:

```
hdcInfo = CreateIC( "DISPLAY", NULL, NULL, NULL );
```

The video display is not the only device which may be available for output. It is probably safe to assume that at least one printer is also attached. Actually, it really doesn't matter if the printer or any other device is physically installed, only if its driver has been installed in Windows.

The file *Win.INI* in the Windows directory contains a variety of initialization and setup information about both active and inactive programs. This is an ASCII file and can be examined by most editors. It is created and modified by Windows when new applications are installed, or when the configuration is modified through the various control panel features.

To open an information context for a device other than the CRT, the first step is to retrieve the profile string describing the device:

```
GetProfileString( "WINDOWS", "DEVICE", "", szPrn
                  sizeof(szPrn) );
```

This will open the *Win.INI* file, searching first for the string *"WINDOWS"* (case is ignored) in the brackets which identify an application name, then, second, for a "*DEVICE*" (key name) entry. The third string parameter, empty in the example, can provide a default string for return. An excerpt from *Win.INI* shows a typical entry:

```
[windows]
  ...
  device=PCL / HP LaserJet,HPPCL,LPT1:
```

After this item is located, the latter portion of the string—*PCL | HP Laser-Jet,HPPCL,LPT1:*—is returned in the *szPrn* variable, identifying the type of printer or other output device installed.

After using the *strtok* function to disassemble this string, the driver name (*HPPCL*), device name (*PCL | HP LaserJet*) and output port (*LPT1:*) are available to create an information context for this device. Once an information context is available, information about the device can be requested.

Device Context Information

Device context information is data about the resolution and capacities of a hardware output device such as a CRT video display, a printer, a plotter, a camera device, or even a metafile (a file consisting of GDI calls in binary format).

The device context contains a variety of information that can be accessed through the 28 identifiers defined in *Windows.INC*. Several of these identifiers return word values composed of bit-flags for further breakdown. Indexes and identifiers are listed in Table 15-1, and demonstrated in the *Devices.C* demo application appearing at the end of this chapter.

Table 15-1: GDI Information Indexes

Index	Meaning	
DRIVERVERSION	version number; as 0x300 for version 3.0	
TECHNOLOGY	device technology	
Value	*Meaning*	
DT_PLOTTER	Vector plotter	
DT_RASDISPLAY	Raster display	
DT_RASPRINTER	Raster printer	
DT_RASCAMERA	Raster camera	
DT_CHARSTREAM	Character stream	
DT_METAFILE	Metafile	

Table 15-1: GDI Information Indexes(cont.)

	Value	Meaning
	DT_DISPFILE	Display file
HORZSIZE		physical display width (in millimeters)
VERTSIZE		physical display height (in millimeters)
HORZRES		display width (in pixels)
index		*meaning*
VERTRES		display height (in raster lines)
LOGPIXELSX		pixels / logical inch (width)
LOGPIXELSY		pixels / logical inch (height)
BITSPIXEL		adjacent color bits for each pixel
PLANES		color planes
NUMBRUSHES		device-specific brushes
NUMPENS		device-specific pens
NUMFONTS		device-specific fonts
NUMCOLORS		entries in the device color table
ASPECTX		relative width of device pixel for line drawing
ASPECTY		relative height of device pixel for line drawing
ASPECTXY		diagonal width of device pixel for line drawing
PDEVICESIZE		size of PDEVICE internal data structure
CLIPCAPS		flag indicating clipping capabilities (1=True / 0=False)

The next three indexes are valid only if *RC_PALETTE* bit is set in *RASTERCAPS* index and available only if driver version is 3.0 or higher.

SIZEPALETTE		entries in the system palette
NUMRESERVED		reserved entries in the system palette
COLORRES		actual color resolution in bits per pixel
RASTERCAPS		bitmask indicating raster capabilities
	Capability	*Meaning*
	RC_BANDING	requires banding support
	RC_BITBLT	capable of transferring bitmaps
	RC_BITMAP64	bitmaps larger than 64K supported
	RC_DI_BITMAP	SetDIBits and GetDIBits supported
	RC_DIBTODEV	SetDIBitsToDevice supported
	RC_FLOODFILL	flood fills supported
	RC_GDI20_OUTPUT	Windows 2.0 features supported
	RC_PALETTE	palette-based device
	RC_SCALING	scaling supported
	RC_STRETCHBLT	StretchBlt supported
	RC_STRETCHDIB	StretchDIBits supported

Table 15-1: GDI Information Indexes(cont.)

CURVECAPS	bitmask indicating curve capabilities
Capability	*Meaning*
CC_CIRCLES	circles
CC_PIE	pie wedges
CC_CHORD	chord arcs
CC_ELLIPSES	ellipses
CC_WIDE	wide borders
CC_STYLED	styled borders
CC_WIDESTYLED	wide and styled borders
CC_INTERIORS	interiors
...	high byte is 0

LINECAPS	bitmask indicating line capabilities
Capability	*Meaning*
LC_POLYLINE	polylines
LC_MARKER	polyline
LC_POLYMARKER	polymarkers
...	bit 3 reserved
LC_WIDE	wide lines
LC_STYLED	styled lines
LC_WIDESTYLED	wide and styled lines
LC_INTERIORS	interiors
...	high byte is 0

POLYGONALCAPS	bitmask indicating polygonal capabilities
Capability	*Meaning*
PC_POLYGON	alternate fill polygon
PC_RECTANGLE	rectangle
PC_TRAPEZOID	winding number fill polygon
PC_SCANLINE	scanline
PC_WIDE	wide borders
PC_STYLED	styled borders
PC_WIDESTYLED	wide and styled borders
PC_INTERIORS	interiors
...	high byte is 0

TEXTCAPS	bitmask indicating text capabilities:
Capability	*Meaning*
TC_OP_CHARACTER	character output precision

Table 15-1: GDI Information Indexes(cont.)

Capability	Meaning
TC_OP_STROKE	stroke output precision
TC_CP_STROKE	stroke clip precision
TC_CR_90	90-degree character rotation
TC_CR_ANY	any character rotation
TC_SF_X_YINDEP	scaling independent of X and Y
TC_SA_DOUBLE	doubled character for scaling
TC_SA_INTEGER	integer multiples for scaling
TC_SA_CONTIN	any multiples for exact scaling
TC_EA_DOUBLE	double-weight characters
TC_IA_ABLE	italicizing
TC_UA_ABLE	underlining
TC_SO_ABLE	strikeouts
TC_RA_ABLE	raster fonts
TC_VA_ABLE	vector fonts
...	high-bit reserved -- must be returned zero

The *GetDeviceCaps* function retrieves one item from the information context as a word value. For example, the driver version number could be retrieved as:

```
j = GetDeviceCaps( hDcInfo, DRIVERVERSION );
```

The value returned in *j* could be further disassembled as *HIBYTE(j)* for the major version number and *LOBYTE(j)* for the minor version. In other instances, the value returned is itself the information or, in the cases of *TEXTCAPS, CURVECAPS, LINECAPS* and *POLYCAPS*, can be treated as an array of flag (bit) values.

The Devices program breaks these value parameters into several arbitrary groupings for display convenience, with the basic display parameters for a VGA video display shown in Figure 15-1, while the same parameters for a LaserJet are shown in Figure 15-2.

As might be expected from Figures 15-1 and 15-2, the resolutions for a VGA video and a laserjet are quite different. The resolutions for different video cards also vary considerably, as shown in Table 15-2, which compares four "standard" video resolutions.

Figure 15-1: CRT Device Information (VGA)

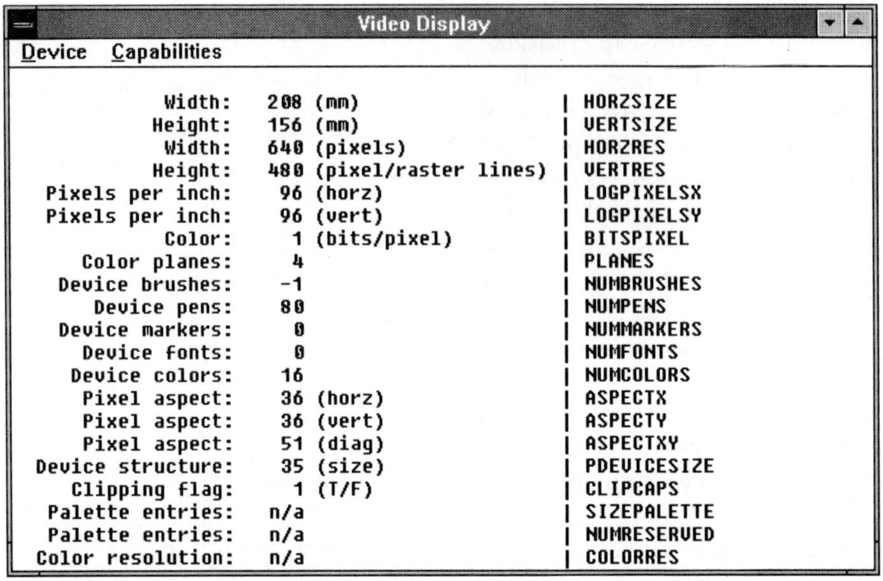

```
┌─────────────────────────────────────────────────────────────────┐
│ ═                          Video Display                    ▼ ▲  │
├───────────────────────────────────────────────────────────────── │
│ Device   Capabilities                                             │
│                                                                   │
│           Width:  208 (mm)                   | HORZSIZE           │
│          Height:  156 (mm)                   | VERTSIZE           │
│           Width:  640 (pixels)               | HORZRES            │
│          Height:  480 (pixel/raster lines)   | VERTRES            │
│  Pixels per inch:  96 (horz)                 | LOGPIXELSX         │
│  Pixels per inch:  96 (vert)                 | LOGPIXELSY         │
│           Color:    1 (bits/pixel)           | BITSPIXEL         │
│    Color planes:    4                        | PLANES             │
│  Device brushes:   -1                        | NUMBRUSHES         │
│     Device pens:   80                        | NUMPENS            │
│  Device markers:    0                        | NUMMARKERS         │
│    Device fonts:    0                        | NUMFONTS           │
│   Device colors:   16                        | NUMCOLORS          │
│    Pixel aspect:   36 (horz)                 | ASPECTX            │
│    Pixel aspect:   36 (vert)                 | ASPECTY            │
│    Pixel aspect:   51 (diag)                 | ASPECTXY           │
│ Device structure:  35 (size)                 | PDEVICESIZE        │
│   Clipping flag:    1 (T/F)                  | CLIPCAPS           │
│  Palette entries:  n/a                       | SIZEPALETTE        │
│  Palette entries:  n/a                       | NUMRESERVED        │
│ Color resolution:  n/a                       | COLORRES           │
└───────────────────────────────────────────────────────────────────┘
```

Figure 15-2: HP LaserJet Device Information

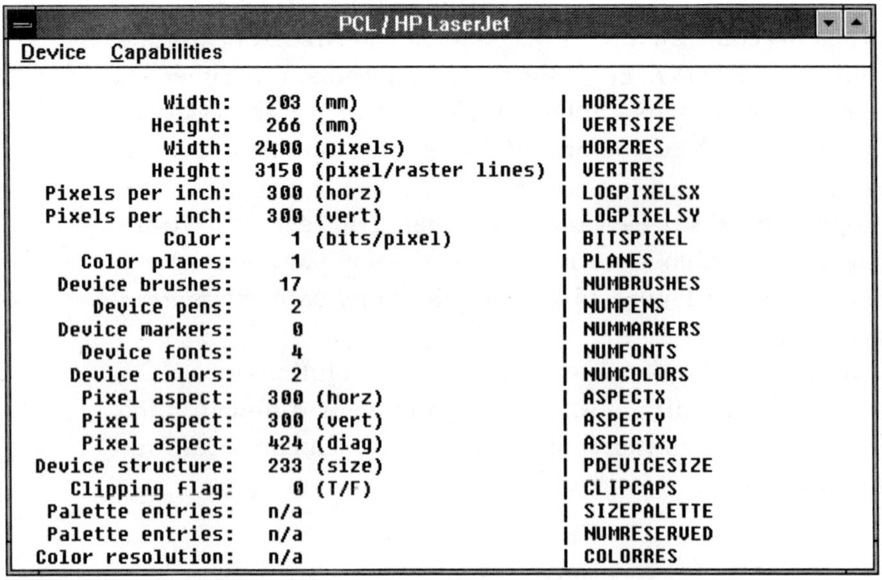

```
┌─────────────────────────────────────────────────────────────────┐
│ ═                        PCL / HP LaserJet                  ▼ ▲  │
├───────────────────────────────────────────────────────────────── │
│ Device   Capabilities                                             │
│                                                                   │
│           Width:   203 (mm)                   | HORZSIZE          │
│          Height:   266 (mm)                   | VERTSIZE          │
│           Width:  2400 (pixels)               | HORZRES           │
│          Height:  3150 (pixel/raster lines)   | VERTRES           │
│  Pixels per inch:  300 (horz)                 | LOGPIXELSX        │
│  Pixels per inch:  300 (vert)                 | LOGPIXELSY        │
│           Color:     1 (bits/pixel)           | BITSPIXEL         │
│    Color planes:     1                        | PLANES            │
│  Device brushes:    17                        | NUMBRUSHES        │
│     Device pens:     2                        | NUMPENS           │
│  Device markers:     0                        | NUMMARKERS        │
│    Device fonts:     4                        | NUMFONTS          │
│   Device colors:     2                        | NUMCOLORS         │
│    Pixel aspect:   300 (horz)                 | ASPECTX           │
│    Pixel aspect:   300 (vert)                 | ASPECTY           │
│    Pixel aspect:   424 (diag)                 | ASPECTXY          │
│ Device structure:  233 (size)                 | PDEVICESIZE       │
│   Clipping flag:     0 (T/F)                  | CLIPCAPS          │
│  Palette entries:  n/a                        | SIZEPALETTE       │
│  Palette entries:  n/a                        | NUMRESERVED       │
│ Color resolution:  n/a                        | COLORRES          │
└───────────────────────────────────────────────────────────────────┘
```

Table 15-2: Video Device Resolutions

GetDeviceCaps	*CGA*	*EGA*	*VGA*	*8514/A*
HORSIZE ((in) mm)	(9.44) 240	(9.44) 240	(8.19)	(11.02) 28
VERTSIZE ((in) mm)	(7.09) 180	(1.89) 175	(6.14) 156	(8.27) 210
HORZREZ (pixels)	640	640	640	1024
VERTREZ (pixels)	200	350	480	760
ASPECTX (horiz)	5	38	36	14
ASPECTZ (vert)	12	48	36	14
(aspect ratio x/y)	*0.416*	*0.791*	*1.000*	*1.000*
ASPECTXY (diagonal)	(13.9) 13	61	51	(19.8) 19
LOGPIXELSX (pixels/inch)	96	96	96	120
LOGPIXELSY (pixels/inch)	48	72	96	120

HORSIZE and *VERTSIZE* are the nominal width and height of the display area in millimeters. These, of course, may or may not correspond to the actual display size, but are based on standard display sizes.

HORZRES and *VERTRES* return the actual pixel width and height of the display area.

ASPECTX, ASPECTY and *ASPECTXY* are the calculated relative width, height, and diagonal size of the pixels. *ASPECTXY* is calculated as $\sqrt{(ASPECTX^2 + ASPECTY^2)}$ rounded (down) to the nearest integer.

Last, *LOGPIXELSX* and *LOGPIXELSY* are the number of pixels per "logical" inch. A logical inch is not a physical inch, and may vary from 1.7 "real" inches (CGA) to near unity (8514/A). Logical inches are a convenience used principally to display rulers with, for example, fixed-width fonts in word-processors such as WORD or WRITE. Figure 15-3 shows an example of a ruler created using "logical" inches.

In general, however, the programmer (and the application) do not need to be particularly concerned with device resolutions and other device-specific capabilities, because these are handled by Windows, not by the application. There are other aspects of Windows graphics programming which are directly relevant to the applications. One of these is mapping modes.

Figure 15-3: An Application Using Logical Inches

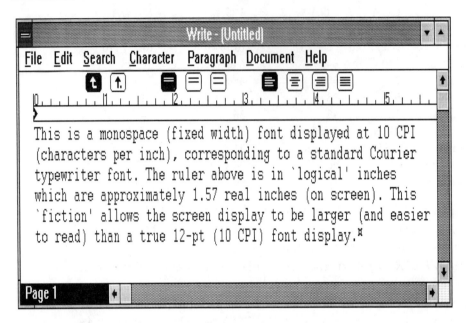

Mapping Modes

With a few exceptions, under DOS all graphics operations have used a single mapping mode in which the logical unit was the screen pixel, and the screen origin—the 0,0—point was located at the upper-left corner. Of course, both text and graphic windows operations could relocate the origin point making operations window relative but, in essence, only one mapping mode was employed.

As an alternative, Windows supports eight separate "mapping modes". Each provides different features, different scalar (logical) units and, except for the *MM_TEXT* mode which is the default and corresponds to the DOS mapping mode, each uses the lower-left corner of the screen as the origin or has a variable origin point. Mapping modes and origin points are illustrated by the *MODES.C* program at the end of this chapter.

The eight mapping modes are defined, briefly, in Table 15-3:

Table 15-3: Windows Mapping Modes

Mapping Mode	Value	Logical Unit	Default Origin x-axis	Default Origin y-axis
MM_TEXT	1	pixel	left	top
MM_LOMETRIC	2	0.1 mm	left	bottom
MM_HIMETRIC	3	0.01 mm	left	bottom
MM_LOENGLISH	4	0.01 inch	left	bottom
MM_HIENGLISH	5	0.001 inch	left	bottom
MM_TWIPS	6	$^1/_{1440}$ inch	left	bottom
MM_ISOTROPIC	7	variable (x=y)	variable	variable
MM_ANISOTROPIC	8	variable (x!=y)	variable	variable

The *MM_TEXT* mode corresponds to the DOS mapping mode and allows applications to work in device pixels. However, as previously discussed, pixel size varies from device to device, as does the size (in pixels, vertically and horizontally). In *MM_TEXT* mode, the default origin lies at the upper-left corner of the screen with x and y coordinates increasing right and down.

The *MM_HIENGLISH, MM_HIMETRIC, MM_LOENGLISH, MM_LOMET-RIC*, and *MM_TWIPS* modes are useful for applications that need to draw in physically meaningful units such as inches or millimeters. At the same time, each of these modes uses Cartesian coordinates, coordinates whose values increase above and to the right of the origin point, with the default origin at the lower-left corner of the client window. The MM_HIMETRIC and *MM_LOMETRIC* mapping modes use units of 0.01 and 0.1 millimeters, providing high and low resolutions respectively. The *MM_HIENGLISH* and *MM_LOENGLISH* mapping modes use units of 0.001 and 0.01 inches, also providing high and low resolutions. The *MM_TWIPS* mapping mode uses logical units that are $^1/_{1440}$ths of an inch, which is also $^1/_{20}$th of a printer's point (72 points = 1 inch). Thus, in *MM_TWIPS* mode, a 10-point typeface can be drawn that is 200 logical units in size, regardless of whether the actual display device is capable of this resolution.

The final two modes, *MM_ISOTROPIC* and *MM_ANISOTROPIC*, provide variable logical units as well as variable origin points. Thus, in either of these modes the 0,0 origin point could be located at the center of the window or at any other point desired.

The difference between these two modes is that the *MM_ISOTROPIC* mode ensures a one-to-one aspect ratio by keeping the x and y logical units equal in size, useful when preserving the exact shape of an image is important. On the other hand, the *MM_ANISOTROPIC* mode allows the x and y logical units to be adjusted independently.

Setting (Getting) Mapping Modes

The various mapping modes can be set or retrieved using the *SetMapMode* and *GetMapMode* functions:

```
SetMapMode( hdc, nMapMode );
nMapMode = GetMapMode( hdc );
```

The *nMapMode* variable, may be one of the eight constants identifying the several modes or may be a byte variable to receive the mode value. The *SetMapMode* function returns, if desired, to the previous mapping mode. The default mapping mode, unless another setting has been made, is always *MM_TEXT*, just like in DOS. Suppose that a different mode such as *MM_LOMETRIC*, has been selected.

First, the origin point is now at the lower-left corner of the client window, and positive y-axis values increase upwards. X-axis values, of course, behave as before, increasing to the right. Instead of pixel coordinates, coordinates are now specified in 0.1 mm increments which, on a VGA monitor, would make the vertical screen resolution 2080 logical units and 1560 logical units horizontally.

Remember, however, that the display capability of the hardware is still only 400 pixels vertical by 640 pixels horizontal, this means that vertically, 5.2 logical units are mapped to one pixel, and horizontally, 2.44 logical units are mapped per pixel. This resolution question—mapping logical to physical units—is not the application's concern. Instead, the GDI uses the mapping mode to convert logical coordinates into the appropriate device coordinates. What is the application's concern (and, of course, the programmer's too) is specifying positions in the appropriate units for the mode in use, and appropriate for the origin used.

Screen (Window) Origins

All mapping modes under Windows have variable origin points which can be selected using the *SetViewportOrg* or *SetWindowOrg* functions to specify a desired 0,0 point.

The *SetViewportOrg* function sets the viewport origin of the specified device context and is declared as:

```
DWORD SetViewportOrg( HDC hdc, int xcoord, int ycoord )
```

The *SetWindowOrg* function sets the window origin of the specified device context and is declared as:

```
DWORD SetWindowOrg( HDC hdc, int xcoord, int ycoord )
```

Together, the device-context viewport and window origin define how the GDI maps points in the logical coordinate system to points in the physical coordinate system of the actual device, i.e., how GDI converts logical coordinates into device coordinates. In both cases, the *xcoord* and *ycoord* parameters are signed integer values, expressed in device units, and must be within the range of the device coordinate system.

Also, *SetViewportOrg* returns a *DWORD* value specifying the previous origin of the viewport in device coordinates with *ycoord* in the high-order word, and *xcoord* in the low-order word. In like fashion, *SetWindowOrg* returns a *DWORD* value with the previous window origin in device coordinates, or the *GetViewportOrg* and *GetWindowOrg* functions can be called to return the current values.

Normally, only one of these two functions would be used. For example:

```
SetViewportOrg( hdc, cxClient / 2, cyClient / 2 );
or
SetWindowOrg( hdc, cxClient / 2, cyClient / 2 );
```

Either of these statements would establish client area coordinates as shown at the left in Figure 15-4, or, using both, would establish client window coordinates as shown at the right in Figure 15-4.

Figure 15-4: Client Area Coordinates

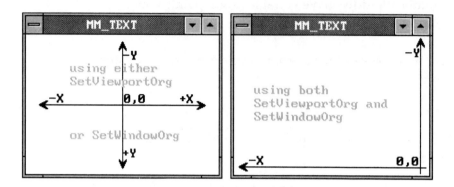

Using Mapping Modes With Physical Units

While the text mode uses coordinates expressed in screen units, all other mapping modes supported by Windows express logical coordinates in terms of physical measurement units, i.e., English, metric and point (TWIPS) measurements. However, as you can see in Table 15-4, all of these modes use units which are higher in resolution than the video display.

Table 15-4: Comparative Device Resolutions

Device	Logical Size	Unit	Inches	Millimeters
EGA Video (H/V)	640/350	pixels	0.014800/0.0197	0.3750/0.5000
VGA Video (H/V)	640/480	pixels	0.012795	0.3250
MM_LOENGLISH	0.01	in	0.010000	0.2540
MM_LOMETRIC	0.1	mm	0.003940	0.1000
LaserJet Printer	300	dpi	0.003333	0.0846
MM_HIENGLISH	0.001	in	0.001000	0.0254
MM_TWIPS	$^1/_{20}$	pt	0.000694	0.0176
Typesetter	2000	dpi	0.000500	0.0127
MM_HIMETRIC 0	.01	mm	0.000394	0.0100

Further, in the case of *MM_HIENGLISH, MM_TWIPS* and *MM_HIMETRIC*, the mapping resolution is still higher than laserjet resolution. Of course, there are still higher output resolution devices such as 2000 DPI typesetters, but these are hardly commonplace and are still exceeded by the *MM_HIMETRIC* resolution. If images calculated in these modes exceed display resolutions, how are these modes used? The answer, of course, is that Windows maps points calculated at high resolutions to the relatively low resolutions of the actual display device(s).

However, the real point of these physical resolution modes is that shapes can be calculated which are constant in aspect, i.e., points on a circle calculated in a metric (or English) mode and then mapped to the video display remain circular rather than becoming an ellipse. For example, a circle with a radius of 100 pixels would, on an EGA display, be (approximately) 175 mm high and 75 mm wide—not very round at all. In other systems, such as the Borland Graphic Interface (BGI), this discrepancy was corrected by calculating the screen aspect ratio for the display device and applying the aspect ratio to the point calculations. For complex shapes, however, applying this type of correction in calculating the displayed points does make the calculations somewhat more complicated.

In Windows, by performing calculations in an essentially isotropic virtual space, no aspect corrections are required. Corrections for translation from the isotropic virtual space to the anisotropic screen space are automatically handled by Windows.

Variable Mapping Modes

Windows also provides the *MM_ISOTROPIC* and *MM_ANISOTROPIC* mapping modes which, unlike the previous modes, permit changing the viewport and window extents, the scaling factors used by Windows to translate logical coordinates to device coordinates. The difference between these two is that *MM_ISOTROPIC* uses the same scale for both the x and y axis while *MM_AN-ISOTROPIC* permits two different scales to be used for the x and y axis.

SetWindowExt and SetViewportExt

The *SetWindowExt* and *SetViewportExt* functions are only valid with the *ISO-TROPIC* and *ANISOTROPIC* mapping modes, and are ignored when the *TEXT, METRIC, ENGLISH,* or *TWIPS* modes are in effect.

The *SetWindowExt* function determines the size of the window in logical units. In Isotropic mapping, the x and y axis extents remain equal even though two extent parameters are still required when setting the range. In Anisotropic mapping, the two extent parameters may specify different ranges for the x and y axis extents.

The *SetViewportExt* function assigns x and y viewport extents that define how much the GDI must stretch or compress units in the logical coordinate system to fit units in the device coordinate system. Again, in Isotropic mapping, the x and y axis extents remain equal while, in Anisotropic mapping, different ranges may be specified for the x and y axis extents.

As an example, if the window x-extent is two and the viewport x-extent is four, the GDI maps two logical units (along the x-axis) to four device units. In similar fashion, if the window y-extent is two and the viewport y-extent is one, the GDI maps two logical units to one device unit along the y-axis.

However, since the viewpoint y-extent is negative and the window y-extent positive, the vertical y-axis coordinates are reversed, and the positive y-axis points in the logical coordinate system are mapped to the negative y-axis in the device coordinate system. If both are positive or both are negative, positive logical coordinates are mapped to positive device coordinates and vice versa.

Note: When Isotropic mode is set, an application must call the *SetWindow-Ext* function before calling the *SetViewportExt* function.

Both of these functions are illustrated in the *MODES.C* program,below.

MODES.C

The *Modes.C* program illustrated in Figure 15-5 shows window sizes using the several mapping modes. The various modes are menu-selected while a second pop-up menu offers a choice of origin as upper-left, centered, or lower-right.

Text mode uses a default origin as upper-left, while the isotropic and anisotropic modes default as centered, and the remaining modes default to lower-right origin. However, in any mode any of the three origins can be selected from the menu and the coordinates shown will change accordingly.

The aspect dialog box is valid only with the isotropic or anisotropic modes, and is grayed out (not selectable) when any other modes are active. In either the isotropic or anisotropic modes, the window and viewport x and y aspects can be altered through the dialog box. If either the x or y viewport aspects are zero, the window settings will be used for the viewport values.

The complete source code for *Modes.C* appears with script files for the menu and dialog box resources. The dialog box for this demo application appears in Figure 15-5 at the lower right. The menu for *MODES* is not shown, but consists of three headers with two pop-up submenus. The third menu header, *Aspect,* calls the aspect dialog box, but is initially grayed out and is only validated (enabled) when the Isotropic or Anisotropic modes are selected.

Figure 15-5: Three Mapping Modes

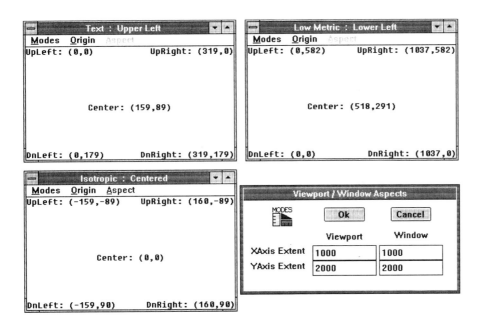

The dialog and menu resources for this application appear as script files, but can be easily created directly using the Resource Toolkit. An icon for the Modes application appears in Figure 15-5 in the dialog box but this, of course, is an optional element.

Summary

As an introduction to the Graphics Device Interface (GDI), demo applications show how device (hardware) information can be derived from the Windows device drivers, and how different mapping modes provide varying environments and resolutions for graphic calculation.

As a bonus, the Modes program also demonstrates two menu handling procedures as menu items are checked and unchecked according to selection.

The Aspects menu item is grayed out when not applicable, or enabled when relevant. In general, mapping modes will not be selected by the user, but will be set by the application according to the programmer's intentions. In like fashion, device information is not normally requested by an application, but is used by Windows in the normal course of transfering information to the output device(s). However, an understanding of how these mechanisms operate and what options are available can be useful in designing your applications.

Figure 15-6 shows the menu structure for the *Devices.C* demo application.

Figure 15-6: Menu for the Devices Demo Application

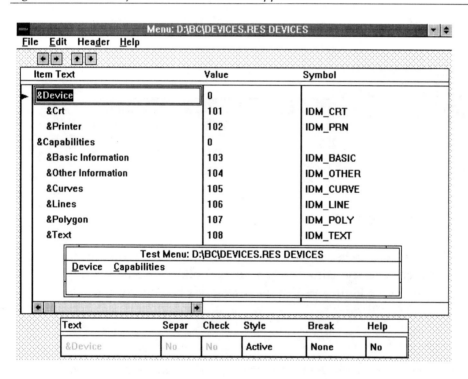

```
//===================================//
//              Devices.C            //
//    C++ Windows Device Capacity    //
//===================================//
```

```
#include <windows.h>
#include <string.h>
#include "devices.h"

typedef struct
{  int   nMask;
   char *szMask;
   char *szDscp;  }  BITS;

int  cxChr, cyChr;

void ListBasic( HDC hdc, HDC hDcInfo )
{
   static struct { int    nIdx;       char *szConst;
                   char *szDscp;   char *szNotes;  } info[] =
   { HORZSIZE,      "HORZSIZE",     "Width",         "(mm)",
     VERTSIZE,      "VERTSIZE",     "Height",        "(mm)",
     HORZRES,       "HORZRES",      "Width",       "(pixels)",
     VERTRES,       "VERTRES",      "Height",
                                      "(pixel/raster lines)",
     LOGPIXELSX,  "LOGPIXELSX",  "Pixels per inch",
                                              "(horz)",
     LOGPIXELSY,  "LOGPIXELSY",  "Pixels per inch",
                                              "(vert)",
     BITSPIXEL,     "BITSPIXEL",    "Color",   "(bits/pixel)",
     PLANES,        "PLANES",       "Color planes",     "",
     NUMBRUSHES,  "NUMBRUSHES",  "Device brushes",      "",
     NUMPENS,       "NUMPENS",      "Device pens",      "",
     NUMMARKERS,  "NUMMARKERS",  "Device markers",      "",
     NUMFONTS,      "NUMFONTS",     "Device fonts",     "",
     NUMCOLORS,     "NUMCOLORS",    "Device colors",    "",
     ASPECTX,       "ASPECTX",      "Pixel aspect", "(horz)",
     ASPECTY,       "ASPECTY",      "Pixel aspect", "(vert)",
     ASPECTXY,      "ASPECTXY",     "Pixel aspect", "(diag)",
     PDEVICESIZE, "PDEVICESIZE", "Device structure",
                                              "(size)",
     CLIPCAPS,      "CLIPCAPS",     "Clipping flag", "(T/F)",
//   Following three indexes valid only if device driver
//   sets the RC_PALETTE bit in the RASTERCAPS index and
//   available only if driver version is 3.0 or higher.
     SIZEPALETTE, "SIZEPALETTE", "Palette entries",    "",
     NUMRESERVED, "NUMRESERVED", "Palette entries",
                                            "(reserved)",
     COLORRES,      "COLORRES",     "Color resolution",  "",
   };
   char  szBuff[80];
```

```
    int    i, nLine;

    for( i=0; i<sizeof(info)/sizeof(info[0]); i++ )
        if( ( info[i].nIdx == SIZEPALETTE ) ||
            ( info[i].nIdx == NUMRESERVED ) ||
            ( info[i].nIdx == COLORRES ) )
            TextOut( hdc, cxChr, cyChr*(i+1), szBuff,
                sprintf( szBuff, "%17s:   n/a %20s | %s",
                        info[i].szDscp, "", info[i].szConst ) );
        else
            TextOut( hdc, cxChr, cyChr*(i+1), szBuff,
                sprintf( szBuff, "%17s: %5d %-20s | %s",
                        info[i].szDscp,
                        GetDeviceCaps( hDcInfo, info[i].nIdx ),
                        info[i].szNotes, info[i].szConst ) );
}

void ListOther( HDC hdc, HDC hDcInfo )
{
    static BITS raster[] =
    {
        RC_BANDING,         "RC_BANDING",
           "Requires banding support",
        RC_BITBLT,          "RC_BITBLT",  "bitmap transfer",
        RC_BITMAP64,        "RC_BITMAP64",
           "bitmaps larger than 64K",
        RC_DI_BITMAP,       "RC_DI_BITMAP",
           "SetDIBits and GetDIBits",
        RC_DIBTODEV,        "RC_DIBTODEV",  "SetDIBitsToDevice",
        RC_FLOODFILL,       "RC_FLOODFILL", "floodfill",
        RC_GDI2O_OUTPUT,    "RC_GDI2O_OUTPUT",
           "Windows 2.0 features",
        RC_PALETTE,         "RC_PALETTE", "Palette-based device",
        RC_SCALING,         "RC_SCALING", "scaling",
        RC_BIGFONT,         "RC_BIGFONT", "fonts larger than 64K",
        RC_STRETCHBLT,      "RC_STRETCHBLT",   "StretchBlt",
        RC_STRETCHDIB,      "RC_STRETCHDIB",    "StretchDIBits"
    };

    static char *szTech[] =
    { "Vector plotter (DT_PLOTTER)",
        "Raster display (DT_RASDISPLAY)",
        "Raster printer (DT_RASPRINTER)",
        "Raster camera (DT_RASCAMERA)",
        "Character stream (DT_CHARSTREAM)",
        "Metafile (DT_METAFILE)",
```

```
     "Display file (DT_DISPFILE)"              };

   char   szBuff[80];
   int    i, j = GetDeviceCaps( hDcInfo, DRIVERVERSION );

   TextOut( hdc, cxChr, cyChr, szBuff,
           sprintf( szBuff, "Driver Version: %2d.%02d",
                    HIBYTE(j), LOBYTE(j) ) );

   TextOut( hdc, cxChr, cyChr*2, szBuff,
      sprintf( szBuff, "   Technology: %s",
        szTech[ GetDeviceCaps( hDcInfo, TECHNOLOGY ) ] ) );
   TextOut( hdc, cxChr, cyChr*4, szBuff,
      sprintf( szBuff,
             "Raster capabilities (RASTERCAPS)" ) );
   for( i=0; i<sizeof(raster)/sizeof(raster[0]); i++ )
      if( ( raster[i].nMask == RC_BANDING ) ||
          ( raster[i].nMask == RC_PALETTE ) )
         TextOut( hdc, cxChr*4, cyChr*(i+6), szBuff,
            sprintf( szBuff, "[%c] %-34s | %s",
                     GetDeviceCaps( hDcInfo, RASTERCAPS ) &
                     raster[i].nMask ? 'X' : ' ',
                     raster[i].szDscp, raster[i].szMask ) );
      else
         TextOut( hdc, cxChr*4, cyChr*(i+6), szBuff,
            sprintf( szBuff, "[%c] Supports %-25s | %s",
                     GetDeviceCaps( hDcInfo, RASTERCAPS ) &
                     raster[i].nMask ? 'X' : ' ',
                     raster[i].szDscp, raster[i].szMask ) );
}

void ListText( HDC hdc, HDC hDcInfo )
{
   static BITS text[] =
   { TC_OP_CHARACTER, "TC_OP_CHARACTER",
       "Character output precision",
     TC_OP_STROKE,    "TC_OP_STROKE",
       "Stroke output precision",
     TC_CP_STROKE,    "TC_CP_STROKE",
       "Stroke clip precision",
     TC_CR_90,        "TC_CR_90",
       "90-degree char rotation",
     TC_CR_ANY,       "TC_CR_ANY",
       "Any character rotation",
     TC_SF_X_YINDEP,  "TC_SF_X_YINDEP",
       "Independent x / y scaling",
```

```
        TC_SA_DOUBLE,      "TC_SA_DOUBLE",
          "Doubled character scaling",
        TC_SA_INTEGER,     "TC_SA_INTEGER",
          "Integer multiple scaling",
        TC_SA_CONTIN,      "TC_SA_CONTIN",
          "Any multiples for exact scaling",
        TC_EA_DOUBLE,      "TC_EA_DOUBLE",
          "Double-weight characters",
        TC_IA_ABLE,        "TC_IA_ABLE",          "Italics",
        TC_UA_ABLE,        "TC_UA_ABLE",          "Underlining",
        TC_SO_ABLE,        "TC_SO_ABLE",          "Strikeouts",
        TC_RA_ABLE,        "TC_RA_ABLE",          "Raster fonts",
        TC_VA_ABLE,        "TC_VA_ABLE",          "Vector fonts"  };
    static char szBuff[80];
    int    i;

    TextOut( hdc, cxChr, cyChr, szBuff,
        sprintf( szBuff, "Text capabilities (TEXTCAPS)" ) );
    for( i=0; i<sizeof(text)/sizeof(text[0]); i++ )
        TextOut( hdc, cxChr, cyChr*(i+3), szBuff,
            sprintf( szBuff, "[%c] %-31s | %s",
                    GetDeviceCaps( hDcInfo, TEXTCAPS ) &
                        text[i].nMask ? 'X' : ' ',
                    text[i].szDscp, text[i].szMask ) );
}

void ListCurve( HDC hdc, HDC hDcInfo )
{
    static BITS curves[] =
    { CC_CIRCLES,        "CC_CIRCLES",          "circles",
      CC_PIE,            "CC_PIE",              "pie wedges",
      CC_CHORD,          "CC_CHORD",            "chord arcs",
      CC_ELLIPSES,       "CC_ELLIPSES",         "ellipses",
      CC_WIDE,           "CC_WIDE",             "wide borders",
      CC_STYLED,         "CC_STYLED",           "styled borders",
      CC_WIDESTYLED,     "CC_WIDESTYLED",
          "wide and styled borders",
      CC_INTERIORS,      "CC_INTERIORS",        "interiors"   };
    static char szBuff[80];
    int    i;

    TextOut( hdc, cxChr, cyChr, szBuff,
        sprintf( szBuff, "Curve capabilities (CURVECAPS)" ) );
    for( i=0; i<sizeof(curves)/sizeof(curves[0]); i++ )
        TextOut( hdc, cxChr, cyChr*(i+3), szBuff,
            sprintf( szBuff, "[%c] Supports %-23s | %s",
```

```
                         GetDeviceCaps( hDcInfo, CURVECAPS ) &
                             curves[i].nMask ? 'X' : ' ',
                         curves[i].szDscp, curves[i].szMask ) );
}

void ListLines( HDC hdc, HDC hDcInfo )
{
    static BITS lines[] =
    {   LC_POLYLINE,       "LC_POLYLINE",        "polylines",
        LC_MARKER,         "LC_MARKER",          "markers",
        LC_POLYMARKER,     "LC_POLYMARKER",      "polymarkers",
        LC_WIDE,           "LC_WIDE",            "wide lines",
        LC_STYLED,         "LC_STYLED",          "styled lines",
        LC_WIDESTYLED,     "LC_WIDESTYLED",
            "wide and styled lines",
        LC_INTERIORS,      "LC_INTERIORS",       "interiors:"   };
    static char szBuff[80];
    int    i;

    TextOut( hdc, cxChr, cyChr, szBuff,
        sprintf( szBuff, "Line Capabilities (LINECAPS)" ) );
    for( i=0; i<sizeof(lines)/sizeof(lines[0]); i++ )
        TextOut( hdc, cxChr, cyChr*(i+3), szBuff,
            sprintf( szBuff, "[%c] Supports %-22s | %s",
                GetDeviceCaps( hDcInfo, LINECAPS ) &
                    lines[i].nMask ? 'X' : ' ',
                lines[i].szDscp, lines[i].szMask ) );
}

void ListPoly( HDC hdc, HDC hDcInfo )
{
    static BITS poly[] =
    {   PC_POLYGON,        "PC_POLYGON",
            "alternate fill polygon",
        PC_RECTANGLE,      "PC_RECTANGLE",       "rectangle",
        PC_TRAPEZOID,      "PC_TRAPEZOID",
            "winding number fill polygon",
        PC_SCANLINE,       "PC_SCANLINE",        "scan lines",
        PC_WIDE,           "PC_WIDE",            "wide borders",
        PC_STYLED,         "PC_STYLED",          "styled borders",
        PC_WIDESTYLED,     "PC_WIDESTYLED",
            "wide and styled polygons",
        PC_INTERIORS,      "PC_INTERIORS",       "interiors"  };
    static char szBuff[80];
    int    i;

    TextOut( hdc, cxChr, cyChr, szBuff,
```

```
            sprintf( szBuff,
                "Polygonal capabilities (POLYGONALCAPS)" ) );
    for( i=0; i<sizeof(poly)/sizeof(poly[0]); i++ )
        TextOut( hdc, cxChr, cyChr*(i+3), szBuff,
            sprintf( szBuff, "[%c] Supports %-27s | %s",
                    GetDeviceCaps( hDcInfo, POLYGONALCAPS ) &
                        poly[i].nMask ? 'X' : ' ',
                    poly[i].szDscp, poly[i].szMask ) );
}

long FAR PASCAL WndProc( HWND hwnd,    WORD msg,
                         WORD wParam, LONG lParam )
{
    static    int    nCurDev = IDM_CRT, nCurInfo = IDM_BASIC;
    char            szPrn[64];
    char            *szDevice, *szDriver, *szOutPut;
    HDC             hdc, hdcInfo;
    HMENU           hMenu;
    PAINTSTRUCT     ps;
    TEXTMETRIC      tm;

    switch( msg )
    {
        case WM_CREATE:
            hdc = GetDC( hwnd );
            SelectObject( hdc,
                          GetStockObject( SYSTEM_FIXED_FONT ) );
            GetTextMetrics( hdc, &tm );
            cxChr = tm.tmAveCharWidth;
            cyChr = tm.tmHeight + tm.tmExternalLeading;
            ReleaseDC( hwnd, hdc );
            return(0);

        case WM_COMMAND:
            hMenu = GetMenu( hwnd );
            switch( wParam )
            {
                case IDM_CRT:      case IDM_PRN:
                    CheckMenuItem( hMenu, nCurDev, MF_UNCHECKED );
                    nCurDev = wParam;
                    CheckMenuItem( hMenu, nCurDev, MF_CHECKED );
                    InvalidateRect( hwnd, NULL, TRUE );
                    return(0);
                case IDM_BASIC:    case IDM_OTHER:
                case IDM_CURVE:    case IDM_LINE:
                case IDM_POLY:     case IDM_TEXT:
```

```
               CheckMenuItem( hMenu, nCurInfo,
                             MF_UNCHECKED );
               nCurInfo = wParam;
               CheckMenuItem( hMenu, nCurInfo, MF_CHECKED );
               InvalidateRect( hwnd, NULL, TRUE );
               return(0);
        } break;

   case WM_DEVMODECHANGE:
      InvalidateRect( hwnd, NULL, TRUE );
      return(0);

   case WM_PAINT:
      hdc = BeginPaint( hwnd, &ps );
      SelectObject( hdc,
                    GetStockObject( SYSTEM_FIXED_FONT ) );
      switch( nCurDev )
      {
         case IDM_CRT:
            hdcInfo = CreateIC( "DISPLAY",
                                 NULL, NULL, NULL );
            SetWindowText( hwnd, "Video Display" );
            break;
         case IDM_PRN:
            GetProfileString( "WINDOWS", "Device", "",
                               szPrn, sizeof( szPrn ) );
            if( ( szDevice = strtok( szPrn, "," ) ) &&
                ( szDriver = strtok( NULL,  "," ) ) &&
                ( szOutPut = strtok( NULL,  "," ) ) )
              hdcInfo = CreateIC( szDriver, szDevice,
                                   szOutPut, NULL );
            else hdcInfo = NULL;
            SetWindowText( hwnd, szPrn );
      }
      if( hdcInfo )
      {
         switch( nCurInfo )
         {
            case IDM_BASIC: ListBasic( hdc, hdcInfo );
                            break;
            case IDM_OTHER: ListOther( hdc, hdcInfo );
                            break;
            case IDM_TEXT:  ListText( hdc, hdcInfo );
                            break;
            case IDM_CURVE: ListCurve( hdc, hdcInfo );
                            break;
```

```
                   case IDM_LINE:   ListLines( hdc, hdcInfo );
                                    break;
                   case IDM_POLY:   ListPoly(  hdc, hdcInfo );
                                    break;
            }
            DeleteDC( hdcInfo );
        }
        EndPaint( hwnd, &ps );
        return(0);

    case WM_DESTROY:
        PostQuitMessage(0);
        return(0);
    }
    return( DefWindowProc( hwnd, msg, wParam, lParam ) );
}

#pragma argsused

int PASCAL WinMain( HANDLE hInstance, HANDLE hPrevInstance,
                    LPSTR  lpszCmdParam, int nCmdShow )
{
    static char szAppName[] = "DEVICES";
    HWND        hwnd;
    MSG         msg;
    WNDCLASS    wc;

    if( ! hPrevInstance )
    {
        wc.hInstance       = hInstance;
        wc.lpfnWndProc     = WndProc;
        wc.cbClsExtra      = 0;
        wc.cbWndExtra      = 0;
        wc.lpszClassName   = szAppName;
        wc.hIcon           = LoadIcon( hInstance, szAppName );
        wc.lpszMenuName    = (LPSTR) szAppName;
        wc.hCursor         = LoadCursor( NULL, IDC_ARROW );
        wc.hbrBackground   = GetStockObject( WHITE_BRUSH );
        wc.style           = CS_HREDRAW | CS_VREDRAW;
        RegisterClass( &wc );
    }
    hwnd = CreateWindow( szAppName,
                         "Hardware Device Capabilites",
                         WS_OVERLAPPEDWINDOW,
                         CW_USEDEFAULT, CW_USEDEFAULT,
                         CW_USEDEFAULT, CW_USEDEFAULT,
                         NULL, NULL, hInstance, NULL  );
```

```
    ShowWindow(    hwnd, nCmdShow );
    UpdateWindow( hwnd );
    while( GetMessage( &msg, NULL, 0, 0 ) )
    {
        TranslateMessage( &msg );
        DispatchMessage(  &msg );
    }
    return( msg.wParam );
}
```

```
                    ;===============;
                    ;  DEVICES.DEF  ;
                    ;===============;

NAME           DEVICES

DESCRIPTION    "DISPLAYS DEVICE CAPABILITIES"
EXETYPE        WINDOWS
STUB           "WINSTUB.EXE"
CODE           PRELOAD MOVEABLE DISCARDABLE
DATA           PRELOAD MOVEABLE MULTIPLE
HEAPSIZE       1024
STACKSIZE      8192
EXPORTS        WndProc
```

```
                    //=============//
                    // DEVICES.H  //
                    //=============//

#define   IDM_CRT        101
#define   IDM_PRN        102
#define   IDM_BASIC      103
#define   IDM_OTHER      104
#define   IDM_CURVE      105
#define   IDM_LINE       106
#define   IDM_POLY       107
#define   IDM_TEXT       108
```

```
                  //===================//
                  //       Modes.C     //
                  //  C++ Windows Modes //
                  //===================//

#include <windows.h>
#include <string.h>
#include "modes.h"
```

```
HANDLE   hInst;
int      XViewAspect, YViewAspect, XWinAspect, YWinAspect;

#pragma argsused

BOOL FAR PASCAL AspectProc( HWND hdlg,    WORD msg,
                            WORD wParam, LONG lParam )
{
    char szAspect[10];

    switch( msg )
    {
        case WM_INITDIALOG:
            sprintf( szAspect, "%d", XViewAspect );
            SendDlgItemMessage( hdlg, IDD_XVIEWASPECT,
                                EM_LIMITTEXT, 10, 0L );
            SetDlgItemText( hdlg, IDD_XVIEWASPECT, szAspect );
            sprintf( szAspect, "%d", YViewAspect );
            SendDlgItemMessage( hdlg, IDD_YVIEWASPECT,
                                EM_LIMITTEXT, 10, 0L );
            SetDlgItemText( hdlg, IDD_YVIEWASPECT, szAspect );
            sprintf( szAspect, "%d", XWinAspect );
            SendDlgItemMessage( hdlg, IDD_XWINASPECT,
                                EM_LIMITTEXT, 10, 0L );
            SetDlgItemText( hdlg, IDD_XWINASPECT, szAspect );
            sprintf( szAspect, "%d", YWinAspect );
            SendDlgItemMessage( hdlg, IDD_YWINASPECT,
                                EM_LIMITTEXT, 10, 0L );
            SetDlgItemText( hdlg, IDD_YWINASPECT, szAspect );
            return( TRUE );

        case WM_COMMAND:
            switch( wParam )
            {
                case IDOK:
                    GetDlgItemText( hdlg, IDD_XVIEWASPECT,
                                    szAspect, 10 );
                    XViewAspect = atoi( szAspect );
                    GetDlgItemText( hdlg, IDD_YVIEWASPECT,
                                    szAspect, 10 );
                    YViewAspect = atoi( szAspect );
                    GetDlgItemText( hdlg, IDD_XWINASPECT,
                                    szAspect, 10 );
                    XWinAspect = atoi( szAspect );
                    GetDlgItemText( hdlg, IDD_YWINASPECT,
                                    szAspect, 10 );
                    YWinAspect = atoi( szAspect );
```

```
                     EndDialog( hdlg, TRUE );
                     break;
                 case IDCANCEL:
                     EndDialog( hdlg, FALSE );
                     break;
                 default:  return( FALSE );
            }
        default: return( FALSE );
}  }

long FAR PASCAL WndProc( HWND hwnd,   WORD msg,
                         WORD wParam, LONG lParam )
{
    static  int  nCurOrg  = IDM_UPLEFT,
                 nCurMode = IDM_TEXT;
    static char *szCurMode[] =
                 { "Text", "Low Metric", "High Metric",
                   "Low English", "High English", "TWIPS",
                   "Isotropic", "Anisotropic" },
                *szCurOrg[]  =
                 { "Upper Left", "Lower Left", "Centered" };
    int          nBuff, xLeft, xRight, xCenter,
                 yTop, yBottom, yCenter, OrgDC,
                 cxChr, cyChr;
    char         szBuff[64];
    HDC          hdc, hdcInfo;
    HMENU        hMenu;
    DWORD        WinSize;
    RECT         rect;
    POINT        pt;
    PAINTSTRUCT  ps;
    TEXTMETRIC   tm;
    FARPROC      lpProc;

    switch( msg )
    {
       case WM_CREATE:
          sprintf( szBuff, "%s  :  %s",
                   szCurMode[nCurMode-IDM_TEXT],
                   szCurOrg[nCurOrg-IDM_UPLEFT] );
          SetWindowText( hwnd, szBuff );
          return(0);

       case WM_COMMAND:
          hMenu = GetMenu( hwnd );
          CheckMenuItem( hMenu, nCurMode, MF_UNCHECKED );
```

```
CheckMenuItem( hMenu, nCurOrg,  MF_UNCHECKED );
switch( wParam )
{
    case IDM_ASPECT:
        lpProc = MakeProcInstance( AspectProc,
                                   hInst );
        DialogBox( hInst, "ASPECT", hwnd, lpProc );
        FreeProcInstance( lpProc );
        break;

    case IDM_TEXT:
        EnableMenuItem( hMenu, IDM_ASPECT,
                        MF_GRAYED );
        DrawMenuBar( hwnd );
        nCurMode = wParam;
        nCurOrg  = IDM_UPLEFT;
        break;

    case IDM_TWIPS:
    case IDM_LOMETRIC:     case IDM_HIMETRIC:
    case IDM_LOENGLISH:    case IDM_HIENGLISH:
        EnableMenuItem( hMenu, IDM_ASPECT,
                        MF_GRAYED );
        DrawMenuBar( hwnd );
        nCurMode = wParam;
        nCurOrg  = IDM_DNLEFT;
        break;

    case IDM_ISOTROPIC:
    case IDM_ANISOTROPIC:
        EnableMenuItem( hMenu, IDM_ASPECT,
                        MF_ENABLED );
        DrawMenuBar( hwnd );
        nCurMode = wParam;
        nCurOrg  = IDM_CENTER;
        break;

    case IDM_UPLEFT:  nCurOrg = IDM_UPLEFT;  break;
    case IDM_DNLEFT:  nCurOrg = IDM_DNLEFT;  break;
    case IDM_CENTER:  nCurOrg = IDM_CENTER;  break;
}
InvalidateRect( hwnd, NULL, TRUE );
CheckMenuItem( hMenu, nCurMode, MF_CHECKED );
CheckMenuItem( hMenu, nCurOrg,  MF_CHECKED );
sprintf( szBuff, "%s  :  %s",
         szCurMode[nCurMode-IDM_TEXT],
         szCurOrg[nCurOrg-IDM_UPLEFT] );
```

```
    SetWindowText( hwnd, szBuff );
    return(0);

case WM_DEVMODECHANGE:
    InvalidateRect( hwnd, NULL, TRUE );
    return(0);

case WM_PAINT:
    hdc = BeginPaint( hwnd, &ps );
    SelectObject( hdc,
                    GetStockObject( SYSTEM_FIXED_FONT ) );
    GetTextMetrics( hdc, &tm );
    cxChr = tm.tmAveCharWidth;
    cyChr = tm.tmHeight + tm.tmExternalLeading;
    OrgDC = SaveDC( hdc );

    SetMapMode( hdc, nCurMode - IDM_TEXT + 1 );
    SetWindowOrg( hdc, 0, 0 );
    switch( nCurMode )
    {
        case IDM_ISOTROPIC:
        case IDM_ANISOTROPIC:
            SetWindowExt( hdc, XWinAspect, YWinAspect );
            if( XViewAspect && YViewAspect )
                SetViewportExt( hdc, XViewAspect,
                                        YViewAspect );
            else SetViewportExt( hdc, XWinAspect,
                                        YWinAspect );
            break;
    }
    GetClientRect( hwnd, &rect );
    DPtoLP( hdc, (LPPOINT) &rect, 2 );
    switch( nCurOrg )
    {
        case IDM_UPLEFT:
            SetWindowOrg( hdc, 0, 0 );
            break;
        case IDM_DNLEFT:
            SetWindowOrg( hdc, 0, -rect.bottom );
            break;
        case IDM_CENTER:
            SetWindowOrg( hdc,
                            -(rect.left+rect.right)/2,
                            -(rect.top+rect.bottom)/2 );
            break;
    }
```

```
        GetClientRect( hwnd, &rect );
        DPtoLP( hdc, (LPPOINT) &rect, 2 );
        xLeft   = rect.left;
        xRight  = rect.right;
        yTop    = rect.top;
        yBottom = rect.bottom;
        xCenter = ( xRight + xLeft ) / 2;
        yCenter = ( yTop + yBottom ) / 2;

        RestoreDC( hdc, OrgDC );
        GetClientRect( hwnd, &rect );
        DPtoLP( hdc, (LPPOINT) &rect, 2 );
        nBuff = sprintf( szBuff, "UpLeft: (%d,%d)",
                         xLeft, yTop);
        TextOut( hdc, rect.left, rect.top, szBuff, nBuff );

        nBuff = sprintf( szBuff, "DnLeft: (%d,%d)",
                         xLeft, yBottom );
        TextOut( hdc, rect.left, rect.bottom-cyChr,
                 szBuff, nBuff );

        nBuff = sprintf( szBuff, "Center: (%d,%d)",
                         xCenter, yCenter );
        TextOut( hdc, (rect.right-rect.left-nBuff*cxChr)/2,
                 (rect.bottom-rect.top)/2,
                 szBuff, nBuff );

        nBuff = sprintf( szBuff, "UpRight: (%d,%d)",
                         xRight, yTop);
        TextOut( hdc, rect.right-(nBuff*cxChr), rect.top,
                 szBuff, nBuff );

        nBuff = sprintf( szBuff, "DnRight: (%d,%d)",
                         xRight, yBottom );
        TextOut( hdc, rect.right-(nBuff*cxChr),
                 rect.bottom-cyChr, szBuff, nBuff );

        EndPaint( hwnd, &ps );
        return(0);

    case WM_DESTROY:
        PostQuitMessage(0);
        return(0);
    }
    return( DefWindowProc( hwnd, msg, wParam, lParam ) );
}
```

```
#pragma argsused

int PASCAL WinMain( HANDLE hInstance,    HANDLE hPrevInstance,
                    LPSTR  lpszCmdParam, int    nCmdShow )
{
    static char szAppName[] = "MODES";
    HWND        hwnd;
    MSG         msg;
    WNDCLASS    wc;

    XViewAspect = YViewAspect = 0;
    XWinAspect = 1000;
    YWinAspect = 2000;
    if( ! hPrevInstance )
    {
        wc.hInstance      = hInstance;
        wc.lpfnWndProc    = WndProc;
        wc.cbClsExtra     = 0;
        wc.cbWndExtra     = 0;
        wc.lpszClassName  = szAppName;
        wc.hIcon          = LoadIcon( hInstance, szAppName );
        wc.lpszMenuName   = (LPSTR) szAppName;
        wc.hCursor        = LoadCursor( NULL, IDC_ARROW );
        wc.hbrBackground  = GetStockObject( WHITE_BRUSH );
        wc.style          = CS_HREDRAW | CS_VREDRAW;
        RegisterClass( &wc );
    }
    hInst = hInstance;
    hwnd = CreateWindow( szAppName, "Mapping Modes",
                         WS_OVERLAPPEDWINDOW,
                         CW_USEDEFAULT, CW_USEDEFAULT,
                         CW_USEDEFAULT, CW_USEDEFAULT,
                         NULL, NULL, hInstance, NULL  );
    ShowWindow(  hwnd, nCmdShow );
    UpdateWindow( hwnd );
    while( GetMessage( &msg, NULL, 0, 0 ) )
    {
        TranslateMessage( &msg );
        DispatchMessage(  &msg );
    }
    return( msg.wParam );
}

                    ;==============;
                    ;  MODES.DEF  ;
                    ;==============;
```

```
NAME           MODES

DESCRIPTION    "WINDOWS MODES"
EXETYPE        WINDOWS
STUB           "WINSTUB.EXE"
CODE           PRELOAD MOVEABLE DISCARDABLE
DATA           PRELOAD MOVEABLE MULTIPLE
HEAPSIZE       1024
STACKSIZE      8192
EXPORTS        WndProc
               AspectProc
```

```
                //====================//
                //    D:\BC\MODES.H    //
                //====================//
```

```
#define    IDM_TEXT                201
#define    IDM_LOMETRIC            202
#define    IDM_HIMETRIC            203
#define    IDM_LOENGLISH           204
#define    IDM_HIENGLISH           205
#define    IDM_TWIPS               206
#define    IDM_ISOTROPIC           207
#define    IDM_ANISOTROPIC         208
#define    IDM_UPLEFT              301
#define    IDM_DNLEFT              302
#define    IDM_CENTER              303
#define    IDM_ASPECT              401
#define    IDD_XVIEWASPECT         501
#define    IDD_YVIEWASPECT         502
#define    IDD_XWINASPECT          503
#define    IDD_YWINASPECT          504
```

```
                //========================//
                //  MODES Dialog Script   //
                //========================//
```

```
ASPECT DIALOG DISCARDABLE LOADONCALL PURE MOVEABLE
   10, 34, 164, 72
STYLE WS_POPUP | WS_CAPTION | 0x80L
CAPTION "Viewport / Window Aspects"
BEGIN
   CONTROL "MODES"          0, "STATIC", WS_CHILD | WS_VISIBLE
      | 0x3L, 22, 5, 16, 16
   CONTROL "XAxis Extent" 0, "STATIC", WS_CHILD | WS_VISIBLE
      | 0x2L,  3, 36, 44, 12
   CONTROL "YAxis Extent" 0, "STATIC", WS_CHILD | WS_VISIBLE
```

```
           | 0x2L,    3, 48, 44, 12
    CONTROL "Viewport"      0, "STATIC", WS_CHILD | WS_VISIBLE
           | 0x1L,  53, 25, 49, 12
    CONTROL "Window"        0, "STATIC", WS_CHILD | WS_VISIBLE
           | 0x1L, 104, 24, 49, 12
    CONTROL "" 501, "EDIT", WS_CHILD | WS_VISIBLE | WS_BORDER
           | WS_TABSTOP,  53, 36, 49, 12
    CONTROL "" 502, "EDIT", WS_CHILD | WS_VISIBLE | WS_BORDER
           | WS_TABSTOP,  53, 48, 49, 12
    CONTROL "" 503, "EDIT", WS_CHILD | WS_VISIBLE | WS_BORDER
           | WS_TABSTOP, 104, 36, 49, 12
    CONTROL "" 504, "EDIT", WS_CHILD | WS_VISIBLE | WS_BORDER
           | WS_TABSTOP, 104, 48, 49, 12
    CONTROL "Ok"      1, "BUTTON", WS_CHILD | WS_VISIBLE
           | WS_TABSTOP,  62, 6, 31, 11
    CONTROL "Cancel" 2, "BUTTON", WS_CHILD | WS_VISIBLE
           | WS_TABSTOP, 113, 6, 31, 11
END


               //=======================//
               //   MODES Menu Script   //
               //=======================//

MODES   MENU LOADONCALL MOVEABLE PURE DISCARDABLE
BEGIN
  POPUP "&Modes"
  BEGIN
    MenuItem   "&Text",        201, CHECKED
    MenuItem   "&LoMetric",    202
    MenuItem   "&HiMetric",    203
    MenuItem   "L&oEnglish",   204
    MenuItem   "Hi&English",   205
    MenuItem   "T&wips",       206
    MenuItem   "&Isometric",   207
    MenuItem   "&Anisometric", 208
  END
  POPUP "&Origin"
  BEGIN
    MenuItem   "&Upper Left",  301, CHECKED
    MenuItem   "&Center",      303
    MenuItem   "&Lower Left",  302
  END
  MenuItem    "&Aspect",        401
END
```

Chapter 16

Colors In Windows

Colors in the Windows environment were discussed in part when we talked about device capabilities and how color information was organized by different device types. This previous discussion, however, was principally introductory and did not cover a number of topics that are integral to developing graphics in Windows. In this chapter, we will look at how color and drawing information are handled under Windows, beginning with how various devices handle color information.

For some devices, color information is organized by color planes, with each plane representing a specific primary color (red, blue, green), and each bit within a plane representing a single pixel. In this arrangement, a pixel's color is determined by a combination of the corresponding bits from the several color planes. In other cases, devices use a single color plane with adjacent bits representing the pixel color.

The *GetDeviceCaps* function is used to query the color planes and bits per pixel, as well as the number of colors supported :

```
nColorPlanes   = GetDeviceCaps( hdc,  PLANES );
nBitsPerPixel = GetDeviceCaps( hdc,  BITSPIXEL );
nColors        = GetDeviceCaps( hdc,  NUMCOLORS );
```

Since most devices use either multiple color planes or multiple color bits, in general a device will return either *nColorPlanes* or *nBitsPerPixel* as one. Table 16-1 shows the results reported for four devices.

Table 16-1: Device Color Capabilities

Device	VGA	8514A	LaserJet	Plotter
nColorPlanes	4	1	1	1
nBitsPerPixel	1	8	1	1
(calculated colors)	16	256	2	2
nColors	16	20	2	8

In theory, the device color capabilities (*nColors*) could be calculated as $2^{nColorPlanes * nBitsPerPixel}$, yielding a result of 16 for the VGA and two for the laser jet. However, for the 8514A monitor and the plotter, as you can readily see, the number of colors reported does not match the calculated result. So, what happened?

The discrepancy is not in the color planes or bits per pixel reported, both of which are accurate, but in the way colors are used. For instance, for the plotter only two colors can be drawn, the pen color or the background color. However, the device driver has reported that the plotter in question has a carousel of eight pens— which,when the paper color is included, makes the actual number of colors nine.

For the 8514A monitor, the 20 colors reported are those reserved for use by Windows, even though the remaining 236 colors can still be assigned and used by Windows programs.

Windows Colors vs Device Colors

The device color limitations are not necessarily limitations on colors that can be used by an application, because Windows will map colors or use dithering (patterns mixing pixels of pure colors) to represent colors which are not directly supported by the device. Thus, on a laserjet printer or a monochrome video, for example, video colors will be mapped to shades of gray. Or, on a VGA which supports on 16 "pure" colors, all other colors are dithered, using two or more supported colors in patterns of mixed pixels.

One good example of dithered colors is found in the Bitmap editor in the Resource Toolkit. The editor supplies a palette of 28 colors consisting of 16 "pure" colors on VGA, and 12 dithered colors. Further examples are shown in Figure 16-2, where the *Colors.C* program is used to demonstrate the full range of Windows colors, and in Figure 16-1 which shows how colors are dithered to supply hues and tones not directly supported by the display device.

Also, note that the colors provided by Windows do not correspond to the standard DOS color palettes. This means, in part, that images transported from Windows to DOS may appear very strange indeed.

Creating Colors

Individual colors in Windows are defined by a long integer (unsigned) in which the three bytes specify intensities of the primary colors: red, green and blue.

Under DOS, a similar arrangement is used, except that the primary colors are specified as flag bits, rather than ranges, and a fourth bit, intensity, is used to create both high and low versions of the eight basic colors.

In a CGA system only eight colors are supported, corresponding to the colors shown in Table 16-2.

Table 16-2: Comparing Color Specifications

color	Windows			DOS (CGA)		
	r	g	b	r	g	b
Black	0	0	0	0	0	0
Blue	0	0	255	0	0	1
Green	0	255	0	0	1	0
Cyan	0	255	255	0	1	1
Red	255	0	0	1	0	0
Magenta	255	0	255	1	0	1
Yellow	255	255	0	1	1	0
White	255	255	255	1	1	1

In an EGA system, a fourth bit is added for intensity, changing the eight principal colors into a 16-color palette with high and low intensity (light and dark) versions of each.

In VGA systems, six flag bits are used, providing one intensity bit for each primary color and supporting a basic palette of sixteen colors. VGA systems, however, are capable of far more than sixteen colors; the Windows device drivers recognize this capacity and use an actual color palette quite different from the standard (DOS) VGA palette.

The actual values for the standard palette(s) under Windows—or names for the corresponding colors—are not important, because any application can redefine colors as desired. Thus, under Windows, several hundred yellows can be defined by varying the relative values of red, green, and blue, while keeping the red and green in the same general range, and keeping the blue value small.

Dithered Colors

In theory, Windows supports 256^3 hues of color, over 16 million shades. However, since few monitors are actually capable of quite such fine color resolution, Windows adapts colors to the device capabilities by displaying selected colors as "dithered" colors, in which an 8x8 grid of "pure" colors simulate the hue desired.

Figure 16-1 shows four dithered colors, three of which are shades of pure red, pure blue, and pure green. On a VGA system, the shading is accomplished by mixing red and dark red, blue and dark blue, and green and dark green. The numerical value shown for each bitmap is the 0..255 value identifying the specific color.

Figure 16-1: Four Dithered Colors (enlarged pixel maps)

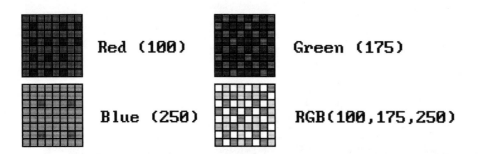

The fourth pixel map is the color generated when the preceding three color values are combined by using the RGB macro to produce a single screen color, a shade of "cloud blue". The 8x8 pixel map shown consists of 23 white pixels (≈36%), 19 light cyan pixels (≈30%), 18 light blue pixels (≈28%) and four dark gray pixels (≈6%). This is only one of literally hundreds of shades of blue . Darker shades of the same color tone could be generated as *RGB(75,150,225)*, *RGB(50,125,200)*, *RGB(25,100,175)*, etc., with 72 other shades falling between the lightest and darkest examples cited.

The *Colors.C* program demonstrates how values for red, green, and blue are combined to yield a Windows color. The four pixel grids shown in Figure 16-1 were derived directly from the default settings in *Color.C* as shown on a VGA monitor.

Colors.C

The *Colors.C* program provides three scrollbars (Figure 16-2) to adjust the red, green, and blue color values that define the background color shown in the lower portion of the client window. Each of these scrollbars can be adjusted for any value from 0 to 255. While the scrollbars themselves show individual red, green, or blue densities, the bottom of the client window background shows the color generated by the combined RGB values.

Figure 16-2:   Creating Colors

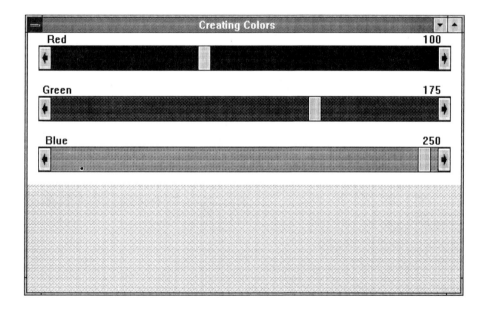

In actual applications when a feature is desired for permit the user to adjust colors interactively in a fashion similiar to Color.C demonstration, a more reasonable approach would be to use a pop-up dialog window rather than employing the main client window for the controls and display. And, using this suggested approach, the pop-up could be created as a dialog box via the Resource Toolkit instead of directly invoking scrollbar creation functions as shown in *Colors.C.*

Still, while more convenient, using WRT to create a dialog box does not absolve the application from setting scrollbar ranges and handling scrollbar events as well as setting the color values both for the individual and resultant colors. Most of the handling demonstrated, however, will be applicable to most scrollbar controls.

Custom Brushes

Adjusting the background color to show color changes is relatively simple,and is accomplished by creating a new brush with the desired color. But before creating a new brush object, the existing brush object should be deleted, as shown here:

```
DeleteObject( GetClassWord( hwnd, GCW_HBRBACKGROUND ) );
SetClassWord( hwnd, GCW_HBRBACKGROUND,
              CreateSolidBrush(
                RGB( CVal[0],CVal[1],CVal[2] ) ) );
InvalidateRect( hwnd, NULL, TRUE );
```

First, *GetClassWord* is called to return a handle to the existing brush, which is then deleted. But before *SetClassWord* creates the new brush object, the *RGB* macro is required to convert the three red, green, and blue values into a single unsigned long integer.

For the scrollbar colors—to make the scrollbars match their individual color settings—a similar operation is used, except that only one of the three color values are set:

```
case WM_CTLCOLOR:
    if( HIWORD( lParam ) == CTLCOLOR_SCROLLBAR )
    {
        i = GetWindowWord( LOWORD( lParam ), GWW_ID );
        DeleteObject( hBrush[i] );
        switch( i )
        {
            case 0: RGBcolor = RGB(CVal[0],0,0); break;
            case 1: RGBcolor = RGB(0,CVal[1],0); break;
            case 2: RGBcolor = RGB(0,0,CVal[2]); break;
        }
```

```
        hBrush[i] = CreateSolidBrush( RGBcolor );
        UnrealizeObject( hBrush[i] );
        return( (DWORD) hBrush[i] );
    }
    break;
```

This operation is executed in response to the *WM_CTLCOLOR* message that is sent by Windows to the parent window of a predefined control or message box when the control or message box is about to be drawn (or redrawn).

The *wParam* value is a handle to display context for the child window and the low-order word (*LOWORD(lParam)*) contains the child window handle while the high-order word (*HIWORD(lParam)*) identifies the control object type as shown in Table 16-3:

Table 16-3: Control Type Identifiers

Value	Control Type
CTLCOLOR_BTN	Button control
CTLCOLOR_DLG	Dialog box
CTLCOLOR_EDIT	Edit control
CTLCOLOR_LISTBOX	List-box control
CTLCOLOR_MSGBOX	Message box
CTLCOLOR_SCROLLBAR	Scroll-bar control
CTLCOLOR_STATIC	Static control

As demonstrated here, this *CTLCOLOR_xxxx* value is useful, when an application needs to intercept redisplay instructions for specific control elements. Alternately, if no specific response is provided to the *WM_CTRLCOLOR* message, as in all previous examples, the DefWindowProc function selects the default system colors.

UnrealizeObject

The *UnrealizeObject* function is called with a handle to an object. If the handle specifies a brush object, the GDI is directed to reset the origin of the brush when next selected. However, a brush specified by the *hObject* parameter must not be the currently selected brush of any display context.

There is a conflict in documentation concerning this function, with some documentation cautioning that when processing the *WM_CTLCOLOR* message, the application must align the origin of the intended brush with the window coordinates by first calling the *UnrealizeObject* function for the brush, and then setting the brush origin to the upper-left corner of the window. UnrealizeObject must also be called whenever a new brush origin is set (by means of the *SetBrushOrg* function). However, the default brush origin is always the upper-left corner of the window (0,0), and does not normally require resetting.

Alternately, *UnrealizeObject* is also used with logical palettes, instructing the GDI to remap the logical palette to the system palette. A palette specified by the object handled can be the currently selected palette of a display context. Caution: The *UnrealizeObject* function should not be used with stock objects.

Normally, return values from functions can be used or ignored as desired, but if an application processes the *WM_CTLCOLOR* message, it must return a handle to the brush that is to be used for painting the control background. Failure to return a valid brush handle will place the system in an unstable state.

Destroying Brushes When Finished

During the execution of this example program, a number of brushes have been created and destroyed, but when operations are finished (i.e., when the *WM_DESTROY* message is received), provisions are needed to destroy these brushes:

```
case WM_DESTROY:
    DeleteObject( GetClassWord( hwnd,
                               GCW_HBRBACKGROUND ) );
    for( i=0; i<=2; i++ ) DeleteObject( hBrush[i] );
    PostQuitMessage(0);
    return(0);
}
```

In previous examples only stock brushes were used, and no provisions were required for destroying custom brushes before the application exited. Each of these custom brushes, however, does require some memory, and if the brush is not deleted prior to exit, it will continue to occupy memory space.

Using Dithered Colors

While dithered colors extend the range of available colors beyond the default palettes, there are some limitations on how dithered colors can be used.

As explained, dithered colors are based on an eight-by-eight pixel array to simulate color hues which are not directly supported. As such, dithered colors can be used for area fill, but cannot be used for pixel drawing operations such as *SetPixel*, or for line drawing operations such as *LineTo* or *LineRel*.

Instead, for pixel or line operations, the *GetNearestColor* function can be used to return the closest pure color supported. *GetNearestColor* is called as:

```
rgbPureColor = GetNearestColor( hdc, rgbDitherredColor );
```

In normal circumstances, of course, Windows will handle this conversion automatically. If necessary, an application can query the device context (*hdc*) for the nearest pure color value.

Colors and Drawing Modes

In conventional DOS graphics, a drawn line simply replaced or wrote over existing screen pixels with a drawing color. In Windows, however, multiple drawing modes are supported in which, again using a line for an example, the line image is combined with the background (existing) image in a variety of fashions.

This type of operation is referred to as a bitwise boolean operation or, in Windows, as a "raster operation", commonly abbreviated as "ROP". Because line operations involve two pixel patterns, the line and the screen display, these are referred to as "ROP2" operations and, in *Windows.H*, sixteen ROP2 operations are defined as shown in Table 16-4.

Table 16-4: Binary Raster Operations

Boolean Mode Constant	(S = Screen P = Pen) Operation	Image Resulting
R2_COPYPEN	P	pen overwrites screen (default)
R2_NOP	S	screen not affected
R2_NOTCOPYPEN	~P	pen inverted
R2_NOT	~S	screen inverted
R2_MASKPEN	P & S	pen ANDed with screen
R2_MASKNOTPEN	~P & S	inverted pen ANDed with screen

Table 16-4: Binary Raster Operations (cont.)

Boolean	(S = Screen	P = Pen)
Mode Constant	Operation	Image Resulting
R2_MASKPENNOT	P & ~S	pen ANDed with inverted screen
R2_NOTMASKPEN	~(P & S)	pen ANDed with screen, result inverted
R2_MERGEPEN	P I S	pen ORed with screen
R2_MERGENOTPEN	~P I S	inverted pen ORed with screen
R2_MERGEPENNOT	*P I ~S*	*pen ORed with inverted screen*
R2_NOTMERGEPEN	~(P I S)	pen ORed with screen, result inverted
R2_XORPEN	P ^ S	pen XORed with screen
R2_NOTXORPEN	~(P ^ S 0)	pen XORed with screen, result inverted
R2_BLACK	0	black line (drawing color ignored)
R2_WHITE	1	white line (drawing color ignored)

The first ROP2 mode shown, *R2_COPYPEN*, is the default mode in which the pen simply overwrites the existing screen, and rewrites screen pixels using the current drawing color. This corresponds to the default DOS drawing mode as well.

The next mode listed, *R2_NOP*, does not affect the screen at all, but is still useful since the current position is still updated by a *LineTo* or *LineRel* operation.

The *R2_NOT* mode insures absolute visibility by simply inverting the existing screen image. Of course, the effectiveness varies according to the screen color, and if the existing screen is roughly 50% gray, the inversion may not be visible.

Rather than attempting to describe all possible interactions, however, Figure 16-3 shows a typical display produced by the *PenDraw.C* demo application where lines are drawn in blue, using all sixteen modes, against a background of both gray-scaled and color panels. The screen illustrated was created by the *PenDraw* demo, which allows selection of pen color from the menu, then draws lines across the background using each of the sixteen drawing modes. The order in which the lines are drawn does not correspond to the listings preceding Table 16-3: instead it follows the value order of the mode constants.

Summary

Colors in the Windows environment are introduced briefly here and will be discussed further. For the moment, two demo programs are provided, which permit further experimentation. However, lines and color selections are only a part of graphics operations, and more sophisticated capabilities will be examined in subsequent chapters.

Figure 16-3: Binary Raster Operations

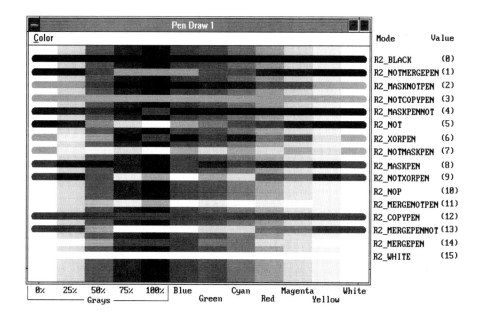

```
//======================//
//        Colors.C       //
//     Windows Colors    //
//======================//

#include <windows.h>
#include <stdlib.h>

#define   CHILD_STYLE    WS_CHILD | WS_VISIBLE

FARPROC   lpScrlFnc[3];
HWND      hwndScrl[3], hwndTag[3], hwndVal[3], hwndRect;
int       nFocus, CVal[3] = { 100, 175, 250 };
char      szBuff[10];

long FAR PASCAL KeybdProc( HWND hwnd,   WORD msg,
```

```
                                    WORD wParam, LONG lParam )
{
    int i = GetWindowWord( hwnd, GWW_ID );

    switch( msg )
    {
        case WM_KEYDOWN:
            if( wParam == VK_TAB )
            {
                if( GetKeyState( VK_SHIFT ) ) i;
                                        else i++;
                if( i < 0 ) i = 2;
                else if( i > 2 ) i = 0;
                SetFocus( hwndScrl[ i % 3 ] );
            } break;
        case WM_SETFOCUS:  nFocus = i;  break;
    }
    return( CallWindowProc( lpScrlFnc[i], hwnd, msg,
                            wParam, lParam ) );
}

long FAR PASCAL WndProc( HWND hwnd,   WORD msg,
                         WORD wParam, LONG lParam )
{
    static HBRUSH   hBrush[3];
    HDC             hdc;
    long            RGBcolor;
    int             i, cxWnd, cyWnd, cyChr, cxChr, vSize;
    TEXTMETRIC      tm;

    switch( msg )
    {
        case WM_CREATE:
            hBrush[0] = CreateSolidBrush( RGB( CVal[0],0,0 ) );
            hBrush[1] = CreateSolidBrush( RGB( 0,CVal[1],0 ) );
            hBrush[2] = CreateSolidBrush( RGB( 0,0,CVal[2] ) );
            return(0);

        case WM_SIZE:
            cxWnd = LOWORD( lParam );
            vSize = HIWORD( lParam ) / 5;
            hdc = GetDC( hwnd );
            GetTextMetrics( hdc, &tm );
            cyChr = tm.tmHeight;
            cxChr = tm.tmAveCharWidth;
            ReleaseDC( hwnd, hdc );
            for( i=0; i<=2; i++ )
```

```
         {
             vSize = i*cyChr*4;
             MoveWindow( hwndTag[i],  2*cxChr,        vSize,
                         cxChr*7,        cyChr, TRUE );
             MoveWindow( hwndVal[i],  cxWnd-9*cxChr, vSize,
                         cxChr*7,        cyChr, TRUE );
             MoveWindow( hwndScrl[i], 2*cxChr, vSize+cyChr,
                         cxWnd-4*cxChr, 2*cyChr, TRUE );
         }
         MoveWindow( hwndRect, 0, 0,
                     cxWnd, vSize+4*cyChr, TRUE );
         SetFocus( hwnd );
         return(0);

    case WM_SETFOCUS:
         SetFocus( hwndScrl[ nFocus ] );
         return(0);

    case WM_HSCROLL:
         i = GetWindowWord( HIWORD( lParam ), GWW_ID );
         switch( wParam )
         {
             case SB_PAGEDOWN:
                 CVal[i] += 15;                   // no break!
             case SB_LINEDOWN:
                 CVal[i]  = min( 255, CVal[i]+1 );  break;
             case SB_PAGEUP:
                 CVal[i] -= 15;                   // no break!
             case SB_LINEUP:
                 CVal[i]  = max(   0, CVal[i]-1 );  break;
             case SB_TOP:
                 CVal[i]  =   0;                     break;
             case SB_BOTTOM:
                 CVal[i]  = 255;                     break;
             case SB_THUMBPOSITION:
             case SB_THUMBTRACK:
                 CVal[i] = LOWORD( lParam );         break;
             default:                               break;
         }
         SetScrollPos( hwndScrl[i], SB_CTL, CVal[i], TRUE );
         SetWindowText( hwndVal[i],
                        itoa( CVal[i], szBuff, 10 ) );
         DeleteObject( GetClassWord( hwnd,
                       GCW_HBRBACKGROUND ) );
         SetClassWord( hwnd, GCW_HBRBACKGROUND,
                       CreateSolidBrush(
```

```
                              RGB( CVal[0],CVal[1],CVal[2] ) ) );
            InvalidateRect( hwnd, NULL, TRUE );
            return(0);

      case WM_CTLCOLOR:
         if( HIWORD( lParam ) == CTLCOLOR_SCROLLBAR )
         {
            i = GetWindowWord( LOWORD( lParam ), GWW_ID );
            DeleteObject( hBrush[i] );
            switch( i )
            {
               case 0: RGBcolor = RGB(CVal[0],0,0); break;
               case 1: RGBcolor = RGB(0,CVal[1],0); break;
               case 2: RGBcolor = RGB(0,0,CVal[2]); break;
            }
            hBrush[i] = CreateSolidBrush( RGBcolor );
            UnrealizeObject( hBrush[i] );
            return( (DWORD) hBrush[i] );
         }
         break;

      case WM_DESTROY:
         DeleteObject( GetClassWord( hwnd,
                              GCW_HBRBACKGROUND ) );
         for( i=0; i<=2; i++ ) DeleteObject( hBrush[i] );
         PostQuitMessage(0);
         return(0);
   }
   return( DefWindowProc( hwnd, msg, wParam, lParam ) );
}

#pragma argsused

int PASCAL WinMain( HANDLE hInst, HANDLE hPrevInst,
                    LPSTR  lpCmd, int     nCmdShow )
{
   static char szAppName[] = "COLORS";
   static char *szColorLabel[] = { "Red", "Green", "Blue" };
   FARPROC     lpKeybdProc;
   HWND        hwnd;
   MSG         msg;
   int         i;
   WNDCLASS    wc;

   if( ! hPrevInst )
   {
      wc.hInstance       = hInst;
```

```
   wc.lpfnWndProc    = WndProc;
   wc.cbClsExtra     = 0;
   wc.cbWndExtra     = 0;
   wc.lpszClassName  = szAppName;
   wc.hIcon          = LoadIcon( hInst, szAppName );
   wc.lpszMenuName   = (LPSTR) szAppName;
   wc.hCursor        = LoadCursor( NULL, IDC_ARROW );
   wc.hbrBackground  = CreateSolidBrush(
                         RGB(CVal[0],CVal[1],CVal[2] ) );
   wc.style          = CS_HREDRAW | CS_VREDRAW;
   RegisterClass( &wc );
}
hwnd = CreateWindow( szAppName, "Creating Colors",
         WS_OVERLAPPEDWINDOW | WS_CLIPCHILDREN,
         CW_USEDEFAULT, CW_USEDEFAULT,
         CW_USEDEFAULT, CW_USEDEFAULT,
         NULL, NULL, hInst, NULL  );
hwndRect = CreateWindow( "static", NULL,
                         CHILD_STYLE | SS_WHITERECT,
                         0, 0, 0, 0,
                         hwnd, 10, hInst, NULL );
lpKeybdProc = MakeProcInstance( (FARPROC) KeybdProc,
                                hInst );
for( i=0; i<=2; i++ )
{
   hwndScrl[i] = CreateWindow( "scrollbar", NULL,
                  CHILD_STYLE | WS_TABSTOP | SBS_HORZ,
                  0, 0, 0, 0, hwnd, i,   hInst, NULL );
   hwndTag[i]  = CreateWindow( "static",
                  szColorLabel[i],
                  CHILD_STYLE | SS_CENTER,
                  0, 0, 0, 0, hwnd, i+4, hInst, NULL );
   hwndVal[i]  = CreateWindow( "static",
                  itoa( CVal[i], szBuff, 10 ),
                  CHILD_STYLE | SS_CENTER,
                  0, 0, 0, 0, hwnd, i+7, hInst, NULL );
   lpScrlFnc[i] = (FARPROC) GetWindowLong( hwndScrl[i],
                                           GWL_WNDPROC );
   SetWindowLong( hwndScrl[i], GWL_WNDPROC,
                  (LONG) lpKeybdProc );
   SetScrollRange( hwndScrl[i], SB_CTL, 0, 255, FALSE );
   SetScrollPos(   hwndScrl[i], SB_CTL, CVal[i], FALSE );
}
ShowWindow(   hwnd, nCmdShow );
UpdateWindow( hwnd );
while( GetMessage( &msg, NULL, 0, 0 ) )
```

```
        {
            TranslateMessage( &msg );
            DispatchMessage(  &msg );
        }
        return( msg.wParam );
    }



                    ;==============;
                    ;  COLORS.DEF  ;
                    ;==============;

NAME            COLORS

DESCRIPTION     "Creating Colors"
EXETYPE         WINDOWS
STUB            "WINSTUB.EXE"
CODE            PRELOAD MOVEABLE DISCARDABLE
DATA            PRELOAD MOVEABLE MULTIPLE
HEAPSIZE        1024
STACKSIZE       8192
EXPORTS         WndProc
                KeybdProc



                //======================//
                //        PenDraw.C      //
                //   C++ Windows Drawing //
                //======================//

#include <windows.h>
#include <string.h>
#include "pendraw.h"

long FAR PASCAL WndProc( HWND hwnd,   WORD msg,
                         WORD wParam, LONG lParam )
{
    static COLORREF lpColor[8] =
                    { RGB(   0,   0,   0 ),      // Black   //
                      RGB(   0,   0, 255 ),      // Blue    //
                      RGB(   0, 255,   0 ),      // Green   //
                      RGB(   0, 255, 255 ),      // Cyan    //
                      RGB( 255,   0,   0 ),      // Red     //
                      RGB( 255,   0, 255 ),      // Magenta //
                      RGB( 255, 255,   0 ),      // Yellow  //
```

```
                    RGB( 255, 255, 255 ) };      // White   //
static   int    nColor = IDM_BLACK;
HDC             hdc;
HMENU           hMenu;
HBRUSH          hBrush;
HPEN            hPen;
PAINTSTRUCT     ps;
RECT            rect;
int             i, j, nMode, HUnits = 60, VUnits = 18;

switch( msg )
{
   case WM_COMMAND:
      hMenu = GetMenu( hwnd );
      CheckMenuItem( hMenu, nColor, MF_UNCHECKED );
      nColor = wParam;
      CheckMenuItem( hMenu, nColor, MF_CHECKED );
      InvalidateRect( hwnd, NULL, FALSE );
      return(0);

   case WM_PAINT:
      hdc = BeginPaint( hwnd, &ps );
      SetMapMode( hdc, MM_ANISOTROPIC );
      GetClientRect( hwnd, &rect );
      SetViewportExt( hdc, rect.right, rect.bottom );
      SetWindowExt( hdc, HUnits, VUnits );

          // Stock Brush Backgrounds //
      for( i=0; i<5; i++ )
      {
         SetRect( &rect, i*5, 0, i*5+5, VUnits );
         FillRect( hdc, &rect, GetStockObject( i ) );
      }
      i*=5;

          // Color Bar Backgrounds //
      for( j=1; j<8; j++ )
      {
         hBrush = CreateSolidBrush( lpColor[ j ] );
         SetRect( &rect, j*5+i-5, 0, j*5+i, VUnits );
         FillRect( hdc, &rect, hBrush );
      }

            // Line Draw Modes //
      for( nMode=R2_BLACK; nMode<=R2_WHITE; nMode++ )
      {
         hPen = CreatePen( PS_SOLID, 1,
```

```
                                  lpColor[nColor-IDM_BLACK] );
            SetROP2( hdc, nMode );
            SelectObject( hdc, hPen );
            MoveTo( hdc, 1, nMode );
            LineTo( hdc, HUnits-1, nMode );
        }

        EndPaint( hwnd, &ps );
        DeleteObject( hPen );
        return(0);

    case WM_DESTROY:
        PostQuitMessage(0);
        return(0);
    }
    return( DefWindowProc( hwnd, msg, wParam, lParam ) );
}

#pragma argsused

int PASCAL WinMain( HANDLE hInstance, HANDLE hPrevInstance,
                    LPSTR  lpszCmdParam, int     nCmdShow )
{
    static char szAppName[] = "PENDRAW";
    HWND        hwnd;
    MSG         msg;
    WNDCLASS    wc;

    if( ! hPrevInstance )
    {
        wc.hInstance      = hInstance;
        wc.lpfnWndProc    = WndProc;
        wc.cbClsExtra     = 0;
        wc.cbWndExtra     = 0;
        wc.lpszClassName  = szAppName;
        wc.hIcon          = LoadIcon( hInstance, szAppName );
        wc.lpszMenuName   = (LPSTR) szAppName;
        wc.hCursor        = LoadCursor( NULL, IDC_ARROW );
        wc.hbrBackground  = GetStockObject( WHITE_BRUSH );
        wc.style          = CS_HREDRAW | CS_VREDRAW;
        RegisterClass( &wc );
    }
    hwnd = CreateWindow( szAppName, "Pen Draw 1",
                         WS_OVERLAPPEDWINDOW,
                         CW_USEDEFAULT, CW_USEDEFAULT,
                         CW_USEDEFAULT, CW_USEDEFAULT,
                         NULL, NULL, hInstance, NULL  );
```

```
    ShowWindow(    hwnd, nCmdShow );
    UpdateWindow( hwnd );
    while( GetMessage( &msg, NULL, 0, 0 ) )
    {
        TranslateMessage( &msg );
        DispatchMessage(  &msg );
    }
    return( msg.wParam );
}
```

```
                    ;===============;
                    ;  PENDRAW.DEF  ;
                    ;===============;

NAME           PENDRAW

DESCRIPTION    "DRAWING WITH PENS"
EXETYPE        WINDOWS
STUB           "WINSTUB.EXE"
CODE           PRELOAD MOVEABLE DISCARDABLE
DATA           PRELOAD MOVEABLE MULTIPLE
HEAPSIZE       1024
STACKSIZE      8192
EXPORTS        WndProc
```

```
                    //=============//
                    // PenDraw.H  //
                    //=============//

#define   IDM_BLACK      300
#define   IDM_BLUE       301
#define   IDM_GREEN      302
#define   IDM_CYAN       303
#define   IDM_RED        304
#define   IDM_MAGENTA    305
#define   IDM_YELLOW     306
#define   IDM_WHITE      307
```

```
                    //======================//
                    // PenDraw Menu Resource //
                    //======================//

PENDRAW   MENU LOADONCALL MOVEABLE PURE DISCARDABLE
BEGIN
  POPUP "&Color"
  BEGIN
```

```
        MenuItem   "&Black",     300, CHECKED
        MenuItem   "B&lue",      301
        MenuItem   "&Green",     302
        MenuItem   "&Cyan",      303
        MenuItem   "&Red",       304
        MenuItem   "&Magenta",   305
        MenuItem   "&Yellow",    306
        MenuItem   "&White",     307
    END
END
```

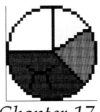

Chapter 17

Drawing Shapes And Figures

An old adage holds that a picture is worth a thousand words. While this adage has been disputed, picked at, and supported in a thousand philosophies as well as used, misused, and outright subverted by everyone from Madison Avenue to political demagogues to would be-tyrants, the truth remains that a picture is, more often than not, preferred to a thousand words.

Frequently in computer applications, the pictures in question are graphics—pictures composed of relatively simple shapes such as bar or pie graphs, flow charts, diagrams or schematic outlines generated by an application to illustrate non-pictorial information—or to bitmapped pictures such as icons or the "wallpaper" bitmaps provided as the background screens in Windows operations in 386 Protected mode. (This is not to belittle bitmapped images. They have their own purposes and also may be usefully combined with graphic images. Bitmapped images, however, will be covered in Chapter 18.)

For the present, the topic will be creating graphic images based on application instructions and/or data internal or external to the application. However, before creating an application, the first step is a look at the tools available.

Graphic Tools

Windows' colors and line drawing modes were introduced in Chapter 16, but Windows also supplies a variety of other drawing features, including standard shapes, line styles, and fill styles.

Beginning with shapes for drawing figures, which may be solid or outlined, Windows provides support with a series of eight functions to create the standard shapes listed in Table 17-1.

Table 17-1: Standard Figures

Function	Shape
Rectangle	rectangle with squared corners
RoundRect	rectangle with rounded corners
Polygon	multisided figure
PolyPolygon	multiple multisided figures
Arc	an open curve
Chord	an arc with the endpoints connected by a chord
Ellipse	ellipse or circle
Pie	pie wedge based on ellipse

Five of these eight figure functions will be demonstrated in the *PenDraw2.C* program; the *Polygon* and *PolyPolygon* functions will be covered later. However, before creating figures, there are also six line (pen) styles defined.

Logical Pens

All shapes are drawn using the current logical pen. The default pen, if no other pen has been created, is a solid black line with a width of one logical unit.

Logical pens (and logical brushes) can be created and selected in two separate steps, as:

```
hPen = CreatePen( nPenStyle,
                  nPenWidth,
                  RGBColor );
SelectObject( hdc, hPen );
```

Or these can be combined in a single step as:

```
hPen = SelectObject( hdc,
        CreatePen( nPenStyle,
                  nPenWidth,
                  RGBcolor ) );
```

The *CreatePen* function specifies the style, width, and color of the custom pen and returns a handle to the new logical pen. The SelectObject function associates a pen or brush with the device context: i.e., makes a specific logical pen (or brush) the currently active drawing object. More than one logical pen and/or brush can be created at any time by using an array of handles and then selecting as needed via the *SelectObject* function. Each logical pen or logical brush created, however, consumes memory, and when no longer in use, should be disposed of via the *DeleteObject* function called as:

```
DeleteObject( hPen );
```

This deletes the logical object from memory. However, a created pen or brush should not be deleted while associated with a device context—unless, of course, the device context is about to be closed.

The pen styles are defined in *Windows.H* and also appear in Appendix A at the end of this book.

Table 17-2: Redefined Pen (Line) Styles

Style ID	Line Type
PS_SOLID	———
PS_DASH	– – – –
PS_DOT	. . . . . .
PS_DASHDOT	–.–.–.–
PS_DASH2DOT	–..–..–..
PS_NULL	none
PS_INSIDEFRAME	(see note following)

While most of these pen styles are self-explanatory, the PS_INSIDEFRAME pen style requires some explanation. For a pen width greater than one logical unit/pixel PS_INSIDEFRAME insures that the line is drawn inside the frame for all primitive shapes except polygons and polylines. Also, if the pen color does not match an available RGB color, the pen is drawn with a dithered (logical) color. Of course, if the pen width is one or less, then PS_INSIDEFRAME is identical to PS_SOLID.

Logical Brushes

When a figure (shape) is drawn, with the exception of the Arc figure which is not closed, the current logical brush is used to fill the figure.

Four types of logical brushes can be created: solid, hollow, hatched, or patterned. For these brush types, separate *Create...Brush* functions are used: *CreateSolidBrush, CreateHatchBrush* or *CreatePatternBrush*. For the present, the *CreateHatchBrush* is used to select from the six fill (hatch) patterns defined as:

Table 17-3: Predefined Hatch Fill Styles

Hatch ID	Hatch Type
HS_HORIZ	horizontal lines
HS_VERT	vertical lines
HS_FDIAG	forward diagonal
HS_BDIAG	backslash diagonal
HS_HCROSS	horizontal crosshatch
HS_DCROSS	diagonal crosshatch

A hatched brush is created in the same fashion as a logical pen and is subject to the same restrictions:

```
hBrush = SelectObject( hdc,
            CreateHatchBrush( nHatchStyle,
                              RGBcolor ) );
```

Please note, however, that in the *PenDraw.C* demo, the handles returned for logical pens and logical brushes are not saved, and no provisions have been made in this example to delete these objects after use. I.e., in *PenDraw.C*, the actual code used appears as:

```
SelectObject( hdc,
    CreateHatchBrush( nHatch-IDM_HORIZ,
                      cColor ) );
```

While this is not the recommended practice and does use memory, which is not recovered until either Windows exits or the system is rebooted, this does demonstrate that there are no guards against this type of error except, of course, for careful programming practices.

Creating Figures

The *PenDraw2.C* program demonstrates six of the eight figure functions using the predefined line and hatchfill styles, and a palette of eight colors corresponding to the DOS CGA color palette. Figures (shapes), line styles, hatch styles, and colors are all menu-selected. The eight colors provided are defined as RGB color values (long integer) as described in Chapter 16 (see Table 16-2).

Rectangles are the simplest of the figures, requiring four parameters specifying the coordinates of the upper-left and lower-right corners:

```
Rectangle( hdc, xUL, yUL, xLR, yLR );
```

Or, to create a square, a special case of *Rectangle* can be used as:

```
Rectangle( hdc, xUL, yUL,
          xUL + min( xLR-xUL, yLR-yUL ),
          yUL + min( yLR-yUL, xLR-xUL ) );
```

The *RoundRect* function is not demonstrated in *PenDraw.C*, but operates in the same fashion as *Rectangle* except for the addition of two parameters defining the elliptical curves for the four corners, as:

```
RoundRect( hdc, xUL, yUL, xLR, yLR,
           xCornerRadius, yCornerRadius );
```

In most cases, you will probably prefer for *xCornerRadius* and *yCornerRadius* to be equal, but the curve describing the corner of a rounded rectangle can be elongated in either dimension as desired. Figure 17-1 shows three corner examples, first with x>y (x=2y), then x=y and, at the right, x<y (2x=y).

Ellipses are drawn much like rectangles, requiring only corner coordinates for a rectangle enclosing the ellipse, thus:

```
Ellipse( hdc, xUL, yUL, xLR, yLR );
```

Also, a circle is simply a special case of an ellipse and can be defined from the *Ellipse* function in the same fashion that a square was created using the *Rectangle* function.

```
Ellipse( hdc, xUL, yUL,                          // circular ellipse //
         xUL + min( xLR-xUL, yLR-yUL ),
         yUL + min( yLR-yUL, xLR-xUL ) );
```

Figure 17-2 shows three ellipses together with the rectangles defining the ellipses. The enclosing rectangles, of course, are not drawn by the *Ellipse* function.

Figure 17-1: Corners Using RoundRect

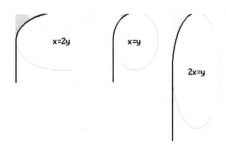

Figure 17-2: Three Elliptical Figures

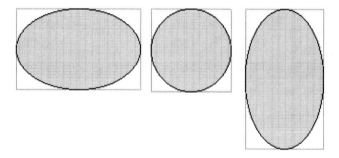

The *Arc, Chord*, and *Pie* functions also use coordinates for an enclosing rectangle. They determine the position and basic curve, but add an additional four parameters: The first pair (of the last four) specifying the beginning position of the arc, and the second pair setting the end position of the arc.

```
Arc(    hdc, xUL, yUL, xLR, yLR, xp1, yp1, xp2, yp2 );
Chord( hdc, xUL, yUL, xLR, yLR, xp1, yp1, xp2, yp2 );
Pie(    hdc, xUL, yUL, xLR, yLR, xp1, yp1, xp2, yp2 );
```

Figure 17-3 shows examples of arc, chord, and pie figures, together with the enclosing rectangles which define the figures and the radii intersecting the begin and end points of the arc segment.

Figure 17-3: Arc, Chord, and Pie Figures

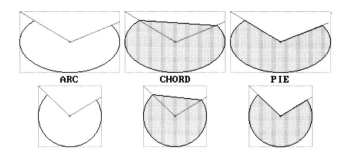

In conventional DOS C++, arc and associated figures are drawn by defining the center point, the radius (or radii), and by defining the begin and end points as angles with the 0° point located horizontally to the right.

In Windows, however, the arc segment is defined by an enclosing rectangle, and the begin and end points for the arc segment are not defined as angles, but as points located anywhere except the center point of the arc. For example, in Figure 17-4, the x/y coordinates specifying the starting angle could lie anywhere along the radii, including the upper-left corner of the rectangle or outside the rectangle itself. The arc itself does not necessarily pass through the point specified. Instead, the actual starting point of the arc is determined by the intersection point of the arc and a radius drawn from the center through the specified point.

For the *Arc* function, the process ends with determining the start and end points for the arc. For the *Chord* function, the next step is to join these endpoints (the arc's endpoints, not the reference endpoints) to produce a closed figure before the completed figure is filled using, in the example, the current hatch-brush.

For the *Pie* function, instead of a chord two lines are drawn from the center point, one to each endpoint of the arc, before filling the closed figure as before.

Figure 17-4: Start and End Points for Arc, Chord, or Pie Figures

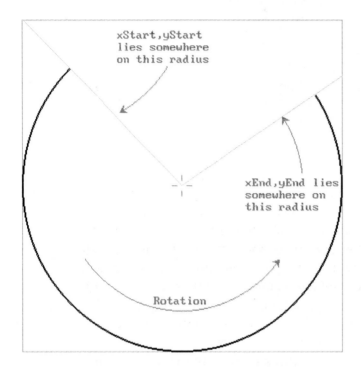

Later, in *PieChart.C*, conventional trigonometry will be used to calculate points which do lie on the arc, since this is easier than calculating appropriate points which do not, but the emphasis here is on the fact that the start and end points are not required to lie on the arc. Even if the mechanisms are different, the end results are the same.

The *PenDraw2.C* program (a complete listingof which appears at the end of this chapter) demonstrates the *Rectangle, Ellipse, Arc, Chord* and *Pie* functions together with pen (line) and hatch-fill styles as shown in Figure 17-5.

Figure 17-5: The PenDraw2.C Application

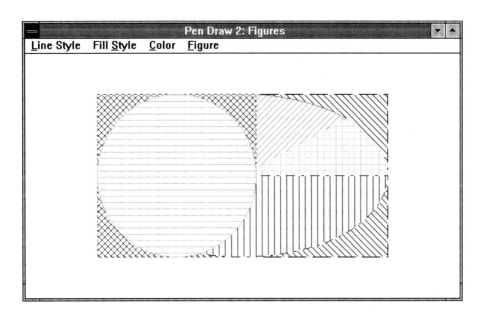

Business Graphs

Business graph displays are one obvious use for the figure-drawing functions. Granted, these are not my favorite topic, and probably not yours either, but business graphs are a common requirement for applications. They can illustrate how the *Rectangle* and *Pie* functions can be used with data sets, and how Pie sections are calculated.

Both the *BarGraph* and *PieGraph* demo programs use arrays of data which are built into the application. In more common circumstances, similar applications would use data values which were either calculated or drawn directly from outside files, but this approach is simpler for demonstration purposes. Note that the same data set is used in both examples.

The *BarGraph* demo charts four years of data in eight categories. It uses a solid brush and colors to identify each year's data, but groups each category in clumps. Since separate vertical and horizontal ranges are useful here, the *MM_ANISOTROPIC* mode is used. The origin point is set near the lower-left corner of the grid, but slightly up and to the right, leaving room for labels below the groups of bars.

Unlike the *PenDraw2.C* program, both *BarGraph* and *PieGraph* delete custom pens and brushes after use, and also save the original (entry) mapping mode, restoring this mode after painting the client window.

The principal elements of the *WM_PAINT* code from *BarGraph* follow:

```
for( j=0; j<4; j++ )
{
   TextOut( hdc, (j+1)*70+20, 2*MaxVal+20, szBuff,
            sprintf( szBuff, "%d", Years[j] ) );
   hPen = SelectObject( hdc, CreatePen( PS_SOLID, 1,
                                        lpColor[j+1] ) );
   hBrush = SelectObject( hdc,
                          CreateSolidBrush( lpColor[j+1] ) );
   Rectangle( hdc, (j+1)*70,      2*MaxVal+20,
                   (j+1)*70+15, 2*MaxVal+5 );
```

This first rectangle is written next to the year label, then the entire year's data is written before another pen and brush color are selected:

```
   for( i=0; i<8; i++ )
      Rectangle( hdc, j*15+1+i*70,     0,
                      (j+1)*15+i*70, 2*Accounts[j][i] );
   DeleteObject( hPen );
   DeleteObject( hBrush );
}
```

Both the pen and brush objects are deleted after use. The alternative would be to create an array of pens and brushes, then use the *SelectObject* function to make each active as needed. Finally,the arrays are deleted before exiting. The *BarGraph* demo is illustrated in Figure 17-6.

For the *PieGraph* demo, a different approach is used, displaying data for only one year at a time data in a piegraph. Since the pie graph should be roughly circular, the *MM_ISOTROPIC* mode is used with the viewport origin in the center of the client window.

Since C does not have a predefined value for pi, PI2 is a macro defined as *(2.0 * 3.14159)*, providing a means of converting values to angles (in radians) before using the angles to calculate points on the circumference.

Figure 17-6: The BarGraph Demo

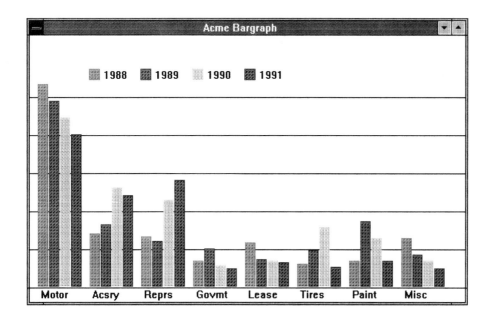

Since the data for the pie graph is an array of individual values, a loop is used to create a series of magnitude values:

```
TotVal[0] = 0;
for( i=0; i<8; i++ )
    TotVal[i+1] = TotVal[i] + Accounts[Year][i];
```

After this is done, *TotVal[i]* no longer describes the magnitude of a category. Instead, it can be used to calculate a percentage of the total and therefore, can calculate a rotation point around the circle:

```
for( i=0; i<8; i++ )
{
    ...
    hPen = SelectObject( hdc, CreatePen( PS_SOLID, 1,
lpColor[i] ) );
    hBrush = SelectObject( hdc, CreateSolidBrush( lpColor[i] )
);
    ...
    Pie( hdc, -Radius, Radius, Radius, -Radius,
```

Since the mapping mode is centered, the enclosing rectangle is defined by two pairs of points: (*-Radius,Radius*) and (*Radius,-Radius*).

The start and end point coordinates for each pie section are calculated as points on the circumference :

```
(int) ( Radius * cos( PI2 * TotVal[i]
                   / TotVal[8] ) ),
(int) ( Radius * sin( PI2 * TotVal[i]
                   / TotVal[8] ) ),
(int) ( Radius * cos( PI2 * TotVal[i+1]
                   / TotVal[8] ) ),
(int) ( Radius * sin( PI2 * TotVal[i+1]
                   / TotVal[8] ) ) );
```

And that's how the hat trick works—each pie section is created as a fraction of the total circle and colored with a different solid brush. The results appear as shown in Figure 17-7.

Source code for both the *BarGraph* and *PieGraph* demos appear at the end of this chapter.

Drawing Polygons

The *Polygon* and *PolyPolygon* functions also draw bordered, closed, and filled figures, but with a few differences. First, the figures drawn can be more complex than simple rectangles but must still be constructed from lines, not curves. Second, the polygon functions require an array of points defining the figures to create:

```
Polygon( hdc, lpPoints, nPoints );
```

The *lpPoints* parameter is a pointer to an array of *POINT*, while *nPoints* is the number of points in the array.

The Polygon function creates a figure by connecting successive pairs of points with straight lines, closing the polygon, if necessary, by connecting the final vertex with the first vertex.

The PolyPolygon function creates a series of closed polygons and is called as:

```
PolyPolygon( hdc, lpPoints, lpPolyCounts, nPolygons );
```

Figure 17-7: The PieGraph Demo

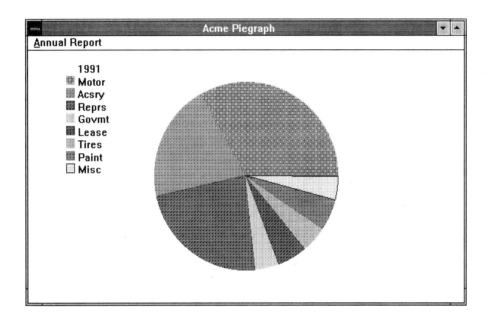

Like the *Polygon* function, the *lpPoints* parameter is a pointer to an array of *POINT* containing coordinates for the position of each vertex. The new parameter, *lpPolyCounts*, is a pointer to an array of integers which specify how many points are in each successive polygon. And, again, *nPolygons* is the total number of polygons—not points—in the *lpPoints* array.

Unlike the *Polygon* function, the *PolyPolygon* vertex arrays must be closed, i.e., the last vertex in each array must be the same as the first vertex—because the *PolyPolygon* function will not automatically close a polygon. Also, multiple polygons are permitted to overlap but are not required to do so. The *Polygon* function is demonstrated in *PenDraw3.C*, following. *PolyPolygon* is not demonstrated.

Polygon Fill Modes

In the previous examples, the figures created were simple closed outlines with continuous interiors that required no special handling to fill. With polygons, however, as will be demonstrated, the interiors of a closed figure may or may not be continuous, and, if not, require a different approach for filling.

For polygons, two fill modes are supported as *ALTERNATE* and *WINDING*, describing the algorithms used to determine which points are inside or outside of the polygon figure. In *ALTERNATE* mode, the default polyfill mode, only regions which are reached by crossing an odd number of boundaries (1, 3, 5, etc., lines) are considered interior and are, therefore, filled.

The *WINDING* mode, on the other hand, is somewhat slower to calculate, but it has the advantage of filling all interior (bounded) regions regardless of the number of boundaries crossed.

As an example, Figure 17-8 shows two polygons as five- and seven-pointed stars where the interiors consist, respectively, of six and fifteen interior regions. In the illustration, the two polygons have been filled using the *ALTERNATE* fill mode. The *WINDING* fill mode can also be selected from the demo's menu and will fill all interior spaces in both figures.

PenDraw3

PenDraw3.C calculates point arrays for the two figures using simple trigonometric operations much the same as used for the *PieGraph* demo:

```
for( i=j=0; i; i++, j=(j+2)%5 )      // five points //
{
   pt[0][i].x = (int)( sin( j*PI2/5 ) * 100 ) - 110;
   pt[0][i].y = (int)( cos( j*PI2/5 ) * 100 );
}
```

For the five-pointed star, the points are calculated in the order 0, 2, 4, 1, 3 using the formula *j=(j+2)%5*. If these same points were calculated in successive order, the result would be a simple pentagon with a single, continuous interior.

For the seven-pointed star, the formula *j=(j+3)%7* serves the same purpose except that the resulting point order is 0, 3, 6, 2, 5, 1, 4:

```
for( i=j=0; i; i++, j=(j+3)%7 )      // seven points //
{
   pt[1][i].x = (int)( sin( j*PI2/7 ) * 100 ) + 110;
   pt[1][i].y = (int)( cos( j*PI2/7 ) * 100 );
}
```

Figure 17-8: PenDraw3—Polygons and Poly Fill Modes

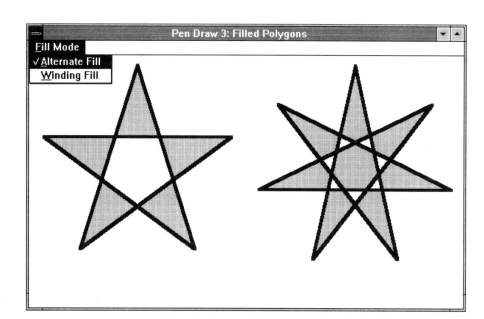

The -110 and +110 constants are supplied simply to position one figure to the left of center and the other to the right.

To use the *PolyPolygon* function, instead of calculating the points for these two stars, a static array of points would be needed:

```
static POINT pt[] =
    { -110, 100, -52, -80, -205, 30, -15,  30, -168, -80,
      -110, 100, 110, 100, 153, -90,  32,  63,  207, -22,
        13, -22, 188,  62,  67, -90, 110, 100  };
static int poly[] = {  6, 8  };
```

The brief array *poly* declares the number of points in each polygon. With these declarations, PolyPolygon could be called as:

```
PolyPolygon( hdc, pt, poly, sizeof(poly) / sizeof(int) );
```

Since PolyPolygon requires closed polygons, instead of the five points calculated for *Polygon,* six points are needed for the five-pointed star, with the final coordinate pair the same as the first point. Likewise, the seven-pointed figure requires eight points for its definition.

If you install this code in the *PenDraw3* listing, be sure to remove the *#include <math.h>* reference. Otherwise, a conflict will occur between the array *poly* and the function *poly* (in *Math.H*) which has quite a different purpose.

Summary

Brush and pen styles and the shape functions are useful but these are only a small part of Windows' graphic capabilities. While business graphs are useful, these may also seem rather pedestrian in view of the other, more elaborate graphics which are possible. In Chapter 18, another aspect of graphics will be demonstrated in the form of bitmapped brushes and paint styles, bimapped images, and, just to round out basic business graphics, a line graph using bitmapped images.

```
//========================//
//        PenDraw2.C       //
//   C++ Windows Drawing   //
//========================//

#include windows.h
#include "pendraw2.h"

long FAR PASCAL WndProc( HWND hwnd,    WORD msg,
                         WORD wParam, LONG lParam )
{
    static COLORREF  cColor = RGB( 0, 0, 0 ),
                     lpColor[8] =
/* Black   */    {  RGB(   0,   0,   0 ),
/* Blue    */       RGB(   0,   0, 255 ),
/* Green   */       RGB(   0, 255,   0 ),
/* Cyan    */       RGB(   0, 255, 255 ),
/* Red     */       RGB( 255,   0,   0 ),
/* Magenta */       RGB( 255,   0, 255 ),
/* Yellow  */       RGB( 255, 255,   0 ),
/* White   */       RGB( 255, 255, 255 ) };
    static   int  cxWnd, cyWnd, xUL, yUL, xRB, yRB,
                  xp1, yp1, xp2, yp2, xp3, yp3,
                  nFigure = IDM_RECT,
                  nHatch  = IDM_HORIZ,
                  nColor  = IDM_BLACK,
                  nPen    = IDM_SOLID;
```

```
HDC          hdc;
HMENU        hMenu;
PAINTSTRUCT  ps;
RECT         rect;
int          i;

switch( msg )
{
   case WM_COMMAND:
      hMenu = GetMenu( hwnd );
      switch( wParam )
      {
         case IDM_BLACK:     case IDM_BLUE:
         case IDM_GREEN:     case IDM_CYAN:
         case IDM_RED:       case IDM_MAGENTA:
         case IDM_YELLOW:    case IDM_WHITE:
            CheckMenuItem( hMenu, nColor, MF_UNCHECKED );
            nColor = wParam;
            cColor = lpColor[nColor-IDM_BLACK];
            CheckMenuItem( hMenu, nColor, MF_CHECKED );
            break;
         case IDM_ARC:       case IDM_CHORD:
         case IDM_CIRCLE:    case IDM_ELLIPSE:
         case IDM_PIE:       case IDM_RECT:
         case IDM_SQUARE:
            CheckMenuItem( hMenu, nFigure, MF_UNCHECKED );
            nFigure = wParam;
            CheckMenuItem( hMenu, nFigure, MF_CHECKED );
            break;
         case IDM_SOLID:     case IDM_DASH:
         case IDM_DOT:       case IDM_DASHDOT:
         case IDM_DASH2DOT:  case IDM_NULL:
         case IDM_INSIDEFRAME:
            CheckMenuItem( hMenu, nPen, MF_UNCHECKED );
            nPen = wParam;
            CheckMenuItem( hMenu, nPen, MF_CHECKED );
            break;
         case IDM_HORIZ:     case IDM_VERT:
         case IDM_FDIAG:     case IDM_BDIAG:
         case IDM_HCROSS:    case IDM_DCROSS:
            CheckMenuItem( hMenu, nHatch, MF_UNCHECKED );
            nHatch = wParam;
            CheckMenuItem( hMenu, nHatch, MF_CHECKED );
            break;
      }
      InvalidateRect( hwnd, NULL, FALSE );
```

```
            return(0);

        case WM_SIZE:
            cxWnd = LOWORD( lParam );
            cyWnd = HIWORD( lParam );
            xRB = cxWnd - ( xUL = cxWnd / 6 );
            yRB = cyWnd - ( yUL = cyWnd / 6 );
            xp1 = yp2 = 0;
            xp3 = ( xp2 = cxWnd ) / 2;
            xp3 = ( yp1 = cyWnd ) / 2;
            return(0);

        case WM_PAINT:
            hdc = BeginPaint( hwnd, &ps );
            SetMapMode( hdc, MM_TEXT );
            GetClientRect( hwnd, &rect );
            SetViewportExt( hdc, rect.right, rect.bottom );
            SetWindowExt( hdc, rect.right, rect.bottom );
            SelectObject( hdc, CreateHatchBrush(
                                nHatch-IDM_HORIZ, cColor ) );
            SelectObject( hdc, CreatePen( nPen-IDM_SOLID, 1,
                                    cColor ) );
            switch( nFigure )
            {
                case IDM_ARC:
                    Arc( hdc, xUL, yUL, xRB, yRB,
                            xp2, yp1, xp1, yp2 );
                    break;
                case IDM_CHORD:
                    Chord( hdc, xUL, yUL, xRB, yRB,
                            xp1, yp1, xp2, yp2 );
                    break;
                case IDM_PIE:
                    Pie( hdc, xUL, yUL, xRB, yRB,
                            xp1, yp1, xp3, yp3 );
                    break;
                case IDM_ELLIPSE:
                    Ellipse( hdc, xUL, yUL, xRB, yRB );
                    break;
                case IDM_CIRCLE:
                    Ellipse( hdc, xUL, yUL,
                            xUL + min( xRB-xUL, yRB-yUL ),
                            yUL + min( yRB-yUL, xRB-xUL ) );
                    break;
                case IDM_RECT:
                    Rectangle( hdc, xUL, yUL, xRB, yRB );
```

```
                    break;
                case IDM_SQUARE:
                    Rectangle( hdc, xUL, yUL,
                                xUL + min( xRB-xUL, yRB-yUL ),
                                yUL + min( yRB-yUL, xRB-xUL ) );
                    break;
            }
            EndPaint( hwnd, &ps );
            return(0);

        case WM_DESTROY:
            PostQuitMessage(0);
            return(0);
    }
    return( DefWindowProc( hwnd, msg, wParam, lParam ) );
}


#pragma argsused

int PASCAL WinMain( HANDLE hInstance,
                    HANDLE hPrevInstance,
                    LPSTR  lpszCmdParam, int nCmdShow )
{
    static char szAppName[] = "PENDRAW2";
    HWND        hwnd;
    MSG         msg;
    WNDCLASS    wc;

    if( ! hPrevInstance )
    {
        wc.hInstance      = hInstance;
        wc.lpfnWndProc    = WndProc;
        wc.cbClsExtra     = 0;
        wc.cbWndExtra     = 0;
        wc.lpszClassName  = szAppName;
        wc.hIcon          = LoadIcon( hInstance, szAppName );
        wc.lpszMenuName   = (LPSTR) szAppName;
        wc.hCursor        = LoadCursor( NULL, IDC_ARROW );
        wc.hbrBackground  = GetStockObject( WHITE_BRUSH );
        wc.style          = CS_HREDRAW | CS_VREDRAW;
        RegisterClass( &wc );
    }
    hwnd = CreateWindow( szAppName, "Pen Draw 2: Figures",
                        WS_OVERLAPPEDWINDOW,
                        CW_USEDEFAULT, CW_USEDEFAULT,
                        CW_USEDEFAULT, CW_USEDEFAULT,
                        NULL, NULL, hInstance, NULL  );
```

```
    ShowWindow(   hwnd, nCmdShow );
    UpdateWindow( hwnd );
    while( GetMessage( &msg, NULL, 0, 0 ) )
    {
        TranslateMessage( &msg );
        DispatchMessage(   &msg );
    }
    return( msg.wParam );
}
```

```
                    ;================;
                    ;  PENDRAW2.DEF  ;
                    ;================;

NAME            PENDRAW2

DESCRIPTION     "DRAWING WITH PENS"
EXETYPE         WINDOWS
STUB            "WINSTUB.EXE"
CODE            PRELOAD MOVEABLE DISCARDABLE
DATA            PRELOAD MOVEABLE MULTIPLE
HEAPSIZE        1024
STACKSIZE       8192
EXPORTS         WndProc
```

```
                    //================//
                    //  PENDRAW2.H    //
                    //================//

#define   IDM_SOLID               100
#define   IDM_DASH                101
#define   IDM_DOT                 102
#define   IDM_DASHDOT             103
#define   IDM_DASH2DOT            104
#define   IDM_NULL                105
#define   IDM_INSIDEFRAME         106

#define   IDM_HORIZ               200
#define   IDM_VERT                201
#define   IDM_FDIAG               202
#define   IDM_BDIAG               203
#define   IDM_HCROSS              204
#define   IDM_DCROSS              205

#define   IDM_BLACK               300
#define   IDM_BLUE                301
#define   IDM_GREEN               302
```

```
#define   IDM_CYAN          303
#define   IDM_RED           304
#define   IDM_MAGENTA       305
#define   IDM_YELLOW        306
#define   IDM_WHITE         307

#define   IDM_RECT          401
#define   IDM_SQUARE        402
#define   IDM_ARC           403
#define   IDM_CHORD         404
#define   IDM_PIE           405
#define   IDM_ELLIPSE       406
#define   IDM_CIRCLE        407


                    //===============//
                    //  PenDraw2.RC  //
                    //  menu script  //
                    //===============//
PENDRAW2   MENU LOADONCALL MOVEABLE PURE DISCARDABLE
BEGIN
    POPUP "&Line Style"
    BEGIN
        MenuItem   "&Solid",        100, CHECKED
        MenuItem   "&Dash",         101
        MenuItem   "D&ot",          102
        MenuItem   "Dash Dot",      103
        MenuItem   "Dash Dot Dot",  104
        MenuItem   "&Null",         105
        MenuItem   "&Inside Frame", 106
    END

    POPUP "Fill &Style"
    BEGIN
        MenuItem   "&Horizontal",           200, CHECKED
        MenuItem   "&Vertical",             201
        MenuItem   "&Forward Diagonal",     202
        MenuItem   "&Backward Diagonal",    203
        MenuItem   "&Crosshatch",           204
        MenuItem   "&Diagonal Crosshatch",  205
    END

    POPUP "&Color"
    BEGIN
        MenuItem   "&Black",    300, CHECKED
        MenuItem   "B&lue",     301
```

```
        MenuItem   "&Green",      302
        MenuItem   "&Cyan",       303
        MenuItem   "&Red",        304
        MenuItem   "&Magenta",    305
        MenuItem   "&Yellow",     306
        MenuItem   "&White",      307
    END

    POPUP "&Figure"
    BEGIN
        MenuItem   "&Rectangle",  401, CHECKED
        MenuItem   "&Square",     402
        MenuItem   "&Arc",        403
        MenuItem   "C&hord",      404
        MenuItem   "&Pie",        405
        MenuItem   "&Ellipse",    406
        MenuItem   "&Circle",     407
    END
END


            //=======================//
            //        BarGraph.C       //
            //   C++ Windows Drawing   //
            //=======================//

#include <windows.h>
#include <stdio.h>

static int    Accounts[4][8] =
            {  133, 35, 33, 17, 29, 15, 17, 32,
               122, 41, 30, 25, 18, 24, 43, 21,
               111, 65, 57, 14, 17, 39, 32, 17,
               100, 60, 70, 12, 16, 13, 17, 12  },
            Years[4] = { 1988, 1989, 1990, 1991 };
static char *AccTypes[9] =
            { "Motor", "Acsry", "Reprs", "Govmt",
              "Lease", "Tires", "Paint", "Misc "  };

long FAR PASCAL WndProc( HWND hwnd,    WORD msg,
                         WORD wParam, LONG lParam )
{
    static COLORREF   lpColor[8] =
                      { RGB(  50,  50,  50 ),    // DarkGray //
                        RGB(  50,  50, 200 ),    // Blue     //
                        RGB(  50, 200,  50 ),    // Green    //
                        RGB(  50, 200, 200 ),    // Cyan     //
```

```
                        RGB( 200,  50,  50 ),    // Red       //
                        RGB( 200,  50, 200 ),    // Magenta   //
                        RGB( 200, 200,  50 ),    // Yellow    //
                        RGB( 200, 200, 200 ) };  // LightGray //
static   int   cxWnd, cyWnd;
HDC            hdc, OrgDC;
HPEN           hPen;
HMENU          hMenu;
HBRUSH         hBrush;
PAINTSTRUCT    ps;
RECT           rect;
int            i, j, MaxVal = 0;
char           szBuff[10];

switch( msg )
{
   case WM_SIZE:
      cxWnd = LOWORD( lParam );
      cyWnd = HIWORD( lParam );
      return(0);

   case WM_PAINT:
      for( i=0; i<8; i++ )
         for( j=0; j<4; j++ )
            MaxVal = max( MaxVal, Accounts[j][i] );
      hdc = BeginPaint( hwnd, &ps );
      OrgDC = SaveDC( hdc );
      SetMapMode(     hdc, MM_ANISOTROPIC );
      SetWindowExt(   hdc, cxWnd,  MaxVal );
      SetViewportExt( hdc, cxWnd, -MaxVal );
      GetClientRect(  hwnd, &rect );
      SetWindowOrg(   hdc, -10, rect.bottom-20 );
      for( i=-1; i<2*MaxVal; i+=50 )
      {
         MoveTo( hdc, -10, i );
         LineTo( hdc, cxWnd, i );
      }
      for( i=0; i<8; i++ )
         TextOut( hdc, i*70+5, -2, szBuff,
                  sprintf( szBuff, "%s", AccTypes[i] ) );
      for( j=0; j<4; j++ )
      {
         TextOut( hdc, (j+1)*70+20, 2*MaxVal+20, szBuff,
                  sprintf( szBuff, "%d", Years[j] ) );
         hPen = SelectObject( hdc,
            CreatePen( PS_SOLID, 1, lpColor[j+1] ) );
```

```
            hBrush = SelectObject( hdc,
                CreateSolidBrush( lpColor[j+1] ) );
            Rectangle( hdc, (j+1)*70,    2*MaxVal+20,
                            (j+1)*70+15, 2*MaxVal+5 );
            for( i=0; i<8; i++ )
                Rectangle( hdc, j*15+1+i*70, 0,
                            (j+1)*15+i*70, 2*Accounts[j][i] );
            DeleteObject( hPen );
            DeleteObject( hBrush );
        }
        RestoreDC( hdc, OrgDC );
        return(0);

    case WM_DESTROY:
        PostQuitMessage(0);
        return(0);
    }
    return( DefWindowProc( hwnd, msg, wParam, lParam ) );
}

#pragma argsused

int PASCAL WinMain( HANDLE hInst,      HANDLE hPrevInst,
                 LPSTR  lpszCmdParam, int nCmdShow )
{
    static char szAppName[] = "BARGRAPH";
    HWND        hwnd;
    MSG         msg;
    WNDCLASS    wc;

    if( ! hPrevInst )
    {
        wc.hInstance      = hInst;
        wc.lpfnWndProc    = WndProc;
        wc.cbClsExtra     = 0;
        wc.cbWndExtra     = 0;
        wc.lpszClassName  = szAppName;
        wc.hIcon          = LoadIcon( hInst, szAppName );
        wc.lpszMenuName   = (LPSTR) szAppName;
        wc.hCursor        = LoadCursor( NULL, IDC_ARROW );
        wc.hbrBackground  = GetStockObject( WHITE_BRUSH );
        wc.style          = CS_HREDRAW | CS_VREDRAW;
        RegisterClass( &wc );
    }
    hwnd = CreateWindow( szAppName, "Acme Bargraph",
                      WS_OVERLAPPEDWINDOW,
                      CW_USEDEFAULT, CW_USEDEFAULT,
```

```
                        CW_USEDEFAULT, CW_USEDEFAULT,
                        NULL, NULL, hInst, NULL );
    ShowWindow(   hwnd, nCmdShow );
    UpdateWindow( hwnd );
    while( GetMessage( &msg, NULL, 0, 0 ) )
    {
        TranslateMessage( &msg );
        DispatchMessage(  &msg );
    }
    return( msg.wParam );
}


                    ;=================;
                    ;  BARGRAPH.DEF   ;
                    ;=================;

NAME            BARGRAPH

DESCRIPTION     "DRAWING BUSINESS GRAPHS"
EXETYPE         WINDOWS
STUB            "WINSTUB.EXE"
CODE            PRELOAD MOVEABLE DISCARDABLE
DATA            PRELOAD MOVEABLE MULTIPLE
HEAPSIZE        1024
STACKSIZE       8192
EXPORTS         WndProc


                //======================//
                //        PieGraph.C    //
                //   C++ Windows Drawing //
                //======================//

#include <windows.h>
#include <stdio.h>
#include <math.h>
#include "piegraph.h"

#define  PI2 ( 3.14159 * 2.0 )

static int   Accounts[4][8] =
             { 133, 35, 33, 17, 29, 15, 17, 32,
               122, 41, 30, 25, 18, 24, 43, 21,
               111, 65, 57, 14, 17, 39, 32, 17,
               100, 60, 70, 12, 16, 13, 17, 12  },
             Years[4] = { 1988, 1989, 1990, 1991 },
             Year = 0;
static char *AccTypes[9] =
```

```
                     { "Motor", "Acsry", "Reprs", "Govmt",
                       "Lease", "Tires", "Paint", "Misc " };

long FAR PASCAL WndProc( HWND hwnd,    WORD msg,
                         WORD wParam, LONG lParam )
{
    static COLORREF   lpColor[8] =
                     { RGB( 100, 100, 100 ),   // DarkGray  //
                       RGB(  50,  50, 200 ),   // Blue      //
                       RGB(  50, 200,  50 ),   // Green     //
                       RGB(  50, 200, 200 ),   // Cyan      //
                       RGB( 200,  50,  50 ),   // Red       //
                       RGB( 200,  50, 200 ),   // Magenta   //
                       RGB( 200, 200,  50 ),   // Yellow    //
                       RGB( 200, 200, 200 ) }; // LightGray //
    static  int  cxWnd, cyWnd;
    HDC          hdc, OrgDC;
    HPEN         hPen;
    HMENU        hMenu;
    HBRUSH       hBrush;
    PAINTSTRUCT  ps;
    RECT         rect;
    int          i, j, Radius, TotVal[9];
    char         szBuff[10];

    switch( msg )
    {
        case WM_COMMAND:
           switch( wParam )
           {
              case Y1988:  case Y1989:
              case Y1990:  case Y1991:
                 CheckMenuItem( hMenu, Year+Y1988,
                                MF_UNCHECKED );
                 Year = wParam - Y1988;
                 CheckMenuItem( hMenu, wParam, MF_CHECKED );
                 break;
           }
           InvalidateRect( hwnd, NULL, TRUE );
           return(0);

        case WM_SIZE:
           cxWnd = LOWORD( lParam );
           cyWnd = HIWORD( lParam );
           return(0);

        case WM_PAINT:
```

```
        TotVal[0] = 0;
        for( i=0; i<8; i++ )
           TotVal[i+1] = TotVal[i] + Accounts[Year][i];
        Radius = 150;
        hdc = BeginPaint( hwnd, &ps );
        OrgDC = SaveDC( hdc );
        SetMapMode(      hdc, MM_ISOTROPIC );
        SetWindowExt(    hdc,     400,       400 );
        SetViewportExt( hdc,    cxWnd,   -cyWnd );
        SetViewportOrg( hdc, cxWnd/2, cyWnd/2 );
        GetClientRect( hwnd, &rect );
        TextOut( hdc, 20-(cxWnd/2), 180, szBuff,
                sprintf( szBuff, "%d", Year+1988 ) );
        for( i=0; i<8; i++ )
        {
            TextOut( hdc, 20-(cxWnd/2), (8-i)*20, szBuff,
                    sprintf( szBuff, "%s", AccTypes[i] ) );
            hPen = SelectObject( hdc,
                CreatePen( PS_SOLID, 1, lpColor[i] ) );
            hBrush = SelectObject( hdc,
                CreateSolidBrush( lpColor[i] ) );
            Rectangle( hdc, -(cxWnd/2),      (8-i)*20,
                            -(cxWnd/2)+15, (8-i)*20-15 );
            Pie( hdc, -Radius, Radius, Radius, -Radius,
                (int) ( Radius * cos( PI2 * TotVal[i]
                                    / TotVal[8] ) ),
                (int) ( Radius * sin( PI2 * TotVal[i]
                                    / TotVal[8] ) ),
                (int) ( Radius * cos( PI2 * TotVal[i+1]
                                    / TotVal[8] ) ),
                (int) ( Radius * sin( PI2 * TotVal[i+1]
                                    / TotVal[8] ) ) );
            DeleteObject( hPen );
            DeleteObject( hBrush );
        }
        RestoreDC( hdc, OrgDC );
        EndPaint (hwnd, Sps);
        return(0);

    case WM_DESTROY:
        PostQuitMessage(0);
        return(0);
    }
    return( DefWindowProc( hwnd, msg, wParam, lParam ) );
}
```

```
#pragma argsused

int PASCAL WinMain( HANDLE hInst,       HANDLE hPrevInst,
                    LPSTR  lpszCmdParam, int nCmdShow )
{
    static char szAppName[] = "PIEGRAPH";
    HWND        hwnd;
    MSG         msg;
    WNDCLASS    wc;

    if( ! hPrevInst )
    {
        wc.hInstance      = hInst;
        wc.lpfnWndProc    = WndProc;
        wc.cbClsExtra     = 0;
        wc.cbWndExtra     = 0;
        wc.lpszClassName  = szAppName;
        wc.hIcon          = LoadIcon( hInst, szAppName );
        wc.lpszMenuName   = (LPSTR) szAppName;
        wc.hCursor        = LoadCursor( NULL, IDC_ARROW );
        wc.hbrBackground  = GetStockObject( WHITE_BRUSH );
        wc.style          = CS_HREDRAW | CS_VREDRAW;
        RegisterClass( &wc );
    }
    hwnd = CreateWindow( szAppName, "Acme Piegraph",
                         WS_OVERLAPPEDWINDOW,
                         CW_USEDEFAULT, CW_USEDEFAULT,
                         CW_USEDEFAULT, CW_USEDEFAULT,
                         NULL, NULL, hInst, NULL  );
    ShowWindow(   hwnd, nCmdShow );
    UpdateWindow( hwnd );
    while( GetMessage( &msg, NULL, 0, 0 ) )
    {
        TranslateMessage( &msg );
        DispatchMessage(  &msg );
    }
    return( msg.wParam );
}

                    ;================;
                    ;  PIEGRAPH.DEF  ;
                    ;================;

NAME         PIEGRAPH

DESCRIPTION  "DRAWING BUSINESS GRAPHS"
EXETYPE      WINDOWS
```

```
STUB            "WINSTUB.EXE"
CODE            PRELOAD MOVEABLE DISCARDABLE
DATA            PRELOAD MOVEABLE MULTIPLE
HEAPSIZE        1024
STACKSIZE       8192
EXPORTS         WndProc

                //==============//
                //  PIEGRAPH.H  //
                //==============//

#define  Y1991   1991
#define  Y1990   1990
#define  Y1989   1989
#define  Y1988   1988


                //======================//
                //         PenDraw3.C    //
                //  C++ Windows Drawing  //
                //======================//

#include <windows.h>
#include <math.h>
#include "pendraw3.h"

#define PI2 ( 2.0 * 3.1415 )
// radians in 360 degrees //

static POINT pt[2][7];

long FAR PASCAL WndProc( HWND hwnd,    WORD msg,
                         WORD wParam, LONG lParam )
{
    static   int    cxWnd, cyWnd, nFillMode = IDM_ALTERNATE;
    HDC             hdc;
    HPEN            hPen;
    HMENU           hMenu;
    PAINTSTRUCT     ps;
    int             i, j;

    switch( msg )
    {
        case WM_CREATE:
            for( i=j=0; i<5; i++, j=(j+2)%5 )      // five points //
            {
                pt[0][i].x = (int)( sin( j*PI2/5 ) * 100 ) - 110;
                pt[0][i].y = (int)( cos( j*PI2/5 ) * 100 );
```

```
        }
        for( i=j=0; i<7; i++, j=(j+3)%7 )    // seven points //
        {
            pt[1][i].x = (int)( sin( j*PI2/7 ) * 100 ) + 110;
            pt[1][i].y = (int)( cos( j*PI2/7 ) * 100 );
        }
        return(0);

    case WM_COMMAND:
        hMenu = GetMenu( hwnd );
        switch( wParam )
        {
            case IDM_ALTERNATE:
            case IDM_WINDING:
                CheckMenuItem( hMenu, nFillMode,
                               MF_UNCHECKED );
                nFillMode = wParam;
                CheckMenuItem( hMenu, nFillMode,
                               MF_CHECKED );
                break;
        }
        InvalidateRect( hwnd, NULL, TRUE );
        return(0);

    case WM_SIZE:
        cxWnd = LOWORD( lParam );
        cyWnd = HIWORD( lParam );
        return(0);

    case WM_PAINT:
        hdc = BeginPaint( hwnd, &ps );
        hPen = CreatePen( PS_SOLID, 3, 0L );
        SelectObject( hdc, hPen );
        SelectObject( hdc, GetStockObject( LTGRAY_BRUSH ) );
        SetMapMode( hdc, MM_ISOTROPIC );
        SetWindowExt(   hdc,   440,  -220 );
        SetViewportExt( hdc, cxWnd, cyWnd );
        SetWindowOrg(   hdc,  -220,   110 );
        SetPolyFillMode( hdc, nFillMode );
        Polygon( hdc, pt[0], 5 );
        Polygon( hdc, pt[1], 7 );
        EndPaint( hwnd, &ps );
        return(0);

    case WM_DESTROY:
        PostQuitMessage(0);
        return(0);
```

```
    }
    return( DefWindowProc( hwnd, msg, wParam, lParam ) );
}

#pragma argsused

int PASCAL WinMain( HANDLE hInst,          HANDLE hPrevInst,
                    LPSTR  lpszCmdParam, int    nCmdShow )
{
    static char szAppName[] = "PENDRAW3";
    HWND        hwnd;
    MSG         msg;
    WNDCLASS    wc;

    if( ! hPrevInst )
    {
        wc.hInstance      = hInst;
        wc.lpfnWndProc    = WndProc;
        wc.cbClsExtra     = 0;
        wc.cbWndExtra     = 0;
        wc.lpszClassName  = szAppName;
        wc.hIcon          = LoadIcon( hInst, szAppName );
        wc.lpszMenuName   = (LPSTR) szAppName;
        wc.hCursor        = LoadCursor( NULL, IDC_ARROW );
        wc.hbrBackground  = GetStockObject( WHITE_BRUSH );
        wc.style          = CS_HREDRAW | CS_VREDRAW;
        RegisterClass( &wc );
    }
    hwnd = CreateWindow( szAppName,
                         "Pen Draw 3: Filled Polygons",
                         WS_OVERLAPPEDWINDOW,
                         CW_USEDEFAULT, CW_USEDEFAULT,
                         CW_USEDEFAULT, CW_USEDEFAULT,
                         NULL, NULL, hInst, NULL  );
    ShowWindow(   hwnd, nCmdShow );
    UpdateWindow( hwnd );
    while( GetMessage( &msg, NULL, 0, 0 ) )
    {
        TranslateMessage( &msg );
        DispatchMessage(  &msg );
    }
    return( msg.wParam );
}
```

```
                    ;================;
                    ;  PENDRAW3.DEF  ;
                    ;================;

NAME            PENDRAW3

DESCRIPTION     "DRAWING WITH PENS"
EXETYPE         WINDOWS
STUB            "WINSTUB.EXE"
CODE            PRELOAD MOVEABLE DISCARDABLE
DATA            PRELOAD MOVEABLE MULTIPLE
HEAPSIZE        1024
STACKSIZE       8192
EXPORTS         WndProc


                    //==============//
                    //  PENDRAW3.H  //
                    //==============//

#define   IDM_ALTERNATE   1
#define   IDM_WINDING     2
```

Chapter 18

Brushes, Bitmaps, BLTs, And DIBs

In previous chapters, both hatched and solid brushes have been used to fill figures. A third type of brush remains to be introduced, the custom patterned brush using a bitmap image for the fill pattern.

Of course, fill patterns are only one of many uses for bitmaps. Other graphic applications will also be examined, including line graphs using bitmapped images, accessing Windows' own bitmaps, device independent bitmaps (DIBs), and block transfers of patterns (BLT functions).

First, however, we will begin with the simplest of these graphic features, using bitmaps to create patterned brushes.

Bitmapped Brushes: I

The first step in creating a bitmapped brush is to create the bitmap itself. For brushes, a minimum 8x8 bitmap image is required. Bitmaps can be defined within your source code as arrays of WORD. For example:

```
static BYTE  wBricks[] =
   {  0xFF, 0x08, 0x08, 0x08, 0xFF, 0x80, 0x80, 0x80  };
```

This defines an 8x8 bit pattern that describes a bitmap similar to the BRICKS image shown in Figure 18-1. It could be used to produce a pattern brush similar to the left half of the pentagonal star in Figure 18-3. Note, however, that these statements are qualified by using the word "similar", because this bitmap is monochrome and the bitmaps and brushes in the illustrations are polychrome. Still, the pattern itself is the same.

Figure 18-1: Three 8x8 Bitmap Patterns

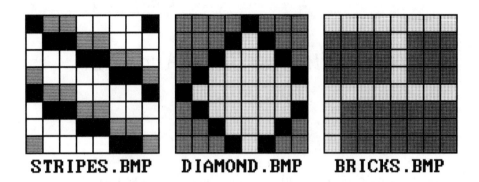

In order to use this bitmap as a brush pattern, the first step is to call CreateBitmap to convert the value array into a bitmap image (in memory):

```
hBitmap = CreateBitmap( 8, 8, 1, 1, (LPSTR) wBricks );
```

The CreateBitmap function creates a device-dependent memory bitmap with the width and height specified by the first two parameters. The third parameter sets the number of color planes in the bitmap (each plane has *nWidth* /*nHeight* /*nBitCount* bits) while the fourth parameter sets the number of color bits per display pixel.

For VGA color monitors please see the"Devices" program in Chapter 15, four color planes are supported with one color bit per pixel (per plane). Changing these parameters, however, would require a change in the bit pattern which has been defined for monochrome. Of course, monochrome is compatible with all devices.

The final parameter required is a pointer to an array of bytes containing the initial bitmap bit values. If *NULL*, the bitmap remains uninitialized.

With the bitmap handle, CreatePatternBrush can be called to create a brush using this pattern:

```
hBrush  = CreatePatternBrush( hBitmap );
SelectObject( hdc, hBrush );
```

The SelectObject function makes the new brush the current brush object.

Don't forget, though, that having created both bitmap and brush, these must be deleted when no longer needed:

```
DeleteObject( hBrush );
DeleteObject( hBitmap );
```

Bitmapped Brushes: II

When bitmaps are defined as arrays of WORD, there are two principal drawbacks: First, that the bitmaps are device-dependent and, second that color bitmaps are difficult to code. However, the Whitewater Resource Toolkit (WRT) provides an excellent bitmap editor (see Chapter 7) that avoids both disadvantages. First, bitmaps created using WRT are device-independent bitmaps (DIBs), and second, since the bitmaps are drawn in color, no coding is required. (DIB structure is explained in Appendix A.)

Since it is device-independent, a bitmap created in color on a VGA color monitor can be displayed in black and white on a monochrome system, or transported to a system using an 8514A video.

This approach does require images created using the WRT Bitmap Editor (or Microsoft's SDK utility), so before proceeding further, you need to create the PENDRAW4.RES resource file containing four bitmap images: BRICKS, CHAINS, DIAMOND and STRIPES. Three of these are shown in Figure 18-1 as 8x8 bitmaps, while the fourth, CHAINS, is illustrated separately in Figure 18-2 as a 24x24 bitmap. The colors used are not particularly important and can easily be adapted to monochrome systems as well.

After the bitmap images have been created as a part of the resource file (.RES), they become part of the compiled and linked .EXE file. However, this does not make these bitmapped images part of the executable application itself. Instead, within the application, an array of HBITMAP is declared globally, and in the *WinMain* procedure, the bitmaps are loaded as external resources:

```
static HBITMAP hBitMap[4];

int PASCAL WinMain...
{
    ...
    if( ! hPrevInst )
    {  ...  }
```

```
hBitMap[0] = LoadBitmap( hInst, "BRICKS"  );
hBitMap[1] = LoadBitmap( hInst, "CHAINS"  );
hBitMap[2] = LoadBitmap( hInst, "DIAMOND" );
hBitMap[3] = LoadBitmap( hInst, "STRIPES" );
...
return( msg.wParam );
}
```

Figure 18-2: A 24x24 Bitmap Pattern (CHAINS)

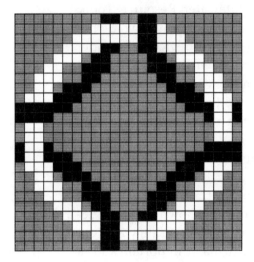

This 24x24 bitmap, if used as 'wallpaper', will produce a screen of interlocking rings.

As a patterned brush, however, the results are not quite as expected.

The LoadBitmap function loads the bitmap resource named by the *lpBitmapName* parameter from the executable file or module specified by the *hInstance* parameter. The *lpBitmapName* is a null-terminated character string naming the bitmap. *LoadBitmap* can also be used to access Windows' predefined bitmaps. In this case, the *hInstance* parameter is passed as NULL, and the *lpBitmapName* parameter must be one of the following values:

Table 18-1: Predefined Windows Bitmaps

OBM_BTNCORNERS	OBM_LFARROW	OBM_RGARROW
OBM_BTSIZE	OBM_LFARROWD	OBM_RGARROWD
OBM_CHECK	OBM_MNARROW	OBM_SIZE
OBM_CHECKBOXES	OBM_REDUCE	OBM_UPARROW

Table 18-1: Predefined Windows Bitmaps (cont.)

OBM_CLOSE	OBM_REDUCED	OBM_UPARROWD
OBM_COMBO	OBM_RESTORE	OBM_ZOOM
OBM_DNARROW	OBM_RESTORED	OBM_ZOOMD
OBM_DNARROWD	OBM_OLD_CLOSE[1]	OBM_OLD_REDUCE
OBM_OLD_UPARROW	OBM_OLD_DNARROW	OBM_OLD_RESTORE
OBM_OLD_ZOOM	OBM_OLD_LFARROW	OBM_OLD_RGARROW

[1] *Bitmap names beginning with OBM_OLD_... represent bitmaps used by Windows versions prior to 3.0.*

The *lpBitmapName* parameter can also be a value created using the MAKEINTRESOURCE macro with the bitmap ID as the low-order word, while the high-order word must be zero. Both custom and predefined bitmap handles should be deleted (use DeleteObject) when no longer needed.

Loading the bitmaps, in either case, is only the first step, because for the *PenDraw4* demo, a brush still needs to be created and selected:

```
hBrush = CreatePatternBrush( hBitMap[ nBitMap ] );
SelectObject( hdc, hBrush );
```

When finished, DeleteObject is called to cancel the brush handle:

```
DeleteObject( hBrush );
```

Also notice that the DeleteObject is not called for the bitmaps themselves, since the CreateBitmap function was never called. In this application, the bitmap handles are a static array, not created on the fly.

PenDraw4.C

PenDraw4 uses four bitmaps to create four different patterned brushes. The brushes are menu-selected and are used to paint the same five- and seven-pointed stars that were created in PenDraw3.

There is one other difference: In PenDraw3, the figures were calculated, but in PenDraw4, a static array of coordinates are used to demonstrate the PolyPolygon function which was discussed (but not shown) in Chapter 17.

Figure 18-3 shows the four bitmapped brushes in a composite illustration. In the actual application, only one brush is used at a time.

Figure 18-3: Four Brushes Using Bitmaps

Using Larger Bitmaps

Earlier, a bitmap used for brushwork had a minimum size of eight pixels by eight pixels and three of the bitmap images used here were 8x8. The fourth bitmap was 24 by 24, and as a tiled image such as wallpaper in Windows, would produce the pattern shown in the left half of Figure 18-4.

When used as a brush pattern, however, the resulting pattern appears as shown in the right half of Figure 18-4. (Note: The two halves of Figure 18-4 are not to the same scale.) What's happening here?

Quite simple. While bitmaps larger than 8x8 can be used for patterned brushes, only the upper left 8x8 bits are actually used. The remainder of the bitmap image is ignored. And that is exactly what has happened here: The upper left 64 bits are used to create a repeating brush pattern, and the remainer is ignored.

Storing Images

In Windows, two quite different methods are used to store image information, bitmap files and metafiles. A bitmap file is, essentially, a pixel-by-pixel copy of an image, while a metafile is a description of an image written as a record of the GDI function calls (such as *Rectangle, MoveTo, Arc, TextOut,* etc.,) used to create the picture. The most important difference between these is the amount of information required.

For example, for a 640x480 pixel color screen, even with data compression, a bitmap requires over 150 Kbytes. Metafile images, in general, create the same screen from a much smaller file of information. Nevertheless, metafiles have their own limitations, as you will see in Chapter 19.

Figure 18-4: Intended VS Actual Bitmap Results

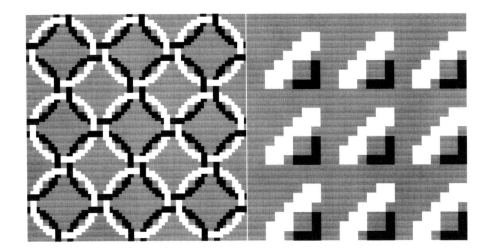

Old-Style Bitmaps

The old-style bitmap format originated with Windows 1.0, and has the principal drawback of being highly device-dependent, i.e., bitmaps are structured for a specific display format and are not readily transported to, or compatible with, other video/device formats.

A monochrome bitmap was described previously using the *CreateBitmap* function and an array of eight *WORD* values defining a simple brick pattern with an 8x8 pixel dimension. Old style bitmaps are not limited in size, though the 8x8 size is the practical limit for brushes. However, all bitmaps—monochrome or color—must be an even number of bytes in width.

Windows provides four functions for creating old-style bitmaps:

```
hBitmap = CreateBitmap( cwWidth, cyHeight,
                        nPlanes, nBitsPixel, lpBits );
hBitmap = CreateBitmapIndirect( &bitmap );
hBitmap = CreateCompatibleBitmap( hdc, cxWidth, cyHeight );
hBitmap = CreateDiscardableBitmap( hdc, cxWidth, cyHeight );
```

The *cxWidth* and *cyHeight* parameters define the width and height of the bitmap in pixels.

The *nPlanes* and *nBitsPixel* parameters, in *CreateBitmap*, define the number of color planes and number of bits per pixel. At least one of these values must be set to one but if both are one, they result in a monochrome bitmap. However, in the *CreateCompatibleBitmap* and *CreateDiscardableBitmap* functions, the device context handle (*hdc*) permits Windows to access the number of color planes and color bits per pixel directly.

Using *CreateBitmap*, if *lpBits* is *NULL*, the bitmap is uninitialized, i.e., it contains random image data. Both the *CreateCompatibleBitmap* and *Create-DiscardableBitmap* functions create uninitialized bitmap images (see *SetBitmap-Bits* and *GetBitmapBits* following).

The *CreateBitmapIndirect* function uses the structure *BITMAP* to define the bitmap data as:

Table 18-2: BITMAP Structure

Field	Type	Description
bmType	int	0
bmWidth	int	width in pixels
bmHeight	int	height in pixels
bmWidthBytes	int	width of bitmap in bytes (even values only)
bmPlanes	BYTE	number of color planes
bmBitsPixel	BYTE	number of color bits / pixel
bmBits	LPSTR	far pointer to array of bits

SetBitmapBits/GetBitmapBits

The *SetBitmapBits* function can be used to copy a character (or *BYTE*) array into an existing bitmap, such as an uninitialized bitmap. For example, *Set-BitmapBits* is called as:

```
SetBitmapBits( hBitmap, dwCount, lpBits );
```

Or an image can be retrieved from an existing bitmap using the *GetBitmap-Bits* function:

```
GetBitmapBits( hBitmap, dwCount, lpBits );
```

The *GetBitmapBits* function copies *dwCount* bits from *hBitmap* to the char (or *BYTE*) array addressed by *lpBits*.

The *GetObject* function can be used to retrieve information about *hBitmap* as:

```
GetObject( hBitmap, sizeof(BITMAP), (LPSTR) &bm );
```

dwCount can be calculated as:

```
dwCount = (DWORD) bm.bmWidthBytes * bm.bmHeight * bm.bmPlanes;
```

Last, since these bitmaps are GDI objects, the *DeleteObject* function should be used to cancel the object when no longer needed:

```
DeleteObject( hBitmap );
```

Monochrome Bitmaps

Monochrome bitmaps were introduced previously with the *wBricks* array, and used to create an 8x8 monochrome brush from an array of eight *WORD* values. For actual bitmaps, of course, the 8x8 bit limitation does not apply, though each scan line of the bitmap must be an even number of bytes (some multiple of 16 bits using zeros to pad right).

For example, a simple bitmap consisting of a square with an x in the center could be defined as:

```
1 1 1 1 1 1 1 1 0 0 0 0 0 0 0 0 = FF 80
1 1 0 0 0 0 0 1 1 0 0 0 0 0 0 0 = C1 80
1 0 1 0 0 0 1 0 1 0 0 0 0 0 0 0 = A2 80
1 0 0 1 0 1 0 0 1 0 0 0 0 0 0 0 = 94 80
1 0 0 0 1 0 0 0 1 0 0 0 0 0 0 0 = 88 80
1 0 0 1 0 1 0 0 1 0 0 0 0 0 0 0 = 94 80
1 0 1 0 0 0 1 0 1 0 0 0 0 0 0 0 = A2 80
1 1 0 0 0 0 0 1 1 0 0 0 0 0 0 0 = C1 80
1 1 1 1 1 1 1 1 0 0 0 0 0 0 0 0 = FF 80
```

In order to make the bitmap 9x9, each scan line is padded with seven zeros for a total width of 16 bits, or two bytes. The actual bitmap structure could be defined as:

```
static BITMAP bm = { 0, 9, 9, 2, 1, 1 };
```

and the data stored in a BYTE array as:

```
static BYTE CheckBox[] = { 0xFF, 0x80, 0xC1, 0x80, 0xA2,
               0x80, 0x94, 0x80, 0x88, 0x80, 0x94, 0x80,
               0xA2, 0x80, 0xC1, 0x80, 0xFF, 0x80 }
```

Note: In the old bitmap style, images are coded from the top down. But in the new DIB style, images are coded from the bottom up.

The simplest method of creating a bitmap from this data is:

```
hBitmap = CreateBitmap( 9, 9, 1, 1, CheckBox );
```

The *CreateBitmapIndirect* function can also be used as:

```
bm.bmBits = (LPSTR) CheckBox;
hBitmap = CreateBitmapIndirect( &bm );
```

There is one limitation to this format: Since Windows may move data around as necessary, the address returned for *CheckBox* may be invalid unless it is used almost immediately after it is accessed.

This potential problem can be avoided, by first creating the bitmap and then transferring the bitmap image:

```
hBitmap = CreateBitmapIndirect( &bm );
SetBitmapBits( hBitmap, (DWORD) sizeof(CheckBox), CheckBox );
```

Color Bitmaps

For color bitmaps, the old Windows style is a bit more complex than for monochrome bitmaps, and it is extremely device-dependent. To show how and why, we will begin by constructing a bitmap similar to *CheckBox*, but using two colors, dark green and white (assuming a standard palette) instead of black and white.

The bitmap image can be calculated as:

```
F F F F F F F F F F 0 0 0 = FF FF FF FF F0 00
F F 2 2 2 2 2 F F 0 0 0 = FF 22 22 2F F0 00
F 2 F 2 2 2 F 2 F 0 0 0 = F2 F2 22 F2 F0 00
F 2 2 F 2 F 2 2 F 0 0 0 = F2 2F 22 F2 F0 00
F 2 2 2 F 2 2 2 F 0 0 0 = F2 22 F2 22 F0 00
F 2 2 F 2 F 2 2 F 0 0 0 = F2 2F 2F 22 F0 00
F 2 F 2 2 2 F 2 F 0 0 0 = F2 F2 22 F2 F0 00
F F 2 2 2 2 2 F F 0 0 0 = FF 22 22 2F F0 00
F F F F F F F F F 0 0 0 = FF FF FF FF F0 00
```

Notice that the bits are still padded to a *WORD* width by adding three zero (black) pixels at the end of each scan line. This array can be defined as:

```
static BYTE CheckBox[] = { 0xFF, 0xFF, 0xFF, 0xFF, 0xF0,
    0x00, 0xFF, 0x22, 0x22, 0x2F, 0xF0, 0x00, 0xF2, 0xF2,
    0x22, 0xF2, 0xF0, 0x00, 0xF2, 0x2F, 0x22, 0xF2, 0xF0,
    0x00, 0xF2, 0x22, 0xF2, 0x22, 0xF0, 0x00, 0xF2, 0x2F,
    0x2F, 0x22, 0xF0, 0x00, 0xF2, 0xF2, 0x22, 0xF2, 0xF0,
    0x00, 0xFF, 0x22, 0x22, 0x2F, 0xF0, 0x00, 0xFF, 0xFF,
    0xFF, 0xFF, 0xF0, 0x00 };
```

For an EGA/VGA device, this bitmap can be interpreted as a marked checkbox image in white against a dark green background with each four bits representing the appropriate palette color for one pixel.

What about an IBM8514/A, which interprets each eight bits as the color value for one pixel? Not only will the image be quite different, but the colors will be different as well. The solution to this quandary is found in the device-independent bitmap format.

Device-Independent Bitmaps

The device-independent bitmap (DIB) format, an extension of the OS/2 Presentation Manager bitmap format, provides device independence, in part by including an RGB color table for all colors used in the bitmap. Device-independent bitmaps can be created automatically by using the WRT Bitmap Editor accompanying Borland C++, as well as the SDKPAINT program in the Windows Software Development Kit, the PaintBrush program included with Windows, and many third party programs.

A sample bitmap file appears in hex format in Figure 18-5, where alternate fields, as defined by the data structures, have been half-toned for ease of identification. The several data sections and structures will be identified further.

Figure 18-5: DIB Bitmap File Dump (BRICKS.BMP)

```
00 │ 42 4D 96 00 00 00 00 00 00 00 76 00 00 00 28 00
10 │ 00 00 08 00 00 00 08 00 00 00 01 00 04 00 00 00
20 │ 00 00 20 00 00 00 00 00 00 00 00 00 00 00 00 00
30 │ 00 00 00 00 00 00 00 00 00 00 00 00 80 00 00 80
40 │ 00 00 00 80 80 00 80 00 00 00 80 00 80 00 80 80
50 │ 00 00 80 80 80 00 C0 C0 C0 00 00 00 FF 00 00 FF
60 │ 00 00 00 FF FF 00 FF 00 00 00 FF 00 FF 00 FF FF
70 │ 00 00 FF FF FF 00 81 11 11 11 81 11 11 11 81 11
80 │ 11 11 88 88 88 88 11 11 81 11 11 11 81 11 11 11
90 │ 81 11 88 88 88 88
```

The DIB Header

The bitmap file begins with a file header containing information about the structure of the file itself (Table 18-3) in the first 14 bytes.

Table 18-3: DIB File Format

Field	——example—— Size	Data	Value	Description
bfType	WORD	42 4D	"BM"	for bitmap
bfSize	DWORD	96 00 00 00	96h	total size of file
reserved1	WORD	00 00 0	h	set to 0
reserved2	WORD	00 00	0h	set to 0
bfOffBits	DWORD	76 00 00 00	76h	offset to bitmap image from first of file

Notice that all data is arranged in *lsb..msb* order, i.e., the data bytes 96 00 00 00 do not represent the value 96000000h but 00000096h.

The BITMAPINFOHEADER Section

The file header information is followed by second header defined by the BITMAPINFOHEADER structure (defined in *Windows.H*, see "Structures For Defining DIBs" in Appendix A). This header contains information about the size and dimensions of the bitmap image, color organization, and data compression. Additional information may be included about device horizontal and vertical resolution, and about any special color information which is contained in the bitmap file.

At the same time, color is represented only as multiple color bits per pixel, regardless of how the physical device handles color, and may specify one bit per pixel for monochrome, four for 16-color bitmaps, eight for 256 color bitmaps, or 24 bits for 16 million colors.

Table 18-4: BITMAPINFOHEADER Structure

Field	Size	—example— Data	Value	Description
biSize	DWORD	28 00 00 00	28h	size of BITMAPINFOHEADER
biWidth	DWORD	08 00 00 00	8h	bitmap pixel width
biHeight	DWORD	08 00 00 00	8h	bitmap pixel height
biPlanes	WORD	01 00	1h	color planes (always 1)
biBitCount	WORD	04 00	4h	color bits per pixel (1, 4, 8, 24)
biCompression	DWORD	00 00 00 00	0h	compression scheme (0 = none)
biSizeImage	DWORD	20 00 00 00	20h	bitmap image size (used only if compression is set)
biXPelsPerMeter	DWORD	00 00 00 00	0h	horizontal resolution (pixels/meter)
biYPelsPerMeter	DWORD	00 00 00 00	0h	vertical resolution (pixels/meter)
biClrUsed	DWORD	00 00 00 00	0h	number of colors used inimage
biClrImportant	DWORD	00 00 00 00	0h	number of important colors

If data compression is used, the data compression scheme is identified together with the actual size of the uncompressed bitmap (in bytes) for a redundancy check in decompressing (see Appendix A, "Constants For The biCompression Field").

The *biClrUsed* and *biClrImportant* may contain additional information about custom colors or multiple color palettes. Zero values in these last four fields simply indicate default values.

The Bitmap Color Table

Following the BITMAPINFOHEADER structure, and enclosed by an outline in Figure 18-5, is the bitmap color table. This consists of a series of RGBQUAD structures. In the order read, the first byte is blue intensity, the second green, the third red, and the fourth byte of each is set to zero.

The number of *RGBQUAD* structures is set by the *biBitCount* field. For a setting of one color bit, two *RGBQUAD* values are required (foreground and background), for four color bits, 16 *RGBQUAD* values are needed (as here), and for eight color bits, 256 *RGBQUAD* values. If the *biClrUsed* field is non-zero, then the *biClrUsed* field reports the number of *RGBQUAD* structures in the color table.

Table 18-5 shows the default color values for a VGA 16-color palette.

Table 18-5: Color Values From BitMap

Palette Entry	Rgbquad Data	Color Value R	G	B	Approximate Color
0	00 00 00 00	00	00	00	Black
1	00 00 80 00	80	00	00	Dark Red
2	00 80 00 00	00	80	00	Dark Green
3	00 80 80 00	80	80	00	Gold Green
4	80 00 00 00	00	00	80	Dark Blue
5	80 00 80 00	80	00	80	Purple
6	80 80 00 00	00	80	80	Blue Gray
7	80 80 80 00	80	80	80	Dark Gray
8	C0 C0 C0 00	C0	C0	C0	Light Gray
9	00 00 FF 00	FF	00	00	Light Red
10	00 FF 00 00	00	FF	00	Light Green
11	00 FF FF 00	FF	FF	00	Yellow
12	FF 00 00 00	00	00	FF	Light Blue
13	FF 00 FF 00	FF	00	FF	Magenta
14	FF FF 00 00	00	FF	FF	Cyan
15	FF FF FF 00	FF	FF	FF	White

The Bitmap Image

The final portion of the bitmap file is the bitmap image itself. The arrangement of this portion of the file is partially dependent on the number of colors used, as reported by the *biBitCount* field, but there are two other elements in the organization of the bitmap image which are constant:

- First, each row of the bitmap image is always some multiple of four bytes (*DWORD*), with the row padded on the right with nulls if necessary. Each row begins, of course, with the left-most pixel.

■ Second, unlike the original bitmap format for device-independent bitmaps, the array of pixels begins with the bottom row of the image, not the top.

For a monochrome bitmap with one color bit per pixel, the bit image begins with the most significant bit of the first byte in each row. If the bit value is zero, the first RGBQUAD color value is used; if it is one, the second RGBQUAD value is used. For a monochrome bitmap, the BRICKS bitmap data would be coded as:

```
80 80 80 FF 08 08 08 FF
```

and would break down as:

```
1 1 1 1 1 1 1 1            //  FF
0 0 0 0 1 0 0 0            //  08
0 0 0 0 1 0 0 0            //  08
0 0 0 0 1 0 0 0            //  08
1 1 1 1 1 1 1 1            //  FF
1 0 0 0 0 0 0 0            //  80
1 0 0 0 0 0 0 0            //  80
1 0 0 0 0 0 0 0            //  80
```

Remember, the bitmap is coded with the bottom row first, working up.

For a sixteen color bitmap—four color bits per pixel—each pixel is represented by a four-bit value that serves as an index to the entries in the color table. Thus, the bitmap image for BRICKS appears as:

```
81 11 11 11 81 11 11 11 81 11 11 11 88 88 88 88
11 11 81 11 11 11 81 11 11 11 81 11 88 88 88 88
```

and is decoded as:

```
8 8 8 8 8 8 8 8
1 1 1 1 8 1 1 1
1 1 1 1 8 1 1 1
1 1 1 1 8 1 1 1
8 8 8 8 8 8 8 8
8 1 1 1 1 1 1 1
8 1 1 1 1 1 1 1
8 1 1 1 1 1 1 1
```

For a 256-color bitmap, each pixel is represented by a byte value indexing the 256 entries in the color table.

Last, for a 24-color-bit-per pixel bitmap, unless the *biClrUsed* field is non-zero, instead of a 16 million entry color table, each pixel is represented by a three- byte *RGBcolor* value. If the *biClrUsed* field is non-zero, then a color table appears and pixels are indexed to the table.

OS/2 Bitmaps

OS/2, version 1.1 and later, uses a bitmap structure very similar to Windows 3.0. The differences are that instead of a BITMAPINFOHEADER structure, a BITMAPCOREHEADER structure is used (see Appendix A), and the color table consists of RGBTRIPLEs instead of RGBQUADs.

Bitmap types (OS/2 vs. Windows) can be identified by identifying the structure used. To do so, examine the first *DWORD* in the structure (the *biSize* or *bcSize* field) for the structure size.

The Dimension Functions

Windows also supplies two bitmap functions dealing with dimensions: *SetBitmapDimension* and *GetBitmapDimension*. These two functions do not, however, have any connection with the pixel dimensions of bitmaps (which can not be changed once defined), but provide a means of setting or retrieving bitmap dimensions in logical units in MM_LOMETRIC mapping mode. These dimensions are not used by the GDI, but can be used by cooperating applications to assist in scaling bitmaps that are exchanged via the clipboard, DDE, or other means. These functions are called as:

```
SetBitmapDimension( hBitmap, xUnits, yUnits );
dwBMSize = GetBitmapDimension( hBitmap );
```

The *xUnits* size is found in the low word of *dwBMSize*; the *yUnits* size in the high word.

Creating and Using Device-Independent Bitmaps

The theory of device-independent bitmaps is all very well, but, in practice, the important consideration is being able to create and display a bitmap. Ideally,

you expect a simple function to be introduced with a name and format
something like:

```
DrawBitmap( hwnd, lpBitmapName, xPos, yPos );
```

However, even though bitmaps are an important and integral part of
Windows' GDI, there are no basic functions provided to display and manip-
ulate bitmap images. Instead, Windows provides a series of bitmap primitives
which can and will be used to create several of the missing high-level bitmap
handlers.

Step One: A Global Instance Handle

Earlier, using bitmaps for brush patterns, several bitmaps were loaded in the
WinMain procedure so that these could be used later to create logical brushes.
The *LoadBitmap* instruction(s) appeared in *WinMain* for the simple reason that
this was the only portion of the program where the *hInst* application instance
handle was available (*hInst* is passed by Windows to *WinMain* as a calling
parameter when the application instance is created). While loading all bitmaps
at the start of the program is possible, it is not the most practical approach, or
the most desireable. Therefore, to give us more flexibility, a global handle is
declared as:

```
HANDLE    hGInst;
```

and is assigned in *WinMain* as:

```
hGInst = hInst;
```

The alternative, of course, would be to pass *hInst* as a calling parameter to
any subprocedures which might need to call *DrawBitmap,* but, as a method of
saving the overhead of a 16-bit global variable, this would be a foolish
approach. With *hGInst* available as a global instance handle, the *LoadBitmap*
function can be relegated to its proper place within our *DrawBitmap* function.

Step Two: Loading The Bitmap

Later, several other bitmap handlers will be demonstrated, but to begin, the
basic form simply displays a bitmap at the coordinates specified, and is called

with four parameters: The window handle, the bitmap name, and the x and y window coordinates for position.

```
BOOL DrawBitmap( HWND hwnd, LPSTR lpName,
                 int xPos, int yPos )
{
```

DrawBitmap is also given the capacity of returning a boolean result to report success or failure, but, as with most C functions, this return value can be used or ignored as desired. Also, for local use, a couple of variables will be needed:

```
HDC     hdc, hdcMem;
BITMAP  bm;
HBITMAP hBitmap;
```

Finally, the function is ready to load the bitmap which, during the final binding, was joined with the .EXE file. Notice that here is where the global *hGInst* handle is used:

```
if( !( hBitmap = LoadBitmap( hGInst, lpName ) ) )
    return( FALSE );
```

If for any reason the load fails, *DrawBitmap* returns *FALSE,* but this is the only error check which will be made. Now that the bitmap is loaded, the next step is to establish an appropriate device context.

Step 3: Device Contexts

In Windows, bitmaps can not be drawn directly to the screen's device context. Instead, a separate device context is created in memory using the *hdcMem* declared earlier as a local variable. At the same time, the application's existing device context cannot be ignored. Therefore, the first step is to retrieve a handle to the application's device context:

```
hdc = GetDC( hwnd );
hdcMem = CreateCompatibleDC( hdc );
```

CreateCompatibleDC is called to create a memory device context compatible with the *hdc* device context. A memory device context is a block of memory representing a display surface, and, as with bitmaps, can be used to prepare an image in memory before copying the image to the actual surface of the compatible device (i.e., the client window or other output device). Note that when a memory device context is created, the GDI automatically assigns a "display surface" with a one by one monochrome bitmap, i.e., the initial device context contains one monochrome pixel, hardly enough space for any real operations. This last deficiency, however, can be corrected immediately by calling *SelectObject* to make the current bitmap the active object for the device context:

```
SelectObject( hdcMem, hBitmap );
SetMapMode( hdcMem, GetMapMode( hdc ) );
```

The *SetMapMode* function assigns the same mode to the memory device context as to the window device context (*hdc*).

Making the bitmap the active object for the device context and setting the map mode is only part of the job, because there is still a lot of information from the selected bitmap that needs to be transferred to the local bitmap record (*bm*).

Step 4: Bitmap Information And Mapping Coordinates

Most of the necessary information can be transferred by calling the *GetObject* function to fill the buffer (*bm*) with the data defining the logical object, the selected bitmap. For a bitmap, GetObject returns the width, height, and color format information. The actual bits of the bitmap image will be retrieved separately:

```
GetObject( hBitmap, sizeof(BITMAP), (LPSTR) &bm );
```

There is still one very important task remaining, because the bitmap image information has not yet been retrieved.

Step 5: Bit Block Transfers

The *BitBlt* function (pronounced "bit-blit"), together with the *PatBlt* and *StretchBlt* functions, comprises Windows' pixel manipulation power operations. Technically, BitBlt stands for "bit-block transfer" but more is involved than simply copying bits from one memory location to another. Instead, the bit transfer involves a choice of raster (logical) operation between three sets of bits (or pixels). While not the simplest of the three, the BitBlt operation is the present operation of choice, and completes the task of writing the bitmap image to the client window:

```
BitBlt( hdc, xPos, yPos, bm.bmWidth, bm.bmHeight,
        hdcMem, 0, 0, SRCCOPY );
```

BitBlt moves a bitmap from the source device (*hdcMem*) to the destination device (*hdc*), with the xSrc and ySrc parameters ((0,0) in the example) specifying the origin in the source device context of the bitmap to be moved. If the *dwRop* parameter (raster operation type) specifies a raster operation which does not include a source, the source device context must be NULL.

The *xPos*, *yPos*, width, and height parameters specify the origin point and size of the rectangle in the destination device context to be filled by the bitmap image. Note that unlike most previous operations, instead of a rectangle (RECT) structure, the origin point is set in device context coordinates, but the width and height values are passed directly, rather than as point coordinates.

The final parameter is a raster-operation code. This defines how the graphics device interface combines colors in output operations which can involve a current brush, a possible source bitmap, and a destination bitmap. For the DrawBitmap operation, the SRCCOPY code copies the source bitmap image directly to the destination (*hdc*).

Table 18-6: Raster Operations Codes

Code	(**P**) Pattern (**S**) Source Bitmap (**D**) Destination Operation	Description
BLACKNESS	0	turns all output black
DSTINVERT	~D	inverts destination
MERGECOPY	P & S	ANDs pattern and source bitmap
MERGEPAINT	~S | D	ORs inverted source bitmap with destination
NOTSRCCOPY	~S	copies inverted source bitmap to destination
NOTSRCERASE	~ (S | D)	ORs destination and source bitmap, then inverts result
PATCOPY	P	copies pattern to destination
PATINVERT	P ^ D	XORs pattern and destination
PATPAINT	P | ~S | D	ORs inverted source bitmap with pattern, then OR s result with destination
SRCAND	S & D	ANDs destination and source bitmaps
SRCCOPY	S	copies source bitmap to destination
SRCERASE	S & ~D	ANDs source bitmap with inverted destination

Table 18-6: Raster Operations Codes (cont.)

Code	(**P**) Pattern (**S**) Source Bitmap Operation	(**D**) Destination Description
SRCINVERT	S ^ D	XORs destination with source bitmaps
SRCPAINT	I D	ORs destination with source bitmap
WHITENESS	1	turns all output white

Note: A total of 256 ROP codes exists but only the preceding 15 ROP codes are identified by name constants. Details for the remaining ROP codes can be found, if desired, in the *Microsoft Windows Programmer's Reference*.

Monochrome operations using ROP codes are relatively straightforward: Bits are either on or off. For color, however, Windows executes separate operations on each color plane or each set of color bits, depending on the organization of the device memory. These operations will be easiest to understand simply by experimentation with the various ROP codes.

Step 6: Clean Up

The *BitBlt* function completed the task of drawing the bitmap, but there is still a bit of clean-up required before the task is finished:

```
    ReleaseDC( hwnd, hdc );
    DeleteDC( hdcMem );
    DeleteObject( hBitmap );
    return( TRUE );
}
```

Once the three local memory allocations are cleaned up, DrawBitmap is free to report success. Everything's done, for this operation, at least.

The DrawBitmap function is demonstrated in PenDraw5.C. Complete source code appears at the end of this chapter.

Stretching Bitmaps

Drawing a bitmap on a one-for-one pixel basis is probably the operation that will be most useful to you. However, there is another bitmap operation that allows you to stretch or distort a bitmap to fit any space desired: the *StretchBlt* function.

In brief, StretchBlt moves a bitmap from a source rectangle to a destination rectangle, stretching or compressing the bitmap as necessary to fit the dimensions of the destination rectangle.

Calling StretchBlt is very similar to calling BitBlt, but with two differences as shown here:

```
BitBlt( hdc, xPos, yPos, bm.bmWidth, bm.bmHeight,
        hdcMem, xOrg, yOrg, SRCCOPY );
StretchBlt( hdc, xPos, yPos, xWidth, yHeight,
        hdcMem, xOrg, yOrg, xOWidth, yOWidth, SRCCOPY);
```

In the StretchBlt example program, a RECT structure has been used to pass the size of the destination rectangle. In the BitBlt example, only a location was passed, and the bitmap's own width and height values were used to set the size.

The second difference is that StretchBlt has four, rather than two, parameters specifying what portion of the source device context to transfer. Further, since the bitmap image is distorted in the process, StretchBlt uses the stretching mode of the destination device context (set by the *SetStretchBltMode* function) to determine how to stretch or compress the bitmap. As with BitBlt, the raster operation specified by the dwRop parameter defines how the source bitmap and the bits already on the destination device are combined (see Table 18-6).

Last, StretchBlt can also create a mirror image of a bitmap if the signs of the source and destination width, or source and destination height, are different. I.e., if the destination width is negative and the source width is positive (or vice versa), StretchBlt creates a mirror image rotated along the x-axis. For the height parameters, the mirror image is rotated along the y-axis.

The SetStretchBltMode

The SetStretchBltMode function sets the stretching mode used by the StretchBlt function. The stretching mode defines which scan lines and/or columns StretchBlt eliminates when contracting a bitmap. The stretch mode is set for the destination device context and is called as:

```
SetStretchBltMode( hdc, nStretchMode );
```

Table 18-7: Stretch Modes

Value	Meaning
BLACKONWHITE	Eliminated lines are ANDed with retained lines, preserving black pixels at the expense of white pixels.
COLORONCOLOR	Eliminated lines are deleted without trying to preserve their information.
WHITEONBLACK	Eliminated lines are ORed with retained lines, preserving white pixels at the expense of black pixels.

BLACKONWHITE and WHITEONBLACK modes are typically used to preserve foreground pixels in monochrome bitmaps. COLORONCOLOR mode is typically used to preserve color in color bitmaps. The return value reports the previous stretching mode.

Demonstrating Bitmap Operations:PenDraw5

The PenDraw5 program demonstrates both the BitBlt and StretchBlt bitmap functions, showing these in several different contexts even though only the two basic functions are used. PenDraw5 requires five bitmaps, four 16x16 pixel bitmaps, and one 40x70 pixel bitmap as illustrated in Figure 18-6. However, any bitmaps desired can be substituted as long as the appropriate name changes are made in the .RES resource file and in the source code.

The DrawBitmap function discussed in this chapter draws the designated bitmap and positions the upper-left corner of the bitmap at the coordinates specified. All five bitmaps are drawn with the four smaller bitmaps placed at the corners of a rectangle within the client window, and the fifth bitmap located at the center.

The DrawCenBitmap function operates in the same fashion as DrawBitmap except that the bitmaps are centered at the coordinates specified.

The LineGraph function uses a brief array of data to position a series of bitmaps in the form of a simple line graph display.

The StretchBitmap function stretches a bitmap to fit a specified rectangle while the StretchBitmap2Client function stretches a bitmap to fill the entire client window.

Last, the MoveBitmap function tracks mouse movement with a bitmap when the left mouse button is down. Note, however, that bitmaps are not particularly well suited to this type of operation, and this is demonstrated more as a curiosity than as a serious suggestion.

If you really need to move bitmaps around the screen, you may find better results by using two bitmaps in combination, with the second bitmap created as a screen mask. This prepares the image background and restores the background when the image is moved.

For hints on how screen masks operate, refer to mouse cursor operations. Some details on this subject can also be found in Chapter 16 of *Graphics Programming In Turbo C++*, published by Addison Wesley.

Figure 18-6: Five Bitmaps For PenDraw5

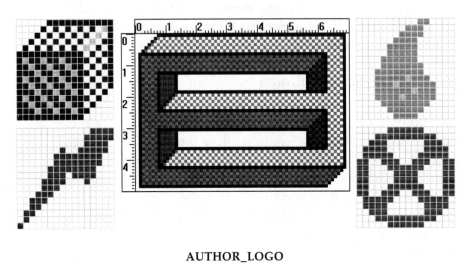

AUTHOR_LOGO

BOX — top left
ELECTRIC — bottom left

OIL_DROP — top right
WHEEL — bottom right

Summary

Bitmap operations are powerful tools, and extend well beyond the few uses demonstrated in this chapter. For example, bitmaps can be copied from the screen, generated or modified off-screen, and pasted from window to window.

However, attempting to demonstrate all of the potentials inherent in bitmap operations would probably try our patience and prevent us from moving on to other important areas.

Recommended reading includes the *Windows 3.0 Programming Primer* by Alan Southerton (published by Addison Wesley) as a source for further bitmap operation examples as well as other interesting subroutines. One caution: the *Programming Primer* was written using Microsoft C rather than Borland C++, and some examples may require minor modifications.

```
//=======================//
//        PenDraw4.C       //
//   C++ Windows Drawing   //
//=======================//

#include <windows.h>
#include <stdio.h>
#include "pendraw4.h"

static HBITMAP hBitMap[4];
static POINT   pt[] =
       { -110, 100, -52, -80, -205,  30, -15, 30, -168, -80,
         -110, 100, 110, 100,  153, -90,  32, 63,  207, -22,
           13, -22, 188,  62,   67, -90, 110, 100   };
static int     ply[] = {  6, 8  };

long FAR PASCAL WndProc( HWND hwnd,    WORD msg,
                         WORD wParam, LONG lParam )
{
    static  int  cxWnd, cyWnd, nBitMap = IDM_BRICK;
    HDC          hdc;
    HMENU        hMenu;
    HBRUSH       hBrush;
    PAINTSTRUCT  ps;
    int          i;

    switch( msg )
    {
        case WM_COMMAND:
            hMenu = GetMenu( hwnd );
            switch( wParam )
            {
                case IDM_BRICK:    case IDM_CHAINS:
                case IDM_DIAMOND:  case IDM_STRIPE:
                    CheckMenuItem( hMenu, nBitMap, MF_UNCHECKED );
                    nBitMap = wParam;
                    CheckMenuItem( hMenu, nBitMap, MF_CHECKED );
                    break;
            }
```

```
            InvalidateRect( hwnd, NULL, TRUE );
            return(0);

        case WM_SIZE:
            cxWnd = LOWORD( lParam );
            cyWnd = HIWORD( lParam );
            return(0);

        case WM_PAINT:
            hdc = BeginPaint( hwnd, &ps );
            hBrush = CreatePatternBrush(
                        hBitMap[ nBitMap-IDM_BRICK ] );
            SelectObject( hdc, hBrush );
            SetMapMode( hdc, MM_ISOTROPIC );
            SetWindowExt(   hdc,    440,   -220 );
            SetViewportExt( hdc, cxWnd, cyWnd );
            SetWindowOrg(   hdc,   -220,    110 );
            SetPolyFillMode( hdc, ALTERNATE );
            PolyPolygon( hdc, pt, ply, 2 );
            DeleteObject( hBrush );
            EndPaint( hwnd, &ps );
            return(0);

        case WM_DESTROY:
            for( i=1; i<3; i++ ) DeleteObject( hBitMap[i] );
            PostQuitMessage(0);
            return(0);
    }
    return( DefWindowProc( hwnd, msg, wParam, lParam ) );
}

#pragma argsused

int PASCAL WinMain( HANDLE hInst,        HANDLE hPrevInst,
                    LPSTR  lpszCmdParam, int nCmdShow )
{
    static char szAppName[] = "PENDRAW4";
    HWND        hwnd;
    MSG         msg;
    WNDCLASS    wc;

    if( ! hPrevInst )
    {
        wc.hInstance      = hInst;
        wc.lpfnWndProc    = WndProc;
        wc.cbClsExtra     = 0;
        wc.cbWndExtra     = 0;
```

```
    wc.lpszClassName = szAppName;
    wc.hIcon          = LoadIcon( hInst, szAppName );
    wc.lpszMenuName  = (LPSTR) szAppName;
    wc.hCursor        = LoadCursor( NULL, IDC_ARROW );
    wc.hbrBackground = GetStockObject( WHITE_BRUSH );
    wc.style          = CS_HREDRAW | CS_VREDRAW;
    RegisterClass( &wc );
}
hBitMap[0] = LoadBitmap( hInst, "BRICKS"  );
hBitMap[1] = LoadBitmap( hInst, "CHAINS"  );
hBitMap[2] = LoadBitmap( hInst, "DIAMOND" );
hBitMap[3] = LoadBitmap( hInst, "STRIPES" );
hwnd = CreateWindow( szAppName,
                     "Pen Draw 4: Bitmapped Brushes",
                     WS_OVERLAPPEDWINDOW,
                     CW_USEDEFAULT, CW_USEDEFAULT,
                     CW_USEDEFAULT, CW_USEDEFAULT,
                     NULL, NULL, hInst, NULL  );
ShowWindow(   hwnd, nCmdShow );
UpdateWindow( hwnd );
while( GetMessage( &msg, NULL, 0, 0 ) )
{
    TranslateMessage( &msg );
    DispatchMessage(  &msg );
}
return( msg.wParam );
}


                    ;================;
                    ;  PENDRAW4.DEF  ;
                    ;================;

NAME            PENDRAW4

DESCRIPTION     "DRAWING WITH BITMAPS"
EXETYPE         WINDOWS
STUB            "WINSTUB.EXE"
CODE            PRELOAD MOVEABLE DISCARDABLE
DATA            PRELOAD MOVEABLE MULTIPLE
HEAPSIZE        1024
STACKSIZE       8192
EXPORTS         WndProc
```

```
                     //==============//
                     //  PENDRAW4.H  //
                     //==============//

#define   IDM_BRICK       100
#define   IDM_CHAINS      101
#define   IDM_DIAMOND     102
#define   IDM_STRIPE      103


                   //==================//
                   //   PenDraw4.RC    //
                   // application menu //
                   //==================//

PENDRAW4   MENU LOADONCALL MOVEABLE PURE DISCARDABLE
BEGIN
    POPUP "&Bitmaps"
    BEGIN
        MenuItem   "&Bricks\t(8x8)",    100, CHECKED
        MenuItem   "&Chain\t(24x24)",   101
        MenuItem   "&Diamonds\t(8x8)",  102
        MenuItem   "&Stripes\t(8x8)",   103
    END
END


                  //=======================//
                  //         PenDraw5.C     //
                  //   C++ Windows Drawing  //
                  //=======================//

#include <windows.h>
#include <stdio.h>
#include "pendraw5.h"

HANDLE    hGInst;                        // global instance handle //
int       BitmapOp    = IDM_DrawBM;
BOOL      bMoveBitmap = FALSE;
HBITMAP   hBitmap;
POINT     ptBitmap;

static    int  LineData[] = { 100, 150, 130, 160, 125, 155,
                              125, 140, 110, 120, 135, 140,
                              150, 155, 145, 130, 120, 100 };


HCURSOR SwitchCursor( LPSTR lpName )
{
```

```
    HCURSOR    hCursor;

    hCursor = LoadCursor( NULL, lpName );
    SetCursor( hCursor );
    return( hCursor );
}

BOOL DrawBitmap( HWND hwnd, LPSTR lpName,
                int xPos, int yPos )
{
    HDC     hdc, hdcMem;
    BITMAP  bm;
    HBITMAP hBitmap;

    if( !( hBitmap = LoadBitmap( hGInst, lpName ) ) )
        return( FALSE );
    hdc = GetDC( hwnd );
    hdcMem = CreateCompatibleDC( hdc );
    SelectObject( hdcMem, hBitmap );
    SetMapMode( hdcMem, GetMapMode( hdc ) );
    GetObject( hBitmap, sizeof(BITMAP), (LPSTR) &bm );
    BitBlt( hdc, xPos, yPos, bm.bmWidth, bm.bmHeight,
            hdcMem, 0, 0, SRCCOPY );
    ReleaseDC( hwnd, hdc );
    DeleteDC( hdcMem );
    DeleteObject( hBitmap );
    return( TRUE );
}

BOOL DrawCenBitmap( HWND hwnd, LPSTR lpName,
                int xPos, int yPos )
{
    HDC     hdc, hdcMem;
    BITMAP  bm;
    HBITMAP hBitmap;

    if( !( hBitmap = LoadBitmap( hGInst, lpName ) ) )
        return( FALSE );
    hdc = GetDC( hwnd );
    hdcMem = CreateCompatibleDC( hdc );
    SelectObject( hdcMem, hBitmap );
    SetMapMode( hdcMem, GetMapMode( hdc ) );
    GetObject( hBitmap, sizeof(BITMAP), (LPSTR) &bm );
    xPos -= bm.bmWidth/2;                        // center bitmap  //
    yPos -= bm.bmHeight/2;                       // on coordinates //
    BitBlt( hdc, xPos, yPos, bm.bmWidth, bm.bmHeight,
```

```
                hdcMem, 0, 0, SRCCOPY );
    ReleaseDC( hwnd, hdc );
    DeleteDC( hdcMem );
    DeleteObject( hBitmap );
    return( TRUE );
}


void LineGraph( HWND hwnd, LPSTR lpName )
{
    int  i;

    for( i=0; i<sizeof(LineData); i++ )
        DrawCenBitmap( hwnd, lpName, i*25+20, LineData[i] );
}


BOOL StretchBitmap( HWND hwnd, LPSTR lpName, RECT rect )
{
    HDC     hdc, hdcMem;
    HBITMAP hBitmap;
    BITMAP  bm;

    if( !( hBitmap = LoadBitmap( hGInst, lpName ) ) )
        return( FALSE );
    hdc = GetDC( hwnd );
    hdcMem = CreateCompatibleDC( hdc );
    SelectObject( hdcMem, hBitmap );
    SetMapMode( hdcMem, GetMapMode(hdc) );
    GetObject( hBitmap, sizeof(BITMAP), (LPSTR) &bm );
    StretchBlt( hdc, rect.left, rect.top,
                     rect.right, rect.bottom,
                hdcMem, 0, 0, bm.bmWidth, bm.bmHeight, SRCCOPY);
    DeleteDC( hdcMem );
    ReleaseDC( hwnd, hdc );
    DeleteObject( hBitmap );
    return( TRUE );
}


BOOL StretchBitMap2Client( HWND hwnd, LPSTR lpName )
{
    HDC     hdc, hdcMem;
    HBITMAP hBitmap;
    BITMAP  bm;
    RECT    rect;

    if( !( hBitmap = LoadBitmap( hGInst, lpName ) ) )
        return( FALSE );
```

```
    hdc = GetDC( hwnd );
    hdcMem = CreateCompatibleDC( hdc );
    SelectObject( hdcMem, hBitmap );
    SetMapMode( hdcMem, GetMapMode(hdc) );
    GetObject( hBitmap, sizeof(BITMAP), (LPSTR) &bm );
    GetClientRect( hwnd, &rect );
    StretchBlt( hdc, rect.left, rect.top,
                     rect.right, rect.bottom,
                hdcMem, 0, 0, bm.bmWidth, bm.bmHeight,
                SRCCOPY );
    DeleteDC( hdcMem );
    ReleaseDC( hwnd, hdc );
    DeleteObject( hBitmap );
    return( TRUE );
}

void MoveBitmap( HWND hwnd, HBITMAP hBitmap, POINT pt )
{
    HDC     hdc, hdcMem;
    BITMAP bm;

    hdc = GetDC( hwnd );
    hdcMem = CreateCompatibleDC( hdc );
    SelectObject( hdcMem, hBitmap );
    SetMapMode( hdcMem, GetMapMode(hdc) );
    GetObject( hBitmap, sizeof(BITMAP), (LPSTR) &bm );
    BitBlt( hdc, pt.x, pt.y, bm.bmWidth, bm.bmHeight,
            hdcMem, 0, 0, SRCCOPY );
    ReleaseDC( hwnd, hdc );
    DeleteDC( hdcMem );
}

Long FAR PASCAL WndProc( HWND hwnd,    WORD msg,
                         WORD wParam, LONG lParam )
{
    static   int   cxStep, cyStep;
    HDC            hdc;
    HMENU          hMenu;
    RECT           rect;
    PAINTSTRUCT    ps;

    switch( msg )
    {
        case WM_COMMAND:
            hMenu = GetMenu( hwnd );
            switch( wParam )
```

```
        {
        case IDM_DrawBM:             case IDM_CenterBM:
        case IDM_StretchBM:          case IDM_Stretch2Client:
        case IDM_BMTrackMouse:   case IDM_BMLineGraph:
            CheckMenuItem( hMenu, BitmapOp,
                            MF_UNCHECKED );
            BitmapOp = wParam;
            CheckMenuItem( hMenu, BitmapOp, MF_CHECKED );
            break;
        }
        switch( BitmapOp )
        {
        case IDM_DrawBM:
            SetWindowText( hwnd,
                "Bitmap Coordinates At UpLeft" );
            break;
        case IDM_CenterBM:
            SetWindowText( hwnd,
                "Bitmap Centered On Coordinates" );
            break;
        case IDM_StretchBM:
            SetWindowText( hwnd,
                "Bitmap Stretched To Fit Rectangle" );
            break;
        case IDM_Stretch2Client:
            SetWindowText( hwnd,
                "Bitmap Stretched To Fit Client Window" );
            break;
        case IDM_BMTrackMouse:
            SetWindowText( hwnd,
                "Bitmap Tracks Mouse (LButton Down)" );
            break;
        case IDM_BMLineGraph:
            SetWindowText( hwnd,
                "Simple Line Graph Using Bitmaps" );
            break;
        }
        InvalidateRect( hwnd, NULL, TRUE );
        return(0);

    case WM_SIZE:
        cxStep = LOWORD( lParam )/4;
        cyStep = HIWORD( lParam )/4;
        return(0);

    case WM_MOUSEMOVE:
```

```
   if( !( wParam && MK_LBUTTON ) ) break;
case WM_LBUTTONDOWN:
   if( BitmapOp == IDM_BMTrackMouse )
   {
      InvalidateRect( hwnd, NULL, TRUE );
      ptBitmap = MAKEPOINT( lParam );
   }
   return(0);

case WM_PAINT:
   hdc = BeginPaint( hwnd, &ps );
   // ...                                    //
   // all other paint operations here //
   // ...                                    //
   EndPaint( hwnd, &ps );
   switch( BitmapOp )
   {
      case IDM_DrawBM:
         DrawBitmap( hwnd, "BOX",
                     cxStep,   cyStep   );
         DrawBitmap( hwnd, "OIL_DROP",
                     cxStep,   cyStep*3 );
         DrawBitmap( hwnd, "ELECTRIC",
                     cxStep*3, cyStep   );
         DrawBitmap( hwnd, "WHEEL",
                     cxStep*3, cyStep*3 );
         DrawBitmap( hwnd, "AUTHOR_LOGO",
                     cxStep*2, cyStep*2 );
         break;

      case IDM_CenterBM:
         DrawCenBitmap( hwnd, "BOX",
                        cxStep,   cyStep   );
         DrawCenBitmap( hwnd, "OIL_DROP",
                        cxStep,   cyStep*3 );
         DrawCenBitmap( hwnd, "ELECTRIC",
                        cxStep*3, cyStep   );
         DrawCenBitmap( hwnd, "WHEEL",
                        cxStep*3, cyStep*3 );
         DrawCenBitmap( hwnd, "AUTHOR_LOGO",
                        cxStep*2, cyStep*2 );
         break;

      case IDM_StretchBM:
         SwitchCursor( IDC_WAIT );
         SetRect( &rect, cxStep, cyStep,
```

```
                        2*cxStep, 2*cyStep );
                StretchBitmap( hwnd, "BOX", rect );
                SwitchCursor( IDC_ARROW );
                break;

            case IDM_Stretch2Client:
                SwitchCursor( IDC_WAIT );
                StretchBitMap2Client( hwnd, "AUTHOR_LOGO" );
                SwitchCursor( IDC_ARROW );
                break;

            case IDM_BMTrackMouse:
                if( !bMoveBitmap )
                {
                    ptBitmap.x = 10;
                    ptBitmap.y = 10;
                    bMoveBitmap = TRUE;
                    hBitmap = LoadBitmap( hGInst, "OIL_DROP" );
                }
                MoveBitmap( hwnd, hBitmap, ptBitmap );
                break;

            case IDM_BMLineGraph:
                LineGraph( hwnd, "ELECTRIC" );
                break;
        }
        return(0);

    case WM_DESTROY:
        PostQuitMessage(0);
        return(0);
    }
    return( DefWindowProc( hwnd, msg, wParam, lParam ) );
}


#pragma argsused

int PASCAL WinMain( HANDLE hInst,       HANDLE hPrevInst,
                    LPSTR  lpszCmdParam, int nCmdShow )
{
    static char szAppName[] = "PENDRAW5";
    HWND        hwnd;
    MSG         msg;
    WNDCLASS    wc;

    if( ! hPrevInst )
```

```
{
    wc.hInstance      = hInst;
    wc.lpfnWndProc    = WndProc;
    wc.cbClsExtra     = 0;
    wc.cbWndExtra     = 0;
    wc.lpszClassName  = szAppName;
    wc.hIcon          = LoadIcon( hInst, szAppName );
    wc.lpszMenuName   = (LPSTR) szAppName;
    wc.hCursor        = LoadCursor( NULL, IDC_ARROW );
    wc.hbrBackground  = GetStockObject( WHITE_BRUSH );
    wc.style          = CS_HREDRAW | CS_VREDRAW;
    RegisterClass( &wc );
}
hGInst = hInst;              // provides global handle to hInst //
hwnd = CreateWindow( szAppName,
                    "Pen Draw 5: Bitmap Images",
                    WS_OVERLAPPEDWINDOW,
                    CW_USEDEFAULT, CW_USEDEFAULT,
                    CW_USEDEFAULT, CW_USEDEFAULT,
                    NULL, NULL, hInst, NULL  );
ShowWindow(   hwnd, nCmdShow );
UpdateWindow( hwnd );
while( GetMessage( &msg, NULL, 0, 0 ) )
{
    TranslateMessage( &msg );
    DispatchMessage(  &msg );
}
return( msg.wParam );
}


                    ;================;
                    ;  PENDRAW5.DEF  ;
                    ;================;

NAME          PENDRAW5

DESCRIPTION   "DRAWING WITH BITMAPS"
EXETYPE       WINDOWS
STUB          "WINSTUB.EXE"
CODE          PRELOAD MOVEABLE DISCARDABLE
DATA          PRELOAD MOVEABLE MULTIPLE
HEAPSIZE      1024
STACKSIZE     8192
EXPORTS       WndProc
```

```
//==============//
//  PENDRAW5.H  //
//==============//

#define   IDM_DrawBM              601
#define   IDM_CenterBM            602
#define   IDM_StretchBM           603
#define   IDM_Stretch2Client      604
#define   IDM_BMTrackMouse        605
#define   IDM_BMLineGraph         606


//==================//
//   PenDraw5.RC    //
//  menu structure  //
//==================//

PENDRAW5  MENU LOADONCALL MOVEABLE PURE DISCARDABLE
BEGIN
    POPUP "&Bitmap Operations"
    BEGIN
        MenuItem  "&Draw Bitmap",              601, CHECKED
        MenuItem  "&Center Bitmap",            602
        MenuItem  "&Stretch Bitmap",           603
        MenuItem  "St&retch Bitmap to Client", 604
        MenuItem  "&Track Mouse Click",        605
        MenuItem  "&Bitmap Line Graph",        606
    END
END
```

Chapter 19

Metafile Operations

Metafiles, mentioned briefly in Chapter 18, are a collection of GDI functions encoded in a binary format and, as such, can be replayed just like a tape recording, recreating the original image. This may sound very nice, but it is not particularly useful. So, what good are metafiles?

First, metafiles provide a means of sharing pictures between applications, either via the clipboard or through disk files. Second, metafiles provide a means of recording a calculated graphic so that it can be repeated without necessarily repeating the calculations. Third, metafiles often require much less space to store than bitmapped images. For example, a 150-byte metafile can easily replace a 3,970-byte image file. Fourth, metafiles are less device-dependent than bitmaps.

Do any of these sound like possibilities?

Granted, metafiles are not miracle solutions which will immediately cure all of your programming problems, but they do offer additional possibilities and potentials.

Recording A Metafile

The first step in creating a metafile is to have an image produced by a series of GDI drawing functions such as the five-or-seven pointed stars originally created in Chapter 17.

For demonstration purposes, we will use the seven-pointed star and enclose it with a circle drawn by the *Ellipse* function. Normally, once the calculations for the points of the star are done, this could be drawn in response to the WM_PAINT message as:

```
SelectObject( hdc, GetStockObject( LTGRAY_BRUSH ) );
Ellipse( hdc, -100, -100, 100, 100 );
SelectObject( hdc, GetStockObject( DKGRAY_BRUSH ) );
SetPolyFillMode( hdc, ALTERNATE );
Polygon( hdc, pt, 7 );
```

Not a particularly onerous task, first drawing a filled circle in light gray, and then drawing the star in dark gray (see the logo above the chapter title), but this will serve to demonstrate metafile operations.

Metafile operations are really not particularly different from conventional drawing operations, but they do require a few additional variables:

```
static HANDLE hMetafile;
HDC           hdc, hdcMeta;
```

The *hdc* variable, of course, has appeared in all of the previous examples, only the *hdcMeta* handle is new.

For the metafile, instead of drawing the image in response to the WM_PAINT command, the image is drawn in response to the WM_CREATE command. The first step, before actually drawing the image, is to open the metafile, as:

```
case WM_CREATE:
    ...  // calculate the points //
    hdcMeta = CreateMetaFile( NULL );
```

Because *CreateMetaFile* has been called with a NULL parameter, the metafile created will be a memory metafile only. I.e., the file will be stored in memory, not in a disk file. (However, disk files can also be created, as alternatives will show presently.)

After creating the metafile and receiving a handle to the file, the GDI operations are carried out in almost exactly the same fashion as if an image was being drawn directly to the screen:

```
hPen = CreatePen( PS_NULL, 1, 0L );
SelectObject( hdcMeta, hPen );
SelectObject( hdcMeta, GetStockObject( LTGRAY_BRUSH ) );
Ellipse( hdcMeta, -100, -100, 100, 100 );
```

```
SelectObject( hdcMeta, GetStockObject( DKGRAY_BRUSH ) );
SetPolyFillMode( hdcMeta, ALTERNATE );
Polygon( hdcMeta, pt, 7 );
```

The differences are fairly obvious: The usual *BeginPaint* instruction is replaced by the *CreateMetaFile* instruction, and, instead of the customary screen device context handle (*hdc*), the metafile device context handle (*hdcMeta*) appears in all graphic drawing instructions. Finally, instead of an *EndPaint* instruction, the metafile receives its own close file instruction:

```
hMetaFile = CloseMetaFile( hdcMeta );
```

In this instance, the *CloseMetaFile* instruction also returns a handle to the metafile which will be needed later to replay the metafile. There are, of course, alternative methods of creating a handle to an existing metafile, and these will be discussed presently.

After closing the metafile, just as during normal screen paint operations, it's time to clean up by deleting any logical objects which were created for use during this process—in this case, the *hPen* object:

```
DeleteObject( hPen );
return(0);
```

The metafile, itself, is also a logical object and, in like fashion, should be disposed of ... but only when the metafile, and the information contained in it, is no longer needed. Therefore, the appropriate point in this application is when the application closes, thus:

```
case WM_DESTROY:
   DeleteMetaFile( hMetaFile );
   PostQuitMessage(0);
   return(0);
```

Simply creating and eventually disposing of the metafile is all very well, but there's also the matter of using this information—replaying the metafile —to actually create an image on screen.

Within the *WinMain* procedure, all normal screen paint operations are carried out in response to the WM_PAINT message, and this case is no exception.

First, however, a few familiar instructions are needed, beginning with a *BeginPaint* instruction to return a device context handle and mapping mode and extent instructions:

```
case WM_PAINT:
   hdc = BeginPaint( hwnd, &ps );
   SetMapMode(   hdc, MM_ANISOTROPIC );
   SetWindowExt(   hdc,   1000,   1000 );
   SetViewportExt( hdc, cxWnd, cyWnd );
```

Remember, when the metafile was created, no specific mapping mode was set, and no window or viewport extent or origin points were set up. Instead, during metafile drawing operations all drawings were done strictly in logical units, and now that these are about to be "played back", the reproduction will be "mapped" onto whatever mapping mode and coordinate system have been established for the output device context.

When the graphics drawing instructions were encoded in the metafile, the drawing was centered around a hypothetical (0,0) origin point. Nothing requires this origin point; it was simply convenient, and the meta-drawing could have been located anywhere in this meta-space i.e., the "image" could have been drawn around some other origin coordinate, and all drawing operations would have been recorded at points relative to this origin and offset from the theoretical 0,0 origin.

For the present, these drawing instructions as recorded are centered around a 0,0 origin. To position the replay within the current device context, the device context window origin point can be changed for each successive replay. This will permit several images to be replayed from a single recording, i.e., the recorded image will be replicated by repeating the instructions necessary to create the image, but changing the window origin point each time:

```
for( i=0; i<3; i++ )
{
    SetWindowOrg( hdc, -200-(i*300), -500 );
    PlayMetaFile( hdc, hMetaFile );
    SetWindowOrg( hdc, -500, -200-(i*300) );
    PlayMetaFile( hdc, hMetaFile );
}
```

This results in six images, though only five will appear on screen since the center image is drawn twice, overlying itself.

Either before or after replaying this or any other metafile, other drawing instructions could be carried out. But remember, these are not images being copied to the screen, these images are being drawn on command, just as any other drawing instructions might be carried out. This could also include ROP instructions affecting how the new image was combined with background images, including other images created by replaying metafiles. Once the drawing instructions are completed, just as in all previous examples, the *EndPaint* instruction closes the process:

```
EndPaint( hwnd, &ps );
return(0);
```

The metafile operations just discussed are demonstrated in the *PenDraw6* program at the end of this chapter, and should adequately illustrate the basic principles of metafile operations, creating the screen display shown in Figure 19-1.

This illustration also shows one possible pitfall in using metafiles, because the figures illustrated are intended to be round. This error is not unique to metafiles, but is caused simply by using the MM_ANISOTROPIC mode; switching to MM_ISOTROPIC would correct the error.

Such errors aside, there remain a few other metafile operations which are worth noting.

Writing Metafiles To Disk

In the preceding example, the metafile created was a memory file. Metafiles can also be written to disk, requiring only one small change in form:

```
hdcMeta = CreateMetaFile( "D:\\METAFILE.WMF" );
```

Neither the filename nor the extension have any particular significance, though you may prefer to use the .WMF extension as a convenient convention. This could also be written with an indirect reference, thus:

```
hdcMeta = CreateMetaFile( (LPSTR) szMetaFileName );
```

where *szMetaFileName* is a null-terminated string specifying the filename and, as desired, drive and path.

Figure 19-1: Metafile Images Produced By PenDraw6

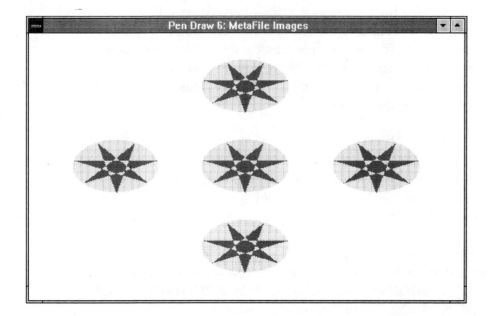

In either case, when the metafile is written to a disk file, the *DeleteMetaFile* instruction which was issued in response to the WM_DESTROY message *does not* affect the disk file itself, only the local handle to the file.

As a further alternative, a temporary file can be created. A temporary file is more ephemeral than a conventional disk file, but less ephemeral than a memory file. To create a temporary file, in response to the WM_CREATE message, the *GetTempFileName* function is called as:

```
GetTempFileName( cDrive, lpPrefixStr, wUnique,
                 lpTempFileName );
```

or, more appropriately, as:

```
GetTempFileName( 0, "MTF", 0, (LPSTR) szMetaFileName );
```

On return, the temporary filename is in the *szMetaFileName* variable.

The *GetTempFileName* function creates a temporary file with a filename which begins with the tilde character (~), followed by an optional prefix (up to three letters), and completed with a unique four-character hexadecimal value created from the *wUnique* parameter. If *wUnique* is zero, a number will be generated.

The *cDrive* parameter is an integer value for the suggested drive for the temporary file. If *cDrive* is passed as zero, the default (current) drive is assumed.

The *szMetaFileName* is an empty string which will receive the drive/path/filename specification for the temporary file. A buffer length of 144 characters is suggested to provide enough room for all possible path specifications, and presumably to allow extra space for the doubled backslash characters ("\\") required by C strings, since DOS pathnames are not permitted to exceed 67 characters (excluding drive and file names).

An example of the returned drive/path/filename might be: D:\WINDOWS\TEMP\~MFT2E12.TMP.

Other than the format and location returned, the tempfile is no different than any other disk file.

However, large numbers of temporary files do tend to clog a hard disk, a fault which is present in many existing Windows applications. The bad news is that your only real recourse is to check the \Windows\Temp directory periodically and erase the fossil files. The good news is that unlike .BAK files, these are all gathered in a single location where they are easy to find and wipe. For your own applications, one small provision can prevent this annoyance: Erase temporary files when no longer needed. This can be accomplished with a very minor revision, as:

```
case WM_DESTROY:
   DeleteMetaFile( hMetaFile );
   unlink( szMetaFileName );                              // add //
   PostQuitMessage(0);
   return(0);
```

The *unlink* function erases most files without requiring a file handle or other handling provisions. Note: Read-Only files can not be unlinked.

Accessing Disk MetaFiles

One of the reasons for creating a metafile is so that another application can access the information contained, or so that the application can access its own metafile(s) created at some previous time. To do so, a means is needed to retrieve or create a metafile handle for a file which was not created by the application, or which was discarded by the *DeleteMetaFile* function. This is provided by the *GetMetaFile* function, which is called as:

```
hMetaFile = GetMetaFile( (LPSTR) szMetaFileName );
```

Once this is done, the metafile can be used as before. When done, the new metafile handle is discarded as before, using the *DeleteMetaFile* function.

Of course, if a metafile is being created by one application for use by a second application, then the creating application should not unlink the disk file, but the second application most definitely should!

Note: Leaving trash files on the disk is simply bad manners for any program, not to mention bad programming.

Metafile Structures

Metafiles are structured records using the METARECORD and METAHEADER structures listed in Appendix A under the heading, "MetaFile Picture Structures". A third structure, the METAFILEPICT, is discussed further in Chapter 22, "Using The Windows Clipboard." For those who are curious, however, Figure 19-2 shows a sample metafile as created by the PenDraw6 demo program.

In general, the metafile begins with an 18-byte record header described by the METAHEADER structure, and is followed by a series of METARECORD records, each consisting of a minimum of three WORD values.

The first two WORDs in each record identify the number of words in the record, including the first DWORD value. This value is, of course, expressed in *lsw,msw* order while each word value is expressed in *lsb,msb* order.

The third WORD in each record is the function identifier while the remaining WORD(s) are parameters (arguments) passed to the function.

Within the function identifier, the low byte identifies the specific GDI function call, while the high byte is normally the number of word parameters passed to the function. Thus the hex value 0418 identifies the (18) Ellipse function which receives (04) four parameters, excluding the *hdcMeta* parameter.

Figure 19-2: Metafile Contents

```
000000   01 00 09 00   00 03 4B 00   00 00 03 00   12 00 00 00   ⊡·o··♥K···♥·↕···
000010   00 00 08 00   00 00 FA 02   05 00 01 00   00 00 00 00   ··▯····⊡◆·⊡····
000020   00 00 04 00   00 00 2D 01   00 00 07 00   00 00 FC 02   ··◆····─⊡··◆···ⁿ⊟
000030   00 00 C0 C0   C0 00 00 00   04 00 00 00   2D 01 01 00   ··LLL··◆····─⊟⊟·
000040   07 00 00 00   18 04 64 00   64 00 9C FF   9C FF 07 00   ◆···↑◆d·d·£ £ ◆·
000050   00 00 FC 02   00 00 40 40   40 00 00 00   04 00 00 00   ··ⁿ⊟·⊡⊡⊡···◆···
000060   2D 01 02 00   04 00 00 00   06 01 01 00   12 00 00 00   ─⊟⊟·◆···◆⊟⊟·↕···
000070   24 03 07 00   00 00 64 00   2B 00 A6 FF   B2 FF 3E 00   $♥·····d·+·ª █ >·
000080   61 00 EA FF   9F FF EA FF   4E 00 3E 00   D5 FF A6 FF   a·Ω ƒ Ω N·>·ᵣ ª
000090   03 00 00 00   00 00                                     ♥·····
```

Metafile codes can be found in Appendix A under the heading "Metafile Constants", both in alphabetical and numerical order. (In Appendix A, to save space, the prefix META_ has been omitted from the individual listings.) Also, the arguments following the function call are in reverse order, i.e., a GDI call which originally appears as:

```
Ellipse( hdcMeta, -100, -100, 100, 100 );
```

appears in the metafile as a seven-word record which, in hexadecimal format, reads as:

```
07 00   00 00   18 04   64 00   64 00   9C FF   9C FF
```

Remember, each WORD value appears here in *lsb,msb* order. Therefore, the seven word values can be rewritten in a more comprehensible format as:

```
00000007   0418   0064   0064   FF9C   FF9C
```

and read as: seven words in length (a double-word value), 418 identifying META_ELLIPSE with four parameters, with the parameters themselves following, in reversed order, as (64h) 100, (64h) 100, (FF9Ch) -100, (FF9Ch) -100.

The complete metafile contents would be deciphered as shown here (note that all values have been normalized for the reader's convenience):

```
0001 0009 0300 0000004B 0003 00000012 0000
METAHEADER
    hPen = CreatePen( PS_NULL, 1, OL );
0000008 02FA 0005 0001 0000 0000 0000
```

```
CREATEPENINDIRECT
    SelectObject( hdcMeta, hPen );
 00000004 012D 0000
SELECTOBJECT
    SelectObject( hdcMeta,
                    GetStockObject( LTGRAY_BRUSH ) );
 00000007 02FC 0000 C0C0 00C0 0000
CREATEBRUSHINDIRECT
 00000004 012D 0001
SELECTOBJECT
    Ellipse( hdcMeta, -100, -100, 100, 100 );
 00000007 0418 0064 0064 FF9C FF9C
ELLIPSE
    SelectObject( hdcMeta,
                    GetStockObject( DKGRAY_BRUSH ) );
 00000007 02FC 0000 4040 0040 0000
CREATEBRUSHINDIRECT
 00000004 012D 0002
SELECTOBJECT
    SetPolyFillMode( hdcMeta, ALTERNATE );
 00000004 0106 0001
SETPOLYFILLMODE
    Polygon( hdcMeta, pt, 7 );
 00000012 0324 0007 0000 0064 002B FFA6
POLYGON
            FFB2 003E 0061 FFEA FF9F FFEA
            004E 003E FFD5 FFA6
 00000003 0000
(NULL RECORD)
```

Notice that the *SelectObject (GetStockObject...* instructions are broken down as two separate meta-instructions, while the final parameter for each of the three *SelectObject* instructions is a sequential object identifier. Also, the *Polygon* meta-instruction includes the complete polygon data point information. And finally, there is one omission to point out, the fact that no *DeletePen* instruction appears in the metafile, even though it did appear in the original instructions. Where the original instruction was *CreatePen,* in the metafile this has become *CreatePenIndirect,* both voiding the need for a delete instruction and voiding any requirement to restore the original pen, brush or other drawing objects.

Happily, of course, you are not personally required to be able to read metafile instruction in order to use metafiles, but occasionally, it may help to be familiar with the metafile organization.

MetaFile Cautions

When using metafiles, there are a few characteristics which you should keep in mind, because an awareness of these may help prevent errors and confusion:

- The metafile is not a true device context. It does not correspond to any actual device, does not include a mapping mode, or window or viewport sizes and origins.
- All parameters entered in the metafile are entered as values, not as formulas. For instance, an argument such as *cxWnd/2* will be recorded as the calculated value at the present time, and will not be affected by future changes in the client window size. (This conflict was avoided in the PenDraw6 example by using the isotropic mapping mode.)
- The metafile is always interpreted in terms of the existing mapping mode, with the exception that the metafile may include instructions setting a specific mapping mode.

There are also instructions which can not be used in metafiles. All permissible instructions begin with a device context parameter (*hdcMeta*) as the first argument.

The following five categories of GDI instruction are not valid in a metafile context:

- Functions treating the metafile device context as if it were an actual device context. These include *CreateCompatibleBitmap*, *CreateCompatibleDC*, *CreateDiscardableBitmap*, *DeleteDC*, *PlayMetaFile* and *ReleaseDC*.
- All functions beginning *Get...*, such as *GetDeviceCaps* or *GetTextMetrics*. All information in the metafile is preset and can not accommodate information returned by such functions.
- Any other functions designed to return information to the program such as *DPtoLP*, *LPtoDP*, etc. Macros, on the other hand, are permissible since these are evaluated at compile time.
- Functions requiring handles to brushes such as: *FillRect* and *FrameRect*.
- Some of the more complex functions including *Drawicon*, *GrayString* and *SetBrushOrg*.

Finally, if you are in doubt about whether a GDI function call is permitted in a metafile, check the table of Metafile Constants in Appendix A. But remember, some GDI functions may not appear simply because the compiler will automatically choose a more compatible variation, such as substituting *CREATEPENINDIRECT* for *CREATEPEN*.

Saving and Restoring The Device Context

When a metafile is played back, operations begin with the device context attributes that were already in effect at the time of the *PlayMetaFile* instruction. However, the metafile is free to change the drawing mode, mapping mode, text colors, etc., but when the metafile is finished, these changes remain in effect for the device context. Therefore, to retain the original device context, two options are possible:

First, before the *PlayMetaFile* instruction is executed, the present device context can be saved as:

```
SaveDC( hdc );
```

and after the metafile is finished, the original device context can be restored as:

```
RestoreDC( hdc, -1 );
```

Second, the metafile itself could include these instructions, and so would save and restore the device context when executed. Remember, each *SaveDC* function call must have a corresponding *RestoreDC* with the -one parameter.

Summary

Metafiles not only provide a powerful means of storing and replaying complex drawing instructions, but also provide a means of transferring graphic information between applications, as will be discussed in Chapter 22. For the present, the PenDraw6 example following provides a convenient platform for experimentation with metafiles, with a second version showing the revisions necessary to create temporary disk files.

For your own understanding and for general practice, you might like to create two new programs for metafiles: One to record a metafile as a disk file, and the other to read the metafile from disk using the *GetMetaFile* instruction and play back the instructions.

```
//=======================//
//       PenDraw6.C      //
//  C++ Windows Drawing  //
//  creating a metafile  //
//=======================//

#include <windows.h>
#include <stdio.h>
#include <math.h>

#define PI2 ( 2.0 * 3.1415 )            // radians in 360 degrees //

long FAR PASCAL WndProc( HWND hwnd,    WORD msg,
                         WORD wParam, LONG lParam )
{
    static int    cxWnd, cyWnd;
    static HANDLE hMetaFile;
    static POINT  pt[7];
    HDC           hdc, hdcMeta;
    HPEN          hPen;
    PAINTSTRUCT   ps;
    int           i, j;

    switch( msg )
    {
      case WM_CREATE:
        for( i=j=0; i<7; i++, j=(j+3)%7 )    // seven points //
        {
            pt[i].x = (int)( sin( j*PI2/7 ) * 100 );
            pt[i].y = (int)( cos( j*PI2/7 ) * 100 );
        }
        hdcMeta = CreateMetaFile( "D:\\METAFILE.MTA" );
        hPen = CreatePen( PS_NULL, 1, 0L );
        SelectObject( hdcMeta, hPen );
        SelectObject( hdcMeta,
                    GetStockObject( LTGRAY_BRUSH ) );
        Ellipse( hdcMeta, -100, -100, 100, 100 );
        SelectObject( hdcMeta,
                    GetStockObject( DKGRAY_BRUSH ) );
        SetPolyFillMode( hdcMeta, ALTERNATE );
        Polygon( hdcMeta, pt, 7 );
        hMetaFile = CloseMetaFile( hdcMeta );
        DeleteObject( hPen );
        return(0);
```

```
        case WM_SIZE:
            cxWnd = LOWORD( lParam );
            cyWnd = HIWORD( lParam );
            return(0);

        case WM_PAINT:
            hdc = BeginPaint( hwnd, &ps );
            SetMapMode(   hdc, MM_ANISOTROPIC );
            SetWindowExt(   hdc,   1000,   1000 );
            SetViewportExt( hdc, cxWnd, cyWnd );
            for( i=0; i<3; i++ )
            {
                SetWindowOrg( hdc, -200-(i*300), -500 );
                PlayMetaFile( hdc, hMetaFile );
                SetWindowOrg( hdc, -500, -200-(i*300) );
                PlayMetaFile( hdc, hMetaFile );
            }
            EndPaint( hwnd, &ps );
            return(0);

        case WM_DESTROY:
            DeleteMetaFile( hMetaFile );
            PostQuitMessage(0);
            return(0);
    }
    return( DefWindowProc( hwnd, msg, wParam, lParam ) );
}

#pragma argsused

int PASCAL WinMain( HANDLE hInst,        HANDLE hPrevInst,
                    LPSTR   lpszCmdParam, int nCmdShow )
{
    static char szAppName[] = "PENDRAW6";
    HWND        hwnd;
    MSG         msg;
    WNDCLASS    wc;

    if( ! hPrevInst )
    {
        wc.hInstance       = hInst;
        wc.lpfnWndProc     = WndProc;
        wc.cbClsExtra      = 0;
        wc.cbWndExtra      = 0;
        wc.lpszClassName   = szAppName;
        wc.hIcon           = LoadIcon( hInst, szAppName );
        wc.lpszMenuName    = (LPSTR) szAppName;
```

```
     wc.hCursor        = LoadCursor( NULL, IDC_ARROW );
     wc.hbrBackground = GetStockObject( WHITE_BRUSH );
     wc.style          = CS_HREDRAW | CS_VREDRAW;
     RegisterClass( &wc );
  }
  hwnd = CreateWindow( szAppName,
                       "Pen Draw 6: MetaFile Images",
                       WS_OVERLAPPEDWINDOW,
                       CW_USEDEFAULT, CW_USEDEFAULT,
                       CW_USEDEFAULT, CW_USEDEFAULT,
                       NULL, NULL, hInst, NULL  );
  ShowWindow(   hwnd, nCmdShow );
  UpdateWindow( hwnd );
  while( GetMessage( &msg, NULL, 0, 0 ) )
  {
     TranslateMessage( &msg );
     DispatchMessage(  &msg );
  }
  return( msg.wParam );
}
```

```
                  ;================;
                  ;  PENDRAW6.DEF  ;
                  ;================;

NAME          PENDRAW6

DESCRIPTION   "DRAWING WITH PENS"
EXETYPE       WINDOWS
STUB          "WINSTUB.EXE"
CODE          PRELOAD MOVEABLE DISCARDABLE
DATA          PRELOAD MOVEABLE MULTIPLE
HEAPSIZE      1024
STACKSIZE     8192
EXPORTS       WndProc
```

```
                  //==============//
                  // PENDRAW6.H  //
                  //==============//

// empty file -- nothing required //
```

```
                  //================//
                  // PENDRAW6.RC  //
                  //================//

// empty file -- no menu defined //
```

```
//========================//
//         PenDraw6.C       //
//    C++ Windows Drawing   //
//                          //
//    alternate version     //
//    for temporary disk    //
//    files                 //
//========================//

#include <windows.h>
#include <stdio.h>
#include <math.h>

#define PI2 ( 2.0 * 3.1415 )

long FAR PASCAL WndProc( HWND hwnd,    WORD msg,
                         WORD wParam, LONG lParam )
{
   ...
   static char    szMetaFileName[67];                      // add //
   ...

   switch( msg )
   {
      case WM_CREATE:
         ...
         GetTempFileName( 0, "MFT", 0,
            (LPSTR) szMetaFileName );                      // add //
         hdcMeta = CreateMetaFile(
                  (LPSTR) szMetaFileName );            // revise //
         ...
         return(0);

      case WM_SIZE:                                   // no changes //

      case WM_PAINT:                                  // no changes //

      case WM_DESTROY:
         DeleteMetaFile( hMetaFile );
         unlink( szMetaFileName );                      // add //
         PostQuitMessage(0);
         return(0);
   }
   return( DefWindowProc( hwnd, msg, wParam, lParam ) );
}
// no further changes //
```

Chapter 20

Graphic Typefaces And Styles

Chapters 2 and 3 have already introduced Windows' basic text-graphic features as well as some aspects of fonts, font selection and the differences between ANSI and ASCII fonts, and functions supporting string conversion between the two forms. Thus far, virtually every application demonstrated has used some text, if only for the caption bar at the top of the window. But now it's time to look at the more advanced elements of text manipulation, including font sizes and styles, justifying text, using text in different device contexts, and the stock fonts supplied with Windows. However, before discussing fonts and typefaces, there are a few aspects of text output remaining to be introduced.

The TextOut and SetTextAlign Functions

Most text output thus far has used the general format:

```
TextOut( hdc, xPos, yPos, lpStr, nCount );
```

or, more conveniently, the format:

```
TextOut( hdc, xPos, yPos, szBuff,
         wsprintf( szBuff, ... ) );
```

where the *wsprintf* function is incorporated to provide both convenience in calculating the length (*nCount*) parameter, and in creating formatted strings.

Thus far, *TextOut* has been viewed as a plain vanilla output function, but when it is combined with the *SetTextAlign* function, it is capable of somewhat more sophisticated performance.

The *SetTextAlign* function is used to control the alignment of output text relative to the *xPos* and *yPos* arguments passed with the *TextOut* and *ExtTextOut* functions and is called as:

```
SetTextAlign( hdc, wFlags );
```

The *wFlags* argument consists of one or more flag specifications. These are combined using the OR operator, which set the relationship between a specific point and a rectangle bounding the text displayed. These flags consist of three groups: horizontal alignment, vertical alignment, and current position, and only one flag can be specified from each group.

Table 20-1: Text Alignment Flags

Flag ID	Meaning
Vertical Alignment At *yPos*	
TA_TOP	aligns the top of the bounding rectangle
TA_BASELINE	aligns the baseline of the chosen font
TA_BOTTOM	aligns the bottom of the bounding rectangle
Horizontal Alignment At *xPos*	
TA_CENTER	aligns the horizontal center of the bounding rectangle (Note: current position is not affected.)
TA_LEFT	aligns the left side of the bounding rectangle
TA_RIGHT	aligns the right side of the bounding rectangle
Current Position Control	
TA_NOUPDATECP	current position is *not* updated after TextOut or ExtTextOut calls
TA_UPDATECP	current position is updated after each TextOut or ExtTextOut call

The default flags are TA_LEFT, TA_TOP, and TA_NOUPDATECP.

SetTextAlign returns a word value reporting the previous text alignment settings with the horizontal alignment in the low byte and the vertical alignment in the high byte. The previous current position flag is not reported.

The ExtTextOut Function

The *ExtTextOut* function uses a RECT specification to write a character string within the region specified. The rectangular region can be set as opaque (ETO_OPAQUE) to be filled with the current background color, and/or can be set as a clipping region (ETO_CLIPPED). *ExtTextOut* also includes a provision to control spacing between characters. By default, the current position is not used or updated by *ExtTextOut*. However, applications can call *SetText-Align* with *wFlags* set to TA_UPDATECP, permitting Windows to use and update the current position each time *ExtTextOut* is called. However, when TA_UPDATECP is set, Windows ignores the X and Y parameters on subsequent *ExtTextOut* calls. Further details on *ExtTextOut* parameters and features can be found by using the Help function.

The TabbedTextOut Function

The *TabbedTextOut* function provides an alternative to *TextOut*, permitting the output string to be tabbed according to column positions specified in the *lpnTabStopPositions* field. The *TabbedTextOut* function is called as:

```
TabbedTextOut( hdc, xPos, yPos, lpStr, nCount,
               nTabPositions, lpnTabStopPositions,
               nTabOrigin );
```

Tabs are included in the *lpStr* string argument by using embedded \t (or 0x09) characters. The *nCount* parameter specifies the number of characters in the string.

nTabPositions is an integer argument specifying the number of tab-stop positions in the *lpnTabStopPositions* array. If *nTabPositions* is zero and *lpnTab-StopPositions* is NULL, tabs are expanded to eight average character widths. If *nTabPositions* is one, all tab stops will be separated by the distance specified by the first value in the *lpnTabStopPositions* array. *lpnTabStopPositions* points to an array of integers containing the tab-stop positions specified in pixels. Tab stops must be sorted in increasing order and back-tabs are not allowed.

If *lpnTabStopPositions* points to more than one value, a tab stop is set for each value in the array, up to the number specified by *nTabPositions*.

The *nTabOrigin* parameter is an integer value specifying the logical x-coordinate from which tabs are expanded.

nTabOrigin allows an application to call *TabbedTextOut* several times for a single line. When *TabbedTextOut* is called repeatedly with *nTabOrigin* set to the same value each time, all tabs are expanded relative to *nTabOrigin*. *Tabbed-TextOut* returns a DWORD value with the height in the high word and the width in the low word.

The DrawText Function

The *DrawText* function draws formatted text in the rectangle specified by the *lpRect* parameter. Flags in the *wFormat* instruction can be set to expand tabs, justify text to the right, left, or center of the rectangle area, or write text as multiple lines.

DrawText uses the device context's selected font, text color, and background color. Unless DT_NOCLIP is used, *DrawText* clips the text displayed to the given rectangle. Also, all formatting is assumed to have multiple lines unless the DT_SINGLELINE format is given. *DrawText* is called as:

```
DrawText( hdc, lpStr, nCount, lpRect, wFormat );
```

lpString is a pointer (LPSTR) to a string or string buffer. Note that if the *nCount* parameter will be passed as -1, this must be a null-terminated (ASCIIZ) string.

The *nCount* parameter is an integer value specifying the number of bytes in the string. If *nCount* is -1, *lpString* is assumed to be a long pointer to a null-terminated (ASCIIZ) string, and the character count is computed automatically.

lpRect is a pointer to a RECT data structure containing the rectangle (in logical coordinates) within which the text is to be formatted. If the selected font is too large for the specified rectangle, *DrawText* does not attempt to substitute a smaller font; depending on the clipflag, only part of the text will be printed.

wFormat is a WORD value containing flag values which set the method of formatting the text. This may be any combination of values shown in Table 20-2:

Table 20-2: DrawText Formats

Value	Meaning
Horizontal Justification	
DT_LEFT	text is aligned flush-left
DT_CENTER	text is aligned centered
DT_RIGHT	text is aligned flush-right
Vertical Justification	
DT_TOP	text is top-justified (single line only)
DT_VCENTER	text is centered vertically (single line only)
DT_BOTTOM	text is bottom-justified; must be combined with DT_SINGLELINE
DT_EXTERNALLEADING	adds font external leading to line height
DT_NOCLIP	clipping to rectangle is disabled, operation is marginally faster
DT_SINGLELINE	sets single line only; carriage returns and line feeds do not break the line
Format Instructions	
DT_EXPANDTABS	expands tab characters (default is 8 characters per tab)
DT_TABSTOP	sets high-order byte of *wFormat* as the number of characters per tab
DT_NOPREFIX	disables processing of prefix characters

Normally DrawText interprets the mnemonic-prefix character "&" as a directive to underscore the character following, and "&&", as a directive to print a single "&".

DT_WORDBREAK	enables word breaks; lines are broken between words if a word would extend past the edge of the rectangle set by the *lpRect* parameter (CR/LF sequences function normally)
Automatic Rectangle Calculation	
DT_CALCRECT	when set, *DrawText* calculates width and height of the rectangle according to the text displayed.

For multiple lines of text, *DrawText* uses the width of the rectangle indicated by *lpRect*, extending the base of the rectangle to bound the last line of text. For a single line of text, *DrawText* modifies the right boundary of the rectangle to bound the last character in the line. In both cases, *DrawText* returns the height of the formatted text but does *not* draw the text.

Note: The DT_CALCRECT, DT_EXTERNALLEADING, DT_INTERNAL, DT_NOCLIP, and DT_NOPREFIX values cannot be used with the DT_TABSTOP value.

Modifying The Device Context

While the choice of output function and flag parameters controls many features of how text is displayed, the active device context also governs several aspects of the display, including not only foreground and background colors, but also how the text display pixels are combined with existing backgrounds.

Using the default device context, the foreground (text) color is black, but it can be changed as desired using the *SetTextColor* function as:

```
SetTextColor( hdc, rgbColor );
```

or,

```
SetTextColor( hdc, GetSysColor( COLOR_WINDOWTEXT ) );
```

In the first instance, the *rgbColor* is, like pen and brush colors, converted to a pure color; dithered colors (which are not directly supported by an output device) are converted to colors that are supported. In the second instance, the window text color reported is presumably already a color which is supported by the device. In either case, the resulting color can be retrieved by calling the *GetTextColor* function.

Drawing text also affects the display background because, in the default OPAQUE background mode, the areas between the character's strokes (or pixels) are filled using the current background color. The background mode is changed using the *SetBkMode* function as:

```
SetBkMode( hdc, nMode );            // OPAQUE or TRANSPARENT //
```

In TRANSPARENT mode, the text is written only as the foreground pixels and the existing background pixels remain unchanged. The background color (white, by default) can be changed using the *SetBkColor* function as:

```
SetBkColor( hdc, rgbColor );
```

or,

```
SetBkColor( hdc, GetSysColor( COLOR_WINDOW ) );
```

Again, if the *rgbColor* value results in a dithered color, it is converted to the nearest pure color supported by the output device.

If the *GetSysColor* function is used to retrieve system color settings, you may want to add a provision to repaint the entire client window if or when these colors are changed, i.e., if the control panel is used to alter the system colors. Such a provision is simple to create, requiring only:

```
case WM_SYSCOLORCHANGE:
    InvalidateRect( hwnd );
    break;
```

Stock Fonts

Windows 3.0 provides a variety of fonts, both bitmapped and stroked. These can be selected, sized, and modified in several fashions as we will see presently. First, however, there are six stock logical font settings which can be selected for text output without the details required for custom fonts.

The six stock logical fonts are defined in Windows.H as:

Table 20-3: Stock Logical Fonts

Constant	Value	Char Set	Typeface*
OEM_FIXED_FONT	10	OEM	Terminal (DOS font)
ANSI_FIXED_FONT	11	ANSI	Courier (typewriter)
ANSI_VAR_FONT	12	ANSI	Helv (Helvetica)
SYSTEM_FONT	13	ANSI	System
DEVICE_DEFAULT_FONT	14	varies, device dependent	varies, device dependent
SYSTEM_FIXED_FONT	16	ANSI	Courier (Windows 2.0 compatible)

* may vary, depending on system and output device

The DEVICE_DEFAULT_FONT, is dependent on the output device's capability. For a CRT output device, such as a VGA video system, this will probably be the Courier font, but for a printer such as an Epson, this will be a typeface internal to the printer. The advantage of using a device font is that output is faster, since Windows does not need to operate the device in graphics mode.

Selecting any of these stock fonts is quite simple: accomplished as:

```
hFont = GetStockObject( StockFontID );
SelectObject( hdc, hFont );
```

The same thing can be accomplished in a single step as:

```
SelectObject( hdc, GetStockObject( StockFontID ) );
```

At this time, both the *SelectObject* and *GetStockObject* functions should be quite familiar, since they have been used repeatedly in previous chapters to select logical objects such as bitmaps, brushes, and pens into the device context. The drawback to using *GetStockObject*, however, is that this gives you very little control over the size, spacing, and typeface selection. Instead of *GetStockObject*, such control requires using custom fonts.

A Brief History of Typefaces

Having (almost) cut my teeth on a pi-stick, a device used by printers in the days before electronic typesetting, to me the word "typeface" still conjures up memories of trays of small compartments containing individual metal characters in various sizes and typeface designs.

Granted, much of the typesetting on the newspaper where I worked beginning at age six (sweeping floors ... but for pay) was accomplished by a huge and intricate machine known as a linotype. However, larger type sizes, such as those used for ads, headlines, and other features, were beyond the capacity of the linotype, and fell to a set of nimble fingers which could choose, arrange, and align individual characters from the appropriate tray with a speed which might have been envied by many typists. This was the only way that different typefaces and different type sizes could be assembled for printing.

Today, of course, these are only the memories of an old-time printer's devil, but please refer back to the dedication, because movable type was a technology that revolutionized the world.

Neither handset nor linotype were compatible with computers so, for a video display, new methods of creating letters were required. The first of these methods, still used today, was known as a bitmapped font.

In a bitmapped font, sometimes called a "raster" font, the data required to display each character is stored as a bit image, an array of bits telling which pixels are on and which are off, just like the bitmapped icons or the bitmapped brushes discussed previously. So bitmapped fonts were and are convenient, because these are easily output to a screen, or to a dot-matrix printer or a laserjet, on a one-bit-to-one-pixel basis, no calculations required. However, bitmapped fonts have shortcomings, as illustrated in the left side of Figure 20-1. They are not easily sized, and when enlarged, are grainy and generally unattractive.

Figure 20-1: Bitmapped vs. Stroked (Vectored) Fonts

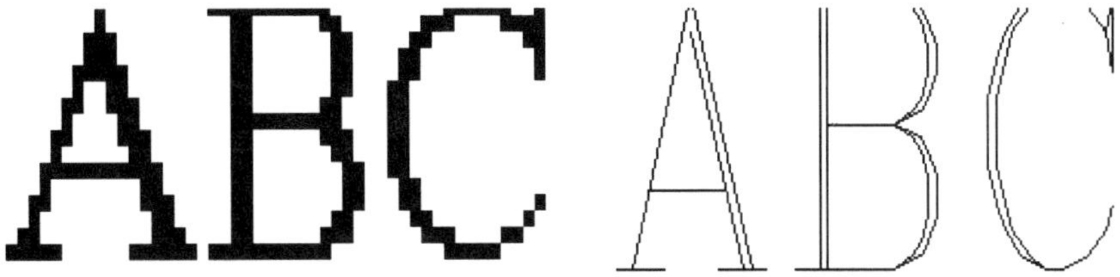

Of course on earlier computers, there was little demand for larger typefaces. Only with the advent of graphic display systems did the advantages of sizable fonts became every bit as obvious as the disadvantages of sizing bitmapped fonts.

One possibility was to create libraries of bitmap fonts in incremental sizes. This was never seriously considered as a solution, because the sheer size of the data required for this approach was also obvious. Instead, a second type of computer font was invented, known as the stroked or vector font. In these fonts, instead of a bitmap image each individual character is described as a series of lines or vectors that form an outline of the character. The advantage is that these stroked fonts can be sized (enlarged or reproportioned) with much less loss of image fidelity, as shown in the right side of Figure 20-1. Still, while stroked fonts provide a number of advantages, one disadvantage is also apparent in Figure 20-1. As you can see, a sufficiently enlarged font is considerably lighter than the equivalent bitmap font, simply because the strokes comprising the character paint only the relatively few pixels which these strokes actually intersect, thus leaving large areas of unpainted pixels within the character.

The original Borland Graphic Interface (BGI) took one approach to circumventing this problem by creating the Triplex font that increased the number of strokes defined for each character.

Other approaches used by various software packages include provisions to paint enclosed regions and, frequently, provisions to smooth enlarged vectors.

In Windows 3.0, some provision is made for increasing the weight of enlarged characters by adding to the number of strokes comprising the character. The results are similar to the BGI Triplex font. However, the large screen characters remain more like outlines than solid figures. Nevertheless, as a trade-off against slowing display speed, these results are acceptable, if not completely ideal. Overall, stroked fonts have other advantages that far outweigh the few disadvantages, since both italics and boldface can be created with results considerably superior to similar operations with bitmapped fonts.

This is not to imply that bitmapped fonts can not be italicized, simply that the results are not always as clear as might be desired. For an example please refer to Figure 20-3, where the Symbol font appears in both standard and italic forms.

A third type of font is also used, in which the characters are described as lines and curves comprising an outline image, which is drawn and then filled. This type, however, requires considerably more computation time to draw, and is generally used only by drafting/typesetting applications such as Corel-Draw, Ventura Publisher, or other elaborate output software/devices requiring high-fidelity, high-quality typefaces.

Typefaces

To a printer or a typographer, the term "typeface" refers to the style of type, differentiating not only between families of type such as Times Roman and Helvetica, but also between the italic, bold, extra bold, condensed, etc., variations within a family of type styles.

The term "font" refers to a complete set (alphabet plus numbers, etc.) of characters in a single size, style, and typeface. Thus a specific font might be referred to as 12pt (size) Helvetica (family) Bold (style).

In computer terms, the specific size of a font is variable, and is determined by several factors, including mapping mode, height, width, and weight, as well as style option settings such as italic.

In Windows 3.0, five families of typeface are provided: Decorative, Modern, Roman, Script, and Swiss. These are not firm descriptions, but general categories based on the appearance of the type style. Depending on the mode and selection, Windows may choose different typefaces regardless of your font selections.

Constants for the six font families are defined in Windows.H as:

Table 20-4: Font Families

Family ID	Characteristics
FF_DONTCARE	don't care or don't know
FF_ROMAN	variable stroke width, serifed as Times Roman, Century Schoolbook, etc
FF_SWISS	variable stroke width, sans-serif as Helvetica, Swiss, etc
FF_MODERN	constant stroke width fonts, may be serif or sans-serif as Pica, Elite, Courier: i.e., typewriter fonts
FF_SCRIPT	cursive, imitating handwriting
FF_DECORATIVE	catch-all, Old English, Symbols, Zapf Dingbats, etc

For example, in Figure 20-2 both the ANSI and OEM character sets are stepped through three pitch selections and five family (font) selections, with the selected typeface resulting shown for each selection on a VGA display. The results are eight different typefaces: Courier, Helvetica, Modern, Roman Script, System, Terminal, and Times Roman. As an example of the potential confusion, the Roman family selection appears using four typefaces: Times Roman, System, Roman and Terminal. At the same time, in the OEM character set, the Roman typeface appears in response both to Roman, Swiss and Don't Care family selections.

However, such idiosyncracies are not worth any particular study. These are simply the font selections which best fit the specified criteria in each case, and when selecting custom fonts for your own applications, such idiosyncracies will not be a problem because your selections can be much more explicit.

Font Resource Files

When Windows is installed on a system, a number of .FON font files are copied to the d:\WINDOWS\SYSTEM subdirectory. Precisely which files are installed depends on your system configuration and hardware (particularly the system video), but the selections will be similar to those shown in Table 20-5:

Table 20-5:   Windows .FON Typeface/Font Files

Filename	Family	Typeface	Charset	Type	Size
VGAFIX	DONTCARE	System	ANSI	Bitmap	5776
VGAOEM	MODERN	Terminal	OEM	Bitmap	5584
VGASYS	SWISS	System	ANSI	Bitmap	6368
MODERN	MODERN	Modern	OEM	Stroked	9728
ROMAN	ROMAN	Roman	OEM	Stroked	14336
SCRIPT	SCRIPT	Script	OEM	Stroked	13312
COURE	MODERN	Courier	ANSI	Bitmap	21360
HELVE	SWISS	Helv	ANSI	Bitmap	59696
TMSRE	ROMAN	Tms Rmn	ANSI	Bitmap	53520
SYMBOLE	DECORATIVE	Symbol	SYMBOL	Bitmap	56912

Three types of fonts are included, beginning with three video specific (i.e., system or terminal) fonts: VGASYS.FON, VGAFIX.FON, and VGAOEM.FON. For a CGA system, the equivalent font files would be designated as CGA-xxx.FON or, for an EGA system, as EGAxxx.FON.

Next are the GDI stroked fonts: MODERN.FON, ROMAN.FON, and SCRIPT.FON. These are installed on all systems.

And, last, the bitmapped typeface fonts: Courier (COURx.FON), Helvetica (HELVx.FON), Times Roman (TMSRx.FON), and Symbol (SYMBOLx.FON). In each case, the last letter of the file name identifies the device (video or printer) the font was designed for, as shown in Table 20-6.

Table 20-6:   Device Font Identifiers

Device	ID	Aspect Ratio	Pixels/Log Inch Horz	Vert
CGA video	A	200	96	48
EGA video	B	133	96	72
Okidata Printers	C	83	60	72
Epson (or IBM) Printers	D	167	120	72
VGA video	E	100	96	96
8514/A video	F	100	120	120

Figure 20-2: Principal Fonts and Styles

ANSI, Default Pitch	Font: Don't Care	Typeface: Courier
ANSI, Default Pitch	Font: Roman	Typeface: Tms Rmn
ANSI. Default Pitch	Font: Swiss	Typeface: Helv
ANSI, Default Pitch	Font: Modern	Typeface: Courier
ANSI, Default Pitch	**Font: Script**	**Typeface: System**
ANSI, Fixed Pitch	Font: Don't Care	Typeface: Courier
ANSI, Fixed Pitch	**Font: Roman**	**Typeface: System**
ANSI, Fixed Pitch	**Font: Swiss**	**Typeface: System**
ANSI, Fixed Pitch	Font: Modern	Typeface: Courier
ANSI, Fixed Pitch	**Font: Script**	**Typeface: System**
ANSI, Variable Pitch	Font: Don't Care	Typeface: Helv
ANSI, Variable Pitch	Font: Roman	Typeface: Tms Rmn
ANSI. Variable Pitch	Font: Swiss	Typeface: Helv
ANSI, Variable Pitch	Font: Modern	Typeface: Courier
ANSI, Variable Pitch	**Font: Script**	**Typeface: System**
OEM. Default Pitch	Font: Don't Care	Typeface: Roman
OEM. Default Pitch	Font: Roman	Typeface: Roman
OEM. Default Pitch	Font: Swiss	Typeface: Roman
OEM, Default Pitch	Font: Modern	Typeface: Modern
OEM, Default Pitch	*Font: Script*	*Typeface: Script*
OEM, Fixed Pitch	**Font: Don't Care**	**Typeface: Terminal**
OEM, Fixed Pitch	**Font: Roman**	**Typeface: Terminal**
OEM, Fixed Pitch	**Font: Swiss**	**Typeface: Terminal**
OEM, Fixed Pitch	**Font: Modern**	**Typeface: Terminal**
OEM, Fixed Pitch	**Font: Script**	**Typeface: Terminal**
OEM, Variable Pitch	Font: Don't Care	Typeface: Roman
OEM, Variable Pitch	Font: Roman	Typeface: Roman
OEM, Variable Pitch	Font: Swiss	Typeface: Roman
OEM, Variable Pitch	Font: Modern	Typeface: Modern
OEM, Variable Pitch	*Font: Script*	*Typeface: Script*

You may also find that 40 and 80 column CGA/EGA fonts have been installed for use in the DOS shell. These are not, however, accessible or needed within Windows applications. These four fonts are named as: CGA40WOA.FON, CGA80WOA.FON, EGA40WOA.FON and EGA80WOA.FON.

The Symbol Font

Figure 20-3 shows a sixth typeface, Symbol, which is simply a Greek character set from the catch-all Decorative family. This family can include any type of symbol set, such as Zapf Dingbats or other special fonts.

The Symbol font is a bitmapped font, and so provides a good example of the effective distortion resulting from generating an italic version of a bitmapped font. With a stroked font, some distortion may still exist, but certainly to a much lesser degree and, in general, the distortion is not visually obvious.

Figure 20-3: The Symbol Character Set

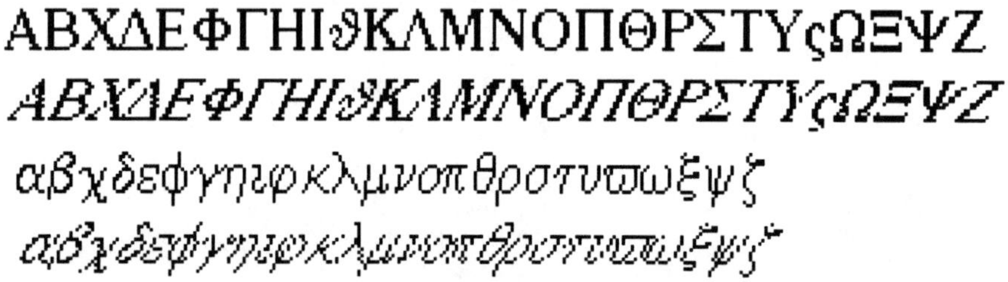

ΑΒΧΔΕΦΓΗΙϑΚΛΜΝΟΠΘΡΣΤΥϚΩΞΨΖ

ΑΒΧΔΕΦΓΗΙϑΚΛΜΝΟΠΘΡΣΤΥϚΩΞΨΖ

αβχδεφγηιφκλμνοπθροτυϖωξψζ

αβχδεφγηιφκλμνοπθροτυϖωξψζ

Using Logical (Custom) Fonts

Logical fonts, while based on the same font files, provide us with the flexibility that is lacking in the stock font objects. For example, using a custom logical font, an application is able to change the characteristics of the font, including height, width, italic and bold faces (weight), and to select explicit typefaces or styles which are not supported as stock logical font objects.

The appearance of a custom logical font is controlled by the fourteen fields in the LOGFONT structure defined in Windows.H:

```
LOGFONT ( struct tagLOGFONT )
{   int    lfHeight;          int    lfWidth;
    int    lfEscapement;      int    lfOrientation;
    int    lfWeight;
    BYTE   lfItalic;
    BYTE   lfUnderline;       BYTE   lfStrikeOut;
    BYTE   lfCharSet;
    BYTE   lfOutPrecision;    BYTE   lfClipPrecision;
    BYTE   lfQuality;
    BYTE   lfPitchAndFamily;
```

```
    BYTE lfFaceName[ LF_FACESIZE ];
}
```

Character Size: lfHeight and lfWidth

The *lfHeight* field defines the height of the font in logical units, including the internal leading but not the external leading. Since the point size of the font is the font height less the internal leading, this value specifies line spacing rather than absolute font size. Negative values of *lfHeight* are treated as absolute values, setting the desired ascent size (font size) instead of the line spacing. A value of zero sets a default size for the font.

The *lfWidth* value sets the character width in logical units. Normally, a zero value would be used to allow Windows to match the font width to the height, but specific values can be set to create condensed or expanded fonts. However, when non-zero values are used, particularly with bitmapped fonts, Windows may select a font designed for an aspect ratio different from the device context where the font is selected.

To review the font height and width characteristics, refer to Chapter Two, Figure 2-1, "Windows' Font Metrics".

Character Orientation: lfEscapement and lfOrientation

The *lfEscapement* value is an angle expressed in $^1/_{10}$th degree increments, beginning with 0° at horizontal, setting the angle at which the string is written.

The *lfOrientation* value is also an angle expressed in $^1/_{10}$th degree increments, again beginning with 0° at horizontal, but now setting the angle of the individual characters.

Table 20-7: Text Orientation

		lfEscapement	*lfOrientation*
Value	*Degrees*	*String Orientation*	*Character Orientation*
0	0°	left to right (default)	normal (default)
900	90°	vertical, rising	rotated 90° counterclockwise
1800	180°	right to left	inverted
2700	270°	vertical, falling	rotated 90° clockwise

Caution: Neither the escapement nor the orientation features work particularly well on screen, though these capabilities may be improved at a future time. Also, before using either feature with an output device (printer, plotter, etc), check the TEXTCAPS index with *GetDeviceCaps* to determine if the device is capable of handling character rotation. (See the Devices.C program in Chapter 15.)

Boldface Fonts: lfWeight

The *lfWeight* integer presently sets normal or boldface with two values recommended: 400 for Normal, or 700 for Boldface. In actual fact, any value from 0.550 is normal, and any greater value is boldface. Future versions of Windows, however, are expected to support a wider range of font weights, so their constants are already included in Windows.H as:

Table 20-8: Font Weights

Value	Font Weight ID
0	FW_DONTCARE
100	FW_THIN
200	FW_EXTRALIGHT or FW_ULTRALIGHT
300	FW_LIGHT
400	FW_NORMAL or FW_REGULAR
500	FW_MEDIUM
600	FW_SEMIBOLD or FW_DEMIBOLD
700	FW_BOLD
800	FW_EXTRABOLD or FW_ULTRABOLD
900	FW_HEAVY or FW_BLACK

Italics

The *lfItalic* field is a byte value used as a flag. When non-zero, Windows creates an italic version of GDI fonts by slanting the characters to the right. With bitmapped fonts, italics tend to appear unusually grainy, particularly when enlarged. For non-video output devices, check the TC_IA_ABLE bit in the TEXTCAPS returned by *GetDeviceCaps* (see Chapter 15).

Underlines and StrikeOuts

The *lfUnderline* and *lfStrikeOut* fields are byte values used as flags. When *lfUnderline* or *lfStrikeOut* are non-zero, underlining or strikeout bars are synthesized for GDI fonts. For other output devices, check the TC_UA_ABLE and TC_SO_ABLE bits in the TEXTCAPS returned by *GetDeviceCaps* (Chapter 15).

Character Sets

The *lfCharSet* field is a byte value selecting the desired character set. Four constants are defined in Windows.H as:

Table 20-9: Character Sets

Value	Character Set ID
0	ANSI_CHARSET
2	SYMBOL_CHARSET
128	SHIFTJIS_CHARSET (Japanese Kanji)
255	OEM_CHARSET

Caution: If an application uses a font with an unknown character set, no attempt should be made to translate or interpret strings which will be rendered with that font. Instead, the strings should be passed directly to the output device driver.

Note: Kanji (Japanese) fonts are not distributed with U.S. and European versions of Windows.

Font Matching: lfOutPrecision

The *lfOutPrecison* byte is not implemented by Windows 3.0 (see *lfQuality*) but will be used to instruct Windows on matching desired font characteristics and sizes with available fonts. Windows.H defines four identifiers as:

Table 20-10: Logical Font Precision

Value	Precision ID
0	OUT_DEFAULT_PRECIS
1	OUT_STRING_PRECIS
2	OUT_CHARACTER_PRECIS
3	OUT_STROKE_PRECIS

Font Clipping

The *lfOutPrecision* byte instructs Windows how to clip characters which would fall partially outside the clipping region. Three options are defined in Windows.H as:

Table 20-11: Clipping Precision

Value	Clipping ID	
0	CLIP_DEFAULT_PRECIS	
1	CLIP_CHARACTER_PRECIS	clip entire character
2	CLIP_STROKE_PRECIS	clip individual strokes

Font Matching: IfQuality

The *lfQuality* byte field tells Windows how to match an actual font to the requested font characteristics (see also *lfOutPrecision*). Three options are defined in Windows.H as:

Table 20-12: Font Matching

Value	Font Matching ID
0	DEFAULT_QUALITY
1	DRAFT_QUALITY
2	PROOF_QUALITY

The PROOF_QUALITY setting instructs Windows not to increase font size to match requested character height or width. While this setting restricts fonts to their optimum size(s), obviously the results may be smaller than requested.

Font Pitch and Family

The *lfPitchAndFamily* byte is a combination of two values with the least significant two bits selecting the pitch setting, and the most significant four bits selecting the typeface family. Pitch and family values are combined using the OR operator. Constants for pitch and family are defined in Windows.H as:

Table 20-13: Pitch and Family Constants

Value	Family ID	Value	Pitch ID
0x00	FF_DONTCARE	0x00	DEFAULT_PITCH
0x10	FF_ROMAN	0x01	FIXED_PITCH

Table 20-13: Pitch and Family Constants (cont.)

Value	Family ID	Value	Pitch ID
0x20	FF_SWISS	0x02	VARIABLE_PITCH
0x30	FF_MODERN		
0x40	FF_SCRIPT		
0x50	FF_DECORATIVE		

Typeface Names

The *lfFaceName* field is an array of byte, defined as:

```
BYTE lfFaceName[ LF_FACESIZE ];
```

This field contains the name of a specific typeface such as Courier, Helvetica, Symbol or Times Roman, which can be retrieved using the *GetTextFace* function as:

```
GetTextFace( hdc, LF_FACESIZE, szFaceName );
```

The constant LF_FACESIZE is defined in Windows.H with a value of 32, the maximum number of characters permitted in a typeface name.

Creating A Logical Font

Speaking of creating a logical font is partially a misnomer, because neither the *CreateFont* nor *CreateFontIndirect* functions actually create a new font. Instead, both functions select the closest match available from the GDI's pool of physical fonts. The matching font is selected on the basis of the information found either in the LOGFONT structure using *CreateFontIndirect*, or in the font specification parameters passed as arguments with the *CreateFont* function. In either case, the first step in loading a specific font is calling either *CreateFont* or *CreateFontIndirect* to return a handle to a font of type HFONT.

Next, after retrieving a handle to a logical font, the *SelectObject* function is called, and responds by selecting the real physical font which is the closest match to the logical font requested. After a font has been selected, the size and characteristics of the actual, physical font can be queried via the *GetTextMetrics* function while the *GetTextFace* function can be used to return the font name.

When the font is no longer needed, the logical font can be deleted using the *DeleteObject* function. However, remember that a logical font (like any other logical object) should never be deleted while in use, i.e., while selected in a valid device context, and, of course, stock logical fonts should never be deleted at all.

CreateFont and CreateFontIndirect

The *CreateFont* function is called with fourteen parameters corresponding to the LOGFONT fields discussed previously, as:

```
CreateFont( nHeight, nWidth, nEscapement, nOrientation,
            nWeight, cItalic, cUnderline, cStrikeOut,
            cCharSet, cOutputPrecision, cClipPrecision,
            cQuality, cPitchAndFamily, lpFacename );
```

The *CreateFontIndirect* function is called with a briefer parameter list. This is only because the *lpLogFont* argument is a long pointer to a structure of LOGFONT type which contains, by assumption, essentially the same information which is passed to *CreateFont* as individual parameters.

```
CreateFontIndirect( lpLogFont )
```

Both functions return a handle to a logical font with the characteristics requested. However, when the font is selected by using the SelectObject function, GDI's font mapper attempts to match the logical font with an existing physical font. If an exact match is not found, an alternative font is returned whose characteristics match as many of the requested characteristics as possible.

The primary fields used for font matching, in approximate order of importance, are shown following:

The *lfCharSet* field is always used, selecting either OEM or ANSI character sets. If stroked fonts are desired, OEM_CHARSET should always be specified, since ANSI_CHARSET selects only raster (bitmapped) fonts.

The *lfFaceName* field is important in specifying exactly which typeface is desired. This field may also be passed as NULL, leaving it to the *lfPitchAnd-Family* field to select the actual typeface. The *lfPitchAndFamily* field, as previously discussed, is actually two fields, but if *lfFaceName* is not set, both the pitch and family specifications will be treated as important.

The *lfHeight* value is always used, with Windows attempting to match the specification even if this requires, as it often does, enlarging the height of an existing font. The resulting character size will always be less than, or equal to, the *lfHeight* specification unless there simply is no smaller font available. For small fonts, the *lfHeight* may take precedence over other considerations, if necessary, to find a font small enough.

The *lfQuality* value can be set to PROOF_QUALITY to prevent font scaling.

The *SetMapperFlags* function controls how Windows matches fonts and aspect ratios, affecting how values of *lfHeight* and *lfWidth* are treated when these do not match the aspect ratio of the device. This is called as:

```
SetMapperFlags( hdc, 1L );
```

Windows is instructed to select only fonts with the same aspect ratio as the output device. Fonts of other aspect ratios can be selected by first restoring the default mapper flag setting as:

```
SetMapperFlags( hdc, 0L );
```

Of course, a hands-on demonstration is always worth a hundred pages of explanation, and the best way to become familiar with the font mapping considerations is to execute the Fonts1.C demo program (the complete listing appears at the end of this chapter) and play with different fonts and settings while using the preceding comments as a guideline.

The Fonts1 Demo Program

The Fonts1 demo program illustrated in Figure 20-4 provides a convenient means of selecting different font parameter settings while watching the resulting output in the bottom of the client window. Note that, particularly for larger type sizes, it may be necessary or helpful to enlarge the application to full screen size.

Most, though not all, of the font selection parameters are included in a modeless dialog box, either as check boxes, as radio buttons, or (for the height, width and weight fields) as edit boxes.

Seven mapping modes are provided, including the conventional Hi and Lo Metric, Hi and Lo English, Text, and TWIPS modes.

The seventh mode, Logical TWIPS, is a custom mode corresponding to conventional TWIPS except that the twenty logical units per point and 72 points per real physical inch in conventional TWIPS are now converted to 1440 logical units per logical inch. This Logical TWIPS mode provides an easy correspondence between the logical inch mapping modes and the font sizes which are expressed in points.

Last, along the right side of the dialog box, the current logical font's text metrics are reported.

For the most part, the Fonts1.C program is simply a dialog handler and contains little that is new except for the Logical TWIPS mapping mode.

Figure 20-4: Fonts and Font Variables

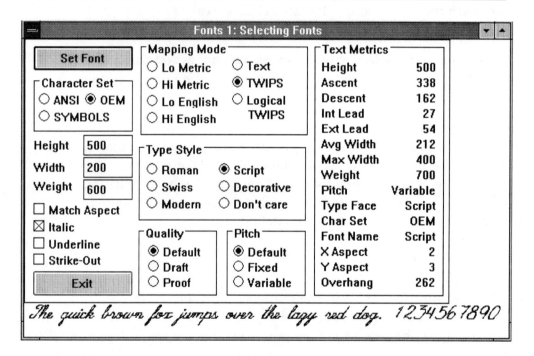

Calculating Point Sizes In Logical TWIPS

The Logical TWIPS mode is set as:

```
SetMapMode( hdc, MM_ANISOTROPIC );
SetWindowExt( hdc, 1440, 1440 );
SetViewport( hdc, GetDeviceCaps( hdc, LOGPIXELSX ),
                  GetDeviceCaps( hdc, LOGPIXELSY ) );
```

With this provision, point-sized fonts can now be written to the screen such that a 72-point font will be one logical inch high, not one physical inch. But remember, the point size still needs to be set in logical units, and therefore for a 30-point line spacing in Logical TWIPS, the *lmHeight* value would be set as 30 (points) times 20 units per point for a height of 600 logical units. More often, however, the point size desired is not the line spacing, but the actual font size, which requires a slightly different calculation. Remember, the *lmHeight* value is *tm.tmHeight* + *tm.tmInternalLeading,* while the typeface point size is determined only by the *tm.tmHeight* value. Therefore, to calculate an actual typeface point size, a little subterfuge is needed, and *lmHeight* can be calculated as:

```
lmHeight = PointSize * ( tm.tmHeight +
                 tm.tmInternalLeading ) / tm.tmHeight
```

Of course, it would probably be more convenient to begin by creating a height ratio for the font as:

```
fnRatio = ( tm.tmHeight + tm.tmInternalLeading ) /
            tm.tmHeight;
```

After all, once a typeface has been selected, *fnRatio* will be a constant for all point sizes in this typeface.

The line spacing (*lmHeight*) can be calculated in a separate step as:

```
lmHeight = fnRatio * PointSize;
```

For example, in Logical TWIPS, the Roman font (OEM) has a height of 274 units with an internal leading of 17 units. This calculates a value for *fnRatio* as 1.06614. Therefore, to create a 30-point font you need to set a value of 640 for *lmHeight* (1.06614 * 30 * 20 = 639.688). Granted, this result is not 100 percent correct, but the results are accurate enough for the display, and certainly well within the available pixel accuracy. In other words, the results are good enough for most practical purposes.

Summary

As demonstrated, Windows 3.0 fonts are both flexible and convenient, even though not all of the features expected are present quite yet, and the quality of the enlarged fonts falls somewhat short of dedicated graphics/drafting/typesetting programs such as Ventura Publisher or CorelDraw. Further, the few short comings mentioned exist largely because of very necessary trade-offs between speed and elaboration, since more elaborate text-graphics would present their own aggravations in the form of slow drawing. Nonetheless, you have seen the basic operations necessary for any type of screen elaboration desired. In Chapter 21, font operations will continue, but with the focus on printer output devices.

```c
//======================//
//        Fonts1.C       //
//   C++ Windows Fonts   //
//======================//

#include <windows.h>
#include "fonts.h"

char     szAppName[] = "FONTS1";
int      nMapMode    = IDD_TEXT;
DWORD    dwAspMatch  = 0L;
HWND     hDlg;
LOGFONT  lf;

void SetMapModeProc( HDC hdc )
{
    if( nMapMode != IDD_LOGTWIPS )
        SetMapMode( hdc, nMapMode - IDD_TEXT + MM_TEXT );
    else
    {
        SetMapMode( hdc, MM_ANISOTROPIC );
        SetWindowExt( hdc, 1440, 1440 );
        SetViewportExt( hdc,
                        GetDeviceCaps( hdc, LOGPIXELSX ),
                        GetDeviceCaps( hdc, LOGPIXELSY ) );
} }

void ShowMetrics( HWND hDlg )
{
    static TEXTMETRIC tm;
    static struct
        {   int  nDlgID;
            int *pTM;    }
        FontData[] =
        {   IDD_TM_HEIGHT,    &tm.tmHeight,
            IDD_TM_ASCENT,    &tm.tmAscent,
            IDD_TM_DESCENT,   &tm.tmDescent,
            IDD_TM_LEADINT,   &tm.tmInternalLeading,
            IDD_TM_LEADEXT,   &tm.tmExternalLeading,
            IDD_TM_WIDTHAVE,  &tm.tmAveCharWidth,
            IDD_TM_WIDTHMAX,  &tm.tmMaxCharWidth,
            IDD_TM_WEIGHT,    &tm.tmWeight,
            IDD_TM_OVER,      &tm.tmOverhang,
            IDD_TM_DIGITX,    &tm.tmDigitizedAspectX,
            IDD_TM_DIGITY,    &tm.tmDigitizedAspectY   };
    static char *szFonts[] =
                { "Don't Care", "Roman", "Swiss",
                  "Modern", "Script", "Decorative" },
              *szCharSet[] = { "ANSI", "SYMBOL", "OEM" };
```

```
    char            szFontName[LF_FACESIZE];
    BOOL            bTrans;
    HFONT           hFont;
    HDC             hdc;
    int             i, CharSet;

    lf.lfHeight     = GetDlgItemInt( hDlg, IDD_HEIGHT,
                                     &bTrans, TRUE );
    lf.lfWidth      = GetDlgItemInt( hDlg, IDD_WIDTH,
                                     &bTrans, FALSE );
    lf.lfWeight     = GetDlgItemInt( hDlg, IDD_WEIGHT,
                                     &bTrans, FALSE );
    lf.lfItalic     = (BYTE)
        IsDlgButtonChecked( hDlg, IDD_ITALIC     );
    lf.lfUnderline = (BYTE)
        IsDlgButtonChecked( hDlg, IDD_UNDERSCORE );
    lf.lfStrikeOut = (BYTE)
        IsDlgButtonChecked( hDlg, IDD_STRIKEOUT  );
    dwAspMatch      = (LONG)
        IsDlgButtonChecked( hDlg, IDD_ASPECT );
    GetDlgItemText( hDlg, IDD_FACENAME,
                    lf.lfFaceName, LF_FACESIZE );
    hdc = GetDC( hDlg );
    SetMapModeProc( hdc );
    SetMapperFlags( hdc, dwAspMatch );
    hFont = SelectObject( hdc, CreateFontIndirect( &lf ) );
    GetTextMetrics( hdc, &tm );
    GetTextFace( hdc, sizeof( szFontName ), szFontName );
    DeleteObject( SelectObject( hdc, hFont ) );
    ReleaseDC( hDlg, hdc );
    for( i=0; i<sizeof(FontData)/sizeof(FontData[0]); i++ )
        SetDlgItemInt( hDlg, FontData[i].nDlgID,
                       *FontData[i].pTM, TRUE );
    SetDlgItemText( hDlg, IDD_TM_PITCH,
                    tm.tmPitchAndFamily & 1 ?
                    "Variable" : "Fixed" );
    SetDlgItemText( hDlg, IDD_TM_FAMILY,
                    szFonts[ tm.tmPitchAndFamily >> 4 ] );
    switch( tm.tmCharSet )
    {
        case ANSI_CHARSET:   CharSet = 0;  break;
        case SYMBOL_CHARSET: CharSet = 1;  break;
        case OEM_CHARSET:    CharSet = 2;  break;
    }
    SetDlgItemText( hDlg, IDD_TM_CHARSET,
                    szCharSet[CharSet] );
    SetDlgItemText( hDlg, IDD_TF_NAME, szFontName );
}

#pragma argsused

BOOL FAR PASCAL DlgProc( HWND hDlg, WORD msg,
```

```
                           WORD wParam, LONG lParam )
{
   switch( msg )
   {
      case WM_INITDIALOG:
         CheckRadioButton( hDlg, IDD_TEXT, IDD_LOGTWIPS,
                           IDD_TEXT );
         CheckRadioButton( hDlg, IDD_ANSI, IDD_OEM,
                           IDD_ANSI );
         CheckRadioButton( hDlg, IDD_QUALDEFAULT,
                           IDD_QUALPROOF, IDD_QUALDEFAULT );
         CheckRadioButton( hDlg, IDD_PITCHDEF,
                           IDD_PITCHVAR,  IDD_PITCHDEF );
         CheckRadioButton( hDlg, IDD_DONTCARE, IDD_DECO,
                           IDD_DONTCARE );
         lf.lfEscapement     = 0;
         lf.lfOrientation    = 0;
         lf.lfOutPrecision   = OUT_DEFAULT_PRECIS;
         lf.lfClipPrecision  = CLIP_DEFAULT_PRECIS;
         ShowMetrics( hDlg );    // fall through to SetFocus //

      case WM_SETFOCUS:
         SetFocus( GetDlgItem( hDlg, IDD_HEIGHT ) );
         return( FALSE );

      case WM_COMMAND:
         switch( wParam )
         {
            case IDD_TEXT:       case IDD_LOMETRIC:
            case IDD_HIMETRIC:   case IDD_LOENGLISH:
            case IDD_HIENGLISH:  case IDD_TWIPS:
            case IDD_LOGTWIPS:
               nMapMode = wParam;    break;

            case IDD_ASPECT:     case IDD_ITALIC:
            case IDD_UNDERSCORE: case IDD_STRIKEOUT:
               // no response //
               break;

            case IDD_ANSI:    lf.lfCharSet = 0;    break;
            case IDD_SYMBOL:  lf.lfCharSet = 2;    break;
            case IDD_OEM:     lf.lfCharSet = 255;  break;

            case IDD_QUALDEFAULT: case IDD_QUALDRAFT:
            case IDD_QUALPROOF:
               lf.lfQuality = (BYTE)
                  (wParam - IDD_QUALDEFAULT);
               break;

            case IDD_PITCHDEF:    case IDD_PITCHFIXED:
            case IDD_PITCHVAR:
               lf.lfPitchAndFamily &= 0xF0;
               lf.lfPitchAndFamily |= (BYTE)
```

```
                            (wParam - IDD_PITCHDEF );
                    break;

            case IDD_ROMAN:        case IDD_SWISS:
            case IDD_MODERN:       case IDD_SCRIPT:
            case IDD_DECO:         case IDD_DONTCARE:
                lf.lfPitchAndFamily &= 0x0F;
                lf.lfPitchAndFamily |= (BYTE)
                    (wParam - IDD_DONTCARE << 4 );

            case IDD_SETFONT:
                ShowMetrics( hDlg );
                InvalidateRect( GetParent(hDlg), NULL, TRUE );
                break;

            case IDD_QUIT:
                PostQuitMessage(0);    break;
        }  break;
    default:  return( FALSE );
    }
    return( TRUE );
}

long FAR PASCAL WndProc( HWND hwnd,   WORD msg,
                         WORD wParam, LONG lParam )
{
    static char szText[] =
        "The quick brown fox jumps over the lazy red dog."
        " 1234567890";
    HANDLE       hInst;
    HDC          hdc;
    HFONT        hFont;
    FARPROC      lpfnDlgProc;
    PAINTSTRUCT  ps;
    RECT         rect;

    switch( msg )
    {
    case WM_CREATE:
        hInst = ( (LPCREATESTRUCT) lParam ) -> hInstance;
        lpfnDlgProc = MakeProcInstance( DlgProc, hInst );
        hDlg = CreateDialog( hInst, szAppName, hwnd,
                             lpfnDlgProc );
        return(0);

    case WM_SETFOCUS:  SetFocus( hDlg );  return(0);

    case WM_PAINT:
        hdc = BeginPaint( hwnd, &ps );
        SetMapModeProc( hdc );
        SetMapperFlags( hdc, dwAspMatch );
        GetClientRect( hDlg, &rect );
        rect.bottom += 1;
        DPtoLP( hdc, (LPPOINT) &rect, 2 );
```

```
        hFont = SelectObject( hdc,
                             CreateFontIndirect( &lf ) );
        TextOut( hdc, rect.left, rect.bottom, szText, 59 );
        DeleteObject( SelectObject( hdc, hFont ) );
        EndPaint( hwnd, &ps );
        return(0);

    case WM_DESTROY:  PostQuitMessage(0);  return(0);
    }
    return( DefWindowProc( hwnd, msg, wParam, lParam ) );
}

#pragma argsused

int PASCAL WinMain( HANDLE hInst,       HANDLE hPrevInst,
                    LPSTR  lpszCmdParam, int nCmdShow )
{
    static char szAppName[] = "FONTS1";
    HWND        hwnd;
    MSG         msg;
    WNDCLASS    wc;

    if( ! hPrevInst )
    {
        wc.hInstance      = hInst;
        wc.lpfnWndProc    = WndProc;
        wc.cbClsExtra     = 0;
        wc.cbWndExtra     = 0;
        wc.lpszClassName  = szAppName;
        wc.lpszMenuName   = (LPSTR) szAppName;
        wc.hIcon          = LoadIcon( hInst, szAppName );
        wc.hCursor        = LoadCursor( NULL, IDC_ARROW );
        wc.hbrBackground  = GetStockObject( WHITE_BRUSH );
        wc.style          = CS_HREDRAW | CS_VREDRAW;
        RegisterClass( &wc );
    }
    hwnd = CreateWindow( szAppName,
                    "Fonts 1: Selecting Fonts",
                    WS_OVERLAPPEDWINDOW |
                    WS_CLIPCHILDREN,
                    CW_USEDEFAULT, CW_USEDEFAULT,
                    CW_USEDEFAULT, CW_USEDEFAULT,
                    NULL, NULL, hInst, NULL  );
    ShowWindow(   hwnd, nCmdShow );
    UpdateWindow( hwnd );
    while( GetMessage( &msg, NULL, 0, 0 ) )
    {
        if( hDlg == 0 || ! IsDialogMessage( hDlg, &msg ) )
        {
            TranslateMessage( &msg );
            DispatchMessage(  &msg );
    }   }
```

```
        return( msg.wParam );
}
                    ;==============;
                    ;  FONTS1.DEF  ;
                    ;==============;
NAME            FONTS1

DESCRIPTION     "WINDOWS TEXT FONTS"
EXETYPE         WINDOWS
STUB            "WINSTUB.EXE"
CODE            PRELOAD MOVEABLE DISCARDABLE
DATA            PRELOAD MOVEABLE MULTIPLE
HEAPSIZE        1024
STACKSIZE       8192
EXPORTS         WndProc
                DlgProc

                    //===========//
                    //  FONTS.H  //
                    //===========//
#define   IDD_SETFONT          1
#define   IDD_QUIT             2

#define   IDD_TEXT             100
#define   IDD_LOMETRIC         101
#define   IDD_HIMETRIC         102
#define   IDD_LOENGLISH        103
#define   IDD_HIENGLISH        104
#define   IDD_TWIPS            105
#define   IDD_LOGTWIPS         106

#define   IDD_HEIGHT           110
#define   IDD_WIDTH            111
#define   IDD_WEIGHT           112
#define   IDD_ITALIC           113
#define   IDD_UNDERSCORE       114
#define   IDD_STRIKEOUT        115
#define   IDD_ASPECT           116

#define   IDD_ANSI             120
#define   IDD_OEM              121
#define   IDD_SYMBOL           122

#define   IDD_QUALDEFAULT      130
#define   IDD_QUALDRAFT        131
#define   IDD_QUALPROOF        132
#define   IDD_PITCHDEF         140
#define   IDD_PITCHFIXED       141
#define   IDD_PITCHVAR         142

#define   IDD_DONTCARE         150
#define   IDD_ROMAN            151
```

```
#define   IDD_SWISS              152
#define   IDD_MODERN             153
#define   IDD_SCRIPT             154
#define   IDD_DECO               155

#define   IDD_FACENAME           160

#define   IDD_TM_HEIGHT          200
#define   IDD_TM_ASCENT          201
#define   IDD_TM_DESCENT         202
#define   IDD_TM_LEADINT         203
#define   IDD_TM_LEADEXT         204
#define   IDD_TM_WIDTHAVE        205
#define   IDD_TM_WIDTHMAX        206
#define   IDD_TM_WEIGHT          207
#define   IDD_TM_PITCH           208
#define   IDD_TM_FAMILY          209
#define   IDD_TM_CHARSET         210
#define   IDD_TM_OVER            211
#define   IDD_TM_DIGITX          212
#define   IDD_TM_DIGITY          213
#define   IDD_TF_NAME            214

                //===============//
                // FONTS1.DLG  //
                //===============//

FONTS1 DIALOG DISCARDABLE LOADONCALL PURE MOVEABLE
      2, 0, 257, 154
STYLE WS_CHILD | WS_VISIBLE | WS_BORDER | 0x1L
BEGIN
   CONTROL "ANSI" 120, "BUTTON",
      WS_CHILD | WS_VISIBLE | 0x9L, 8, 29, 26, 12
   CONTROL "OEM" 121, "BUTTON",
      WS_CHILD | WS_VISIBLE | 0x9L, 36, 29, 26, 12
   CONTROL "Default" 140, "BUTTON",
      WS_CHILD | WS_VISIBLE | WS_GROUP | 0x9L,
      127, 118, 38, 12
   CONTROL "Fixed" 141, "BUTTON",
      WS_CHILD | WS_VISIBLE | 0x9L, 127, 127, 38, 12
   CONTROL "Variable" 142, "BUTTON",
      WS_CHILD | WS_VISIBLE | 0x9L, 127, 136, 38, 12
   CONTROL "Default" 130, "BUTTON",
      WS_CHILD | WS_VISIBLE | WS_GROUP | 0x9L, 75, 118, 42, 12
   CONTROL "Draft" 131, "BUTTON",
      WS_CHILD | WS_VISIBLE | 0x9L, 75, 127, 42, 12
   CONTROL "Proof" 132, "BUTTON",
      WS_CHILD | WS_VISIBLE | 0x9L, 75, 136, 42, 12
   CONTROL "Roman" 151, "BUTTON",
      WS_CHILD | WS_VISIBLE | WS_GROUP | 0x9L, 74, 70, 39, 12
   CONTROL "Script" 154, "BUTTON",
      WS_CHILD | WS_VISIBLE | 0x9L, 118, 70, 50, 12
```

```
CONTROL "Swiss" 152, "BUTTON",
    WS_CHILD | WS_VISIBLE | 0x9L, 74, 80, 39, 12
CONTROL "Decorative" 155, "BUTTON",
    WS_CHILD | WS_VISIBLE | 0x9L, 118, 80, 50, 12
CONTROL "Modern" 153, "BUTTON",
    WS_CHILD | WS_VISIBLE | 0x9L, 74, 90, 39, 12
CONTROL "Don't care" 150, "BUTTON",
    WS_CHILD | WS_VISIBLE | 0x9L, 118, 90, 50, 12
CONTROL "Lo Metric" 101, "BUTTON",
    WS_CHILD | WS_VISIBLE | WS_GROUP | 0x9L, 74, 10, 46, 12
CONTROL "Text" 100, "BUTTON",
    WS_CHILD | WS_VISIBLE | 0x9L, 126, 10, 40, 10
CONTROL "Hi Metric" 102, "BUTTON",
    WS_CHILD | WS_VISIBLE | 0x9L, 74, 20, 46, 12
CONTROL "TWIPS" 105, "BUTTON",
    WS_CHILD | WS_VISIBLE | 0x9L, 126, 20, 40, 10
CONTROL "Lo English" 103, "BUTTON",
    WS_CHILD | WS_VISIBLE | 0x9L, 74, 30, 46, 12
CONTROL "Logical " 106, "BUTTON",
    WS_CHILD | WS_VISIBLE | 0x9L, 126, 30, 40, 10
CONTROL "Hi English" 104, "BUTTON",
    WS_CHILD | WS_VISIBLE | 0x9L, 74, 40, 46, 12
CONTROL "TWIPS" 215, "STATIC",
    WS_CHILD | WS_VISIBLE | 0x2L, 126, 40, 32, 9
CONTROL "Height" -1, "STATIC",
    WS_CHILD | WS_VISIBLE | WS_GROUP, 5, 58, 30, 8
CONTROL "" 110, "EDIT",
    WS_CHILD | WS_VISIBLE | WS_BORDER | WS_TABSTOP,
    35, 56, 30, 12
CONTROL "Width" -1, "STATIC",
    WS_CHILD | WS_VISIBLE | WS_GROUP, 5, 71, 30, 8
CONTROL "" 111, "EDIT",
    WS_CHILD | WS_VISIBLE | WS_BORDER | WS_TABSTOP,
    35, 69, 30, 12
CONTROL "Weight" -1, "STATIC",
    WS_CHILD | WS_VISIBLE | WS_GROUP, 5, 82, 30, 8
CONTROL "" 112, "EDIT",
    WS_CHILD | WS_VISIBLE | WS_BORDER | WS_TABSTOP,
    35, 82, 30, 12
CONTROL "Mapping Mode" -1, "BUTTON",
    WS_CHILD | WS_VISIBLE | 0x7L, 70, 0, 102, 56
CONTROL "Match Aspect" 116, "BUTTON",
    WS_CHILD | WS_VISIBLE | WS_TABSTOP | 0x3L, 5, 94, 60, 11
CONTROL "Italic" 113, "BUTTON",
    WS_CHILD | WS_VISIBLE | WS_TABSTOP | 0x3L,
    5, 104, 60, 11
CONTROL "Underline" 114, "BUTTON",
    WS_CHILD | WS_VISIBLE | WS_TABSTOP | 0x3L,
    5, 114, 60, 11
CONTROL "Strike-Out" 115, "BUTTON",
    WS_CHILD | WS_VISIBLE | WS_TABSTOP | 0x3L,
```

```
    5, 123, 60, 12
CONTROL "Character Set" -1, "BUTTON",
    WS_CHILD | WS_VISIBLE | 0x7L, 5, 20, 60, 34
CONTROL "Quality" -1, "BUTTON",
    WS_CHILD | WS_VISIBLE | 0x7L, 69, 108, 48, 42
CONTROL "Pitch" -1, "BUTTON",
    WS_CHILD | WS_VISIBLE | 0x7L, 123, 108, 48, 42
CONTROL "Type Style" -1, "BUTTON",
    WS_CHILD | WS_VISIBLE | 0x7L, 69, 59, 102, 47
CONTROL "Set Font" 1, "BUTTON",
    WS_CHILD | WS_VISIBLE | WS_TABSTOP | 0x1L, 5, 4, 60, 14
CONTROL "Text Metrics" -1, "BUTTON",
    WS_CHILD | WS_VISIBLE | 0x7L, 176, 0, 78, 150
CONTROL "Height" -1, "STATIC",
    WS_CHILD | WS_VISIBLE | WS_GROUP, 180, 12, 44, 8
CONTROL "Ascent" -1, "STATIC",
    WS_CHILD | WS_VISIBLE | WS_GROUP, 180, 21, 44, 8
CONTROL "Descent" -1, "STATIC",
    WS_CHILD | WS_VISIBLE | WS_GROUP, 180, 30, 44, 8
CONTROL "Int Lead" -1, "STATIC",
    WS_CHILD | WS_VISIBLE | WS_GROUP, 180, 39, 44, 8
CONTROL "Ext Lead" -1, "STATIC",
    WS_CHILD | WS_VISIBLE | WS_GROUP, 180, 48, 44, 8
CONTROL "Avg Width" -1, "STATIC",
    WS_CHILD | WS_VISIBLE | WS_GROUP, 180, 57, 44, 8
CONTROL "Max Width" -1, "STATIC",
    WS_CHILD | WS_VISIBLE | WS_GROUP, 180, 66, 44, 8
CONTROL "Weight" -1, "STATIC",
    WS_CHILD | WS_VISIBLE | WS_GROUP, 180, 75, 44, 8
CONTROL "Pitch" -1, "STATIC",
    WS_CHILD | WS_VISIBLE | WS_GROUP, 180, 84, 44, 8
CONTROL "Type Face" -1, "STATIC",
    WS_CHILD | WS_VISIBLE | WS_GROUP, 180, 93, 44, 8
CONTROL "Char Set" -1, "STATIC",
    WS_CHILD | WS_VISIBLE | WS_GROUP, 180, 102, 44, 8
CONTROL "Overhang" -1, "STATIC",
    WS_CHILD | WS_VISIBLE | WS_GROUP, 180, 138, 44, 8
CONTROL "X Aspect" -1, "STATIC",
    WS_CHILD | WS_VISIBLE | WS_GROUP, 180, 120, 44, 8
CONTROL "Y Aspect" -1, "STATIC",
    WS_CHILD | WS_VISIBLE | WS_GROUP, 180, 129, 44, 8
CONTROL "Font Name" -1, "STATIC",
    WS_CHILD | WS_VISIBLE | WS_GROUP, 180, 111, 44, 8
CONTROL "0" 200, "STATIC",
    WS_CHILD | WS_VISIBLE | WS_GROUP | 0x2L, 234, 12, 15, 8
CONTROL "0" 201, "STATIC",
    WS_CHILD | WS_VISIBLE | WS_GROUP | 0x2L, 234, 21, 15, 8
CONTROL "0" 202, "STATIC",
    WS_CHILD | WS_VISIBLE | WS_GROUP | 0x2L, 234, 30, 15, 8
CONTROL "0" 204, "STATIC",
    WS_CHILD | WS_VISIBLE | WS_GROUP | 0x2L, 234, 39, 15, 8
```

```
CONTROL "0" 203, "STATIC",
    WS_CHILD | WS_VISIBLE | WS_GROUP | 0x2L, 234, 48, 15, 8
CONTROL "0" 205, "STATIC",
    WS_CHILD | WS_VISIBLE | WS_GROUP | 0x2L, 234, 57, 15, 8
CONTROL "0" 206, "STATIC",
    WS_CHILD | WS_VISIBLE | WS_GROUP | 0x2L, 234, 66, 15, 8
CONTROL "0" 207, "STATIC",
    WS_CHILD | WS_VISIBLE | WS_GROUP | 0x2L, 234, 75, 15, 8
CONTROL "" 208, "STATIC",
    WS_CHILD | WS_VISIBLE | WS_GROUP | 0x2L, 215, 84, 34, 8
CONTROL "" 209, "STATIC",
    WS_CHILD | WS_VISIBLE | WS_GROUP | WS_TABSTOP | 0x2L,
    215, 93, 34, 8
CONTROL "" 210, "STATIC",
    WS_CHILD | WS_VISIBLE | WS_GROUP | 0x2L, 215, 102, 34, 8
CONTROL "0" 211, "STATIC",
    WS_CHILD | WS_VISIBLE | WS_GROUP | 0x2L, 234, 138, 15, 8
CONTROL "0" 212, "STATIC",
    WS_CHILD | WS_VISIBLE | WS_GROUP | 0x2L, 234, 120, 15, 8
CONTROL "0" 213, "STATIC",
    WS_CHILD | WS_VISIBLE | WS_GROUP | 0x2L, 234, 129, 15, 8
CONTROL "" 214, "STATIC",
    WS_CHILD | WS_VISIBLE | WS_GROUP | 0x2L, 215, 111, 34, 8
CONTROL "Exit" 2, "BUTTON",
    WS_CHILD | WS_VISIBLE | WS_TABSTOP, 5, 136, 60, 14
CONTROL "SYMBOLS" 122, "BUTTON",
    WS_CHILD | WS_VISIBLE | 0x9L, 8, 39, 46, 12
END
```

Chapter 21

The Printer Device Context

Thus far, we've spent quite a bit of time talking about device independence, including device-independent bitmaps (DIBs), and device-independent video displays using the isotropic mapping mode and automatic dithering of colors. These are all devices used by Windows to make applications transportable from one system to another.

But what about printers? After all, printer capacities vary even more than video displays, ranging from 9-pin to 24-pin dot matrix printers to daisy-wheels and spin writers to laser jet and ink jet devices—quite a diversity, not only in mechanisms but also in print resolutions and device capacities. In the past, it has been quite a headache trying to guess what escape codes were supported by any specific printer.

Previous solutions to the mystery printer problem have ranged from treating all printers as "bare-bones" systems supporting virtually nothing except the simplest character output to elaborate printer support libraries which queried the user about types and features. Neither extreme was an ideal solution to the problem. Unfortunately, Windows 3.0 does not have an ideal solution either, but it does provide a better solution than previously available.

Under Windows, a variety of printers are supported by printer device drivers that provide largely device-independent operation for both text and graphic operations. These are not miracle device drivers, and they do not make non-graphic devices suddenly graphics-capable. Also, these drivers do not support absolutely every printer available, although they do support almost all contemporary printers. Most important, using the Windows drivers, your application does not need to worry about printer control sequences, communications protocols, and interpreting error messages, because these are tasks handled by the drivers. Of course, the question always remains, did the end-user install the correct printer driver(s) to match their hardware? But under Windows, this question occurs only once, (when Windows is installed), and is no longer the application programmer's concern.

Printers vs. Video

While Windows has provided a high degree of video independence, even with device-independent printer drivers, applications using the printer must still have some consideration for device limitations.

When dealing with screen graphics, we could count on two certainties: First, that the video was graphics capable, and second, that the correct graphics driver was installed, since, if either were not the case, Windows itself wouldn't execute.

With printers, however, these conditions can be hoped for but not assumed. A printer may function quite well with Windows in text modes, but not support graphics at all. It might have only limited graphics support or, like a plotter, might support vectored graphics very well, but be almost useless for both text and bitmapped images. Further, unlike video systems, printers:

- Use a one-shot display surface which can not be rewritten or corrected, i.e., a page must be written as a single image;
- are relatively slow to execute;
- may run out of paper;
- may be off line;
- may return error reports.

In Windows, however, both device output and error messages are handled by a single function, the Escape function, which will be discussed presently. First, however, the topic will be setting up printer operations:

Initiating Printer Operations

Under Windows, printing operations involve a number of Windows modules, including the printer device driver library (.DRV), the Windows Print Manager (PRINTMAN.EXE), and GDI library module.

As a first step in printer operations, the application calls for a handle to a printer device context using the *CreateDC* function. In turn, Windows loads the printer device driver library module (if it is not presently in memory), instructing the driver to initialize itself.

The second step in the application is to call the *Escape* function, handled by the GDI module, requesting the Escape subfunction STARTDOC to initiate a new print task. In turn, the GDI module calls the *Control* function in the printer driver, telling the printer driver to execute any appropriate initialization routines before it returns to the GDI module with an *OpenJob* request. And, after this, the GDI module loads the Print Manager (spooler) program.

At this point, Windows is ready for printer operations, but remember that the output is not being sent directly to the printer device. Instead, Windows will create one or more temporary files to where the actual output will be held. Two types of files are created: Metafiles with the filename format ~MF-xxxx.TMP for graphics instructions, and text files with the format ~SPL-xxxx.TMP. Both types of file are written to the subdirectory indicated by the TEMP variable (in WIN.INI), or to the root directory of the first fixed disk if no TEMP specification exists. When printer output is finished, these temporary files will be erased automatically.

For text output, each page (as written by the printer) will be stored in a separate file. For graphics metafiles, a similar format is used except that output may be separated by bands rather than pages (see"Banding", following). Most of this, however, is invisible to both the application and the programmer.

Output To A Printer Device Context

Most of an application's output to a printer device is not particularly different from writing to the video device. The principal difference is simply the device context handle where the operations are directed. For example, the instructions:

```
fgets( Buffer, sizeof( Buffer ), File );
TextOut( hdcPrn, 0, nLineCnt * nLineVert,
         (LPSTR) Buffer, strlen( Buffer ) );
```

read from the input file into *Buffer,* and then write the contents of *Buffer* to the printer (*hdcPrn*).

The only difference between writing the output to the screen instead of the printer would be the device driver handle, i.e., changing *hdcPrn* to *hdc*.

Graphics instructions can be written to the printer in a similar fashion. For an example, in Chapter 17, five- and seven-pointed stars were written to the client window to demonstrate the difference in the winding and alternate fill modes. With a few minor revisions, these same two diagrams could be written to the printer. The first change required would be replacing the instruction:

```
hdc = BeginPaint( hwnd, &ps );
```

with a printer device instruction as:

```
hdcPrn = GetPrinterDC( hwnd );
```

Subsequent drawing instructions require virtually no revision except for changing *hdc* to *hdcPrn* as:

```
hPen = CreatePen( PS_SOLID, 3, 0L );
SelectObject( hdcPrn, hPen );
SelectObject( hdcPrn, GetStockObject( LTGRAY_BRUSH ) );
SetMapMode( hdcPrn, MM_ISOTROPIC );
SetWindowExt(    hdcPrn,    440,   -220 );
SetViewportExt( hdcPrn, cxWnd, cyWnd );
SetWindowOrg(    hdcPrn,   -220,    110 );
SetPolyFillMode( hdcPrn, nFillMode );
Polygon( hdcPrn, pt[0], 5 );
Polygon( hdcPrn, pt[1], 7 );
```

Of course, when you are finished, the device context needs to be closed, but instead of:

```
EndPaint( hwnd, &ps );
```

the appropriate instruction is:

```
DeleteDC( hdcPrn );
```

This section has been a bit over-simplified because there are some printer-specific instructions which have been omitted here, but which will be discussed in a moment.

Escape Subfunctions

One very important element is missing in the preceding examples: The *Escape* function calls which are used to send printer specific instructions to the printer driver.

The *Escape* function allows applications to access facilities belonging to a specific device which are not directly available through GDI functions. While *Escape* is a single function, sixty-five subfunctions are defined in Windows.H, making calling *Escape* rather like calling a DOS *Interrupt 21h* function. Only a few of these subfunctions will be discussed here. For a complete list, see **GDI Escapes** in Appendix A.

The *Escape* function is called with five parameters as:

```
Escape( hdcPrn, nEscape, nCount, lpInData, lpOutData );
```

The *hdcPrn* parameter identifies the device context, and the *nEscape* parameter identifies the subfunction requested. *lpInData* is a LPSTR pointer to a structure containing the input data required by the escape subfunction, while *nCount* indicates the number of bytes in the input structure. Last, *lpOutData* points to a data structure receiving data returned by the subfunction. In most of the examples discussed here, *nCount* is zero, while the *lpInData* and *lpOut-Data* parameters will be NULL.

Escape calls made by an application are translated and sent to the device driver by Windows, returning an integer value specifying the outcome of the function. If successful, a positive value is returned. The exception is the QUERYESCSUPPORT escape, which checks implementation only, and returns zero if the escape is not implemented.

A negative value indicates an error with five error codes defined as:

Table 21-1: Spooler Error Codes

Constant	Value	Meaning
SP_ERROR	-1	general error
SP_APPABORT	-2	application abort
SP_USERABORT	-3	job user terminated through Print Manager
SP_OUTOFDISK	-4	insufficient disk space currently available for spooling /no more space expected to become available
SP_OUTOFMEMORY	-5	insufficient memory available for spooling

Amending The Output Example

In Chapter 17, an example was given showing how a portion of a routine could be converted for printer output, concluding with the comment that printer-specific instructions had been omitted. Now that you've met, however briefly, the *Escape* function, it's time to amend the example and show how printer-specific instructions would be included.

The first instruction needed, after getting the printer device context, is an *Escape* STARTDOC subfunction call as:

```
hdcPrn = GetPrinterDC( hwnd );
if( Escape( hdcPrn, STARTDOC,
            sizeof(szDoc)-1, szDoc, NULL ) > 0 )
{
    ... drawing instructions ...
```

The STARTDOC subfunction tells the printer—(or, more correctly, the spooler)—to initiate a new document. In this case, two additional parameters are being passed: First, the *nCount* parameter which specifies the size of the *szDoc* array, and second, the *szDoc* data itself, which, for STARTDOC, is simply a string that Print Manager will use to identify the document. Note that this label will not be printed and is only used within Print Manager to identify the document being processed. The value returned by the *Escape* function is tested, proceeding with the drawing instructions only if the result of the STARTDOC call is positive.

Following the drawing instructions, a second *Escape* function call is made, but this time for the NEWFRAME subfunction, advancing the printer to a new page, i.e., ejecting the finished page:

```
    if( Escape( hdcPrn, NEWFRAME, 0, NULL, NULL ) > 0 )
        Escape( hdcPrn, ENDDOC,  0, NULL, NULL );
}
DeleteDC( hdcPrn );
```

After the NEWFRAME instruction, but before closing the device context, an *Escape* ENDDOC function call is made to tell the spooler that the document is finished.

Note that the ENDDOC call is made only if all previous *Escape* functions have reported *no error*. If any of the prior *Escape*s have reported an error, the GDI will already have aborted the current document. Requesting an ENDDOC subfunction without an active document may result in the spooler and/or printer being reset.

Gaining Direct Access To The Printer

To begin, **don't!**

That is the brief but blunt fact. You can, if you insist, use C functions to access the printer port directly, assuming that you can identify which port is being used (said information is available from WIN.INI), and send anything you want directly to the port. But there are a few small problems with this: First, other applications may have the present output queue and your application would be stepping on another application's output. Second, your application will not know what information is appropriate. I.e., is the actual printer a dot matrix? A spinwriter or daisy-wheel? A laser jet? A PostScript printer? Remember, control codes differ greatly for different device types. Therefore, leave the print handling to the Print Manager.

Last, **don't** tamper!

Banding Graphics Output

A full page of graphics on a 300 dpi laser jet may easily require a megabyte or more of data. At the same time, many laser jet printers may have 512K of RAM (or less). And, while using lower resolutions, dot-matrix printers which support graphics usually lack adequate memory to hold an entire bitmapped page. Thus, because many print devices may lack sufficient memory for full page images, a technique called "banding" is employed, allowing a page of graphics to be printed as a series of separately constructed rectangles which are called bands. When printed, these bands compose a single image and do not present any break or other differentiation between the separate bands. They do, however, provide a means of circumventing device limitations.

Of primary importance to the programmer is understanding that an application does not need to be responsible for banding operations. When an output device requires banding, but the application makes no provisions for specific banding operations, the GDI uses banding techniques transparently by first storing the image as a metafile. It then employs banding to set clipping regions to define the band area before replaying the metafile to the output device driver. The application can also provide its own banding operations using the *Escape* NEXTBAND subfunction.

However, if the GDI can handle this type of operation on its own, why use explicit banding? There are two principal reasons: First, explicit banding can increase printing speed because the application only needs to call graphics functions affecting each specific band. This is often faster than replaying an entire metafile for each band. Second, banding can reduce the disk space required for .TMP files. For example, if large bitmaps are being printed and banding is not used, the GDI creates a single large metafile which is the same size as the eventual printer output file. With banding, a series of smaller metafiles are created, but only one at a time.

Using Banding

When using explicit banding to print a page, the first thing to remember is that the GDI will be responsible for setting the individual band areas. To use this, you will need to declare a variable of type RECT, as:

```
RECT    rect;
```

After calling STARTDOC, the output process begins with an *Escape* NEXTBAND function call to retrieve the first *rect* coordinates:

```
hdcPrn = GetPrinterDC( hwnd );
if( Escape( hdcPrn, STARTDOC,
            sizeof(szDoc)-1, szDoc, NULL ) > 0 )
{
    Escape( hdcPrn, NEXTBAND, 0, NULL, (LPSTR) &rect );
```

At this point, the NEXTBAND call has not only returned *rect* coordinate, but also has set the clipping region to the *rect* coordinates.

Before any graphics operations are carried out, the *IsRectEmpty* function is called to determine if *rect* is empty, i.e., if the width and/or the height are zero:

```
    while( ! IsRectEmpty( &rect ) )
    {
```

If *rect* is empty, this is a indication that the page is finished and there is no point in repeating the graphics operations again. If *rect* is not empty, then graphics operations continue for the current band:

```
        ... drawing instructions ...
        Escape( hdcPrn, NEXTBAND, 0, NULL, (LPSTR) &rect );
    }
```

The loop concludes with a repeat *Escape* NEXTBAND call. This serves two purposes: First, it tells the GDI that the present band is completed, and second, it retrieves the coordinates for the next band.

This loop will continue until an empty *rect* is returned by the NEXTBAND call, indicating that the page is completed.

Now, in the previous example, graphics operations for a page were concluded with a final pair of *Escape* functions as:

```
if( Escape( hdcPrn, NEWFRAME, 0, NULL, NULL ) > 0 )
    Escape( hdcPrn, ENDDOC,   0, NULL, NULL );
}
DeleteDC( hdcPrn );
```

With banding, however, the NEWFRAME subfunction should not be used, since it will only result in a blank page being ejected after the completed page. Instead, only the *Escape* ENDDOC subfunction is called as:

```
    Escape( hdcPrn, ENDDOC,   0, NULL, NULL );
}
DeleteDC( hdcPrn );
```

You will recall that you were warned earlier about the potential problem of making an ENDDOC call if printing had already been aborted for any other reason. This version lacks any conditional provisions to prevent an inappropriate ENDDOC call. So, what now?

Well, having brought the problem to your attention, the answer to this quandary must be deferred temporarily while another topic is introduced: Abort procedures.

Printer Abort Procedures

While you should not tamper directly with the printer output, there are provisions which can be made within an application to allow you some additional control over the printing process.

The most useful example is an abort process that can interrupt data output if or when the spooler reports an error. As you know, output is written first to a disk file. An SP_OUTOFDISK error code is the most common error to occur, but just which error is not important.

What is important is, first, providing an exported function which Windows can call to report an error; second, within the application, making provisions to register the exported procedure; and third, making provisions for checking for an error report.

The first step is creating the abort procedure, commonly called *AbortProc* and defined as:

```
int FAR PASCAL AbortProc( HDC hdcPrn, int nPrnStat )
{
```

```
MSG    msg;
while( !bAbortPrn &&
        PeekMessage( &msg, NULL, 0, 0, PM_REMOVE ) )
if( !IsDialogMessage( hAbortDlg, &msg ) )
{
    TranslateMessage( &msg );
    DispatchMessage( &msg );
}
return( !bAbortPrn );
}
```

Of course, this function must also be listed in the EXPORTS section of your .DEF file and, within the main application, you will also need two global declarations as:

```
FARPROC   lpAbortProc;
BOOL      bAbortPrn;
```

The first declaration, *lpAbortProc*, will provide a pointer to *AbortProc*, while the second, *bAbortProc*, provides a flag used both by *AbortProc* and by another procedure to be introduced for general error conditions.

Windows includes two provisions for establishing an abort procedure. The first is *MakeProcInstance*, which is called as:

```
lpAbortProc = MakeProcInstance( AbortProc, hInst );
```

The second, the *Escape* SETABORTPROC subfunction, registers the abort procedure with the Print Manager:

```
Escape( hdcPrn, SETABORTPROC, 0,
        (LPSTR) lpAbortProc, NULL );
```

The SETABORTPROC subfunction is called before the STARTDOC call. Note, however, that it is not necessary to "unregister" the abort procedure when printing is finished. This is essentially all that is necessary because after this, it is up to the GDI to process graphics or text output instructions to build output files, and to transfer these files to the actual device. During this process, the GDI repeatedly calls the exported abort procedure to peek at messages which are actually intended for the Print Manager.

The purpose of this, while difficult to explain, is to allow the Print Manager (or the GDI if the spooler is not loaded) opportunities to transfer temporary disk files to the output device, freeing more space for new temporary disk files, or, if a problem occurs, halting operations that would create new disk files.

If this explanation seems sketchy, what is needed most is simply to know how to create an abort procedure ... and then leave it alone and let Windows continue on its own convoluted way.

An Abort Dialog

In addition to the abort procedure used by the GDI to halt operations, two other provisions are needed: First, to show that printing is continuing, and second, to provide a means for the user to interrupt (abort) printing. Both of these can be accomplished in a single package by creating an abort dialog box (Figure 21-1) that identifies the current operation and, at the same time, contains an interrupt provision, i.e., a Cancel button. This second abort provision is also declared in the .DEF EXPORTS and requires two further global declarations as:

```
FARPROC    lpAbortDlg;
HWND       hAbortDlg;
```

And, like *AbortProc*, *AbortDlg* is created as:

```
lpAbortDlg  = MakeProcInstance( AbortDlg, hInst );
```

Figure 21-1: A User-Abort Dialog Box

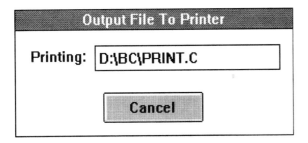

But beyond this point, the similarity ends. *AbortProc* was registered for use by Windows, but *AbortDlg* is intended only for the application user's benefit and, to be useful, must be displayed:

```
bAbortPrn = FALSE;
if( !( hwndDlg = CreateDialog( hInst, "PRINT_DLG",
```

```
                                          hwnd, lpAbortDlg ) ) )
        return( NULL );
    ShowWindow( hAbortDlg, SW_NORMAL );
    EnableWindow( hwnd, FALSE );
    return( hwndDlg );
```

The dialog box is defined in the resource file (.RES) with the name PRINT_DLG, and is created at the same time as the *AbortProc* function. However, creating the dialog is only half the process. It concludes with *ShowWindow* to make the dialog visible, and *EnableWindow(...FALSE)* to disable the main client window.

The reason for the first step should be obvious—a dialog box isn't much good unless it is displayed—but why disable the main window? Principally because this application, at the time this dialog box is displayed, is now engaged in a printing operation and cannot respond to any other processes until printing is finished. The main client window is disabled partially to show the user that the application is busy, and partially to prevent futile (or abortive) attempts to use the mouse or keyboard to operate other features of the main window.

Granted, in this example, the main client window does not implement any other features, but as long as it is disabled, the user cannot attempt to switch focus away from the *AbortDlg* dialog box. This does not prevent activating some other application and placing this one in the background, but this at least is perfectly in keeping with Windows multitasking. Further, if a long print job is involved—long in terms of sending the output to the Print Manager for spooling—the user is free to switch over to play a game of Solitaire while waiting. Try it.

When the print job is finished, i.e., when all output has been sent to the spooler, the *AbortDlg* dialog box is erased and the application's client window is enabled again.

AbortDlg performs two tasks: First, it displays the name of the file being printed, and second, it responds to the Cancel button by setting the boolean *bAbortPrn* flag. It does not directly interrupt the printing process. This is left to the original *AbortProc* procedure which, if you remember, returns *!bAbortPrn*. However, when *AbortDlg* changes the setting for *bAbortPrn*, this results indirectly in *AbortProc* returning a new result, and the operation is aborted as desired.

As you can see, the two abort processes, *AbortProc* and *AbortDlg*, are designed to work together, one providing the GDI with an abort process, and the other providing the user with an abort process.

Does any of this solve the potential problem mentioned earlier with calling *Escape* ENDDOC when using print banding? It should, because the problem statement can now be written with a conditional test as:

```
    if( !bAbortPrn )
        Escape( hdcPrn, ENDDOC,  0, NULL, NULL );
}
DeleteDC( hdcPrn );
```

In this fashion, if the print job has been aborted, then ENDDOC is not called.

Caution: Thus far, only part of the preventive process has been described because *AbortProc* does not set a new value for *bAbortPrn*. However, if you will examine the listing for Print.C, you will find a second provision insuring that *bAbortPrn* is set when either process calls for an abort. Hint: First look for the *Escape* ABORTDOC statement.

Aborting A Document

The *Escape* ABORTDOC subfunction is used to terminate a specific print job and is called as:

```
Escape( hdcPrn, ABORTDOC, 0, NULL, NULL );
```

This instruction not only tells the Print Manager to terminate the current document print job, but also, if no other jobs are in the spooler, closes the Print Manager. If, however, any other applications are using the Print Manager, or if the present application has another job in the Print Manager, only the current job is terminated. Very useful.

Now, having shown you how to interrupt print jobs, we will return to the subject of outputting print.

Text Output

Like graphics, text output to the printer is essentially quite simple, and is demonstrated in the PRINT.C program as:

```
while( ! feof( File ) )
{
    fgets( Buffer, sizeof( Buffer ), File );
    TextOut( hdcPrn, 0, nLineCnt * nLineVert,
```

```
                    (LPSTR) Buffer, strlen( Buffer ) );
    if( ++nLineCnt > nLinesPg )
    {
        nLineCnt = 1;
        nPrnStat = Escape( hdcPrn, NEWFRAME,
                             0, NULL, NULL );
    }
```

The only provision here that would not be found in a screen output program is a test to reset the line number position, and to issue an *Escape* NEWFRAME subfunction call when each page is filled.

The Print.C program (a complete listing appears at the end of this chapter) is designed to read its own source file, writing 65 lines per page to the printer. It does this very well ... with one or two exceptions:

Within Print.C, provisions are included for the program to query the printer driver to determine the page sizes and to query the font size (of the output device, not the screen) to adjust line spacing. But there are other provisions which have not been made but are left as an exercise—and an object lesson— for the reader.

First, as you should note when executing this program (at least on a laser jet), all carriage returns in the source file are printed as characters on the output. Second, tab characters are not expanded as spaces, but are also printed as characters. In both cases, the result on my own laser jet for both the carriage returns and the tabs are half-tone block characters. On a dot-matrix, of course, the results are likely to be quite different and, as a wild guess, you might expect to see tabs fully and correctly expanded, while the carriage returns, depending on the printer, might result in double spacing. The best solution is not to depend on happy circumstance, but to provide appropriate filtering. Of course, you may also need to provide ANSI/OEM conversion, but both of these are left for your own implementation.

Available Fonts and Device Capabilities

One problem with output to a printer or plotter device is determining available fonts. Retrieving TEXTMETRIC information—information about device capabilities and features—has been demonstrated and used many times in this book, beginning in Chapter 2.

While it is useful, the TEXTMETRIC information is only part of the story. It tells us nothing about fonts which may or may not be internal to a printer

or even to Windows itself. Font information can be retrieved from the printer
device driver(s) through the *EnumFonts* function. *EnumFonts* is called as:

```
EnumFonts( HDC hdc, LPSTR lpFaceName,
           FARPROC lpFontFunc, LPSTR lpData );
```

Note that the *EnumFonts* function parameters include a FARPROC pointer
to another function which is known as a "callback" function, which will be
explained presently.

The *lpFaceName* parameter is a pointer to a null-terminated, ASCIIZ, character string specifying the typeface name of the desired font(s). If *lpFaceName*
is NULL, *EnumFonts* randomly selects and enumerates one font from each
available typeface.

The *lpData* parameter is a pointer to application-supplied data which is
passed to the callback function along with the font information.

Last, *EnumFonts* returns a value which is the last value returned to *Enum-
Fonts* by the callback function. The meaning of the returned value is user-defined with one exception: *EnumFonts* continues enumeration until there are no
more fonts, or until the callback function returns zero.

The Callback Function

The callback function is called by *EnumFonts*, but must be supplied by the
application. The *lpFontFunc* declaration is only a place holder, and does not
identify an actual function. Instead, the callback function defined in the
application is required to actually process the font information retrieved by
EnumFonts and passed, not to the calling application, but to the callback
function.

Three restrictions exist for callback functions: The address passed as the
lpFontFunc parameter must be created by using the *MakeProcInstance* function;
the function must use Pascal calling conventions and must be declared FAR;
and the function must be declared in the application's EXPORTS list (in the
.DEF file).

The callback function is declared as:

```
int FAR PASCAL FontFunc( LPLOGFONT lpLF, LPTEXTMETRICS lpTM,
                         int nFontType,   LPSTR lpData )
```

An example of a callback function is:

```
int FAR PASCAL EnumFontTypes( LPLOGFONT lf,  LPTEXTMETRIC tm,
                              int nFontType,
                              ENUMDATA FAR *EnumData )
{
   FONTDATA FAR *font;

   if( ! GlobalReAlloc( EnumData->hGlobal,
                        (DWORD) sizeof( FONTDATA ) *
                          ( 1 + EnumData->nCount ),
                        GMEM_MOVEABLE ) )
      return( FALSE );
   font = (FONTDATA FAR *)
      GlobalLock( EnumData->hGlobal ) + EnumData->nCount;
   font->nFontType = nFontType;
   font->lf = *lf;
   font->tm = *tm;
   GlobalUnlock( EnumData->hGlobal );
   EnumData->nCount++;
   return( TRUE );
}
```

In this example, the *lpData* parameter is declared as a FAR pointer to an ENUMDATA structure. The actual callback function begins by dynamically allocating memory for a copy of the data supplied by *EnumFonts*, then copying the entire data structure—the *tm*, *lf* and *nFontType* arguments—into the memory structure. Afterwards, this data is directly available to other functions within the application.

As an alternative, the callback function can simply create an array, either static or dynamically allocated, of such selected data as the application may require. How the application uses this data, and which data the application chooses to employ, is entirely up to the application. However, to assist in creating your own applications, a partial example of a program using two exported callback functions, *EnumFontTypes* and *EnumTypeFaces*, appears at the end of this chapter.

Two final comments on *EnumFonts*: Remember, the *EnumFonts* function is also useful for retrieving Windows (GDI) font information, not just printer font information. Also remember that the information retrieved is only what the device driver knows about. For a laserjet, for example, *EnumFonts* cannot report on fonts that are supplied by a plug-in cartridge.

The System Menu Entry

In most previous examples, an application menu has been used to select operations. In this example, however, only one option is needed and, instead of creating an application menu, the single entry required is added to the system menu.

And this is a very simple process accomplished, first, by retrieving a handle to the system menu and then calling *AppendMenu* to add a separator line and the option label "Print File", thus:

```
case WM_CREATE:
   hMenu = GetSystemMenu( hwnd, FALSE );
   AppendMenu( hMenu, MF_SEPARATOR, 0, NULL );
   AppendMenu( hMenu, 0, SC_PRINT, "&Print File" );
   return(0);
```

In brief, using *AppendMenu* is a very simple process requiring four parameters: the menu handle, a WORD flags value specifying information about the initial state of the menu item, a WORD item ID specifying the command ID returned by the menu item or, if MF_POPUP is set, the handle for a pop-up menu and, last, a LPSTR value setting the menu entry, normally a string but can be, optionally, a bitmap or an owner-draw item.

AppendMenu can also be used with application menus but does make it more difficult to later revise the menu (using the Resource Editors) for transport, for example, to another language.

Summary

Printer output (or plotter or other device types) does require a few consideration which were not required for screen displays. At the same time, Windows has supplied features and functions that make output to a variety of devices both easier to manage, and almost device-independent.

Following are the source listings for the Print.C demo application, as well as a partial listing showing one example of how the *EnumFonts* function can be called. In both cases, experimentation is suggested.

```
//===============================//
//             Print.C           //
//   C++ Windows Printer Support //
//===============================//

#include <windows.h>
#include <string.h>
```

```
#include <stdio.h>
#include "print.h"

static FARPROC lpAbortDlg;
static FARPROC lpAbortProc;

HANDLE hInst;
char    szAppName[]  = "Print";
char    szCaption[]  = "Prints Source File";
char    szFileName[] = "D:\\BC\\PRINT.C";
BOOL    bAbortPrn;
HWND    hAbortDlg;

#pragma argsused

int FAR PASCAL AbortDlg( HWND hwndDlg, WORD msg, WORD wParam,
LONG lParam )
{
    switch( msg )
    {
        case WM_INITDIALOG:
            SetDlgItemText( hwndDlg, IDD_FILENAME, szFileName );
            SetFocus( GetDlgItem( hwndDlg, IDCANCEL ) );
            return( TRUE );

        case WM_COMMAND:
            switch( wParam )
            {
                case IDCANCEL:  bAbortPrn = TRUE;   break;
                default:        bAbortPrn = FALSE;
            }
            return( TRUE );
    }
    return( FALSE );
}

#pragma argsused

int FAR PASCAL AbortProc( HDC hdcPrn, int nPrnStat )
{
    MSG    msg;

    while( ! bAbortPrn &&
            PeekMessage( &msg, NULL, 0, 0, PM_REMOVE ) )
    if( !IsDialogMessage( hAbortDlg, &msg ) )
    {
        TranslateMessage( &msg );
        DispatchMessage( &msg );
    }
    return( !bAbortPrn );
}

HWND CreateAbortDlg( HWND hwnd,     HDC hdcPrn,
                     HANDLE hInst, LPSTR Text )
```

```
{
    HWND hwndDlg;

    lpAbortDlg  = MakeProcInstance( AbortDlg, hInst );
    lpAbortProc = MakeProcInstance( AbortProc, hInst );
    Escape( hdcPrn, SETABORTPROC, 0, lpAbortProc, NULL );
    if( Escape( hdcPrn, STARTDOC, 4, Text, 0L ) < 0 )
    {
        FreeProcInstance( lpAbortDlg );
        FreeProcInstance( lpAbortProc );
    }
    bAbortPrn = FALSE;
    if( !( hwndDlg = CreateDialog( hInst, "PRINT_DLG",
                                   hwnd, lpAbortDlg ) ) )
        return( NULL );
    ShowWindow( hAbortDlg, SW_NORMAL );
    EnableWindow( hwnd, FALSE );
    return( hwndDlg );
}

#pragma argsused

HDC GetPrinterDC( HWND hwnd )
{
    static char  szPrinter[40];
           char *szDevice, *szDriver, *szOutput;

    GetProfileString( "windows", "device", ",,,",
                      szPrinter, 80 );
    if( ( szDevice = strtok( szPrinter, "," ) ) &&
        ( szDriver = strtok( NULL,      "," ) ) &&
        ( szOutput = strtok( NULL,      "," ) ) )
        return( CreateDC( szDriver, szDevice,
                          szOutput, NULL ) );
    return(0);
}

BOOL PrintFile( HWND hwnd, HDC hdcPrn, LPSTR lpszFileName )
{
    TEXTMETRIC tm;
    FILE       *File;
    char       Buffer[255];
    int        nPageLen, nLineVert, nLinesPg,
               nLineCnt, nPrnStat;

    GetTextMetrics( hdcPrn, &tm );
    nLineVert = tm.tmHeight + tm.tmExternalLeading;
    nPageLen  = GetDeviceCaps( hdcPrn, VERTRES );
    nLinesPg  = nPageLen / nLineVert - 1;
    if( !( File = fopen( lpszFileName, "r" ) ) )
        return( FALSE );
    nLineCnt = 1;
    while( ! feof( File ) )
```

```
    {
        fgets( Buffer, sizeof( Buffer ), File );
        TextOut( hdcPrn, 0, nLineCnt * nLineVert,
                 (LPSTR) Buffer, strlen( Buffer ) );
        if( ++nLineCnt > nLinesPg )
        {
            nLineCnt = 1;
            nPrnStat = Escape( hdcPrn, NEWFRAME,
                               0, NULL, NULL );
        }
        if( nPrnStat < 0 || bAbortPrn )
        {
            Escape( hdcPrn, ABORTDOC, 0, NULL, NULL );
            MessageBox( hwnd, "Print Aborted!",
                        szAppName, MB_OK | MB_ICONSTOP );
            bAbortPrn = TRUE;
            break;
    }   }
    if( !bAbortPrn )
    {
        if( Escape( hdcPrn, NEWFRAME, 0, NULL, NULL ) > 0 )
            Escape( hdcPrn, ENDDOC,   0, NULL, NULL );
        MessageBox( hwnd, "Print Completed...",
                    szAppName, MB_OK | MB_ICONEXCLAMATION );
    }
    fclose( lpszFileName );
    return( TRUE );
}

BOOL SetPrnFile( HWND hwnd, HANDLE hInst, LPSTR lpszText )
{
    HDC     hdcPrn;

    if( !( hdcPrn = GetPrinterDC( hwnd ) ) ) return( FALSE );
    if( !( hAbortDlg = CreateAbortDlg( hwnd, hdcPrn,
                                       hInst, lpszText ) ) )
    {
        DeleteDC( hdcPrn );
        return( FALSE );
    }
    if( !PrintFile( hwnd, hdcPrn, szFileName ) )
        return( FALSE );
    EnableWindow( hwnd, TRUE );
    DestroyWindow( hAbortDlg );
    FreeProcInstance( lpAbortDlg );
    FreeProcInstance( lpAbortProc );
    DeleteDC( hdcPrn );
    return( TRUE );
}

long FAR PASCAL WndProc( HWND hwnd,   WORD msg,
                         WORD wParam, LONG lParam )
```

```
{
    HMENU   hMenu;

    switch( msg )
    {
        case WM_CREATE:
            hMenu = GetSystemMenu( hwnd, FALSE );
            AppendMenu( hMenu, MF_SEPARATOR, 0, NULL );
            AppendMenu( hMenu, 0, SC_PRINT, "&Print File" );
            return(0);

        case WM_SYSCOMMAND:
            if( wParam == SC_PRINT )
            {
                MessageBox( hwnd, "Ready to print?",
                            szAppName, MB_OK | MB_ICONQUESTION );
                if( ! SetPrnFile( hwnd, hInst, szFileName ) )
                    MessageBox( hwnd, "Can't print file",
                        szAppName, MB_OK | MB_ICONEXCLAMATION );
                return(0);
            }
            break;

        case WM_DESTROY:
            PostQuitMessage(0);
            return(0);
    }
    return( DefWindowProc( hwnd, msg, wParam, lParam ) );
}

#pragma argsused

int PASCAL WinMain( HANDLE hInstance, HANDLE hPrevInstance,
                    LPSTR  lpszCmdParam, int nCmdShow )
{
    HWND        hwnd;
    MSG         msg;
    WNDCLASS    wc;

    if( ! hPrevInstance )
    {
        wc.hInstance      = hInstance;
        wc.lpfnWndProc    = WndProc;
        wc.cbClsExtra     = 0;
        wc.cbWndExtra     = 0;
        wc.lpszClassName  = szAppName;
        wc.hIcon          = LoadIcon( hInstance, szAppName );
        wc.lpszMenuName   = (LPSTR) szAppName;
        wc.hCursor        = LoadCursor( NULL, IDC_ARROW );
        wc.hbrBackground  = GetStockObject( WHITE_BRUSH );
        wc.style          = CS_HREDRAW | CS_VREDRAW;
        RegisterClass( &wc );
    }
```

```
    hInst = hInstance;
    hwnd = CreateWindow( szAppName, szCaption,
                         WS_OVERLAPPEDWINDOW,
                         CW_USEDEFAULT, CW_USEDEFAULT,
                         CW_USEDEFAULT, CW_USEDEFAULT,
                         NULL, NULL, hInstance, NULL  );
    ShowWindow(    hwnd, nCmdShow );
    UpdateWindow( hwnd );
    while( GetMessage( &msg, NULL, 0, 0 ) )
    {
        TranslateMessage( &msg );
        DispatchMessage(  &msg );
    }
    return( msg.wParam );
}


                      ;=============;
                      ;  Print.DEF  ;
                      ;=============;

NAME          PRINT

DESCRIPTION   "Print Program"
EXETYPE       WINDOWS
STUB          "WINSTUB.EXE"
CODE          PRELOAD MOVABLE DISCARDABLE
DATA          PRELOAD MOVABLE MULTIPLE
HEAPSIZE      1024
STACKSIZE     8192
EXPORTS       WndProc
              AbortDlg
              AbortProc


                     //=============//
                     //  PRINT.DLG  //
                     //=============//

PRINT_DLG DIALOG DISCARDABLE LOADONCALL PURE MOVEABLE
          41, 41, 133, 49
STYLE WS_POPUP | WS_VISIBLE | WS_CAPTION
CAPTION "Output File To Printer"
BEGIN
  CONTROL "Printing:" -1, "STATIC",
    WS_CHILD | WS_VISIBLE | WS_GROUP | 0x2L,
    4, 8, 30, 11
  CONTROL "Cancel"     2, "BUTTON",
    WS_CHILD | WS_VISIBLE | WS_GROUP | WS_TABSTOP,
    42, 29, 48, 14
  CONTROL ""          101, "EDIT",
    WS_CHILD | WS_VISIBLE | WS_BORDER | 0x8L,
    38, 7, 89, 12
END
```

```
                    //==========//
                    //  PRINT.H //
                    //==========//
#define   SC_PRINT      100
#define   IDD_FILENAME  101

        //======================================//
        //                 PRINT2.C             //
        //   partial example showing retrieval  //
        //   of printer font information using  //
        //   the EnumFonts function . . .       //
        //======================================//
typedef struct {  GLOBALHANDLE hGlobal;
                  int          nCount; }  ENUMDATA;
typedef struct {  int          nFontType;
                  LOGFONT      lf;
                  TEXTMETRIC   tm;       }  FONTDATA;

#pragma argsused

int FAR PASCAL EnumTypeFaces( LPLOGFONT lf,  LPTEXTMETRIC tm,
                              int nFontType,
                              ENUMDATA FAR *EnumData )
{
    LPSTR lpFaces;

    if( ! GlobalReAlloc( EnumData->hGlobal,
                         (DWORD) LF_FACESIZE *
                             ( 1 + EnumData->nCount ),
                         GMEM_MOVEABLE ) )
        return( FALSE );
    lpFaces = GlobalLock( EnumData->hGlobal );
    lstrcpy( lpFaces + EnumData->nCount * LF_FACESIZE,
             lf->lfFaceName );
    GlobalUnlock( EnumData->hGlobal );
    EnumData->nCount++;
    return( TRUE );
}

#pragma argsused

int FAR PASCAL EnumFontTypes( LPLOGFONT lf,  LPTEXTMETRIC tm,
                              int nFontType,
                              ENUMDATA FAR *EnumData )
{
    FONTDATA FAR *font;

    if( ! GlobalReAlloc( EnumData->hGlobal,
                         (DWORD) sizeof( FONTDATA ) *
                             ( 1 + EnumData->nCount ),
                         GMEM_MOVEABLE ) )
        return( FALSE );
```

```
    font = (FONTDATA FAR *)
        GlobalLock( EnumData->hGlobal ) + EnumData->nCount;
    font->nFontType = nFontType;
    font->lf = *lf;
    font->tm = *tm;
    GlobalUnlock( EnumData->hGlobal );
    EnumData->nCount++;
    return( TRUE );
}

HDC GetPrinterIC()
{
    char  szPrinter[64];
    char *szDevice, *szDriver, *szOutput;

    GetProfileString( "windows", "device",
                      "", szPrinter, 64 );
    if( ( szDevice = strtok( szPrinter, "," ) ) &&
        ( szDriver = strtok( NULL,      "," ) ) &&
        ( szOutput = strtok( NULL,      "," ) ) )
        return( CreateIC( szDriver, szDevice,
                          szOutput, NULL ) );
    return( NULL );
}

long FAR PASCAL WndProc( HWND hwnd,    WORD msg,
                         WORD wParam, LONG lParam )
{
    ...
    static ENUMDATA    EnumData1, EnumData2;
    static FARPROC     lpfnEnumTypeFaces, lpfnEnumFontTypes;
    ...
    LPSTR              lpFaces;
    TEXTMETRIC         tm;
    PAINTSTRUCT        ps;
    int                i;
    BOOL               bRetrieved;

    switch( msg )
    {
        case WM_CREATE:
            ...
            hInstance = ((LPCREATESTRUCT) lParam)->hInstance;
            lpfnEnumFontTypes =
                MakeProcInstance( EnumFontTypes, hInstance );
            lpfnEnumTypeFaces =
                MakeProcInstance( EnumTypeFaces, hInstance );
            ...
            return(0);

        case WM_PAINT:
            if( ! bRetrieved )
```

```
        {
            if( EnumData2.hGlobal )
               GlobalFree( EnumData2.hGlobal );
            EnumData1.hGlobal  = GlobalAlloc( GHND, 1L );
            EnumData1.nCount = 0;
            EnumData2.hGlobal  = GlobalAlloc( GHND, 1L );
            EnumData2.nCount = 0;
            hdc = GetPrinterIC();
            if( hdc )
            {
                lpFaces = GlobalLock( EnumData1.hGlobal );
                for( i=0; i<EnumData1.nCount; i++ )
                    if( ! EnumFonts( hdc,
                                     lpFaces + i * LF_FACESIZE,
                                     lpfnEnumFontTypes,
                                     (LPSTR) &EnumData2 ) )
                        ... memory error ... out of memory ...
                GlobalUnlock( EnumData1.hGlobal );
                EnumData2.nCount;  // check double minus //
                DeleteDC( hdc );
                bRetrieved = TRUE;
            }
            GlobalFree( EnumData1.hGlobal );
        }
        ...
        EndPaint( hwnd, &ps );
        return(0);

    case WM_DESTROY: ...
    }
    return( DefWindowProc( hwnd, msg, wParam, lParam ) );
}

#pragma argsused

int PASCAL WinMain( HANDLE hInstance, HANDLE hPrevInstance,
                    LPSTR  lpszCmdParam, int nCmdShow )
{
    ....
}
```

Chapter 22

Clipboard Data Transfers

The Windows Clipboard is actually two quite different entities: One clipboard is an application: titled ClipBrd.EXE, which is actually a clipboard viewer, while the real clipboard is a feature of the Windows USER module that provides a series of functions used to facilitate the transfer of information between applications. The subject of this chapter will be the clipboard facilities provided by the USER module. First, a brief look at the ClipBrd.EXE program.

The Clipboard Viewer: ClipBrd.EXE

The ClipBrd.EXE program distributed with Windows 3.0 is a clipboard viewer that provides a means of checking (viewing) material which has been copied to the USER clipboard facilities. As such, ClipBrd can be useful for testing your own clipboard routines or, in other circumstances, can be used to capture the contents of the real clipboard by saving these contents as a disk file. Remember, this is not the real clipboard. The real clipboard will be introduced in a moment.

Using The Real Clipboard

The real clipboard is a series of features that provide a platform to transfer material between applications. To use the clipboard, one application, the source, must copy material to the clipboard using either one of the predefined formats, which will be discussed presently, or using a custom format. Once material has been copied to the clipboard, any application can access the clipboard, inquire what type of material is present, and, if desired, copy the material from clipboard.

The ClipBrd.EXE application, if active, does this automatically. It watches to see if any material is written to the clipboard and, if there is, determines the data format. If possible, it displays the material in its own client window. ClipBrd.EXE normally only retrieves a copy of the material, and does not alter or erase the contents of the clipboard.

Clipboard Drawbacks

The clipboard works very well, but it does have two particular disadvantages: First, there is only one clipboard, and second, material written to the clipboard is public, i.e., accessible to any application. Even if all applications are well behaved, the two elements can still present definite potential for error.

The first problem is that there is only one clipboard, and all applications wanting access to a clipboard must use the single facility. Because of this, if application A has written, for example, a bitmap to the clipboard and application B needs to write a block of text data, the bitmap written by A is erased.

Now, if the destination application had already retrieved the bitmap data, everything would be fine ... but "if" is not a guarantee against problems.

The second problem is that the clipboard is always public. There is no way for Application A to write something to the clipboard with a directive that this can only be retrieved by Application X, and therefore cannot be accessed, erased, or otherwise affected by any other application.

Because of these potentials for error, a strong recommendation is made that applications using the clipboard should not transfer data in or out of the clipboard, or erase the clipboard contents except under explicit instructions from the user.

All of these problems, however, are minor and, as you will see in Chapter 23, can be circumvented by using Dynamic Data Exchange. Further, irregular and generally unlikely problems aside, the clipboard remains a useful and convenient method of exchanging data—many types of data—between applications.

How The Clipboard Functions

In brief, the Windows clipboard functions by taking control of globally allocated memory blocks by altering memory allocation flags.

To use the clipboard, applications begin by using the *GlobalAlloc* function and the GHND flag (defined as GMEM_MOVEABLE and GMEM_ZEROINIT) to initiate a memory block which, for the moment, belongs to the application instance. Normally, when the application instance exits, the memory block is deleted by Windows.

However, when an application calls *SetClipboardData* with the global handle to the memory block, Windows transfers ownership of the memory block from the application to itself, i.e., to the clipboard feature, by modifying the memory allocation flags for the global memory block.

To transfer ownership, Windows uses the *GlobalReAlloc* function as:

```
GlobalReAlloc( hMemory, NULL, GMEM_MODIFY | GMEM_DDESHARE );
```

At this point, the transferred memory block no longer belongs to the original application, and can be accessed only by calling the clipboard through the *GetClipboardData* function. Normally, calling *GetClipboardData* grants an application temporary access to the clipboard data via a handle to the global memory block. However, ownership of the data remains with Windows, not with an application accessing the memory block. Therefore the clipboard data can only be deleted by calling *EmptyClipboard*. There is an exception to this which will be discussed later, but it is not recommended.

Clipboard Data Formats

Windows supports nine standard clipboard formats. These are defined in Windows.H as: CF_BITMAP, CF_DIB, CF_DIF, CF_METAFILEPICT, CF_OEMTEXT, CF_PALETTE, CF_SYLK, CF_TEXT, and CF_TIFF. These are options, not limitations, and there is nothing to prevent you from defining your own clipboard data format(s), but for most purposes, the standard formats should serve. (Note: Four additional formats and several special flags are defined in Windows.H. See "Predefined Clipboard Formats" in Appendix A.)

The standard clipboard formats are defined as:

CF_TEXT

The simplest clipboard format is the CF_TEXT format, consisting of null-terminated ANSI character strings, each ending with a carriage return (0x0D) / line feed (0x0A). In CF_TEXT format, data is stored in a global memory block, and the handle to the memory block is transferred from the source application to the clipboard, or from the clipboard to the destination application. Once transferred, the memory block becomes the property of the clipboard, and the application originally generating the memory block should not attempt to access the block further. At this point, the memory block belongs to the USER module.

CF_OEMTEXT

The CF_OEMTEXT format is the same as the CF_TEXT format, except that the OEM character set is used instead of the ANSI character set.

CF_METAFILEPICT

The CF_METAFILEPICT format is used to transfer memory (not disk) metafiles between applications. The CF_METAFILEPICT format uses the METAFILEPICT structure defined in Windows.H as:

```
struct tagMETAFILEPICT
    {    int     mm;       int     xExt;
         int     yExt;     HANDLE hMF;   } METAFILEPICT;
```

The *hMF* metafile handle is a handle to the METAFILE structure introduced in Chapter 19.

The differences between a clipboard metafile transfer and a metafile within an application are found in the remaining three parameters which indicate the mapping mode (*mm*), and the x and y extent fields (*xExt* and *yExt*) that define the height and width of the metafile image. As with clipboard text formats, metafile images are transferred to the clipboard as a global memory block. Once transferred, the originating application should not attempt to use either the global memory block or the original metafile handle.

CF_BITMAP

The CF_BITMAP format is used to transfer Windows 2.0 compatible bitmaps by transferring the bitmap handle to the clipboard. As always, the originating application should not attempt to use the bitmap handle after transfer to the clipboard.

CF_DIB

The CF_DIB format is used to transfer Windows 3.0 device-independent bitmaps to the clipboard. The DIB bitmap is transferred as a global memory block, beginning with a BITMAPINFO structure and followed by the bitmap data. The BITMAPINFO structure is defined in Windows.H as:

```
struct  tagBITMAPINFO
   {     BITMAPINFOHEADER    bmiHeader;
         RGBQUAD             bmiColors[1];   }   BITMAPINFO;
```

Bitmap structures were introduced in Chapter 7.

Again, once the global memory block handle has been transferred to the clipboard, the originating application should not attempt to access either the memory block or the bitmap handle.

CF_PALETTE

The CF_PALETTE format is used to transfer a handle to a color palette, and is used in conjunction with CF_DIB to define the color palette used by the bitmap.

Special Purpose Formats

Windows 3.0 also defines three special clipboard formats, originally created for use by specific applications. They are:

CF_SYLK

The CF_SYLK format uses a global memory block to transfer data in the Microsoft "Symbol Link" format. It was designed to exchange data between Microsoft's Multiplan (spread sheet), Chart, and Excel applications. The format is an ASCII string format, with each line terminated by a carriage return /line feed pair.

CF_DIF

The CF_DIF format uses a global memory block to transfer data using the Data Interchange Format (DIF). This was created by Software Arts for use with the VisiCalc spreadsheet program, but is now controlled by Lotus Corporation (Lotus 1-2-3). The format is an ASCII string format, with each line terminated by a carriage return/line feed pair.

While both the CF_SYLK and CF_DIF formats are similar to the CF_TEXT format, the strings transferred are not always null-terminated. Instead, the format defines the end of the data.

For further information on these two formats, consult *File Formats For Popular PC Software* by Jeff Walden, published by John Wiley & Sons.

CF_TIFF

The CF_TIFF format uses a global memory block to transfer data in the Tag Image File Format (TIFF), a format devised jointly by Aldus, Hewlett-Packard, and Microsoft, together with hardware manufacturers. Details on the TIFF format are available from Hewlett-Packard Company.

Clipboard Access

Allowing access to the clipboard by only one application at a time is one mechanism that prevents a conflict of purposes. The *OpenClipboard* function is used to request access, and returns a boolean value indicating that the clipboard is available and opened, or that access is denied because another appication has the current access. When finished with the clipboard, *CloseClipboard* is called to relinquish access, yielding the clipboard access to anyone else.

Note that the *OpenClipboard* function is always matched with a *CloseClipboard* call. Emphasis is on **ALWAYS!** An application should never—ever—attempt to hold the clipboard open, and should always relinquish control of the clipboard as quickly as possible.

An example of a clipboard transfer function (copying to the clipboard):

```
BOOL TransferToClipBD( HWND hwnd, HANDLE hMemBlock,
                       WORD FormatCB )
{
   if( OpenClipboard( hwnd ) )
   {
      EmptyClipboard();
      SetClipboardData( FormatCB, hMemBlock );
      CloseClipboard();
      return( TRUE );
   }
   return( FALSE );
}
```

The *TransferToClipBD* function is used in the ClipBd.C demo program. It begins by requesting access to (opening) the clipboard, then copies a single memory block to the clipboard before closing the clipboard and relinquishing further access. *TransferToClipBD* is quite generic and accepts any type of handle, but it does require the *FormatCB* parameter to specify the format type used.

In other cases you may want to copy more than one memory block to the clipboard. Note, however, that the term "memory block" does not specify a size. The size of the block was set by the *GlobalAlloc* function and could contain paragraphs of text, multiple records, or other data.

Suppose that your application needs to transfer a bitmap, a metafile and a block of text. What then?

Actually, the process is quite simple. First, each item is copied separately to globally allocated memory with handles to each memory block as, for example, *hBitmap*, *hMetafile* and *hText*. Next, the clipboard is opened and emptied, and each of these handles is transferred to the clipboard:

```
if( OpenClipboard( hwnd ) )
{
    EmptyClipboard();
    SetClipboardData( CF_METAFILEPICT, hMetafile );
    SetClipboardData( CF_BITMAP, hBitmap );
    SetClipboardData( CF_TEXT, hText );
    CloseClipboard();
}
```

Last, the clipboard is closed again. However, there are a few restrictions on clipboard operations:

First, before an item can be copied to the clipboard, *EmptyClipboard* must be called to erase the present contents, if any, of the clipboard. Remember, simply accessing the clipboard does not change (assign) ownership of the existing clipboard contents. On the other hand, the *EmptyClipboard* function does assign ownership and, at the same time, clears any existing contents.

And, while any application can access the contents of the clipboard, only the clipboard owner can write material to the clipboard ... and the clipboard can have only one owner at any time. Previous owner's contents are simply discarded.

Second, while multiple items can be copied to the clipboard, they must all be transferred in a single operation. The clipboard cannot be opened, one item copied in, closed, and then reopened to transfer another item ... at least, not without erasing the first item transferred.

Third, only one item of each type can be transferred at any time, simply because there is no means of distinguishing between multiple items of a given type. However, when multiple items have been transferred to the clipboard, another application can request only one item, or several items, or all items, but it must request each item separately. It may also open the clipboard repeatedly to request different items, or to request the same item more than once.

In general, however, when an item is requested from the clipboard, the best option is to make a local copy of the desired item, rather than attempting to request the same item repeatedly. After all, there is nothing to insure that the data item desired will remain available indefinitely.

Determining Item Availability

When using the clipboard, an important item is to be able to find out if the clipboard contains a particular data type. Different data types require different handling on retrieval, and applications need to know if the data type desired is available.

One method would be to ask for data of the desired type and see if anything was returned. This approach is neither elegant nor efficient. Instead, there are two methods—functions—which can be used to ask about the clipboard contents.

The first method uses the *IsClipboardFormatAvailable* function, which returns a boolean result indicating whether the clipboard contains a particular data format. *IsClipboardFormatAvailable* is called as:

```
if( IsClipboardFormatAvailable( CF_xxtypexx ) ) ...
```

The second method is to query all available clipboard formats, using the *EnumClipboardFormats* function. *EnumClipboardFormats* can be called in two different fashions, either with a type parameter requesting a specific format, or with a zero parameter requesting any format. For example, to request a list of all formats available, the following code could be used:

```
wFormat = 0;
OpenClipboard( hwnd );
while( wFormat = EnumClipboardFormats( wFormat ) )
{
    ... code handling various formats ...
}
CloseClipboard();
```

The first value returned to *wFormat* is used for the next call, causing *EnumClipboardFormats* to step through the list. If necessary, the *wFormat* value could be reset to any value to repeat the list from that point. When no further formats are found, or if the clipboard is empty, *EnumClipboardFormats* will return zero. Note that the assignment in the conditional statement used here will return the probably-familiar compiler warning message: *Possibly incorrect assignment....* This, of course, is not an error here, but often is in other cases.

The number of formats available in the clipboard can be obtained by calling:

```
nFormats = CountClipboardFormats();
```

Retrieving Clipboard Data

Retrieving clipboard data actually consists of two different operations: First, retrieving a handle to the clipboard data memory block, and second, doing something with the data after retrieving the handle.

The first is quite simple. The second, which is dependent on the data type, will be deferred for the present and illustrated later for three data types.

Retrieving a handle to a clipboard data block is quite simple, and can be handled by a subprocedure as:

```
HANDLE RetrieveCB( HWND hwnd, WORD FormatCB )
{
    HANDLE  hCB;

    if( ! IsClipboardFormatAvailable( FormatCB ) )
        return( NULL );
    OpenClipboard( hwnd );
    hCB = GetClipboardData( FormatCB );
    CloseClipboard();
    return( hCB );
}
```

In actual practice, and in the ClipBd.C demo program and the examples derived from this demo, a slightly different format is used. Nonetheless, the preceding offers a generic subroutine that will return an untyped handle to a clipboard memory block. If the requested type is not available, the subprocedure returns NULL.

The ClipBd.C Demo

The ClipBd.C program demonstrates three types of clipboard operation: text, bitmap, and metafile. ClipBd.C uses a simple menu with two initial menu options: *Data To Clipboard* and *Data From Clipboard*. Each of these has a three-item submenu with such equally imaginative options as *Write-datatype-* and *Retrieve-datatype-*.

There is one exception: Under *Data To Clipboard* for bitmaps, the menu item reads *Capture Bitmap*. This is because the demo program uses a simple screen capture procedure that allows you to grab and store a portion of the screen as a bitmap image. Thus, when *Capture Bitmap* is selected, the mouse cursor is changed to a cross mark, then, when the left mouse button is pressed, bitmap capture begins. It is completed when the button is released. The captured bitmap will not be displayed in the client window, only stored in the clipboard until the *Retrieve Bitmap* option is selected.

A simple text sample is provided for the text demo. For the metafile demo, the metafile from PenDraw6 has been adapted. Please note that in this demo program, provisions are made to store only one item on the clipboard at any time.

Text Clipboard Operations

Perhaps the simplest type of clipboard operation is text operation. The first step is to transfer text information to the clipboard. While the text chosen is brief but hardly original, it does serve to demonstrate the principles involved.

The mechanism of actually transferring the text to the clipboard is accomplished by a subprocedure that is called with two parameters, a handle to the application (*hwnd*) and a pointer to the text (*lpTxt*):

```
BOOL TextToClipboard( HWND hwnd, LPSTR lpTxt )
{
```

Within the *TextToClipboard* subroutine, four local variables are needed, but only two, *hGMem* and *lpGMem*, should require any explanation:

```
    int          i, wLen;
    GLOBALHANDLE hGMem;
    LPSTR        lpGMem;
```

The *hGMem* variable provides a global handle to a block of memory which has not yet been allocated. The *lpGMem* variable is a long pointer which will be used as a pointer into the memory block.

After the *wLen* variable is initialized with the length of text parameter, *hGMem* becomes a pointer to sufficient globally-allocated memory to hold a copy of the text. Notice that *wLen* is increased by one to provide allocation for a null terminator because clipboard text is always stored in an ASCIIZ (or ANSIZ) format:

```
wLen = strlen( lpTxt );
hGMem = GlobalAlloc( GHND, (DWORD) wLen + 1 );
lpGMem = GlobalLock( hGMem );
```

Last, *lpGMem* becomes a pointer to the memory block via the *GlobalLock* function. The *GlobalLock* function serves two purposes because, in addition to returning a pointer to the memory block, it also locks the memory block, preventing it from being moved by Windows. Remember that normally, memory allocations are declared as moveable.

At this point, the memory allocated is empty, or, more correctly, has been entirely zeroed out because the GHND specification includes the GMEM_ZEROINIT (initialize as zeros) flag. Therefore, the next step is to copy the local string, pointed to by *lpTxt*, into the memory block:

```
    for( i=0; i<wLen; i++ ) *lpGMem++ = *lpTxt++;
    GlobalUnlock( hGMem );
    return( TransferToClipBD( hwnd, hGMem, CF_TEXT ) );
}
```

After copying the text information, *GlobalUnlock* is called to release the memory block on *hGMem*, making it again moveable and relocatable. However, if the memory block had been moved while the local text information was being copied, the *lpGMem* pointer would not have remained valid.

Last, the *hGMem* block, the CF_TEXT flag, and the window handle are passed to the *TransferToClipBD* subroutine described earlier, completing the process of transferring a block of text to the clipboard.

Retrieving text from the clipboard is almost as simple and very similar, but instead of a subroutine, in the ClipBd.C demo, the text retrieval operations are included in the response to the WM_PAINT message. For retrieval, operations begin by opening the clipboard, and continue by calling *GetClipboardData* to return a handle to the memory block:

```
OpenClipboard( hwnd );
hTextMem = GetClipboardData( CF_TEXT );
lpText = GlobalLock( hTextMem );
```

Just as during the transfer to the clipboard, *GlobalLock* locks the memory block and returns a pointer to the memory address which is held by *lpText*.

This time, however, instead of using a loop, the *lstrcpy* function is used to copy the string contents from the memory address (*lpText*) to the local variable *TextStr*:

```
lstrcpy( TextStr, lpText );
GlobalUnlock( hTextMem );
CloseClipboard();
```

To finish up, *GlobalUnlock* releases the lock on the memory block, and *CloseClipboard* completes operations. Note: A memory block should never be left locked. Always call *GlobalUnlock* after calling *GlobalLock*.

Bitmap Clipboard Transfers

For the text clipboard transfer, a subprocedure was used with the text passed as a parameter. For the bitmap image, because screen capture is being used to supply the bitmap image, operations begin with two point pairs, *pt1* and *pt2*, which describe the area to be captured.

The first step is to create a compatible device context, i.e., compatible with the present window (screen) context:

```
hdcMem = CreateCompatibleDC( hdc );
hBitmap =
    CreateCompatibleBitmap( hdc, abs(pt2.x),
                                 abs(pt2.y) );
```

The second step is to get a handle to a bitmap using *CreateCompatibleBitmap* and the absolute value of *pt2*, because this point is an offset from *pt1* and therefore, defines the size of the image to be captured.

Next, *SelectObject* is called to select the bitmap (*hBitmap*) into the device context (*hdcMem*):

```
if( hBitmap )
{
    SelectObject( hdcMem, hBitmap );
```

However, the actual image has not yet been copied, so *StretchBlt* copies the image from *hdc* to *hdcMem*, using the inital coordinates in *pt1* and the image size in *pt2*:

```
StretchBlt( hdcMem, 0, 0, abs(pt2.x), abs(pt2.y),
            hdc, pt1.x, pt1.y, pt2.x, pt2.y,
            SRCCOPY );
```

Now the bitmap image has been copied to *hdcMem* and *hBitmap* has provided a handle for it. Now *hwnd*, *hBitmap*, and the format specification CF_BITMAP, are passed to *TransferToClipBD*, just as was done for the text demo:

```
      TransferToClipBD( hwnd, hBitmap, CF_BITMAP );
}
DeleteDC( hdcMem );
ReleaseDC( hwnd, hdc );
```

In this case, a bit of cleanup remains because, while the memory block has been transferred, the temporary device context needs to be deleted, and of course the screen device context also needs to be released.

Retrieving the bitmap image from the clipboard is relatively simple, as well as quite similar to the process of storing the bitmap. As usual, the operation begins by opening the clipboard and then retrieving a handle to the bitmap memory block:

```
OpenClipboard( hwnd );
hBitmap = GetClipboardData( CF_BITMAP );
hdcMem = CreateCompatibleDC( hdc );
```

A compatible memory device context is also needed, after which the *SelectObject* function selects the bitmap into the device context:

```
SelectObject( hdcMem, hBitmap );
SetMapMode( hdcMem, GetMapMode( hdc ) );
```

The mapping mode also needs to be set for the memory device context before the actual image can be copied from the clipboard memory block.

GetObject gives us the dimensions of the bitmap:

```
GetObject( hBitmap, sizeof(BITMAP), (LPSTR) &bm );
BitBlt( hdc, 0, 0, bm.bmWidth, bm.bmHeight,
        hdcMem, 0, 0, SRCCOPY );
```

This leaves only the image information to be copied. Since all that's wanted is a one-to-one copy, the *BitBlt* function is quite adequate, and the image is positioned at the origin (upper left) of ClipBd's client window.

This leaves only cleanup (releasing and deleting device contexts) and closing the clipboard:

```
ReleaseDC( hwnd, hdc );
DeleteDC( hdcMem );
CloseClipboard();
```

Actually, the clipboard could have been closed earlier, as soon as a handle had been retrieved to the memory block because, remember, closing the clipboard does not delete the memory block. Pretty simple, wasn't it?

The remaining clipboard operation, for metafiles, has a few new wrinkles to demonstrate.

Metafile Clipboard Transfers

Transferring metafiles involves a couple of complexities which simply weren't relevant in the discussion of text and bitmap transfers. For metafiles, not only is the mapping mode needed under which the metafile was originally created, but also the application replaying the metafile may need extent or size information which is not inherent in the metafile.

With text, metric, English, and TWIPS mapping modes, mapping scale is fixed. The MM_ISOTROPIC and MM_ANISOTROPIC mapping modes, which have popular advantages for metafiles, also present a need for special information to accompany the metafiles. For these reasons, the METAFILEPICT record is the clipboard storage format, and includes a record of the mapping mode used, and x and y extent information as well as the metafile script itself.

Before examining how this information will be used, however, transferring a metafile to the clipboard will illustrate how the information is generated. For convenience, a subroutine (*DrawMetafile*) is used in the ClipBd.C demo program, beginning with these local variables:

```
{
    LPMETAFILEPICT    lpMFP;
    GLOBALHANDLE      hGMem;
    HDC               hdc, hdcMeta;
```

lpMFP provides a pointer to the METAFILEPICT structure that will be generated, and *hGMem* provides the usual global memory handle. *hdcMeta*, of course, is a handle to the metafile itself.

The process of actually creating the metafile has been omitted here but differs from previous examples only in the metafile creation declaration, as:

```
    hdcMeta = CreateMetaFile( NULL );
```

The window extent and origin are set just as if this were a normal metafile, and the metafile drawing operations are carried out exactly as in previous examples.

Now it's time to create the memory block which will be transferred to the clipboard, beginning by allocatiing memory. This should be familar by now:

```
hGMem = GlobalAlloc( GHND, (DWORD) sizeof(METAFILEPICT) );
lpMFP = (LPMETAFILEPICT) GlobalLock( hGMem );
lpMFP->mm = MM_ISOTROPIC;
```

The allocated memory is locked, returning a pointer (*lpMFP*) before the mapping mode is copied to the *lpMFP->mm* field.

The two extent fields are also important, and these receive the suggested size of the metafile image in MM_HIMETRIC units:

```
lpMFP->xExt = 200;
lpMFP->yExt = 200;
lpMFP->hMF = hMetaFile;
```

Last, the *hMF* handle is given the handle of the metafile proper (*hMetaFile*).

This finishes setting up the metafile for transfer. The allocated memory is unlocked, and *TransferToClipBD* is called to complete the transfer to the clipboard, reporting the results back to the calling process:

```
GlobalUnlock( hGMem );
return( TransferToClipBD( hwnd, hGMem,
                          CF_METAFILEPICT ) );
}
```

Thus far, setting up and transferring the metafile hasn't been that difficult. In a moment, when the metafile is retrieved, a new element will be introduced.

The process begins by opening the clipboard, asking for a handle to the memory block containing the metafile, and locking the block while returning a pointer:

```
OpenClipboard( hwnd );
hGMem = GetClipboardData( CF_METAFILEPICT );
lpMFP = (LPMETAFILEPICT) GlobalLock( hGMem );
```

Now that we have a pointer to the metafile, it's time to do something with it. The first step is to save the present device context. Next, a call to a subroutine, *CreateMapMode*, sets the appropriate mapping mode for this metafile. This is a new element to which we will return in a moment:

```
SaveDC( hdc );
CreateMapMode( hdc, lpMFP, cxWnd, cyWnd );
PlayMetaFile( hdc, lpMFP->hMF );
RestoreDC( hdc, - 1 );
```

Once the appropriate mapping mode is set, *PlayMetaFile* executes the metafile. This done, the original device context can be restored. To finish, the memory block is unlocked and the clipboard closed:

```
GlobalUnlock( hGMem );
CloseClipboard();
```

The *CreateMapMode* subroutine is the key to replaying the metafile and is called with four parameters: The device context (*hdc*), a pointer to the METAFILEPICT structure (*lpMFP*), and the client window sizes (*cxWnd* and *cyWnd*):

```
BOOL CreateMapMode( HDC hdc,    LPMETAFILEPICT lpMFP,
                    int cxWnd, int cyWnd )
{
    long   lMapScale;
    int    nHRes, nVRes, nHSize, nVSize;
```

For convenience, there can be several local variables, but *lMapScale* is the critical value that may need to be calculated. The operational word is "may", because not all metafiles will require this calculation. In all cases, the first step is to set the map mode indicated by the *lpMFP->mm* field:

```
SetMapMode( hdc, lpMFP->mm );
if( lpMFP->mm != MM_ISOTROPIC &&
    lpMFP->mm != MM_ANISOTROPIC )
    return( TRUE );
```

If the mode is neither MM_ISOTROPIC nor MM_ANISOTROPIC, then the step above is all that is necessary, and the subroutine can return right now.

For the isotropic or anisotropic mapping modes, additional information is needed, and is obtained by calling *GetDeviceCaps* for the horizontal and vertical resolution, and the size of the device:

```
nHRes  = GetDeviceCaps( hdc, HORZRES );
nVRes  = GetDeviceCaps( hdc, VERTRES );
nHSize = GetDeviceCaps( hdc, HORZSIZE );
nVSize = GetDeviceCaps( hdc, VERTSIZE );
```

Granted, this is the same device where the metafile was created and none of these values have changed, but the application still needs this information for calculating the appropriate viewport extents.

There are three circumstances under which the viewport extents can be calculated: First, the *xExt* and *yExt* parameters (both are assumed to have the same sign or general magnitude) are positive, and therefore are a suggested metafile image size. Note that the word is "suggested", not absolute, and the size is expressed in MM_HIMETRIC units (0.01mm):

```
if( lpMFP->xExt > 0 )
    SetViewportExt( hdc,
        (int)((long) lpMFP->xExt * nHRes / nHSize / 100 ),
        (int)((long) lpMFP->yExt * nHRes / nHSize / 100 ) );
```

The calculations are relatively straightforward as shown, and once the viewport extent is set, the application is ready to play back the metafile.

The second case is a negative value for *xExt* (and, presumably, for *yExt*), which means that the values are a suggested aspect ratio rather than a metafile image size:

```
else
if( lpMFP->xExt < 0 )
{
    lMapScale =
        min( ( 100L * (long) cxWnd *
                nHSize / nHRes / -lpMFP->xExt ),
              ( 100L * (long) cyWnd *
                nVSize / nVRes / -lpMFP->yExt ) );
    SetViewportExt( hdc,
            (int) ( (long) -lpMFP->xExt * lMapScale *
                            nHRes / nHSize / 100 ),
            (int) ( (long) -lpMFP->yExt * lMapScale *
                            nVRes / nVSize / 100 ) );
}
```

In this case, the calculations are slightly more involved, but still relatively simple.

In the third case, *xExt* and, by presumption, *yExt*, are both zero, in which circumstance the viewport extent is simply set to the present client window width and height:

```
    else SetViewportExt( hdc, cxWnd, cyWnd );
    return( TRUE );
}
```

This is moderately complicated but, happily, it does not present the computer with anythingthat the CPU can not handle quite readily. After all, these are minor calculations compared with the image mapping required during the actual replay.

Other Clipboard Formats

We have covered three of the nine clipboard formats. These three are representative of the processes involved, and using any of the remaining six principal clipboard formats should present no special difficulty.

This does not exhaust the clipboard formats that are available. Windows also defines private data formats as: CF_DSPTEXT, CF_DSPBITMAP, and CF_DSPMETAFILEPICT (DSP is for "display"). These correspond in format to the CF_TEXT, CF_BITMAP, and CF_METAFILEPICT formats, but with a difference: Applications asking for the normal formats will not access these private formats.

The assumptions are, first, that this type of data is for exchange between two instances of the same program, and second, that these clipboard files contain private information as, for example, formatting and font information used by the Windows WRITE program.

Obviously, two instances of the same application should understand their own private formats, or two companion programs could use these private formats to communicate. When these private formats are used, the question will arise as to where a CF_DSPxxxx format clipboard entry originated. Did this come from another instance of the current application, or from a companion program? Or was it generated by an entirely different application which just happens to be using the same format? Provisions have also been made for this eventuality, and the originator of the clipboard contents can be obtained by calling:

```
hwndCBOwner = GetClipboardOwner();
```

Remember, when *EmptyClipboard* was called preparatory to copying material to the clipboard, this function assigned the calling application as the clipboard owner. Regardless of who accesses the clipboard, only another clipboard owner can copy new material into the clipboard—which means erasing the previous material.

Of course, the *hwndCBOwner* parameter does not in itself tell you very much, but it does provide a handle to find out the application's class name, as:

```
GetClassName( hwndCBOwner, &szClassName, 16 );
```

With this information, *szClassName* can be compared to the current application's classname (or to a copy of a companion application's classname) to identify the source of the clipboard information.

Delayed Clipboard Rendering

Copying data to the clipboard frequently involves passing a copy of the data to the clipboard while keeping the original data, and this, of course, means expending memory on duplicate data blocks. In many circumstances this is not particularly important, simply because the amount of memory used is small. In the case of the ClipBd.C demo, no copy of the data is retained and this also avoids the memory problem.

There is also a third approach which is especially appropriate when large data blocks—bitmaps, metafiles, text or custom data—are involved: Delayed rendering of the clipboard data.

For delayed rendering, instead of passing a global memory block handle to the clipboard, only a format specification is passed, and the handle parameter is passed as NULL, as:

```
SetClipboardData( wFormat, NULL );
```

If more than one item needs to be passed to the clipboard, some items may be passed as data, and others passed as NULL for delayed rendering.

When an application calls for data which was passed as NULL, Windows recognizes that the data has been delayed and calls the clipboard owner, the application which last called *EmptyClipboard*, with a WM_RENDERFORMAT message. WM_RENDERFORMAT is an instruction requesting the delayed data with the format type requested contained in *wParam*.

In response to WM_RENDERFORMAT, instead of calling *OpenClipboard* and *EmptyClipboard*, the only call required is *SetClipboardData* with the global memory block handle, and, of course, the format identifier.

If, however, another application calls the clipboard with an *EmptyClipboard* call, taking ownership of the clipboard away from the original application, the original clipboard owner receives a WM_DESTROYCLIPBOARD message, simply indicating that ownership has been lost.

The final special message is WM_RENDERALLFORMATS. When an application is ready to terminate itself but is still the current clipboard owner, and the clipboard contains NULL data handles, Windows sends the WM_RENDERALLFORMATS message. In response, the owner application has two choices: Either clear the clipboard, or replace the NULL data handles with the actual data blocks.

Normally, the latter choice would be preferred. After all, if another instance or application was expected to retrieve the data from the clipboard in the first place, presumably this data will still be wanted. Further, since the reason for using a NULL handle in the first place was to avoid duplicating memory, transferring the data to the clipboard before the original application exits serves essentially the same purpose.

Note, however, that the response to a WM_RENDERALLFORMATS message is not the same as the WM_RENDERFORMAT message. Instead, the appropriate response to the WM_RENDERALLFORMATS message is essentially the same as creating normal clipboard entries: Opening the clipboard, erasing the previous contents, writing new data block(s) without using null handles, and, closing the clipboard, just as if delayed rendering had never been used at all.

Owner Displayed Clipboard Data

A fourth, very private, clipboard format is also declared as:

```
SetClipboardData( CF_OWNERDISPLAY, NULL );
```

In this format, the global memory handle is passed as NULL, just as it is with delayed rendering. But because the clipboard owner is directly responsible for the display, Windows does not send a WM_RENDERFORMAT request. Instead, messages are sent to the clipboard owner from the clipboard viewer, requesting the originating application to provide the actual display and, granting the originating appication access to the destination application's display.

The five messages which can be sent from the destination window are: WM_ASKCBFORMATNAME, WM_HSCROLLCLIPBOARD, WM_PAINT-CLIPBOARD, WM_SIZECLIPBOARD, and WM_VSCROLLCLIPBOARD.

- WM_ASKCBFORMATNAME is sent by the clipboard viewer to request a copy of the format name from the clipboard owner. Remember, the clipboard itself contains only the CF_OWNERDISPLAY format identifier. The *wParam* argument specifies the maximum number of bytes to copy, and the *lParam* argument points to the destination buffer.

- WM_PAINTCLIPBOARD is sent to request repainting part or all of the clipboard viewer's client area. The *wParam* argument supplies a handle to the destination window, while the low-order word of *lParam* identifies a PAINTSTRUCT data structure defining the portion of the client area to be painted. The high-order word of *lParam* is not used.

To determine whether all or part of the client area requires repainting, the clipboard owner must compare the dimensions of the drawing area specified in the *rcpaint* field of the PAINTSTRUCT with the dimensions in the most recent WM_SIZECLIPBOARD message. The PAINTSTRUCT data should be globally locked during use and, unlocked when finished.

- WM_SIZECLIPBOARD is sent to indicate that the clipboard application window has changed size. *wParam* contains a handle to the application window, while the low-order word in *lParam* identifies a RECT data structure containing the new window size. A WM_SIZECLIPBOARD message sent with a null rectangle (0,0,0,0) as the new size indicates that the clipboard application is about to be destroyed or minimized, and permits the clipboard owner to free its display resources.
- WM_HSCROLLCLIPBOARD and WM_VSCROLLCLIPBOARD messages are sent when an event occurs in the clipboard-application's vertical scroll bar. *wParam* contains a handle to the clipboard application window, while *lParam* contains the scrollbar code in the low-order word. If the scrollbar code is SB_THUMBPOSITION, the high-order word in *lParam* contains the thumb position. This is the same as *lParam*'s low-order word in normal scrollbar messages. Otherwise, the high-order word is not used.

In response to either message, the clipboard owner should use the *InvalidateRect* function, or repaint as desired. Also, the scrollbar position should be reset.

Other Uses For Private Formats

Applications can also define their own private clipboard formats, registering a new clipboard format by calling:

```
wFormat = RegisterClipboardFormat( lpszFormatTitle );
```

The returned *wFormat* identifier will be a value between 0xC000 and 0xFFFF, and can be used subsequently as the format parameter in *SetClipboard-Data* and *GetClipboardData*. However, before another application or instance can retrieve data from the clipboard, this same *wFormat* id is required, although it could be passed via the clipboard as CF_TEXT format.

EnumClipboardFormats, discussed previously, can also be used to return all format identifiers. The *GetClipboardFormatName* function can then obtain the ASCII name of the format, as:

```
GetClipboardFormatName( wFormat, lpszBuffer, nCharCount );
```

The identifiers CF_PRIVATEFIRST...CF_PRIVATELAST (0x0200..0x02FF) can also be used as a range of integer values for private format identifiers. Note that data handles associated with formats in this range will not be freed automatically; any data handles must be freed by the application before the application terminates, or when a WM_DESTROYCLIPBOARD message is received.

Summary

The clipboard is a useful method of exchanging data between separate instances of a single application, and between different applications. A variety of different standard formats are available, as are custom formats that applications can define for themselves.

There are also a few disadvantages which, while not major, should still be given appropriate consideration. These disadvantages, however, can be circumvented using the Dynamic Data Exchange methods discussed in Chapter 23.

The complete source code for the ClipBd demo program follows, demonstrating text, bitmap, and metafile transfers via the Windows clipboard utility.

```
//========================//
//          ClipBd.C          //
//   C++ Windows Drawing   //
//    creating a metafile   //
//========================//

#include <windows.h>
#include <stdio.h>
#include <math.h>
#include <clipbd.h>

HANDLE    hGInst;
HANDLE    hMetaFile;
```

```
#define PI2 ( 2.0 * 3.1415 )          // radians in 360 degrees //

BOOL TransferToClipBD( HWND hwnd, HANDLE hMemBlock,
                       WORD FormatCB )
{
   if( OpenClipboard( hwnd ) )
   {
      EmptyClipboard();
      SetClipboardData( FormatCB, hMemBlock );
      CloseClipboard();
      return( TRUE );
   }
   return( FALSE );
}

BOOL TextToClipboard( HWND hwnd, LPSTR Txt )
{
   int           i, wLen;
   GLOBALHANDLE  hGMem;
   LPSTR         lpGMem;

   wLen = strlen( Txt );
   hGMem = GlobalAlloc( GHND, (DWORD) wLen + 1 );
   lpGMem = GlobalLock( hGMem );
   for( i=0; i<wLen; i++ ) *lpGMem++ = *Txt++;
   GlobalUnlock( hGMem );
   return( TransferToClipBD( hwnd, hGMem, CF_TEXT ) );
}

void FlashRect( HWND hwnd, POINT pt1, POINT pt2 )
{
   HDC  hdc;

   hdc = CreateDC( "DISPLAY", NULL, NULL, NULL );
   ClientToScreen( hwnd, &pt1 );
   PatBlt( hdc, pt1.x, pt1.y, pt2.x, pt2.y, DSTINVERT );
   PatBlt( hdc, pt1.x, pt1.y, pt2.x, pt2.y, DSTINVERT );
   DeleteDC( hdc );
}

BOOL CreateMapMode( HDC hdc,   LPMETAFILEPICT lpMFP,
                    int cxWnd, int cyWnd )
{
   long  lMapScale;
   int   nHRes, nVRes, nHSize, nVSize;

   SetMapMode( hdc, lpMFP->mm );
   if( lpMFP->mm != MM_ISOTROPIC &&
       lpMFP->mm != MM_ANISOTROPIC )
      return( TRUE );                    // mode's set, that's all //

   nHRes  = GetDeviceCaps( hdc, HORZRES );
   nVRes  = GetDeviceCaps( hdc, VERTRES );
   nHSize = GetDeviceCaps( hdc, HORZSIZE );
```

```
    nVSize = GetDeviceCaps( hdc, VERTSIZE );
            // positive values = suggested      //
            // image size in MM_HIMETRIC units //
    if( lpMFP->xExt > 0 )
        SetViewportExt( hdc,
            (int)((long) lpMFP->xExt * nHRes / nHSize / 100 ),
            (int)((long) lpMFP->yExt * nHRes / nHSize / 100 ) );
    else
            // negative values = suggested //
            // aspect ratio, not size      //
    if( lpMFP->xExt < 0 )
    {
        lMapScale =
            min( ( 100L * (long) cxWnd *
                    nHSize / nHRes / -lpMFP->xExt ),
                 ( 100L * (long) cyWnd *
                    nVSize / nVRes / -lpMFP->yExt ) );
        SetViewportExt( hdc,
            (int) ( (long) -lpMFP->xExt * lMapScale *
                            nHRes / nHSize / 100 ),
            (int) ( (long) -lpMFP->yExt * lMapScale *
                            nVRes / nVSize / 100 ) );
    }
            // zero extent = neither size //
            // nor aspect ratio suggested  //
    else SetViewportExt( hdc, cxWnd, cyWnd );
    return( TRUE );
}

BOOL DrawMetafile( HWND hwnd, int cxWnd, int cyWnd )
{
    LPMETAFILEPICT   lpMFP;
    GLOBALHANDLE     hGMem;
    POINT            pt[7];
    HDC              hdc, hdcMeta;
    HPEN             hPen;
    int              i, j;
                    // calculate points //
    for( i=j=0; i<7; i++, j=(j+3)%7 )          // seven points //
    {
        pt[i].x = (int)( sin( j*PI2/7 ) * 100 );
        pt[i].y = (int)( cos( j*PI2/7 ) * 100 );
    }
                    // create METAFILE //
    hdcMeta = CreateMetaFile( NULL );
    SetMapMode(      hdcMeta, MM_ISOTROPIC );
    SetWindowExt(    hdcMeta, 1000, 1000 );
    SetViewportExt(  hdcMeta, cxWnd, cyWnd );
    SetWindowOrg(    hdcMeta, -300, -300 );
    hPen = CreatePen( PS_NULL, 1, 0L );
```

```
        SelectObject( hdcMeta, hPen );
        SelectObject( hdcMeta, GetStockObject( LTGRAY_BRUSH ) );
        Ellipse( hdcMeta, -100, -100, 100, 100 );
        SelectObject( hdcMeta, GetStockObject( DKGRAY_BRUSH ) );
        SetPolyFillMode( hdcMeta, ALTERNATE );
        Polygon( hdcMeta, pt, 7 );
        hMetaFile = CloseMetaFile( hdcMeta );
        DeleteObject( hPen );
                        // create METAFILEPICT //
        hGMem = GlobalAlloc( GHND, (DWORD) sizeof(METAFILEPICT) );
        lpMFP = (LPMETAFILEPICT) GlobalLock( hGMem );
        lpMFP->mm = MM_ISOTROPIC;
        lpMFP->xExt = 200;                      // suggested size in //
        lpMFP->yExt = 200;                      // MM_HIMETRIC units //
        lpMFP->hMF = hMetaFile;
        GlobalUnlock( hGMem );
                        // copy to clipboard //
        return( TransferToClipBD( hwnd, hGMem,
                                  CF_METAFILEPICT ) );
}

long FAR PASCAL WndProc( HWND hwnd,    WORD msg,
                         WORD wParam, LONG lParam )
{
    static BOOL      bCaptEnable, bCapturing;
    static POINT     pt1, pt2;
    static int       cxWnd, cyWnd, nClipRetrieve;
    char             TextStr[80];
    int              i, j;
    LPMETAFILEPICT   lpMFP;
    LPSTR            lpText;
    GLOBALHANDLE     hGMem;
    PAINTSTRUCT      ps;
    BITMAP           bm;
    HBITMAP          hBitmap;
    HANDLE           hTextMem;
    HMENU            hMenu;
    HDC              hdc, hdcMeta, hdcMem;

    switch( msg )
    {
        case WM_CREATE:
            nClipRetrieve = bCaptEnable = bCapturing = 0;
            return(0);

        case WM_LBUTTONDOWN:
            if( bCaptEnable )
            {
                bCapturing = TRUE;
                pt1 = MAKEPOINT( lParam );
            }
            return(0);
```

```
      case WM_MOUSEMOVE:
        if( bCaptEnable )
          SetCursor( LoadCursor( NULL, IDC_CROSS ) );
        if( bCapturing )
        {
          pt2 = MAKEPOINT( lParam );
          pt2.x -= pt1.x;
          pt2.y -= pt1.y;
          FlashRect( hwnd, pt1, pt2 );
        }
        return(0);
      case WM_LBUTTONUP:
        if( ! bCapturing ) return(0);
        if( ! pt2.x || ! pt2.y ) return(0);
        hdc = GetDC( hwnd );
        hdcMem = CreateCompatibleDC( hdc );
        hBitmap =
          CreateCompatibleBitmap( hdc, abs(pt2.x),
                                       abs(pt2.y) );
        if( hBitmap )
        {
          MessageBeep(0);
          SelectObject( hdcMem, hBitmap );
          StretchBlt( hdcMem, 0, 0, abs(pt2.x), abs(pt2.y),
                      hdc, pt1.x, pt1.y, pt2.x, pt2.y,
                      SRCCOPY );
          TransferToClipBD( hwnd, hBitmap, CF_BITMAP );
          InvalidateRect( hwnd, NULL, TRUE );
        }
        DeleteDC( hdcMem );
        ReleaseDC( hwnd, hdc );
        bCaptEnable = bCapturing = FALSE;
        SetCursor( LoadCursor( NULL, IDC_ARROW ) );
        ReleaseCapture();
        return(0);
      case WM_COMMAND:
        switch( wParam )
        {
          case IDM_PUT_BITMAP:
            if( ! bCaptEnable )
            {
              bCaptEnable = TRUE;
              SetCapture( hwnd );
              SetCursor( LoadCursor( NULL, IDC_CROSS ) );
            }
            else
            {
              bCaptEnable = FALSE;
              ReleaseCapture();
              SetCursor( LoadCursor( NULL, IDC_ARROW ) );
```

```
            }
            MessageBeep(0);
            return(0);

        case IDM_PUT_METAFILE:
            DrawMetafile( hwnd, cxWnd, cyWnd );
            MessageBeep(0);
            break;

        case IDM_PUT_TEXT:
            TextToClipboard( hwnd,
                "The quick brown fox jumped "
                "over the lazy red dog" );
            MessageBeep(0);
            break;

        case IDM_GET_METAFILE:
        case IDM_GET_BITMAP:
        case IDM_GET_TEXT:
            nClipRetrieve = wParam;
            InvalidateRect( hwnd, NULL, TRUE );
            break;
    }
    return(0);

case WM_SIZE:
    cxWnd = LOWORD( lParam );
    cyWnd = HIWORD( lParam );
    return(0);

case WM_PAINT:
    InvalidateRect( hwnd, NULL, TRUE );
    hdc = BeginPaint( hwnd, &ps );
    switch( nClipRetrieve )
    {
        case IDM_GET_TEXT:
            nClipRetrieve = 0;
            if( IsClipboardFormatAvailable( CF_TEXT ) )
            {
                MessageBeep(0);
                OpenClipboard( hwnd );
                hTextMem = GetClipboardData( CF_TEXT );
                lpText = GlobalLock( hTextMem );
                lstrcpy( TextStr, lpText );
                GlobalUnlock( hTextMem );
                CloseClipboard();
                TextOut( hdc, 10, 10, TextStr,
                         strlen( TextStr ) );
            } break;

        case IDM_GET_BITMAP:
            nClipRetrieve = 0;
            if( IsClipboardFormatAvailable( CF_BITMAP ) )
```

```
                    {
                        MessageBeep(0);
                        OpenClipboard( hwnd );
                        hBitmap = GetClipboardData( CF_BITMAP );
                        SetCursor( LoadCursor( NULL, IDC_WAIT ) );
                        hdcMem = CreateCompatibleDC( hdc );
                        SelectObject( hdcMem, hBitmap );
                        SetMapMode( hdcMem, GetMapMode( hdc ) );
                        GetObject( hBitmap, sizeof(BITMAP),
                                    (LPSTR) &bm );
                        BitBlt( hdc, 0, 0, bm.bmWidth, bm.bmHeight,
                                    hdcMem, 0, 0, SRCCOPY );
                        SetCursor( LoadCursor( NULL, IDC_ARROW ) );
                        ReleaseDC( hwnd, hdc );
                        DeleteDC( hdcMem );
                        CloseClipboard();
                    } break;
                case IDM_GET_METAFILE:
                    nClipRetrieve = 0;
                    if( IsClipboardFormatAvailable(
                            CF_METAFILEPICT ) )
                    {
                        MessageBeep(0);
                        OpenClipboard( hwnd );
                        hGMem = GetClipboardData(
                                    CF_METAFILEPICT );
                        lpMFP =
                            (LPMETAFILEPICT) GlobalLock( hGMem );
                        SaveDC( hdc );
                        CreateMapMode( hdc, lpMFP, cxWnd, cyWnd );
                        PlayMetaFile( hdc, lpMFP->hMF );
                        RestoreDC( hdc, - 1 );
                        GlobalUnlock( hGMem );
                        CloseClipboard();
                    } break;

                default:  break;
            }
            EndPaint( hwnd, &ps );
            return(0);

        case WM_DESTROY:  PostQuitMessage(0);
                            return(0);
    }
    return( DefWindowProc( hwnd, msg, wParam, lParam ) );
}

#pragma argsused

int PASCAL WinMain( HANDLE hInst,        HANDLE hPrevInst,
                    LPSTR  lpszCmdParam, int nCmdShow )
{
```

```
    static char szAppName[] = "CLIPBD";
    HWND        hwnd;
    MSG         msg;
    WNDCLASS    wc;

    hGInst = hInst;
    if( ! hPrevInst )
    {
        wc.hInstance      = hInst;
        wc.lpfnWndProc    = WndProc;
        wc.cbClsExtra     = 0;
        wc.cbWndExtra     = 0;
        wc.lpszClassName  = szAppName;
        wc.lpszMenuName   = (LPSTR) szAppName;
        wc.hIcon          = LoadIcon( hInst, szAppName );
        wc.hCursor        = LoadCursor( NULL, IDC_ARROW );
        wc.hbrBackground  = GetStockObject( WHITE_BRUSH );
        wc.style          = CS_HREDRAW | CS_VREDRAW;
        RegisterClass( &wc );
    }
    hwnd = CreateWindow( szAppName, "ClipBoard Demo",
                         WS_OVERLAPPEDWINDOW,
                         CW_USEDEFAULT, CW_USEDEFAULT,
                         CW_USEDEFAULT, CW_USEDEFAULT,
                         NULL, NULL, hInst, NULL  );
    ShowWindow(   hwnd, nCmdShow );
    UpdateWindow( hwnd );
    while( GetMessage( &msg, NULL, 0, 0 ) )
    {
        TranslateMessage( &msg );
        DispatchMessage(  &msg );
    }
    return( msg.wParam );
}


                    ;==============;
                    ;  CLIPBD.DEF  ;
                    ;==============;

NAME          CLIPBD

DESCRIPTION   "CLIPBOARD OPERATIONS"
EXETYPE       WINDOWS
STUB          "WINSTUB.EXE"
CODE          PRELOAD MOVEABLE DISCARDABLE
DATA          PRELOAD MOVEABLE MULTIPLE
HEAPSIZE      1024
STACKSIZE     8192
EXPORTS       WndProc
```

```
                    //============//
                    //  ClipBd.H  //
                    //============//

#define   IDM_PUT_BITMAP      101
#define   IDM_PUT_METAFILE    102
#define   IDM_PUT_TEXT        103
#define   IDM_GET_BITMAP      201
#define   IDM_GET_METAFILE    202
#define   IDM_GET_TEXT        203

                    //========================//
                    //  ClipBd.RC menu file    //
                    //========================//

CLIPBD   MENU LOADONCALL MOVEABLE PURE DISCARDABLE
BEGIN
    POPUP "Data To Clipboard"
    BEGIN
        MenuItem    "Capture &Bitmap",      101
        MenuItem    "Write &Metafile",      102
        MenuItem    "Write &Text",          103
    END
    POPUP "Data From Clipboard"
    BEGIN
        MenuItem    "Retrieve &Bitmap",     201
        MenuItem    "Retrieve &Metafile",   202
        MenuItem    "Retrieve &Text",       203
    END
END
```

Chapter 23

Dynamic Data Exchange (DDE)

In Chapter 22, the Clipboard was presented as a means of exchanging data between two applications: This is only one of the data transfer facilities which Windows 3.0 offers. Now it's time to take a look at a second process: the Dynamic Data Exchange process. (A third process also exists—shared memory in dynamic link libraries—but is not discussed here.)

The DDE is based on a message system. Managed by Windows, this system permits applications to send messages either broadcast (i.e., to any application which will respond), or to post messages directly to another application. Using global memory blocks similar to those which were introduced in Chapter 22 for the clipboard, blocks of data can also be exchanged between applications.

Unlike clipboard traffic, using Dynamic Data Exchange (DDE) methods ensures that messages and data are passed directly between applications without the data becoming general, and without the possibility of data becoming lost if the clipboard is preempted by another application. Further, unlike the clipboard, data traffic between two applications can be carried on without requesting (requiring) permission from the user.

An Introduction To DDE

DDE message traffic is a conversation between two applications and, like human conversations, consists of both protocols and redundancies. While less than 100% theoretically efficient, the conversations provide a high degree of surety. Under the DDE, conversations are always dialogs, with the application initiating the conversation taking the role of *client*, while the second application, known as the *server*, responds to requests from the client application.

In actual practice, any one application can carry on multiple DDE conversations with one or more other applications. An application can act as client in one conversation and server in another, even if both conversations are being carried on with the same second application. Or, a single client might be conversing with several servers or a single server might be conversing with several clients, each in separate conversations. In general, when multiple conversations are used, in order to keep these conversations separate and unique, the application will create a hidden child window—i.e., a window ID—for each conversation. However, for demonstration and discussion, only a single DDE conversation will be used, and one application will always be the client in converse with a dedicated server.

DDE Terminology

In order to carry on a conversation, DDE applications require three identifiers, or character strings. These are the "application name", the data "topic", and the data "item".

- The application name is a familiar item from all the application examples shown in this book. In DDE applications, however, the application name will be used in a new fashion, to identify the applications themselves within the conversation, or to identify a specific server to which a message is addressed.
- The topic name is a new element introduced by DDE applications. All DDE conversations involve at least one "topic", though individual server applications may provide data for several different topics.
- The item name is an identifier within a topic, specifying a specific item of data.

In the example programs DDE_DATA and DDE_MAIN, the DDE_DATA is a dedicated server which supplies information on a single topic titled "Item_Stocks". In this example program, the available data under this topic consists of a series of item names, part numbers, and quantities, all of which are provided as static data.

In actual applications, of course, the types of data that might be exchanged are not limited to text and number data but, like the clipboard, could include bitmaps, metafiles, or custom data types. At the same time, the server could be a database application, a spreadsheet, some other utility such as a graphics program, or even a device-driver/data converter. Nevertheless, the static data used here is adequate to demonstrate principles without adding unnecessary complications.

Before we go into details about the example programs, first we will look at the types of DDE conversations which are possible. In general, DDE conversations can be broken down as three types: cold link, warm link, or hot link conversations. (Dde_Data and Dde_Main demonstrate hot link conversations.)

Cold Link DDE Conversations

A cold link conversation is initiated by a client application which broadcasts a WM_DDE_INITIATE message that identifies the called application and the type of data requested. Both the application ID and topic can be specified as NULL if any available server or subject is acceptable.

A server application supporting the requested topic sends a reply to the client with a WM_DDE_ACK message (see Figure 23-1). The WM_DDE_ACK acknowledgment is assumed to contain a positive confirmation at this time (see Table 23-1, DDE Window Messages, for details on message structures). Otherwise the server would not reply. The response also includes the server's identification, which can be used for subsequent message traffic.

After receiving the acknowledgment, the client sends a WM_DDE_RE-QUEST message that includes an item identifier specifying the information desired. The server replies with a WM_DDE_DATA message, after which the client confirms receipt with its own WM_DDE_ACK message. At this point, the conversation is, temporarily, complete, but the channels of communication remain open, and the client can, as desired, send another WM_DDE_RE-QUEST message.

If, however, the server is out of data—i.e., has no further data to supply—the server may (as illustrated) respond with a negative WM_DDE_ACK message. Or, if the client desires no further details, the client can send a WM_DDE_TERMINATE message. The server will respond to this using its own ID and repeating the same message, thus terminating the conversation.

Note that the server might also initiate the WM_DDE_TERMINATE message, and that it would be the client's responsibility to respond.

Figure 23-1: Cold Link Message Traffic

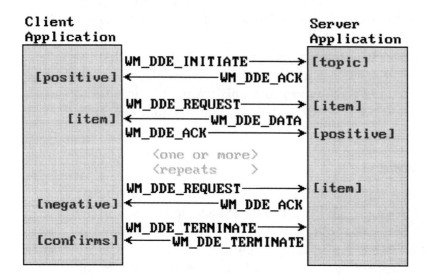

Hot Link DDE Communications

The limitation on cold link conversations is that the server is not free to let the client know that it (the server) has updated information available which would be of interest to the client. The hot link conversation circumvents this problem by permitting the server to initiate data transmissions.

As you can see in Figure 23-2, the conversation begins in the same fashion as the cold link, i.e., with a WM_DDE_INITIATE and a WM_DDE_ACK exchange. Next, instead of a WM_DDE_REQUEST message, the client sends a WM_DDE_ADVISE message, again requesting information about a specific item. Before responding with the data, the server replies with a positive acknowledge message (WM_DDE_ACK), saying that it can supply the requested data, or negative acknowledge message if it cannot.

The WM_DDE_ACK message is followed with a WM_DDE_DATA message containing the actual information, and the client confirms receipt with its own WM_DDE_ACK message. At this point, however, the server has accepted an obligation to notify the client at any time that previously transmitted data has changed.

Figure 23-2: Hot Link Message Traffic

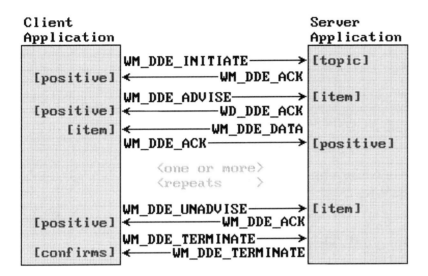

Notification of a change is made by the server with another WM_DDE_DATA message that may contain a flag requesting acknowledgment, or may simply be sent without needing a receipt.

Alternatively, the client application may choose to send a WM_DDE_UNADVISE message, cancelling any further notification of changes. The server would confirmthis message, and, finally, the conversation can be terminated as before.

Warm Link DDE Communications

A warm link combines features of both the cold and hot link formats and is initiated, as always, with a WM_DDE_INITIATE / WM_DDE_ACK message pair.

Again, a WM_DDE_ADVISE message is sent by the client application, but this time with a difference, because the advise message includes a deferred update flag. This flag informs the server that the client should be notified of changes, but defers receipt of the updated information. Thus, for a warm link, when a change does occur, the server still sends a WM_DDE_DATA message, but with a NULL data block. As before, the client application responds with a WM_DDE_ACK message. Remember, however, that the changing data has not yet been received.

Figure 23-3: Warm Link Message Traffic

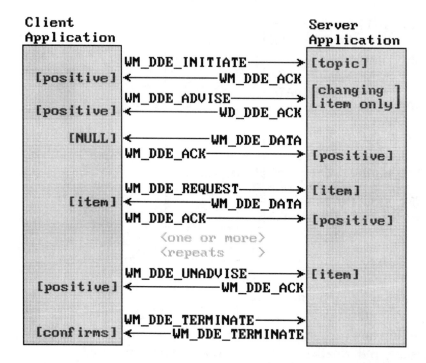

By using warm link protocol, the client has been notified of a change and, when ready, sends a WM_DDE_REQUEST message, just like in the cold link, and this time receives from the server a WM_DDE_DATA response with the changed data. As in a hot link, a WM_DDE_UNADVISE message may be sent to cancel notification of changes. Last, a pair of WM_TERMINATE messages are exchanged to end the conversation.

DDE Conversations: Atoms and Character Strings

Earlier, you were told that in order to carry on a conversation, DDE applications require three identifiers in the form of character strings. These provide the application name, the data topic, and the data item. However, these strings are not passed directly between applications as a part of the message traffic.

Instead, the actual strings are stored in an atom table in the application's default data segment. The message traffic passes "atoms", WORD values that ignore case and uniquely identify the string values. Atom variables are declared as:

```
ATOM   aItem, aName;
```

and strings are included in the atom table as:

```
aItem = AddAtom( lpItemStr );
aName = AddAtom( lpNameStr );
```

If the character string specified does not exist in the atom table, *AddAtom* adds the string to the atom table. If the string does exist in the atom table, the existing string's reference count, initially one, is incremented. In either case, *AddAtom* returns a unique number in the range 0xC000..0xFFFF to identify the string.

When no longer needed, strings can also be removed from the atom table by calling the *DeleteAtom* function, as:

```
DeleteAtom( aItem );
```

However, calling *DeleteAtom* does not immediately remove a string from the atom table. Instead, calling *DeleteAtom* decrements the string's reference count by one, but the string itself is removed only when the reference count reaches zero.

Two functions are provided to access the contents of the string table: *FindAtom* and *GetAtomName*.

The function *FindAtom* searches the atom table to retrieve the ATOM (WORD) value associated with a specific string, but does not increment the string's reference count. *FindAtom* is called as:

```
aItem = FindAtom( lpItemStr );
```

The return value identifies the atom associated with the given string, and returns NULL if the string is not in the atom table.

To use the atom value to retrieve the string value, the *GetAtomName* function is called as:

```
GetAtomName( aItem, lpBuff, sizeof( lpBuff ) );
```

GetAtomName retrieves a copy of the character string associated with the *aItem* parameter and places the string in the buffer indicated. The third parameter specifies the maximum number of characters which can be copied, i.e., the size of the buffer. *GetAtomName* returns the actual number of bytes copied to the buffer, or zero if the specified atom is not valid. Again, the string's reference count is not affected.

Global Access For Atom Tables

Atom tables within an application are all very well, but these are not hash tables, and there is no guarantee that an atom code for one application's atom table will match another application's atom table. Therefore, when atom codes are to be exchanged between applications, as in DDE message traffic, a shared atom table is needed, and for this purpose the *Global...Atom* functions provide global access.

Four global atom functions are defined as *GlobalAddAtom*, *GlobalDelete-Atom*, *GlobalFindAtom* and *GlobalGetAtomName*. Each is called in the same fashion as their local versions, and operates in the same fashion. There is a single exception, and the exception is the reason for using the *Global...Atom*. In these cases, the atom table is not local to the application, but is stored in a dynamic link library within Windows. It is therefore common to all Windows applications. However, by storing string information in the global atom table, applications can exchange application, topic, and item strings indirectly by exchanging atom values.

Other DDE Communications Elements

All Windows DDE communications begin with one of a series of message type identifiers which are defined in the DDE.H header file as shown in Table 23-1.

Two of these messages which have not been illustrated in preceding conversation are the WM_DDE_POKE message, used by a server to pass unsolicited data to a client, and the WM_DDE_EXECUTE message, used by a client application to send a command string to a server application. These two, however, are not commonly employed.

The DDE.H header file also defines the four data structures used with various messages: DDEACK, DDEADVISE, DDEDATA, and DDEPOKE.

Table 23-1: DDE Window Messages

Constant	Definition	Value
WM_DDE_FIRST	0x03E0	0x03E0
WM_DDE_INITIATE	(WM_DDE_FIRST)	0x03E0
WM_DDE_TERMINATE	(WM_DDE_FIRST+1)	0x03E1
WM_DDE_ADVISE	(WM_DDE_FIRST+2)	0x03E2
WM_DDE_UNADVISE	(WM_DDE_FIRST+3)	0x03E3
WM_DDE_ACK	(WM_DDE_FIRST+4)	0x03E4
WM_DDE_DATA	(WM_DDE_FIRST+5)	0x03E5
WM_DDE_REQUEST	(WM_DDE_FIRST+6)	0x03E6
WM_DDE_POKE	(WM_DDE_FIRST+7)	0x03E7
WM_DDE_EXECUTE	(WM_DDE_FIRST+8)	0x03E8
WM_DDE_LAST	(WM_DDE_FIRST+8)	0x03E8

DDEACK Message Record

The DDEACK message record is sent with WM_DDE_ACK messages in response to WM_DDE_DATA, WM_DDE_REQUEST, WM_DDE_POKE, WM_DDE_ADVISE, or WM_DDE_UNADVISE messages, and is contained in the low word of *lParam* (LOWORD(lParam)). All data fields are bit fields as shown by the DDEACK structure definition:

```
DDEACK (struct)
    {   unsigned  bAppReturnCode:8,
                  reserved:6,
                  fBusy:1,
                  fAck:1;          }
```

The DDEACK structure begins with an eight-bit (byte) *bAppReturnCode*, which could be used for any privately defined message information desired or, more commonly, passed as zero.

The *fBusy* and *fAck* fields are one-bit boolean flags. By convention *fBusy*, is set to indicate that the server is otherwise occupied, while the *fAck* field is set at one for a positive acknowledgment or clear (0) for a negative acknowledgment.

The six-bit *reserved* field is undefined, but could be used to pass custom flag values if necessary.

DDEADVISE Message Record

The DDEADVISE message record is contained in the low word of the *lParam* parameter (LOWORD(lParam)). Except for the *cfFormat* field, which is an integer value, all fields are bit values as defined by the DDEADVISE structure:

```
DDEADVISE (struct)
      {  unsigned  reserved:14,
                   fDeferUpd:1,
                   fAckReq:1;
         int       cfFormat;    }
```

The DDEADVISE structure consists of three fields, beginning with the one-bit boolean *fDeferUpd* (deferred update) specification. This is used in the warm link protocol to request only notification of change. The *fAckReq* (acknowledgment required) field indicates whether the sender expects a WM_DDE_ACK response. The *cfFormat* field is an integer value that follows the same conventions as the format specifications used with the clipboard.

DDEDATA Structure

The actual size of the WM_DDE_DATA parameter structure for hData (LOWORD(lParam)) depends on the size of the Value array:

```
DDEDATA (struct)       <new version>
      { unsigned unused:12,
                 fResponse:1,
                 fRelease:1,
                 reserved:1,
                 fAckReq:1;
        int      cfFormat;
        BYTE     Value[1];     }
```

An old version of essentially the same structure was defined in Windows 2.0, and for compatibility it is still valid. However, it is not suggested for use other than for support of 2.0 applications:

```
DDEUP (struct)         <old version>
      {  unsigned unused:12,
                  fAck:1,
                  fRelease:1,
                  fReserved:1,
                  fAckReq:1;
         int      cfFormat;
         BYTE     rgb[1];       }
```

DDEPOKE Structure

The actual size of the WM_DDE_POKE parameter structure for hData (LOWORD(lParam)) depends on the size of the Value array:

```
DDEPOKE (struct)      <new version>
     {  unsigned  unused:13,
                   fRelease:1,
                   fReserved:2;
        int        cfFormat;
        BYTE       Value[1];  }
```

The DDEPOKE structure is used with the WM_DDE_POKE message only. A Windows 2.0 version, DDELN, continues to be valid, but is supplied only for backwards compatibility:

```
DDELN (struct)        <old version>
     {  unsigned  unused:13,
                   fRelease:1,
                   fDeferUpd:1,
                   fAckReq:1;
        int        cfFormat;   }
```

Note that the DDEPOKE structure typedef'ed in earlier versions of DDE.H did not correctly define the bit positions.

The Dde_Data and Dde_Main Programs

Theory is well and good, but a practical example of DDE communications is always better. The Dde_Data.C and Dde_Main.C programs demonstrate hot link DDE communications, with Dde_Data acting as a dedicated server, and Dde_Main as the client application displaying data provided by the server.

For demonstration purposes, a brief data set has been defined in both examples as a series of item names and part numbers but, where Dde_Data has initial quantities defined for each item, the corresponding data in Dde_Main has only zero values. To demonstrate hot link communications, the server application will, at five second intervals, choose one or more data items, randomly changing the quantity for each, and reporting, via hot link, the changed values to the client. Each application is compiled separately, and produces separate .EXE files, even though both use a single resource file (DDEDEMO.RES) that provides two icons.

Perhaps the most noticeable difference between these two programs is that when Dde_Main is executed, Dde_Main begins by initiating a conversation directed to Dde_Data. Since Dde_Data is not active, i.e., has not been loaded, Windows searches the current directory and the directories specified in the PATH statement, looking for Dde_Data and loading the server program automatically.

The server program, however, is loaded as an icon, not as a full-sized window, and actually can neither be restored nor maximized. Since the server, in this example, exists only to communicate with the client application, the server does not require display space (a client window), and includes no WM_PAINT provisions to manage a display.

Figure 23-4 shows Dde_Main with the Dde_Data icon (DDE Server Demo) superimposed in the lower-right corner. Normally, of course, the Dde_Data icon would appear at the bottom of the screen and not within the Dde_Main window.

The Dde_Data Server

Aside from using DDE message handling, the Dde_Data server program differs from previous examples in several fashions, beginning in the *WinMain* procedure.

One of the first differences is that Dde_Data can not have more than one instance of the application active at any time. This provision is not normally made but is accomplished as:

```
int PASCAL WinMain( HANDLE hInst,       HANDLE hPrevInst,
                    LPSTR  lpszCmdParam, int nCmdShow )
{
    ...
    if( hPrevInst ) return( FALSE );
```

In all of the previous examples, the *hPrevInst* parameter was tested to decide if this was the first instance of the application, and the window class needed to be registered. In this application, not only should only the first instance register the window class(es), but any attempted second instance should not be allowed to load at all.

Where previous examples have registered a single window class in the *WinMain* procedure, the Dde_Data application registers two separate window classes. The first window class registered is the regular window class. It is similar to previous examples, but has a couple of provisions to allow for the fact that this application will never have a client window or scrollbars, menu or background color:

```
wc.style            = 0;                    // note: no style flags
wc.lpfnWndProc      = WndProc;
wc.cbClsExtra       = 0;
wc.cbWndExtra       = 0;
wc.hInstance        = hInst;
wc.lpszClassName    = szAppName;
wc.lpszMenuName     = NULL;
wc.hIcon            = LoadIcon( hInst, szAppName );
wc.hCursor          = LoadCursor( NULL, IDC_ARROW );
wc.hbrBackground    = GetStockObject( WHITE_BRUSH );
RegisterClass( &wc );
```

Of course, Dde_Data does have an icon, but this is about all of Dde_Data which will be visible.

It is the second window class registered that is really different, because this window class is used for the ServerProc, an exported subprocedure which handles the DDE communications with the client application:

```
              // register window for DDE server //
wc.hInstance        = hInst;
wc.lpfnWndProc      = ServerProc;
wc.cbClsExtra       = 0;
wc.cbWndExtra       = 2 * sizeof( WORD );
wc.lpszClassName    = szServerClass;
wc.lpszMenuName     = NULL;
wc.hIcon            = NULL;
wc.hCursor          = NULL;
wc.hbrBackground    = NULL;
wc.style            = 0;
RegisterClass( &wc );
```

This window class consists of very little except the ClassName and the exported WndProc (*ServerProc*). However, since Dde_Data will create a separate server instance in the form of a "hidden" window for each client conversing with Dde_Data, the *cbWndExtra* field is declared as a two WORD value. It provides one word in memory to store the window handle that identifies each server window's client, while the second word is used for a handle to the global memory block containing the application's data.

Next, the *CreateWindow* provision, which is essentially the same as in any other application, is followed by provisions to set a timer which uses another exported procedure.

Figure 23-4: DDE_MAIN and Server

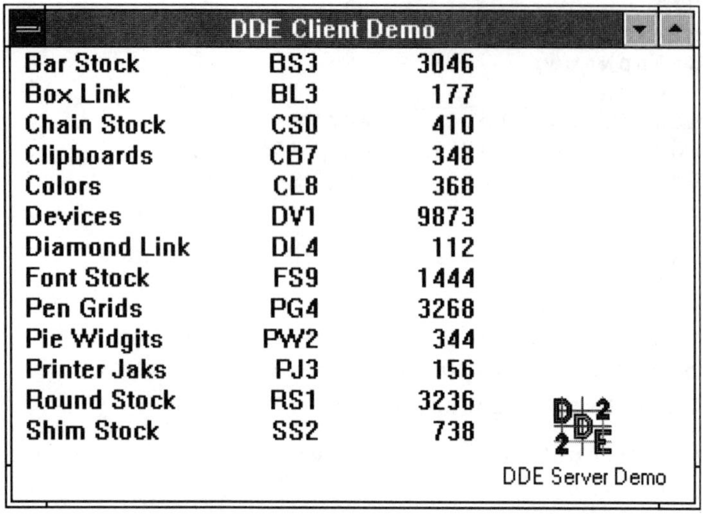

DDE Client Demo		
Bar Stock	BS3	3046
Box Link	BL3	177
Chain Stock	CS0	410
Clipboards	CB7	348
Colors	CL8	368
Devices	DV1	9873
Diamond Link	DL4	112
Font Stock	FS9	1444
Pen Grids	PG4	3268
Pie Widgits	PW2	344
Printer Jaks	PJ3	156
Round Stock	RS1	3236
Shim Stock	SS2	738

DDE Server Demo

If the *CreateWindow* provision is familiar, the *ShowWindow* instruction used is not, and insures that the application remains an inactive icon as:

```
ShowWindow( hwnd, SW_SHOWMINNOACTIVE );
```

Within the exported *WndProc* function, a second provision is in the form:

```
case WM_QUERYOPEN:   return(0);
```

and insures that Dde_Data remains displayed as an icon. Remember, just because the window remains minimized and cannot be activated does not mean that the application is not active!

The remainder of *WinMain* follows the same format as previous examples with a single additional provision: Before the application exits, kill the timer registered with Windows.

Now, if only one instance of Dde_Data can be active at one time, the same is not true of the Dde_Main application. Multiple instances of Dde_Main can be served by a single instance of Dde_Data, though Dde_Data does create a separate *ServerProc* for each dialog.

DDE Message Traffic

In the Dde_Data application, most of the DDE message traffic is handled by the exported *ServerProc*, while in the Dde_Main application, the *WndProc* procedure handles both conventional and DDE message traffic. Where the DDE messages are handled, however, is less important than the information accompanying each message. The first message sent, in any dialog, is a WM_DDE_INITIATE message.

Tracking DDE Message Traffic

A WM_DDE_INITIATE message is always issued by the client window. Before the initiate message is sent, the server application (*szServer*) and topic (*szTopic*) are added to the global atom table, returning *aApp* and *aTopic* as the atom identifiers. With this preparation completed, the message is sent as:

```
SendMessage( 0xFFFF, WM_DDE_INITIATE, hwnd,
             MAKELONG( aApp, aTopic ) );
```

The 0xFFFF value for the addressee makes this a broadcast message because, at this point, the server application's handle is not known. It may not even be established yet if Dde_Data has not yet been loaded.

Remember, though, that Dde_Data has been identified by the *aApp* atom identifier, and Windows will, if possible, load Dde_Data in response to this message. When Dde_Data receives the initiate message (in Dde_Data's *WndProc* procedure), the client window's handle (Dde_Main) appears in *wParam*, but instead of immediately retrieving the two atoms from *lParam*, Dde_Data insures that its own application name (*szAppName*) and topic (*szTopic*) are included in the global atom table:

```
case WM_DDE_INITIATE:
   hClient = wParam;
   aApp = GlobalAddAtom( szAppName );
   aTopic = GlobalAddAtom( szTopic );
```

Once these strings are included in the global atom table and two local atoms (values) are returned, instead of retrieving strings which the calling process placed in the atom table, a simpler test can be made using the atom values as:

```
if( ( !LOWORD(lParam) || LOWORD(lParam) == aApp ) &&
    ( !HIWORD(lParam) || HIWORD(lParam) == aTopic ) )
```

In this example, the test is written to accept either a match on the requested application (the server) and the topic, or to accept a null (wild-card) on either parameter. If there's a match, the server application creates a hidden window that uses *szServerClass* to handle communications with the client:

```
{
    hServer = CreateWindow( szServerClass, NULL,
                            WS_CHILD, 0, 0, 0, 0,
                            hwnd, NULL, hGInst, NULL );
    SetWindowWord( hServer, 0 , hClient );
    SendMessage( wParam, WM_DDE_ACK, hServer,
                 MAKELONG( aApp, aTopic ) );
}
```

Last, a WM_DDE_ACK message is returned, addressed explicitly to the caller using the calling processes' handle in *wParam*, and now including the server application's window handle (*hServer*) with the original *aApp* and *aTopic* atoms in *lParam*.

If this is not a match, i.e., if this server cannot respond appropriately, then Dde_Data calls *GlobalDeleteAtom* to remove the *aApp* and *aTopic* atoms:

```
else
{
    GlobalDeleteAtom( aApp );
    GlobalDeleteAtom( aTopic );
}
return(0);
```

This is how a conversation is initiated, but at this point, the conversation is in the client's court. The server will not act further until it receives a WM_DDE_REQUEST or WM_DDE_ADVISE message.

Next, since the Dde_Main application is using hot link protocols, the client responds with a series of WM_DDE_ADVISE messages specifying all of the items on the stocklist for which information is requested:

```
for( i=0; i<STOCK_ITEMS; i++ )
{
    hDdeAdvise = GlobalAlloc( GHND | GMEM_DDESHARE,
                             sizeof( DDEADVISE ) );
    lpDdeAdvise = ( DDEADVISE FAR * )
                  GlobalLock( hDdeAdvise );
    lpDdeAdvise->fAckReq   = TRUE;
```

```
lpDdeAdvise->fDeferUpd = FALSE;
lpDdeAdvise->cfFormat  = CF_TEXT;
GlobalUnlock( hDdeAdvise );
```

The first step in the process involves setting up a global memory block for each item on the list, then adding each of the stock numbers to the atom list, receiving *aItem* as the identifier for each:

```
aItem = GlobalAddAtom( stocks[i].szStkNum );
if( ! PostMessage( hServer, WM_DDE_ADVISE, hwnd,
            MAKELONG( hDdeAdvise, aItem ) ) )
```

A *PostMessage* call is made to send a WM_DDE_ADVISE message for each item with the memory block handle (*hDdeAdvise*) and stock number atom (*aItem*) in *lParam*. Because *PostMessage* is used instead of *SendMessage,*, an immediate response is returned reporting the receipt of each message.

Note that this response only means that the server process has received the message. It is not the same as the requested *WM_DDE_ACK* message. If the message is not received, then the *hDdeAdvise* memory block is freed and the *aItem* atom deleted, because communications have broken down, i.e., the server is suddenly unavailable for further services.

```
    {
        GlobalFree( hDdeAdvise );
        GlobalDeleteAtom( aItem );
        break;
    }
```

As long as communications continue, the client process will wait up to three seconds for a confirmation response from the server:

```
    DdeAck.fAck = FALSE;
    dwTime = GetCurrentTime();
    while( GetCurrentTime() - dwTime < 3000 )
        if( PeekMessage( &msg, hwnd, WM_DDE_ACK,
                        WM_DDE_ACK, PM_REMOVE ) )
        {
            GlobalDeleteAtom( HIWORD( msg.lParam ) );
            DdeAck = *( DDEACK *) & LOWORD(msg.lParam);
            if( ! DdeAck.fAck ) GlobalFree( hDdeAdvise );
                break;
        }
    ...
}
```

If positive acknowledgment is not received (! *DdeAck.fAck*), again the global memory block containing the request is freed. For a computer, even a slow 12 MHz model, three seconds is a long time. If a response is not received within this time, the only reasonable assumption is that something is wrong and it's time to quit waiting.

Normally, of course, the response will be received within a relatively short time (a few CPU cycles, not fractions of a second), and the total time, even for a long list of WM_DDE_ADVISE messages, should not be particularly noticeable. Still, requests should be made only for data which is needed at the present time, and not made willy-nilly for all possible data regardless of need.

When the server application receives each WM_DDE_ADVISE message, the client ID is contained in *wParam*, with the handle for the memory block (*hDdeAdvise*) in the low-order word of *lParam*, and the stock number atom (*aItem*) in the high-order word of *lParam*. The server begins by identifying the item request, making sure that it does have data available and appropriate to the request, and reporting accordingly via a WM_DDE_ACK message.

Again, since *PostMessage* rather than *SendMessage* is used, acknowledging the receipt of the message is immediate. The server application continues by calling its own *PostDataMsg* subprocedure to send the requested data via a WM_DDE_DATA message.

The actual data transmission is handled via a subprocedure, because this procedure will be called not only from the WM_DDE_ADVISE response, but also in response to timer events which are used to direct Dde_Data to provide updates of the data.

As far as the Dde_Main application is concerned, at this point the WM_DDE_ADVISE messages have been posted, and there is nothing to do except wait for WM_DDE_DATA messages to be returned by the server (Dde_Data) application.

If you have been following the rather complicated maze of events which are actually taking place here, you've already realized that, while Dde_Main is still sending WM_DDE_ADVISE messages, Dde_Data is already responding with WM_DDE_ACK messages as well as WM_DDE_DATA messages containing the requested data. On receipt of the WM_DDE_DATA messages, Dde_Main is expected to return its own WM_DDE_ACK acknowledgements to Dde_Data, which is still receiving WM_DDE_ADVISE messages. Complicated isn't it? And aren't you glad that it's up to the computer to keep track of it all?

If you really want to track the intricacies of this traffic, the Dde_Data.C and Dde_Main.C examples that follow will lead you through the major part of the maze. If and when you get too confused, refer back to Figures 23-1 thru 23-3. However, in the long run the DDE maze isn't really that complicated, just tedious.

Summary

Between the growing interest in multitasking environments and the demand for individual applications to handle more and more complexity, there is also a very real need to subdivide tasks between semi-independent or even completely independent applications.

In the past, there has been a determined attempt on the part of many applications to become multitask systems, with word processors attempting to integrate typesetting and spread sheets and databases and drafting utilities and virtually anything else that anyone can imagine a use for—all in one package.

The result, of course, is a completely unwieldy and generally unworkable package.

There is a second approach which began, in a primitive fashion, with the Windows clipboard. This allowed separate applications to execute concurrently, and to share data in several different forms between themselves. Thus far, this inter-application cooperation has not yet set the world on fire and is generally limited in cooperative examples but nonetheless, it is still a direction which should be watched carefully for future developments. The DDE processes provide tools toward this aim.

```
//====================//
//     DDE_DATA.C     //
//   DDE Server Demo  //
//====================//

#include <windows.h>
#include <dde.h>
#include <string.h>
#include <stdlib.h>
#include <time.h>

static char szAppName[]     = "DDE_DATA";
static char szServerClass[] = "DDE_DATA.Server";
```

```
struct  {  char *szItemName;
           char *szStkNum;
           long  lQuantity;  }
    stocks[] = { "Bar Stock",      "BS3",   3926,
                 "Box Link",       "BL3",    246,
                 "Chain Stock",    "CS0",    406,
                 "Clipboards",     "CB7",    319,
                 "Colors",         "CL8",    358,
                 "Devices",        "DV1",  13010,
                 "Diamond Link",   "DL4",    150,
                 "Font Stock",     "FS9",   1283,
                 "Pen Grids",      "PG4",   3380,
                 "Pie Widgits",    "PW2",    350,
                 "Printer Jaks",   "PJ3",    134,
                 "Round Stock",    "RS1",   3926,
                 "Shim Stock",     "SS2",    717  };

#define  NUM_ITEMS  ( sizeof(stock ) / sizeof(stocks[0]) )

typedef struct {  unsigned  int  fAdvise:1;
                  unsigned  int  fDeferUpd:1;
                  unsigned  int  fAckReq:1;
                  unsigned  int  undefined:13;
                  long           lQuantity;  }  STOCKRPT;

HANDLE hGInst;

#pragma argsused

BOOL FAR PASCAL TimerProc( HWND hwnd, LONG lParam )
{
    SendMessage( hwnd, WM_TIMER, 0, 0L );
    return( TRUE );
}

#pragma argsused

BOOL FAR PASCAL CloseProc( HWND hwnd, LONG lParam )
{
    SendMessage( hwnd, WM_CLOSE, 0, 0L );
    return( TRUE );
}

long FAR PASCAL ServerProc( HWND hwnd,   WORD msg,
                            WORD wParam, LONG lParam )
{
    ATOM            aItem;
    char            szItem[10], szStkNum[3];
    long            lSize;
    DDEACK          DdeAck;
    DDEADVISE FAR  *lpAdvise;
    DDEDATA   FAR  *lpDdeData;
    DWORD           dwTime;
    GLOBALHANDLE    hStkReport, hDdeData, hDdeAdvise,
```

```
                hDdeCmnds,  hDdePoke;
int             i;
HWND            hClient;
MSG             mMsg;
STOCKRPT FAR    *lpStkReport;
WORD            cfFormat, wStatus;

switch( msg )
{
    case WM_CREATE:
        hStkReport = GlobalAlloc( GHND, NUM_ITEMS *
                                    sizeof( STOCKRPT ) );
        if( ! hStkReport ) DestroyWindow( hwnd );
        else SetWindowWord( hwnd, 2, hStkReport );
        return( 0 );

    case WM_DDE_REQUEST:
        hClient  = wParam;
        cfFormat = LOWORD( lParam );
        aItem    = HIWORD( lParam );
        if( cfFormat == CF_TEXT )
        {
            GlobalGetAtomName( aItem, szItem,
                                sizeof( szItem ) );
            for( i=0; i<NUM_ITEMS; i++ )
                if( ! strcmp( szItem, stocks[i].szStkNum ) )
                    break;
            if( i<NUM_ITEMS )
            {
                GlobalDeleteAtom( aItem );
                PostDataMsg( hwnd, hClient,
                            TRUE, FALSE, FALSE, i );
                return(0);
        }   }
        DdeAck.bAppReturnCode = 0;
        DdeAck.reserved       = 0;
        DdeAck.fBusy          = FALSE;
        DdeAck.fAck           = FALSE;
        wStatus = *( WORD *) & DdeAck;
        if( ! PostMessage( hClient, WM_DDE_ACK, hwnd,
                            MAKELONG( wStatus, aItem ) ) )
            GlobalDeleteAtom( aItem );
        return(0);

    case WM_DDE_ADVISE:
        hClient    = wParam;
        hDdeAdvise = LOWORD( lParam );
        aItem      = HIWORD( lParam );
        lpAdvise = (DDEADVISE FAR *)
                    GlobalLock( hDdeAdvise );
        if( lpAdvise->cfFormat == CF_TEXT )
        {
```

```
            GlobalGetAtomName( aItem, szItem,
                            sizeof(szItem) );
            for( i=0; i<NUM_ITEMS; i++ )
               if( ! strcmp( szItem, stocks[i].szStkNum ) )
                  break;
            if( i < NUM_ITEMS )
            {
               hStkReport = GetWindowWord( hwnd, 2 );
               lpStkReport = (STOCKRPT FAR *)
                            GlobalLock( hStkReport );
               lpStkReport[i].fAdvise   = TRUE;
               lpStkReport[i].fDeferUpd =
                                  lpAdvise->fDeferUpd;
               lpStkReport[i].fAckReq   = lpAdvise->fAckReq;
               lpStkReport[i].lQuantity =
                                  stocks[i].lQuantity;
               GlobalUnlock( hDdeAdvise );
               GlobalFree( hDdeAdvise );
               DdeAck.bAppReturnCode = 0;
               DdeAck.reserved       = 0;
               DdeAck.fBusy          = FALSE;
               DdeAck.fAck           = TRUE;
               wStatus = *( WORD *) & DdeAck;
               if( ! PostMessage( hClient, WM_DDE_ACK, hwnd,
                           MAKELONG( wStatus, aItem ) ) )
                  GlobalDeleteAtom( aItem );
               else
                  PostDataMsg( hwnd, hClient, FALSE,
                           lpStkReport[i].fAckReq,
                           lpStkReport[i].fDeferUpd, i );
               GlobalUnlock( hStkReport );
               return( 0 );
         }  }
         GlobalUnlock( hDdeAdvise );
         DdeAck.bAppReturnCode = 0;
         DdeAck.reserved       = 0;
         DdeAck.fBusy          = FALSE;
         DdeAck.fAck           = FALSE;
         wStatus = *( WORD *) &DdeAck;
         if( ! PostMessage( hClient, WM_DDE_ACK, hwnd,
                           MAKELONG( wStatus, aItem ) ) )
         {
            GlobalFree( hDdeAdvise );
            GlobalDeleteAtom( aItem );
         }
         return(0);

      case WM_DDE_UNADVISE:
         hClient  = wParam;
         cfFormat = LOWORD( lParam );
         aItem    = HIWORD( lParam );
```

```
   DdeAck.bAppReturnCode = 0;
   DdeAck.reserved       = 0;
   DdeAck.fBusy          = FALSE;
   DdeAck.fAck           = TRUE;
   hStkReport  = GetWindowWord( hwnd, 2 );
   lpStkReport = (STOCKRPT FAR *)
                    GlobalLock( hStkReport );
   if( ! cfFormat || cfFormat == CF_TEXT )
   {
       if( ! aItem )
          for( i=0; i<NUM_ITEMS; i++ )
             lpStkReport[i].fAdvise = FALSE;
       else
       {
           GlobalGetAtomName( aItem, szItem,
                               sizeof(szItem) );
           for( i=0; i<NUM_ITEMS; i++ )
              if( !strcmp( szItem, stocks[i].szStkNum) )
                 break;
           if( i<NUM_ITEMS )
               lpStkReport[i].fAdvise = FALSE;
           else DdeAck.fAck = FALSE;
   }  }
   else DdeAck.fAck = FALSE;
   wStatus = *( WORD *) & DdeAck;
   if( ! PostMessage( hClient, WM_DDE_ACK, hwnd,
                    MAKELONG( wStatus, aItem ) ) )
      if( aItem ) GlobalDeleteAtom( aItem );
   GlobalUnlock( hStkReport );
   return(0);

case WM_DDE_EXECUTE:
   hClient   = wParam;
   hDdeCmnds = HIWORD( lParam );
   DdeAck.bAppReturnCode = 0;
   DdeAck.reserved       = 0;
   DdeAck.fBusy          = FALSE;
   DdeAck.fAck           = FALSE;
   wStatus = *( WORD *) & DdeAck;
   if( ! PostMessage( hClient, WM_DDE_ACK, hwnd,
                    MAKELONG( wStatus, hDdeCmnds ) ) )
      GlobalFree( hDdeCmnds );
   return(0);

case WM_DDE_POKE:
   hClient  = wParam;
   hDdePoke = LOWORD( lParam );
   aItem    = HIWORD( lParam );
   DdeAck.bAppReturnCode = 0;
   DdeAck.reserved       = 0;
   DdeAck.fBusy          = FALSE;
   DdeAck.fAck           = FALSE;
```

```
        wStatus = *( WORD *) & DdeAck;
        if( ! PostMessage( hClient, WM_DDE_ACK, hwnd,
                            MAKELONG( wStatus, aItem ) ) )
        {
            GlobalFree( hDdePoke );
            GlobalDeleteAtom( aItem );
        }
        return(0);

    case WM_DDE_TERMINATE:
        hClient = wParam;
        PostMessage( hClient, WM_DDE_TERMINATE, hwnd, 0L );
        DestroyWindow( hwnd );
        return(0);

    case WM_TIMER:
        hClient     = GetWindowWord( hwnd, 0 );
        hStkReport  = GetWindowWord( hwnd, 2 );
        lpStkReport = (STOCKRPT FAR *)
                        GlobalLock( hStkReport );
        for( i=0; i<NUM_ITEMS; i++ )
            if( lpStkReport[i].fAdvise )
                if( lpStkReport[i].lQuantity !=
                    stocks[i].lQuantity )
                {
                    if( ! PostDataMsg( hwnd, hClient, FALSE,
                        lpStkReport[i].fAckReq,
                        lpStkReport[i].fDeferUpd, i ) )
                        break;
                    lpStkReport[i].lQuantity =
                                        stocks[i].lQuantity;
                }
        GlobalUnlock( hStkReport );
        return(0);

    case WM_CLOSE:
        hClient = GetWindowWord( hwnd, 0 );
        PostMessage( hClient, WM_DDE_TERMINATE, hwnd, 0L );
        dwTime = GetCurrentTime();
        while( GetCurrentTime() - dwTime < 3000 )
            if( PeekMessage( &mMsg, hwnd, WM_DDE_TERMINATE,
                            WM_DDE_TERMINATE, PM_REMOVE ) )
                break;
        DestroyWindow( hwnd );
        return(0);

    case WM_DESTROY:
        hStkReport = GetWindowWord( hwnd, 2 );
        GlobalFree( hStkReport );
        return(0);
    }
    return( DefWindowProc( hwnd, msg, wParam, lParam ) );
```

```
}
long FAR PASCAL WndProc( HWND hwnd,    WORD msg,
                         WORD wParam, LONG lParam )
{
    static FARPROC  lpTimerProc, lpCloseProc;
    static char     szTopic[] = "Item_Stocks";
    ATOM            aApp, aTopic;
    HWND            hClient, hServer;
    int             i;

    switch( msg )
    {
        case WM_CREATE:
            lpTimerProc = MakeProcInstance( TimerProc, hGInst );
            lpCloseProc = MakeProcInstance( CloseProc, hGInst );
            return(0);

        case WM_DDE_INITIATE:
            hClient = wParam;
            aApp = GlobalAddAtom( szAppName );
            aTopic = GlobalAddAtom( szTopic );
            if( ( !LOWORD(lParam) || LOWORD(lParam) == aApp ) &&
                ( !HIWORD(lParam) ||
                    HIWORD(lParam) == aTopic ) )
            {
                hServer = CreateWindow( szServerClass, NULL,
                                    WS_CHILD, 0, 0, 0, 0,
                                    hwnd, NULL, hGInst, NULL );
                SetWindowWord( hServer, 0 , hClient );
                SendMessage( wParam, WM_DDE_ACK, hServer,
                            MAKELONG( aApp, aTopic ) );
            }
            else
            {
                GlobalDeleteAtom( aApp );
                GlobalDeleteAtom( aTopic );
            }
            return(0);

        case WM_TIMER:
        case WM_TIMECHANGE:
            for( i=0; i<NUM_ITEMS; i++ )
            {
                if( ! random(3) )
                    stocks[i].lQuantity = (long)
                        ( stocks[i].lQuantity *
                        ( 90 + random(20) ) / 100 );
            }
            EnumChildWindows( hwnd, lpTimerProc, 0L );
            return(0);

        case WM_QUERYOPEN:  return(0);
```

```
        case WM_CLOSE:
            EnumChildWindows( hwnd, lpCloseProc, 0L );
            break;

        case WM_DESTROY:
            PostQuitMessage(0);
            return(0);
    }
    return( DefWindowProc( hwnd, msg, wParam, lParam ) );
}

BOOL PostDataMsg( HWND hServer,    HWND hClient,
                  BOOL fResponse, BOOL fAckReq,
                  BOOL fDeferUpd, int  iState )
{
    ATOM           aItem;
    char           szPop[10];
    DDEACK         DdeAck;
    DDEDATA FAR    *lpDdeData;
    DWORD          dwTime;
    GLOBALHANDLE   hDdeData;
    MSG            mMsg;

    aItem = GlobalAddAtom( stocks[iState].szStkNum );
    if( ! fDeferUpd )
    {
        wsprintf( szPop, "%1d\r\n", stocks[iState].lQuantity );
        hDdeData = GlobalAlloc( GHND | GMEM_DDESHARE,
                             sizeof( DDEDATA ) +
                             strlen( szPop ) );
        lpDdeData = (DDEDATA FAR *) GlobalLock( hDdeData );
        lpDdeData->fResponse = fResponse;
        lpDdeData->fRelease  = TRUE;
        lpDdeData->fAckReq   = fAckReq;
        lpDdeData->cfFormat  = CF_TEXT;
        lstrcpy( (LPSTR) lpDdeData->Value, szPop );
        GlobalUnlock( hDdeData );
    }
    else hDdeData = NULL;
    if( !PostMessage( hClient, WM_DDE_DATA, hServer,
                    MAKELONG( hDdeData, aItem ) ) )
    {
        if( hDdeData ) GlobalFree( hDdeData );
        GlobalDeleteAtom( aItem );
        return( FALSE );
    }
    if( fAckReq )
    {
        DdeAck.fAck = FALSE;
        dwTime = GetCurrentTime();
        while( GetCurrentTime() - dwTime < 3000 )
            if( PeekMessage( &mMsg, hServer, WM_DDE_ACK,
```

```
                            WM_DDE_ACK, PM_REMOVE ) )
        {
            DdeAck = *( DDEACK *) & LOWORD( mMsg.lParam );
            aItem = HIWORD( mMsg.lParam );
            GlobalDeleteAtom( aItem );
            break;
        }
        if( ! DdeAck.fAck )
        {
            if( hDdeData ) GlobalFree( hDdeData );
            return( FALSE );
    }  }
    return( TRUE );
}

#pragma argsused

int PASCAL WinMain( HANDLE hInst,        HANDLE hPrevInst,
                    LPSTR  lpszCmdParam, int nCmdShow )
{
    HWND          hwnd;
    MSG           mMsg;
    WNDCLASS      wc;

    if( hPrevInst ) return( FALSE );
    hGInst = hInst;
                    // register window class //
    wc.style          = 0;
    wc.lpfnWndProc    = WndProc;
    wc.cbClsExtra     = 0;
    wc.cbWndExtra     = 0;
    wc.hInstance      = hInst;
    wc.lpszClassName  = szAppName;
    wc.lpszMenuName   = NULL;
    wc.hIcon          = LoadIcon( hInst, szAppName );
    wc.hCursor        = LoadCursor( NULL, IDC_ARROW );
    wc.hbrBackground  = GetStockObject( WHITE_BRUSH );
    RegisterClass( &wc );

                    // register window for DDE server //
    wc.hInstance      = hInst;
    wc.lpfnWndProc    = ServerProc;
    wc.cbClsExtra     = 0;
    wc.cbWndExtra     = 2 * sizeof( WORD );
    wc.lpszClassName  = szServerClass;
    wc.lpszMenuName   = NULL;
    wc.hIcon          = NULL;
    wc.hCursor        = NULL;
    wc.hbrBackground  = NULL;
    wc.style          = 0;
    RegisterClass( &wc );

    hwnd = CreateWindow( szAppName, "DDE Server Demo",
```

```
                              WS_OVERLAPPEDWINDOW,
                              CW_USEDEFAULT, CW_USEDEFAULT,
                              CW_USEDEFAULT, CW_USEDEFAULT,
                              NULL, NULL, hInst, NULL  );
    SendMessage( hwnd, WM_TIMER, 0, 0L );
    if( ! SetTimer( hwnd, 101, 5000, NULL ) )
    {
        MessageBox( hwnd, "Too many clocks or timers!",
                    szAppName, MB_OK | MB_ICONEXCLAMATION );
        return( FALSE );
    }
    ShowWindow(   hwnd, SW_SHOWMINNOACTIVE );
    UpdateWindow( hwnd );
    while( GetMessage( &mMsg, NULL, 0, 0 ) )
    {
        TranslateMessage( &mMsg );
        DispatchMessage(  &mMsg );
    }
    KillTimer( hwnd, 101 );
    return( mMsg.wParam );
}

                    ;=================;
                    ;  DDE_DATA.DEF   ;
                    ;=================;
NAME           DDE_DATA

DESCRIPTION    "DDE Server Demo"
EXETYPE        WINDOWS
STUB           "WINSTUB.EXE"
CODE           PRELOAD MOVEABLE DISCARDABLE
DATA           PRELOAD MOVEABLE MULTIPLE
HEAPSIZE       1024
STACKSIZE      8192
EXPORTS        WndProc
               ServerProc
               TimerProc
               CloseProc

                    //===================//
                    //    DDE_MAIN.C     //
                    //  DDE Server Demo  //
                    //===================//

#include <windows.h>
#include <dde.h>
#include <stdlib.h>
#include <string.h>
static char szAppName[] = "DDE_MAIN";

struct  {  char *szItemName;
           char *szStkNum;
```

```
            long    lQuantity;  }
     stocks[] = { "Bar Stock",      "BS3", 0,
                  "Box Link",       "BL3", 0,
                  "Chain Stock",    "CS0", 0,
                  "Clipboards",     "CB7", 0,
                  "Colors",         "CL8", 0,
                  "Devices",        "DV1", 0,
                  "Diamond Link",   "DL4", 0,
                  "Font Stock",     "FS9", 0,
                  "Pen Grids",      "PG4", 0,
                  "Pie Widgits",    "PW2", 0,
                  "Printer Jaks",   "PJ3", 0,
                  "Round Stock",    "RS1", 0,
                  "Shim Stock",     "SS2", 0  };

#define  STOCK_ITEMS    ( sizeof(stocks) / sizeof(stocks[0]) )
#define  WM_USER_INIT   ( WM_USER + 1 )

long FAR PASCAL WndProc( HWND hwnd,    WORD wMsg,
                         WORD wParam, LONG lParam )
{
    static BOOL     bInitiate  = TRUE;
    static char     szServer[] = "DdeFiles",
                    szTopic[]  = "Item_Stocks";
    static HWND     hServer = NULL;
    static int      cxChr, cyChr;
    ATOM            aApp, aTopic, aItem;
    char            szBuff[24], szPop[16], szItem[16];
    DDEACK          DdeAck;
    DDEDATA   FAR   *lpDdeData;
    DDEADVISE FAR   *lpDdeAdvise;
    DWORD           dwTime;
    GLOBALHANDLE    hDdeAdvise, hDdeData;
    HDC             hdc;
    MSG             msg;
    PAINTSTRUCT     ps;
    int             i;
    TEXTMETRIC      tm;
    WORD            wStatus, cfFormat;

    switch( wMsg )
    {
        case WM_CREATE:
            hdc = GetDC( hwnd );
            GetTextMetrics( hdc, &tm );
            cxChr = tm.tmAveCharWidth;
            cyChr = tm.tmHeight + tm.tmExternalLeading;
            ReleaseDC( hwnd, hdc );
            return(0);

        case WM_USER_INIT:
            aApp = GlobalAddAtom( szServer );
```

```
aTopic = GlobalAddAtom( szTopic );
SendMessage( 0xFFFF, WM_DDE_INITIATE, hwnd,
             MAKELONG( aApp, aTopic ) );
if( ! hServer )
{
   WinExec( szServer, SW_SHOWMINNOACTIVE );
   SendMessage( 0xFFFF, WM_DDE_INITIATE, hwnd,
                MAKELONG( aApp, aTopic ) );
}
GlobalDeleteAtom( aApp );
GlobalDeleteAtom( aTopic );
bInitiate = FALSE;
if( ! hServer )
{
   MessageBox( hwnd, "Server does not respond!",
      szAppName, MB_OK | MB_ICONEXCLAMATION );
   return(0);
}
for( i=0; i<STOCK_ITEMS; i++ )
{
   hDdeAdvise = GlobalAlloc( GHND | GMEM_DDESHARE,
                             sizeof( DDEADVISE ) );
   lpDdeAdvise = ( DDEADVISE FAR * )
                 GlobalLock( hDdeAdvise );
   lpDdeAdvise->fAckReq  = TRUE;
   lpDdeAdvise->fDeferUpd = FALSE;
   lpDdeAdvise->cfFormat  = CF_TEXT;
   GlobalUnlock( hDdeAdvise );
   aItem = GlobalAddAtom( stocks[i].szStkNum );
   if( ! PostMessage( hServer, WM_DDE_ADVISE, hwnd,
                MAKELONG( hDdeAdvise, aItem ) ) )
   {
      GlobalFree( hDdeAdvise );
      GlobalDeleteAtom( aItem );
      break;
   }
   DdeAck.fAck = FALSE;
   dwTime = GetCurrentTime();
   while( GetCurrentTime() - dwTime < 3000 )
      if( PeekMessage( &msg, hwnd, WM_DDE_ACK,
                     WM_DDE_ACK, PM_REMOVE ) )
      {
         GlobalDeleteAtom( HIWORD( msg.lParam ) );
         DdeAck = *( DDEACK *) & LOWORD(msg.lParam);
         if(!DdeAck.fAck) GlobalFree( hDdeAdvise );
         break;
      }
   if( ! DdeAck.fAck ) break;
   while( PeekMessage( &msg, hwnd, WM_DDE_FIRST,
                     WM_DDE_LAST, PM_REMOVE ) )
      DispatchMessage( &msg );
```

```
      }
   if( i < STOCK_ITEMS )
      MessageBox( hwnd, "WM_DDE_ADVISE msg failure!",
         szAppName, MB_OK | MB_ICONEXCLAMATION );
   return(0);
case WM_DDE_ACK:
   if( bInitiate )
   {
      hServer = wParam;
      GlobalDeleteAtom( LOWORD( lParam ) );
      GlobalDeleteAtom( HIWORD( lParam ) );
   }
   return(0);
case WM_DDE_DATA:
   hDdeData   = LOWORD( lParam );
   lpDdeData  = (DDEDATA FAR *) GlobalLock( hDdeData );
   aItem      = HIWORD( lParam );
   DdeAck.bAppReturnCode = 0;
   DdeAck.reserved       = 0;
   DdeAck.fBusy          = FALSE;
   DdeAck.fAck           = FALSE;
   if( lpDdeData->cfFormat == CF_TEXT )
   {
      GlobalGetAtomName( aItem, szItem,
                         sizeof( szItem ) );
      for( i=0; i<STOCK_ITEMS; i++ )
         if( ! strcmp( szItem, stocks[i].szStkNum ) )
            break;
      if( i<STOCK_ITEMS )
      {
         lstrcpy( szPop, lpDdeData->Value );
         stocks[i].lQuantity = atol( szPop );
         InvalidateRect( hwnd, NULL, FALSE );
         DdeAck.fAck = TRUE;
   } }
   if( lpDdeData->fAckReq )
   {
      wStatus = *( WORD *) &DdeAck;
      if( ! PostMessage( wParam, WM_DDE_ACK, hwnd,
                         MAKELONG( wStatus, aItem ) ) )
      {
         GlobalDeleteAtom( aItem );
         GlobalUnlock( hDdeData );
         GlobalFree( hDdeData );
         return(0);
   } }
   else GlobalDeleteAtom( aItem );
   if( lpDdeData->fRelease || ! DdeAck.fAck )
   {
      GlobalUnlock( hDdeData );
```

```
        GlobalFree( hDdeData );
     }
     else GlobalUnlock( hDdeData );
     return(0);

 case WM_PAINT:
     hdc = BeginPaint( hwnd, &ps );
     for( i=0; i<STOCK_ITEMS; i++ )
     {
         SetTextAlign( hdc, TA_LEFT | TA_TOP );
         TextOut( hdc, cxChr, i*cyChr, szBuff,
                 wsprintf( szBuff, "%-20s",
                     (LPSTR) stocks[i].szItemName ) );
         SetTextAlign( hdc, TA_RIGHT | TA_TOP );
         TextOut( hdc, cxChr*25, i*cyChr, szBuff,
                 wsprintf( szBuff, "%-5s",
                     (LPSTR) stocks[i].szStkNum   ) );
         TextOut( hdc, cxChr*36, i*cyChr, szBuff,
                 wsprintf( szBuff, "%10d",
                             stocks[i].lQuantity  ) );
     }
     SetTextAlign( hdc, TA_LEFT | TA_TOP );
     EndPaint( hwnd, &ps );
     return(0);
 case WM_DDE_TERMINATE:
     PostMessage( hServer, WM_DDE_TERMINATE,
                 hwnd, NULL );
     hServer = NULL;
     return(0);
 case WM_CLOSE:
     if( ! hServer )  break;
     PostMessage( hServer, WM_DDE_UNADVISE, hwnd,
                 MAKELONG( CF_TEXT, NULL ) );
     dwTime = GetCurrentTime();
     while( GetCurrentTime() - dwTime < 3000 )
         if( PeekMessage( &msg, hwnd, WM_DDE_ACK,
                     WM_DDE_ACK, PM_REMOVE ) ) break;
     PostMessage( hServer, WM_DDE_TERMINATE, hwnd, OL );
     dwTime = GetCurrentTime();
     while( GetCurrentTime() - dwTime > 3000 )
         if( PeekMessage( &msg, hwnd, WM_DDE_TERMINATE,
                     WM_DDE_TERMINATE, PM_REMOVE ) )
             break;
     break;
  case WM_DESTROY:
     PostQuitMessage(0);
     return(0);
}
return( DefWindowProc( hwnd, wMsg, wParam, lParam ) );
}
```

```
#pragma argsused
int PASCAL WinMain( HANDLE hInst,        HANDLE hPrevInst,
                    LPSTR  lpszCmdParam, int nCmdShow )
{
    HWND        hwnd;
    MSG         msg;
    WNDCLASS    wc;
    if( ! hPrevInst )
    {
        wc.hInstance      = hInst;
        wc.lpfnWndProc    = WndProc;
        wc.cbClsExtra     = 0;
        wc.cbWndExtra     = 0;
        wc.lpszClassName  = szAppName;
        wc.lpszMenuName   = (LPSTR) szAppName;
        wc.hIcon          = LoadIcon( hInst, szAppName );
        wc.hCursor        = LoadCursor( NULL, IDC_ARROW );
        wc.hbrBackground  = GetStockObject( WHITE_BRUSH );
        wc.style          = CS_HREDRAW | CS_VREDRAW;
        RegisterClass( &wc );
    }
    hwnd = CreateWindow( szAppName, "DDE Client Demo",
                         WS_OVERLAPPEDWINDOW,
                         CW_USEDEFAULT, CW_USEDEFAULT,
                         CW_USEDEFAULT, CW_USEDEFAULT,
                         NULL, NULL, hInst, NULL  );
    ShowWindow(   hwnd, nCmdShow );
    UpdateWindow( hwnd );
    SendMessage( hwnd, WM_USER_INIT, 0, 0L );
    while( GetMessage( &msg, NULL, 0, 0 ) )
    {
        TranslateMessage( &msg );
        DispatchMessage(  &msg );
    }
    return( msg.wParam );
}
                    ;=================;
                    ;  DDE_MAIN.DEF   ;
                    ;=================;
NAME          DDE_MAIN
DESCRIPTION   "DDE Client"
EXETYPE       WINDOWS
STUB          "WINSTUB.EXE"
CODE          PRELOAD MOVEABLE DISCARDABLE
DATA          PRELOAD MOVEABLE MULTIPLE
HEAPSIZE      1024
STACKSIZE     8192
EXPORTS       WndProc
```

Appendix A

Constants/Flags/Macros/Structures

Index To Structure Definitions

General Purpose Definitions

Boolean Constants

FALSE	0	TRUE	1

Type Equivalents

FAR	far	NEAR	near
LONG	long	VOID	void
PASCAL	pascal		
BOOL	int	BYTE	unsigned char
WORD	unsigned int	DWORD	unsigned long
COLORREF	DWORD		
HANDLE	WORD	GLOBALHANDLE	HANDLE
HBITMAP	HANDLE	HBRUSH	HANDLE
HCURSOR	HANDLE	HDC	HANDLE
HFONT	HANDLE	HICON	HANDLE
HMENU	HANDLE	HPALETTE	HANDLE
HPEN	HANDLE	HRGN	HANDLE
HSTR	HANDLE	HWND	HANDLE
LOCALHANDLE	HANDLE		

```
LPBYTE     (pointer)   BYTE FAR              LPDWORD  (pointer)  DWORD
FAR
LPHANDLE   (pointer)   HANDLE FAR            LPINT    (pointer)  int FAR
LPLONG     (pointer)   long FAR              LPSTR    (pointer)  char FAR
LPVOID     (pointer)   void FAR              LPWORD   (pointer)  WORD FAR
NPSTR      (pointer)   char NEAR             PBYTE    (pointer)  BYTE
NEAR
PDWORD     (pointer)   DWORD NEAR            PHANDLE  (pointer)  HANDLE
PINT       (pointer)   int NEAR             PLONG    (pointer)  long
NEAR
PSTR       (pointer)   char NEAR             PWORD    (pointer)  WORD
NEAR
SPHANDLE   (pointer)   HANDLE NEAR
FARPROC() (pointer)   (FAR PASCAL) int     NEARPROC() (pointer)  (NEAR
PASCAL) int
```

Macro Definitions

```
max(a,b)        (((a) > (b)) ? (a) : (b))
min(a,b)        (((a) < (b)) ? (a) : (b))
MAKELONG(a,b)   ((LONG)(((WORD)(a)) | (((DWORD)((WORD)(b))) << 16)))
LOWORD(l)       ((WORD)(l))
HIWORD(l)       ((WORD)(((DWORD)(l) >> 16) & 0xFFFF))
LOBYTE(w)       ((BYTE)(w))
HIBYTE(w)       ((BYTE)(((WORD)(w) >> 8) & 0xFF))
```

Screen (Window) Coordinates

```
RECT ( struct tagRect )
{ int left;  int top;   int right;  int bottom;  }
PRECT   (pointer)  RECT              NRECT   (pointer)  RECT NEAR
LPRECT  (pointer)  RECT FAR

POINT ( struct tagPOINT )
{ int x;   int y;  }
PPOINT  (pointer)  POINT             NPPOINT (pointer)  POINT NEAR
LPPOINT (pointer)  POINT FAR
```

OpenFile() Structure and Pointers

```
OFSTRUCT ( struct tagOFSTRUCT )
{  BYTE   cBytes;        BYTE   fFixedDisk;
   WORD   nErrCode;      BYTE   reserved[4];
   BYTE   szPathName[128];   }
POFSTRUCT  (pointer)  OFSTRUCT        NPOFSTRUCT  (pointer)  OFSTRUCT
NEAR
LPOFSTRUCT (pointer)  OFSTRUCT FAR
```

OpenFile() Flags

OF_READ	0x0000	OF_PARSE	0x0100
OF_READWRITE	0x0002	OF_CREATE	0x1000
OF_WRITE	0x0001	OF_DELETE	0x0200
OF_SHARE_COMPAT	0x0000	OF_PROMPT	0x2000
OF_SHARE_EXCLUSIVE	0x0010	OF_VERIFY	0x0400
OF_SHARE_DENY_WRITE	0x0020	OF_EXIST	0x4000
OF_SHARE_DENY_READ	0x0030	OF_CANCEL	0x0800
OF_SHARE_DENY_NONE	0x0040	OF_REOPEN	0x8000

GetTempFileName() Flag

TF_FORCEDRIVE	0x80	(BYTE)

GetDriveType Return Values

DRIVE_REMOVABLE	2	DRIVE_FIXED	3	DRIVE_REMOTE	4

Global Memory Flags /Macros

GMEM_FIXED	0x0000	GMEM_DISCARDABLE	0x0100
GMEM_MOVEABLE	0x0002	GMEM_NOT_BANKED	0x1000
GMEM_NOCOMPACT	0x0010	GMEM_SHARE	0x2000
GMEM_NODISCARD	0x0020	GMEM_DDESHARE	0x2000
GMEM_ZEROINIT	0x0040	GMEM_NOTIFY	0x4000
GMEM_MODIFY	0x0080		
GMEM_LOWER	GMEM_NOT_BANKED		
GHND	(GMEM_MOVEABLE | GMEM_ZEROINIT)		
GPTR	(GMEM_FIXED | GMEM_ZEROINIT)		
GlobalDiscard(h)	GlobalReAlloc(h, OL, GMEM_MOVEABLE)		

Flags Returned By GlobalFlags (in addition to GMEM_DISCARDABLE)

GMEM_DISCARDED	0x4000	GMEM_LOCKCOUNT	0x00FF
LockData(dummy)	LockSegment(0xFFFF)		
UnlockData(dummy)	UnlockSegment(0xFFFF)		

Local Memory Flags

LMEM_FIXED	0x0000	LMEM_NODISCARD	0x0020
LMEM_MOVEABLE	0x0002	LMEM_ZEROINIT	0x0040
LMEM_NOCOMPACT	0x0010	LMEM_MODIFY	0x0080
LMEM_DISCARDABLE	0x0F00		
LHND	==>	(LMEM_MOVEABLE | LMEM_ZEROINIT)	
LPTR	==>	(LMEM_FIXED | LMEM_ZEROINIT)	
NONZEROLHND	==>	(LMEM_MOVEABLE)	
NONZEROLPTR	==>	(LMEM_FIXED)	
LNOTIFY_OUTOFMEM	0	LNOTIFY_DISCARD	2
LNOTIFY_MOVE	1		
LocalDiscard(h)	LocalReAlloc(h, O, LMEM_MOVEABLE)		

Flags Returned By LocalFlags

LMEM_DISCARDABLE	0x0F00	LMEM_DISCARDED	0x4000
LMEM_LOCKCOUNT	0x00FF		
UnlockResource(h)	GlobalUnlock(h)		
MAKEINTRESOURCE(i)	(LPSTR)((DWORD)((WORD)(i)))		

Predefined Resource Types

RT_CURSOR	MAKEINTRESOURCE(1)	RT_STRING	MAKEINTRESOURCE(6)
RT_BITMAP	MAKEINTRESOURCE(2)	RT_FONTDIR	MAKEINTRESOURCE(7)
RT_ICON	MAKEINTRESOURCE(3)	RT_FONT	MAKEINTRESOURCE(8)
RT_MENU	MAKEINTRESOURCE(4)	RT_ACCELERATOR	MAKEINTRESOURCE(9)
RT_DIALOG	MAKEINTRESOURCE(5)	RT_RCDATA	MAKEINTRESOURCE(10)

ATOM   WORD

MAKEINTATOM(i)   (LPSTR)((DWORD)((WORD)(i)))

Catch() and Throw()

int   CATCHBUF[9];   int FAR   *LPCATCHBUF;

Mode /Hardware Constants

WF_PMODE	0x0001	WF_WIN386	0x0020
WF_CPU286	0x0002	WF_CPU086	0x0040
WF_CPU386	0x0004	WF_CPU186	0x0080
WF_CPU486	0x0008	WF_LARGEFRAME	0x0100
WF_STANDARD	0x0010	WF_SMALLFRAME	0x0200
WF_WIN286	0x0010	WF_80x87	0x0400
WF_ENHANCED	0x0020		

WEP fSystemExit Flag Values

WEP_SYSTEM_EXIT	1	WEP_FREE_DLL	0

OEM Resource Ordinal Numbers

OBM_CLOSE	32754	OBM_CHECK	32760
OBM_UPARROW	32753	OBM_CHECKBOXES	32759
OBM_DNARROW	32752	OBM_BTNCORNERS	32758
OBM_RGARROW	32751	OBM_OLD_REDUCE	32757
OBM_LFARROW	32750	OBM_OLD_ZOOM	32756
OBM_REDUCE	32749	OBM_OLD_RESTORE	32755
OBM_ZOOM	32748	OCR_NORMAL	32512
OBM_RESTORE	32747	OCR_IBEAM	32513
OBM_REDUCED	32746	OCR_WAIT	32514
OBM_ZOOMD	32745	OCR_CROSS	32515
OBM_RESTORED	32744	OCR_UP	32516
OBM_UPARROWD	32743	OCR_SIZE	32640
OBM_DNARROWD	32742	OCR_ICON	32641
OBM_RGARROWD	32741	OCR_SIZENWSE	32642
OBM_LFARROWD	32740	OCR_SIZENESW	32643
OBM_MNARROW	32739	OCR_SIZEWE	32644
OBM_COMBO	32738	OCR_SIZENS	32645
OBM_OLD_CLOSE	32767	OCR_SIZEALL	32646
OBM_SIZE	32766	OCR_ICOCUR	32647
OBM_OLD_UPARROW	32765	OIC_SAMPLE	32512
OBM_OLD_DNARROW	32764	OIC_HAND	32513
OBM_OLD_RGARROW	32763	OIC_QUES	32514
OBM_OLD_LFARROW	32762	OIC_BANG	32515
OBM_BTSIZE	32761	OIC_NOTE	32516

GDI Section

Binary Raster Ops

R2_BLACK	1	R2_MASKPEN	9
R2_NOTMERGEPEN	2	R2_NOTXORPEN	10
R2_MASKNOTPEN	3	R2_NOP	11
R2_NOTCOPYPEN	4	R2_MERGENOTPEN	12
R2_MASKPENNOT	5	R2_COPYPEN	13
R2_NOT	6	R2_MERGEPENNOT	14
R2_XORPEN	7	R2_MERGEPEN	15
R2_NOTMASKPEN	8	R2_WHITE	16

Ternary Raster Operations

- Note: values are DWORD (32-bit) hex.

SRCCOPY	00CC 0020	MERGEPAINT	00BB 0226
SRCPAINT	00EE 0086	PATCOPY	00F0 0021
SRCAND	0088 00C6	PATPAINT	00FB 0A09
SRCINVERT	0066 0046	PATINVERT	005A 0049
SRCERASE	0044 0328	DSTINVERT	0055 0009
NOTSRCCOPY	0033 0008	BLACKNESS	0000 0042
NOTSRCERASE	0011 00A6	WHITENESS	00FF 0062
MERGECOPY	00C0 00CA		

StretchBlt() Modes

BLACKONWHITE	1	WHITEONBLACK	2	COLORONCOLOR	3

PolyFill() Modes

ALTERNATE	1	WINDING	2

Text Alignment Options

TA_NOUPDATECP	0	TA_UPDATECP	1		
TA_LEFT	0	TA_RIGHT	2	TA_CENTER	6
TA_TOP	0	TA_BOTTOM	8	TA_BASELINE	24
ETO_GRAYED	1	ETO_OPAQUE	2	ETO_CLIPPED	4
ASPECT_FILTERING	0x0001				

Metafile Constants

- Note: all MetaFile constant names begin as **META_xxxxxxxxxx**

ANIMATEPALETTE	0x0436	POLYLINE	0x0325
ARC	0x0817	POLYPOLYGON	0x0538
BITBLT	0x0922	REALIZEPALETTE	0x0035
CHORD	0x0830	RECTANGLE	0x041B
CREATEBITMAP	0x06FE	RESIZEPALETTE	0x0139
CREATEBITMAPINDIRECT	0x02FD	RESTOREDC	0x0127
CREATEBRUSH	0x00F8	ROUNDRECT	0x061C
CREATEBRUSHINDIRECT	0x02FC	SAVEDC	0x001E
CREATEFONTINDIRECT	0x02FB	SCALEVIEWPORTEXT	0x0412
CREATEPALETTE	0x00F7	SCALEWINDOWEXT	0x0400
CREATEPATTERNBRUSH	0x01F9	SELECTCLIPREGION	0x012C
CREATEPENINDIRECT	0x02FA	SELECTOBJECT	0x012D
CREATEREGION	0x06FF	SELECTPALETTE	0x0234
DELETEOBJECT	0x01F0	SETBKCOLOR	0x0201
DIBBITBLT	0x0940	SETBKMODE	0x0102
DIBCREATEPATTERNBRUSH	0x0142	SETDIBTODEV	0x0D33

DIBSTRETCHBLT	0x0B41	SETMAPMODE	0x0103
DRAWTEXT	0x062F	SETMAPPERFLAGS	0x0231
ELLIPSE	0x0418	SETPALENTRIES	0x0037
ESCAPE	0x0626	SETPIXEL	0x041F
EXCLUDECLIPRECT	0x0415	SETPOLYFILLMODE	0x0106
EXTTEXTOUT	0x0A32	SETRELABS	0x0105
FILLREGION	0x0228	SETROP2	0x0104
FLOODFILL	0x0419	SETSTRETCHBLTMODE	0x0107
FRAMEREGION	0x0429	SETTEXTALIGN	0x012E
INTERSECTCLIPRECT	0x0416	SETTEXTCHAREXTRA	0x0108
INVERTREGION	0x012A	SETTEXTCOLOR	0x0209
LINETO	0x0213	SETTEXTJUSTIFICATION	0x020A
MOVETO	0x0214	SETVIEWPORTEXT	0x020E
OFFSETCLIPRGN	0x0220	SETVIEWPORTORG	0x020D
OFFSETVIEWPORTORG	0x0211	SETWINDOWEXT	0x020C
OFFSETWINDOWORG	0x020F	SETWINDOWORG	0x020B
PAINTREGION	0x012B	STRETCHBLT	0x0B23
PATBLT	0x061D	STRETCHDIB	0x0F43
PIE	0x081A	TEXTOUT	0x0521
POLYGON	0x0324		

GDI Escapes

NEWFRAME	1	SETDIBSCALING	32
ABORTDOC	2	EPSPRINTING	33
NEXTBAND	3	ENUMPAPERMETRICS	34
SETCOLORTABLE	4	GETSETPAPERMETRICS	35
GETCOLORTABLE	5	POSTSCRIPT_DATA	37
FLUSHOUTPUT	6	POSTSCRIPT_IGNORE	38
DRAFTMODE	7	GETEXTENDEDTEXTMETRICS	256
QUERYESCSUPPORT	8	GETEXTENTTABLE	257
SETABORTPROC	9	GETPAIRKERNTABLE	258
STARTDOC	10	GETTRACKKERNTABLE	259
ENDDOC	11	EXTTEXTOUT	512
GETPHYSPAGESIZE	12	ENABLERELATIVEWIDTHS	768
GETPRINTINGOFFSET	13	ENABLEPAIRKERNING	769
GETSCALINGFACTOR	14	SETKERNTRACK	770
MFCOMMENT	15	SETALLJUSTVALUES	771
GETPENWIDTH	16	SETCHARSET	772
SETCOPYCOUNT	17	STRETCHBLT	2048
SELECTPAPERSOURCE	18	BEGIN_PATH	4096
DEVICEDATA	19	CLIP_TO_PATH	4097
PASSTHROUGH	19	END_PATH	4098
GETTECHNOLOGY	20	EXT_DEVICE_CAPS	4099
SETENDCAP	21	RESTORE_CTM	4100
SETLINEJOIN	22	SAVE_CTM	4101
SETMITERLIMIT	23	SET_ARC_DIRECTION	4102
BANDINFO	24	SET_BACKGROUND_COLOR	4103
DRAWPATTERNRECT	25	SET_POLY_MODE	4104
GETVECTORPENSIZE	26	SET_SCREEN_ANGLE	4105
GETVECTORBRUSHSIZE	27	SET_SPREAD	4106
ENABLEDUPLEX	28	TRANSFORM_CTM	4107
GETSETPAPERBINS	29	SET_CLIP_BOX	4108
GETSETPRINTORIENT	30	SET_BOUNDS	4109
ENUMPAPERBINS	31	SET_MIRROR_MODE	4110

Spooler Error Codes

SP_NOTREPORTED	0x4000	PR_JOBSTATUS	0x0000
SP_ERROR	−1	SP_OUTOFDISK	−4
SP_APPABORT	−2	SP_OUTOFMEMORY	−5
SP_USERABORT	−3		

Object Definitions for EnumObjects()

```
OBJ_PEN   1              OBJ_BRUSH      2
```

Bitmap Header Definition

```
BITMAP ( struct tagBITMAP )
{  int    bmType;        int    bmWidth;      int    bmHeight;
   int    bmWidthBytes;  BYTE   bmPlanes;     BYTE   bmBitsPixel;
   LPSTR bmBits;        }
PBITMAP   (pointer)  BITMAP;              NPBITMAP  (pointer)  BITMAP NEAR
LPBITMAP  (pointer)  BITMAP FAR

RGBTRIPLE ( struct tagRGBTRIPLE )
{  BYTE  rgbtBlue;      BYTE  rgbtGreen;     BYTE  rgbtRed;         }

RGBQUAD ( struct tagRGBQUAD )
{  BYTE  rgbBlue;  BYTE  rgbGreen;  BYTE  rgbRed;  BYTE  rgbReserved;
}
```

Structures for Defining DIBs

```
BITMAPCOREHEADER ( struct tagBITMAPCOREHEADER )
{  DWORD    bcSize;                        // used to get to color table
   WORD   bcWidth;      WORD   bcHeight;
   WORD   bcPlanes;     WORD   bcBitCount;  }
PBITMAPCOREHEADER   (pointer)  BITMAPCOREHEADER
LPBITMAPCOREHEADER  (pointer)  BITMAPCOREHEADER FAR

BITMAPINFOHEADER ( struct tagBITMAPINFOHEADER )
{  DWORD   biSize;         DWORD   biWidth;      DWORD   biHeight;
   WORD    biPlanes;       WORD    biBitCount;   DWORD   biCompression;
   DWORD   biSizeImage;    DWORD   biXPelsPerMeter;
   DWORD   biYPelsPerMeter; DWORD   biClrUsed;    DWORD   biClrImportant;
}
LPBITMAPINFOHEADER  (pointer)  FAR BITMAPINFOHEADER
PBITMAPINFOHEADER   (pointer)  BITMAPINFOHEADER
```

Constants for the biCompression Field

```
BI_RGB   0L            BI_RLE8   1L            BI_RLE4   2L
BITMAPINFO ( struct tagBITMAPINFO )
{  BITMAPINFOHEADER    bmiHeader;   RGBQUAD    bmiColors[1]; }
LPBITMAPINFO (pointer)  BITMAPINFO FAR
PBITMAPINFO  (pointer)  BITMAPINFO

BITMAPCOREINFO ( struct tagBITMAPCOREINFO )
{  BITMAPCOREHEADER    bmciHeader;  RGBTRIPLE bmciColors[1]; }
LPBITMAPCOREINFO (pointer)  BITMAPCOREINFO FAR
PBITMAPCOREINFO  (pointer)  BITMAPCOREINFO

BITMAPFILEHEADER ( struct tagBITMAPFILEHEADER )
{  WORD   bfType;        DWORD   bfSize;
   WORD   bfReserved1;   WORD   bfReserved2;   DWORD   bfOffBits;  }
LPBITMAPFILEHEADER (pointer)  BITMAPFILEHEADER FAR
PBITMAPFILEHEADER  (pointer)  BITMAPFILEHEADER

MAKEPOINT(l)   (*((POINT FAR *)&(l)))
```

Clipboard Metafile Picture Structure

```
HANDLETABLE ( struct tagHANDLETABLE )
{  HANDLE objectHandle[1];  }
PHANDLETABLE   (pointer)  HANDLETABLE
```

```
LPHANDLETABLE  (pointer)  HANDLETABLE FAR

METARECORD ( struct tagMETARECORD )
{ DWORD  rdSize;  WORD  rdFunction;  WORD  rdParm[1];  }
PMETARECORD  (pointer)  METARECORD
LPMETARECORD  (pointer)  METARECORD FAR

METAFILEPICT ( struct tagMETAFILEPICT )
{ int   mm;     int    xExt;    int yExt;   HANDLE  hMF;  }
LPMETAFILEPICT  (pointer)  METAFILEPICT

METAHEADER ( struct tagMETAHEADER )
{ WORD  mtType;     WORD  mtHeaderSize;    WORD  mtVersion;
  DWORD  mtSize;    WORD  mtNoObjects;    DWORD  mtMaxRecord;
  WORD  mtNoParameters;  }

TEXTMETRIC ( struct tagTEXTMETRIC )
{ int   tmHeight;            int  tmAscent;    int  tmDescent;
  int   tmInternalLeading;   int  tmExternalLeading;
  int   tmAveCharWidth;      int  tmMaxCharWidth;
  int   tmWeight;            BYTE tmItalic;    BYTE tmUnderlined;
  BYTE  tmStruckOut;         BYTE tmFirstChar;
  BYTE  tmLastChar;          BYTE tmDefaultChar;
  BYTE  tmBreakChar;         BYTE tmPitchAndFamily;
  BYTE  tmCharSet;           int  tmOverhang;
  int   tmDigitizedAspectX;  int  tmDigitizedAspectY;  }
PTEXTMETRIC   (pointer)  TEXTMETRIC
NPTEXTMETRIC  (pointer)  TEXTMETRIC NEAR
LPTEXTMETRIC  (pointer)  TEXTMETRIC FAR
```

GDI Logical Objects

Pel Array

```
PELARRAY ( struct tagPELARRAY )
{ int  paXCount;    int  paYCount;
  int  paXExt;      int  paYExt;      BYTE paRGBs;  }
PPELARRAY  (pointer)  PELARRAY;       NPPELARRAY  (pointer)  PELARRAY
NEAR
LPPELARRAY  (pointer)  PELARRAY FAR
```

Logical Brush (or Pattern)

```
LOGBRUSH ( struct tagLOGBRUSH )
{ WORD  lbStyle;    DWORD lbColor;    int  lbHatch;  }
PLOGBRUSH  (pointer)  LOGBRUSH       NPLOGBRUSH  (pointer)  LOGBRUSH
NEAR
LPLOGBRUSH  (pointer)  LOGBRUSH FAR    PATTERN     (pointer)  LOGBRUSH
PPATTERN   (pointer)  PATTERN        NPPATTERN   (pointer)  PATTERN
NEAR
LPPATTERN   (pointer)  PATTERN FAR
```

Logical Pen

```
LOGPEN ( struct tagLOGPEN )
{ WORD  lopnStyle;     POINT lopnWidth;   DWORD lopnColor;   }
PLOGPEN  (pointer)  LOGPEN            NPLOGPEN  (pointer)  LOGPEN NEAR
LPLOGPEN  (pointer)  LOGPEN FAR
```

Logical Palettes

```
PALETTEENTRY ( struct tagPALETTEENTRY )
```

```
{  BYTE   peRed;      BYTE   peGreen;     BYTE   peBlue;     BYTE   peFlags;
}
LPPALETTEENTRY  (pointer)          PALETTEENTRY FAR

LOGPALETTE ( struct tagLOGPALETTE )
{  WORD    palVersion;    WORD    palNumEntries;    PALETTEENTRY
palPalEntry[1];   }
PLOGPALETTE    (pointer)   LOGPALETTE
NPLOGPALETTE   (pointer)   LOGPALETTE NEAR
LPLOGPALETTE   (pointer)   LOGPALETTE FAR
```

Logical Font

```
LOGFONT ( struct tagLOGFONT )
{   int   lfHeight;        int    lfWidth;    int   lfEscapement;
    int   lfOrientation;   int    lfWeight;  BYTE  lfItalic;
    BYTE  lfUnderline;     BYTE   lfStrikeOut;
    BYTE  lfCharSet;       BYTE   lfOutPrecision;     BYTE
lfClipPrecision;
    BYTE  lfQuality;       BYTE   lfPitchAndFamily;   BYTE
lfFaceName[LF_FACESIZE];   }
PLOGFONT   (pointer)   LOGFONT
NPLOGFONT  (pointer)   LOGFONT NEAR    LPLOGFONT  (pointer)   LOGFONT FAR
```

LF_FACESIZE	32		
OUT_DEFAULT_PRECIS	0	OUT_CHARACTER_PRECIS	2
OUT_STRING_PRECIS	1	OUT_STROKE_PRECIS	3
CLIP_DEFAULT_PRECIS	0	CLIP_STROKE_PRECIS	2
CLIP_CHARACTER_PRECIS	1	PROOF_QUALITY	2
DEFAULT_QUALITY	0	DRAFT_QUALITY	1
DEFAULT_PITCH	0	FIXED_PITCH	1
ANSI_CHARSET	0	SHIFTJIS_CHARSET	128
SYMBOL_CHARSET	2	OEM_CHARSET	255
VARIABLE_PITC	2		

Font Families

FF_DONTCARE	(0<<4)	FF_SWISS	(2<<4)	FF_SCRIPT	(4<<4)
FF_ROMAN	(1<<4)	FF_MODERN	(3<<4)	FF_DECORATIVE	(5<<4)

Font Weights

FW_DONTCARE	0	FW_NORMAL	400	FW_EXTRABOLD	800
FW_THIN	100	FW_MEDIUM	500	FW_HEAVY	900
FW_EXTRALIGHT	200	FW_SEMIBOLD	600		
FW_LIGHT	300	FW_BOLD	700		
FW_ULTRALIGHT	==>	FW_EXTRALIGHT			
FW_REGULAR	==>	FW_NORMAL			
FW_DEMIBOLD	==>	FW_SEMIBOLD			
FW_ULTRABOLD	==>	FW_EXTRABOLD			
FW_BLACK	==>	FW_HEAVY			

EnumFonts Masks

RASTER_FONTTYPE	0x0001	DEVICE_FONTTYPE	0x0002

```
RGB(r,g,b)
((DWORD)(((BYTE)(r)|((WORD)(g)<<8))|(((DWORD)(BYTE)(b))<<16)))
PALETTERGB(r,g,b)          (0x02000000UL | RGB(r,g,b))
PALETTEINDEX(i) ((DWORD)(0x01000000UL | (WORD)(i)))
GetRValue(rgb)   ((BYTE)(rgb))
GetGValue(rgb)   ((BYTE)(((WORD)(rgb)) >> 8))
GetBValue(rgb)   ((BYTE)((rgb)>>16))
```

Background Modes

TRANSPARENT	1	OPAQUE		2

Mapping Modes

MM_TEXT	1	MM_LOENGLISH	4	MM_ISOTROPIC	7
MM_LOMETRIC	2	MM_HIENGLISH	5	MM_ANISOTROPIC	8
MM_HIMETRIC	3	MM_TWIPS	6		

Coordinate Modes

ABSOLUTE	1	RELATIVE		2

Stock Logical Objects

WHITE_BRUSH	0	NULL_PEN	8
LTGRAY_BRUSH	1	OEM_FIXED_FONT	10
GRAY_BRUSH	2	ANSI_FIXED_FONT	11
DKGRAY_BRUSH	3	ANSI_VAR_FONT	12
BLACK_BRUSH	4	SYSTEM_FONT	13
NULL_BRUSH	5	DEVICE_DEFAULT_FONT	14
WHITE_PEN	6	DEFAULT_PALETTE	15
BLACK_PEN	7	SYSTEM_FIXED_FONT	16
HOLLOW_BRUSH	==>	NULL_BRUSH	

Brush Styles

BS_SOLID	0	BS_HATCHED	2	BS_INDEXED	4
BS_NULL	1	BS_PATTERN	3	BS_DIBPATTERN	5
BS_HOLLOW	==>	BS_NULL			

Hatch Styles

HS_HORIZONTAL	0	HS_FDIAGONAL	2	HS_CROSS	4
HS_VERTICAL	1	HS_BDIAGONAL	3	HS_DIAGCROSS	5

Pen Styles

PS_SOLID	0	PS_DASHDOT	3	PS_INSIDEFRAME	6
PS_DASH	1	PS_DASHDOTDOT	4		
PS_DOT	2	PS_NULL	5		

Device Parameters for GetDeviceCaps()

DRIVERVERSION	0	NUMMARKERS	20	ASPECTX	40
TECHNOLOGY	2	NUMFONTS	22	ASPECTY	42
HORZSIZE	4	NUMCOLORS	24	ASPECTXY	44
VERTSIZE	6	PDEVICESIZE	26	LOGPIXELSX	88
HORZRES	8	CURVECAPS	28	LOGPIXELSY	90
VERTRES	10	LINECAPS	30	SIZEPALETTE	104
BITSPIXEL	12	POLYGONALCAPS	32	NUMRESERVED	106
PLANES	14	TEXTCAPS	34	COLORRES	108
NUMBRUSHES	16	CLIPCAPS	36		
NUMPENS	18	RASTERCAPS	38		

Device Capability Masks:

Device Technologies

DT_PLOTTER	0	DT_RASCAMERA	3	DT_DISPFILE	6	// Vector plotter
DT_RASDISPLAY	1	DT_CHARSTREAM	4			

| DT_RASPRINTER | 2 | DT_METAFILE | 5 |

Curve Capabilities

CC_NONE	0	CC_CHORD	4	CC_STYLED	32
CC_CIRCLES	1	CC_ELLIPSES	8	CC_WIDESTYLED	64
CC_PIE	2	CC_WIDE	16	CC_INTERIORS	128

Line Capabilities

LC_NONE	0	LC_POLYMARKER	8	LC_WIDESTYLED	64
LC_POLYLINE	2	LC_WIDE	16	LC_INTERIORS	128
LC_MARKER	4	LC_STYLED	32		

Polygonal Capabilities

PC_NONE	0	PC_WINDPOLYGON	4	PC_STYLED	32
PC_POLYGON	1	PC_SCANLINE	8	PC_WIDESTYLED	64
PC_RECTANGLE	2	PC_WIDE	16	PC_INTERIORS	128

Polygonal Capabilities

| CP_NONE | 0 | CP_RECTANGLE | 1 |

Text Capabilities

TC_OP_CHARACTER	0x0001	TC_SA_CONTIN	0x0100
TC_OP_STROKE	0x0002	TC_EA_DOUBLE	0x0200
TC_CP_STROKE	0x0004	TC_IA_ABLE	0x0400
TC_CR_90	0x0008	TC_UA_ABLE	0x0800
TC_CR_ANY	0x0010	TC_SO_ABLE	0x1000
TC_SF_X_YINDEP	0x0020	TC_RA_ABLE	0x2000
TC_SA_DOUBLE	0x0040	TC_VA_ABLE	0x4000
TC_SA_INTEGER	0x0080	TC_RESERVED	0x8000

Raster Capabilities

RC_BITBLT	1	RC_SCALING	4
RC_BANDING	2	RC_BITMAP64	8
RC_GDI20_OUTPUT	0x0010	RC_BIGFONT	0x0400
RC_DI_BITMAP	0x0080	RC_STRETCHBLT	0x0800
RC_PALETTE	0x0100	RC_FLOODFILL	0x1000
RC_DIBTODEV	0x0200	RC_STRETCHDIB	0x2000

Palette Entry Flags

| PC_RESERVED | 0x01 | PC_EXPLICIT | 0x02 | PC_NOCOLLAPSE | 0x04 |

DIB Color Table Identifiers

| DIB_RGB_COLORS | 0 | DIB_PAL_COLORS | 1 |

Constants for Get/SetSystemPaletteUse()

| SYSPAL_STATIC | 1 | SYSPAL_NOSTATIC | 2 |

Constants for CreateDIBitmap

| CBM_INIT | 0x04L | // initialize bitmap |

DrawText() Format Flags

| DT_TOP | 0x0000 | DT_EXPANDTABS | 0x0040 |

DT_LEFT	0x0000	DT_TABSTOP	0x0080
DT_CENTER	0x0001	DT_NOCLIP	0x0100
DT_RIGHT	0x0002	DT_EXTERNALLEADING	0x0200
DT_VCENTER	0x0004	DT_CALCRECT	0x0400
DT_BOTTOM	0x0008	DT_NOPREFIX	0x0800
DT_WORDBREAK	0x0010	DT_INTERNAL	0x1000
DT_SINGLELINE	0x0020		

ExtFloodFill Style Flags

FLOODFILLSURFACE	1	FLOODFILLBORDER	0

USER Section

Scroll Bar Constants

SB_HORZ	0	SB_CTL	2
SB_VERT	1	SB_BOTH	3

Scroll Bar Commands

SB_LINEUP	0	SB_THUMBTRACK	5
SB_LINEDOWN	1	SB_TOP	6
SB_PAGEUP	2	SB_BOTTOM	7
SB_PAGEDOWN	3	SB_ENDSCROLL	8
SB_THUMBPOSITION	4		

ShowWindow() Commands

SW_HIDE	0	SW_SHOWNOACTIVATE	4
SW_SHOWNORMAL	1	SW_SHOW	5
SW_NORMAL	1	SW_MINIMIZE	6
SW_SHOWMINIMIZED	2	SW_SHOWMINNOACTIVE	7
SW_SHOWMAXIMIZED	3	SW_SHOWNA	8
SW_MAXIMIZE	3	SW_RESTORE	9

Old ShowWindow() Commands

HIDE_WINDOW	0	SHOW_FULLSCREEN	3
SHOW_OPENWINDOW	1	SHOW_OPENNOACTIVATE	4
SHOW_ICONWINDOW	2		

Identifiers for WM_SHOWWINDOW Message

SW_PARENTCLOSING	1	SW_PARENTOPENING	3
SW_OTHERZOOM	2	SW_OTHERUNZOOM	4

Region Flags

ERROR	0	SIMPLEREGION	2
NULLREGION	1	COMPLEXREGION	3

CombineRgn() Styles

RGN_AND	1	RGN_XOR	3	RGN_COPY	5
RGN_OR	2	RGN_DIFF	4		

Virtual Keys, Standard Set

VK_LBUTTON	0x01	VK_MENU	0x12	VK_UP	0x26
VK_RBUTTON	0x02	VK_PAUSE	0x13	VK_RIGHT	0x27
VK_CANCEL	0x03	VK_CAPITAL	0x14	VK_DOWN	0x28

VK_MBUTTON	0x04	VK_ESCAPE	0x1B	VK_SELECT	0x29
VK_BACK	0x08	VK_SPACE	0x20	VK_PRINT	0x2A
VK_TAB	0x09	VK_PRIOR	0x21	VK_EXECUTE	0x2B
VK_CLEAR	0x0C	VK_NEXT	0x22	VK_SNAPSHOT	0x2C
VK_RETURN	0x0D	VK_END	0x23	VK_INSERT	0x2D
VK_SHIFT	0x10	VK_HOME	0x24	VK_DELETE	0x2E
VK_CONTROL	0x11	VK_LEFT	0x25	VK_HELP	0x2F

VK_A thru VK_Z are the same as their ASCII equivalents: 'A' thru 'Z'
VK_0 thru VK_9 are the same as their ASCII equivalents: '0' thru '9'

VK_NUMPAD0	0x60	VK_ADD	0x6B	VK_F7	0x76
VK_NUMPAD1	0x61	VK_SEPARATOR	0x6C	VK_F8	0x77
VK_NUMPAD2	0x62	VK_SUBTRACT	0x6D	VK_F9	0x78
VK_NUMPAD3	0x63	VK_DECIMAL	0x6E	VK_F10	0x79
VK_NUMPAD4	0x64	VK_DIVIDE	0x6F	VK_F11	0x7A
VK_NUMPAD5	0x65	VK_F1	0x70	VK_F12	0x7B
VK_NUMPAD6	0x66	VK_F2	0x71	VK_F13	0x7C
VK_NUMPAD7	0x67	VK_F3	0x72	VK_F14	0x7D
VK_NUMPAD8	0x68	VK_F4	0x73	VK_F15	0x7E
VK_NUMPAD9	0x69	VK_F5	0x74	VK_F16	0x7F
VK_MULTIPLY	0x6A	VK_F6	0x75	VK_NUMLOCK	0x90

SetWindowsHook() Codes

WH_MSGFILTER	−1	WH_CALLWNDPROC	4
WH_JOURNALRECORD	0	WH_CBT	5
WH_JOURNALPLAYBACK	1	WH_SYSMSGFILTER	6
WH_KEYBOARD	2	WH_WINDOWMGR	7
WH_GETMESSAGE	3		

Hook Codes

HC_LPLPFNNEXT	−2	HC_GETNEXT	1	HC_NOREMOVE	3
HC_LPFNNEXT	−1	HC_SKIP	2	HC_SYSMODALON	4
HC_ACTION	0	HC_NOREM	3	HC_SYSMODALOFF	5

CBT Hook Codes

HCBT_MOVESIZE	0	HCBT_MINMAX	1	HCBT_QS2

WH_MSGFILTER Filter Proc Codes

MSGF_DIALOGBOX	0	MSGF_MENU	2	MSGF_SIZE	4
MSGF_MESSAGEBOX	1	MSGF_MOVE	3	MSGF_SCROLLBAR	5
				MSGF_NEXTWINDOW	6

Window Manager Hook Codes

WC_INIT	1	WC_MOVE	5
WC_SWP	2	WC_SIZE	6
WC_DEFWINDOWPROC	3	WC_DRAWCAPTION	7
WC_MINMAX	4		

Message Structure Used In Journaling

```
EVENTMSG ( struct tagEVENTMSG )
{ WORD      message;   WORD      paramL;   WORD paramH;   DWORD   time;   }
PEVENTMSG   (pointer)   EVENTMSGMSG
NPEVENTMSG  (pointer)   EVENTMSGMSG NEAR     LPEVENTMSG   (pointer)
EVENTMSGMSG FAR

WNDCLASS ( struct tagWNDCLASS )
{ WORD  style;
    LONG (FAR PASCAL *lpfnWndProc)( HWND, WORD, WORD, LONG );
    int      cbClsExtra;      int      cbWndExtra;
```

```
    HANDLE   hInstance;      HICON   hIcon;
    HCURSOR  hCursor;        HBRUSH  hbrBackground;
    LPSTR    lpszMenuName;  LPSTR   lpszClassName;  }
WNDCLASS  (pointer)  WNDCLASS
WNDCLASS  (pointer)  WNDCLASS NEAR   WNDCLASS  (pointer)   WNDCLASS FAR
```

Message Structure

```
MSG ( struct tagMSG )
{  HWND    hwnd;        WORD    message;       WORD    wParam;
   LONG    lParam;      DWORD   time;          POINT   pt;          }
PMSG   (pointer)   MSG
NPMSG  (pointer)   MSG NEAR    LPMSG  (pointer)   MSG FAR
```

Window Field Offsets for GetWindowLong() and GetWindowWord()

GWL_WNDPROC	−4	GWW_ID	−12
GWW_HINSTANCE	−6	GWL_STYLE	−16
GWW_HWNDPARENT	−8	GWL_EXSTYLE	−20

Class Field Offsets for GetClassLong() and GetClassWord()

GCL_MENUNAME	−8	GCW_CBWNDEXTRA	−18
GCW_HBRBACKGROUND	−10	GCW_CBCLSEXTRA	−20
GCW_HCURSOR	−12	GCL_WNDPROC	−24
GCW_HICON	−14	GCW_STYLE	−26
GCW_HMODULE	−16		

Window Messages

WM_NULL	0x0000		
WM_CREATE	0x0001	WM_KEYFIRST	0x0100
WM_DESTROY	0x0002	WM_KEYDOWN	0x0100
WM_MOVE	0x0003	WM_KEYUP	0x0101
WM_SIZE	0x0005	WM_CHAR	0x0102
WM_ACTIVATE	0x0006	WM_DEADCHAR	0x0103
WM_SETFOCUS	0x0007	WM_SYSKEYDOWN	0x0104
WM_KILLFOCUS	0x0008	WM_SYSKEYUP	0x0105
WM_ENABLE	0x000A	WM_SYSCHAR	0x0106
WM_SETREDRAW	0x000B	WM_SYSDEADCHAR	0x0107
WM_SETTEXT	0x000C	WM_KEYLAST	0x0108
WM_GETTEXT	0x000D	WM_INITDIALOG	0x0110
WM_GETTEXTLENGTH	0x000E	WM_COMMAND	0x0111
WM_PAINT	0x000F	WM_SYSCOMMAND	0x0112
WM_CLOSE	0x0010	WM_TIMER	0x0113
WM_QUERYENDSESSION	0x0011	WM_HSCROLL	0x0114
WM_QUIT	0x0012	WM_VSCROLL	0x0115
WM_QUERYOPEN	0x0013	WM_INITMENU	0x0116
WM_ERASEBKGND	0x0014	WM_INITMENUPOPUP	0x0117
WM_SYSCOLORCHANGE	0x0015	WM_MENUSELECT	0x011F
WM_ENDSESSION	0x0016	WM_MENUCHAR	0x0120
WM_SHOWWINDOW	0x0018	WM_ENTERIDLE	0x0121
WM_CTLCOLOR	0x0019	WM_MOUSEFIRST	0x0200
WM_WININICHANGE	0x001A	WM_MOUSEMOVE	0x0200
WM_DEVMODECHANGE	0x001B	WM_LBUTTONDOWN	0x0201
WM_ACTIVATEAPP	0x001C	WM_LBUTTONUP	0x0202
WM_FONTCHANGE	0x001D	WM_LBUTTONDBLCLK	0x0203
WM_TIMECHANGE	0x001E	WM_RBUTTONDOWN	0x0204
WM_CANCELMODE	0x001F	WM_RBUTTONUP	0x0205
WM_SETCURSOR	0x0020	WM_RBUTTONDBLCLK	0x0206
WM_MOUSEACTIVATE	0x0021	WM_MBUTTONDOWN	0x0207
WM_CHILDACTIVATE	0x0022	WM_MBUTTONUP	0x0208
WM_QUEUESYNC	0x0023	WM_MBUTTONDBLCLK	0x0209
WM_GETMINMAXINFO	0x0024	WM_MOUSELAST	0x0209

WM_PAINTICON	0x0026	WM_PARENTNOTIFY	0x0210
WM_ICONERASEBKGND	0x0027	WM_MDICREATE	0x0220
WM_NEXTDLGCTL	0x0028	WM_MDIDESTROY	0x0221
WM_SPOOLERSTATUS	0x002A	WM_MDIACTIVATE	0x0222
WM_DRAWITEM	0x002B	WM_MDIRESTORE	0x0223
WM_MEASUREITEM	0x002C	WM_MDINEXT	0x0224
WM_DELETEITEM	0x002D	WM_MDIMAXIMIZE	0x0225
WM_VKEYTOITEM	0x002E	WM_MDITILE	0x0226
WM_CHARTOITEM	0x002F	WM_MDICASCADE	0x0227
WM_SETFONT	0x0030	WM_MDIICONARRANGE	0x0228
WM_GETFONT	0x0031	WM_MDIGETACTIVE	0x0229
WM_QUERYDRAGICON	0x0037	WM_MDISETMENU	0x0230
WM_COMPAREITEM	0x0039	WM_CUT	0x0300
WM_COMPACTING	0x0041	WM_COPY	0x0301
WM_NCCREATE	0x0081	WM_PASTE	0x0302
WM_NCDESTROY	0x0082	WM_CLEAR	0x0303
WM_NCCALCSIZE	0x0083	WM_UNDO	0x0304
WM_NCHITTEST	0x0084	WM_RENDERFORMAT	0x0305
WM_NCPAINT	0x0085	WM_RENDERALLFORMATS	0x0306
WM_NCACTIVATE	0x0086	WM_DESTROYCLIPBOARD	0x0307
WM_GETDLGCODE	0x0087	WM_DRAWCLIPBOARD	0x0308
WM_NCMOUSEMOVE	0x00A0	WM_PAINTCLIPBOARD	0x0309
WM_NCLBUTTONDOWN	0x00A1	WM_VSCROLLCLIPBOARD	0x030A
WM_NCLBUTTONUP	0x00A2	WM_SIZECLIPBOARD	0x030B
WM_NCLBUTTONDBLCLK	0x00A3	WM_ASKCBFORMATNAME	0x030C
WM_NCRBUTTONDOWN	0x00A4	WM_CHANGECBCHAIN	0x030D
WM_NCRBUTTONUP	0x00A5	WM_HSCROLLCLIPBOARD	0x030E
WM_NCRBUTTONDBLCLK	0x00A6	WM_QUERYNEWPALETTE	0x030F
WM_NCMBUTTONDOWN	0x00A7	WM_PALETTEISCHANGING	0x0310
WM_NCMBUTTONUP	0x00A8	WM_PALETTECHANGED	0x0311
WM_NCMBUTTONDBLCLK	0x00A9	WM_USER	0x0400

NOTE: All Message Numbers below 0x0400 are RESERVED.

WM_SYNCTASK Commands

ST_BEGINSWP	0	ST_ENDSWP	1

WinWhere() Area Codes

HTERROR	−2	HTMENU	5	HTTOP	12
HTTRANSPARENT	−1	HTHSCROLL	6	HTTOPLEFT	13
HTNOWHERE	0	HTVSCROLL	7	HTTOPRIGHT	14
HTCLIENT	1	HTREDUCE	8	HTBOTTOM	15
HTCAPTION	2	HTZOOM	9	HTBOTTOMLEFT	16
HTSYSMENU	3	HTLEFT	10	HTBOTTOMRIGHT	17
HTGROWBOX	4	HTRIGHT	11		
HTSIZE		HTGROWBOX			
HTSIZEFIRST		HTLEFT		HTSIZELAST	HTBOTTOMRIGHT

WM_MOUSEACTIVATE Return Codes

MA_ACTIVATE	1	MA_NOACTIVATE	3
MA_ACTIVATEANDEAT	2		

Size Message Commands

SIZENORMAL	0	SIZEFULLSCREEN	2	SIZEZOOMHIDE	4
SIZEICONIC	1	SIZEZOOMSHOW	3		

Key State Masks for Mouse Messages

MK_LBUTTON	0x0001	MK_CONTROL	0x0008
MK_RBUTTON	0x0002	MK_MBUTTON	0x0010

MK_SHIFT   0x0004

Window Styles

WS_OVERLAPPED	0x00000000L	WS_DLGFRAME	0x00400000L
WS_POPUP	0x80000000L	WS_VSCROLL	0x00200000L
WS_CHILD	0x40000000L	WS_HSCROLL	0x00100000L
WS_MINIMIZE	0x20000000L	WS_SYSMENU	0x00080000L
WS_VISIBLE	0x10000000L	WS_THICKFRAME	0x00040000L
WS_DISABLED	0x08000000L	WS_GROUP	0x00020000L
WS_CLIPSIBLINGS	0x04000000L	WS_TABSTOP	0x00010000L
WS_CLIPCHILDREN	0x02000000L	WS_MINIMIZEBOX	0x00020000L
WS_MAXIMIZE	0x01000000L	WS_MAXIMIZEBOX	0x00010000L
WS_BORDER	0x00800000L		
WS_CAPTION	0x00C00000L		`// WS_BORDER	WS_DLGFRAME`

WS_TILED	==>	WS_OVERLAPPED
WS_ICONIC	==>	WS_MINIMIZE
WS_SIZEBOX	==>	WS_THICKFRAME

Common Window Styles

WS_OVERLAPPEDWINDOW	==>	(WS_OVERLAPPED | WS_CAPTION | WS_SYSMENU | WS_THICKFRAME | WS_MINIMIZEBOX | WS_MAXIMIZEBOX)
WS_POPUPWINDOW	==>	(WS_POPUP | WS_BORDER | WS_SYSMENU)
WS_CHILDWINDOW	==>	(WS_CHILD)
WS_TILEDWINDOW	==>	(WS_OVERLAPPEDWINDOW)

Extended Window Styles

WS_EX_DLGMODALFRAME   0x00000001L   WS_EX_NOPARENTNOTIFY   0x00000004L

Class styles

CS_VREDRAW	0x0001	CS_PARENTDC	0x0080
CS_HREDRAW	0x0002	CS_NOKEYCVT	0x0100
CS_KEYCVTWINDOW	0x0004	CS_NOCLOSE	0x0200
CS_DBLCLKS	0x0008	CS_SAVEBITS	0x0800
//no longer used //	0x0010	CS_BYTEALIGNCLIENT	0x1000
CS_OWNDC	0x0020	CS_BYTEALIGNWINDOW	0x2000
CS_CLASSDC	0x0040	CS_GLOBALCLASS	0x4000

Predefined Clipboard Formats

CF_TEXT	1	CF_SYLK	4	CF_OEMTEXT	7
CF_BITMAP	2	CF_DIF	5	CF_DIB	8
CF_METAFILEPICT	3	CF_TIFF	6	CF_PALETTE	9
CF_OWNERDISPLAY	0x0080	CF_DSPBITMAP	0x0082		
CF_DSPTEXT	0x0081	CF_DSPMETAFILEPICT	0x0083		

■ "Private" formats don't get GlobalFree()'d
CF_PRIVATEFIRST   0x0200   CF_PRIVATELAST   0x02FF
■ "GDIOBJ" formats do get DeleteObject()'d
CF_GDIOBJFIRST   0x0300   CF_GDIOBJLAST   0x03FF

```
PAINTSTRUCT ( struct tagPAINTSTRUCT )
{ HDC    hdc;         BOOL   fErase;      RECT  rcPaint;
  BOOL   fRestore;    BOOL   fIncUpdate;  BYTE  rgbReserved[16]; }
PPAINTSTRUCT  (pointer)  PAINTSTRUCT
NPPAINTSTRUCT (pointer)  PAINTSTRUCT NEAR
LPPAINTSTRUCT (pointer)  PAINTSTRUCT FAR

CREATESTRUCT ( struct tagCREATESTRUCT )
{ LPSTR  lpCreateParams;   HANDLE hInstance;
```

```
    HANDLE  hMenu;              HWND    hwndParent;
    int     cy;     int  cx;    int     y;      int     x;
    LONG    style;              LPSTR   lpszName;
    LPSTR   lpszClass;          DWORD   dwExStyle;    }
LPCREATESTRUCT  (pointer)  CREATESTRUCT FAR
```

Owner Draw Control Types / Actions / State Flags

```
ODT_MENU            1           ODT_COMBOBOX      3
ODT_LISTBOX         2           ODT_BUTTON        4
ODA_DRAWENTIRE      0x0001      ODA_SELECT        0x0002    ODA_FOCUS     0x0004
ODS_SELECTED        0x0001      ODS_DISABLED      0x0004    ODS_FOCUS     0x0010
ODS_GRAYED          0x0002      ODS_CHECKED       0x0008
MEASUREITEMSTRUCT ( struct tagMEASUREITEMSTRUCT )
{  WORD CtlType;       WORD   CtlID;        WORD   itemID;
   WORD itemWidth;     WORD   itemHeight;   DWORD  itemData;   }
PMEASUREITEMSTRUCT   (pointer)   MEASUREITEMSTRUCT NEAR
LPMEASUREITEMSTRUCT  (pointer)   MEASUREITEMSTRUCT FAR

DRAWITEMSTRUCT ( struct tagDRAWITEMSTRUCT )
{  WORD   CtlType;     WORD   CtlID;        WORD   itemID;
   WORD   itemAction;  WORD   itemState;    HWND   hwndItem;
   HDC    hDC;         RECT   rcItem;       DWORD  itemData;    }
PDRAWITEMSTRUCT   (pointer)   DRAWITEMSTRUCT NEAR
LPDRAWITEMSTRUCT  (pointer)   DRAWITEMSTRUCT FAR

DETETEITEMSTRUCT ( struct tagDELETEITEMSTRUCT )
{  WORD   CtlType;     WORD   CtlID;     WORD   itemID;
   HWND   hwndItem;    DWORD  itemData;    }
PDELETEITEMSTRUCT   (pointer)   DELETEITEMSTRUCT NEAR
LPDELETEITEMSTRUCT  (pointer)   DELETEITEMSTRUCT FAR

COMPAREITEMSTRUCT ( struct tagCOMPAREITEMSTRUCT )
{  WORD   CtlType;     WORD   CtlID;    HWND   hwndItem;
   WORD   itemID1;     DWORD  itemData1;
   WORD   itemID2;     DWORD  itemData2;    }
PCOMPAREITEMSTRUCT   (pointer)   COMPAREITEMSTRUCT NEAR
LPCOMPAREITEMSTRUCT  (pointer)   COMPAREITEMSTRUCT FAR
```

PeekMessage() Options

```
PM_NOREMOVE 0x0000     M_REMOVE       0x0001     PM_NOYIELD    0x0002
READ        0          WRITE          1          READ_WRITE    2
CW_USEDEFAULT          ((int)0x8000)
```

SetWindowPos Flags

```
SWP_NOSIZE              0x0001      SWP_DRAWFRAME          0x0020
SWP_NOMOVE              0x0002      SWP_SHOWWINDOW         0x0040
SWP_NOZORDER            0x0004      SWP_HIDEWINDOW         0x0080
SWP_NOREDRAW            0x0008      SWP_NOCOPYBITS         0x0100
SWP_NOACTIVATE          0x0010      SWP_NOREPOSITION       0x0200
DLGWINDOWEXTRA          30                    // needed for private dialog classes
```

GetSystemMetrics() Codes

```
SM_CXSCREEN      0      SM_CXCURSOR        13     SM_RESERVED3  26
SM_CYSCREEN      1      SM_CYCURSOR        14     SM_RESERVED4  27
SM_CXVSCROLL     2      SM_CYMENU          15     SM_CXMIN      28
SM_CYHSCROLL     3      SM_CXFULLSCREEN    16     SM_CYMIN      29
SM_CYCAPTION     4      SM_CYFULLSCREEN    17     SM_CXSIZE     30
SM_CXBORDER      5      SM_CYKANJIWINDOW   18
SM_CYBORDER      6      SM_MOUSEPRESENT    19     SM_CYSIZE     31
SM_CXDLGFRAME    7      SM_CYVSCROLL       20     SM_CXFRAME    32
```

SM_CYDLGFRAME	8	SM_CXHSCROLL	21	SM_CYFRAME	33
SM_CYVTHUMB	9	SM_DEBUG	22	SM_CXMINTRACK	34
SM_CXHTHUMB	10	SM_SWAPBUTTON	23	SM_CYMINTRACK	35
SM_CXICON	11	SM_RESERVED1	24	SM_CMETRICS	36
SM_CYICON	12	SM_RESERVED2	25		

MessageBox() Flags

MB_OK	0x0000	MB_DEFBUTTON1	0x0000
MB_OKCANCEL	0x0001	MB_DEFBUTTON2	0x0100
MB_ABORTRETRYIGNORE	0x0002	MB_DEFBUTTON3	0x0200
MB_YESNOCANCEL	0x0003	MB_APPLMODAL	0x0000
MB_YESNO	0x0004	MB_SYSTEMMODAL	0x1000
MB_RETRYCANCEL	0x0005	MB_TASKMODAL	0x2000
MB_ICONHAND	0x0010	MB_NOFOCUS	0x8000
MB_ICONQUESTION	0x0020	MB_TYPEMASK	0x000F
MB_ICONEXCLAMATION	0x0030	MB_ICONMASK	0x00F0
MB_ICONASTERISK	0x0040	MB_DEFMASK	0x0F00
		MB_MODEMASK	0x3000
		MB_MISCMASK	0xC000
MB_ICONINFORMATION	==>	MB_ICONASTERISK	
MB_ICONSTOP	==>	MB_ICONHAND	

Color Types

CTLCOLOR_MSGBOX	0	CTLCOLOR_DLG	4
CTLCOLOR_EDIT	1	CTLCOLOR_SCROLLBAR	5
CTLCOLOR_LISTBOX	2	CTLCOLOR_STATIC	6
CTLCOLOR_BTN	3	CTLCOLOR_MAX	8
COLOR_SCROLLBAR	0	COLOR_ACTIVEBORDER	10
COLOR_BACKGROUND	1	COLOR_INACTIVEBORDER	11
COLOR_ACTIVECAPTION	2	COLOR_APPWORKSPACE	12
COLOR_INACTIVECAPTION	3	COLOR_HIGHLIGHT	13
COLOR_MENU	4	COLOR_HIGHLIGHTTEXT	14
COLOR_WINDOW	5	COLOR_BTNFACE	15
COLOR_WINDOWFRAME	6	COLOR_BTNSHADOW	16
COLOR_MENUTEXT	7	COLOR_GRAYTEXT	17
COLOR_WINDOWTEXT	8	COLOR_BTNTEXT	18
COLOR_CAPTIONTEXT	9		
COLOR_ENDCOLORS	==>	COLOR_BTNTEXT	

GetWindow() Constants

GW_HWNDFIRST	0	GW_HWNDNEXT	2	GW_OWNER	4
GW_HWNDLAST	1	GW_HWNDPREV	3	GW_CHILD	5

Menu flags for Add/Check/EnableMenuItem()

MF_INSERT	0x0000	MF_USECHECKBITMAPS	0x0200
MF_CHANGE	0x0080	MF_STRING	0x0000
MF_APPEND	0x0100	MF_BITMAP	0x0004
MF_DELETE	0x0200	MF_OWNERDRAW	0x0100
MF_REMOVE	0x1000	MF_POPUP	0x0010
MF_BYCOMMAND	0x0000	MF_MENUBARBREAK	0x0020
MF_BYPOSITION	0x0400	MF_MENUBREAK	0x0040
MF_SEPARATOR	0x0800	MF_UNHILITE	0x0000
MF_ENABLED	0x0000	MF_HILITE	0x0080
MF_GRAYED	0x0001	MF_SYSMENU	0x2000
MF_DISABLED	0x0002	MF_HELP	0x4000
MF_UNCHECKED	0x0000	MF_MOUSESELECT	0x8000
MF_CHECKED	0x0008		

Menu Item Resource Format

```
MENUITEMTEMPLATEHEADER ( struct )
{  WORD versionNumber;   WORD offset;              }

MENUITEMTEMPLATE ( struct )
{  WORD  mtOption;   WORD  mtID;   char  mtString[1]; }
```

MF_END   0x0080

System Menu Command Values

SC_SIZE	0xF000	SC_VSCROLL	0xF070
SC_MOVE	0xF010	SC_HSCROLL	0xF080
SC_MINIMIZE	0xF020	SC_MOUSEMENU	0xF090
SC_MAXIMIZE	0xF030	SC_KEYMENU	0xF100
SC_NEXTWINDOW	0xF040	SC_ARRANGE	0xF110
SC_PREVWINDOW	0xF050	SC_RESTORE	0xF120
SC_CLOSE	0xF060	SC_TASKLIST	0xF130
SC_ICON	SC_MINIMIZE		
SC_ZOOM	SC_MAXIMIZE		

Standard Cursor IDs

```
IDC_ARROW      MAKEINTRESOURCE(32512)        IDC_IBEAM
MAKEINTRESOURCE(32513)
IDC_WAIT       MAKEINTRESOURCE(32514)        IDC_CROSS
MAKEINTRESOURCE(32515)
IDC_UPARROW    MAKEINTRESOURCE(32516)        IDC_SIZE
MAKEINTRESOURCE(32640)
IDC_ICON       MAKEINTRESOURCE(32641)        IDC_SIZENWSE
MAKEINTRESOURCE(32642)
IDC_SIZENESW   MAKEINTRESOURCE(32643)        IDC_SIZEWE
MAKEINTRESOURCE(32644)
IDC_SIZENS     MAKEINTRESOURCE(32645)
```

ORD_LANGDRIVER   1

Standard Icon IDs

```
IDI_APPLICATION MAKEINTRESOURCE(32512)       IDI_HAND
MAKEINTRESOURCE(32513)
IDI_QUESTION   MAKEINTRESOURCE(32514)        IDI_EXCLAMATION
MAKEINTRESOURCE(32515)
IDI_ASTERISK   MAKEINTRESOURCE(32516)
CP_HWND        0                CP_OPEN         1    CP_DIRECT2
```

VK From The Keyboard Driver

VK_KANA	0x15	VK_HIRAGANA	0x18
VK_ROMAJI	0x16	VK_KANJI	0x19
VK_ZENKAKU	0x17		

VK To Send To Applications

VK_CONVERT	0x1C	VK_ACCEPT	0x1E
VK_NONCONVERT	0x1D	VK_MODECHANGE	0x1F

Conversion Function Numbers

KNJ_START	0x01	KNJ_NEXT	0x22
KNJ_END	0x02	KNJ_PREVIOUS	0x23
KNJ_QUERY	0x03	KNJ_ACCEPT	0x24
KNJ_LEARN_MODE	0x10	KNJ_LEARN	0x30

KNJ_GETMODE	0x11	KNJ_REGISTER	0x31
KNJ_SETMODE	0x12	KNJ_REMOVE	0x32
KNJ_CODECONVERT	0x20	KNJ_CHANGE_UDIC	0x33
KNJ_CONVERT	0x21		

```
NOTE:  DEFAULT = 0          JIS1KATAKANA  = 4
       JIS1 = 1             SJIS2HIRAGANA = 5
       JIS2 = 2             SJIS2KATAKANA = 6
       SJIS2 = 3            OEM = F
```

KNJ_JIS1toJIS1KATAKANA	0x14	KNJ_JIS1toDEFAULT	0x10
KNJ_JIS1toSJIS2	0x13	KNJ_JIS1toSJIS2OEM	0x1F
KNJ_JIS1toSJIS2HIRAGANA	0x15	KNJ_JIS2toSJIS2	0x23
KNJ_JIS1toSJIS2KATAKANA	0x16	KNJ_SJIS2toJIS2	0x32
KNJ_MD_ALPHA	0x01	KNJ_MD_JIS	0x08
KNJ_MD_HIRAGANA	0x02	KNJ_MD_SPECIAL	0x10
KNJ_MD_HALF	0x04		
KNJ_CVT_NEXT	0x01	KNJ_CVT_JIS1	0x05
KNJ_CVT_PREV	0x02	KNJ_CVT_SJIS2	0x06
KNJ_CVT_KATAKANA	0x03	KNJ_CVT_DEFAULT	0x07
KNJ_CVT_HIRAGANA	0x04	KNJ_CVT_TYPED	0x08

```
KANJISTRUCT, FAR *LPKANJISTRUCT  ( struct )
{   int     fnc;          int     wParam;
    LPSTR   lpSource;     LPSTR   lpDest;     int     wCount;
    LPSTR   lpReserved1;  LPSTR   lpReserved2;
}
```

Dialog Box Command IDs

IDOK	1	IDRETRY	4	IDNO7
IDCANCEL	2	IDIGNORE	5	
IDABORT	3	IDYES	6	

Control Manager Structures and Definitions

Edit Control Styles

ES_LEFT	0x0000	ES_PASSWORD	0x0020
ES_CENTER	0x0001	ES_AUTOVSCROLL	0x0040
ES_RIGHT	0x0002	ES_AUTOHSCROLL	0x0080
ES_MULTILINE	0x0004	ES_NOHIDESEL	0x0100
ES_UPPERCASE	0x0008	ES_OEMCONVERT	0x0400
ES_LOWERCASE	0x0010		

Edit Control Notification Codes

EN_SETFOCUS	0x0100	EN_ERRSPACE	0x0500
EN_KILLFOCUS	0x0200	EN_MAXTEXT	0x0501
EN_CHANGE	0x0300	EN_HSCROLL	0x0601
EN_UPDATE	0x0400	EN_VSCROLL	0x0602

Edit Control Messages

EM_GETSEL	(WM_USER)	EM_LINELENGTH	(...+17)
EM_SETSEL	(...+1)	EM_REPLACESEL	(...+18)
EM_GETRECT	(...+2)	EM_SETFONT	(...+19)
EM_SETRECT	(...+3)	EM_GETLINE	(...+20)
EM_SETRECTNP	(...+4)	EM_LIMITTEXT	(...+21)
EM_SCROLL	(...+5)	EM_CANUNDO	(...+22)
EM_LINESCROLL	(...+6)	EM_UNDO	(...+23)
EM_GETMODIFY	(...+8)	EM_FMTLINES	(...+24)
EM_SETMODIFY	(...+9)	EM_LINEFROMCHAR	(...+25)
EM_GETLINECOUNT	(...+10)	EM_SETWORDBREAK	(...+26)

EM_LINEINDEX	(...+11)	EM_SETTABSTOPS	(...+27)
EM_SETHANDLE	(...+12)	EM_SETPASSWORDCHAR	(...+28)
EM_GETHANDLE	(...+13)	EM_EMPTYUNDOBUFFER	(...+29)
EM_GETTHUMB	(...+14)	EM_MSGMAX	(...+30)

Button Control Styles

BS_PUSHBUTTON	0x00L	BS_GROUPBOX	0x07L
BS_DEFPUSHBUTTON	0x01L	BS_USERBUTTON	0x08L
BS_CHECKBOX	0x02L	BS_AUTORADIOBUTTON	0x09L
BS_AUTOCHECKBOX	0x03L	BS_PUSHBOX	0x0AL
BS_RADIOBUTTON	0x04L	BS_OWNERDRAW	0x0BL
BS_3STATE	0x05L	BS_LEFTTEXT	0x20L
BS_AUTO3STATE	0x06L		

User Button Notification Codes

BN_CLICKED	0	BN_HILITE	2	BN_DISABLE	4		
BN_PAINT	1	BN_UNHILITE	3	BN_DOUBLECLICKED	5		

Button Control Messages

BM_GETCHECK	(WM_USER+0)		
BM_SETCHECK	(...+1)	BM_SETSTATE	(...+3)
BM_GETSTATE	(...+2)	BM_SETSTYLE	(...+4)

Static Control Constants

SS_LEFT	0x00L	SS_BLACKFRAME	0x07L
SS_CENTER	0x01L	SS_GRAYFRAME	0x08L
SS_RIGHT	0x02L	SS_WHITEFRAME	0x09L
SS_ICON	0x03L	SS_USERITEM	0x0AL
SS_BLACKRECT	0x04L	SS_SIMPLE	0x0BL
SS_GRAYRECT	0x05L	SS_LEFTNOWORDWRAP	0x0CL
SS_WHITERECT	0x06L		
SS_NOPREFIX	0x80L	**// Don't do & character translation**	

Dialog Styles

DS_ABSALIGN	0x01L	DS_SETFONT	0x40L
DS_SYSMODAL	0x02L	DS_MODALFRAME	0x80L
DS_LOCALEDIT	0x20L	DS_NOIDLEMSG	0x100L
DM_GETDEFID	(WM_USER)	DM_SETDEFID	(...+1)
DC_HASDEFID	0x534B		

Dialog Codes

DLGC_WANTARROWS	0x0001	DLGC_UNDEFPUSHBUTTON	0x0020
DLGC_WANTTAB	0x0002	DLGC_RADIOBUTTON	0x0040
DLGC_WANTALLKEYS	0x0004	DLGC_WANTCHARS	0x0080
DLGC_WANTMESSAGE	0x0004	DLGC_STATIC	0x0100
DLGC_HASSETSEL	0x0008	DLGC_BUTTON	0x2000
DLGC_DEFPUSHBUTTON	0x0010	LB_CTLCODE	0L

Listbox Return Values / Notification Codes / Messages

LBN_ERRSPACE	−2	LBN_SELCHANGE	1	LBN_SETFOCUS	4
LB_ERR	−1	LBN_DBLCLK	2	LBN_KILLFOCUS	5
LB_OKAY	0	LBN_SELCANCEL	3		
LB_ADDSTRING	(WM_USER+1)				
LB_INSERTSTRING	(...+2)	LB_FINDSTRING	(...+16)		
LB_DELETESTRING	(...+3)	LB_GETSELCOUNT	(...+17)		
LB_RESETCONTENT	(...+5)	LB_GETSELITEMS	(...+18)		

LB_SETSEL	(...+6)	LB_SETTABSTOPS	(...+19)
LB_SETCURSEL	(...+7)	LB_GETHORIZONTALEXTENT	(...+20)
LB_GETSEL	(...+8)	LB_SETHORIZONTALEXTENT	(...+21)
LB_GETCURSEL	(...+9)	LB_SETCOLUMNWIDTH	(...+22)
LB_GETTEXT	(...+10)	LB_SETTOPINDEX	(...+24)
LB_GETTEXTLEN	(...+11)	LB_GETITEMRECT	(...+25)
LB_GETCOUNT	(...+12)	LB_GETITEMDATA	(...+26)
LB_SELECTSTRING	(...+13)	LB_SETITEMDATA	(...+27)
LB_DIR	(...+14)	LB_SELITEMRANGE	(...+28)
LB_GETTOPINDEX	(...+15)	LB_MSGMAX	(...+33)

Listbox Styles

LBS_NOTIFY	0x0001L	LBS_HASSTRINGS	0x0040L
LBS_SORT	0x0002L	LBS_USETABSTOPS	0x0080L
LBS_NOREDRAW	0x0004L	LBS_NOINTEGRALHEIGHT	0x0100L
LBS_MULTIPLESEL	0x0008L	LBS_MULTICOLUMN	0x0200L
LBS_OWNERDRAWFIXED	0x0010L	LBS_WANTKEYBOARDINPUT	0x0400L
LBS_OWNERDRAWVARIABLE	0x0020L	LBS_EXTENDEDSEL	0x0800L
LBS_STANDARD	==>	(LBS_NOTIFY | LBS_SORT |	
		WS_VSCROLL | WS_BORDER)	

Combo Box Return Values

CB_OKAY	0	CB_ERR	−1	CB_ERRSPACE	−2

Combo Box Notification Codes

CBN_ERRSPACE –	1	CBN_SETFOCUS	3	CBN_EDITUPDATE	6
CBN_SELCHANGE	1	CBN_KILLFOCUS	4	CBN_DROPDOWN	7
CBN_DBLCLK	2	CBN_EDITCHANGE	5		

Combo Box Styles

CBS_SIMPLE	0x0001L	CBS_AUTOHSCROLL	0x0040L
CBS_DROPDOWN	0x0002L	CBS_OEMCONVERT	0x0080L
CBS_DROPDOWNLIST	0x0003L	CBS_SORT	0x0100L
CBS_OWNERDRAWFIXED	0x0010L	CBS_HASSTRINGS	0x0200L
CBS_OWNERDRAWVARIABLE	0x0020L	CBS_NOINTEGRALHEIGHT	0x0400L

Combo Box Messages

CB_GETEDITSEL	(WM_USER+0)		
		CB_INSERTSTRING	(...+10)
CB_LIMITTEXT	(...+1)	CB_RESETCONTENT	(...+11)
CB_SETEDITSEL	(...+2)	CB_FINDSTRING	(...+12)
CB_ADDSTRING	(...+3)	CB_SELECTSTRING	(...+13)
CB_DELETESTRING	(...+4)	CB_SETCURSEL	(...+14)
CB_DIR	(...+5)	CB_SHOWDROPDOWN	(...+15)
CB_GETCOUNT	(...+6)	CB_GETITEMDATA	(...+16)
CB_GETCURSEL	(...+7)	CB_SETITEMDATA	(...+17)
CB_GETLBTEXT	(...+8)		
CB_GETDROPPEDCONTROLRECT		(...+18)	
CB_GETLBTEXTLEN	(...+9)	CB_MSGMAX	(...+19)

Scroll Bar Styles

SBS_HORZ	0x0000L	SBS_RIGHTALIGN	0x0004L
SBS_VERT	0x0001L	SBS_SIZEBOXTOPLEFTALIGN	0x0002L
SBS_TOPALIGN	0x0002L		
SBS_SIZEBOXBOTTOMRIGHTALIGN		0x0004L	
SBS_LEFTALIGN	0x0002L	SBS_SIZEBOX	0x0008L
SBS_BOTTOMALIGN	0x0004L		

Parity Codes

NOPARITY	0	EVENPARITY	2	SPACEPARITY	4	
ODDPARITY	1	MARKPARITY	3			
ONESTOPBIT	0	ONE5STOPBITS	1	TWOSTOPBITS	2	
IGNORE	0			INFINITE	0xFFFF	

Error Flags

CE_RXOVER	0x0001	CE_CTSTO	0x0020	CE_IOE	0x0400	
CE_OVERRUN	0x0002	CE_DSRTO	0x0040	CE_DNS	0x0800	
CE_RXPARITY	0x0004	CE_RLSDTO	0x0080	CE_OOP	0x1000	
CE_FRAME	0x0008	CE_TXFULL	0x0100	CE_MODE	0x8000	
CE_BREAK	0x0010	CE_PTO	0x0200			
IE_BADID	−1	IE_MEMORY	−4	IE_BYTESIZE	−11	
IE_OPEN	−2	IE_DEFAULT	−5	IE_BAUDRATE	−12	
IE_NOPEN	−3	IE_HARDWARE	−10			

Events

EV_RXCHAR	0x0001	EV_DSR	0x0010	EV_RING	0x0100
EV_RXFLAG	0x0002	EV_RLSD	0x0020	EV_PERR	0x0200
EV_TXEMPTY	0x0004	EV_BREAK	0x0040		
EV_CTS	0x0008	EV_ERR	0x0080		

Escape Functions

SETXOFF	1	CLRRTS	4	RESETDEV	7
SETXON	2	SETDTR	5	LPTx	0x80
SETRTS	3	CLRDTR	6		

```
DCB ( struct tagDCB )
{   BYTE  Id;             WORD  BaudRate;         BYTE  ByteSize;
    BYTE  Parity;         BYTE  StopBits;         WORD  RlsTimeout;
    WORD  CtsTimeout;     WORD  DsrTimeout;
    BYTE  fBinary: 1;     BYTE  fRtsDisable:1;    BYTE  fParity: 1;
    BYTE  fOutxCtsFlow:1; BYTE  fOutxDsrFlow:1;
    BYTE  fDummy: 2;      BYTE  fDtrDisable:1;    BYTE  fOutX: 1;
    BYTE  fInX: 1;        BYTE  fPeChar: 1;       BYTE  fNull: 1;
    BYTE  fChEvt: 1;      BYTE  fDtrflow: 1;      BYTE  fRtsflow: 1;
    BYTE  fDummy2: 1;     char  XonChar;          char  XoffChar;
    WORD  XonLim;         WORD  XoffLim;          char  PeChar;
    char  EofChar;        char  EvtChar;          WORD  TxDelay;   }
COMSTAT ( struct tagCOMSTAT )
{   BYTE  fCtsHold: 1;    BYTE  fDsrHold: 1;      BYTE  fRlsdHold: 1;
    BYTE  fXoffHold: 1;   BYTE  fXoffSent: 1;     BYTE  fEof: 1;
    BYTE  fTxim: 1;       WORD  cbInQue;          WORD  cbOutQue;  }
MDICREATESTRUCT ( struct tagMDICREATESTRUCT )
{   LPSTR szClass;       LPSTR szTitle;       HANDLE hOwner;
    int   x, y;          int  cx, cy;         LONG   style;    LONG  lParam;  }
                                                  // app-defined stuff

LPMDICREATESTRUCT    (pointer)  MDICREATESTRUCT FAR
CLIENTCREATESTRUCT ( struct tagCLIENTCREATESTRUCT )
{   HANDLE hWindowMenu;   WORD idFirstChild;  }
```

Help Engine Section

Commands to Pass WinHelp()

HELP_CONTEXT	0x0001	HELP_HELPONHELP	0x0004		
HELP_QUIT	0x0002	HELP_SETINDEX	0x0005		
HELP_INDEX	0x0003	HELP_KEY	0x0101	HELP_MULTIKEY	0x0201

```
MULTIKEYHELP ( struct tagMULTIKEYHELP )
{   WORD   mkSize;      BYTE   mkKeylist;     BYTE   szKeyphrase[1];  }
```

Index